FOURTH CANADIAN EDITION

Human Resource Management

FOURTH CANADIAN EDITION

Human Resource Management

Sandra L. Steen
University of Regina

Raymond A. Noe
Ohio State University

John R. Hollenbeck
Michigan State University

Barry Gerhart
University of Wisconsin—Madison

Patrick M. Wright
Cornell University

McGraw Hill Education

HUMAN RESOURCE MANAGEMENT
Fourth Canadian Edition

The Internet addresses listed in the text were accurate at the time of publication. The inclusion of a website does not indicate an endorsement by the authors or McGraw-Hill Ryerson, and McGraw-Hill Ryerson does not guarantee the accuracy of information presented at these sites.

ISBN-13: 978-1-25-908756-1

ISBN-10: 1-25-908756-5

5 6 7 8 9 WEB 22 21 20 19 18

Printed and bound in Canada.

Care has been taken to trace ownership of copyright material contained in this text; however, the publisher will welcome any information that enables it to rectify any reference or credit for subsequent editions.

Director of Product Management: *Rhondda McNabb*
Group Product Manager: *Kim Brewster*
Marketing Manager: *Cathie Lefebvre*
Product Developer: *Tracey Haggert*
Product Team Associate: *Stephanie Giles*
Supervising Editor / Plant Production Coordinator: *Michelle Saddler*
Full Service Project Manager: *SPi Global*
Copy Editor: *Erin Moore*
Manufacturing Production Coordinator: *Emily Hickey*
Cover and Interior Design: *Katherine Strain*
Cover Photo: *Blend Images / Getty Images*
Composition: *SPi Global*
Printer: *Webcom, Inc.*

Dedication

In tribute to the lives of Walter and Alice Yung, and to my husband, Aaron, and our children, Matt and Jess

—S.L.S.

In tribute to the lives of Raymond and Mildred Noe

—R.A.N.

To my parents, Harold and Elizabeth, my wife, Patty, and my children, Jennifer, Marie, Timothy, and Jeffrey

—J.R.H.

To my parents, Robert and Shirley, my wife, Heather, and my children, Chris and Annie

—B.G.

To my parents, Patricia and Paul, my wife, Mary, and my sons, Michael and Matthew

—P.M.W.

About the Authors

Sandra L. Steen teaches in the Paul J. Hill School of Business and the Kenneth Levene Graduate School of Business at the University of Regina. Sandra also leads executive education and professional development sessions with the Centre for Management Development, Faculty of Business Administration. Sandra has an integrated education and background in both Human Resource Management and Organizational Behaviour. She received her MBA from the University of Regina and has more than 25 years of leading, managing, teaching, and consulting across a wide range of organizations in the private, public, and not-for-profit sectors. Sandra teaches in the undergraduate, MBA, and Executive MBA programs at the University of Regina. Along with co-authoring *Human Resource Management,* Fourth Canadian Edition, Sandra is also co-author with Steven McShane (University of Western Australia) and Kevin Tasa (York University) of *Canadian Organizational Behaviour,* Ninth Edition (2015). Sandra holds the designation of Certified Human Resources Professional (CHRP) and she is a member of the Saskatchewan Association of Human Resource Professionals. She is a former Commissioner of the Saskatchewan Public Service Commission, the central human resource agency for the provincial government. Sandra has received recognition for her teaching accomplishments including "Inspiring Teacher Award—Business Administration." In her leisure time, Sandra enjoys spending time at the lake with her husband Aaron, and their children, Matt and Jess.

Raymond A. Noe is the Robert and Anne Hoyt Professor of Management at Ohio State University. He was previously a professor in the Department of Management at Michigan State University and the Industrial Relations Center of the Carlson School of Management, University of Minnesota. He received his B.S. in Psychology from Ohio State University and his M.A. and Ph.D. in Psychology from Michigan State University. Professor Noe conducts research and teaches undergraduate as well as MBA and Ph.D. students in human resource management, managerial skills, quantitative methods, human resource information systems, training, employee development, and organizational behavior. He has published articles in the *Academy of Management Journal, Academy of Management Review, Journal of Applied Psychology, Journal of Vocational Behavior,* and *Personnel Psychology.* Professor Noe is currently on the editorial boards of several journals including *Personnel Psychology, Journal of Applied Psychology,* and *Journal of Organizational Behavior.* Professor Noe has received awards for his teaching and research excellence, including the Herbert G. Heneman Distinguished Teaching Award in 1991 and the Ernest J. McCormick Award for Distinguished Early Career Contribution from the Society for Industrial and Organizational Psychology in 1993. He is also a fellow of the Society for Industrial and Organizational Psychology.

John R. Hollenbeck is currently the Eli Broad Professor of Management at the Eli Broad Graduate School of Business Administration at Michigan State University. He received his Ph.D. in Management from New York University in 1984 and joined the Michigan State faculty that year. Dr. Hollenbeck has published over 60 articles and book chapters, with more than 35 of these appearing in the most highly cited refereed outlets (*Journal of Applied Psychology, Academy of Management Journal, Personnel Psychology,* and *Organizational Behavior and Human Decision Processes*). Dr. Hollenbeck was the acting editor at *Organizational Behavior and Human Decision Processes* in 1995, the associate editor at *Decision Sciences* from 1999 to 2004, and the editor of *Personnel Psychology* between 1996 and 2002. Prior to serving as editor, he served on the editorial board of these journals, as well as the boards of the *Academy* *of Management Journal, Academy of Management Review, Journal of Applied Psychology,* and *Journal of Management.* Dr. Hollenbeck was the first recipient of the Ernest J. McCormick Award for Early Contributions to the field of Industrial and Organizational Psychology in 1992, and is a Fellow of the American Psychological Association.

Barry Gerhart is Professor of Management and Human Resources, the Bruce R. Ellig Distinguished Chair in Pay and Organizational Effectiveness, and Director of the Strategic Human Resources Program, School of Business, University of Wisconsin–Madison. His previous faculty appointments include serving as Area Coordinator of the Organization Studies area at Vanderbilt University's Owen Graduate School of Management and as Chair of the Department of Human Resource Studies, Cornell University. His major fields of interest are human resource management and strategy, compensation, and business performance. Professor Gerhart received his B.S. in Psychology from Bowling Green State University and his Ph.D. in Industrial Relations from the University of Wisconsin–Madison. Current and past editorial board appointments include the *Academy of Management Journal, Administration Science Quarterly, Industrial and Labor Relations Review,* the *International Journal of Human Resource Management,* the *Journal of Applied Psychology,* and *Personnel Psychology.* In 1991, Professor Gerhart received the Scholarly Achievement Award from the Human Resources Division, Academy of Management. He is also a Fellow of the American Psychological Association and of the Society for Industrial and Organizational Psychology. Professor Gerhard is co-author of the book, *Compensation: Theory, Evidence, and Strategic Implications,* as well as co-editor of *Compensation in Organizations.*

Patrick M. Wright is Professor of Human Resource Studies and Director of the Center for Advanced Human Resource Studies in the School of Industrial and Labor Relations, Cornell University. He holds a B.A. in Psychology from Wheaton College, and an MBA and Ph.D. in Organizational Behavior/Human Resource Management from Michigan State University. Professor Wright teaches, conducts research, and consults in the area of Strategic Human Resource Management (SHRM), particularly focusing on how firms use people as a source of competitive advantage. He has published over 50 articles in journals such as *Academy of Management Journal, Academy of Management Review, Strategic Management Journal, Organizational Behavior and Human Decision Processes, Journal of Applied Psychology, Personnel Psychology,* and *Journal of Management,* as well as over 20 chapters in books and edited volumes such as *Research in P/HRM* and *Handbook of I/O Psychology.* He currently serves on the editorial boards of *Personnel Psychology, Human Resource Management Journal, Human Resource Management Review, Journal of Management, Human Resource Planning, Management and Organization Review, Journal of Management Studies,* and *Journal of Managerial Issues.* He has co-authored two textbooks, and has co-edited a number of special issues of journals dealing with the future of Strategic HRM as well as Corporate Social Responsibility. He has taught in Executive Development programs, and conducted programs and/or consulted for a number of large public- and private-sector organizations. Dr. Wright served as Chair of the HR Division of the Academy of Management, and on the Board of Directors for SHRM Foundation, World at Work, and Human Resource Planning Society.

Brief Contents

PART 4

Compensating and Rewarding Human Resources *279*

PART 5

Meeting Other HR Goals *326*

Contents

CHAPTER 2

The Legal Context for HRM and Creating Safe and Healthy Workplaces *45*

Contents

PART 2

Preparing for and Acquiring Human Resources *83*

Contents

PART 3

Managing Talent   *185*

CHAPTER 6
Training, Learning, and Development   *186*

CHAPTER 7

Managing Employees' Performance   236

PART 4

Compensating and Rewarding Human Resources *279*

Contents

PART 5

Meeting Other HR Goals *326*

CHAPTER 9
Collective Bargaining and Labour Relations *327*

Contents

Preface

Welcome to the fourth Canadian edition of *Human Resource Management.* This book was created to provide you with a focused introduction to HRM in Canada that is rich in content and relevant in its strategic application. The 11 chapters balance theory and practical application, and present the material in a manner that is intended to be engaging as well as thought-provoking.

Whether you are a prospective or current employee, supervisor, manager, entrepreneur, executive, or HR professional, this fourth edition is even more focused on supporting your need for foundational Human Resource Management thought leadership and applied insight necessary to perform and thrive in organizations today.

New to this edition are additional resources designed to bring real-world relevance to the study of human resource management. New **Experiencing HR** in each chapter, provides experiential exercises to encourage students to explore real-world HR topics and situations in both individual and group settings.

Engaging, Focused, and Applied

Managing human resources is a critical component of any company's overall mission to provide value to customers, shareholders, employees, and the communities in which it does business. Value includes not only profits, but also employee growth and engagement, creation of new jobs, protection of the environment, and contributions to community programs. All aspects of human resource management including acquiring, preparing for, developing, and rewarding employees can help organizations meet their competitive challenges, create value, and provide competitive advantages in the global marketplace. In addition, effective human resource management requires being mindful of broader contextual issues such as economic conditions, legal issues, and globalization. Both the media and academic research show that effective human resource management practices result in greater value for stakeholders, including employees. For example, in this edition, you will find a broad range of examples featuring organizations throughout Canada that are leading the way in effective human resource management.

An important feature of this book is that it is rich with examples and provides practical applications. Regardless of the direction of your career aspirations, and whether or not you directly manage other employees now or will in the future, effective human resource management has never been more critical to achieving organizational success as well as personal success and satisfaction. As described in detail in the guided tour of the book, each chapter contains several features that encourage analysis and evaluation of human resource-related situations and applies the chapter concepts.

The author team believes that the engaging, focused, and applied approach distinguishes this book from others that have similar coverage of HR topics. The book has timely coverage of important HR issues, is easy to read, and provides the content, tools, and resources to demonstrate the relevance of HR from the perspective of future and current employees, managers, entrepreneurs, executives, and HR professionals.

Organization of the Fourth Edition

- **Part 1** (Chapters 1–2) discusses several aspects of the human resource environment. To be effective, human resource management must begin with an awareness of the trends and challenges shaping this field, including changes in the workforce, technology, and society as well as the profession of HR itself. Such trends and issues are the topic of *Chapter 1*. On a more detailed level, human resource management must also ensure that the organization's actions comply with and exceed legal requirements in the effort to meet goals such as diversity, protecting employees' human rights, privacy, and health and safety at work—the focus of *Chapter 2*.

- **Part 2** (Chapters 3–5) explores the responsibilities involved in preparing for and acquiring human resources. *Chapter 3* covers the topics of analyzing work and designing jobs. *Chapter 4* explains how to plan for human resource needs and recruit candidates to meet those needs. *Chapter 5* discusses the selection of employees and their placement into jobs or teams.

- In **Part 3** (Chapters 6–7), the discussion turns to managing the organization's talent. *Chapter 6* addresses various ways organizations stimulate learning by training and developing employees to perform their jobs, prepare for future jobs, and help establish career paths that take into account work interests, goals, values, and other career issues. *Chapter 7* describes the various requirements involved in managing performance, including establishing performance expectations, coaching and providing feedback, as well as making performance appraisals effective and meaningful.

- An important element of attracting, retaining, and engaging human resources is rewarding employees for the work performed and accomplishments achieved. **Part 4** (Chapter 8) addresses several topics related to compensation and rewards. *Chapter 8* explores decisions related to the organization's overall pay structure, discusses ways organizations can use pay to recognize individual and group contributions to the organization's performance, considers benefits and services—forms of total compensation other than pay—and looks at how to create a total rewards culture.

- **Part 5** (Chapters 9–11) addresses a number of important HR topics. *Chapter 9* discusses human resource management in organizations where employees have or are seeking union representation. *Chapter 10* explores issues that arise when the organization has people working globally. And *Chapter 11*, the last chapter, addresses HR's role in creating and maintaining high-performance organizations.

MARKET LEADING TECHNOLOGY

Learn without Limits

McGraw-Hill Connect® is an award-winning digital teaching and learning platform that gives students the means to better connect with their coursework, with their instructors, and with the important concepts that they will need to know for success now and in the future. With Connect, instructors can take advantage of McGraw-Hill's trusted content to seamlessly deliver assignments, quizzes, and tests online. McGraw-Hill Connect is a learning platform that continually adapts to each student, delivering precisely what they need, when they need it, so class time is more engaging and effective. Connect makes teaching and learning personal, easy, and proven.

Connect Key Features:

SmartBook®

As the first and only adaptive reading experience, SmartBook is changing the way students read and learn. SmartBook creates a personalized reading experience by highlighting the most important concepts a student needs to learn at that moment in time. As a student engages with SmartBook, the reading experience continuously adapts by highlighting content based on what each student knows and doesn't know. This ensures that he or she is focused on the content needed to close specific knowledge gaps, while it simultaneously promotes long-term learning.

Connect Insight®

Connect Insight is Connect's new one-of-a-kind visual analytics dashboard—now available for instructors—that provides at-a-glance information regarding student performance, which is immediately actionable. By presenting assignment, assessment, and topical performance results together with a time metric that is easily visible for aggregate or individual results, Connect Insight gives instructors the ability to take a just-in-time approach to teaching and learning, which was never before available. Connect Insight presents data that helps instructors improve class performance in a way that is efficient and effective.

Simple Assignment Management

With Connect, creating assignments is easier than ever, so instructors can spend more time teaching and less time managing.

- Assign SmartBook learning modules.
- Instructors can edit existing questions and create their own questions.
- Draw from a variety of text specific questions, resources, and test bank material to assign online.
- Streamline lesson planning, student progress reporting, and assignment grading to make classroom management more efficient than ever.

Smart Grading

When it comes to studying, time is precious. Connect helps students learn more efficiently by providing feedback and practise material when they need it, where they need it.

- Automatically score assignments, giving students immediate feedback on their work and comparisons with correct answers.
- Access and review each response; manually change grades or leave comments for students to review.
- Track individual student performance—by question, assignment, or in relation to the class overall—with detailed grade reports.
- Reinforce classroom concepts with practise tests and instant quizzes.
- Integrate grade reports easily with Learning Management Systems including Blackboard, D2L, and Moodle.

Instructor Library

The Connect Instructor Library is a repository for additional resources to improve student engagement in and out of the class. It provides all the critical resources instructors need to build their course.

- Access instructor resources.
- View assignments and resources created for past sections.
- Post your own resources for students to use.

Instructors' Resources

To ensure maximum consistency with the text material, all of the instructor resources have been prepared by the lead text author, Sandra Steen, making Connect a one-stop shop for quality instructor resources, including:

- **Instructor's Manual:** The Instructor's Manual accurately represents the text's content and supports instructors' needs. Each chapter includes the learning objectives, glossary of key terms, a chapter synopsis, complete lecture outline, and solutions to the end-of-chapter critical thinking questions, cases, and other exercises.
- **Computerized Test Bank:** This flexible and easy to use electronic testing program allows instructors to create tests from book specific items. The Test Bank contains a broad selection of multiple choice, true/false, and essay questions and instructors may add their own questions as well. Each question identifies the relevant page reference and difficulty level. Multiple versions of the test can be created and printed.
- **PowerPoint® Presentations:** These robust presentations offer high quality visuals from the text and highlight key concepts from each chapter to bring key HR concepts to life.
- **Video Presentations:** This video package contains exclusive videos from Canada's leading HR publication, the *HR Reporter*. It is an excellent supplement to lectures and useful for generating in-class discussion. Video summary information and teaching notes have been prepared to accompany the video package and that can be integrated with course planning using the Instructor's Manual.

MANAGER'S HOTSEAT ONLINE

The Manager's HotSeat allows students to watch over 14 real managers apply their years of experience to confront daily issues such as ethics, diversity, teamwork, and the virtual workplace. Students are prompted for their feedback throughout each scenario and then submit a reporting critiquing the manager's choices while defending their own. The Manager's HotSeat is ideal for group or classroom discussion.

CCH CANADIAN BUSINESSWORKS©

Use the tools the professionals use! **CCH Canadian BusinessWorks,©** available on Connect, provides a snapshot of the BusinessWorks information database. This online resource gives students and instructors access to laws, regulations, and developments in all major areas of human resource management, including health and safety, employment standards, and industrial relations.

Acknowledgments

The fourth Canadian edition of *Human Resource Management* represents the efforts of an extraordinary publishing team at McGraw-Hill Ryerson. Kim Brewster, our group product manager, guided the vision for the book, put the team and resources in place, and navigated all the strategic considerations in concert with Tracey Haggert, product developer. For all four editions, Tracey has guided the overall framework, orchestrating and managing the entire writing and review process. Tracey's wisdom, expertise, foresight, enthusiasm, good judgment, and commitment continue to inspire and focus our efforts and outcomes. We also appreciate the expertise and leadership demonstrated by Indu Arora throughout the photo research and permissions process. We could not be more delighted to have Erin Moore return once again as copy editor. Erin's keen eye, keen wit, and articulate good humour define this edition. Thank you to Katherine Strain for composing a compelling and crisp design for the book. Thank you to Cathie Lefebvre, marketing manager, for all of her great work to keep us current and connected to the higher education and learning community. For this edition, we are also very grateful for the contributions of Michelle Saddler, our supervising editor, who guided the production process.

We would also like to extend our sincere appreciation to all of the professors and students who shared their experiences, both teaching from and learning with, this product. Through focus groups, informal reviews, and conversations, their suggestions, insights, and comments helped us develop and shape this new edition.

Features

Each of these features has been designed to take human resource management into the real world—with either a practical exercise, a visit to the Web, a headline news feature, an example of a best practice, innovation, or even an awkward situation in the workplace.

WHAT DO I NEED TO KNOW?

Assurance of learning:

- Learning objectives open each chapter.
- Learning objectives are referenced in the text where the relevant discussion begins.
- The chapter summary is written around the same learning objectives.
- Quizzes and exercises in Connect are tagged to the learning objectives they cover.

WHAT DO I NEED TO KNOW?

After reading this chapter, you should be able to:

LO1	Summarize how the growth in international business activity affects human resource management.
LO2	Identify the factors that most strongly influence HRM in international markets.
LO3	Discuss how differences among countries affect workforce planning at organizations with international operations.
LO4	Describe how companies select and train human resources in a global labour market.
LO5	Discuss challenges related to managing performance and rewarding employees globally.
LO6	Explain how employers prepare employees for international assignments and for their return home.

HR OOPS!

Engages conversations about HR missteps. Discussion questions at the end of most examples encourage analysis of the situation. Examples include: "Hiring Clones," "When a Contractor Isn't a Contractor," and "How to Recruit a Public Outcry."

HR Oops!

Starbucks Brews Up Controversy with "Race Together" Campaign

"Here's a venti caramel macchiato for Jake — and has anyone told you about our 'Race Together' initiative? Uh huh. Uh huh. No, I'm sorry sir. No, it's not because you're bl — No, I just have to give out 30 of these today and —No, you're right, it's stupid and I'm sorry. Oh, your drink is the wrong size? Sorry, I'm just so nervous. . . ." The following is a scenario of an awkward barista-customer exchange during Starbucks' (www.starbucks.ca) controversial 'Race Together' campaign.

Starbucks is well known for its commitment to social responsibility according to Manda Cuthbertson, director of operations and delivery at employer branding firm Blu Ivy Group (www.bluivygroup.com) in Toronto, however, the social campaign that had baristas writing the words, 'Race Together' on customers' cups, was met with skepticism and criticism, particularly on social media. CEO Howard Schultz said the intent of the campaign was to "stimulate conversation, compassion, and actions around race." However, in the wake of the response, senior vice-president for global communication, Corey duBrowa, even temporarily deleted his personal Twitter account. "I felt personally attacked in a cascade of negativity. I got overwhelmed by the volume and tenor of the discussion."

Asking employees to start conversations around core values invited scrutiny around Starbucks own track record of limited diversity of senior leadership and racial diversity. In addition, questions were raised about how baristas were trained and prepared for the conversations. A spokesperson for Starbucks said the CEO "delivered a video through a retail portal to all the company's employees on the initiative, but no formal training" was provided.

Questions

1. Why do you think Starbucks received such harsh criticism for its 'Race Together' campaign?
2. What advice do you have for CEO Howard Schultz about engaging and supporting employees in interactions with customers that extend beyond the usual duties and expectations of their jobs?

Sources: Liz Bernier, "Brewing Up Controversy," *Canadian HR Reporter*, April 20, 2015, p. I, II; Nancy Wartik, "Readers Respond to Starbucks 'Race Together' Initiative," *New York Times*, www.nytimes.com/2015/03/21/business/readers-respond-to-starbucks-race-together-initiative.html?_r=0, March 21, 2015, retrieved May 12, 2015; and Sydney Ember, "What Was Starbucks Thinking? 'Race Together' Campaign Generates Hostile Responses," *The National Post*, March 19, 2015, http://news.nationalpost.com/news/what-was-starbucks-thinking-race-together-campaign-generates-hostile-responses, retrieved May 12, 2015.

DID YOU KNOW?

Shares thought-provoking statistics related to chapter topics. Examples include: "Millenials & Gen X Prefer Praise to Corrective Feedback," "Top Seven Dangers for Young Workers (in B.C.)," and "Telecommuters Viewed as More Productive."

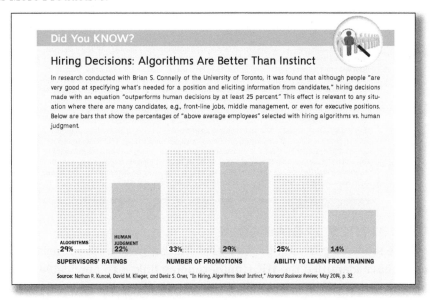

THINKING ETHICALLY

Focused on ethics. The "Thinking Ethically" feature at the end of each chapter offers challenging ethical issues about human resources that require making and validating decisions. Examples include: "Is Social Score Mixing Business and Pleasure?" and "What Boundaries, If Any, Should Employers Set for Social Media?"

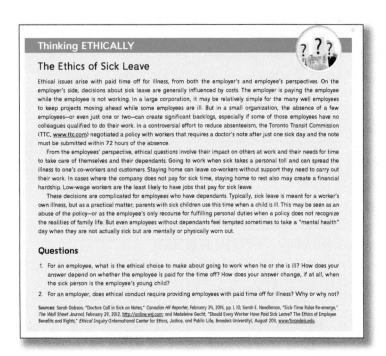

CHAPTER OPENING VIGNETTES

Each chapter opens with a look at events and people in real organizations to encourage critical evaluation and application of each situation to the chapter content.

Measuring Results of TELUS's Work Styles Program

TELUS (www.telus.com) is Canada's second largest telecommunications company with 13.9 million customer connections, and more than $12 billion in annual revenues. TELUS offers a program called *Work Styles* that provides employees the ability to work in the office, at a mobile site, or at home. Sandy McIntosh, VP Human Resources for TELUS Customer Solutions explains the "goal is to have 40 percent of our team members working on a mobile basis, 30 percent working within TELUS buildings, and another 30 percent working from home full time." Benefits of the Work Styles program include increased engagement, productivity, and business results as well as significant cost savings for the company. Andrea Goertz, Chief Communications & Sustainability Officer, explains that at TELUS, employee engagement has gone from 53 percent in 2007 to 83 per cent in 2014—the highest score worldwide for a company of its size and workforce mix—according to global HR organization Aon Hewitt (www.aon.com/canada/). TELUS also reports that the Work Styles program has significant environmental sustainability and organizational benefits including a reduction of more than 5.6 million kg of carbon emissions since the program was implemented in 2010; projected net cash flow savings of $63.5 million over the next 13 years for travel related expenses; as well as projected 20-year net cash flow savings of $166 million for corporate real estate.[1]

CHRP Competency Framework

HRC For those students pursuing the Certified Human Resources Professional (CHRP) designation, we have identified the **HR Competencies** linked to applicable content areas with an HRC icon. The Competency Framework, comprised of 44 discipline specific professional competencies, is the foundation on which the CHRP designation rests. We have followed the Canadian Council of Human Resources Associations' (CCHRA) grouping of nine functional knowledge areas and the HRC references appear in the text as follows:

HRC 1—Strategy

HRC 2—Professional Practice

HRC 3—Engagement

HRC 4—Workforce Planning and Talent Management

HRC 5—Labour and Employee Relations

HRC 6—Total Rewards

HRC 7—Learning and Development

HRC 8—Health, Wellness, and Safe Workplace

HRC 9—Human Resources Metrics, Reporting, and Financial Management

Outcomes of a High-Performance Work System

HRC 2

Consider the practices of steel minimills (which produce steel to make a limited quantity of products for the construction industry). Some minimills have strategies based on keeping their costs below competitors' costs; low costs let them operate at a profit while winning customers with low prices. Other

KEY TERMS

Key terms and definitions appear in the text, so terms are highlighted where they are discussed for easy review and in order to introduce the language of HRM.

company that has a policy of not employing any part-time employees appears to have a policy that can be equally applied to all applicants and existing employees. However, the effect of this policy is not neutral—someone who has family responsibilities would be denied employment or denied the opportunity to reduce their work hours.

direct discrimination
Policies or practices that clearly make a distinction on the basis of a prohibited ground.

indirect discrimination
Policies or practices that appear to be neutral but have an adverse effect on the basis of a prohibited ground.

HR BEST PRACTICES

Real-world examples of what is working well in HRM. Examples include: "Reining in Rising Health Care Costs," "The Forest Products Industry's 'Green Dream Contest,'" and "The YMCA of Greater Toronto: Competency Modelling."

E-HRM

Examples of how technology is used in HR on a daily basis. Each E-HRM feature is highlighted in the chapter and hotlinked as pop-up text when clicked within the ebook. Examples include: "Gamification in HR," "Social Learning," and "Social Networks Can Also be Career Networks."

HR HOW-TO

Specific steps and methods to implement HRM initiatives. This feature provides the context for understanding typical responsibilities of managers and/or human resources professionals. Examples include: "Writing a Job Description," "Aligning Incentive Programs with Company Strategy," and "Supporting Line Management."

CHAPTER SUMMARIES

Recap the "What Do I Need to Know?" objectives from the beginning of each chapter with brief summary discussions.

SUMMARY

LO1 Summarize the elements of work flow analysis and how work flow relates to an organization's structure.

The analysis identifies the amount and quality of a work unit's outputs (products, parts of products, or services). Next, the analyst determines the work processes required to produce the outputs, breaking down tasks into those performed by each person. Finally, the work flow analysis identifies the inputs used to carry out the processes and produce the outputs. Within an organization, units and individuals must cooperate to create outputs, and the organization's structure brings people together for this purpose. The structure may be centralized or decentralized, and people may be grouped according to function or into divisions focusing on particular products or customer groups.

LO2 Discuss the significance, recent trends, and outcomes of job analysis.

Job analysis is the process of getting detailed information about jobs. Job analysis provides a foundation for carrying out many HRM responsibilities. To broaden traditional approaches to job analysis in support of talent management, organizations develop competency models. Because today's workplace requires a high degree of adaptability, job tasks and requirements are subject to constant change. Organizations are also adopting project-based structures and teamwork, which also require flexibility and the ability to handle broad responsibilities. Outcomes of job analysis include job descriptions and job specifications.

EXPERIENCING HR—NEW!

These experiential exercises encourage students to explore real-world HR topics and situations in both individual and group settings.

Experiencing HR

Divide into groups of about six students each. Visit the website for *Canada's Top 100 Employers* (www.canadastop100.com/national/). Scan the complete list of companies, and then choose a company that interests your group. Click the link for the company information. Read the reasons for selecting this company as one of the best, and take notes on what you learn. Next, visit the Glassdoor website (www.glassdoor.ca) and use its search function to look up company information for the company you selected. On the company page, use the Reviews link to read the information employees have posted about what it is like to work at this company. Look for patterns, and take notes on what you learn.

As a group, discuss what these two sources tell you about employee engagement and job satisfaction at the company you selected. What criteria does the Top 100 Employers list use for selecting organizations? What criteria do the reviewers on Glassdoor use for reporting their satisfaction or dissatisfaction? What criteria from this chapter are not mentioned? Imagine you work in HR at the company you evaluated. What would you do to address any dissatisfaction you observe in the Glassdoor reviews? Be prepared to summarize your discussion in class (or, if your instructor directs, write a one-page summary of your discussion).

CRITICAL THINKING QUESTIONS

At the end of each chapter assist in opening conversations and discussions about the concepts in the chapter.

Critical Thinking Questions

1. Why do employees join unions? Did you ever belong to a union? If you did, do you think union membership benefited you? If you did not, do you think a union would have benefited you? Why or why not?

2. Why do managers at most companies prefer that unions not represent their employees? Can unions provide benefits to an employer? Explain.

3. Can highly effective human resource management practices make unions unnecessary? Explain.

4. How has union membership in Canada changed over the past few decades? How does union membership in Canada compare with union membership in other countries? How might these patterns in union membership affect the HR decisions of an international company?

5. What legal responsibilities do employers have regarding unions? What are the legal requirements affecting unions?

6. "Management gets the kind of union it deserves." Discuss.

CASES

In each chapter apply the concepts by looking at companies and how their practices illustrate chapter content. They provide external examples to bring into the classroom, along with questions for assignments or discussion.

Case Study 7.2:

How Google Searches for Performance Measures

If there's one thing Google knows, it's how to use software to wade through massive amounts of data and find what is most relevant. So it should come as no surprise that when the information

---

CRHA CASE

A CRHA Case is also featured. This case was used in Excalibur, the Canadian University Tournament in Human Resources.

CANADIAN HR REPORTER TV VIDEO CASES

At the end of each part, these cases, which are hotlinked within the text, include summaries and challenging questions about current HRM issues. Teaching notes to the video cases are included in the Instructor's Manual.

VIDEO CASES PART 1

Video Case: What CEOs Want from HR Professionals (www.hrreporter.com/students/videodisplay/201-what-ceos-want-from-hr-professionals)

President and CEO of Ricoh Canada, Glenn Laverty suggests that HR has tended to be positioned functionally rather than strategically in most organizations. Although HR has many regulatory and administrative responsibilities, he wants to see HR thinking outside the box and taking the role of strategic partner to the business. Establishing that role at the executive level provides HR the opportunity to establish credibility and create ability to execute for each and every department.

Laverty suggests that HR needs the CEO's assistance to break through the mindset that still exists in some organizations that HR is just a function and work to open up a true partnership relationship for HR with other departments. He says that should begin with HR being present at strategic planning sessions where HR can put forward their strategies and be highly involved in understanding how they can help leaders in the organization accomplish their strategies. This means that HR needs to be at the executive level, at the strategic planning sessions, and recognize what it takes to partner with the organization to achieve the firm's goals.

Questions

1. What competencies do you think HR professionals need to fulfill the expectations this CEO has for HR?
2. Does this role for HR sound like the kind of career you would like to have? Why or Why not?

Source: Based on "What CEOs Want from HR Professionals," *Canadian HR Reporter TV*, November 23, 2011.

Video Case: Competing Human Rights Claims in the Workplace (www.hrreporter.com/videodisplay/367-competing-human-rights-claims-in-the-workplace)

As workplaces become increasingly diverse it becomes inevitable that organizations will face a competing human rights claim. Cherie Robertson, a senior policy analyst at the Ontario Human

---

The Human
Resource Environment

CHAPTER 1

Strategies, Trends, and Challenges in Human Resource Management

WHAT DO I NEED TO KNOW?

After reading this chapter, you should be able to:

LO1	Define human resource management, identify the roles and responsibilities of human resource departments, and explain how HRM contributes to an organization's performance.
LO2	Summarize areas in which human resource management can support organizational strategies.
LO3	Summarize the types of competencies needed for human resource management.
LO4	Explain the role of supervisors and managers in human resource management.
LO5	Describe typical careers in human resource management.
LO6	Describe trends in the labour force composition and how they affect human resource management.
LO7	Discuss the role of high-performance work systems and how technological developments are affecting human resource management.
LO8	Explain how the nature of the employment relationship is changing and how the need for flexibility affects human resource management.

Google has been ranked multiple times as #1 on *Fortune's* "Best Companies to Work For."

Earning a Reputation as a Great Employer

What do Labatt Breweries of Canada (www.labatt.com), George Brown College (www.georgebrown.ca), Manitoba Hydro (www.hydro.mb.ca), the City of Vancouver (www.vancouver.ca), and Google (www.google.ca) have in common? They have all been recently recognized as excellent employers with progressive human resource management practices. The list of employment awards is growing, raising the bar on what it takes to attract, retain, and engage top talent. As labour markets become increasingly competitive, human resources professionals are being called upon to provide people management practices that not only support the organization's priorities but also provide for competitive success in a global marketplace. Organizations strive to create an employment brand that attracts top talent and earns a reputation as a great place to work.

In addition to Mediacorp's "Canada's Top 100 Employers" (www.canadastop100.com), there are several additional annual competitions, including "Canada's Top Employers for Young People," "Canada's Greenest Employers," "Canada's Best Diversity Employers," and "Canada's Top Family-Friendly Employers." Organizations are also considered for regional recognition including "Greater Toronto's Top Employers," "Atlantic Canada's Top Employers," and "Alberta's Top Employers."

Perhaps no organization has received more attention or has a stronger employment brand than Google. Google is known for its people practices and employee-first culture that directly contribute to its success. The work environment provides Googlers free, healthy, gourmet food at all times of the day, lap pools, onsite massages, free fitness classes and gyms, laundry service, and the ability to bring pets to work. Google's "20-percent time" gives employees 20 percent of their day to work on "passion projects they believe will help the company"—and tangible organizational outcomes often result. For example, Gmail came about from one Google employee's 20-percent time efforts. Perhaps it is no surprise that Google receives over one million résumés in a year and is able to attract and retain some of the world's top talent.[1]

L○1 Define human resource management, identify the roles and responsibilities of human resource departments, and explain how HRM contributes to an organization's performance.

Introduction

HRC 1, 2, 3

Organizations of all sizes and in all industries are increasingly recognizing the importance of people. "This is a time of rapid change in the market—a time when Canadian organizations are constantly trying to keep pace and remain competitive. In today's knowledge-based economy, we rely on people to generate, develop, and implement ideas"[2] and the "human resource function has an important role in ensuring that organizations have the people capacity to execute strategic objectives."[3]

Human resource management (HRM), centres on the practices, policies, and systems that influence employees' behaviours, attitudes, and performance. Many companies refer to HRM as "people practices." Figure 1.1 emphasizes there are many important HRM practices that support the organization's business strategy: analyzing work and designing jobs, determining how many employees with specific knowledge and skills are needed (workforce planning), attracting potential employees (recruiting), choosing employees (selection), preparing employees to perform their jobs and for the future (training, learning, and development), supporting their performance (performance management), rewarding employees (total rewards), and creating a positive work environment (employee and labour relations).

FIGURE 1.1

Human Resource Management Practices

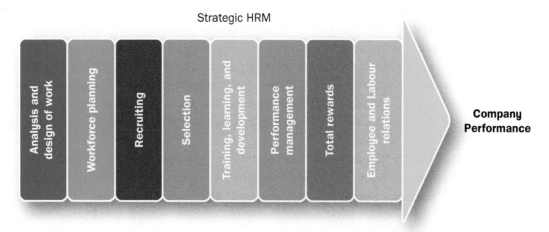

In addition, HRM has responsibility for providing safe and healthy work environments and proactively meeting legal requirements. An organization performs best when all of these practices are managed systemically. At companies with effective HRM, employees and customers tend to be more satisfied, and the companies tend to be more innovative, have greater productivity, and develop a more favourable reputation in the community.[4]

human resource management (HRM)
The practices, policies, and systems that influence employees' behaviours, attitudes, and performance.

In this chapter, we introduce the scope of human resource management, including the ways HRM facilitates and supports organizational strategy. We begin by discussing why human resource management is an essential element of an organization's success. We then turn to the elements of managing human resources: the roles and capabilities needed for effective human resource management. Next, the chapter describes how all managers, not just human resources professionals, participate in the functions and processes of human resource management. We then provide an overview of careers in human resource management and the highlights of practices covered in the remainder of the book. The chapter concludes by discussing a variety of trends and developments that impact HRM.

Why Are People So Valuable?

Managers and economists traditionally have seen human resource management as a necessary expense, rather than as a source of value to their organizations. Economic value is usually associated with *capital*—cash, equipment, technology, and facilities. However, "in the changing corporate environment, more and more organizations are awakening to the importance of human capital as the next competitive advantage."[5] A barrier to business expansion is not only availability of financial capital but also access to talent—that is, human capital. In summary, people are crucial to organizational success and the human and intellectual capital of an organization's workforce provides an opportunity for substantial competitive advantage. "As the 'resident people experts,' HR leaders are ideally suited to advise their organization on the best means for realizing their objectives."[6] Decisions such as whom to hire, what to pay, what training to offer, and how to evaluate employee performance directly affect employees' motivation, engagement, and ability to provide goods and services that customers value. Companies that attempt to increase their competitiveness by investing in new technology and promoting quality throughout the organization also invest in state-of-the-art staffing, training, and compensation practices.[7] These types of practices indicate that employees are viewed as valuable investments.[8]

The concept of "human resource management" implies that employees are *resources* of the employer. As a type of resource, **human capital** means the organization's employees, described in terms of their training, experience, judgment, intelligence, relationships, and insight—the employee characteristics that can add economic value to the organization. In other words, whether it assembles vehicles or forecasts the weather, for an organization to succeed at what it does, it needs employees with certain qualities, such as particular kinds of skills and experience. This view means employees in today's organizations are not interchangeable, easily replaced parts of a system but the source of the company's success or failure. By influencing *who* works for the organization and *how* those people work, human resource management contributes to fundamental measures of an organization's success such as quality, profitability, and customer satisfaction. Figure 1.2 shows this relationship.

human capital
An organization's employees, described in terms of their training, experience, judgment, intelligence, relationships, and insight.

Human resource management is critical to the success of organizations, because human capital has certain qualities that make it valuable. In terms of business strategy, an organization can succeed if it has a *sustainable competitive advantage* (is better than competitors at something, and can hold that advantage over a sustained period of time). Therefore, we can conclude that organizations need the kind of resources that will give them such an advantage. Human resources have these necessary qualities:

● Human resources are *valuable*. High-quality employees provide a needed service as they perform many critical functions.

FIGURE 1.2

Impact of Human Resource Management

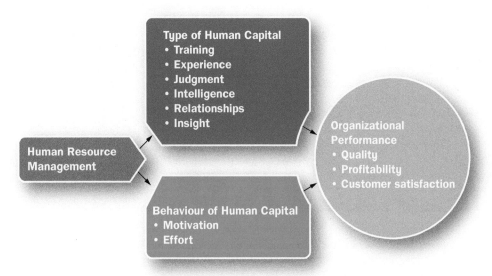

- Human resources are *rare* in the sense that a person with high levels of the needed skills and knowledge is not common. An organization might spend months looking for a talented and experienced manager or technician.

- Human resources *cannot be imitated*. To imitate human resources at a high-performing competitor, you would have to figure out which employees are providing the advantage and how. Then you would have to recruit people who can do precisely the same thing and set up the systems that enable those people to imitate your competitor.

- Human resources have *no good substitutes*. When people are well trained and highly motivated, they learn, develop their abilities, and care about customers. It is difficult to imagine another resource that can match committed and talented employees.

These qualities imply that human resources have enormous potential. As demonstrated in the "Did You Know?" box, an organization realizes this potential through the ways it practises human resource management.

Effective management of human resources can form the foundation of a **high-performance work system**—an organization in which technology, organizational structure, people, and processes all work together to give an organization an advantage in the competitive environment. As technology changes the ways organizations manufacture, transport, communicate, and keep track of information, human resource management must ensure that the organization has the right kinds of people to meet the new challenges. Maintaining a high-performance work system might include development of training programs, recruitment of people with new skill sets, and establishment of rewards for such behaviours as teamwork, flexibility, and learning. Chapter 11 examines high-performance work systems in greater detail.

high-performance work system
An organization in which technology, organizational structure, people, and processes all work together to give an organization an advantage in the competitive environment.

At WestJet (www.westjet.com), a key focus is on keeping employees engaged, motivated, trained, and rewarded effectively. In turn, there is a low turnover rate and a high rate of customer satisfaction.

Engaged and Enabled Employees Deliver Organizational Results

Comparing companies where employees are highly engaged (commitment and discretionary effort) and highly enabled (optimized roles and supportive environment) with low-engagement, low-enablement companies, the HayGroup found significant performance differences.

Revenue Growth

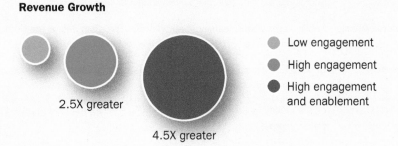

Low engagement

High engagement

High engagement and enablement

2.5X greater

4.5X greater

Source: HayGroup (www.haygroup.com), "Are You Missing Something? Engaging and Enabling Employees for Success," www.haygroup.com/downloads/ca/hay_group_employee_engagement_are_you_missing_something.pdf, retrieved January 5, 2015.

What Are the Responsibilities of HR Departments?

In all but the smallest organizations, a human resource department is responsible for the functions of human resource management. On average, an organization has roughly two full-time HR staff persons for every hundred employees on the payroll.[9] One way to define the responsibilities of HR departments is to think of HR as a business within the organization with three product lines:[10]

1. *Administrative services and transactions*—Handling administrative tasks (for example, processing tuition reimbursement applications and responding to questions about benefits) efficiently and with a commitment to quality. This requires expertise in the particular tasks.

2. *Business partner services*—Developing effective HR systems that help the organization meet its goals for attracting, keeping, and developing people with the skills it needs. For the systems to be effective, HR professionals must understand the business so it can understand what the business needs.

3. *Strategic partner*—Contributing to the company's strategy through an understanding of its existing and needed human resources and ways HR practices can give the company a competitive advantage. For strategic ideas to be effective, HR professionals must understand the business, its industry, and its competitors.

Another way to think of HR responsibilities is in terms of specific activities. Table 1.1 details the responsibilities of human resource departments. These responsibilities include the practices introduced in Figure 1.1 plus additional two areas of accountability that support those practices: (1) establishing and administering human resource policies, ensuring compliance with legal requirements, and implementing and maintaining HR technology, and (2) developing strategy.

TABLE 1.1

Typical Responsibilities of HR Departments

Function	Responsibilities
Analysis and design of work	Workflow analysis; job analysis; job design; job descriptions; job specifications
Workforce planning	Labour demand and supply forecasts; labour surplus and shortage projections; succession planning
Recruitment and selection	Recruiting; testing; screening; interviewing; background checking
Training, learning, and development	Needs assessment; learning methodologies; program design, delivery, and evaluation; career management systems; orientation/onboarding
Performance management	Organizational framework and criteria; goal-setting, appraisal, feedback, and performance improvement tools and processes
Total rewards	Compensation plans; incentive programs; employee benefits and services; pension plans; payroll
Employee and labour relations	Satisfaction and engagement surveys; communications; labour relations
HR polices, compliance, and systems	Policy development and implementation; health and safety; reporting; record keeping; HR information systems
Strategy	Adviser to senior management/board; change management; talent management; human capital metrics and analytics

Source: Based on Canadian Council of Human Resources Associations National Standards for Human Resources Professionals, www.cchra-caarh.ca/en/phaselreport/, retrieved March 22, 2004.

Although the human resource department has responsibility for these areas, many of the requirements are performed by supervisors or others inside or outside the organization. No two human resource departments have precisely the same roles, because of differences in organization size and characteristics of the workforce, the industry, and management's values. In some organizations, the HR department handles all the activities listed in Table 1.1. In others, it may share the roles and duties with managers and supervisors of other departments such as finance, operations, or information technology. In some companies, the HR department actively advises top management. In others, the department responds to top-level management decisions and implements staffing, training, and rewards activities in light of company strategy and policies. When managers and supervisors actively perform a variety of HR activities, the HR department usually retains responsibility for consistency and compliance with all legal requirements.

Let's take an overview of the HR functions and some of the options available for carrying them out. Human resource management involves both the selection of which options to use and the activities related to implementation. Later chapters will explore each function in greater detail.

Analyzing and Designing Jobs

To produce their given product or service (or set of products or services), companies require that a number of tasks be performed. The tasks are grouped in various combinations to form jobs. Ideally, the tasks should be grouped in ways that help the organization to operate efficiently and to obtain people with the right qualifications to do the jobs well. This function involves the activities of job analysis and job design. **Job analysis** is the process of getting detailed information about jobs. **Job design** is the process of defining the way work will be performed and the tasks that a given job requires.

job analysis
The process of getting detailed information about jobs.

job design
The process of defining the way work will be performed and the tasks that a given job requires.

Recruiting and Hiring Employees

Based on job analysis and job design, an organization can determine the kinds of employees it needs. With this knowledge, it carries out the function of recruiting and hiring employees. **Recruitment** is the process through which the organization seeks applicants for potential employment. **Selection** refers to the process by which the organization attempts to identify applicants with the necessary knowledge, skills, abilities, and other characteristics that will help the organization achieve its goals. An organization makes selection decisions in order to add employees to its workforce, as well as to transfer existing employees to new positions.

recruitment
The process through which the organization seeks applicants for potential employment.

selection
The process by which the organization attempts to identify applicants with the necessary knowledge, skills, abilities, and other characteristics that will help the organization achieve its goals.

Approaches to recruiting and selection involve a variety of alternatives. Some organizations may actively recruit from many external sources using job postings on their corporate websites, social media, and campus recruiting events. Other organizations may rely heavily on internal job postings relying upon the availability of current employees with the necessary skills.

At some organizations, the selection process may focus on specific skills, such as experience with a particular technology or type of equipment. At others, selection may focus on general abilities, such as the ability to work as part of a team or find creative solutions. The focus an organization favours will affect many choices, from the way the organization assesses skills, to the questions it asks in interviews, to the sources it uses to attract candidates. Table 1.2 lists the top five skills/qualities that employers say they are looking for in job candidates.

Training, Learning, and Development

Although organizations base hiring decisions on candidates' existing qualifications, most organizations provide ways for their employees to engage in learning to reinforce, broaden or deepen their knowledge,

TABLE 1.2

Top Skills/Qualities Employers Look for in Employees

1. Teamwork skills
2. Verbal communication skills
3. Decision making, problem solving
4. Gathering/processing information
5. Planning, prioritizing tasks

Source: Based on National Association of Colleges and Employers, "Job Outlook: The Candidate Skills/Qualities Employers Want," *Spotlight for Career Services Professionals,* October 2, 2011, www.naceweb.org.

skills, and abilities. To do this, organizations provide for employee training, learning, and development. **Training** is a planned effort to enable employees to learn job-related knowledge, skills, and behaviours. For example, many organizations offer safety training to teach employees safe work habits. **Development** involves acquiring knowledge, skills, and behaviour that improve employees' ability to meet the challenges of a variety of new or existing jobs, including preparing employees to work in diverse work teams. Development programs often focus on preparing employees for management responsibility.

training
A planned effort to enable employees to learn job-related knowledge, skills, and behaviours.

development
The acquisition of knowledge, skills, and behaviours that improve an employee's ability to meet the challenges of a variety of new or existing jobs.

Performance Management

Managing human resources includes assessing how well employees are performing relative to objectives such as job descriptions and goals for a particular position. The process of ensuring that employees' activities and outputs match the organization's goals is called **performance management**. The activities of performance management include specifying the tasks and outcomes of a job that contribute to the organization's success; providing timely feedback and coaching; and comparing the employee's actual performance and behaviours over some time period with the desired performance and behaviours. Often, rewards—the topic of the next section—are developed to encourage good performance.

performance management
The process of ensuring that employees' activities and outputs match the organization's goals.

Total Rewards

The pay and benefits that employees earn play an important role in motivation. This is especially true when rewards such as bonuses are linked to the individual's or team's performance. Decisions about pay and benefits can also support other aspects of an organization's strategy. For example, a company that wants to provide an exceptional level of service or be exceptionally innovative might pay significantly more than competitors in order to attract and keep the best employees. At other companies, a low-cost strategy requires knowledge of industry norms, so that the company does not spend more than market rates of pay for similar positions. Planning pay and benefits involves many decisions, often complex and based on knowledge of a multitude of legal requirements. An important decision is how much to offer in salary or wages, as opposed to bonuses, commissions, and other performance-related pay. Other decisions involve which benefits to offer, from retirement plans to various kinds of insurance to other more intangible rewards such as opportunities for learning and personal growth. All such decisions have implications for the organization's bottom line, as well as for employee motivation.

Administering pay and benefits is another big responsibility. Organizations need systems for keeping track of each employee's earnings and benefits. Employees need information about their health plans, retirement plan, and other benefits. Keeping track of this involves extensive record keeping and reporting to management, employees, and others, while ensuring compliance with all applicable legislation.

Maintaining Positive Employee and Labour Relations

Organizations often depend on human resources professionals to help them identify and perform many of the responsibilities related to providing satisfying and engaging work environments and maintaining positive relations with employees. This function often includes providing for communications to employees including maintaining a website on the organization's intranet. The human resource department can also expect to handle certain kinds of communications from individual employees. Employees turn to the HR department for answers to questions about benefits and company policy. If employees feel they have been discriminated against, see safety hazards, or have other issues and are dissatisfied with their supervisor's response, they may turn to the HR department for help. Members of the department should be prepared to address such issues.

In organizations where employees belong to a union, labour relations entails additional responsibilities. The organization periodically conducts collective bargaining to negotiate an employment contract with union members. The HR department also maintains communication with union representatives to ensure that issues are resolved as they arise.

Establishing and Administering Human Resource Policies

All the human resource activities described so far require fair and consistent decisions, and most require substantial record keeping. Organizations depend on their HR department to help establish policies related to hiring, discipline, promotions, benefits, and the other activities of human resource management. For example, with a policy in place about acceptable use of company-provided vehicles, the company can handle inappropriate vehicle use more fairly and consistently than if it addressed such incidents on a case-by-case basis. The company depends on its HR professionals to help develop and then communicate the policy to every employee, so that everyone knows its importance. Developing fair and effective policies requires strong decision-making skills, the ability to think ethically, and a broad understanding of business activities that will be covered by the policies. Therefore, human resource management requires the ability to communicate through a variety of channels e.g., presentations, social media posts.

Managing and Using Human Resource Data

All aspects of human resource management require careful and discreet record keeping, from screening job applications, to performance appraisals, benefits enrolment, and government-mandated reports. Handling records about employees requires accuracy as well as sensitivity to employee privacy. Whether the organization keeps records in file cabinets or on a sophisticated information system, it must have methods for ensuring accuracy and for balancing privacy concerns with easy accesses for those who need information and are authorized to see it.

Thanks to technology, employee-related information is not just an administrative responsibility; it also can be the basis for knowledge that gives organizations an edge over their competitors. Data about employees can show, for example, which of the company's talent has the most promise for future leadership, what kinds of employees tend to perform best in particular positions, and in which departments the need for hiring will be most pressing. To use the data for answering questions such as these, many organizations have set up human resource information systems with predictive capabilities. They may engage in **human capital analytics**, which is the use of quantitative tools and scientific methods to analyze data from human resource databases and other sources to make evidence-based decisions that support business goals. Later in the chapter, we will take a closer look at how developments in technology are enabling sophisticated analysis of employee data to support decision making.

human capital analytics
The use of quantitative tools and scientific methods to analyze data from human resource databases and other sources to make evidence-based decisions that support business goals.

Ensuring Compliance with Federal and Provincial/Territorial Legislation

As we will discuss in later chapters, especially in Chapter 2, governments have many laws and regulations concerning the treatment of employees. These laws govern such matters as human rights, employment equity, employee safety and health, employee compensation and benefits, and employee privacy. Most managers depend on human resources professionals to help them keep up to date and on track with these requirements. Ensuring compliance with laws requires that human resources professionals keep watch over a rapidly changing legal landscape. For example, the increased use of social media by employees and employers suggest that legislation may be needed to protect employee privacy rights. As the age of the workforce increases, as described later in this chapter, the number of cases dealing with age discrimination in layoffs, promotions, and benefits will likely rise. Employers will need to review recruitment practices and performance evaluation systems, revising them if necessary to ensure that they do not discriminate on the basis of age.

Why Focus on Strategy?

HRC 1, 2, 4, 9

At one time, human resource management was primarily an administrative function. The HR department focused on filling out forms and processing paperwork. As more organizations have come to appreciate the significance of highly skilled human resources, many HR departments have taken on a more active role in supporting the organization's strategy. As a result, today's HR professionals need to understand the organization's business operations, project how business trends might affect the business, reinforce positive aspects of the organization's culture, develop talent for present and future needs, craft effective HR strategies, and make a case for them to top management. Evidence for greater involvement in strategy comes from interviews with finance and HR executives who say they are more interested than ever in collaborating to strengthen their companies.[11] Finance leaders can see that employees are a major budget item, so they want to make sure they are getting the best value for that expense. HR leaders, for their part, are learning to appreciate the importance of using quantitative tools to measure performance. For some practical ideas on how to approach human resource management from a strategic perspective, see "HR How-To."

LO2 Summarize areas in which human resource management can support organizational strategies.

An important element of this responsibility is **workforce planning**, identifying the numbers and types of employees the organization will require in order to meet its objectives. Using these estimates, the human resource department helps the organization forecast its needs for hiring, training, and reassigning employees. Planning also may show that the organization will need fewer employees to meet anticipated needs. In that situation, workforce planning includes how to handle or avoid layoffs. Workforce planning provides important information for **talent management**—a systematic, planned effort to train, develop, and engage the performance of highly skilled employees and managers. Approaching these accountabilities in terms of talent management is one way HR professionals are making the link to organizational strategy.

workforce planning
Identifying the numbers and types of employees the organization will require to meet its objectives.

talent management
A systematic, planned effort to train, develop, and engage the performance of highly skilled employees and managers.

HR How-To

Aligning HR with the Organization's Strategy

HR employees often start their careers with a focus on a particular specialty, such as developing training programs or administering payroll. Especially as they move into management roles, they need a broader view of human resource management as supporting the organization's strategy. To think strategically about human resource management, try these ideas:

- Before deciding *how* to complete a project, ask yourself or your team *what* you are supposed to accomplish. For example, don't start with how to present the new benefits package to employees, but with what you want to accomplish by making the presentation. Answering that question might open up new avenues that are more effective and efficient.

- Ask goal-related questions: Where do you envision your team and your company in the next year? The next three years? To meet goals related to human resource management, what in the organization—not just the HR department—would be different?

- In meetings, especially with higher level managers, pay attention to the participants who think strategically. Notice the kinds of questions they ask and the issues they focus on.

- Read about the field of human resources and the industry in which your organization operates. Get involved in professional and industry associations. Keep abreast of the latest research and trends.

- Learn ways to measure the results of human resource management, such as changes in productivity and employee turnover. When communicating with other managers, talk in terms of these results.

- Learn about your own organization's strategy; pay close attention to goals expressed by other managers. For example, when change is afoot in any part of the organization, it will affect the organization's people. Think about how the HR department can support the change—say, by assessing employees' attitudes, communicating with and training employees, and hiring the right talent for new kinds of work. Help the organization anticipate these issues and incorporate them into the plan for the change.

- Seek out work assignments and volunteer opportunities that include planning for an organization's future. These roles offer practical experience in thinking strategically.

Sources: Eric Krell, "Change Within," *HR Magazine,* August 2011, pp. 43–50; Jill Fowler and Jeanette Savage, "Ask 'What,' Not 'How,'" *HR Magazine,* August 2011, pp. 85–86.

As part of its strategic role, one of the key contributions HR can make is to engage in evidence-based HR. **Evidence-based HR** refers to demonstrating that human resource practices have a positive influence on the company's profits or key stakeholders (employees, customers, community, shareholders). This practice helps show that the resources invested in HR programs is justified and that HR is contributing to the company's goals and objectives. For example, data collected on the relationship between HR practices and productivity, turnover, workplace injuries, and employee engagement may show that HR functions are as important to the business as finance, accounting, and marketing.

evidence-based HR
Collecting and using data to show that human resource practices have a positive influence on the company's bottom line or key stakeholders.

Often, an organization's strategy requires some type of change—for example, adding, moving, or closing facilities, applying new technology, or entering markets in other regions or countries. Common reactions to change include fear, anger, and confusion. The organization may turn to its human resource department for help in managing the change process. Skilled human resources professionals can apply knowledge of human behaviour, along with performance management tools, to help the organization manage change constructively.

Another strategic challenge tackled by a growing number of companies is how to seek profits in ways that communities, customers, and suppliers will support over the long run. This concern is called **sustainability**—broadly defined as an organization's ability to profit without depleting its resources, including employees, natural resources, and the support of the surrounding community. Success at sustainability comes from meeting the needs of the organization's **stakeholders**, all the parties that have an interest in the company's success. Typically, an organization's stakeholders include shareholders, the community, customers, and employees. Sustainable organizations meet their needs by minimizing their environmental impact, providing high-quality products and services, ensuring workplace health and safety, offering fair compensation, and delivering an adequate return to investors. Sustainability delivers a strategic advantage when it boosts the organization's image with customers, opens access to new markets, and helps attract and retain talented employees. In an organization with a sustainable strategy, HR departments focus on employee development and empowerment rather than short-term costs, on long-term planning rather than smooth turnover and outsourcing, and on justice and fairness over short-term profits.[12] At IBM (www.ibm.com/ca/en), human resource management sustainably addresses the company's global presence and drive for innovation in several ways. Diversity training helps people work productively in teams regardless of ethnicity, gender, or other differences. Global Enablement Teams address employee development needs in various regions by sending employees from highly developed nations to mentor employees in developing nations; the mentors teach business skills while learning about these high-potential markets. IBM's *Smarter Planet* projects to lower resource use and pollution attract talented innovators; job candidates are excited about the chance to be part of this effort.[13]

sustainability
An organization's ability to profit without depleting its resources, including employees, natural resources, and the support of the surrounding community.

stakeholders
The parties with an interest in the company's success (typically, shareholders, the community, customers, and employees).

Productivity Improvement

To compete in today's global economy, companies need to enhance productivity. The relationship between an organization's outputs (products, information, or services) and its inputs (e.g., people, facilities, equipment, data, and materials) is referred to as **productivity**. Canada's record of productivity growth has underperformed the United States over the past two decades. The Conference Board of Canada reported noteworthy results of a productivity model simulation to establish how much better off Canada would be if its labour productivity growth had kept up with the United States during the past 20 years. The simulation revealed that if Canada's productivity had kept pace with the United States, per capita personal disposable income would have been $7,500 higher, corporate profits would have been 40 percent higher, and federal government revenues would have been more than 30 percent higher.[14] This productivity gap between Canada and the United States also threatens Canada's ability to compete globally.

productivity
The relationship between an organization's outputs (products, information, or services) and its inputs (e.g., people, facilities, equipment, data, and materials).

Expanding Into Global Markets

Companies are finding that to survive and prosper they must compete in international markets as well as fend off foreign competitors' attempts to gain ground in Canada. To meet these challenges, Canadian businesses must develop global markets, keep up with competition from overseas, hire from an international labour pool, and prepare employees for global assignments.

Companies that are successful and widely admired not only operate on a multinational scale, but also have workforces and corporate cultures that reflect their global markets. McDonald's (www.mcdonalds.ca) opened 165 stores in China in 2010 and laid plans to open 1,000 more. In support of that strategy, McDonald's built a new Hamburger University near Shanghai. The Shanghai Hamburger University will train future Chinese managers in store operations, leadership, and staff management.[15]

The Global Workforce

For today's and tomorrow's employers, talent comes from a global workforce. Organizations with international operations hire at least some of their employees in the foreign countries where they operate. And even small businesses that stick close to home hire qualified candidates who are immigrants to Canada. For an organization to operate in other countries, its HR practices must take into consideration differences in culture and business practices.

Even hiring at home may involve selection of employees from other countries. The 21st century, like the beginning of the previous century, have been years of significant immigration. Figure 1.3 shows the distribution of immigration by continent of origin. Canada's foreign-born population accounts for one in five of Canada's total population—the highest proportion in almost a century.[16] The impact of immigration is especially significant in some regions of Canada. The vast majority of the foreign-born population lives in Ontario, British Columbia, Quebec, and Alberta—most live in Toronto, Montreal, and Vancouver.[17] Statistics Canada projects that by 2031, nearly one-half (46 percent) of Canadians aged 15 and over will be foreign-born or have at least one foreign-born parent.[18]

Because of declining population and labour shortages predicted for the future, employers will increasingly turn to immigrants to fill available job openings. For example, a growing number of employers in tight labour markets such as Nova Scotia, Saskatchewan, Newfoundland and Labrador, New Brunswick, and Prince Edward Island have undertaken recruiting efforts in recession-battered Ireland.[19]

FIGURE 1.3

Where Do Immigrants (Permanent Residents) to Canada Come From? (2012)

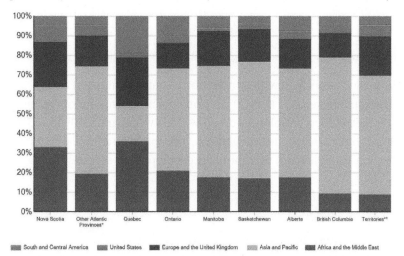

Source: Facts and Figures 2012, Immigration Overview, Permanent and Temporary Residents, Government of Canada, Figure, Permanent Residents by Province or Territory and Source Area, 2012, page 38, http://publications.gc.ca/collections/collection_2013/cic/Cil-8-2012-eng.pdf. Reproduced with permission from Citizenship and Immigration Canada.

International Assignments

Besides hiring an international workforce, organizations must be prepared to send employees to other countries. This requires HR expertise in selecting employees for international assignments and preparing them for those assignments. Employees who take assignments in other countries are called **expatriates**.

expatriates
Employees who take assignments in other countries.

Canadian companies must prepare employees to work in other countries. Canadian companies must carefully select employees to work abroad on the basis of their ability to understand and respect the cultural and business norms of the host country. Qualified candidates also need language skills and technical ability. In Chapter 10, we discuss practices for training employees to understand other cultures.

Outsourcing

Many organizations are increasingly outsourcing and offshoring business activities. **Outsourcing** refers to the practice of having another company (a vendor, third-party provider, or consultant) provide services. For instance, a manufacturing company might outsource its accounting and transportation functions to businesses that specialize in these activities. Outsourcing gives the company access to in-depth expertise and is often more economical as well. In addition to manufacturing, software development and support, as well as call centre operations are other functions typically considered for outsourcing. **Offshoring**, on the other hand, refers to setting up a business enterprise in another country, for example, setting up a factory in China to manufacture products at less cost than in Canada. Increasingly, organizations are *offshore outsourcing*, that is, the company providing outsourced services is located in another country rather than the organization's home country. For example, The Portables (www.theportables.com), a trade-show display and exhibits maker based in Richmond, B.C., have increased annual sales dramatically since starting its use of offshore outsourcing. Hanif Mulijinai, president and CEO, says offshore outsourcing was never the plan for his company. "But we find with some of the newer products, it's a lot easier to get some of the products manufactured in China. It's a lot quicker and less expensive," he says. "Some of the quality of the work they do is very scary, it's so good."[20]

outsourcing
The practice of having another company (a vendor, third-party provider, or consultant) provide services.

offshoring
Setting up a business enterprise in another country (e.g., building a factory in China).

Not only do HR departments help with a transition to outsourcing, but many HR functions are being outsourced. Benefits Canada reports that 59 percent of Canadian employers outsourced some or all HR services and another 10 percent plan to do so within two years.[21] HR functions being outsourced are increasingly expanding from benefits, pension, and payroll administration to including recruiting, relocation, absence management, learning and development, succession planning, and workforce analysis.[22]

Mergers and Acquisitions

Often, organizations join forces through mergers (two companies becoming one) and acquisitions (one company buying another). These deals do not always meet expectations, and often failures may be due to "people issues." Recognizing this, some companies now heavily weigh the other organization's culture before they embark on a merger or acquisition. HRM should have a significant role in carrying out a merger or acquisition. Differences between the businesses involved in the deal make conflict inevitable. Training efforts should therefore include development of skills in conflict resolution. Also, HR professionals have to sort out differences in the two companies' practices with regard to rewards, performance management, and other HR systems. Settling on a consistent structure to meet the combined organization's goals may help to bring employees together. HR's role in engaging top talent and keeping them on board with challenging opportunities following a merger or acquisition will be explored further in Chapter 11.

LO3 Summarize the types of competencies needed for human resource management.

What Competencies Do HR Professionals Need?

HRC2

With such varied responsibilities, human resources professionals need to bring together a large pool of competencies. These competencies fall into the six basic groupings shown in Figure 1.4. Members of the HR department need to be:

1. *Credible activists*—are so well-respected in the organization that they can influence the positions taken by managers. HR professionals who are competent in this area have the most influence over the organization's success, but to build this competency, they have to gain credibility by mastering all the others.

2. *Cultural and change steward*—understands the organization's culture and helps to build and strengthen or change that culture by identifying and expressing its values through words and actions.

3. *Talent manager/organizational designer*—knows the ways that people join the organization and move to different positions within it. To do this effectively requires knowledge of how the organization is structured and how that structure might be adjusted to help it meet its goals for developing and using employees' talents.

4. *Strategic architect*—requires awareness of business trends and an understanding of how they might affect the business, as well as opportunities and threats they might present. A person with this capability spots ways effective management of human resources can help the company seize opportunities and confront threats to the business.

5. *Business allies*—know how the organization achieves its success, who its customers are, and why customers support what the company provides.

6. *Operational executors*—at the most basic level carry out particular HR functions such as handling the selection, training, or compensation of employees and communicating through a variety of media. All of the other HR skills require some ability as operational executor, because this is the level at which policies and transactions deliver results by legally, ethically, and efficiently acquiring, developing, motivating, and deploying human resources.

All of these competencies require interpersonal skills. Successful HR professionals must be able to share information, build relationships, and influence persons inside and outside the organization. See the numbered HRC icons (Human Resource Competency) throughout the book to see how the content links to the nine areas of expertise identified in the Canadian Council of Human Resources Associations' (CCHRA) Competency Framework.

FIGURE 1.4

Six Competencies for the HR Profession

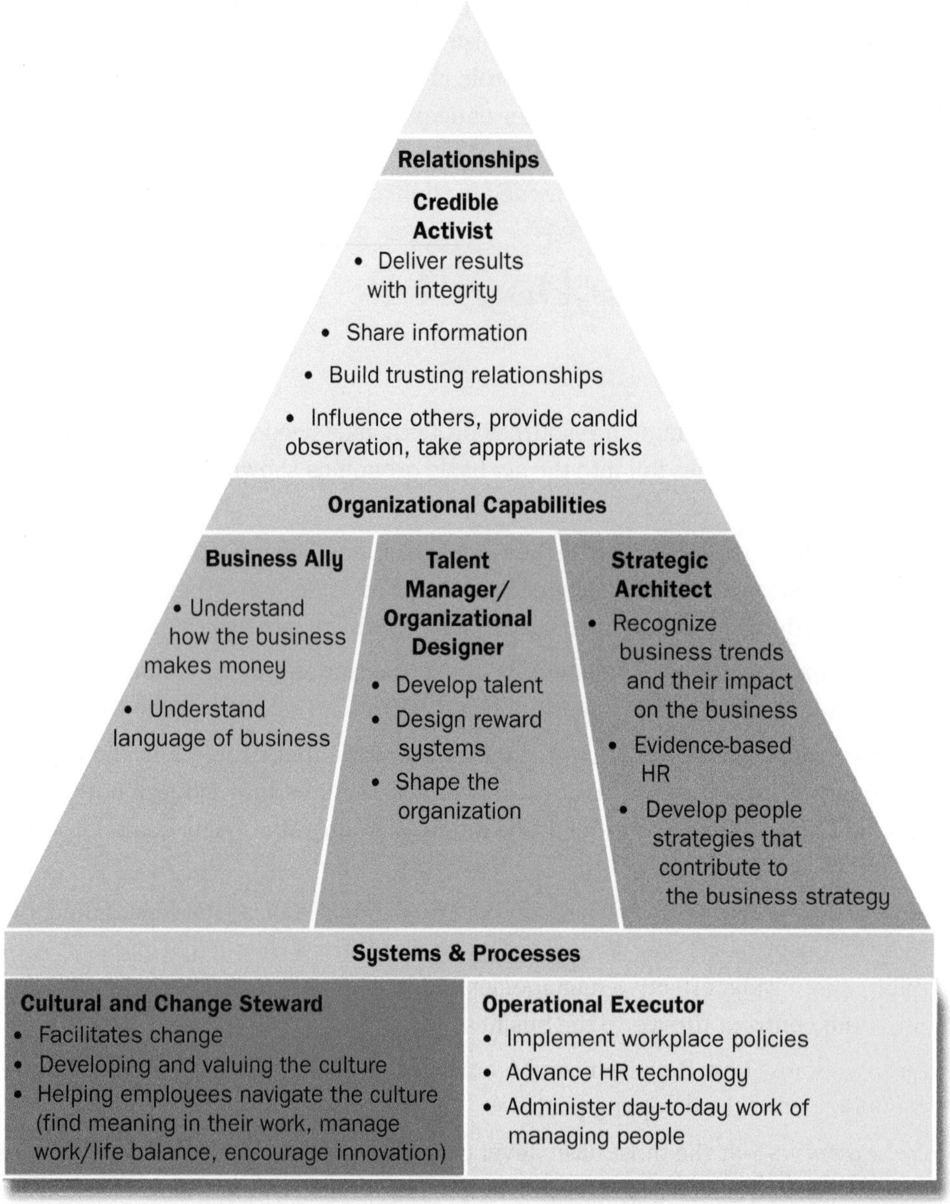

Relationships

Credible Activist
• Deliver results with integrity
• Share information
• Build trusting relationships
• Influence others, provide candid observation, take appropriate risks

Organizational Capabilities

Business Ally
• Understand how the business makes money
• Understand language of business

Talent Manager/ Organizational Designer
• Develop talent
• Design reward systems
• Shape the organization

Strategic Architect
• Recognize business trends and their impact on the business
• Evidence-based HR
• Develop people strategies that contribute to the business strategy

Systems & Processes

Cultural and Change Steward
• Facilitates change
• Developing and valuing the culture
• Helping employees navigate the culture (find meaning in their work, manage work/life balance, encourage innovation)

Operational Executor
• Implement workplace policies
• Advance HR technology
• Administer day-to-day work of managing people

Sources: Based on R. Grossman, "New Competencies for HR," *HR Magazine* (June 2007): pp. 58–62; D. Ulrich, W. Bruckbank, D. Johnson, K. Sandholtz, and J. Younger, "HR Competencies; Mastery at the Intersection of People and Business" (Alexandria, VA: Society for Human Resource Management +/RBL Group, 2008).

Ethics in Human Resource Management

HRC 2

Whenever people's actions affect one another, ethical issues arise, and business decisions are no exception. **Ethics** refers to fundamental principles of right and wrong; ethical behaviour is behaviour that is consistent with those principles. Business decisions, including HRM decisions, should be ethical, but the evidence suggests that is not always what happens. Recent surveys indicate that the general public and managers do not have positive perceptions of the ethical conduct of businesses. For example, in a Gallup poll on honesty and ethics in 21 professions, only 12 percent of respondents rated business executives high or very high; close to twice as many rated them low or very low. And within organizations, a recent survey of workers found that 45 percent had witnessed some form of unethical conduct at their workplace.[23]

ethics
The fundamental principles of right and wrong.

The "HR Best Practices" box provides the Code of Ethics for the Canadian Council of Human Resources Associations (CCHRA) that identifies standards for professional and ethical conduct of HR practitioners. For human resource practices to be considered ethical, they must satisfy the three basic

HR Best Practices

CCHRA's National Code of Ethics

1. *Preamble.* As HR practitioners in the following categories:
   - Certified Human Resources Professionals
   - CHRP Candidates, or
   - CHRP Exam Registrants,

   We commit to abide by all requirements of the Code of Ethics of the Canadian Council of Human Resources Associations (CCHRA), as listed in this document. (Where provincial codes are legislated, those will prevail.)

2. *Competence.* Maintain competence in carrying out professional responsibilities and provide services in an honest and diligent manner. Ensure that activities engaged in are within the limits of one's knowledge, experience, and skill. When providing services outside one's level of competence, or the profession, the necessary assistance must be sought so as not to compromise professional responsibility.

3. *Legal requirements.* Adhere to any statutory acts, regulation, or by-laws which relate to the field of human resources management, as well as all civil and criminal laws, regulations, and statutes that apply in one's jurisdiction. Not knowingly or otherwise engage in or condone any activity or attempt to circumvent the clear intention of the law.

4. *Dignity in the workplace.* Support, promote and apply the principles of human rights, equity, dignity and respect in the workplace, within the profession, and in society as a whole.

5. *Balancing interests.* Strive to balance organizational and employee needs and interests in the practice of the profession.

6. *Confidentiality.* Hold in strict confidence all confidential information acquired in the course of the performance of one's duties, and not divulge confidential information unless required by law and/or where serious harm is imminent.

7. *Conflict of interest.* Either avoid or disclose a potential conflict of interest that might influence or might be perceived to influence personal actions or judgments.

8. *Professional growth and support of other professionals.* Maintain personal and professional growth in human resources management by engaging in activities that enhance the credibility and value of the profession.

9. *Enforcement.* The Canadian Council of Human Resources Associations works collaboratively with its Member Associations to develop and enforce high standards of ethical practice among all its members.

Source: © Reproduced with permission by the Canadian Council of Human Resources Associations. www.chrp.ca/?page=Code_of_Ethics, retrieved January 21, 2015.

standards summarized in Figure 1.5.[24] First, HRM practices must result in the greatest good for the greatest number of people. Second, HRM practices must respect legal requirements including human rights and privacy. Third, managers must treat employees and customers equitably and fairly. To explore how ethical principles apply to a variety of decisions, we will highlight ethical dilemmas in HRM practices throughout the book.

Closely related to the discussion of ethics and ethical practices is HR's role in organizational values including sustainability. For example, "there is increasing evidence that interest in environmental issues is motivating people's behaviour as consumers, employees and jobseekers."[25] In Chapter 11, we will explore this subject in more depth including a discussion of how greener firms may have an edge in their ability to attract, retain, and engage top talent.

L○4 Explain the role of supervisors and managers in human resource management.

What Are the HR Responsibilities of Supervisors and Managers?

Although many organizations have human resource departments with specialists responsible for developing effective HR practices, *implementation* of these practices ultimately resides with the organization's supervisors and managers.

Figure 1.6 shows some HR responsibilities that supervisors and managers are likely to have. Organizations depend on supervisors to help them determine what kinds of work need to be done (job analysis and design) and in what quantities (workforce planning). Supervisors and managers typically interview job candidates and participate in the decisions about which candidates to hire. Many organizations expect supervisors to train employees in some or all aspects of the employees'

FIGURE 1.5

Standards for Identifying Ethical Practices

FIGURE 1.6

Typical Areas of Involvement of Supervisors and Managers in HRM

jobs. Supervisors work with employees to set goals, provide performance feedback, appraise performance, and may recommend pay increases. And, of course, supervisors and managers play a key role in employee relations, because they are most often the voice of management for their employees, representing the company on a day-to-day basis. In all of these activities, supervisors and managers can participate in HRM by taking into consideration how decisions and policies will affect their employees. Understanding the principles of communication, motivation, and other elements of human behaviour can help supervisors and managers engage and inspire the best from the organization's human resources.

LO5 Describe typical careers in human resource management.

Careers in Human Resource Management

HRC 1, 2

There are many different types of jobs in the HRM profession. Figure 1.7 shows selected HRM positions and their median salaries and bonuses. The salaries vary according to education and experience, as well as the type of industry in which the person works.

As you can see from Figure 1.7, some positions involve work in specialized areas of HRM such as recruiting, training, or compensation. Other positions call for generalists to perform a full range of HRM activities, including recruiting, training, compensation, and employee relations. The vast majority of HRM professionals have a university or college degree, and many also have completed postgraduate work. The typical field of study is business (especially human resources or industrial relations), but some HRM professionals have degrees in the social sciences (economics or psychology), the humanities, and law programs. Those who have completed graduate work have master's degrees in HR management, business management, or a similar field. This is important because to be successful in HR, you need to speak the same language as people in the other business functions. You have to have credibility as a business leader, so you must be able to understand finance and to build a business case for HR activities. Many recent entrants have a university degree or college diploma.

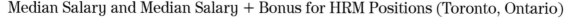

FIGURE 1.7

Median Salary and Median Salary + Bonus for HRM Positions (Toronto, Ontario)

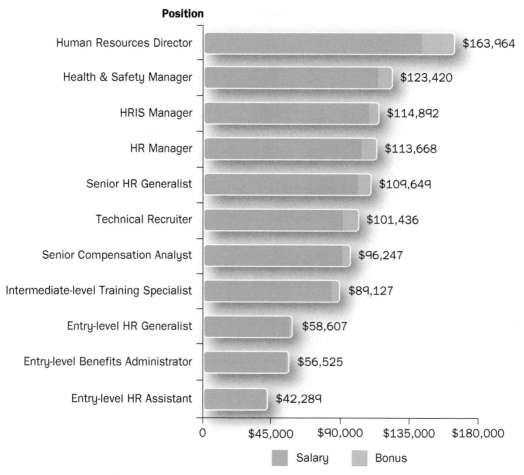

Source: Data from Salary Wizard Canada, Salary.com, http://swz.salary.com/CanadaSalaryWizard/layoutscripts/cswzl_newsearch.aspx, retrieved January 7, 2015.

CHRP Designation

The CHRP (Certified Human Resources Professional) designation is the national designation that recognizes achievement and capability. In Canada, the CHRP designation is guided by the Canadian Council of Human Resources Associations (CCHRA)—a national federation with representatives from human resources associations across Canada. Candidates for certification require specific educational requirements (a minimum of a bachelor's degree in any discipline), assessed proficiency in human resources knowledge—National Knowledge Exam® (NKE), professional experience (three or more years), as well as membership in a provincial HR Association. In Ontario, the Human Resources Professionals Association (HRPA) works independently and has recently established a tiered certification framework that includes two additional designations for HR professionals in addition to the CHRP—CHRL (Certified Human Resources Leader) and CHRE (Certified Human Resources Executive).[26]

The HRPA recently engaged PayScale (www.payscale.com/hr), a global company that creates compensation profiles, to examine the relationship between pay levels and career trajectories for HR professionals with a CHRP designation compared to HR professionals without a CHRP. In addition to overall higher levels for pay for HR professionals with the CHRP designation, the resulting report concluded that

HRPA (Human Resources Professionals Association) regulates the HR profession in Ontario and provides education, information services (such as conferences), seminars, government and media representation, online services, and publications such as *HR Professional*.

professionals with the CHRP designation are "promoted more frequently and move into higher positions more than those without a CHRP."[27] See Figure 1.8.

How Is the Labour Force Changing?

HRC4

The *labour force* is a general way to refer to all the people willing and able to work. For an organization, the **internal labour force** consists of the organization's workers—its employees and the people who work

FIGURE 1.8

With CHRP & Without CHRP: Percentage Receiving Promotions Within Five Years

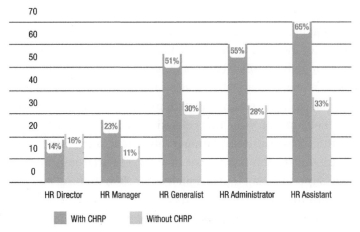

Source: "The 2013 Market Value of CHRP Certification," PayScale, http://resources.payscale.com/rs/payscale/images/research_PayScale-CHRP-market-value.pdf, retrieved January 10, 2015.

Adrian Joseph (in photo), a Sri Lankan immigrant with a strong financial and accounting background lacked Canadian work experience but was hired as CFO (chief financial officer) by Toronto's Steam Whistle Brewing (www.steamwhistle.ca) only three weeks after his arrival in Canada.

at the organization. This internal labour force is drawn from the organization's **external labour market**, that is, individuals who are actively seeking employment. The number and kinds of people in the external labour market determine the kinds of human resources available to an organization (and their cost). Human resources professionals need to be aware of trends in the composition of the external labour market, because these trends affect the organization's options for creating a well-skilled, motivated internal labour force.

internal labour force
An organization's workers (its employees and the people who work at the organization).

external labour market
Individuals who are actively seeking employment.

L○6 Describe trends in the labour force composition and how they affect human resource management.

An Aging Workforce

Canada's population and its labour force are aging. The only age group growing in numbers between 2014 and 2033 is the 55+ age group. The 25- to 54-year-old group will decrease as a proportion of the total population, so its share of the total workforce will fall. And young workers, between the ages of 15 and 24 will also be proportionately smaller. This combination of trends will cause the overall workforce to age. Figure 1.9 shows the change in age distribution from Canada's actual 2014 population to Statistics Canada's 2033 projection (using a medium growth projection). Human resources professionals will therefore spend much of their time on concerns related to creating a work environment that supports the needs of a multigenerational workforce, planning retirement, and reskilling workers. Organizations will struggle with ways to control the rising cost of health-related and other benefits, and many of tomorrow's managers will supervise employees much older than themselves. At the same time, organizations will have to find ways to attract, retain, and prepare the younger generations in the workforce.

Today's older generation includes many people who are in no hurry to retire. They may enjoy making a contribution at work, have ambitious plans for which they want to earn money, or simply be among

FIGURE 1.9

Age Distribution of the Canadian Population 2014 (Actual) and Projected 2033 (Medium Growth Scenario)

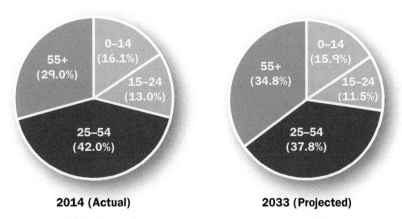

2014 (Actual)   2033 (Projected)

Note: Percentages may not add up to 100 due to rounding

Source: Data from Statistics Canada website, "Population by Sex and Age Group," www.statcan.gc.ca/tables-tableaux/sum-som/l0l/cst0l/demol0a-eng.htm, and "Projected Population by Age Group According to Three Projection Scenarios," www.statcan.gc.ca/tables-tableaux/sum-som/l0l/cst0l/demo08c-eng.htm, retrieved January 7, 2015.

the many who have inadequate savings for full retirement. More older workers are asking to work part-time or for only a few months at a time as a way to transition to full retirement.

With older workers continuing to hold jobs at least part-time, today's workplaces often bring together employees representing three or even four generations. This creates a need for understanding the values and work habits that tend to characterize each generation.[28] For example, members of the silent generation (born between 1925 and 1945) tend to value income and employment security and avoid challenging authority. Baby boomers (born between 1946 and 1964) tend to value unexpected rewards, opportunities for learning, and time with management. Members of Generation X (1965–1980) tend to be pragmatic and cynical, and they have well-developed self-management skills. Those born from 1981 to 1995, often called millennials, or Generation Y, are comfortable with the latest technology, and they want to be noticed, respected, and involved. Some say millennials work to live, while baby boomers live to work. Some generational differences can be addressed through effective human resource management. For example, organizations train managers to provide frequent feedback to members of Generation Y, and they show respect for older generations' hard work and respect for authority by asking them to mentor younger workers.

A Diverse Workforce

Another change affecting the Canadian population and labour force is that it is growing more diverse. More than 200 ethnic groups were reported in the 2011 National Household Survey, conducted by Statistics Canada. According to a recent study by the Association for Canadian Studies, 80 percent of Canadians aged 18 to 24 describe their school or workplace as ethnically diverse. Jack Jedwab, the association's executive director says this diversity is helping to make Canadians among the world's most tolerant people. The four-country survey also reveals that "the more diverse your workplace or school, the more accepting you will be of diversity in other areas of life, like the friends you choose and the neighbourhood you live in."[29]

"I think the main difference between us and some other Canadian companies is that when we look at a résumé, first of all we don't put Canadian experience as a criteria," says Cam Heaps, Steam Whistle co-founder. "We don't discredit or put a lower value on a new Canadian's résumé because their experience might have been outside of the country. Actually, we might put a bit of a premium on it because if anything it brings a fresh perspective. You're tapping into a whole other strategy experience when you bring people in from different regions."[30]

Employment equity is now recognized as an effective Canadian tool for efficient use of skilled human resources—and is increasingly borrowed by many industrialized countries. The four designated groups under the federal Employment Equity Act (women, Aboriginal peoples, persons with disabilities, and members of visible minorities) represent a strategic resource in Canada's labour force. Employment equity considerations will be discussed in more detail in Chapter 2.

New data from Statistics Canada show that more than 1.4 million people in Canada report having an Aboriginal identity (4.3 percent of the total Canadian population). The Aboriginal population is young— 28 percent of the total Aboriginal population are children under the age of 15 years, in contrast with 16.5 percent of the non-Aboriginal population,[31] thus providing opportunities for a significant source of skilled workers for the future. Persons with disabilities comprise a productive but historically overlooked sector of the workforce. Some persons with disabilities require accommodation on the job to be effective; however, more often than not, this accommodation can be provided at little or no cost, for example, by providing large print software or arranging the office environment to promote ease of access.[32]

Throughout this book, we will show how diversity affects HRM practices. For example, from a staffing perspective, it is important to ensure that tests used to select employees are objective and unbiased. From the perspective of work design, employees need flexible schedules that allow them to meet non-work needs. In terms of training, learning, and development, it is clear that employees must be made aware of the damage that stereotypes can do. With regard to total rewards, organizations are providing benefits such as child and elder care as a way to accommodate the needs of a diverse workforce.

Skill Deficiencies of the Workforce

The increasing use of computers to do routine tasks has shifted the kinds of skills needed for employees. Such qualities as physical strength and mastery of a particular piece of machinery are no longer important for many jobs. More employers are looking for mathematical, verbal, and interpersonal skills, such as the ability to solve math or other problems or reach decisions as part of a team. Often, when organizations are looking for technical skills, they are looking for skills related to using technology. When employees lack advanced literacy and thinking skills, they may be unable to perform their jobs competently and will experience difficulty adjusting to changes in the workplace.[33] Today's employees must be able to handle a variety of responsibilities, interact with customers, and think creatively.

To find such employees, many organizations are looking for educational achievements. A college diploma, university degree, or skilled trades certificate is a basic requirement for many jobs today. Competition for qualified college, university, and skilled trades graduates in many fields is intense. At the other extreme, workers with less education often have to settle for low-paying jobs. Some companies are unable to find qualified employees and instead rely on training to correct skill deficiencies.[34]

L○7 Discuss the role of high-performance work systems and how technological developments are affecting human resource management.

What Is a High-Performance Work System?

HRC**1**

Human resource management is playing an important role in helping organizations gain and keep an advantage over competitors by becoming high-performance work systems. These are organizations that have the best possible fit between their social system (people and how they interact) and technical system (equipment and processes).[35] As the nature of the workforce and the technology available to organizations have changed, so have the requirements for creating a high-performance work system. Customers are demanding high quality and customized products, employees are seeking flexible work arrangements, and employers are looking for ways to tap people's creativity and interpersonal skills. Such demands require that organizations make full use of their people's knowledge and skill, and skilled human resource management can help organizations do this.

Among the trends that are occurring in today's high-performance work systems are reliance on knowledge workers, employee engagement, the use of teamwork, and the increasing levels of education of the workforce. The following sections describe these four trends. HR professionals who keep up with change are well positioned to help create high-performance work systems. Chapter 11 will further explore the elements and outcomes of a high-performance work system.

Knowledge Workers

To meet their human capital needs, companies are increasingly trying to attract, develop, and retain knowledge workers. **Knowledge workers** are employees whose main contribution to the organization is specialized knowledge, such as knowledge of customers, a process, or a profession. Knowledge workers are especially needed for jobs in health services, business services, social services, engineering, and management.

knowledge workers
Employees whose main contribution to the organization is specialized knowledge, such as knowledge of customers, a process, or a profession.

Knowledge workers are in a position of power, because they own the knowledge that the company needs in order to produce its products and services, and they must share their knowledge and collaborate with others in order for their employer to succeed. An employer cannot simply order these employees to perform tasks. Managers depend on the employees' willingness to share information. Furthermore, skilled knowledge workers have many job opportunities, even in a slow economy. If they choose, they can leave a company and take their knowledge to another employer. Replacing them may be difficult and time-consuming.

Recently, the idea that only some of an organization's workers are knowledge workers has come under criticism.[36] To the critics, this definition is no longer realistic in a day of computerized information systems and computer-controlled production processes. For the company to excel, everyone must know how their work contributes to the organization's success. At the same time, employees—especially younger generations, which grew up with the Internet—will expect to have wide access to information. From this perspective, successful organizations treat *all* their workers as knowledge workers. They let employees know how well the organization is performing, and they invite ideas about how the organization can do better.

Employee Engagement

HRC3

To completely benefit from employees' knowledge, organizations need a management style that focuses on developing and engaging employees. **Employee engagement** refers to the extent that an employee experiences full involvement in one's work and commitment to one's job and organization.

Knowledge workers are employees whose value to their employers stems primarily from what they know. Employees such as the ones pictured here have in-depth knowledge of their profession and are hard to replace because of their special knowledge.

employee engagement
Full involvement in one's work and commitment to one's job and organization.

HRM practices such as performance management, training and development, career management, work design, and employee relations are important for sustaining employee engagement. Engagement is associated with higher productivity, better customer service, and lower turnover.[37]

Jobs must be designed to give employees the necessary latitude for making a variety of decisions. Employees must be properly trained to exert their wider authority and use information resources, as well as tools for communicating information. Employees also need feedback to help them evaluate their success. Pay and other rewards should reflect employees' accountabilities and accomplishments. In addition, for engagement to occur, managers must be trained to link employees to resources within and outside the organization, such as customers, co-workers in other departments, and websites with needed information. Managers must also encourage employees to interact with staff throughout the organization, ensure that employees receive the information they need, and reward collaboration.

As with the need for knowledge workers, employee engagement shifts the recruiting focus away from technical skills and toward general cognitive and interpersonal skills. Employees who have responsibility for a final product or service must be able to listen to customers, adapt to changing needs, and creatively solve a variety of problems. Chapter 11 will explore employee engagement practices and outcomes in more detail.

Teamwork

Modern technology places the information that employees need for improving quality and providing customer service right at the point of sale or production. As a result, the employees engaging in selling and producing must also be able to make decisions about how to do their work. Organizations need to set up work in a way that gives employees the authority and ability to make those decisions. One of the most popular ways to increase employee responsibility and control is to assign work to teams. **Teamwork** is the assignment of work to groups of employees with various skills who interact to assemble a product or provide a service. In some organizations, technology is enabling teamwork even when workers are at different locations at different times. These organizations use *virtual teams*—teams that rely on communications technologies to keep in touch and coordinate activities.

teamwork
The assignment of work to groups of employees with various skills who interact to assemble a product or provide a service.

Increasing Levels of Education

The educational attainment of Canada's population is increasing—31.4 percent of Canada's population 15 years and older had a college or trade certification and 22.2 percent had a university degree. These figures are up from 28.7 and 16.4 percent respectively from 2002, and 22.3 and 11.9 percent in 1992.[38] See Figure 1.10.

FIGURE 1.10

Level of Education, 15 Years of Age and Over (Percent)

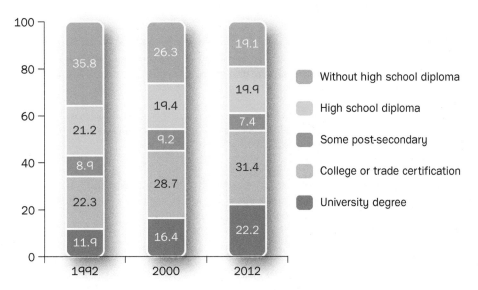

Note: Percentages may not add up to 100 due to rounding

Source: "Learning—Educational Attainment/Indicators of Well-being in Canada, Employment and Social Development Canada, http://well-being.esdc.gc.ca/misme-iowb/.3ndic.1t.4r@-eng.jsp?iid=29#M], retrieved January 9, 2015. HRSDC calculations based on Statistics Canada. Table 282-0004—Labour Force Survey Estimates (LFS), by Educational Attainment, Sex and Age Group, Annual (persons unless otherwise noted), CANSIM (database).

In a survey conducted for a TD Bank Financial Group paper, economists Craig Alexander and Eric Lascalles examined the work of a dozen researchers to discover the rate of return of postsecondary education. The rate of return was calculated using the present value difference between the lifetime earnings of a postsecondary graduate and those of a high-school graduate, factoring in the cost of tuition, academic fees, and lost earnings while students were in school. Annual rates of return for a university degree ranged from 12 percent to 17 percent for men and 16 percent to 20 percent for women; for a college diploma, rates of return were between 15 percent and 28 percent for men, and 18 percent and 28 percent for women.[39]

How Is Technological Change Impacting HRM?

HRC 2

Advances in computer-related technology have had a major impact on the use of information for managing human resources. Large quantities of employee data (including training records, skills, pay rates, and benefits usage and cost) can easily be stored on personal computers and manipulated with user-friendly spreadsheets or statistical software. Often these features are combined in a **human resource information system (HRIS)**, a computer system used to acquire, store, manipulate, analyze, retrieve, and distribute information related to an organization's human resources.[40] An HRIS can support strategic decision making, help the organization avoid lawsuits, provide data for evaluating programs or policies, and support day-to-day HR decisions. Table 1.3 describes some of the technologies that may be included in an organization's HRIS.

human resource information system (HRIS)
A computer system used to acquire, store, manipulate, analyze, retrieve, and distribute information related to an organization's human resources.

TABLE 1.3

New Technologies Influencing HRM

Technology	What It Does	Example
Internet portal	Combines data from several sources into a single site; lets user customize data without programming skills.	A company's manager can track labour costs by work group.
Shared service centres	Consolidate different HR functions into a single location; eliminate redundancy and reduce administrative costs; process all HR transactions at one time.	AlliedSignal combined more than 75 functions, including finance and HR, into a shared service centre.
Cloud computing, such as application service providers (ASP)	Lets companies rent space on a remote computer system and use the system's software to manage its HR activities, including security and upgrades.	KPMG Consulting uses an ASP to host the company's computerized learning program.
Business intelligence	Provides insight into business trends and patterns and helps businesses improve decisions.	Managers use the system to analyze labour costs and productivity among different employee groups.
Data mining	Uses powerful computers to analyze large amounts of data, such as data about employee traits, pay, and performance.	Managers can identify high-potential employees throughout a large organization and offer them development opportunities.

The support of an HRIS can help HR professionals think strategically. As strategies are planned, implemented, and changed, the organization must be constantly prepared to have the right talent in place at all levels. This requires keeping track of an enormous amount of information related to employees' skills, experience, and training needs, as well as the organization's shifting needs for the future. An HRIS can support talent management by integrating data on recruiting, performance management, and training. Integrating the data means, for example, that the HRIS user can see how specific kinds of recruiting, hiring, and training decisions relate to performance success. This helps HR professionals identify how to develop the organization's talent and where to recruit new talent so that an ongoing supply of human resources is available to fill new positions or new openings in existing positions.[41]

Electronic Human Resource Management (E-HRM)

Many HRM activities have moved onto the Internet. Electronic HRM applications let employees enrol in and participate in training programs online. Employees can go online to select from items in a benefits package and enrol in the benefits they choose. They can look up answers to HR-related questions and read company news, perhaps downloading it as a podcast. This processing and transmission of digitized HR information is called **electronic human resource management (E-HRM)**.

electronic human resource management (E-HRM)
The processing and transmission of digitized HR information, especially using computer networking and the Internet.

E-HRM has the potential to change all traditional HRM functions. For example, employees in different geographic areas can work together. Use of the Internet lets companies search for talent without geographic limitations. Recruiting can include online job postings, applications, and candidate screening from the company's website or the websites of companies that specialize in online recruiting, such as Monster (www.monster.ca) or CareerBuilder (www.careerbuilder.ca). Employees from different geographic locations can all receive the same training over the company's computer network.

The Internet and E-HRM are helpful for employees who work outside the office because they can receive and share information online easily. The benefits of products such smartphones is enormous, but is it possible to be too accessible?

Technology trends that are shaping Internet use are also shaping E-HRM. One example is *social networking*. Table 1.4 identifies some ways that creative organizations are applying social networking tools to human resource management.

Another recent technology trend is *cloud computing*, which generally refers to arrangements in which remote server computers do the user's computing tasks. Thus, an organization that once owned a big mainframe computer to process data for payroll and performance data could contract with a service provider to do the data processing on its computer network and make the results available online. Access to cloud computing makes powerful HRIS tools available even to small organizations with limited computer hardware. Some organizations specialize in offering such services. An example is Workday (www.workday.com), which hosts software for human resource management, including workforce planning, job design, analysis of compensation to make sure it is aligned with performance, and assessment of the organization's skills and training needs.[42]

 E-HRM

Gamification in HR—See how organizations are embedding game thinking and game technologies in HR functions to engage employees and potential employees.

Privacy is an important issue in E-HRM. A great deal of HR information is confidential and not suitable for posting on a website for everyone to see. Therefore, E-HRM typically is set up on an *intranet*, which is a network that uses Internet tools but limits access to authorized users in the organization. With any E-HRM application, however, the organization must ensure that it has sufficient security measures in place to protect employees' privacy.

TABLE 1.4

HRM Applications for Social Networking

Application	Purpose
Sites for capturing, sharing, storing knowledge	Preserving knowledge that otherwise could be lost when employees retire
Online surveys to gather employees' opinions	Increasing employees' engagement with the jobs and the organization
Networking tools to create online expert communities	Identifying employee expertise and making it available to those who can apply it
Online discussions, such as commenting tools	Promoting creativity and innovation
Sites where users can post links to articles, webinars, training programs, and other information	Reinforcing lessons learned during training and on-the-job experience
Instant messaging and other communication tools to use with mentors and coaches	Providing employee development through mentoring and coaching
Site where the HR department posts job openings and responds to candidates' questions	Identifying and connecting with promising job candidates

Sources: P. Brotherson, "Social Networks Enhance Employee Learning," *T + D*, April 2011, pp. 18–19; T. Bingham and M. Connor, *The New Social Learning* (Alexandria, VA: American Society for Training and Development, 2010); M. Derven, "Social Networking: A Frame for Development," *T + D*, July 2009, pp. 58–63; M. Weinstein, "Are You Linked In?" *Training*, September/October 2010, pp. 30–33.

Sharing of Human Resource Information

Information technology is changing the way HR departments handle record keeping and information sharing. Today, HR employees use technology to automate much of their work in managing employee records and giving employees access to information and enrolment forms for training, benefits, and other programs. As a result, HR employees play a smaller role in maintaining records, and employees now get information through **self-service**. This means employees have online access to information about HR issues such as training, benefits, rewards, and contracts; go online to enrol themselves in programs and services; and provide feedback through online surveys. Today, employees routinely look up workplace policies and information about their benefits online, and they may receive electronic notification when deposits are made directly to their bank accounts.

self-service
System in which employees have online access to information about HR issues and go online to enrol themselves in programs and provide feedback through surveys.

A growing number of companies are combining employee self-service with *management self-service,* such as the ability to go online to authorize pay increases, approve expenses, and transfer employees to new positions. More sophisticated systems extend management applications to decision making in areas such as compensation and performance management. To further support management decisions, the company may create an *HR dashboard,* or a display of how the company is performing on specific HR metrics, such as productivity and absenteeism. For example, Cisco Systems helps with talent management by displaying on its HR dashboard how many of its people move and why.[43] The data can help management identify divisions where the managers are successfully developing new talent.

In the age of social networking, information sharing has become far more powerful than simply a means of increasing efficiency through self-service. Creative organizations are enabling information sharing online to permit a free flow of knowledge among the organization's people. Essilor International (www.essilor.ca) uses social networking to improve learning in the 40 countries where it makes and sells optometric lens. Trainers share knowledge of what is working best for them: for example, a Thai lens-processing centre came up with a game to teach workers to understand lens shapes and then made it available online.[44]

How Is the Employment Relationship Changing?
HRC3

Trends and developments we have described in this chapter require managers at all levels to make rapid changes in response to new opportunities, competitive challenges, and customer demands. These changes are most likely to succeed in flexible, forward-thinking organizations, and the employees who will thrive in such organizations need to be flexible and open to change as well. In this environment, employers and employees have begun to reshape the employment relationship.[45]

L○8 Explain how the nature of the employment relationship is changing and how the need for flexibility affects human resource management.

A New Psychological Contract

We can think of that relationship in terms of a **psychological contract**, a description of what an employee expects to contribute in an employment relationship and what the employer will provide the employee in exchange for those contributions.[46] Unlike a written sales contract, the psychological contract is not formally put into words. Instead, it describes unspoken expectations that are widely held by employers and employees. In the traditional version of this psychological contract, organizations expected their employees to contribute time, effort, skills, abilities, and loyalty. In return, the organizations would provide job security and opportunities for promotion.

psychological contract
A description of what an employee expects to contribute in an employment relationship and what the employer will provide the employee in exchange for those contributions.

However, this arrangement is being replaced with a new type of psychological contract. Companies expect employees to take more responsibility for their own careers, from seeking training to balancing work and family. These expectations result in less job security for employees, who can count on working for several companies over the course of a career. In exchange for top performance and working longer hours without job security, employees want companies to provide flexible work schedules, comfortable working conditions, more control over how they accomplish work, training and development opportunities, and financial incentives based on how the organization performs. (Figure 1.11 provides a humorous look at an employee who seems to have benefited from this modern psychological contract by obtaining a family friendly work arrangement.) Employees realize that companies cannot provide employment security, so they want *employability*. This means they want their company to provide training and job experiences to help ensure that they can find other employment opportunities.

Flexibility

The new psychological contract largely results from the HRM challenge of building a committed, productive workforce in turbulent economic conditions that offer opportunity for financial success but can also quickly turn sour, making any employee expendable. From the organization's perspective, the key

FIGURE 1.11

A Family-Friendly Work Arrangement

to survival in a fast-changing environment is flexibility. Organizations want to be able to change as fast as customer needs and economic conditions change. Flexibility in human resource management includes flexible staffing levels and flexible work schedules.

Flexible Staffing Levels

A flexible workforce is one the organization can quickly reshape and resize to meet its changing needs. To be able to do this without massive hiring and firing campaigns, organizations are using more **alternative work arrangements**. Alternative work arrangements are methods of staffing other than the traditional hiring of full-time employees. There are a variety of methods, the following being most common:

> **alternative work arrangements**
> Methods of staffing other than the traditional hiring of full-time employees (e.g., use of independent contractors, on-call workers, temporary workers, and contract company workers).

- *Independent contractors* are self-employed individuals with multiple clients.
- *On-call workers* are persons who work for an organization only when they are needed.
- *Temporary workers* are employed by a temporary agency; client organizations pay the agency for the services of these workers.
- *Contract company workers* are employed directly by a company for a specific time specified in a written contract.

More workers are choosing these arrangements, but preferences vary. Most independent contractors and contract workers have this type of arrangement by choice, however as discussed in the "HR Oops!" box,

HR Oops!

When a Contractor Isn't a Contractor

Signing up contract workers instead of having employees can look like a good deal, because the company doesn't have to pay employee benefits like Canada Pension Plan and Employment Insurance (EI) required for employees on the company's payroll. They can also get around laws designed to protect employees such as minimum wages and notice periods to terminate the employment relationship.

Although the classification may be a judgment call in some cases, it's not just a matter of opinion. For example, when La-Z-Boy Canada Ltd. terminated a long-term employee who had been working as an "independent contractor" for the past eight years, the Ontario Court of Appeal considered the individual's career working for La-Z-Boy Canada before being required to incorporate his own company and sign an independent contractor's agreement. In making its decision, the Ontario Court of Appeal considered factors such as: the individual worked exclusively and full-time for La-Z-Boy; La-Z-Boy reviewed his sales; and maintained control over the territory, products sold, and pricing. The Ontario Court of Appeal determined that the individual was an employee, not a contractor and was entitled to notice of termination consistent with his 22 years of employment with La-Z-Boy rather than the 60 days' notice provided in his contractor's agreement.

Questions

1. Why might a company legitimately want to hire contractors rather than employees?
2. Given that employers may not direct the details of when and how contractors do their work, what HR challenges could result from relying on contractors rather than employees?

Source: "Winter 2011: Labour & Employment Update," MacPherson, Leslie & Tyerman LLP, p. l.

incorrectly calling someone a contractor can result in significant issues and liabilities. In contrast, temporary agency workers and on-call workers are likely to prefer traditional full-time employment. With flexible staffing, organizations can more easily modify the number of their employees. Continually adjusting staffing levels is especially cost-effective for an organization that has fluctuating demand for its products and services. And when an organization downsizes by laying off temporary and part-time employees, the damage to morale among permanent full-time workers is likely to be less severe.

Flexible Work Schedules

The globalization of the work economy and the development of e-commerce have made the notion of a 40-hour workweek obsolete. As a result, companies need to be staffed 24 hours a day, seven days a week. Employees in manufacturing environments and call centres are being asked to work 12-hour days or to work afternoon or midnight shifts. Similarly, professional employees face long hours and work demands that spill over into their personal lives.

Thinking ETHICALLY

What Boundaries, If Any, Should Employers Set for Social Media?

As more and more millennials enter the labour force, more of an organization's employees will have grown up with the Internet and social media. These employees are unlikely to comprehend being separated from their mobile devices or Internet access. They expect to be able to send a quick text, post on Twitter or Instagram, or reward themselves with a funny video after wrapping up a report. And as these technologies become mainstream, more of their older colleagues share this attitude.

Employers, in contrast, have tended to greet each new social media application as a new form of time wasting. Organizations are under intense pressure to improve their performance month after month, and the thought of employees checking out photos on Facebook while at work horrifies many managers. In this view, most uses of social media amount to theft of time from employers, not a reasonable break or a valuable way to stay connected to co-workers and customers as well as family and friends.

Recently, the Ethics Resource Center added to managers' discomfort with a study showing that employees categorized as "active social networkers" are much more likely than their co-workers to say they experience pressure to compromise ethical standards. And when asked about ethically questionable actions, such as taking home company software or keeping personal copies of confidential company information for future career use, the active social networkers are more likely to say these actions are acceptable.

Questions

1. How much time on social media is reasonable at work before it becomes time wasting or a theft of the employer's time? Does your answer depend on whether the employee has met his or her goals? Does it depend on how many hours he or she has worked?

2. Why do you think the heavy social media users surveyed by the Ethics Resource Center were more likely than other employees to believe employees are justified in making personal use of company software and confidential data? How would you respond to that attitude if you were a human resources manager?

Sources: Andrew McIlvaine, "The Word for Today Is . . . ," *Human Resource Executive Online*, January 23, 2012, http://blog.hronline.com; Colleen Taylor, "Study: Social Networkers Have More Ethics Problems at Work," *GigaOM*, January 6, 2012, http://gigaom.com; Liz Ryan, "Five Destructive Company HR Policies," *Bloomberg Businessweek*, April 16, 2010, www.businessweek.com; Craig Matsuda, "The Debate over Social Media at the Office," *Entrepreneur*, February 16, 2010, www.entrepreneur.com.

Companies including NetFlix, SurveyMonkey, and Virgin Group have recently simplified their vacation polices to permit salaried staff to "take off whenever they want for as long as they want," in recognition that technology enabled employees work at all hours and everywhere they can receive a business email or text message. As Daniel Jacobson, Netflix's vice-president for engineering, wrote on his website last year, "Netflix does not have an unlimited vacation policy." Rather, the company trusts that everyone will get their work done, and it has no interest in monitoring their hours, either at work or away from the office.[47]

Many organizations are taking steps to provide more flexible work schedules, to protect employees' free time, and to more productively use employees' work time. Workers consider flexible schedules a valuable way to ease the pressures and conflicts of trying to balance work and nonwork activities. Employers are using flexible schedules to recruit and retain employees and to increase satisfaction and productivity.

How Is This Book Organized?

This chapter has provided an overview of human resource management as well as a summary of challenges and trends impacting Canadian organizations, employees, and HR professionals. In this book, the topics are organized according to the broad areas of human resource management shown in Table 1.5. The numbers in the table refer to the part and chapter numbers.

Along with examples highlighting how HRM helps a company maintain high performance, the chapters offer various other features to help you connect the principles to real-world situations. "HR Best Practices" boxes tell success stories related to the chapter's topics. "HR Oops!" boxes identify situations gone wrong and invite you to find better alternatives. "HR How-To" boxes provide details about how to carry out a practice in each HR area. "Did You Know?" boxes are snapshots of interesting statistics related to chapter topics. All chapters also include an "E-HRM" feature identifying ways that human resources professionals are applying information technology and the Internet to help their organizations excel in the fast-changing world. Finally, the "Thinking Ethically" box at the end of each chapter demonstrates ethical issues in managing human resources. New to this edition, is also the inclusion of "Experiencing HR," experiential exercises that encourage students to explore real-word HR topics and situations in both individual and group settings.

SUMMARY

LO1 Define human resource management, identify the roles and responsibilities of human resource departments, and explain how human resource management contributes to an organization's performance.

Human resource management consists of an organization's "people practices"—the policies, practices, and systems that influence employees' behaviours, attitudes, and performance. HRM influences who works for the organization and how those people work. These human resources, if well-managed, have the potential to be a source of sustainable competitive advantage, contributing to basic objectives such as quality, profits, and customer satisfaction.

LO2 Summarize areas in which human resource management can support organizational strategies.

HR professionals need a solid understanding of the organizational strategy and may even play a role in developing the strategy. Specific HR practices vary according to the type of strategy. Workforce planning informs talent management—an important way HR professionals are making the link to organizational strategy. As part of its strategic role, HR can demonstrate the impact of human resource practices on company results, by engaging in evidence-based HR. Strategic challenges of sustainability by meeting the needs of diverse stakeholders is another strategic challenge. When organizations with international operations hire employees in other countries where they operate, they need to be mindful of the differences in culture and business practices. Outsourcing and off-shoring require effective job design, planning, recruitment and selection, and rewards practices to realize the potential benefits. Mergers and acquisitions also demand HRM to take a significant role.

LO3 Summarize the types of competencies needed for human resource management.

Human resource management requires substantial and varied competencies. Human resources professionals are required to uphold high ethical standards. Some areas in which ethical issues arise include adherence to legislation, protecting confidentiality, and main-taining professional competence.

LO4 Explain the role of supervisors and managers in human resource management.

Although many organizations have human resource departments, supervisors and manag-ers must be familiar with HRM and their own role with regard to managing human resources and implementing HR processes. Supervisors and managers typically have responsibilities related to all the HR functions. Supervisors help analyze work, interview job candidates, participate in selection decisions, provide training, set goals, provide feedback, conduct performance appraisals, and recommend pay increases. On a day-to-day basis, supervisors and line managers represent the company to their employees, so they also play an import-ant role in employee and labour relations.

LO5 Describe typical careers in human resource management.

Careers in HRM may involve specialized work in fields such as recruiting, training, or labour relations. HR professionals may also be generalists, performing the full range of HR activities described in this chapter. People in these positions usually have a university degree or college diploma in business or the social sciences. Many human resources pro-fessionals have achieved the national designation, Certified Human Resources Professional (CHRP).

LO6 Describe trends in the labour force composition and how they affect human resource management.

An organization's internal labour force comes from its external labour market—individuals who are actively seeking employment. In Canada, this labour market is aging and becom-ing more diverse. To compete for talent, organizations must be flexible enough to meet the varying needs of workers, must recruit from a diverse population, establish bias-free HR systems, and help employees understand and appreciate cultural differences. Organi-zations also need employees with skills in decision making, customer service, and team-work, as well as technical skills. The competition for such talent is intense. Organizations facing a skills shortage often hire employees who lack certain skills, then train them for their jobs.

LO7 Discuss the role of high-performance work systems and how technological developments are affecting human resource management.

HRM can help organizations find and keep the best possible fit between their social system and technical system. Recruiting and selection decisions are especially important for organizations that rely on knowledge workers. Job design and appropriate systems for assessment and rewards have a central role in supporting employee engagement and teamwork. Information systems have become a important tool for HR professionals, and often these systems are provided through the Internet. The widespread use of the Internet includes HRM applications. Organizations search for talent globally using online job postings and screening candidates online. Organizations' websites feature information directed toward potential employees. Employees may receive training online. At many companies, online information sharing enables employee self-service for many HR needs.

LO8 Explain how the nature of the employment relationship is changing and how the need for flexibility affects human resource management.

The employment relationship takes the form of a "psychological contract" that describes what employees and employers expect from the employment relationship. Traditionally, organizations expected employees to contribute their skills and loyalty in exchange for job security and opportunities for promotion. Today, organizations are requiring top performance and longer work hours but often cannot provide job security. Organizations seek flexibility in staffing through non-standard work arrangements. They may use outsourcing as well as temporary and contract workers. The use of such workers can affect job design, as well as the motivation of the organization's permanent employees.

Critical Thinking Questions

1. How can human resource management contribute to a company's success and sustainability?

2. How does engaging in evidence-based HR including the use of human capital analytics change the role and competency requirements of the human resources professionals?

3. What skills are important for success in human resource management? Which of these skills are already strengths of yours? Which would you like to develop further?

4. Why do all managers and supervisors need knowledge and skills related to human resource management?

5. Does a career in human resource management, based on this chapter's description appeal to you? Why or why not?

6. How does each of the following labour force trends affect HRM?
    a. Aging of the workforce
    b. Diversity
    c. Skill deficiencies
    d. Higher levels of education

7. Suppose you have been hired to manage human resources for a small company that offers business services including customer service calls and business report preparation. The 20-person company has been preparing to expand from serving a few local clients that are well known to the company's owners. The owners believe that their experience and reputation will help them expand to serve more and larger clients. What challenges will you need to prepare the company to meet? How will you begin?

8. What HRM functions could an organization provide through self-service? What are some advantages and disadvantages of using self-service for these functions?

9. How is the employment relationship that is typical of today's organizations different from the relationship of a generation ago?

Experiencing HR

This chapter described trends shaping human resource management, including the aging of the workforce and the impact of social media. Alone or with a partner, list three of the trends that interest you. Then select a manager or employee who would be willing to talk about these trends for about 15 minutes—someone in human resource management or in a different field that interests you.

With your partner if you have one, interview the person. Summarize each trend you listed, and ask your interviewee to describe any impact of that trend that he or she has observed at work. Take notes.

In a paragraph, summarize what you learned. In a second paragraph, analyze the impact on human resource management. If your interviewee noted negative impacts, suggest how HR professionals might help the organization cope. If your interviewee noted positive impacts, consider how human resource management might have contributed to, or could enhance, the positives.

CASE STUDY 1.1:

Do Companies Need HR?

When Glen Laverty was VP, Marketing at Ricoh, he saw HR as a fairly basic functional role in the organization that provided service and support for processes such as staffing and performance management. Now, as president and CEO of Ricoh, based in Mississauga, Ontario, he suggests that he had a "pretty basic view of HR back then." "Once you transform into the role of CEO, you recognize what you have (in HR) isn't the function but the role of a strategic partner to take a look at the organization from a people perspective," says Laverty. Speaking at a Strategic Capability Network event in Toronto he describes how HR serves as a strategic business partner to each department and holds a prominent role on the executive team. "(HR's plan outlines) what they're going to do in the organization, how they're going to provide a partner to the business, what they're going to bring to the party in terms of enlightening or changing or challenging the leadership within the organization to move in the right direction as it relates to people," he said.

However, in other organizations, HR has been accused of getting tied up in too much transactional red tape and having a reputation for not thinking outside the box. Boon Poon Tip, founder of

Toronto-based sustainable global travel company, G Adventures (formerly Gap Adventures) eliminated the HR function in his company. "I wanted a company that celebrated winning and I couldn't get that out of HR," he explains. "HR takes away people's freedoms, and is really just used to try to avoid errors," Boon Poon Tip adds.

A less controversial but perhaps inspired solution to address some CEOs' disappointment in their HR people, is to split HR into "two strands." One strand would report to the CFO and would manage administrative functions and the other strand would report to the CEO and would focus on enhancing people capabilities.

In many firms, technology is also transforming the role of HR professionals. Many tasks such as payroll, staffing, training, and collecting employee information can be automated and handled online. A recent study by Towers Watson revealed that companies are significantly increasing investment in HR technologies. And HR outsourcing is becoming more prevalent in Canada. In 2005, only one-third of Canadian employers outsourced any HR administration, but by 2010, 59 percent outsourced all or some HR services. For example, IBM recently announced an eight-year deal with Air Canada to handle a broad range of Air Canada's HR services. Under the deal, IBM will manage Air Canada's HR contact centre, employee data management, employee travel support, recruiting services, benefits administration, leave management, and payroll.

Questions

1. Why might these senior leaders have such varying views of the role and relevance of HR?

2. Should organizations outsource, split, perhaps even "fire" their HR departments? Why or why not?

Sources: Ram Charan, "It's Time to Split HR," *Harvard Business Review*, July/August 2014, Vol. 92 Issue 7/8, p. 34; Danielle Harder, "Air Canada Outsources HR to IBM," *Canadian HR Reporter*, November 7, 2011, pp. 2 and 6; Paul McDougall, "IBM Lands $80 Million Air Canada HR Deal," *Information Week*, October 7, 2011; Jean-Francois Potvin, "HR Outsourcing is Gaining Ground," *Benefits Canada*, November 23, 2010, www.benefitscanada.com/news/hr-outsourcing-is-gaining-ground-570?print, retrieved January 21, 2012; Jacqueline Nelson, "Should You Fire Your HR Department?" *Canadian Business*, November 3, 2011, www.canadianbusiness.com/print/54587, retrieved January 18, 2012.

CASE STUDY 1.2:

SpiderWeb Inc.

SpiderWeb, a telecommunications company founded in 2008, has posted rapid growth in recent months following the launch of a new smartphone based on leading-edge interactive technology.

SpiderWeb has a total workforce of 150 people, most of whom belong to Generation Y. The organization's head office in Montreal is staffed by 50 employees, while a new plant in the Vancouver suburbs employs 100 people in production and distribution. The company is financially sound and plans to double its workforce over the next two years through developing the American and world markets.

SpiderWeb is strongly influenced by the entrepreneurial management style of its two founders. Still active in the organization, they are responsible in particular for the HR function. To support the firm's anticipated growth, they have decided to create a new position of HR director. After a rigorous selection process, you have been hired to fill this position and are to be in charge of HR at SpiderWeb's two locations.

At your first meetings with the executive committee, composed of the founders and four key managers from Montreal and Vancouver (the finance director, R&D director, operations director, and CEO of the Vancouver plant), you realize that they are fairly apprehensive and uninformed about the new HR function and its strategic dimension, which is of some concern to you.

Findings

A few days after joining the company, you hold a number of meetings with managers and employees from both sites. Your initial findings are striking:

- at first glance, the employees generally seem to be motivated and happy to work for Spider-Web, particularly since the launch of the new smartphone, which everyone is proud of;
- the company has no HR management policy;
- its senior managers are assigned their duties and the management of major projects on an arbitrary basis;
- this is the first management experience for most of the company's managers;
- up to now supply and demand have served as a guideline for compensation, which is inconsistent and inequitable. This practice is not unanimously approved of and is a source of discontent among employees and executives alike.

The Issues

Many managers confided that they would like to see the company move forward and institute a new and equitable compensation policy. The executive committee also informed you that recruitment is the main HR issue. The scarcity of talent in cutting-edge technology and the low level of awareness of the employer brand, given that the company was established only a few years ago, add to the challenges you face.

You also note several issues that are specific to the Vancouver plant. Its CEO, whose responsibilities include HR management, is the brother of one of the founders. However, he lacks the relevant training and experience to fulfill this function. Many of the plant's employees have spoken to you about his lack of organization and management skills. Nonetheless, the two founders would like to see him continue these duties and want you to assist him in his professional development.

After a brief analysis of the key HR indicators, you realize that there are some serious problems at the Vancouver plant:

- turnover is far too high when compared to the industry average;
- there are numerous disability cases;
- absenteeism is high.

As well, you heard employees at the plant's distribution centre discussing a proposal to apply for union certification. You talked this over with the plant manager, who doesn't seem to be worried or interested in the matter. In his view, the workers in questions are mainly isolated cases, troublemakers that he plans to take care of. He believes that engagement levels among most of the plant's employees are high.

When you return to Montreal, you hear a rumour about the strategic R&D team. Apparently its members fail to comply with the guidelines respecting the protection of intellectual property and lack the sense of professional ethics their role requires. You also hear that some of them have met with competitors outside the workplace.

Lastly, despite the considerable respect the employees have for the founders, several more experienced executives shared their concern about the founders' lack of medium- and long-term vision and planning. Moreover, the founders themselves are the first to admit that they've never really taken the time to think about the priorities and strategic directions that would ensure the company's survival. They realize that this situation should be remedied as soon as possible and admit that they have focused exclusively on the company's growth from the start.

Note: *The names and characters in this case study are fictitious and any resemblance to actual persons living or dead is purely coincidental.*

Your Mandate

In view of the analyses performed and your meetings with senior management, executives, and employees:

1. Indicate what concrete actions you will take in the next three months to ensure that:

   a. The executive committee understands the strategic role you wish to play (at least four concrete actions);

   b. You establish your credibility with senior management (at least four concrete actions).

2. Identify the three main issues that should be incorporated into your HR management plan in the next year and develop an action plan for one of them. The plan should:

   a. Include strategic and operational elements (at least five elements);

   b. Include communication activities and follow-up;

   c. Be logically implemented over time;

   d. Be creative and feasible in the context of a young SME run by young entrepreneurs.

Source: www.portailrh.org/excalibur/en/case/2011_Epreuve1.pdf, retrieved January 21, 2012. Case is adapted from the short case used in the Semi-Final 2011 Event I of Excalibur (the Canadian University Tournament of Human Resources). Reprinted with the permission of CRHA.

CHAPTER 2

The Legal Context for HRM and Creating Safe and Healthy Workplaces

WHAT DO I NEED TO KNOW?

After reading this chapter, you should be able to:

Lo1	Discuss the importance of valuing diversity and safety.
Lo2	Describe the legal framework for human resource management in Canada.
Lo3	Explain the importance of human rights and the implications for HRM.
Lo4	Discuss privacy, employment/labour standards, and pay equity and their relevance for HRM.
Lo5	Explain the context for workplace health and safety.
Lo6	Identify the responsibilities of employers, and managers or supervisors, as well as employees' rights and responsibilities related to workforce health and safety.
Lo7	Discuss the ways employers promote worker health and safety.

The Willow Bean Café provides meaningful employment in a supportive setting for people with mental health challenges.

The Willow Bean Café

Willow Bean Café in Vancouver General Hospital is a partnership between Vancouver Coastal Health (www.vch.ca), the Burnaby Branch of the Canadian Mental Health Association (www.cmha.ca), and Sodexo Canada (www.sodexo.ca). Sodexo Canada is an integrated food and facilities management company with more than 10,000 employees and is recognized as one of Canada's Best Diversity Employers. The Willow Bean Café employs people with mental health issues. Individuals interested in working at the café participate in a competitive hiring process held by Sodexo who manages the café and its employees. Baristas work part-time hours, which provides a gradual transition back to the workplace. After six months spent developing their skills, experience, and confidence, they move on to their next position. "It can be tough having a regular job sometimes," says barista, Caer Weber, who's living with post-traumatic stress and depression. "But working at Willow Bean has changed that. I love making the cappuccinos and lattes."

Sodexo's goal for the enterprise is to provide a supportive environment that increases employees' confidence and "lead to more employment opportunities, particularly with Sodexo." Barry Telford, vice-president of health care and education services at Sodexo in Burlington, Ontario explains, "We are very committed as an organization to supporting diversity and inclusion at every level we possibly can. When this opportunity came up, we were very proud to participate."[1]

Introduction

As we saw in Chapter 1, human resource management takes place in the context of the company's goals and society's expectations for how a company should operate. In Canada, the federal, provincial, and territorial governments have set some limits on how an organization can practise human resource management. Among these limits are requirements intended to foster fairness in hiring and employment practices and to protect the health and safety of workers while they are on the job. Questions about a company's performance in these areas can result in employee turnover, human rights complaints, lawsuits, and negative publicity that often cause serious problems for a company's success and survival. Conversely, a company can gain a competitive advantage over its competitors by going beyond just legal compliance to find ways of linking fair and respectful employment and worker safety to business goals such as building a workforce that is highly motivated and attuned to customers.

One point to make at the outset is that managers often want a list of dos and don'ts that will keep them out of legal trouble. Some managers rely on strict rules such as "Don't ever ask a female applicant if she is married," rather than learning the reasons behind those rules. Clearly, certain practices are illegal or at least inadvisable, and this chapter will discuss these areas. However, managers who merely focus on how to avoid breaking the law are not thinking about how to be ethical or how to acquire and engage people in the best way to carry out the company's mission. This chapter introduces ways to think proactively about employment and workplace safety.

LO1 Discuss the importance of valuing diversity and safety.

Valuing Diversity and Inclusion

HRC **1,2**

As we mentioned in Chapter 1, Canada is a diverse nation, and becoming more so. In addition, many Canadian companies have customers and operations in more than one country. Managers differ in how they approach the opportunities and challenges related to this diversity. Some define a diverse workforce as a competitive advantage that brings them a wider pool of talent and greater insight into the needs and behaviours of their diverse customers. These organizations have a policy of *valuing diversity* and *inclusion*. Canada's Top 100 Employers includes a specific category to recognize employers that provide the most inclusive workplaces—"Canada's Best Diversity Employers." Employers recently recognized include Cargill Ltd. (www.cargill.ca; Winnipeg), BC Hydro (www.bchydro.com; Vancouver), Saskatchewan Government Insurance (www.sgi.com; Regina), Dalhousie University (www.dal.ca; Halifax), and Mount Sinai Hospital (www.mountsinai.on.ca; Toronto).[2]

The practice of valuing diversity has no single form; it is not written into law or business theory. One of the concerns about diversity is that "the majority of Canadian organizations rank diversity as a priority, but 42 percent of them have no strategic plan to foster it" according to a report from the Conference Board of Canada.[3]

Organizations that value diversity may also actively work to meet employment equity goals, which will be discussed later in this chapter. Bell Canada speaks to the benefits of diversity: "Business objectives, and our objectives for diversity and employment equity go hand in hand. And as we apply our considerable strengths to achieving our business goals with a strong diversity focus, we see no limits to what we are able to accomplish as individuals, as a company, and even as a nation."[4] Organizations may try to hire, reward, and promote employees who demonstrate respect for others. They may have policies stating their value of understanding and respecting differences. They may sponsor training programs designed to teach employees about differences among groups. Whatever their form, these efforts are intended to ensure every employee is respected. Also, these actions can support diversity by cultivating an environment in which individuals feel valued and able to perform to their potential.

Employers are recognized for being Canada's most inclusive workplaces.

Creating a Culture of Health and Safety

HRC 1, 8

The protection of employee health and safety is regulated by the government, however, the effective management of health and safety in the workplace includes more than legal compliance. NB Power (www.nbpower.ca) takes a holistic approach to health and safety and makes it one of the eight integrated HR functions. The other seven functions are recruitment, compensation, diversity, leadership, relationship management, well-being, and labour relations.[5]

Increasingly, organizations are taking a strategic approach to occupational health and safety by adopting a values-based commitment to safe operations as a way to protect people. Additional benefits to business include cost savings by reducing worker injuries, fatalities, occupational disease, and property damage as well as improved employee relations, reliability, and productivity improvement.[6]

Employers and employees share responsibility for creating and maintaining safe and healthy work environments. Employer–employee partnerships are put in place to create a climate and culture of safety in the organization in addition to ensuring compliance.[7] Ultimately, however, employers have a legal duty to provide their employees with a physically and psychologically safe work environment.

L○2 Describe the legal framework for human resource management in Canada.

The Legal Framework for Human Resource Management

HRC 1,2

Federal, provincial, and territorial governments in Canada all play an important role in creating the legal environment for human resource management. Approximately 94 percent of Canadian employers and their employees are covered by provincial and territorial legislation. The remaining 6 percent are covered by federal legislation. Table 2.1 summarizes the types of organizations that fall under federal and provincial/territorial legislation.

TABLE 2.1

What Types of Organizations Are Regulated by the Provinces and Territories versus the Federal Government?

Organizations Regulated by the Federal Government	Organizations Regulated by Provinces and Territories
• Banks	All other businesses not listed. Examples include:
• Marine shipping, ferry and port services	• Retail and hospitality businesses, such as a store, a restaurant, a hotel, etc.
• Air transportation, including airports, aerodromes, and airlines	• Hospitals and health care providers
• Railway and road transportation that involves crossing provincial or international borders	• Schools, colleges, and universities
• Canals, pipelines, tunnels, and bridges (crossing provincial borders)	• Most manufacturers
• Telephone, telegraph, and cable systems	
• Radio and television broadcasting	
• Grain elevators, feed, and seed mills	
• Uranium mining and processing	
• Businesses dealing with the protection of fisheries	
• Many First Nation activities	
• Federal departments, agencies, and most federal Crown corporations	

Sources: "Federally Regulated Businesses and Industries," www.labour.gc.ca/eng/regulated, retrieved June 24, 2015; "Canadian Human Rights Commission Overview," www.chrc-ccdp.ca/discrimination/federally_regulated-en.asp, retrieved April 13, 2008; Anti-Discrimination Casebook, p. 1, www.chrc-ccdp.ca/legis&poli, retrieved February 18, 2004; and Human Resource Management Laws and Regulations Government of Canada, http://hrmanagement.gc.ca, retrieved February 18, 2004.

Federal, provincial, and territorial employment-related laws tend to mirror one another; however, some differences exist. It is important for employers to be aware of and comply with all legal requirements. For organizations with workers in more than one province, territory, or industry it can be time-consuming and challenging to maintain compliance with this web of legal requirements. As mentioned previously in the chapter, many proactive human resource departments and their organizations are moving beyond a mindset of compliance and are recognizing the strategic importance of valuing the various goals pursued through the legislation, for example, diversity, health and safety of employees, and privacy.

L○3 Explain the importance of human rights and the implications for HRM.

Protecting Human Rights

All the jurisdictions have human rights legislation. The purpose of human rights legislation is to remove discrimination. **Discrimination** means "treating someone differently, negatively, or adversely because of their race, age, religion, sex, or other prohibited ground."[8]

> **discrimination**
> Treating someone differently, negatively, or adversely because of their race, age, religion, sex, or other prohibited ground.

Direct discrimination involves policies or practices that clearly make a distinction on the basis of a prohibited ground (see Figure 2.1). **Indirect discrimination** involves policies or practices that appear to be neutral but have an *adverse effect* on the basis of a prohibited ground. For example, a company that has a policy of not employing any part-time employees appears to have a policy that can be equally applied to all applicants and existing employees. However, the effect of this policy is not neutral—someone who has family responsibilities would be denied employment or denied the opportunity to reduce their work hours.

> **direct discrimination**
> Policies or practices that clearly make a distinction on the basis of a prohibited ground.

> **indirect discrimination**
> Policies or practices that appear to be neutral but have an adverse effect on the basis of a prohibited ground.

In summary, all individuals have a right to an equal chance to be hired, keep a job, get a promotion, or receive other work benefit regardless of personal characteristics including race, colour, national or ethnic origin, religion, sexual orientation, age, marital status, sex, family status, and physical or mental disability.

How Would You Know?

How would you know if you had been discriminated against? Decisions about human resources are so complex that discrimination is often difficult to identify and prove. However, legal scholars and court rulings have arrived at some ways to show evidence of discrimination.

Differential Treatment

One sign of discrimination is **differential treatment**—differing treatment of individuals, where the differences are based on a prohibited ground such as the individuals' race, colour, religion, sex, national origin, age, or disability. For example, differential treatment would include hiring or promoting one

FIGURE 2.1

Prohibited Grounds of Discrimination in Employment

Prohibited Ground	Federal	BC	AB	SK	MB	ON	QC	NB	NS	PEI	NL	NWT	YT	NU
Race	*	*	*	*		*	*	*	*	*	*	*	*	*
National or ethnic origin	*		*	*	*	*	*	*	*	*	*	*	*	*
Colour	*	*	*	*		*	*	*	*	*	*	*	*	*
Religion or creed	*	*	*	*	*	*	*	*	*	*	*	*	*	*
Age	*	*	*	*	*	*	*	*	*	*	*	*	*	*
Sex (gender; pregnancy; gender identity)	*	*	*	*	*	*	*	*	*	*	*	*	*	*
Sexual orientation	*	*	*	*	*	*	*	*	*	*	*	*	*	*
Marital status	*	*	*	*	*	*	*	*	*	*	*	*	*	*
Family status	*	*	*	*	*	*	*		*	*	*	*	*	*
Disability (physical or mental)	*	*	*	*	*	*	*	*	*	*	*	*	*	*
Pardoned conviction	*	*			*		*			*		*	*	*
Ancestry or place of origin		*	*	*	*	*	*		*			*	*	*
Political belief (or activity)		*			*		*	*	*	*	*	*	*	
Source of income (social condition) e.g., receipt of public assistance			*	*	*	*	*	*	*	*	*	*	*	*

Note: This chart is for quick reference purposes; for interpretation and/or application of specific details, contact the relevant Human Rights Commission(s).

Sources: From "Prohibited Grounds of Discrimination in Canada," pp. 1–3, Canadian Human Rights Commission, 1998. Reproduced with the permission of the Minister of Public Works and Government Services Canada, 2004, www.chrc-ccdp.ca/discrimination/grounds-en.asp, retrieved December 6, 2004. *Updates:* "What is Discrimination? www.chrc-ccdp.gc.ca/eng/content/what-discrimination, retrieved March 23, 2015; "Mandatory Retirement in Canada," www.hrsdc.gc.ca/en/lp/spila/clli/eslc/19mandatory_retirement.shtml, retrieved April 13, 2008; and "Retiring Mandatory Retirement," February 21, 2008, www.cbc.ca/newsbackground/retirement/mandatory/retirement.html, retrieved April 19, 2009.

person over an equally qualified person because of the individual's race. Suppose a company fails to hire women with school-age children (claiming the women will be frequently absent) but hires men with school-age children. In that situation, the women are victims of differential treatment, because they are being treated differently on the basis of their sex.

differential treatment
Differing treatment of individuals where the differences are based on a prohibited ground.

To avoid complaints of differential treatment, companies can evaluate the questions and investigations they use in making employment decisions. These should be applied consistently. For example, if the company investigates conviction records of job applicants, it should investigate them for all applicants, not just for applicants from certain groups. Companies may want to avoid some types of questions altogether. For example, questions about marital status can cause problems, because interviewers may unfairly make different assumptions about men and women. (Common stereotypes about women have been that a married woman is less flexible or more likely to get pregnant than a single woman, in contrast to the assumption that a married man is more stable and committed to his work.)

Is differential treatment ever legal? The courts have held that in some situations, a factor such as sex or race may be a **bona fide occupational requirement (BFOR)**, that is, a necessary (not merely preferred) qualification for performing a job. A typical example is a job that includes handing out towels in a locker room. Requiring that employees who perform this job in the women's locker room be female is a BFOR. However, it is very difficult to think of many jobs where criteria such as sex and race are BFORs. In some cases, a core function of the job may be related to a protected ground. For example, a job may require a specified level of visual capability to be performed effectively and safely, thereby eliminating someone who does not meet this requirement. Employers should seek ways to perform the job so that these restrictions are not needed.

bona fide occupational requirement (BFOR)
A necessary (not merely preferred) requirement for performing a job.

It is the employer's responsibility to prove the existence of a BFOR if any complaint of discrimination should arise. In the widely publicized *Meiorin* case from 1999, Tawny Meiorin, a female forest firefighter, lost her job when she failed to meet a required aerobic fitness standard that had been established by the British Columbia Public Service Employee Relations Commission. This standard had been put in place as a minimum requirement for all firefighters. She lost her job after failing *one* aspect of a minimum fitness standard—taking 49.4 seconds too long to complete a 2.5 kilometre run.[9] She filed a complaint stating that the fitness standard discriminated against women because women usually have less aerobic capability than men. Although the employer argued the standard was a bona fide occupational requirement of the job, the Supreme Court of Canada ultimately ruled the standard was not a BFOR—the fitness standard was not reasonably necessary to fulfill a legitimate work-related purpose.[10] Ms. Meiorin was reinstated to her job and received compensation for lost wages and benefits.

Mandatory Retirement

The practice of forcing an employee to retire for the reason of age is a human rights issue and falls under the protection of human rights legislation. All jurisdictions in Canada have legislation that makes mandatory retirement discriminatory unless there is a bona fide occupational requirement due to a specific employment requirement.[11]

What Is the Employer's Duty to Accommodate?

An employer has a duty to consider how an employee's characteristic such as disability, religion, or sex can be accommodated and to take action so that the employee can perform the job. See Figure 2.2. This duty is referred to as the **duty to accommodate**.

FIGURE 2.2

Looking for an individual's abilities

Cornered
by Mike Baldwin

3-26 © 2012 Mike Baldwin/Dist. by Universal Uclick www.cornered.com
urcornered@gmail.com
BALdwin

"We believe in seeing ability, not disability.
In your case, we see neither."

duty to accommodate
An employer's duty to consider how an employee's characteristic such as disability, religion, or sex can be accommodated and to take action so the employee can perform the job.

The employer's duty to accommodate has been evolving since it became a part of human rights law in the 1980s. Although the employee is generally considered responsible for requesting accommodation, there may be circumstances where the employer has responsibility to initiate the action to provide accommodation. For example if an employee tells his supervisor: "I need a half day a week off for the next six weeks to get treatment for a medical problem," the supervisor needs to pursue this as a request for medical accommodation.[12]

Accommodation may even require that the employee perform another job within their capabilities. Employers' duty to accommodate extends to the point of *undue hardship*—"undue" meaning only if it is so high that the very survival of the organization or business would be threatened or essentially changed.[13]

In the context of religion, this principle recognizes that for some individuals, religious observations and practices may present a conflict with work duties, dress codes, or company practices. For example, some religions require head coverings, or to be able to pray at a particular time, or individuals might need time off to observe the Sabbath or other holy days, when the company might have them scheduled to work. When the employee has a legitimate religious belief requiring accommodation, the employee should communicate this need to the employer. Assuming that it would not present an undue hardship, employers are required to accommodate such religious practices. They may have to adjust schedules so

Steven Fletcher, Canada's first quadriplegic MP and Member of Cabinet was a two-time Manitoba kayaking champion and recent geological engineering graduate when in 1996 at the age of 23, his car collided with a moose while driving to work. Steven was paralyzed from the neck down, however, within one year of the accident, he was accepted into the University of Manitoba's MBA program. Two years later (1999), he was president, University of Manitoba Students Union and after serving for two years was elected president, Progressive Conservative Party of Manitoba. In 2004, Steven won his competitive Winnipeg riding and became a federal member of parliament. Since then, he has won the riding three more times.[14]

that employees do not have to work on days when their religion forbids it, or they may have to alter dress or grooming requirements.

For employees with disabilities, accommodations also vary according to the individuals' needs—increasingly, however, the emphasis is placed on *abilities* and capabilities rather than focusing on disabilities. For example, Sodexo has a "disABILITY" strategy that advances the inclusion of adults with disabilities. "We find people with disabilities are absolutely fantastic at the jobs we put them in. They want to be part of the organization, they stay in the organization, they grow within the organization, so it works very well for us and for those employees," explains Dean Johnson, president and CEO of Sodexo Canada.[15]

As shown in Figure 2.3, employers may restructure jobs, make facilities in the workplace more accessible, modify equipment, or reassign an employee to a job that the person can perform. In some situations, an individual may provide his or her own accommodation, which the employer permits, as in the case of a blind worker who brings a service dog to work.

When Steven Fletcher (in photo above) was elected in a competitive Winnipeg riding as Canada's first quadriplegic MP, one of his first impacts was directly on the House of Commons where aisles were too narrow and elevators too small for his motorized wheelchair. Some of the buildings are more than 150 years old and are not as accessible as one might expect. Because Fletcher needs help to perform the day-to-day aspects of his job—for example, turning the pages of a report—an aide is by his side. But Steven is focused on his ability to contribute, "I made the decision to use what I have. What's important is from the neck up." A variety of necessary arrangements were needed for him to do his job as a parliamentarian. These accommodations included not only building adaptations such as lifts and ramps,

FIGURE 2.3

Examples of Accommodations

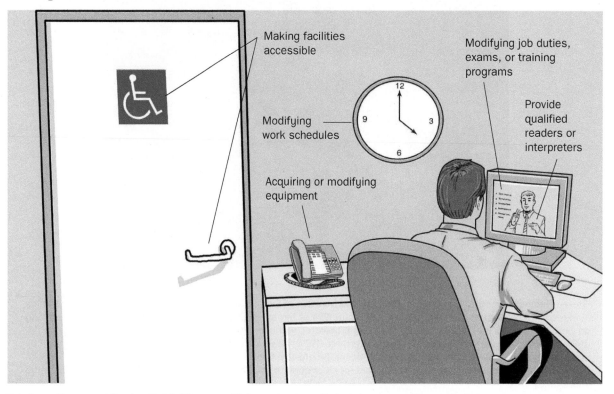

Making facilities accessible

Modifying job duties, exams, or training programs

Modifying work schedules

Provide qualified readers or interpreters

Acquiring or modifying equipment

Note: Reasonable accommodations do not include hiring an unqualified person, lowering quality standards, or compromising co-workers' safety.

Source: Equal Employment Opportunity Commission, "The ADA: Questions and Answers," www.eeoc.gov/facts/adaqa1.html, retrieved August 28, 2008.

but also information technology needs such as wireless voice-activated dialing for his phone system and use of a head mouse for his computer. Although the initial focus was on accommodating Steven Fletcher's needs to allow him to do his job, his legacy already includes a long list of accomplishments achieved for others. "Let's lay the foundation so we'll see people in wheelchairs contributing . . . and it's natural," adds Steven.[16]

What About Harassment?

HRC 8

Human rights legislation also prohibits all forms of **harassment**. Harassment is "a form of discrimination. It involves any unwanted physical or verbal behaviour that offends or humiliates you."[17] Recent research from the Queen's School of Business at Queen's University in Kingston, Ontario found that 31 percent of female and 22 percent of male respondents "had experienced or were currently experiencing workplace harassment." These numbers had decreased slightly since 2012. Dr. Jane Raver, the study's lead, theorizes that an increased public interest in the topic evidenced from media coverage to government legislation has likely led to the decline, however workplace harassment remains a problem in Canada. She recommends employers establish clear policies supported by education. "Actually outline a code of conduct. Do some training. Let people understand what this looks like and where people cross the line."[18]

harassment
A form of discrimination that involves any unwanted physical or verbal behaviour that offends or humiliates you.

For example here is Seneca College's Discrimination & Harassment Policy Statement:

"It is the Policy of Seneca College that all employees and students have a right to work and study in an environment that asserts the personal worth and dignity of each individual. In order to achieve this objective, Seneca College will not tolerate any form of discrimination and/or harassment in its employment, educational, accommodation or business dealings. Every member of the College community has the right to file a complaint of discrimination/harassment."[19]

Sexual harassment refers to unwelcome behaviour that is of a sexual nature or is related to a person's sex (gender or gender identity).

sexual harassment
Unwelcome behaviour that is of a sexual nature or is related to a person's sex (gender or gender identity).

In general, the most obvious examples of sexual harassment involve *quid pro quo harassment*, meaning that a person makes a benefit (or punishment) contingent on an employee's submitting to (or rejecting) sexual advances. For example, a manager who promises a raise to an employee who will participate in sexual activities is engaging in *quid pro quo* harassment. Likewise, it would be sexual harassment to threaten to reassign someone to a less desirable job if that person refuses sexual advances.

A more subtle but more common form of sexual harassment is to create or permit a *hostile (or poisoned) work environment*. Although the following list is not exhaustive it is intended to provide illustrative samples of behaviours that may be considered hostile (or poisoned) work environment sexual harassment:[20]

- derogatory language and/or comments toward women (or men, depending on the circumstances)
- sex-specific derogatory names
- leering or inappropriate staring
- displaying or circulating pornography, sexual pictures or cartoons, or other sexual images (including online)
- sexual jokes, including circulating written sexual jokes (e.g., by email)
- unnecessary physical contact, including unwanted touching
- rough and vulgar humour or language related to gender
- spreading sexual rumours (including online)
- suggestive or offensive remarks or innuendo about members of a specific gender
- bragging about sexual prowess
- questions or discussions about sexual activities
- paternalistic behaviour based on gender that a person feels undermines their status or position of responsibility.

As noted above, paternalistic behaviour based on gender, which a person feels undermines their status or position of responsibility may also be determined to be sexual harassment. For example, a "tribunal found an employer's repeated use of terms including "sweetheart," "little lady," "hun," "sweetie," and "dear" to be "terms of diminishment," and that, within the broader context of his other sexualized overtures, the use of these terms created a poisoned work environment.[21] Although a large majority of sexual harassment complaints involve women being harassed by men, sexual harassment can affect anyone.

To ensure a workplace free from harassment, organizations can follow some important steps. Federally regulated employees are required to develop an anti-harassment policy making it very clear that harassment will not be tolerated in the workplace. Second, all employees need to be made aware of the policy and receive training. In addition, the organization can develop a mechanism for reporting harassment in a way that encourages people to speak out. Finally, management can prepare to act promptly to discipline those who engage in harassment, as well as to protect the victims of harassment. Despite these types of efforts, many employees continue to face harassment in the workplace. For example, it was recently reported that "almost 20 percent of [federal] public servants say they were harassed on the job over the past two years and the main culprits were their bosses and co-workers."[22] These numbers were better than the results from the survey conducted three years prior, which found that almost 30 percent of all employees said "they had faced some type of harassment over the previous two years."[23]

Rare is the business owner or manager who wants to wait for the government to identify that his or her organization has failed to meet its legal requirements to treat employees fairly. Instead, out of motives ranging from concern for employee well-being to the desire to avoid costly lawsuits and negative publicity, most companies recognize the importance of complying with these laws and creating safe and respectful workplaces. Often, management depends on the expertise of human resources professionals to help to ensure employees are not exposed to behaviours that could be psychologically harmful. Keeping the workplace psychologically safe and healthy will be discussed in more detail later in this chapter.

Figure 2.4 discusses each of the prohibited grounds of discrimination and provides an example of an allegation of discrimination or harassment made in a work-related situation along with the settlement that the complainant received.

Employment Equity

HRC 2, 9

Canada's employment equity policy was inspired by a report written in 1984 by Justice Rosalie Abella. Employment equity legislation focuses on eliminating employment barriers to the four designated groups who are viewed to have been historically disadvantaged in their employment relationships. The four designated groups are:

- **Women**
- **Aboriginal peoples** ("An Aboriginal person is a North American Indian or a member of a First Nation, Métis, or Inuit. North American Indians or members of a First Nation include treaty, status, or registered Indians, as well as non-status and non-registered Indians.")[24]
- **Members of visible minorities** ("A person in a visible minority group is someone, other than an Aboriginal person as defined above, who is non-white in colour/race, regardless of place of birth.")[25]
- **Persons with disabilities** ("A person with a disability has a long term or recurring physical, mental, sensory, psychiatric, or learning impairment.")[26]

Employment equity promotes equitable workforce representation for each of the designated groups. Reporting progress examines *representation*—the share of designated groups in a given labour market (e.g., the entire federally regulated private sector workforce, a specific industry, or a specific organization), relative to *labour market availability* (LMA)—the share of designated group members in the workforce from which the employer(s) could hire. Figure 2.5 provides the progress in representation over time of the four designated employment equity groups in the federally regulated private sector. "Members of visible minorities have seen the most progress with their representation, which increased from 5.0%

FIGURE 2.4

Human Rights Allegations and Settlements (Federal Prohibited Grounds)

Prohibited Ground	Description	Allegation	Settlement
Race, colour, and national or ethnic origin	These three grounds are related, and it is often difficult to draw clear distinctions between them. They are intended to get at the societal problem referred to as "racism."	The complainant alleged that a disgruntled customer used a distasteful tone and made racial slurs. She alleged that the respondent (employer) asked her to deal with the situation by hiding whenever the customer entered her area. Her employment was subsequently terminated for poor performance.	• Letter of reference • Financial compensation for general damages • Financial compensation for pain and suffering • Reimbursement of legal fees • Assistance with job search
Religion or creed	Discrimination has occurred because of knowledge of one's religion or a perception of that religion. *Note:* When an individual alleges adverse effect discrimination from some policy or decision the following three questions must be answered "yes": • Is the belief sincerely held? • Is it religious? • Is it the cause of the objection being made?	The complainant cannot work on Saturdays because of her religious beliefs. She alleged that, because of this, her supervisor required her to work every Saturday. Eventually, her employment was terminated.	• Financial compensation for general damages • Letter of regret
Age	The ground can refer to: • An individual's actual age. • Membership in a specific age-group, e.g., over 55. • A generalized characterization of his or her age, e.g., too old, or too young.	The complainant, who is 47 years old, alleged that he was denied education assistance normally provided to younger employees. The complainant also alleged that remarks about his age were made and written comments included in his personnel file.	• Removal from the complainant's file of all reference to his age or to the number of years he could remain as an employee • Assurance that having filed a complaint will not negatively affect his employment • Financial compensation for future tuition and books • Reimbursement for tuition and books for past courses
Sex (including pregnancy and gender identity)	Refers to the condition of being: • Male or female	The complainant handed in her resignation at one point because of an excessive workload, but her employer refused to accept it and she continued working. After she announced that she was pregnant two months later, she alleged that her employer suddenly decided to accept her resignation.	• Financial compensation for lost wages and general damages • Letter of recommendation
Sexual orientation	Refers to: • Heterosexuality • Homosexuality • Bisexuality	The complainant alleged that, during a job interview, he was asked inappropriate questions about his sexual orientation. In the end, the complainant got the job.	• Letter of regret • Training for all interviewers on the Canadian Human Rights Act

(continued on next page)

FIGURE 2.4

Human Rights Allegations and Settlements (Federal Prohibited Grounds) (*continued*)

Prohibited Ground	Description	Allegation	Settlement
Marital status	Condition of being: • Single • Legally married • Common-law spouses (opposite-sex or same-sex) • Widowed • Divorced	The complainant and his partner filed separate complaints alleging that the respondent did not take action against a co-worker who made defamatory and harassing remarks about their personal relationship. They allege that the respondent did not provide a harassment-free work environment. *Note:* This allegation included two grounds: marital status and sex.	• Development of protocol for future instances of sexual harassment • Joint management and union anti-harassment and human rights training • Posting of the respondent's human rights and employment equity policy, and relevant provisions of the collective agreement • Financial compensation for pain and suffering
Family status	Refers to the interrelationship that arises as a result of marriage, legal adoption, ancestral relationship, as well as the relationships between spouses, siblings, uncles or aunts, cousins, etc.	The complainant alleged that her employer denied her several career-enhancing opportunities when she returned to work from maternity leave, and that it ultimately terminated her employment on the pretext that it was downsizing and that her job no longer existed. *Note:* This allegation included two grounds: family status and sex.	• Expression of regret to the complainant • Financial compensation for general damages
Physical or mental disability	Disability is defined as being either: • Physical or mental • Previous or existing • Including dependence on alcohol or a drug *Note:* A disability can be either permanent or temporary (e.g., a temporary impairment as a result of an accident, or a treatable illness).	The complainant, who has multiple sclerosis, alleged that her employer, by refusing her a work schedule recommended by her doctor, failed to accommodate her disability.	• Adjustment of the complainant's work schedule to reflect the doctor's recommendations • Briefing session for employees on multiple sclerosis and non-visible disabilities • Occupational training, with half of the training program to be determined by one of the two parties • Reinstatement of leave • Letter of regret • Withdrawal of related grievances
Pardoned criminal conviction	A conviction for which a pardon has been granted by any authority under law.	The complainant is a truck driver who was required to travel to the U.S. Although he had been granted a pardon for a conviction in Canada, he was nevertheless denied entry in the U.S. Consequently, his employer laid him off on the ground that he could not fulfill all the requirements of the job.	• Financial compensation

Sources: Settlement Examples, www.chrc-ccdp.ca/disputeresolution_reglementdifferends/settlements_ententes-eng.aspx; Discrimination and Harassment, www.chrc-ccdp.ca/discrimination/act_actes-eng.aspx. Canadian Human Rights Commission. Reproduced with the permission of the Minister of Public Works and Government Services, 2012.

FIGURE 2.5

Progress in Representation Over Time in the Federally Regulated Private Sector (Banking, Communication, Transportation, and Other)

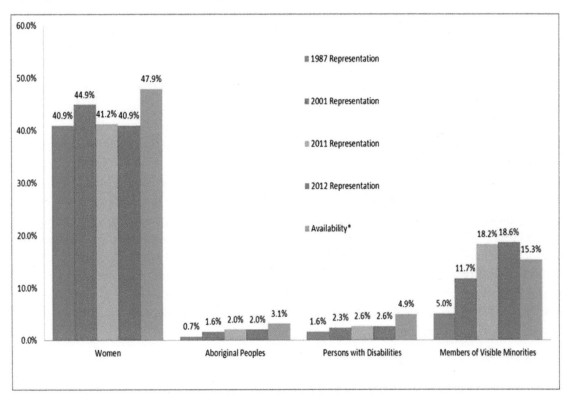

Source: "Employment Equity Act: Annual Report *2013*, Chart I: Progress in Representation Over Time in the Federally Regulated Private Sector," *Employment and Social Development Canada*, December II, 20I4, p. 3.

in 1987 to 18.6% in 2012, surpassing the group's LMA of 15.3%. This is the only designated group in the federally regulated private sector whose overall representation surpasses its LMA."[27] The application of employment equity to workforce planning will be discussed in Chapter 4.

L○4 Discuss privacy, employment/labour standards, and pay equity and their relevance for HRM.

Protection of Privacy

HRC 2

All of the jurisdictions—provinces, territories, and federal, have privacy laws that regulate how personal information is handled, for example, personal health information and personal financial information. The following section will discuss privacy requirements that connect most directly to the employer–employee relationship.

Personal Information Protection and Electronic Documents Act (PIPEDA)

The **Personal Information Protection and Electronic Documents Act (PIPEDA)** is a federal law that "sets out ground rules for how private sector organizations may collect, use, or disclose personal information in the course of commercial activities. This law also gives individuals the right to access and request correction of the personal information these organizations may have collected about them."[28] PIPEDA applies to personal information of employees who work in the federally regulated private sector (e.g., banking, communications, transportation, other).

> **Personal Information Protection and Electronic Documents Act (PIPEDA)**
> Federal law that sets out ground rules for how private sector organizations may collect, use, or disclose personal information.

The Act's ten principles establish standards for privacy practices and have implications for human resource departments and their responsibilities to safeguard employee privacy. Decisions made by the federal Privacy Commissioner have confirmed that although employers can collect information on employees about performance, attendance, and potential for advancement there is little an employer can keep from an employee.

For example, an employee of the federal public service demanded to see all the information obtained about her during an assessment review. The employee wanted to see the notes made by the contractor hired to conduct the assessment. These notes contained feedback and comments from other employees. The federal Privacy Commissioner ruled the employee was entitled to this information and that employees cannot be promised confidentiality when they make statements about another person.[29]

Alberta and British Columbia have privacy laws recognized as "substantially similar" to PIPEDA. In these provinces the relevant Personal Information Privacy Act (PIPA), e.g., PIPA Alberta and PIPA BC applies. The "HR How-To" box discusses some of the responsibilities HR departments have in protecting employees' personal information.

Employment/Labour Standards

Federal, provincial, and territorial laws are in place to provide minimum standards for employees. Some of the areas covered typically include:

- Minimum wage
- Overtime pay
- Hours of work and work scheduling
- General holidays
- Annual vacations
- Benefits for part-time workers
- Parental leave
- Layoff procedures
- Terminations and severance pay

Each jurisdiction has relevant laws to provide minimum employment/labour standards.

A variety of changes to employment/labour standards laws have recently been made in several jurisdictions. For example, Ontario has amended its Employment Standards Act to create three new job-protected leaves to provide care or support to a family member with a serious medical condition, to provide care to a critically ill child, and for parents whose child is missing or has died as a result of a crime; Nova Scotia created a new statutory holiday (Nova Scotia Heritage Day—third Monday in February); minimum wages have increased in several provinces; federal legislation was enacted to provide workers

HR How-To

Protecting Employees' Personal Information

PIPEDA's ten principles serve as a guide to organizations and HR professionals as to how to maintain legal compliance when collecting and using employee information needed for administration and decision making. HR professionals need to consider the following principles when collecting and using employee personal information in the course of all HR activities:

1. *Accountability.* The employer is responsible for personal information it controls. Start by appointing a privacy officer(s).

2. *Identifying purpose.* Before collecting information, the organization needs to identify why they are collecting the information and how it will be used. Conduct a "privacy audit" to determine what information is collected and why it is collected.

3. *Consent.* The organization is responsible for ensuring that employees know and consent to the collection, use, and/or disclosure of personal information. Consider what type of consent is needed for each type of information on the basis of criteria such as the sensitivity of the information.

4. *Limiting collection.* Care must be taken to make sure that the collection of personal information is limited to what is needed for the stated purpose. Use a "reasonable person" test to determine what is considered appropriate.

5. *Limiting use, disclosure, and retention.* Personal information cannot be used or disclosed to others without consent and information can only be retained to meet the stated purpose(s) for which it was collected. Additional care must be taken when HR functions are outsourced. Create minimum and maximum retention times for information collected.

6. *Accuracy.* Information of employees must be current and correct. Keep information accurate and introduce a process to correct errors in a timely way.

7. *Safeguards.* Security protection needs to be put in place. Implement both technical and physical security measures to safeguard employee information.

8. *Openness.* Communicate privacy policies and practices. Consider developing training materials, brochures, or other means of communication about the organization's approach to privacy protection.

9. *Individual access.* Be responsive to employees when they request access to information the organization holds about them. Have a method in place to deal with employee concerns about the accuracy and completeness of information.

10. *Compliance challenges.* Individuals have the power to challenge what the organization does to comply with the principles just described. Be open to employee concerns and be willing to adapt policies and practices to ensure compliance with all aspects.

Sources: "Application of the *Personal Information Protection and Electronic Documents Act* to Employee Records, *Office of the Privacy Commissioner of Canada,* www.priv.gc.ca/resource/fs-fi/02_05_d_l8_e.asp, retrieved March 25, 2015; Dianne Rinehart, "The ABC's of the New Privacy Legislation," *Small Business Canada Magazine* 6, no. 2 (Spring 2004), p. 7; and "The l0 Principles of the Federal Privacy Law," *Canadian HR Reporter,* March 6, 2004, p. G7.

quick payment of unpaid wages in cases of bankruptcy or receivership; in British Columbia, the Employment Standards Act was amended in order to introduce compassionate care benefits; and the federal Employment Insurance Act has expanded the list of persons for whom an employee can claim compassionate care benefits.[30]

Controversies

A current controversy with respect to employment/labour standards relates to the use of unpaid interns. In a variety of industries including politics, technology, fashion, and journalism, it seems that several years of unpaid labour may be needed to finally achieve "paid status." These young and inexperienced interns may be particularly vulnerable to being exploited because they are unlikely to complain due to fear of jeopardizing future employment or securing a good reference.[31] The "HR Oops!" feature further explores the scrutiny the federal government and other employers face over unpaid interns.

Another area of employment/labour standards controversy emerged in the form of class-action lawsuits over unpaid overtime. For example, CIBC, Scotiabank, and KPMG have faced class-action lawsuits on behalf of employees over allegations of unpaid overtime. CIBC faced a potential $600 million lawsuit involving as many as 10,000 current and former employees from across Canada. The suit alleged that front-line employees such as tellers, account executives, and commercial and personal bankers were given workloads too heavy to be handled in regular working hours and claimed that CIBC failed to pay for overtime work that was required or at least permitted, in contravention to the Canada Labour Code. CIBC maintained it has a "clearly defined" overtime policy that "exceeds legislative requirements," and have continued its legal battle. In contrast, KPMG reached a relatively timely out-of-court settlement and Scotia Bank recently reached a tentative settlement with its current and former employees that will cover unpaid overtime worked between January 1, 2000 and December 1, 2013.[32]

An even more recent class-action lawsuit before the courts was filed on behalf of all current and some former hockey players in the OHL, WHL, and QMJHL seeking compensation for their "back-wages, overtime pay, holiday pay and vacation pay which should have been paid to them while they played in one or more of the leagues." The statement of claim alleges the players are actually employees who sign standard form league contracts and are paid only a weekly fee of between $35 and $120 per week for spending 35–40 hours of time each week on team business. "If the court decides that the players are employees, then the fee violates minimum wage legislation in every province where the teams play hockey."[33]

HR Oops!

Are Unpaid Internships a Violation of Minimum Employment Standards?

The federal government has been facing "uncomfortable questions" about its extensive use of unpaid interns. A reported 961 interns have been used in federal departments between 2008 and 2014, however only 22 were actually hired after their internship terms ended. "It's shocking, it's disappointing but unfortunately it means that these opportunities aren't actually benefiting the interns," says Member of Parliament, Laurin Liu. Liu estimates there are 300,000 unpaid interns in Canada. "But there is no official data from StatsCan to prove this. So if we want to deal with the issue of unpaid interns in Canada. . . . we need to measure the problem."

Under the Ontario Employment Standards Act, the Ontario Ministry of Labour has been cracking down on unpaid internships by establishing six criteria for an unpaid internship to be legal. If all of the criteria are not met, the intern is determined to be an employee and must be paid at least minimum wage. Magazines including *Toronto Life* and the *Walrus* have stopped "employing" unpaid interns after they were informed their practice of bringing in aspiring journalists, designers, as well as others, was in violation of Ontario's Employment Standards Act. And Bell Mobility recently scrapped its unpaid intern program in the wake of "a growing public outcry" although other federally regulated companies in the telecommunications and banking sectors continue to use unpaid interns.

Sources: Liz Bernier, "Feds Facing Scrutiny Over Unpaid Interns," *Canadian HR Reporter,* February 9, 2015, pp. l, 7; Lee-Ann Goodman, "Federal Officials to Discuss Unpaid Interns With Youth Work Advocates," *The Globe and Mail,* January 26, 2015, www.theglobeandmail.com, retrieved March 26, 2015; Simon Houpt, "End to Unpaid Internships Shakes Up Magazine Industry," *The Globe and Mail,* March 27, 2014, www.theglobeandmail.com, retrieved March 26, 2015; and Zane Schwartz, "Unpaid Internships Are Just Wrong," *The Globe and Mail,* May 3, 2013, www.theglobeandmail.com, retrieved March 26, 2015.

Pay Equity

Pay equity legislation requires that employers are responsible to provide equal pay for work of equal value. **Pay equity** is a principle of nondiscrimination in wages that requires men and women doing work of equal value to the employer to be paid the same. In addition to the federal model, several provinces, as well as Australia, Scandinavian countries, and many U.S. states, have laws to ensure women and men working in female-dominated jobs, for example, nursing, clerical, and retail sales, are paid fairly. The four criteria usually applied are *skill, effort, responsibility,* and *working conditions.* Chapter 8 includes a discussion of job evaluation, which applies these criteria to measure the relative value of jobs in the effort to ensure that jobs are paid fairly relative to one another within an organization.

pay equity
The concept of "equal pay for work of equal value."

Pay equity legislation is intended to address the *pay gap*—the difference between the earnings of women working full-time versus the earnings of men working full-time. Although many Canadian believe that the gender income tap has been successfully dealt with, the Conference Board of Canada reports the gap in income between men and women in Canada is 19 percent. This ties Canada with the U.S. at 11th spot in its peer countries (earns a "C" grade). The gender income gap ranges from a low of 8 percent (Norway) to a high of 29 percent (Japan).[34]

The irony is that men and women tend to begin their career on an approximately equal footing; however, women fall behind later—often after time away from paid employment to have children. As a result, men end up with more experience. Also, men tend to work longer hours, have more education, and are less likely than women to work part-time.[35] Cumulatively, however, these factors do not explain the entire wage gap or earnings gap between men and women. For example, Statistics Canada reported the results of a study of 29 universities related to the salaries of male and female professors. The study revealed that "male university professors earned on average up to $17,300 more than female colleagues."[36] According to the Canadian Association of University Teachers (CAUT), one reason for the wage gap is that women are underrepresented in the highest-paying position of full professor.[37]

How Are the Laws Enforced?

Human Rights Commissions

At minimum, employers must comply with the legal requirements of their jurisdictions. To provide oversight and enforce these laws, the federal government, provinces, and territories have Human Rights Commissions. For example, the *Canadian Human Rights Commission (CHRC)* provides individuals under federal jurisdiction a means to resolve complaints of discrimination. The CHRC has the power to receive and address allegations of discrimination or harassment complaints based on the 11 prohibited grounds outlined in the Canadian Human Rights Act. The CHRC tries to resolve complaints using mediation and conciliation; however, some complaints only get resolved by using a tribunal. Cases may also be ultimately appealed all the way to the Supreme Court of Canada for final resolution.

The Canadian Human Rights Commission is also responsible for auditing federally regulated employers to ensure compliance with the federal Employment Equity Act. In addition, the CHRC enforces pay equity requirements.[38] For example, in Canada's longest-running pay equity case, the initial complaint was filed back in 1983 by the Public Service Alliance of Canada on behalf of 2,300 Canada Post clerical workers, mostly female. The complaint argued the clerical workers performed work that was comparable to the mostly male letter-carriers and sorters, however they earned substantially less. Despite hearings and decisions made by the Canadian Human Rights Tribunal, the Federal Court, and the Federal Court of Appeal, Canada Post appealed the decisions until ultimately the Supreme Court ruled unanimously in the union's favour in 2011 after hearing 20 minutes of oral arguments. Even then, payments were delayed until 2013 when Canada Post agreed to pay interest on 90 percent of the settlement, which goes back to the wage gap from 1982–2002. By January 2015, it was reported that 10,000 individuals (or their estates) had received compensation from Canada Post, however, thousands more could still be eligible. Canada Post is taking out newspaper ads across the country to alert additional potential recipients as well as working with the Canada Revenue Agency to reach out to others who may be eligible for payments.[39]

Privacy Commissioners

The Office of the Privacy Commissioner of Canada is responsible for ensuring compliance with federal privacy legislation including the Personal Information Protection and Electronic Documents Act (PIPEDA) and the Privacy Act. The Office of the Privacy Commissioner of Canada has the power to investigate complaints and recommend solutions to employers. To ensure compliance, the Commissioner can publicly identify organizations violating individuals' privacy rights and take the complaint to the Federal Court of Canada. If unable to resolve the complaint, the Court can order the organization to take specific actions and can also award damages.[40] Other jurisdictions also have Privacy Commissioners responsible for ensuring compliance with their respective relevant provincial/territorial legislation.

One area of interest and concern for both individuals and organizations is the growing use of social media and specifically the growing practice of HR professionals conducting social media background checks on both current and prospective employees. For example, The Office of the Information Privacy Commissioner of Alberta published "Guidelines for Social Media Background Checks" (see Table 2.2).

LO5 Explain the context for workplace health and safety.

Workplace Health and Safety

HRC8

At the beginning of this chapter we briefly introduced the importance of taking a strategic approach to health and safety. The protection of employee health and safety is regulated by the government. Many elements are similar in all the jurisdictions across Canada, however the details of the Occupational Health and Safety (OH&S) legislation and the ways the laws are enforced vary. Some provisions in the laws and

---

TABLE 2.2

Guidelines for Social Media Background Checks

1. Determine what the business purpose is for performing a social media background check. Do you reasonably require personal information that cannot be obtained through traditional means such as interviews or reference checks?

2. Recognize that any information that is collected about an individual is personal information or personal employee information and is subject to privacy laws.

3. Consider the risks of using social media to perform a background check. Conduct a privacy impact assessment to assess the risks.

Source: "Guidelines for Social Media Background Checks," Office of the Information and Privacy Commissioner of Alberta, December 2011, www.oipc.ab.ca/downloads/documentloader.ashx?id=3539, retrieved March 23, 2015.

All workers have a right to return home each day safe and sound.

regulations also vary, e.g., "mandatory" vs. "discretionary."[41] The effective management of health and safety in the workplace includes more than legal compliance. Increasingly, organizations are approaching health and safety with a values-based commitment to safe operations as a way to protect people: "All workers have the right to return home each day safe and sound."[42] See the "Did You Know?" box.

Internal Responsibility System

In Canada, safety in the workplace is based on the foundation of an **internal responsibility system**. The internal responsibility system is a philosophy of occupational health and safety in which employers and employees share responsibility for creating and maintaining safe and healthy work environments. Employer–employee partnerships are put in place to ensure compliance and create a culture of safety in the organization.[43]

internal responsibility system
Philosophy of occupational health and safety whereby employers and employees share responsibility for creating and maintaining safe and healthy work environments.

Health and Safety Committees

Health and safety committees, a key feature of the internal responsibility system, are jointly appointed by the employer and employees at large (or union) to address health and safety issues in a workplace. For example, under federal regulations, a workplace health and safety committee is required for every workplace that has 20 or more employees. The committee must consist of at least two persons and is required to meet at least nine times a year, at regular intervals, during normal working hours.[44] The premise is that it is the people employed in a particular workplace who know the most about hazards and unhealthy conditions. Figure 2.6 outlines the role of a health and safety committee.

health and safety committees
A committee jointly appointed by the employer and employees at large (or union) to address health and safety issues in a workplace.

Top Seven Dangers for Young Workers (in B.C.)

Young workers are at significant risk of injury in a number of industries as a result of lifting objects; at risk of falls when working at elevated levels; and working with knives, food slicers, and hot substances or objects when employed as cooks, waiters, and food preparers in the hospitality and services industry.

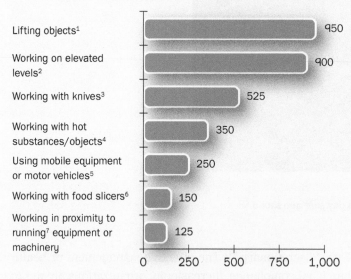

Lifting objects[1] — 950
Working on elevated levels[2] — 900
Working with knives[3] — 525
Working with hot substances/objects[4] — 350
Using mobile equipment or motor vehicles[5] — 250
Working with food slicers[6] — 150
Working in proximity to running[7] equipment or machinery — 125

(x-axis: 0, 250, 500, 750, 1,000)

[1] Lifting objects—overexertion causing sprains, strains, tears.
[2] Working at elevated levels—sprains, strains, tears, and fractures.
[3] Working with knives—cuts and lacerations.
[4] Working with hot substances/objects—burns.
[5] Using mobile equipment or motor vehicles—sprains, strains, tears, and fractures.
[6] Working with food slicers—cuts and lacerations.
[7] Working in proximity to running equipment or machinery—cuts, lacerations, and fractures.

Source: From WorkSafeBC "Top 7 Dangers for Young Workers," www2.worksafebc.com/Topics/YoungWorker/Top-Seven-Dangers.asp, retrieved March 23, 2015. © WorkSafeBC. Used with permission. WorkSafeBC.com.

FIGURE 2.6

Role of a Health and Safety Committee

The role of a health and safety committee includes:
- Act as an advisory body
- Identify hazards and obtain information about them
- Recommend corrective actions
- Assist in resolving work refusal cases
- Participate in accident investigations and workplace inspections
- Make recommendations to the management regarding actions required to resolve health and safety concerns

Source: "OH&S Legislation in Canada—Basic Responsibilities," *Canadian Centre for Occupational Health and Safety,* www.ccohs.ca/oshanswers/legisl/responsi.html, retrieved March 29, 2015.

LO6 Identify the responsibilities of employers, and managers or supervisors, as well as employees' rights and responsibilities related to workforce health and safety.

What Are the Responsibilities of Employers, and Managers or Supervisors?

Employers, managers and supervisors have a *duty* to provide a safe workplace. An employer must:

● establish and maintain a health and safety committee, or cause workers to select at least one health and safety representative

- take every reasonable precaution to ensure the workplace is safe

- train employees about any potential hazards and in how to safely use, handle, store, and dispose of hazardous substances and how to handle emergencies

- supply personal protective equipment and ensure workers know how to use the equipment safely and properly

- immediately report all critical injuries to the government department responsible for OH&S

- appoint a competent supervisor who sets the standards for performance, and who ensures safe working conditions are always observed[45]

Employers need to assess and be alert to workplace hazards and safety issues. For example, "a study published in the *British Medical Journal* found drivers talking on a cellphone are four times more likely to be involved in a serious crash." In another study, psychologists concluded that "using a hands-free cellphone while driving could impair drivers as much as having a blood-alcohol level of 0.08 percent."[46] The Ontario Ministry of Labour also provides the cautionary finding that "when drivers take their eyes off the road for more than two seconds, their crash risk doubles."[47] However, hazards associated with the use of devices is not limited to driving. Kevin Hayes, corporate safety manager for the Canadian operations of Acciona Infrastructure (www.acciona.ca), a global construction and engineering firm explains: "There are more cellular phone subscribers in the world today than landline phone subscribers. People are communicating in real-time and, unfortunately, with this need to communicate instantly, new hazards are being created." Hayes discusses a workplace fatality he was tasked to investigate at one of his company's construction projects. A road worker had been hit and killed by a dump truck and it was concluded that cellphone use was a significant factor that resulted in the fatal accident. Hayes's company has since enforced a cellphone use policy that prescribes acceptable and unacceptable use of the cellphone while at work. In particular, Hayes said, workers are prohibited from using their cellphones while performing safety-sensitive tasks, like operating heavy equipment.[48]

Employee Rights and Responsibilities

All Canadian workers have three fundamental rights that are protected by occupational health and safety legislation:

- *The right to refuse* unsafe work.

- *The right to participate* in the workplace health and safety activities through a health and safety committee or as a worker health and safety representative.

- *The right to know*, or the right to be informed about, actual and potential dangers in the workplace.[49]

An employee can refuse work if he or she believes that the situation is unsafe to either himself/herself or his/her co-workers. When the employee believes that a work refusal should be made the employee must report to his/her supervisor that he/she is refusing the work and state why the situation is unsafe. The resulting investigation will involve the employee, supervisor, and a health and safety committee member (or employee representative). Mutual agreement that the problem is solved is needed before the employee returns to this work. However, if the problem is not resolved, a government health and safety inspector will be called in to investigate and provide a written decision.[50]

Although employers and their managers and supervisors are responsible for protecting workers from health and safety hazards, employees have responsibilities as well. Employees' responsibilities include:

- working in compliance with OH&S acts and regulations

- using personal protective equipment and clothing as directed by the employer

- reporting workplace hazards and dangers
- working in a manner as required by the employer and using the prescribed safety equipment[51]

WHMIS

The Workplace Hazardous Materials Information System or WHMIS is related to the worker's "right to know." "WHMIS is Canada's national hazard communication program consisting of symbols and warning labels for consumers and material-specific safety data sheets that guide the handling of dangerous substances in the workplace, as well as related worker education and training."[52] WHMIS is implemented through coordinated federal, provincial, and territorial laws to ensure that hazardous products are properly labelled, used, stored, handled, and disposed of safely. In 2015, WHMIS was modified to incorporate the Globally Harmonized System of Classification and Labelling of Chemicals (GHS) for workplace chemicals and is now referred to as *WHMIS 2015*. The transition to WHMIS 2015 will be accomplished in a phased approach that will be fully implemented in 2018.[53]

Organizations must have **safety data sheets (SDSs)** for hazardous products that employees are exposed to. An SDS form details the hazards associated with a chemical; the chemical's producer or importer is responsible for identifying these hazards and detailing them on the form. Employers must ensure that all containers of hazardous chemicals are labelled with information about the hazards, prepare workplace labels and SDSs (as necessary), educate and train employees in safe handling of the chemicals, and ensure appropriate control methods are in place to protect the health and safety of workers.

safety data sheets (SDSs)
Detailed hazard information concerning a controlled (hazardous) product.

Enforcement of Occupational Health and Safety Regulations

Enforcement responsibilities exist within the federal, provincial, and territorial governments. Occupational health and safety officers/inspectors have the authority to inspect workplaces and issue orders to

WHMIS 2015: Pictograms of Hazard Classes & Categories

Exploding bomb (for explosion or reactivity hazards)	**Flame** (for fire hazards)	**Flame over circle** (for oxidizing hazards)
Gas cylinder (for gases under pressure)	**Corrosion** (for corrosive damage to metals, as well as skin, eyes)	**Skull and Crossbones** (can cause death or toxicity with short exposure to small amounts)
Health hazard (may cause or suspected of causing serious health effects)	**Exclamation mark** (may cause less serious health effects or damage the ozone layer)	**Environment** (may cause damage to the aquatic environment)
Biohazardous Infectious Materials (for organisms or toxins that can cause diseases in people or animals)		

Source: Reproduced with permission from the Canadian Centre for Occupational Health & Safety, www.ccohs.ca/oshanswers/chemicals/whmis_ghs/pictograms.html, retrieved March 30, 2015.

employers and workers. In some serious cases, charges may also be laid by law enforcement under a section of the Canada Criminal Code that was amended to 2004 to create additional legal duties on employers to ensure the safety of workers and the public. This amendment, **Bill C-45 (Westray Bill)**, named after the Nova Scotia mining disaster in 1992 that killed 26 workers, makes organizations and anyone who directs the work of others criminally liable for safety offences. Maximum fines were increased to $100,000 from $25,000 for less serious offences and provides an unlimited fine for more serious offences. Anyone who directs the work of others can also face serious charges—criminal conviction, a criminal record, and even life imprisonment for failing to provide for health and safety in the workplace.[54] The chapter-ending Case Study 2.2 discusses criminal convictions handed down since the amendments came into force.

> **Bill C-45 (Westray Bill)**
> Amendment to the Criminal Code making organizations and anyone who directs the work of others criminally liable for safety offences.

Psycholgical Safety

Ensuring a safe physical working environment for employees has long been recognized as an essential organizational responsibility, however, psychological safety has more recently become a significant focus. As discussed earlier in the chapter, human rights legislation prohibits behaviours such as harassment. Workplace violence is a broad problem, particularly for certain occupational groups. According to the Canadian Centre for Occupational Health and Safety, health care workers, correctional officers, social service employees, teachers, and retail employees are some of the occupational groups more at risk.[55] In addition to harassment, workplace violence includes:

- Threatening behaviour, e.g., throwing objects, or destroying property;
- Verbal or written threats, e.g., expressing intent to inflict harm
- Verbal abuse, e.g., swearing and insults
- Physical attacks, e.g., hitting, pushing, or kicking[56]

More than two-thirds of 1,381 EMS workers surveyed in Ontario and Nova Scotia reported being subjected to on-the-job verbal, physical, or sexual abuse.[57] Employees exposed to workplace violence, including harassment may develop conditions considered occupational injuries, e.g., depression, anxiety, and burnout. Judges, arbitrators, and commissioners now identify that action needs to be taken under both human rights and occupational health and safety laws and regulations to protect the psychological well-being and safety of employees.[58] The case of a former British Columbia RCMP officer serves to illustrate the significant consequences. Ex-Mountie Nancy Sulz was awarded $950,000 by the B.C. Supreme Court for "damages, lost wages, and loss of future earnings" after finding her Staff Sgt. and two subordinate officers caused Sulz "serious psychological harm" related to incidents arising after the birth of a child.[59]

Impact of Occupational Health and Safety Legislation

HRC8,9

Legislation has unquestionably succeeded in raising the level of awareness of occupational safety. The rate of workforce fatalities increased by more than 50 percent between 1996 and 2005, however, workplace fatalities have been reduced by almost 18 percent between 2005 and 2013 (see Figure 2.7). Although on every second day in 2013, approximately one less person lost their life due to work than in 2005—905 lives were lost to workplace fatalities in 2013. In addition, there has been a relatively significant reduction in time-loss injuries experienced in recent years relative to 1996–2008 levels (Figure 2.8).

FIGURE 2.7

Workplace Fatalities in Canada, 1996–2013

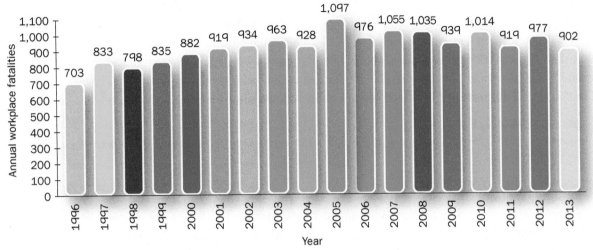

Source: Association of Workers' Compensation Boards of Canada, "Table 22: Number of Fatalities, by Jurisdiction, 1993–2013," www.awcbc.org, retrieved March 25, 2015. Reprinted with permission.

FIGURE 2.8

Time-Loss Injuries in Canada, 1996–2013

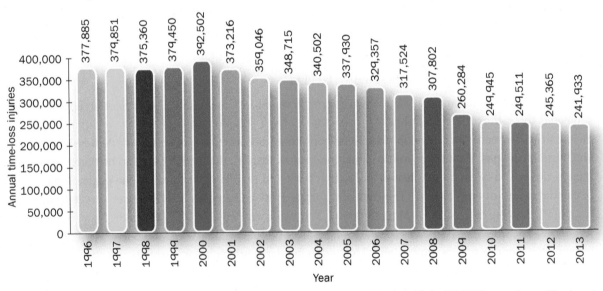

Source: Association of Workers' Compensation Boards of Canada, "Table 1: Number of Accepted Time-Loss Injuries, by Jurisdiction, 1982–2013," www.awcbc.org, retrieved March 25, 2015. Reprinted with permission.

Many workplace accidents are a product of unsafe behaviours, not unsafe working conditions. Because legislation does not directly regulate employee behaviour, little change can be expected unless employees are convinced of the standards' importance.[60] Because conforming to the law alone does not necessarily guarantee their employees will be safe, many employers go beyond the letter of the law. In the next section we examine various kinds of employer-initiated safety awareness programs that comply with, and in some cases exceed, legal requirements.

L○7 Discuss the ways employers promote worker health and safety.

Employer-Sponsored Health and Safety Programs

HRC 8

Many employers establish safety awareness programs to go beyond mere compliance with occupational health and safety regulations and attempt to instill an emphasis on safety. A safety awareness program has three primary components: identifying and communicating hazards, reinforcing safe practices, and promoting safety internationally. See the nearby "HR Best Practices" box.

Identifying and Communicating Job Hazards

Employees, supervisors, and other knowledgeable sources need to sit down and discuss potential problems related to safety. One method for doing this is the **job hazard analysis technique**.[61] With this technique, each job is broken down into basic elements, and each of these is rated for its potential for harm or injury. If there is agreement that some job element has high hazard potential, the group isolates the element and considers possible technological or behaviour changes to reduce or eliminate the hazard.

job hazard analysis technique
Safety promotion technique that involves breaking down a job into basic elements, then rating each element for its potential for harm or injury.

 E-HRM

"Health and Safety To Go" Podcasts—Subscribe on iTunes to access free content from The Canadian Centre for Occupational Health & Safety.

Another means of isolating unsafe job elements is to study past accidents. The **technic of operations review (TOR)** is an analysis method for determining which specific element of a job led to a past accident.[62] The first step in a TOR analysis is to establish the facts surrounding the incident. To accomplish this, all members of the work group involved in the accident give their initial impressions of what happened. The group must then, through discussion, come to an agreement on the single, systematic failure that most likely contributed to the incident, as well as two or three major secondary factors that contributed to it.

technic of operations review (TOR)
Method of promoting safety by determining which specific element of a job led to a past accident.

McShane Construction Company (www.mcshane.com) combined job analysis with mobile computing technology when it signed on with Field ID (www.fieldid.com) to provide the software for its safety inspections. When safety inspectors visit construction sites, they use a mobile device to scan a bar code or read a radio frequency identification (RFID) tag on each piece of equipment. The code calls up a checklist of safety measures for that equipment, and the inspector simply checks off or scores the items one by one. The mobile device then transmits the inspection data to a Field ID database, where information can easily be retrieved if the company ever needs to study the cause of an accident.[63]

To communicate with employees about job hazards, managers should talk directly with their employees about safety. Written communications are also important because it helps establish a "paper trail"

HR Best Practices

County of Wellington: Gold Winner in the Psychological Safety Category

County of Wellington is the gold winner in the psychological safety category for Canada's Safest Employers Awards

Through a range of programs and policies, the County of Wellington shows its employees that preserving their mental health is just as important as preventing slips and falls. "We really do put all our health and safety policies into action. We do walk the talk," says Andrea Lawson, human resources director at the municipal government in southwest Ontario.

The County of Wellington is the winner of the very first Canada's Safest Employers Psychological Safety Award. Michele Richardson, health and safety co-ordinator, says the county puts a great deal of effort into education and communication on the importance of psychological safety. From the time they're hired, employees are trained in respectful workplace, verbal de-escalation, and workplace violence policies. Training, including online programs, continues on a regular basis. The county recently introduced a mental health tool kit, part of mandatory training for all staff.

While workers learn to report unhealthy psychological situations to their managers, managers are trained to investigate issues and, if required, take corrective action. At quarterly managers' meetings, they often discuss a topic regarding psychological health and safety. "We work hard to give them the skills they need to identify employees who may be struggling with mental health issues and the skills they need to initiate a conversation with them," Richardson says. Consistency of manager training is important, says Melanie Shaye, human resources supervisor. The county's 800 employees work at 50 offices spread across 2,590 square kilometres. "We have people working in very remote locations and in different businesses—solid waste, roads, libraries. But because managers have this training and can deliver it to rural as well as urban staff all employees get the same message," she says. Workers can go to Richardson for support, who is an occupational health nurse, or they can also consult trained mental health first-aiders who work on site.

Absenteeism reports, worker complaints, results of exit interviews and employee and family assistance program (EFAP) quarterly reports are used to set objectives when the health and safety team develops its psychological health and safety management system, Richardson says. It also promotes prevention in areas with high EFAP usage. The County of Wellington council, senior staff, and chief administrative officer, Scott Wilson, are extremely supportive of a psychologically healthy workplace, which is a central reason for the county's success, Lawson says.

Source: "Psychological Safety 2014: County of Wellington," October 20, 2014, www.cos-mag.com/safety/safety-stories/4173-psychological-safety-2014-county-of-wellington.html, retrieved March 27, 2015. Reprinted by permission of Canadian Occupational Safety. © Copyright Thomson Reuters Canada Ltd., October 20, 2014, Toronto, Ontario 1800-387-5164. Web: www.cos-mag.com

that can later document a history of the employer's concern regarding the job hazard. Posters, especially if placed near the hazard, serve as a constant reminder, reinforcing other messages.

In communicating risk, managers should recognize that different groups of individuals may constitute different audiences. "Young and new workers are particularly vulnerable to workplace injury or illness, many of the injuries occurring in the first month on the job."[64] "Full of energy and enthusiasm, young workers can be a valuable asset to an organization. Yet this spirit, coupled with an eagerness to please and a lack of experience, may increase the risk of workplace injuries or illnesses."[65]

A recent study showed a high correlation between shift work in nurses and the risk of developing Type 2 diabetes. Shift workers are also considered at greater risk for obesity. "The relationship now between shift work and Type 2 diabetes is much clearer, the evidence is much stronger and therefore, we need to start looking at ways to intervene and the workplace is an obvious place for that to start," said Jocalyn Clark, a Toronto-based senior editor at the publication, *PLOS Medicine*.[66]

Experienced employees sometimes need retraining to jar them from complacency about the real dangers associated with their work.[67] This is especially the case if the hazard in question poses a greater threat to older employees. For example, accidents that involve falling off a ladder are a greater threat to older workers than to younger ones. Over 20 percent of such falls lead to a fatality for workers in the 55-to-65 age group, versus 10 percent for all other workers.[68]

So you think hearing protection is boring...

think again.

think safety   WORK SAFE BC   HearSafe

If you have questions about workplace safety, call WorkSafeBC's Call Centre at 604 276-3100, or toll-free in B.C. at 1 888 621-SAFE (7233).

WorkSafeBC produces a variety of posters and other resources to communicate job hazards and promote working safely.

Reinforcing Safe Practices

To ensure safe behaviours, employers should not only define how to work safely but also reinforce the desired behaviour. One common technique for reinforcing safe practices is implementing a *safety incentive program* to reward workers for their support of and commitment to safety goals. Such programs start by focusing on monthly or quarterly goals or by encouraging suggestions for improving safety. Goals might include good housekeeping practices, adherence to safety rules, and proper use of protective equipment. Later, the program expands to include more wide-ranging, long-term goals. Typically, the employer distributes awards in highly public forums, such as company or department meetings. Using merchandise for prizes, instead of cash, provides a lasting symbol of achievement. A good deal of evidence suggests that such incentive programs are effective in reducing the number and cost of injuries.[69]

Besides focusing on specific jobs, organizations can target particular types of injuries or disabilities, especially those for which employees may be at risk. For example, the CNIB (www.cnib.ca) reports that every day 700 Canadian workers sustain eye injuries on the job, often resulting in lost time and, in some cases, either temporary or permanent vision loss.[70] Organizations can prevent such injuries through a combination of job analysis, written policies, safety training, protective eyewear, rewards and sanctions for safe and unsafe behaviour, and management support for the safety effort.

Industries and occupational groups also provide organizational safety awards. For example, the Canadian Association of Petroleum Producers—CAPP (www.capp.ca) presents annual awards to oil and gas companies for innovative health and safety accomplishments. Talisman Energy Inc. (www.talisman-energy.com) was recently given an award for its "Cypress 3D Seismic Program," a large-scale, low-environmental impact, geophysical exploration program near Fort St. John, British Columbia. The program's study included the potential to improve helicopter safety while also protecting migratory birds.[71]

Employee Health and Wellness Programs

Another way to improve the well-being and overall health of employees is to offer an **employee health and wellness program**, a set of communications, activities, and facilities designed to change health-related behaviours in ways that reduce health risks. Typically, wellness programs aim at specific health risks, such as high blood pressure, high cholesterol levels, smoking, and obesity, by encouraging preventive measures such as exercise and good nutrition. However, many organizations are adopting an integrated strategic approach to wellness that promotes a corporate culture to support employees in taking responsibility for their health and overall wellness. Many organizations are also using incentives to create more interest in their program. "Incentives create more interest in the program and inspire people who aren't usually active to get involved," says Kathleen Jones, business solutions manager at Fraser & Hoyt Incentives (www.fh-incentives.ca) in Halifax. Examples of wellness incentives include exercise-themed prizes like yoga mats, iPods, and even big-ticket items like trips and TVs.[72]

> **employee health and wellness program**
> A set of communications, activities, and facilities designed to change health-related behaviours in ways that reduce health risks.

Organizations that place a strategic emphasis on corporate wellness achieve economic benefits including reduced injury and disability insurance costs, enhanced productivity and service, and reduced costs due to a reduction in employee absenteeism and turnover.[73] Some organizations are also attempting to measure the return on investment (ROI) of health and wellness programs. For example, Desjardins Group (www.desjardins.com/ca) reports "a return on investment of between $1.50 and $3 for every dollar invested in their program in addition to other positive employee self-reported outcomes including making healthier food choices, lower stress, and engaging in more physical activity.[74]

Wellness programs are either *passive* or *active*. Passive programs provide information and services, but no formal support or motivation to use the program. Examples include health education (such as lunchtime courses) and fitness facilities. These programs are considered passive because they rely on employees to identify the services they need and act on their own to obtain the services, such as participating in classes. Active wellness programs assume that behaviour change requires support and reinforcement along with awareness and opportunity. These programs provide for outreach and follow-up. For example, the program may include counsellors who tailor programs to individual employees' needs, take baseline measurements (e.g., blood pressure and weight), and take follow-up measures for comparison to the baseline. Active programs often set goals and provide symbolic rewards as individuals make progress toward meeting their goals. In general, passive health education programs cost less than active wellness programs.[75] All these variations have had success in reducing risk factors associated with cardiovascular disease (obesity, high blood pressure, smoking, lack of exercise), but the follow-up method is most successful.

The Town of Conception Bay South, Newfoundland and Labrador, is a growing municipality located just minutes away from St. John's, the provincial capital. After senior leaders noted a significant increase in Workplace Health, Safety, and Compensation Commission claims and premiums, they decided to create a health and wellness program. After seeking feedback from all employees on health and wellness concerns, a health and wellness program with several components was implemented. Employees receive free use of all recreational facilities e.g., swimming, tennis, skating, and squash; they are encouraged to use the employee assistance program (EAP), attend luncheon sessions, and access the monthly wellness newsletters. Some of the outcomes experienced to date include annual savings of $45,000 in sick leave, significant and sustained savings in WHSCC premiums due to a significant decline in claims, and achieving a score of over 90 percent on its occupational health and safety audit, a considerable improvement from its initial audit score of 38 percent.[76]

Employee Assistance Program (EAP)

An **employee assistance program (EAP)** is a confidential, short term, counselling service for employees with personal problems that affect their work performance.[77] EAPs began in the 1950s with a focus on treating alcoholism, and in the 1980s they expanded into drug treatment. Today, many EAP providers offer a very broad range of services that may overlap with health, wellness, and lifestyle-related services, e.g., dealing with stress. Many organizations also extend these services to family members. Left untreated, these issues may cause employees to lose their ability to cope and their work performance and safety may suffer. Employees must be able to feel confident the program respects their confidentiality. In addition to services provided, other considerations include proximity to counsellors, client references, and availability of effectiveness reporting measures.[78]

employee assistance program (EAP)
Confidential, short term, counselling service for employees with personal problems that affect their work performance.

The City of Calgary (www.calgary.ca) recently launched a three-year mental health strategy. One element of the strategy is to improve depression care—from short-term to long-term counselling, with a maximum of 20 sessions, said Cindy Munn, the city's HR business partner for employee wellness. The counselling sessions are provided as part of the EAP.[79]

Promoting Safety Internationally

Given the increasing focus on international management, organizations also need to consider how to ensure the safety of their employees regardless of the nation in which they operate. Cultural differences may make this more difficult than it seems. For example, a study examined the impact of one standardized corporation-wide safety policy on employees in three different countries: the United States, France, and Argentina. The results of this study indicate that employees in the three countries interpreted the policy differently because of cultural differences. The individualistic, control-oriented culture of the United States stressed the role of top management in ensuring safety in a top-down fashion. However, this policy failed to work in Argentina, where the culture is more "collectivist" (emphasizing the group). Argentine employees tend to feel that safety is everyone's joint concern, so the safety programs needed to be defined from the bottom of the organization up.[80]

Another challenge in promoting safety internationally is that laws, enforcement practices, and political climates vary from country to country. With the increasing use of offshoring, described in Chapter 1, more companies have operations in countries where employment and labour standards are far less strict than Canada. Managers and employees in these countries may not think the company is serious about protecting workers' health and safety. In that case, strong communication and oversight will be necessary if the company intends to adhere to the ethical principle of valuing its global workers' safety as much as the safety of its Canadian workers. For example, The Gap (www.gapcanada.ca) treats this issue as part of its corporate social responsibility. The company views its supply chain as socially sustainable only when working conditions and factory conditions meet acceptable business practices. According to Eva Sage-Gavin, Gap's executive vice-president of human resources and corporate communications, "We know that better factory working conditions lead to better factories, and better factories make better products."[81]

Thinking ETHICALLY

Simple Questions Cause Awkward Situations

"What did you do on the weekend?" It sounds like a simple question that managers might ask their employees in order to build a team atmosphere and show interest in their lives outside work. But for lesbian, gay, bisexual, or transgender (LGBT) employees who may not be "out" to their bosses, it can be one of the hardest questions to answer. According to 72 percent of respondents to a survey released by the Canadian Gay and Lesbian Chamber of Commerce (CGLCC), attitudes toward LGBT people in the workplace have improved over the last five years. However, two-fifths of respondents said they have faced discrimination in the workplace. The survey of 983 LGBT employees from across the country reported that ridicule (42 percent) and social exclusion (43 percent) were the most common forms of discrimination.

Companies that promote diversity emphasize hiring, training, and retention of people protected by human rights and employment equity legislation. Some companies take diversity efforts further. For example, IBM Canada has nine diversity network groups. These network groups share information, provide coaching and mentoring, participate in community outreach activities, and plan and implement social, cultural, and educational events. An example of how these groups contribute to building an inclusive work environment is found in the activity of IBM's LGBT Network Group.

The group has been active in Canada since the early 1990s. At first, its work involved advising the human resource department in establishing benefit rights for partners and creating a forum for sharing with fellow LGBT members. As the group evolved, it has taken on a larger mandate of community involvement. One of the most successful examples of this is the executive breakfast series hosted by members of the LGBT group. The program is designed to educate IBM executives on the sensitivities of working with a member of the LGBT constituency who may not be "out" in the workplace. Since LGBT employees are less identifiable, the group felt it was important to be more visible and provide names and faces that can help drive home issues. The sessions are designed so executive participants can "walk in the shoes" of a LGBT member.

When Esther Dryburgh, a partner in business consulting services at IBM in Toronto, was asked by a friend to speak at one of the executive breakfasts about what it was like to be gay, but in the closet at work, she had a big decision to make. If she spoke at the breakfast she would reveal her "secret." She decided to go ahead, make the speech and serve as a role model for others. "It was amazing. It was a very positive experience for me, coming out at work, bring my full self at work," Esther said. "All of the executives were so supportive—it was almost like a religious experience for them." One of the reasons Dryburgh hesitated to come out at work was a concern that it might affect her career, she said. "People tend to network, mentor and promote people who are similar to them so, as a result LGBT people work hard, make their numbers like every other employee but they are at a disadvantage," said Dryburgh. "We just don't have equal representation (in leadership) of folks that are like us."

Apple CEO Tim Cook recently announced in a column he wrote that he "is proud to be gay." As the first openly gay CEO of a Fortune 500 company, his ongoing impact on the experiences of LGBT people may be significant. "I've come to realize that my desire for personal privacy has been holding me back from doing something more important," he said in *Bloomberg Businessweek*. "If hearing that the CEO of Apple is gay can help someone struggling to come to terms with who he or she is, or bring comfort to anyone who feels alone, or inspire people to insist on their equality, then it's worth the trade-off with my own privacy."

Questions

1. Is IBM's policy toward LGBT employees good business? Is it good ethics? Should a company pursue a diversity policy that goes beyond legal requirements? Why or why not?

2. What impact, if any, do you think Apple CEO Tim Cook's announcement will have on creating workplaces where LGBT (and transgender) employees are less likely to feel they need to hide their sexual orientation (gender identity) or endure harassment?

Sources: Sarah Dobson, "Out and Proud at Work," *Canadian HR Reporter,*" December 1, 2014, pp. 1-2; Timothy Cook, "Tim Cook Speaks Up," *Bloomberg Business,* October 30, 2014, www.bloomberg.com/news/articles/2014-10-30/tim-cook-speaks-up, retrieved March 30, 2014; Amanda Silliker, "LGBT Staff Still Face Bias," *Canadian HR Reporter,* December 19, 2011, pp. 1, 9; "IBM Canada Ltd.: Diversity & Inclusion at IBM," January 2007, www-03.ibm.com/employment/ca/en/newhire/diversity_faq.pdf, retrieved March 25, 2012; and Susan Turner, "Simple Questions and Awkward Situations: The Impact of the Closet at Work," *Canadian HR Reporter,* December 20, 2004, p. 10.

SUMMARY

L○1 Discuss the importance of valuing diversity and safety.

Although the practice of valuing diversity has no single form, organizations that value diversity are likely to be mindful of the benefits of diversity and work actively to create a work environment in which individuals feel valued and able to perform to their potential. Increasingly, organizations are taking a strategic approach to occupational health and safety by adopting a values-based commitment to safe and healthy operations.

L○2 Describe the legal framework for human resource management in Canada.

Approximately 94 percent of Canadian employees are covered by provincial and territorial legislation. The remaining 6 percent are covered by federal legislation. Although jurisdictional differences exist, laws tend to mirror one another.

L○3 Explain the importance of human rights and the implications for HRM.

Employers can avoid discrimination by avoiding differential treatment of job applicants and employees. Organizations can develop and enforce practices and policies that demonstrate a high value placed on diversity. To provide accommodation, companies should recognize individuals' needs. Employers may need to make such accommodations as adjusting schedules or dress codes, making the workplace more accessible, or restructuring jobs.

Organizations can prevent harassment by developing policies, training employees to recognize and avoid this behaviour, and providing the means for employees to be protected. Employment equity initiatives may remove employment barriers to the designated groups.

L○4 Discuss privacy, employment/labour standards, and pay equity and their relevance for HRM.

The Personal Information Protection and Electronic Documents Act (PIPEDA) provides rules about how organizations can collect, use, and disclose information about you. Employment/labour standards legislation deals with the minimum standards an employee will receive.

Pay equity provisions help assure equal pay for work of equal value. Human Rights Commissions are responsible for enforcing human rights legislation in their respective jurisdictions. Privacy Commissioners are responsible for enforcing privacy legislation in their jurisdictions.

L○5 Explain the context for workplace health and safety

All jurisdictions in Canada have occupational health and safety legislation. Canada's approach to safety in the workplace is based on the internal responsibility system whereby both employers and employees are responsible for safety.

L○6 Identify the responsibilities of employers, and managers or supervisors, as well as employees' rights and responsibilities related to workforce health and safety.

Employers and managers and supervisors have a duty to provide a safe workplace. Canada's workers have three fundamental rights that are protected by occupational health and safety legislation as well as specific responsibilities.

Bill C-45, an amendment to the Criminal Code, has created a legal duty on employers to ensure the safety of workers. Employees also have responsibilities including following safety rules and reporting hazardous conditions. Psychological safety has also become a significant workplace health and safety issue.

LO7 Discuss the ways employers promote worker health and safety.

Besides complying with occupational health and safety regulations, employers often establish safety awareness programs designed to instill an emphasis on safety. Employers may identify and communicate hazards through the job hazard analysis technique or the technic of operations review. They may adapt communications and training to the needs of different employees, such as differences in experience levels or cultural differences from one country to another. Employers may also establish incentive programs to reward safe behaviour.

Critical Thinking Questions

1. "Organizations that value diversity and inclusiveness are more likely to meet their employment equity goals." Do you agree or disagree with this statement? Why or why not?

2. On the basis of your knowledge of diverse religious practices, what types of accommodations should an employer be prepared to provide?

3. What is sexual harassment? What are some types of behaviour likely considered to be sexual harassment in a workplace?

4. Research minimum wages across various jurisdictions in Canada, for example, Alberta, New Brunswick, and Ontario. Also, conduct online research regarding advertised salaries at traditionally "minimum wage" service-sector jobs such as retail sales and fast-food restaurants in Alberta, New Brunswick, and Ontario. What are your observations and conclusions?

5. Do you think that employers violate current or prospective employees' privacy rights when they use social media sites such as Facebook, Twitter, and LinkedIn to conduct background checks? Why or why not?

6. Have you ever been injured on the job or experienced workplace violence? What are jobs that you think may be hazardous? What types of hazards and hazardous activities might workers experience in these jobs?

7. What effect does Bill C-45 (Westray Bill) likely have on supervisors' behaviours and attitudes related to workplace safety?

8. Why do you think younger workers are more likely to be injured on the job?

9. Due to demands of your job or expectations of your manager, have you ever felt pressured to text or answer a call while driving (or performing safety-sensitive work)? What were the circumstances? Would you do anything differently in the future? Why or why not?

10. For each of the following occupations, identify at least one possible hazard and at least one action employees could take to minimize the risk of any injury or illness related to that hazard.

   a. Server in a restaurant

   b. House painter

   c. Computer programmer

   d. Worker in a care home for seniors

Experiencing HR

Form groups of three students. Assign three roles for a role-playing exercise: a human resources manager, an employee in his or her mid-50s, and the employee's supervisor.

Background: The supervisor is concerned about an employee that reports to her. The employee is responsible for shipping and receiving freight at a large privately owned manufacturing company. The employee has been experiencing severe back pain that is making it impossible for her to perform her job. The employee has just provided the supervisor a medical assessment that states that the employee cannot lift more than 10 kg.

Role-play a meeting in which the supervisor discusses the employee's situation with the HR manager. Then, as a group, decide who should meet with the employee and what should be said. Role-play that meeting. Finally, discuss the outcome of the meetings. Was the meeting with the employee conducted in a way that will avoid accusations of age (or other) discrimination? Write a paragraph to summarize what you have learned.

CASE STUDY 2.1:

Airport Screener Suspended for Altering Uniform to Comply with Her Religious Beliefs

Halima Muse, 33, a practising Muslim, immigrated to Canada from Somalia and had been employed for six years with Garda, a company contracted by the Canadian Air Transport Security Authority (CATSA) to screen passengers and their luggage at Toronto's Pearson International Airport. At the airport, security employees are provided a standard uniform. Female employees had a choice of wearing either a knee-length skirt or slacks. Muse had been wearing slacks, because knee-length skirts violate the modesty standards of her religion. However, due to her Islamic beliefs she also felt uncomfortable exposing the shape of her body by wearing slacks and always wore a blazer to cover her hips. Finally, she asked her employer if she could wear a non-standard loose-fitting skirt that she had made of similar colour and fabric. She received approval to wear the ankle-length skirt; however, several months later, the Canadian Air Transport Security Authority insisted that she wear one of the two standard uniforms, that is, slacks or knee-length skirt. When she refused to give up the ankle-length skirt she was suspended. Although she filed a grievance with her union, Teamsters 847, her employer advised her that CATSA, not Garda, controlled the policy related to uniforms.

CATSA defended its strict policy regarding uniforms on the grounds that maintaining a professional image in airport security was very important.

Questions

1. By offering Muse a choice of slacks or a knee-length skirt do you feel CATSA provided a reasonable accommodation to this employee? Justify your answer.

2. Because Muse agreed to wear slacks for several years before telling her employer about her concerns should there be any reduced duty on her employer or CATSA to accommodate? Explain.

3. If you had been Muse's supervisor, how would you have handled her request? Is there anything you would have done differently?

Sources: Jeffrey R. Smith, "Airport Screener Suspended for Wearing Long Skirt," *Canadian HR Reporter,* December 17, 2007, pp. I, II; "Suspended Muslim Airport Screener Offered New Job," *The Globe and Mail,* November 22, 2007, p. A17; and John Goddard, "Guard to Get Back Pay Pending Uniform Review: Airport Screener Will Do Alternative Work During Uniform Assessment," *Toronto Star,* November 21, 2007, p. A14.

CASE STUDY 2.2:

Employers Found Guilty of Criminal Negligence Causing Death

Metron Construction Corporation was the first Ontario firm to be convicted under the Criminal Code after making a guilty plea to a charge of "criminal negligence causing death" after four workers were killed and another was seriously injured when a swing stage scaffold collapsed while they were repairing concrete balconies on an apartment building in Toronto. Metron's president also pleaded guilty to four charges under the Occupational Health and Safety Act, for failing "as a director to take all reasonable care to ensure the health and safety of Metron's workers." Metron was fined $200,000 plus a victim surcharge of $30,000 and its president was fined $90,000 plus a victim surcharge of $22,500. The total of the fines ($342,500) represented three times Metron's net earnings in the year prior to the accident.

The first conviction under Bill C-45 was handed down in Quebec when a Quebec court in 2008 ordered a company convicted of criminal negligence in the death of a worker to pay $110,000. Transpavé, a paving-stone manufacturer in Saint-Eustache, Quebec, pleaded guilty to criminal negligence in the 2005 death of 23-year-old Steve L'Écuyer. L'Écuyer had been crushed by a machine that stacks concrete blocks after pallets with concrete had backed up on the conveyer belt. Inspectors found the machine's safety guard had been disabled for nearly two years.

In his ruling, the judge said the company, managers, and employees weren't aware that the safety guard wasn't working and that there was no intent on the company's part for the system to be down. He also stated the fine reflected the company's willingness to take responsibility for the incident and the $500,000 in safety upgrades the company has made since the accident to bring the plant in line with European standards, which are more stringent than North American standards.

The second employer convicted of criminal negligence under the amendments to the Criminal Code was Pasquale Scrocca, a landscape contractor, who admitted that he did not check the brake fluid on a backhoe and had not had the equipment checked by a certified mechanic. Scrocca was operating the backhoe when it failed to brake and pinned one of his employees, Ariello Boccanfuso, to a wall, causing his death. After the incident, a mechanical inspection determined the backhoe had "no braking capacity in the front two wheels, no reservoir, and a total braking capacity of less than 30 percent." Despite Scrocca's argument that he was not aware of the braking issue, the court applied a "conditional sentence of two years imprisonment, less a day" with the sentence to be served in the community.

In the more than ten years since Bill C-45 was passed, there have been relatively few prosecutions—ten in total. It should also be noted that the average number of fatalities has only decreased modestly since Bill C-45 came into law.

Questions

1. Do you think company managers should be held accountable for a workplace fatality? Why or why not?

2. Do you think these criminal convictions described in the case will have any lasting effect on improving the safety of workplaces in Canada? Why or why not?

Sources: Norm Keith, "After 10 Years, Bill C-45 Yields Few Prosecutions," *Canadian Occupational Safety,* www.cos-mag.com/legal/legal-columns/3900-after-10-years-bill-c-45-yields-few-prosecutions.html, April 23, 2014, retrieved March 27, 2015; Norm Keith, "Canadian Employers Hit with Record-Setting Safety Fines," October 21, 2013, *SHRM website,* www.shrm.org/hrdisciplines/safetysecurity/articles/pages/canadian-employers-safety-fines.aspx, retrieved March 27, 2015, Kathleen Chevalier, "Metron Construction Accident Results In Criminal Conviction and $200k Fine," *Strikeman Elliott–Canadian Employment & Pension Law,* September 27, 2012, www.canadianemploymentpensionlaw.com/employment-standards/metron-construction-accident-results-in-criminal-conviction-and-20000000-fine/, retrieved March 27, 2015; Norm Keith and Anna Abbott, "Criminal Conviction in Death of Worker," *Canadian HR Reporter,* October 10, 2011, p. 25; "Safety Update: Employer Convicted of Bill C-45 Charge Following Trial," www.ecompliance.com/about-us/safety-updates/2011/10/13/safety-update-employer-convicted-of-bill-c-45-charge-following-trial, retrieved March 24, 2012; Chris Doucette, "4 Workers Killed in Scaffolding Collapse," *The Toronto Sun,* December 25, 2009, www.torontosun.com/news/torontoandgta/2009/12/25/12266386.html, retrieved March 24, 2012; and "Quebec Company Fined $110,000 in Worker's Death," *Canadian HR Reporter,* March 18, 2008.

VIDEO CASES PART 1

Video Case: What CEOs Want from HR Professionals (www.hrreporter.com/students/videodisplay/201-what-ceos-want-from-hr-professionals)

President and CEO of Ricoh Canada, Glenn Laverty suggests that HR has tended to be positioned functionally rather than strategically in most organizations. Although HR has many regulatory and administrative responsibilities, he wants to see HR thinking outside the box and taking the role of strategic partner to the business. Establishing that role at the executive level provides HR the opportunity to establish credibility and create ability to execute for each and every department.

Laverty suggests that HR needs the CEO's assistance to break through the mindset that still exists in some organizations that HR is just a function and work to open up a true partnership relationship for HR with other departments. He says that should begin with HR being present at strategic planning sessions where HR can put forward their strategies and be highly involved in understanding how they can help leaders in the organization accomplish their strategies. This means that HR needs to be at the executive level, at the strategic planning sessions, and recognize what it takes to partner with the organization to achieve the firm's goals.

Questions

1. What competencies do you think HR professionals need to fulfill the expectations this CEO has for HR?

2. Does this role for HR sound like the kind of career you would like to have? Why or Why not?

Source: Based on "What CEOs Want from HR Professionals," *Canadian HR Reporter TV,* November 23, 2011. Reprinted by permission of Canadian HR Reporter. © Copyright Thomson Reuters Canada Ltd., November 23, 2011, Toronto, Ontario 1800-387-5164. Web: www.hrreporter.com

Video Case: Competing Human Rights Claims in the Workplace (www.hrreporter.com/videodisplay/367-competing-human-rights-claims-in-the-workplace)

As workplaces become increasingly diverse it becomes inevitable that organizations will face a competing human rights claim. Cherie Robertson, a senior policy analyst at the Ontario Human

Rights Commission, explains how creating a competing human rights policy can prevent conflicts from escalating.

The Ontario Human Rights Commission introduced a policy and framework on competing human rights, which is intended to be a useful tool for employers. It is recommended that employers have their own internal competing rights policy so they educate themselves and their staff should a competing human rights issue emerge.

Cherie describes a scenario in which a college professor with a visual disability has a service dog in the classroom to assist with his/her needs, however a student has a severe allergy to dogs and as a result is not able to attend the college professor's lectures. In this case the professor's code-protected right of disability conflicts with the student's code-protected right of disability. She recommends that an organization facing a competing human rights issue educate the parties on each other's rights and see if the parties can work together to brainstorm a solution consistent with legal principles and respects the rights of both parties. If an organization does not have a policy on competing rights it becomes vulnerable to having a human rights complaint filed and this can be costly as well as damaging to workplace morale.

Questions (Consider the sample situation of the student and professor described in the video)

1. Competing rights issues are likely to generate strong emotions. What advice would you have for an HR professional from the college who is preparing to meet with both parties to discuss their rights and possible solutions?

2. What do you think would be a fair and reasonable solution that would respect the rights of both parties?

Source: Based on "Competing Human Rights Claims in the Workplace," *Canadian HR Reporter TV*, March 31, 2014. Reprinted by permission of Canadian HR Reporter. © Copyright Thomson Reuters Canada Ltd., March 31, 2014, Toronto, Ontario 1800-387-5164. Web: www.hrreporter.com

Preparing for and
Acquiring Human Resources

CHAPTER 3

Analyzing Work and Designing Jobs

WHAT DO I NEED TO KNOW?

After reading this chapter, you should be able to:

LO1	Summarize the elements of work flow analysis and how work flow relates to an organization's structure.
LO2	Discuss the significance, recent trends, and outcomes of job analysis.
LO3	Tell how to obtain information for a job analysis.
LO4	Describe methods for designing a job so that it can be done efficiently.
LO5	Identify approaches to designing a job to make it motivating.
LO6	Explain how organizations apply ergonomics to design safe jobs.
LO7	Discuss how organizations can plan for the mental demands of a job.

What is a "good" or "best" job? What type of job would it take to retain your loyalty. . . even after winning the lottery?

Would You Keep Working If You Won the Lottery?

CareerBuilder (www.careerbuilder.ca) recently polled 3,372 workers asking them if they would keep working even if they won the lottery. More than one-half of those surveyed said they would keep working, even if they didn't need a job for financial reasons and 30 percent of those surveyed said they would *keep their current job.*

So what does it take for a job to be "good" or "best?" One perspective of "best jobs" is advanced by Glassdoor (www.glassdoor.ca) in their "10 Best Jobs for People in Their 20s." Glassdoor looked at three years of job reviews posted on their site by employees between the ages of 20 and 29 to create their list: #1: Marketing Manager; #2: Software Engineer; #3: Mechanical Engineer; #4: Research Associate; and #5: Business Analyst. Another large annual survey bases its assessment of "best jobs" by using a combination of weighted elements including ten-year growth volume, ten-year growth percentage, median salary, job prospects, employment rate, stress levels, and work/life balance.

It has been suggested that a *good* job "offers financial stability, financial security, safe working conditions, a degree of challenge, opportunity for growth, and should interest but not necessarily inspire—the worker." Understanding the organization's jobs and careful consideration of how to effectively design jobs is important work for managers and HR professionals. . . before the next lottery office pool![1]

Introduction

Broad responsibilities, duties like analyzing legal documents, acting as a company representative at career fairs, or providing feedback on First Nations issues—may all be elements of an internship or regular position in an HR department. These elements give rise to the types of skills and characteristics required for success, and they in turn help to define the people who will succeed in the position. Consideration of such elements is at the heart of analyzing work, whether in a startup enterprise, a multinational corporation, or a government agency.

This chapter discusses the analysis and design of work and, in doing so, lays out some considerations that go into making informed decisions about how to create and link jobs. The chapter begins with a look at the big-picture issues related to analyzing work flow and organizational structure. The discussion then turns to the more specific issues of analyzing and designing jobs. Traditionally, job analysis has emphasized the study of existing jobs in order to make decisions such as employee selection, training, and rewards. In contrast, job design has emphasized making jobs more efficient or more motivating. However, as this chapter shows, the two activities are interrelated.

Informed decisions about jobs take place in the context of the organization's overall work flow. Through the process of **work flow design**, managers analyze the tasks needed to produce a product or service. With this information, they assign these tasks to specific jobs and positions. (A **job** is a set of related duties. A **position** is the set of duties performed by one person. A school has many teaching *positions;* the person filling each of those positions is performing the *job* of teacher.) Basing these decisions on work flow design can lead to better results than the more traditional practice of looking at jobs individually.

work flow design
The process of analyzing the tasks necessary for the production of a product or service.

job
A set of related duties.

position
The set of duties (job) performed by a particular person.

Firefighters work as a team. They and their equipment are the "inputs" (they do the work), and the "output" is an extinguished fire and the rescue of people and pets. In any organization or team, workers need to be cross-trained in several skills to create an effective team. If these firefighters are trained to do any part of the job, the chief can deploy them rapidly as needed.

L○1 Summarize the elements of work flow analysis and how work flow relates to an organization's structure.

What Is Work Flow Analysis?

HRC4

Before designing its work flow, the organization's planners need to analyze what work needs to be done. Figure 3.1 shows the elements of a work flow analysis. For each type of work, such as producing a product or providing a support service (accounting, legal support, and so on), the analysis identifies the output of the process, the activities involved, and three categories of inputs: raw inputs (materials and information), equipment, and human resources.

Outputs are the products of any work unit, say department or team. Outputs may be tangible, as in the case of a restaurant meal or finished part. They may be intangible, such as building security or an answered question about employee benefits. In identifying the outputs of particular work units, work flow analysis considers both quantity and quality. Thinking in terms of these outputs gives HRM professionals a clearer view of how to increase each work unit's effectiveness.

Work flow analysis next considers the *work processes* used to generate the outputs identified. Work processes are the activities that a work unit's members engage in to produce a given output. They are described in terms of operating procedures for every task performed by each employee at each stage of the process. Specifying the processes helps HRM professionals design efficient work systems by clarifying which tasks are necessary. Knowledge of work processes also can guide staffing changes when work is automated, outsourced, or restructured. The nearby "HR Oops!" feature describes when work flow analysis may have gone into too much detail.

Finally work flow analysis identifies the *inputs* required to carry out the work processes. As shown in Figure 3.1, inputs fall into three categories: raw inputs (materials and information), equipment, and human resources (knowledge, skills, and abilities.) At manufacturing companies in North America, there has

FIGURE 3.1

Developing a Work Flow Analysis

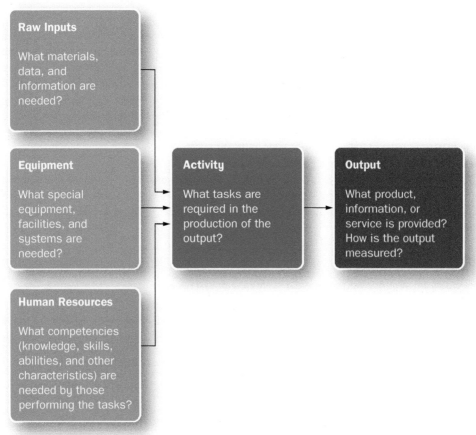

been a shift in the kinds of inputs needed for success. Most low-wage, low-skill manufacturing processes have been moved to parts of the world where the cost of labour is low. In North America, successful manufacturers now emphasize innovation and short runs of specialized products. This kind of work calls for greater use of computerized equipment, which is run by lean workforces of highly skilled technicians.[2]

How Does the Work Fit with the Organization's Structure?

HRC**1**

Work flow takes place in the context of an organization's structure. It requires the cooperation of individuals and groups. Ideally, the organization's structure brings together the people who must collaborate to produce the desired outputs efficiently. The structure may do this in a way that is highly centralized (i.e., with authority concentrated in a few people at the top of the organization) or decentralized (with authority spread among many people). The organization may group jobs according to functions (e.g., welding, painting, packaging), or it may set up divisions to focus on products or customer groups.

Although there are an infinite number of ways to combine the elements of an organization's structure, we can make some general observations about structure and work design. If the structure is strongly based on function, workers tend to have low authority and to work alone at highly specialized jobs. Jobs that involve teamwork or broad responsibility tend to require a structure based on divisions other than functions. When the goal is to empower employees, companies therefore need to set up structures and

HR Oops!

How to Brew Coffee?

An eight-step set of detailed instructions "directing staff how to properly brew a pot of coffee" that appeared on the Saskatchewan Health Quality Council (HCQ) office refrigerator stirred renewed controversy about the province's $39 million Lean consulting initiative. The instructions were written on the consulting firm's work order and were also branded with the province's "Putting Patients First" health care logo. Under criticism, the HQC initially explained: "It's part of HQC staff learning how to apply tools/techniques that others in system are learning/using." Later, the interim HQC director explained the eight-step process was "simply instructions written on a . . . work order for staff members unfamiliar with the coffee machine." According to the Saskatchewan Health Quality Council website, the HQC is "a team of individuals with many different skills committed to helping Saskatchewan's health system make care better and safer for the people of Saskatchewan."

Saskatchewan's Opposition Party says "a document that gives health workers step-by-step instructions on how to brew a pot of coffee is disrespectful and silly," and that "making coffee is a very straightforward simple task that. . . people know how to do." They also suggested that the instructions had been updated and revised—"This is not some random, one-of thing."

Questions

1. Did this organization go too far in preparing (and apparently revising) detailed instructions for its employees about "how to properly brew a pot of coffee"? Why or why not?

2. What advice would you offer management about the potential pitfalls of providing detailed instructions for employees who work in jobs that involve teamwork and/or broad responsibility?

Sources: M. Mandryk, "Mandryk: Lean Brews Micro-Management Mess," *The Leader Post*, www.leaderpost.com/life/Mandryk+Lean+brews+micro+management+mess/10724248/story.html, January 13, 2015; J. Charlton, "NDP Stirs Pot with Coffee Criticism," *The Star Phoenix*, January 10, 2015, www.thestarphoenix.com/life/stirs+with+coffee+criticism/10718035/story.html, retrieved January 18, 2015; "Lean Goes Too Far with Steps for Making Coffee, Sask. NDP says," *CBC News*, January 9, 2015, www.cbc.ca/news/canada/saskatoon/lean-goes-too-far-with-steps-for-making-coffee-sask-ndp-says-1.2895284, retrieved January 18, 2015; C. Clancy, "Health Workers Instructed on Coffee-Making: NDP," National *Newswatch*, January 9, 2015, www.nationalnewswatch.com/2015/01/09/saskatchewan-health-care-workers-instructed-on-coffee-making-ndp/#.VLyPhjnrfdk, retrieved January 18, 2015; "Our Story: Who is the Health Quality Council?" http://hqc.sk.ca/about/story/, retrieved January 18, 2015.

jobs that enable broad responsibility, such as jobs that involve employees in serving a particular group of customers or producing a particular product, rather than performing a narrowly defined function. The organization's structure also affects managers' jobs. Managing a division responsible for a product or customer group tends to require more experience and cognitive (thinking) ability than managing a department that handles a specific function.[3]

Work design often emphasizes the analysis and design of jobs, as described in the remainder of this chapter. Although all of these approaches can succeed, each focuses on one isolated job at a time. These approaches do not necessarily consider how that single job fits into the overall work flow or structure of the organization. To use these techniques effectively, human resources professionals should also understand their organization as a whole.

L○2 Discuss the significance, recent trends, and outcomes of job analysis.

Job Analysis

HRC1,4

To achieve high-quality performance, organizations have to understand and match job requirements and people. This understanding requires job analysis, the process of getting detailed information about jobs. Analyzing jobs and understanding what is required to carry out a job provide essential knowledge for staffing, training, performance management, and many other HR activities (see Figure 3.2). For instance, a supervisor's assessment of an employee's work should be based on performance relative to job requirements. In very small organizations, managers may perform a job analysis, but usually the work is done by a human resources professional. A large company may have a compensation management or total rewards function that includes *job analysts*. Organizations may also contract with firms that provide this service.

Importance of Job Analysis

Job analysis is so important that it has been called the building block of everything that HR does.[4] The fact is that almost every human resource management process requires some type of information gleaned from job analysis:[5]

- *Work redesign.* Often an organization seeks to redesign work to make it more efficient or to improve quality. The redesign requires detailed information about the existing job(s). In addition, preparing the redesign is similar to analyzing a job that does not yet exist.

- *Workforce planning.* As planners analyze human resource needs and how to meet those needs, they must have accurate information about the levels of skill required in various jobs, so that they can tell what kinds of human resources will be needed.

FIGURE 3.2

Job Analysis Provides Information for HR Processes

- *Selection.* To identify the applicants most likely to be the highest performers in various positions, decision makers need to know what tasks the individuals must perform, as well as the necessary knowledge, skills, and abilities.

- *Training, learning, and development.* Almost every employee hired by an organization will require training and/or development. Any learning initiative requires knowledge of the tasks performed in a job, so that the learning is related to the necessary knowledge and skills.

- *Performance management.* Performance management requires information about how well each employee is performing in order to reward employees who perform well and to improve their performance. Job analysis helps in identifying the behaviours and the results associated with effective performance.

- *Career planning.* Matching an individual's skills and aspirations with career opportunities requires that those responsible for developing career planning processes know the skill requirements of the various jobs. This facilitates matching of individuals to jobs in which they will succeed and be satisfied.

- *Job evaluation.* The process of job evaluation involves assessing the relative value of each job to the organization in order to set up fair pay structures. If employees do not believe pay structures are fair, they will become dissatisfied and may quit, or they will not see much benefit in striving for advancement. To put values on jobs, it is necessary to get information about different jobs and compare them.

Job analysis is also important from a legal standpoint. As we saw in Chapter 2, governments impose requirements related to human rights and pay equity. Detailed, accurate, objective job analysis information helps decision makers comply with these requirements by keeping the focus on tasks and abilities. Employers have a legal obligation to eliminate discrimination against employees and prospective employees with disabilities. Job redesign may be required to consider the needs of the job applicant to ensure that accommodation is provided. When accommodation is discussed with the employee or job applicant, it is important to use language that focuses on the person's abilities, rather than the person's disability. For example, ask all employees regardless of whether they have a disability, "Will you require accommodation to perform this task?" rather than, "Can you perform this task?"[6]

Besides helping human resources professionals, job analysis helps supervisors and managers carry out their duties. Data from job analysis can help managers identify the types of work in their units, as well as provide information about the work flow process, so that managers can evaluate whether work is done in the most efficient way. Job analysis information also supports managers as they make hiring decisions, review performance, and recommend rewards.

Trends in Job Analysis

HRC**2**

As we noted in the earlier discussion of work flow analysis, organizations have been appreciating the need to analyze jobs in the context of the organization's structure and strategy. In addition, organizations are recognizing that today's workplace must be adaptable and is constantly subject to change. Thus, although we tend to think of "jobs" as something stable, they actually tend to change and evolve over time. Those who occupy or manage jobs often make minor adjustments to match personal preferences or changing conditions.[7] Indeed, although errors in job analysis can have many sources, most of the inaccuracy is likely to result from job descriptions being outdated. For this reason, job analysis must not only define jobs when they are created, but also detect changes in jobs as time passes.

With global competitive pressure and economic downturns, one corporate change that has affected many organizations is downsizing. Research suggests that successful downsizing efforts almost always entail changes in the nature of jobs, not just their number.

These changes in the nature of work and the expanded use of "project-based" organizational structures require the type of broader understanding that comes from an analysis of work flows. Because the work can change rapidly and it is impossible to rewrite job descriptions every week, job descriptions and specifications need to be flexible. At the same time, legal requirements (as discussed in Chapter 2) may discourage organizations from writing flexible job descriptions. This means organizations must balance the need for flexibility with the need for legal documentation. This presents one of the major challenges to be faced by HRM departments in the next decade.

Outcome of Job Analysis: Job Descriptions

A key outcome of job analysis is the creation of job descriptions. A **job description** is a list of the tasks, duties, and responsibilities (TDRs) that a job entails. TDRs are observable actions. For example, a news photographer's job requires the job holder to use a camera to take photographs. If you were to observe someone in that position for a day, you would almost certainly see some pictures being taken. When a manager attempts to evaluate job performance, it is most important to have detailed information about the work performed in the job (i.e., the TDRs). This information makes it possible to determine how well an individual is meeting each job requirement.

job description
A list of the tasks, duties, and responsibilities (TDRs) that a particular job entails.

A job description typically has the format shown in Figure 3.3. It includes the job title, an overview of the job, and a list of the main duties. Although organizations may modify this format according to their needs, all job descriptions within an organization should follow the same format. This helps the organization make consistent decisions about such matters as pay and promotions. It also helps the organization show that it makes human resource decisions fairly.

Whenever the organization creates a new job, it needs to prepare a job description, using a process such as the one detailed in the nearby "HR How-To" box. Job descriptions should be reviewed periodically (say once a year) and updated if necessary. Performance appraisals can provide a good opportunity for updating job descriptions, as the employee and supervisor compare what the employee has been doing against the details of the job description.

When organizations prepare many job descriptions, the process can become repetitive and time-consuming. To address this challenge, a number of companies have developed software that provides forms into which the job analyst can insert details about the specific job. Typically, the job analyst would use a library of basic descriptions, selecting one that is for a similar type of job and then modifying it to fit the organization's needs.

Organizations should provide each newly hired employee his or her job description. This helps the employee to understand what is expected, but it shouldn't be presented as limiting the employee's commitment to quality and customer satisfaction. Ideally, employees will want to go above and beyond the listed duties when the situation and their abilities call for that. Many job descriptions include the phrase *and other duties as required* as a way to remind employees not to tell their supervisor, "But that's not part of my job."

Outcome of Job Analysis: Job Specifications

Whereas the job description focuses on the activities involved in carrying out a job, a **job specification** looks at the qualities or requirements that person performing the job must possess. It is a list of the

Sample Job Description

FINANCIAL AND INVESTMENT ANALYSTS

Financial and investment analysts collect and analyze financial information such as economic forecasts, trading volumes and the movement of capital, financial backgrounds of companies, historical performances, and future trends of stocks, bonds, and other investment instruments to provide financial and investment or financing advice for their company or their company's clients. Their studies and evaluations cover areas such as takeover bids, private placements, mergers, or acquisitions.

Main Duties

Financial analysts perform some or all of the following duties:

- Evaluate financial risk, prepare financial forecasts, financing scenarios, and other documents concerning capital management, and write reports and recommendations
- Plan short- and long-term cash flows and assess financial performance
- Analyze investment projects
- Advise on and participate in the financial aspects of contracts and calls for tender
- Follow up on financing projects with financial backers
- Develop, implement, and use tools for managing and analyzing financial portfolios
- Prepare a regular risk profile for debt portfolios

Investment analysts perform some or all of the following duties:

- Collect financial and investment information about companies, stocks, bonds, and other investments using daily stock and bond reports, economic forecasts, trading volumes, financial periodicals, securities manuals, company financial statements, and other financial reports and publications
- Examine and analyze financial and investment information collected, including profiles of companies, stock and bond prices, yields, and future trends and other investment information
- Provide investment advice and recommendations to clients, senior company officials, pension fund managers, securities agents, and associates
- Prepare company, industry and economic outlooks, analytical reports, briefing notes, and correspondence

Source: Human Resources and Skills Development Canada, 1112 Financial and Investment Analysts, www5.hrsdc.gc.ca/noc/english/noc/2011/ProfileQuickSearch.aspx?val=1&vall=1112&val65=*, retrieved January 16, 2015.

competencies, that is, knowledge, skills, abilities, and other characteristics associated with effective performance. These competencies may also become part of a *competency model* or *competency framework* that describes competencies for success in a particular occupation, or set of jobs. Organizations may create competency models for occupational groups, levels of the organization, or even the entire organization.

job specification
A list of the competencies an individual must have to perform a particular job.

competencies
Knowledge, skills, abilities, and other characteristics associated with effective performance.

Competency models help HR professionals ensure that all aspects of talent management are aligned with the organization's strategy. Looking at the competencies needed for a particular occupational group, department, or the organization as a whole shows which candidates will be the best to fill open positions. Not only can the organization select those who can carry out a particular job today, but it can spot those with competencies they can develop further to assume greater responsibility in the future. Competency models for a career path or for success in management show the organization which competencies

HR How-To

Writing a Job Description

Preparing a job description begins with gathering information from sources who can identify the details of performing a task—for example, persons already performing the job and, the supervisor, or team leader, or, if the job is new, managers who are creating the new position. Other sources of information may include the company's human resource files, such as past job advertisements and job descriptions, as well as general sources of information about similar jobs, such as Human Resources and Skills Development Canada's National Occupational Classification (NOC) system.

Based on the information gathered, the next step is to identify which activities are essential duties of the job. These include mental and physical tasks, as well as any particular methods and equipment to be used in carrying out those tasks. When possible, these should be stated in terms that are broad and goal oriented enough for the person in the position to innovate and improve. For example, "Developing and implementing a system for ordering supplies efficiently" implies a goal (efficiency) as well as a task.

From these sources, the writer of the description obtains the important elements of the description:

- *Title of the job*—The title should be descriptive and, if appropriate, indicate the job's level in the organization.

- *Administrative information about the job*—The job description may identify a division, department, supervisor's title, date of the analysis, name of the analyst, and other information for administering the company's human resource activities.

- *Statement of the job's purpose*—This should be brief and describe the position in broad terms.

- *Essential duties of the job*—These should be listed in order of importance to successful performance and should include details such as physical requirements (e.g., the amount of weight to be lifted), the persons with whom an employee in this job interacts, and the results to be accomplished. This section should include every duty that the job analysis identified as essential.

- *Additional responsibilities*—The job description may state that the position requires additional responsibilities as requested by the supervisor.

Sources: Small Business Administration, "Writing Effective Job Descriptions," *Small Business Planner*, www.sba.gov/small businessplanner/, accessed March 10, 2010; and "How to Write a Job Analysis and Description," *Entrepreneur*, www.entrepreneur.com, accessed March 10, 2010.

to emphasize in plans for development of high-potential employees. And competency models identify the important capabilities to measure in performance evaluations and to reward. The "HR Best Practices" box, found later in this chapter, discusses the use of competency modelling at the YMCA of Greater Toronto (www.ymcagta.org).

Knowledge refers to factual or procedural information necessary for successfully performing a task. For example, this course is providing you with knowledge in how to manage human resources. A *skill* is an individual's level of proficiency at performing a particular task—the capability to perform it well. With knowledge and experience, you could acquire skill in the task of preparing job specifications. *Ability,* in contrast to skill, refers to a more general enduring capability that an individual possesses. A person might have the ability to collaborate with others or to write clearly and concisely. Finally, *other characteristics* might be personality traits such as persistence or motivation to achieve. Some jobs also have legal requirements, such as licensing or certification. Figure 3.4 gives a set of sample job specifications for the job description in Figure 3.3.

In developing job specifications, it is important to consider all of the elements of the competencies. As with writing a job description, the information can come from a combination of people performing the job, people supervising or planning for the job, and trained job analysts. At Acxiom Corporation (www.acxiom.com), job specifications are based on an analysis of employees' roles and competencies (what they must be able to do), stated in terms of behaviours. To reach these definitions, groups studied

FIGURE 3.4

Sample Job Specifications

FINANCIAL AND INVESTMENT ANALYSTS
Employment Requirements

- A bachelor's degree in commerce, business administration, or economics *and* on-the-job training and industry courses and programs are usually required.

- A master's degree in business administration (MBA—concentration in finance) or in finance may be required.

- The Chartered Financial Analyst (CFA) designation, available through a program conducted by the Institute of Chartered Financial Analysts in the United States, may be required.

Source: Human Resources and Skills Development Canada, 1112 Financial and Investment Analysts, www5.hrsdc.gc.ca/noc/english/noc/2011/ProfileQuickSearch. aspx?val=1&vall=1112&val65=*, retrieved January 16, 2015.

what the company's good performers were doing and looked for the underlying abilities. A study by ACT's Workforce Development Division interviewed manufacturing supervisors to learn what they do each day and what skills they rely on. The researchers learned that the supervisors spend much of their day monitoring their employees to make sure the workplace is safe, product quality is maintained, and work processes are optimal. Also, they rely heavily on their technical knowledge of the work processes they supervise.[8] Based on this information, job specifications for a manufacturing supervisor would include skill in observing how people work, as well as in-depth knowledge of manufacturing processes and tools.

In contrast to tasks, duties, and responsibilities, competencies are characteristics of people and are observable only when individuals are carrying out the TDRs of the job—and afterward, if they can show the product of their work. Thus, if someone applied for a job as a news photographer, you could not simply look at the individual to determine whether he or she can spot and take effective photos. However, you would be able to draw conclusions later about the person's skills by looking at examples of his or her photos.

Accurate information about competencies is especially important for making decisions about who will fill a job. A manager attempting to fill a position needs information about the characteristics required, and about the characteristics of each applicant. Interviews and selection decisions should therefore focus on competencies.

The identification of competencies is also being implemented widely in the public sector. The federal government's "Middle Management Competency Profile" identifies five competencies and includes behaviours associated with each competency. Competencies identified for middle managers in the federal public sector include *leadership* (e.g., facilitating); *rigorous thinking* (e.g., continuous learning); *positive interaction* (e.g., team work); *results orientation* (e.g., client service orientation); and *personal competencies* (e.g., resilience).[9]

Operations that need to run 24 hours a day have special job requirements. For example, shutting down certain equipment at night may be inefficient or cause production problems; and some industries, such as security and health care, may have customers who need services 24/7. Globalization often means that operations take place across many time zones, requiring management at all hours. When a job entails working night shifts, job specifications should reflect this requirement.

Competency requirements of a job may be more stable and long-lasting than the tasks, duties, and responsibilities associated with that job.

L○3 Tell how to obtain information for a job analysis.

Sources of Job Information

Information for analyzing an existing job often comes from *incumbents*, that is, people who currently hold that position in the organization. They are a logical source of information, because they are most acquainted with the details of the job. Incumbents should be able to provide very accurate information.

A drawback of relying solely on incumbents' information is that they may have an incentive to exaggerate what they do, to appear more valuable to the organization. Information from incumbents should therefore be supplemented with information from observers, such as supervisors. Supervisors should review the information provided by incumbents, looking for a match between what incumbents are doing and what they are supposed to do. Research suggests that supervisors may provide the most accurate estimates of the importance of job duties, while incumbents may be more accurate in reporting information about the actual time spent performing job tasks and safety-related risk factors.[10] For analyzing skill levels, the best source may be external job analysts who have more experience rating a wide range of jobs.[11]

The federal government also provides background information for analyzing jobs. Employment and Social Development Canada (www.esdc.gc.ca) working with Statistics Canada maintains the **National Occupational Classification (NOC)** to provide standardized sources of information about jobs in Canada's labour market. The NOC is a tool that uses a four-digit code to classify occupations based on the types and levels of skills required. The NOC classification system supports the needs of employers, individual job seekers, as well as career counsellors, statisticians, and labour market analysts, by providing a consistent way to identify and interpret the nature of work. A recent addition to the site is a publication titled "Job Descriptions: An Employers' Handbook" that may be particularly helpful to managers and human resources professionals.

National Occupational Classification (NOC)
Tool created by the federal government to provide a standardized source of information about jobs in Canada's labour market.

Position Analysis Questionnaire

After gathering information, the job analyst uses the information to analyze the job. One of the broadest and best-researched instruments for analyzing jobs is the **Position Analysis Questionnaire (PAQ)**, a standardized tool containing 194 items that represent work behaviours, work conditions, and job characteristics that apply to a wide variety of jobs, and are organized into six sections concerning different aspects of the job:

Position Analysis Questionnaire (PAQ)
A standardized job analysis questionnaire containing 194 questions about work behaviours, work conditions, and job characteristics that apply to a wide variety of jobs.

1. *Information input.* Where and how a worker gets information needed to perform the job.
2. *Mental processes.* The reasoning, decision making, planning, and information processing activities involved in performing the job.
3. *Work output.* The physical activities, tools, and devices used by the worker to perform the job.
4. *Relationships with other persons.* The relationships with other people required in performing the job.

5. *Job context.* The physical and social contexts where the work is performed.

6. *Other characteristics.* The activities, conditions, and characteristics other than those previously described that are relevant to the job.

The person analyzing a job determines whether each item on the questionnaire applies to the job being analyzed. The analyst rates each item on six scales: extent of use, amount of time, importance to the job, possibility of occurrence, applicability, and special code (special rating scales used with a particular item). PAQ headquarters scores the questionnaire and generates a report that describes the scores on the job dimensions.

Using the PAQ provides an organization with information that helps in comparing jobs, even when they are dissimilar. The PAQ also has the advantage that it considers the whole work process, from inputs through outputs. However, the person who fills out the questionnaire must have postsecondary-level reading skills, and the PAQ is meant to be completed only by job analysts trained in this method. In fact, the ratings of job incumbents tend to be less reliable than ratings by supervisors and trained analysts.[12] Also, the descriptions in the PAQ reports are rather abstract, so the reports may not be useful for writing job descriptions or redesigning jobs.

Fleishman Job Analysis System

To gather information about worker requirements, the **Fleishman Job Analysis System** asks subject-matter experts (typically job incumbents) to evaluate a job in terms of the abilities required to perform the job.[13] The survey is based on 52 categories of abilities, ranging from written comprehension to deductive reasoning, manual dexterity, stamina, and originality. As in the example in Figure 3.5, the survey items are arranged into a scale for each ability. Each begins with a description of the ability and a comparison to related abilities. Below this is a seven-point scale with phrases describing extremely high and low levels of the ability. The person completing the survey indicates which point on the scale represents the level of the ability required for performing the job being analyzed.

> **Fleishman Job Analysis System**
> Job analysis technique that asks subject-matter experts to evaluate a job in terms of the abilities required to perform the job.

HR Best Practices

The YMCA of Greater Toronto: Competency Modelling

Competency modelling identifies the specific competencies required by employees to support an organization's vision, values, and strategic direction. Melanie Laflamme, vice-president of human resources and organizational development of the YMCA of Greater Toronto was recently recognized for her leadership role in HR including the development of a competency model that serves as a key element of the YMCA's employment brand. "It's very exciting to see the work that's being done in HR and, in particular, in non-profit is being acknowledged," said Laflamme when she was named the top HR leader for organizations with more than 500 employees at the annual Toronto Business Excellence Rewards. The YMCA of Greater Toronto's competency model consists of seven association-wide competencies and seven leadership competencies that form the foundation for all HR processes including the development of job descriptions, recruitment and selection, training and development, performance appraisal, and succession planning.

Sources: Joan Hill, "Competency Model Helps HR Add Value," *Canadian HR Reporter*, January 30, 2012, pp. 20–21; Rahul Gupta, "Awards Recognize Top CEOs, Human Resource Leaders," *Inside Toronto.com*, November 25, 2010, www.insidetoronto.com/news/business/article/908329—awards-recognize-top-coos-human-resource-leaders, retrieved March 15, 2012; Shannon Klie, "Awards Honour Top Toronto Leaders," *Canadian HR Reporter*, December 13, 2010, pp. 1 and 13; and www.ymcagta.org.

FIGURE 3.5

Example of an Ability from the Fleishman Job Analysis System

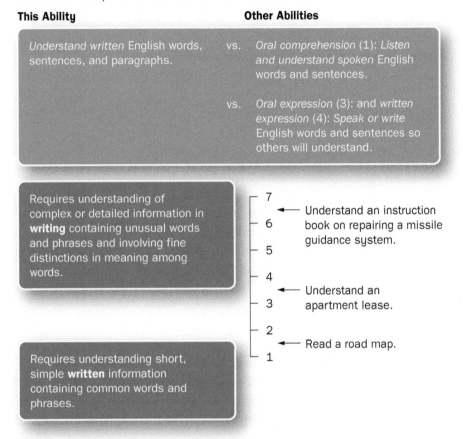

Written Comprehension

This is the ability to understand written sentences and paragraphs.
How written comprehension is different from other abilities:

This Ability		Other Abilities
Understand written English words, sentences, and paragraphs.	vs.	*Oral comprehension* (1): *Listen and understand spoken* English words and sentences.
	vs.	*Oral expression* (3): and *written expression* (4): *Speak or write* English words and sentences so others will understand.

Requires understanding of complex or detailed information in **writing** containing unusual words and phrases and involving fine distinctions in meaning among words.

7
6 ← Understand an instruction book on repairing a missile guidance system.
5
4
3 ← Understand an apartment lease.
2
1 ← Read a road map.

Requires understanding short, simple **written** information containing common words and phrases.

Source: From E.A. Fleishman and M. D. Mumford, "Evaluating Classifications of Job Behavior: A Construct Validation of the Ability Requirements Scales," *Personnel Psychology* 44 (1991), pp. 523-576. The complete set of ability requirement scales, along with instructions for their use, may be found in E. A. Fleishman, *Fleishman Job Analysis Survey (F-JAS)* (Palo Alto, CA: Consulting Psychologists Press, 1992). Used with permission.

Job Design

HRC4

Although job analysis, as just described, is important for an understanding of existing jobs, organizations also must plan for new jobs and periodically consider whether they should revise existing jobs. When an organization is expanding, supervisors and human resources professionals must help plan for new or growing work units. When an organization is trying to improve quality or efficiency, a review of work units and processes may require a fresh look at how jobs are designed.

These situations call for job design, the process of defining the way work will be performed and the tasks that a given job requires, or *job redesign*, a similar process that involves changing an existing job design. To design jobs effectively, a person must thoroughly understand the job itself (through job analysis) and its place in the larger work unit's work flow process (through work flow analysis). Having a detailed knowledge of the tasks performed in the work unit and in the job, a manager then has many alternative ways to design a job. As shown in Figure 3.6, the available approaches emphasize different aspects of the job: the mechanics of doing a job efficiently, the job's impact on motivation, the use of safe work practices, and the mental demands of the job.

 E-HRM

The Hospital for SickKids' (www.sickkids.ca) aSk HR Help-Desk gives clients the ability to connect by email and instant message, in addition to in person and by phone.

L○4 Describe methods for designing a job so that it can be done efficiently.

Designing Efficient Jobs

If workers perform tasks as efficiently as possible, not only does the organization benefit from lower costs and greater output per worker, but workers should be less fatigued. This point of view has for years formed the basis of classical **industrial engineering**, which looks for the simplest way to structure work in order to maximize efficiency. Typically, applying industrial engineering to a job reduces the complexity of the work, making it so simple that almost anyone can be trained quickly and easily to perform the job. Such jobs tend to be highly specialized and repetitive.

industrial engineering
The study of jobs to find the simplest way to structure work in order to maximize efficiency.

In practice, the scientific method traditionally seeks the "one best way" to perform a job by performing time-and-motion studies to identify the most efficient movements for workers to make. Once the engineers have identified the most efficient sequence of motions, the organization should select workers based on their ability to do the job, then train them in the details of the "one best way" to perform that job. The company also should offer pay structured to motivate workers to do their best. (Chapter 8 discusses total rewards.)

FIGURE 3.6

Approaches to Job Design

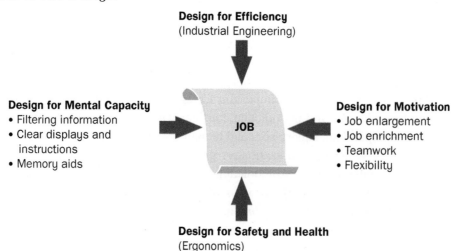

Design for Efficiency
(Industrial Engineering)

Design for Mental Capacity
- Filtering information
- Clear displays and instructions
- Memory aids

JOB

Design for Motivation
- Job enlargement
- Job enrichment
- Teamwork
- Flexibility

Design for Safety and Health
(Ergonomics)

Industrial engineering provides measurable and practical benefits. However, a focus on efficiency alone can create jobs that are so simple and repetitive that workers get bored. Workers performing these jobs may feel their work is meaningless. Hence, most organizations combine industrial engineering with other approaches to job design.

L○5 Identify approaches to designing a job to make it motivating.

Designing Jobs That Motivate

Especially when organizations have to compete for employees, depend on skilled knowledge workers, or need a workforce that cares about customer satisfaction, a pure focus on efficiency will not achieve human resource objectives. These organizations need jobs that employees find interesting and satisfying, and job design should take into account factors that make jobs motivating to employees.

A model that shows how to make jobs more motivating is the Job Characteristics Model, developed by Richard Hackman and Greg Oldham. This model describes jobs in terms of five characteristics:[14]

1. *Skill variety*—The extent to which a job requires a variety of skills to carry out the tasks involved.

2. *Task identity*—The degree to which a job requires completing a "whole" piece of work from beginning to end (e.g., building an entire component or resolving a customer's complaint).

3. *Task significance*—The extent to which the job has an important impact on the lives of other people.

4. *Autonomy*—The degree to which the job allows an individual to make decisions about the way the work will be carried out.

5. *Feedback*—The extent to which a person receives clear information about performance effectiveness from the work itself.

As shown in Figure 3.7, the more of each of these characteristics a job has, the more motivating the job will be, according to the Job Characteristics Model. The model predicts that a person with such a job will be more satisfied and will produce more and better work. For example, to increase the meaningfulness of making artery stents (devices that are surgically inserted to promote blood flow), the maker of these products invites its production workers to an annual party, where they meet patients whose lives were saved by the products they helped to manufacture.[15]

FIGURE 3.7

Characteristics of a Motivating Job

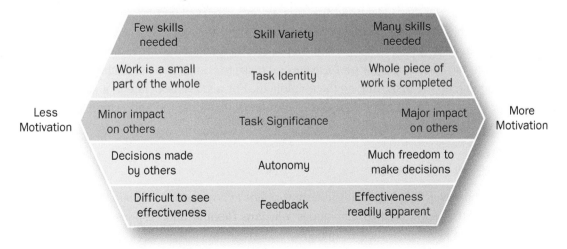

Applications of the job characteristics approach to job design include job enlargement, job enrichment, self-managing work teams, flexible work schedules, and telework.

Job Enlargement

In a job design, **job enlargement** refers to broadening the types of tasks performed. The objective of job enlargement is to make jobs less repetitive and more interesting. Jobs also become enlarged when organizations add new goals or ask fewer workers to accomplish work that had been spread among more people. Methods of job enlargement include job extension and job rotation.

job enlargement
Broadening the types of tasks performed in a job.

Organizations that use job enlargement to make jobs more motivational employ techniques such as job extension and job rotation. **Job extension** is enlarging jobs by combining several relatively simple jobs to form a job with a wider range of tasks. An example might be combining the jobs of receptionist, data entry clerk, and records clerk into jobs containing all three kinds of work. This approach to job enlargement is relatively simple, but if all the tasks are dull, workers will not necessarily be more motivated by the redesigned job.

job extension
Enlarging jobs by combining several relatively simple jobs to form a job with a wider range of tasks.

Job rotation does not actually redesign the jobs themselves, but moves employees among several different jobs. This approach to job enlargement is common among production teams. During the course of a week, a team member may carry out each of the jobs handled by the team. Team members might assemble components one day and pack products into cases another day. As with job extension, the enlarged jobs may still consist of repetitious activities, but with greater variation among those activities.

job rotation
Enlarging jobs by moving employees among several different jobs.

Job Enrichment

The idea of **job enrichment**, or engaging workers by adding more decision-making authority to their jobs, comes from the work of Frederick Herzberg. According to Herzberg's two-factor theory, individuals are motivated more by the intrinsic aspects of work (e.g., the meaningfulness of a job) than by extrinsic rewards such as pay. Herzberg identified five factors he associated with motivating jobs: achievement, recognition, growth, responsibility, and performance of the entire job. Thus, ways to enrich a manufacturing job might include giving employees authority to stop production when quality standards are not being met and having each employee perform several tasks to complete a particular stage of the process, rather than dividing up the tasks among the employees. For a sales associate in a store, job enrichment might involve the authority to resolve customer problems, including the authority to decide whether to issue refunds or replace merchandise.

job enrichment
Engaging workers by adding more decision-making authority to jobs.

In practice, however, it is important to note that not every worker responds positively to enriched jobs. These jobs are best suited to employees who are flexible and responsive to others; for these employees, enriched jobs can dramatically improve motivation.[16]

Self-Managing Work Teams

HRC 1, 3

Instead of merely enriching individual jobs, some organizations engage employees by designing work to be done by self-managing work teams. As described in Chapter 1, these teams have authority for an entire work process or segment. Team members typically have authority to schedule work, hire team members, resolve problems related to the team's performance, and perform other duties traditionally handled by management. Teamwork can give a job such motivating characteristics as autonomy, skill variety, and task identity.

Because team members' responsibilities are great, their jobs usually are defined broadly and include sharing of work assignments. Team members may, at one time or another, perform every duty of the team. The challenge for the organization is to provide enough training so that the team members can learn the necessary skills. Another approach, when teams are responsible for particular work processes or customers, is to assign the team responsibility for the process or customer, then let the team decide which members will carry out which tasks.

A study of work teams at a large financial services company found that the right job design was associated with effective teamwork.[17] In particular, when teams are self-managed and team members are highly involved in decision-making, teams are more productive, employees more satisfied, and managers more satisfied with performance. Teams also tend to do better when each team member performs a variety of tasks and when team members view their effort as significant.

Flexible Work Schedules

One way an organization can give employees some say in how their work is structured is to offer flexible work schedules. Depending on the requirements of the organization and the individual jobs, organizations may be able to be flexible in terms of when employees work. As introduced in Chapter 1, types of flexibility include flextime and job sharing. Figure 3.8 illustrates alternatives to the traditional 40-hour workweek.

Flextime is a scheduling policy in which full-time employees may choose starting and ending times within guidelines specified by the organization. The flextime policy may require that employees be at work

Employees who have enriched jobs and/or work in self-managed teams can be engaged and motivated when they have decision-making authority.

FIGURE 3.8

Alternatives to the 8-to-5 Job

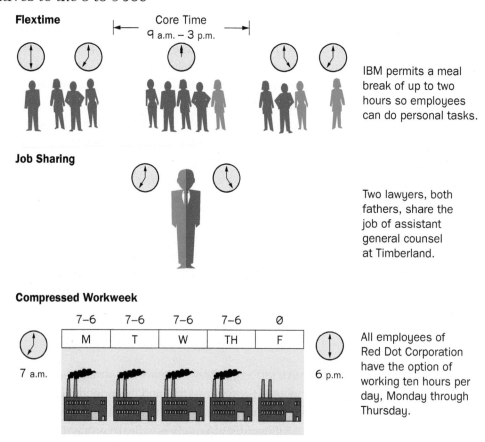

Flextime

Core Time
9 a.m. – 3 p.m.

IBM permits a meal break of up to two hours so employees can do personal tasks.

Job Sharing

Two lawyers, both fathers, share the job of assistant general counsel at Timberland.

Compressed Workweek

7–6	7–6	7–6	7–6	0
M	T	W	TH	F

7 a.m.

6 p.m.

All employees of Red Dot Corporation have the option of working ten hours per day, Monday through Thursday.

between certain hours, say, 10:00 a.m. and 3:00 p.m. Employees work additional hours before or after this period in order to work the full day. One employee might arrive early in the morning in order to leave at 3:00 p.m. to pick up children after school. Another employee might need to check in on an aging parent in the morning, or prefer going to the gym before arriving for work at 10:00 a.m. and work until 6:00, 7:00, or even later in the evening. A flextime policy may also enable workers to adjust a specific day's hours in order to make time for outside appointments, family activities, or volunteer work. A work schedule that allows time for personal, community, and family interests can be extremely motivating for some employees.

flextime
A scheduling policy in which full-time employees may choose starting and ending times within guidelines specified by the organization.

Job sharing is a work option in which two part-time employees carry out the tasks associated with a single job. Such arrangements can enable an organization to attract or retain valued employees who want more time to attend school, care for family members, or allocate time to personal interests. The job requirements in such an arrangement include the ability to work cooperatively and coordinate the details of one's job with another person.

job sharing
A work option in which two part-time employees carry out the tasks associated with a single job.

Although not strictly a form of flexibility on the level of individual employees, another scheduling alternative is the *compressed workweek*. A compressed workweek is a schedule in which full-time workers complete their weekly hours in fewer than five days. For example, instead of working eight hours a day for five days, the employees might complete 40 hours of work in four 10-hour days. This alternative is most common, but some companies use other alternatives, such as scheduling 80 hours over nine days (with a three-day weekend every other week) or reducing the workweek from 40 to 38 or 36 hours. Employees may appreciate the extra days available for leisure, family, or volunteer activities. An organization might even use this schedule to offer a kind of flexibility—for example, letting workers choose whether they want a compressed workweek during the summer months. This type of schedule has a couple of drawbacks, however. One is that employees may become exhausted on the longer workdays. Another is that if the arrangement involves working more than a specific number of hours during a week, employment/labour standards legislation may require the payment of overtime wages to nonsupervisory employees.

Remote Work Arrangements

Flexibility can extend to work locations as well as work schedules. Before the Industrial Revolution, most people worked either close to or inside their own homes. Mass production technologies changed all this, separating work life from home life, as people began to travel to centrally located factories and offices. Today, however escalating prices for office space, combined with drastically reduced prices for computers and communication technologies and easy access to the Internet—seem to reverse this trend. The broad term for doing one's work away from a centrally located office is *remote work, telework,* or *telecommuting.* Recently, the concept known as *distributed work* has been increasingly made available to employees in

Did You KNOW?

Telecommuters Viewed As More Productive

Two thirds (65 percent) of more than 11,000 online employees polled by global research company Ipsos for Reuters News responded that telecommuters are more productive because the flexibility allows them to work when they are most focused and/or because having control over their work environment results in job satisfaction.

Source: "The World of Work: Global Study of Online Employees," January 23, 2012, www.ipsos-na.com/news-polls/pressrelease.aspx?id=5486, retrieved March 11, 2012.

Agree that Telecommuters Are More Productive

Argentina, India, Mexico, Saudi Arabia, Canada, Great Britain, South Korea, Japan companies including Bell Canada's (www.bell.ca) *FlexSpace*, Boeing's (www.boeing.ca) *Virtual Office*, and TELUS's (www.telus.com) *Agent Anywhere.*™ **Distributed work** is "a combination of work options, including work from the corporate office, work from home, work from a satellite office or work from another remote location."[18] Distributed work programs might require employees to give up a dedicated office space.

> **distributed work**
>
> A combination of work options, including work from the corporate office, work from home, work from a satellite office, or work from another remote location.

For employers, advantages of distributed work include less need for office space and the ability to offer greater flexibility to employees. The employees using telework arrangements may have less absences from work than employees with similar demands who must commute to work. Telecommuting can also support a strategy of sustainability because these employees do not produce the greenhouse gas emissions that result from commuting by vehicle. Telework is easiest to implement for people in managerial, professional, or sales jobs, especially those that involve working and communicating on a computer. A telework arrangement is generally difficult to set up for manufacturing workers. A recent survey by WorldatWork found that more than half of teleworkers were men, their median age was 40, and three-quarters had at least some college education. WorldatWork sees in the demographic data evidence that teleworkers tend to be knowledge workers taking advantage of the ability to work wherever they have Internet and computer access.[19]

"The demographic skills crunch is coming. More employees, particularly the baby boomers, are interested in flexible work arrangements but, ironically, so are Generations X and Y. So you have three generations right now, for different reasons, looking for flexible work arrangements," says George Horhota, co-founder of SuiteWorks (www.suiteworks.ca), a Barrie, Ontario–based provider of satellite office space. "Employees love distributed work. It empowers them to have a choice as to where they work best today."[20] As is illustrated in Figures 3.9 and 3.10, *where* work is being performed is being transformed from the traditional office setting to a variety of remote locations including clients' offices, airplanes, airport lounges, hotels, cottages and vacation properties, coffee shops, homes, and satellite offices located close to employees' homes.[21]

FIGURE 3.9

Distributed Work—Working Where You Are

"You know your problem, Harlan? You need to get in touch with your 'inner beach bum.'"

FIGURE 3.10

Evolution of the Workplace

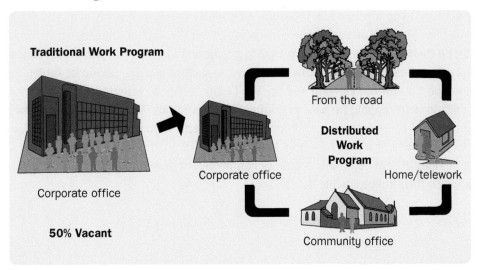

Source: SuiteWorks, Inc.

L○6 Explain how organizations apply ergonomics to design safe jobs.

Designing Ergonomically Correct Jobs

HRC4, 8

The way people use their bodies when they work—whether lifting heavy furniture into a moving truck or sitting quietly before a computer screen—affects their physical well-being and may affect how well and how long they can work. The study of the interface between individuals' physiology and the characteristics of the physical work environment is called **ergonomics**. The goal of ergonomics is to minimize physical strain on the worker by structuring the physical work environment around the way the human body works. Ergonomics therefore focuses on outcomes such as reducing physical fatigue, aches and pains, and health complaints. Ergonomic research includes the context in which work takes place, such as the lighting, space, and hours worked.[22]

ergonomics
The study of the interface between individuals' physiology and the characteristics of the physical work environment.

Ergonomic job design has been applied in redesigning equipment used in jobs that are physically demanding. Such redesign is often aimed at reducing the physical demands of certain jobs so that more people are able to perform them. In addition, many interventions focus on redesigning machines and technology—for instance, adjusting the height of a computer keyboard to minimize occupational illnesses, such as carpal tunnel syndrome. The design of chairs and desks to fit posture requirements is very important in many office jobs. One study found that having employees participate in an ergonomic redesign effort significantly reduced the number and severity of repetitive strain injuries (injuries that result from performing the same movement over and over), lost production time, and restricted-duty days.[23]

A recent ergonomic challenge comes from the popularity of mobile devices. As workers find more and more uses for these devices, they are at risk from repetitive-stress injuries (RSIs). Typing with one's thumbs to send frequent text messages on a smartphone can result in inflammation of the tendons that move the thumbs. Laptop and notebook computers are handy to carry, but because the screen and keyboard are attached in a single device, the computer can't be positioned to the ergonomically correct standards of screen at eye level and keyboard low enough to type with arms bent at a 90-degree angle. Heavy users of these devices must therefore trade off eyestrain against physical strain to wrists, unless they can hook up their device to an extra, properly positioned keyboard or monitor. Touchscreens pose their own risks. They are typically part of a flat device such as a smartphone or tablet, and these are difficult to position for optimal viewing and typing. Using vertically oriented touchscreens causes even more muscle strain than tapping on a screen lying flat. In addition, because touchscreens usually lack the tactile feedback of pressing keys on a keyboard, users tend to strike them with more force than they use on real keys. Attaching a supplemental keyboard addresses this potential source of strain. When using mobile devices or any computer, workers can protect themselves by taking frequent breaks and paying attention to their posture while they work.[24]

L○7 Discuss how organizations can plan for the mental demands of a job.

Designing Jobs That Meet Mental Capabilities and Limitations

Just as the human body has capabilities and limitations, addressed by ergonomics, the mind, too, has capabilities and limitations. As more and more work activities become information processing activities, the need to consider *cognitive ergonomics* is likely to be an emerging trend.[25] Besides hiring people with certain mental skills, organizations can design jobs so that they can be accurately and safely performed given the way the brain processes information. Generally, this means reducing the information processing requirements of a job. In these simpler jobs, workers may be less likely to make mistakes or have accidents. Of course, the simpler jobs may also be less motivating. Research has found that challenging jobs tend to fatigue and dissatisfy workers when they feel little control over their situation, lack social support, and feel motivated mainly to avoid errors. In contrast, they may enjoy the challenges of a difficult job where they have some control and social support, especially if they enjoy learning and are unafraid of making mistakes.[26] Because of this drawback to simplifying jobs, it can be most beneficial to simplify jobs

Ergonomically designed workstations have adjustable components, enabling the employee to modify the workstation to accommodate various job and physical requirements.

Thinking ETHICALLY

Should Employers Fret About Making Employees Happy?

One consideration in job design is to increase job satisfaction. The expectation is that employees with high job satisfaction will be motivated to do their best. Some managers are interested in taking this idea a step further. They are applying research into what conditions are associated with happiness. By using our knowledge about what makes people happy, the thinking goes, organizations can try to establish the conditions for a happy workforce.

During the past two decades, psychologists have become much more involved in the study of emotions, especially happiness. As one would expect, they have learned that happiness is greater under conditions such as good health and strong relationships. But the difference that comes from any single condition is not large or long lasting. People do, however, sustain happiness when they experience frequent positive events, even minor ones. Therefore, people can add to their happiness with positive activities such as meditation, exercise, good deeds for others, and social interaction. This logic suggests that organizations could add to employees' happiness by building positive experiences into each day—praise from supervisors, for example, or a time for employees to describe where they have seen acts of kindness at work.

But should employers even take on employee happiness as another project? Time for feel-good activities could take away time from productive activities. And managers might worry that if employees are *too* comfortable, they won't be motivated to try hard. Psychology professor Daniel Gilbert has one response to those concerns: "people are happiest when they're appropriately challenged." People who aren't challenged get bored, and boredom reduces happiness. Former Verizon CEO Denny Strigl would agree. He notes, "Good results make happy employees—and not the other way around."

Questions

1. What ethical responsibilities do organizations have with regard to employees' health? To their happiness?

2. If designing work so that employees will be happier will also make employees more engaged in challenging assignments, should employers address happiness in job design? Should they address happiness if it will instead distract employees from their work? Why or why not?

Sources: Gardiner Morse, "The Science behind the Smile," *Harvard Business Review*, January–February 2012, pp. 85–90 (interview with Daniel Gilbert); Denny Strigl, "Results Drive Happiness," *HR Magazine*, October 2011, p. 113.

where employees will most appreciate having the mental demands reduced (as in a job that is extremely challenging) or where the costs of errors are severe (as in the job of a surgeon or air-traffic controller).

There are several ways to simplify a job's mental demands. One is to limit the amount of information and memorization the job requires. Organizations can also provide adequate lighting, easy-to-understand gauges and displays, simple-to-operate equipment, and clear instructions. Often, employees try to simplify some of the mental demands of their own jobs by creating checklists, charts, or other aids. Finally, every job requires some degree of thinking, remembering, and paying attention, so for every job, organizations need to evaluate whether their employees can handle the job's mental demands.

Changes in technology sometimes reduce job demands and errors, but in some cases, technology has made the problem worse. Some employees try to juggle information from several sources at once—say, browsing the Internet for information during a team member's business presentation, or repeatedly stopping work on a project to check email or text messages. In these cases, the smartphone or device, and email or text messages are distracting the employees from their primary task. They may convey important information, but they also break the employee's train of thought, reducing performance, and increasing the likelihood of errors. The problem may be aggravated by employees downplaying the significance of these interruptions. Research by a firm called Basex, which specializes in the knowledge economy, found that a big part of the information overload problem is *recovery time,* that is, the time it takes a person's thinking to switch back from an interruption to the task at hand. The Basex researchers found that recovery time is from 10 to 20 times the length of the interruption. For example, after a 30-second pause to check a Twitter feed, the recovery time could be five minutes or longer.[27]

SUMMARY

LO1 Summarize the elements of work flow analysis and how work flow relates to an organization's structure.

The analysis identifies the amount and quality of a work unit's outputs (products, parts of products, or services). Next, the analyst determines the work processes required to produce the outputs, breaking down tasks into those performed by each person. Finally, the work flow analysis identifies the inputs used to carry out the processes and produce the outputs. Within an organization, units and individuals must cooperate to create outputs, and the organization's structure brings people together for this purpose. The structure may be centralized or decentralized, and people may be grouped according to function or into divisions focusing on particular products or customer groups.

LO2 Discuss the significance, recent trends, and outcomes of job analysis.

Job analysis is the process of getting detailed information about jobs. Job analysis provides a foundation for carrying out many HRM responsibilities. To broaden traditional approaches to job analysis in support of talent management, organizations develop competency models. Because today's workplace requires a high degree of adaptability, job tasks and requirements are subject to constant change. Organizations are also adopting project-based structures and teamwork, which also require flexibility and the ability to handle broad responsibilities. Outcomes of job analysis include job descriptions and job specifications.

LO3 Tell how to obtain information for a job analysis.

Information for analyzing an existing job often comes from incumbents and their supervisors. The federal government provides background information about jobs in the National Occupational Classification (NOC). Job analysts, employees, and managers may complete a Position Analysis Questionnaire or fill out a survey for the Fleishman Job Analysis System.

LO4 Describe methods for designing a job so that it can be done efficiently.

The basic technique for designing efficient jobs is industrial engineering, which looks for the simplest way to structure work in order to maximize efficiency. Through methods such as time-and-motion studies, the industrial engineer creates jobs that are relatively simple and typically repetitive. These jobs may bore workers because they are so simple.

LO5 Identify approaches to designing a job to make it motivating.

According to the Job Characteristics Model, jobs are more motivating if they have greater skill variety, task identity, task significance, autonomy, and feedback about performance effectiveness. Ways to create such jobs include job enlargement (through job extension or job rotation) and job enrichment. Self-managing work teams offer greater skill variety and task identity. Flexible work schedules and remote work arrangements offer greater autonomy.

L○6 Explain how organizations apply ergonomics to design safe jobs.

The goal of ergonomics is to minimize physical strain on the worker by structuring the physical work environment around the way the human body works. Ergonomic design may involve modifying equipment to reduce the physical demands of performing certain jobs or redesigning the jobs themselves to reduce strain. Ergonomic design may target working conditions associated with injuries.

L○7 Discuss how organizations can plan for the mental demands of a job.

Employers may seek to reduce mental as well as physical strain. The job design may limit the amount of information and memorization involved. Adequate lighting, easy-to-read gauges and displays, simple-to-operate equipment, and clear instructions can also minimize mental strain. Although technology may be used to reduce job demands and errors, technology may also distract employees from primary tasks, e.g., as they retrieve and generate text messages and emails. Finally, organizations can select employees with the necessary abilities to handle a job's mental demands.

Critical Thinking Questions

1. Assume you are the manager/owner of a local coffee house. What are the outputs of your work unit? What are the activities required to produce those outputs? What are the inputs?

2. Based on Question 1, consider the barista's job of the local coffee house. What are the outputs, activities, and inputs for that job?

3. Consider the "job" of university or college student. Perform a job analysis on this job. What tasks are required in the job? What competencies are necessary to perform those tasks?

4. Discuss how the following trends are changing the skill requirements for managerial jobs in Canada:
   a. Increasing use of social media
   b. Increasing global competition
   c. Increasing job demands including the need to be reachable at all times

5. Suppose you have taken a job as a training and learning specialist for a large bank that has created competency models for its various departments. How could the competency models help you implement training, learning, and development initiatives at the bank? How could the competency models help you succeed in your career at the bank?

6. Consider the job of a customer service representative for a telecommunications provider who handles calls from residential customers for billing inquires and routine service requests. What measures can the employer take to design this job to make it efficient? What might be some drawbacks or challenges of designing this job for efficiency?

7. How might the job in Question 6 be designed to make it more motivating? Would these considerations apply to the barista's job in Question 2?

8. What ergonomic considerations might apply to each of the following jobs? For each job, what kinds of costs would result from addressing ergonomics? What costs might result from failing to address ergonomics?

   a. A computer programmer

   b. A UPS delivery person

   c. A child care worker

9. What advice do you have for a supervisor who is concerned that employees appear to be distracted during meetings and while performing job tasks due to use of devices such as smartphones to retrieve and create text and email messages and monitor their social media applications?

10. Consider a job you hold now or have held recently. Would you want this job to be redesigned to place more emphasis on efficiency, motivation, ergonomics, or mental processing? What changes would you want, and why? (Or why do you *not* want the job to be redesigned?)

Experiencing HR

Divide into groups of four. In your group, develop a job description for your professor's job. Use your knowledge and assumptions about the tasks, duties, and responsibilities you think are involved. If you have been given time for research, review the chapter for additional ideas on where to gather information for your job description, and use it to improve your job description. Then use your completed job description as a basis for listing job specifications for your professor's job.

With the whole class, share which tasks, duties, and responsibilities you included in your job description and what you included in your job specifications. Discuss what requirements you define as important and what your professor defines as important. Ask your professor how closely your job description and job specifications match the school's actual expectations. Was your professor given a job description? Would professors at your school be more effective if the school used the job descriptions and specifications written by you and your classmates? Why or why not? How would you adjust your team's job description and specifications, based on what you learned from this discussion? Turn in your job description and job specifications for credit on the assignment.

CASE STUDY 3.1:

Job Design for Drivers Keeps UPS on the Road to Energy Efficiency

United Parcel Service (www.ups.com/canada) is famous for its brown-uniformed drivers behind the wheel of brown delivery trucks. But when it comes to energy consumption, UPS is all green. The company is constantly looking for better fuel-efficient vehicles. Its fleet includes electric, hybrid, and natural-gas vehicles, as well as its standard gasoline-powered trucks.

UPS drivers are expected to follow very specific guidelines for how to deliver packages. These aim to complete each route in the fastest, most efficient way possible. The company details the route that each vehicle is to follow; the routes avoid left turns, which require time and gas to idle while the driver waits for oncoming traffic to clear. At each stop, drivers are supposed to walk at a "brisk pace" of 2.5 paces per second as they move to and from their truck. They keep this up as they make an average of up to 20 stops an hour to deliver about 500 packages a day.

Until recently, drivers were supposed to carry their key ring on their ring finger, so they would never need to spend time fumbling around in pockets. Now the company has improved on that method: Drivers no longer need to waste time pulling keys out of the ignition and using them to unlock the door to the packages. Instead, UPS is giving drivers a digital-remote fob to wear on their belts. With the new keyless system, drivers stop the truck and press a button to turn off the engine and unlock the bulkhead door. The changes will save 1.75 seconds at each stop. That's equivalent to an average of 6.5 minutes per driver per day. Besides saving time, the changes save motions by the driver, thus reducing fatigue.

Specific requirements such as these are the result of relentless efforts to improve efficiency. Throughout each day, computers installed in each truck gather data about the truck's activities: how long it idled, how often it backed up, how far it travelled when it was time for the driver's break. The computers also record whether drivers wore their seat belts. At the end of each delivery day, industrial engineers analyze the day's data and look for ways they can save more time, fuel, and money.

The demand to maintain a "brisk pace" is only one reason why jobs for drivers and other workers at UPS can be physically demanding. Besides being able to move quickly, workers are expected to be able to lift packages weighing up to 70 pounds without assistance. Joe Korziuk told a reporter that in more than two decades with UPS, he has enjoyed his jobs driving and washing trucks, but it has taken a toll. He says the surgeries he has had on both knees and a shoulder and the bulging disks in his back are all results of working conditions: "They're always harping on you and pushing you to go faster and faster." As a result, he said, he also was injured when boxes fell on his head, causing a concussion. According to workers, UPS promoted safety and higher efficiency at the same time. Workers trying to keep up with the pace were unable to meet the safety goals. UPS's response has been that safety is a top priority and injury rates are low for the messenger and courier industry. Officials note that when employees experience even minor on-the-job injuries, they receive training in how to prevent similar injuries in the future.

Despite the safety complaints, UPS is a good employer in the opinion of many workers. Drivers appreciate what they consider to be good wages and benefits.

Questions

1. How do UPS's goals for environmental sustainability affect its job design?

2. How well does UPS take worker safety into account in its job design? How could the company better incorporate safety into job design in a way that is consistent with the company's business strategy?

3. Based on the information given, what role would you say motivation plays in the design of drivers' jobs at UPS? How could the company make its jobs more motivational?

Sources: Jennifer Levitz, "Deliver Drivers to Pick Up Pace by Surrendering Keys," *The Wall Street Journal*, September 16, 2011, http://online.wsj.com; Kari Lydersen, "UPS Workers Demand New Approach to Safety," *The New York Times*, May 6, 2011, Business & Company Resource Center, http://galenet.galegroup.com; Seth Skydel, "Makes Good Sense," *Fleet Equipment*, July 2011, Business & Company Resource Center, http://galenet.galegroup.com; David R. Baker, "100 Brown UPS Trucks Going Greener on Inside," *San Francisco Chronicle*, August 25, 2011, Business & Company Resource Center, http://galenet.galegroup.com.

CASE STUDY 3.2:

Creative Jobs at W. L. Gore

When the husband-and-wife team of Bill and Vieve Gore founded W. L. Gore & Associates (www.gore.com), their aim was not just to make and sell products from high-tech materials. Rather, they believed they could create a thriving, creative organization by giving smart people a chance to fully use their talents and ideas. They believed creativity could be stifled by rigid structure and hierarchy, so they built their company without managers, assigning teams of employees to work on opportunities. Today, W. L. Gore remains a privately held company with annual sales of more than $3 billion and more than 10,000 "associates" (employees).

At W. L. Gore, work flow is often about ideas as well as products. To produce good ideas, the company needs scientists and engineers with a profound understanding of their field of expertise, be it chemistry or the fabrication of a new prototype. At the same time, the company's long-term success requires that it back only ideas that will meet real market needs, so expertise must extend to business knowledge coupled with a willingness to terminate projects that have little chance of success. This pairing of skill sets is especially powerful when an innovation isn't working out because Gore employees are gifted at analyzing the idea to see what aspects can be carried over into new projects, so the company builds on ideas. Also related to business skills, Gore associates must be good at communicating with customers, who can help the company identify needs and assess the value of ideas. This combination of skills is broad because jobs at Gore are broadly defined; in contrast, at many other companies, scientists and engineers communicate mainly with other technical experts, leaving customer communication and market knowledge to the sales force.

The basic principle for organizing work at Gore is the team, established to meet a particular opportunity. Thus, each team includes a variety of functions and areas of expertise. As a result, team members see how different viewpoints are necessary to meet the team's objectives. Teams appoint a leader, so leadership is accountable to the team, rather than to corporate hierarchy.

Team members are expected to balance autonomy in how they work with responsibility for meeting team goals. They also must balance time spent on existing, known business requirements with time spent on ideas for creating value in new ways. To help employees maintain the balance, Gore assigns a "sponsor" to each individual, even the chief executive. The sponsor is someone who has made a commitment to the sponsored employee's success and provides the employee with learning opportunities, such as meeting a customer, building relationships with others in the company, or getting involved in a particular project. Sponsors also advocate for their employees' ideas and help them obtain resources to develop those ideas.

The Gore emphasis on teams provides fertile ground for creative thinking. For example, one of the company's biochemical engineers routinely collaborates with an excellent prototyper to develop innovations. The practice of building, reviewing, and discussing prototypes engages more people in thinking about an idea, so it can be improved and made practical in its early stages. Collaboration across teams and functions is encouraged, too. One employee says he can find an answer to any question from someone in the company in three phone calls or less. Facilities are kept relatively small and incorporate all the functions for a particular line of business, making it easier for employees to know who they work with across various functions. Of course, the company also needs to provide enough lab space and other physical resources. Employees feel reinforced by

Gore's culture of trusting them to develop new ideas and tackle big challenges. They report feeling able to create something unique and valuable.

For HR staffers, working for W. L. Gore entails knowing the business unit they support and protecting the organizational culture so carefully laid out by Bill and Vieve Gore. As you might expect, the emphasis is less on forms and structure. When new employees are hired, HR provides them with an orientation and three-day workshop that teaches how work is done at the company. Employees are paired up with their sponsor at the beginning as well. The transition to Gore's culture is tricky for some people who are used to the traditional hierarchy they've experienced at other companies. Some need guidance on how to be influential when they can't rely on their position in a hierarchy.

Questions

1. According to the information given, what basic inputs, work activities (processes), and outputs can you identify for work at W. L. Gore?

2. What are some strengths of designing work around teams, as Gore has done? What are some challenges for managing this structure?

3. If you worked in HR for W. L. Gore, what are some of the competencies you would include in the company's job descriptions?

Sources: "About Gore," www.gore.com/en_xx/aboutus/index.html, retrieved January 17, 2015; "Who We Are," www.gore.com/en_xx/careers/whoweare/about-gore.html, retrieved January 17, 2015; Debra Ricker France, "Creating Compelling Environments for Innovation," *Research-Technology Management,* November-December 2009, pp. 33-38; and "The World is Flat," *Personnel Today,* July 22, 2008, Business & Company Resource Center, http://galenet.galegroup.com.

CHAPTER 4

Planning for and Recruiting Human Resources

WHAT DO I NEED TO KNOW?

After reading this chapter, you should be able to:

LO1	Discuss how to plan for the human resources needed to carry out the organization's strategy.
LO2	Determine the demand for and supply of workers in various job categories.
LO3	Summarize the advantages and disadvantages of ways to eliminate a labour surplus and avoid a labour shortage.
LO4	Identify the steps in the process of succession planning.
LO5	Discuss aspects of recruiting including employment branding and other recruitment policies organizations use to make job vacancies more attractive.
LO6	List and compare sources of job applicants.
LO7	Describe the recruiter's role in the recruitment process, including limits and opportunities.

Diversity and inclusion are at the core of Sodexo's employment brand.

Sodexo's Employment Brand: Diversity

Sodexo is a food and facilities management company with 750 locations and more than 10,000 (approximately 6,000 full-time and over 4,000 part-time) employees in Canada and 420,000 full-time employees globally. Some of Sodexo's recent accomplishments include same year recognition as one of Canada's Top 100 Diversity Employers, Canada's Greenest Employers, and Canada's Top Employers for Young People, Gold Level Progressive Aboriginal Relations—Canadian Counsel for Aboriginal Business, and a 100 percent rating in Human Rights Campaigns' 2014 Corporate Equality Index. Sodexo is known for taking on big projects, e.g., foodservices for Toronto's 2015 Pan American and Parapan American Games—serving up 18,000 meals a day in one dining room for athletes and officials. However, Sodexo also actively engages in less visible but significant initiatives aligned with its "disABILITY" strategy such as the Willow Bean Café discussed in Chapter 2— a partnership with the Canadian Mental Health Association (Burnaby branch) and Vancouver Coastal Health, "to provide real world training opportunities for mental health consumers in a coffee kiosk setting."[1]

Introduction

Trends and events that affect the economy and organizations create opportunities and problems in obtaining human resources. When customer demand rises (or falls), organizations may need more (or fewer) employees. When the labour market changes—as when more people pursue postsecondary education or when a sizable share of the population retires—the supply of qualified workers may grow, shrink, or change in nature. Organizations recently have had difficulty filling information technology jobs, because the demand for people with these skills outstrips the supply. To prepare for and respond to these challenges, organizations engage in *workforce planning*—defined in Chapter 1 as identifying the numbers and types of employees the organization will require to meet its objectives.

This chapter describes how organizations carry out workforce planning. In the first part of the chapter, we lay out the steps that go into developing and implementing a workforce plan. Throughout each section, we focus especially on recent trends and practices, including downsizing, employing temporary workers, and outsourcing. The remainder of the chapter explores the process of recruiting. We discuss the importance of employment branding in attracting potential employees, the process by which organizations look for people to fill job openings, and the usual sources of job candidates. Finally, we discuss the role of recruiters.

LO1 Discuss how to plan for the human resources needed to carry out the organization's strategy.

What Is Workforce Planning?

HRC 1, 2, 4, 9

Organizations should carry out *workforce planning* so as to meet business objectives and gain an advantage over competitors. To do this, organizations need a clear idea of the strengths and weaknesses of their existing internal labour force. They also must know what they want to be doing in the future—what size they want the organization to be, what products and services it should be producing, and so on. This knowledge helps them define the number and kinds of employees they will need. Workforce planning compares the present state of the organization with its goals for the future, then identifies what changes it must make in its human resources to meet those goals. The changes may include downsizing, training existing employees in new skills, or hiring new employees. The overall goal of workforce planning is to ensure the organization has the right people with the right skills in the right places at the right time.

These activities give a general view of workforce planning. They take place in the workforce planning process shown in Figure 4.1. The process consists of three stages: forecasting, goal setting and strategic planning, and program implementation and evaluation.

Forecasting

The first step in workforce planning is **forecasting**, as shown in the top portion of Figure 4.1. In forecasting, the HR professional tries to determine the *supply* of and *demand* for various types of human resources. The primary goal is to predict which areas of the organization will experience labour shortages or surpluses.

forecasting
The attempts to determine the supply of and demand for various types of human resources to predict areas within the organization where there will be labour shortages or surpluses.

Forecasting supply and demand can use statistical methods or judgment. Statistical methods capture historic trends in a company's demand for labour. Under the right conditions, these methods predict demand and supply more precisely than a human forecaster can using subjective judgment. But many important events in the labour market have no precedent. When such events occur, statistical methods are of little use. To prepare for these situations, the organization must rely on the subjective judgments of experts. Pooling their "best guesses" is an important source of ideas about the future.

LO2 Determine the demand for and supply of workers in various job categories.

Forecasting the Demand for Labour

Usually, an organization forecasts demand for specific job categories or skill areas. After identifying the relevant job categories or skills, the planner investigates the likely demand for each. The planner must forecast whether the need for people with the necessary skills and experience will increase or decrease. There are several ways of making such forecasts.

FIGURE 4.1

Overview of the Workforce Planning Process

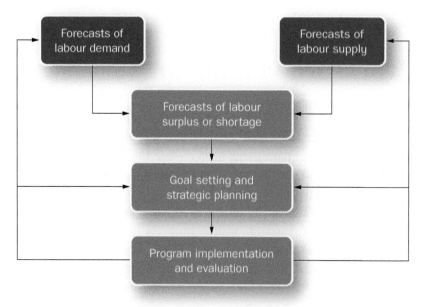

At the most sophisticated level, an organization might use **trend analysis**, constructing and applying statistical models that predict labour demand for the next year, given relatively objective statistics from the previous year. These statistics are called **leading indicators**—objective measures that accurately predict future labour demand. They might include measures of the economy (such as sales or inventory levels), actions of competitors, changes in technology, and trends in the composition of the workforce and overall population. For example, hospitals need to be aware of trends that may shape the demand for medical care because that demand will drive their need for nurses and other health care professionals.

trend analysis
Constructing and applying statistical models that predict labour demand for the next year, given relatively objective statistics from the previous year.

leading indicators
Objective measures that accurately predict future labour demand.

Statistical planning models are useful when there is a long, stable history that can be used to reliably detect relationships among variables. However, these models almost always have to be complemented with subjective judgments of experts. There are simply too many "once in a lifetime" changes to consider, and statistical models cannot capture them.

Forecasting the Available Supply of Labour

Once a company has forecast the demand for labour, it needs an indication of the firm's available labour supply. Determining the internal labour supply calls for a detailed analysis of how many people are currently in various job categories or have specific skills within the organization. The planner then modifies this analysis to reflect changes expected in the near future as a result of retirements, promotions, transfers, voluntary turnover, and terminations.

As the average age of many workers in skilled trades increases, the growing demand for workers in many trades is expected to outstrip supply. There is a potential for employers in some areas to continue to experience a labour shortage because of this. What should HR do to avoid shortages of labour?

One type of statistical procedure that can be used for this purpose is the analysis of a **transitional matrix**, which is a chart that lists job categories held in one period and shows the proportion of employees in each of those job categories in a future period. It answers two questions: "Where did people who were in each job category go?" and "Where did people now in each job category come from?" Table 4.1 is an example of a transitional matrix.

> **transitional matrix**
> A chart that lists job categories held in one period and shows the proportion of employees in each of those job categories in a future period.

This example lists job categories for an auto parts manufacturer. The jobs listed at the left were held in 2012; the numbers across show what happened to the people in 2015. The numbers represent proportions. For example, 0.95 means 95 percent of the people represented by a row in the matrix. The column headings under 2015 refer to the row numbers. The first row is sales manager, so the numbers under column (1) represent people who became sales managers. Reading across the first row, we see that 95 percent of the people who were sales managers in 2012 are still sales managers in 2015. The other 5 percent correspond to column (8), "Not in organization," meaning that 5 percent of people who are not still sales managers have left the organization. In the second row are sales representatives. Of those who were sales reps in 2012, 5 percent were promoted to sales manager, 60 percent are still sales reps, and 35 percent have left the organization. In row (3) half (50 percent) of sales apprentices are still in that job, but 20 percent are now sales reps, and 30 percent have left the organization. This pattern of jobs shows a career path from sales apprentice to sales representative to sales manager. Of course, not everyone is promoted, and some of the people leave instead.

Reading down the columns provides another kind of information: the sources of employees holding the positions in 2015. In the first column, we see that most sales managers (95 percent) held that same job three years earlier. The other 5 percent were promoted from sales representative positions. Skipping over to column (3), half the sales apprentices on the payroll in 2015 held the same job three years before, and the other half were hired from outside the organization. This suggests that the organization fills sales manager positions primarily through promotions, so planning for this job would focus on preparing sales representatives. In contrast, planning to meet the organization's needs for sales apprentices would emphasize recruitment and selection of new employees.

TABLE 4.1

Transitional Matrix: Example for an Auto Parts Manufacturer

2012	2015							
	(1)	(2)	(3)	(4)	(5)	(6)	(7)	(8)
(1) Sales manager	0.95							0.05
(2) Sales representative	0.05	0.60						0.35
(3) Sales apprentice		0.20	0.50					0.30
(4) Assistant plant manager				0.90	0.05			0.05
(5) Production manager				0.10	0.75			0.15
(6) Production assembler					0.10	0.80		0.10
(7) Clerical							0.70	0.30
(8) Not in organization	0.00	0.20	0.50	0.00	0.10	0.20	0.30	

Matrices like this are extremely useful for charting historical trends in the company's supply of labour. More important, if conditions remain somewhat constant, they can also be used to plan for the future. For example, if we believe we are going to have a surplus of labour in the production assembler job category in the next three years, we can plan to avoid layoffs. Still, historical data may not always reliably indicate future trends. Planners need to combine statistical forecasts of labour supply with expert judgments. For example, managers in the organization may see that a new training program will likely increase the number of employees qualified for new openings. Forecasts of labour supply also should take into account the organization's pool of skills. Many organizations include inventories of employees' skills in an HR database. When the organization forecasts that it will need new skills in the future, planners can consult the database to see how many existing employees have those skills.

Besides looking at the labour supply within the organization, the planner should examine trends in the external labour market. The planner should keep abreast of labour market forecasts, including the size of the labour market, the unemployment rate, and the kinds of people who will be in the labour market. For example, we saw in Chapter 1 that the labour market is aging and that immigration is an important source of new workers. Important sources of data on the external labour market are available from Statistics Canada. Details and news (releases from *The Daily*) are available at the Statistics Canada website (www.statcan.ca).

Determining Labour Surplus or Shortage

Based on the forecasts for labour demand and supply, the planner can compare the figures to determine whether there will be a shortage or surplus of labour for each job category. Determining expected shortages and surpluses allows the organization to plan how to address these challenges.

Issues related to a labour surplus or shortage can pose serious challenges for the organization. Manufacturers, for example, expect to have difficulty filling skilled-trades positions such as jobs for ironworkers, machinists, plumbers, and welders. Demand for these jobs is strong and is likely to continue as important infrastructure such as bridges and tunnels age. Although, the average age of tradespeople is rising above 55, and young people have tended to be less attracted to these jobs, assuming, often incorrectly, that manufacturing-related jobs will be difficult to find or will not pay well.[2]

LO3 Summarize the advantages and disadvantages of ways to eliminate a labour surplus and avoid a labour shortage.

Goal Setting and Strategic Planning

The second step in workforce planning is goal setting and strategic planning, as shown in the middle of Figure 4.1. The purpose of setting specific numerical goals is to focus attention on the issue and provide a basis for measuring the organization's success in addressing labour shortages and surpluses. The goals should come directly from the analysis of labour supply and demand. They should include a specific figure indicating what should happen with the job category or skill area and a specific timetable for when the results should be achieved.

For each goal, the organization must choose one or more human resource strategies. A variety of strategies are available for handling expected shortages and surpluses of labour. The top of Table 4.2 shows major options for reducing an expected labour surplus, and the bottom of the table lists options for avoiding an expected labour shortage.

This planning stage is critical. The options differ widely in their expense, speed, and effectiveness. Options for reducing a labour surplus cause differing amounts of human suffering. The options for avoiding a labour shortage differ in terms of how easily the organization can undo the change if it no longer faces a labour shortage. For example, an organization probably would not want to handle every

TABLE 4.2

HR Strategies for Addressing a Labour Shortage or Surplus

Options for Reducing a Surplus		
Option	Speed of Results	Amount of Suffering Caused
Downsizing	Fast	High
Pay reductions	Fast	High
Demotions	Fast	High
Transfers	Fast	Moderate
Reducing hours	Fast	Moderate
Hiring freeze	Slow	Low
Natural attrition	Slow	Low
Early retirement	Slow	Low
Retraining	Slow	Low
Options for Avoiding a Shortage		
Option Later	Speed of Results	Ability to Change Later
Overtime	Fast	High
Temporary employees	Fast	High
Outsourcing	Fast	High
Retrained transfers	Slow	High
Turnover reductions	Slow	Moderate
New external hires	Slow	Low
Technological innovation	Slow	Low

expected labour shortage by hiring new employees. The process is relatively slow and involves expenses to find and train new employees. Also, if the shortage becomes a surplus, the organization will have to consider laying off some of the employees. Layoffs involve another set of expenses, such as severance pay, and they are costly in terms of human suffering.

Another consideration in choosing an HR strategy is whether the employees needed will contribute directly to the organization's success. Organizations are most likely to benefit from hiring and retaining as employees who have competencies that are part of the organization's competency framework (model) discussed in Chapter 3.

Organizations try to anticipate labour surpluses far enough ahead that they can freeze hiring and let natural attrition (people leaving on their own) reduce the labour force. Unfortunately for many workers, organizations often stay competitive in a fast-changing environment by responding to a labour surplus with downsizing, which delivers fast results. The impact is painful for those who lost jobs, as well as those left behind to carry on without them. To handle a labour shortage, organizations typically hire temporary employees or use outsourcing. Because downsizing, using temporary employees, and outsourcing are most common, we will look at each of these in greater detail in the following sections.

Downsizing

As we discussed in Chapter 1, **downsizing** is the planned elimination of large numbers of employees with the goal of enhancing the organization's competitiveness. For example, BlackBerry (http://ca.blackberry.com/) (the former Research In Motion—which in 2007, based on market capitalization, was the most valuable company in Canada) embarked upon an extended period of downsizing beginning in 2011 when it cut 2,000 jobs—10 percent of its workforce. In the wake of product delays, service interruptions, increased competition, and declining market share, another 4,500 jobs, equivalent to 40 percent of its remaining workforce were eliminated in 2013–2014.[3] The "HR Oops!" box shows how a recent downsizing at Tim Hortons was handled.

downsizing
The planned elimination of large numbers of employees with the goal of enhancing the organization's competitiveness.

The primary reason organizations engage in downsizing is to promote future competitiveness. According to surveys, they do this by meeting four objectives:

1. *Reducing costs*—Labour is a large part of a company's total costs, so downsizing is an attractive place to start cutting costs.

2. *Replacing labour with technology*—Closing outdated factories, automating, or introducing other technological changes reduces the need for labour. Often, the labour savings outweigh the cost of the new technology.

3. *Mergers and acquisitions*—When organizations combine, they often need less bureaucratic overhead, so they lay off managers and some professional staff members.

4. *Moving to more economical locations*—In recent years, many Canadian firms have shifted jobs to other countries, including Mexico, India, and China, where wages are lower.

Although downsizing has an immediate effect on costs, much of the evidence suggests that it hurts long-term organizational effectiveness. This is especially true for certain kinds of companies, such as those that emphasize research and development and where employees have extensive contact with

The iconic Tim Hortons confirmed scores of head office and regional office layoffs in 2015.

When a "Double-Double" Means Downsized and Disgruntled

There is likely no good way to lay off employees but how Tim Hortons handled the cut of 350 employees at its headquarters in Oakville, Ontario, as well as regional offices in British Columbia, Alberta, Quebec, Nova Scotia, Ontario, has received media scrutiny. The layoffs came following a $12.5 billion takeover and had been speculated for some time when a story in the *Financial Post* stated "that a significant staff reduction was imminent." Then, "days of damage control as speculation about job cuts mounted, until finally, their disgruntled—and suddenly former—employees vented to reporters." A corporate statement emailed by Alexandra Cygal, spokesperson for the recently formed Restaurant Brands International (Tim Hortons parent company), confirmed the layoffs and said, "This comprehensive process has created tremendous opportunities for some of our employees in new roles and promotions."

A laid-off Tim Hortons manager from Oakville who didn't want her name published, said, "workers didn't see the cuts coming." "It was just really sour, really ominous. You could see a steady flow of people being escorted from the building." Ms. Cygal described the decision as "difficult but necessary" and that the company is "treating departing employees with the utmost respect, while providing generous and enhanced severance packages, continuing health benefits and outplacement services."

Questions

1. Why might management be reluctant to confirm impending layoffs? What are the pitfalls of not doing so?

2. What advice do you have to management about communication with and treatment of employees during a downsizing?

Sources: Stephen Ewert, "Tim Hortons Job Cut Strategy Leaves A Sour Taste," *Calgary Herald,* January 30, 2015, http://calgaryherald.com/business/energy/tim-hortons-job-cuNt-strategy-leaves-a-sour-taste, retrieved February 3, 2015; Sophia Harris, "Tim Hortons Confirms 350 Layoffs As Workers Say They Were Blindsided," January 29, 2015, www.cbc.ca/news/business/tim-hortons-confirms-350-layoffs-as-workers-say-they-were-blindsided-1.2935454?cmp=rss, retrieved February 7, 2015; Hollie Shaw, "Tim Hortons Inc. Confirms Scores of Head Office Layoffs," *Financial Post,* January 28, 2015, http://business.financialpost.com/2015/01/27/tim-hortons-inc-confirms-head-office-layoffs/, retrieved January 31, 2015; and Nicola Middlemiss, "Tim Hortons Lay-Offs Labelled "Tremendous Opportunity," *HRM Online,* January 28, 2015, www.hrmonline.ca/hr-news/tim-hortons-layoffs-labelled-tremendous-opportunity-187550.aspx, retrieved January 31, 2015.

customers.[4] The negative effect of downsizing was especially high among firms that engaged in high-involvement work practices, such as the use of teams and performance-related pay incentives. As a result, the more a company tries to compete through its human resources, the more layoffs hurt productivity.[5]

Why do so many downsizing efforts fail to meet expectations? There seem to be several reasons. First, although the initial cost savings give a temporary boost to profits, the long-term effects of an improperly managed downsizing effort can be negative. Downsizing leads to a loss of talent, and it often disrupts the social networks through which people are creative and flexible.[6]

Unless the downsizing is managed well, employees feel confused, demoralized, and even less willing to stay with the organization. Organizations may not take (or even know) the steps that can counter these reactions—for example, demonstrating how they are treating employees fairly, building confidence in the company's plans for a stronger future, and showing the organization's commitment to behaving responsibly with regard to all its stakeholders, including employees, customers, and the community.[7] Also, many companies wind up rehiring. Downsizing campaigns often eliminate people who turn out to be irreplaceable. In one survey, 80 percent of the firms that had downsized wound up replacing some of the very people they had laid off. However, recent trends in employment suggests that companies will not rehire employees for many of the jobs eliminated when they restructured, introduced automation, or moved work to lower-cost regions.[8]

Finally, downsizing efforts often fail, because employees who survive the purge become self-absorbed and afraid to take risks. Motivation drops, because any hope of future promotions—or any future—with the company dies. Many employees start looking for other employment opportunities. The negative publicity associated with a downsizing campaign can also hurt the company's image in the labour market, so it is harder to recruit employees later.

Many problems with downsizing can be reduced with better planning. Instead of slashing jobs across the board, successful downsizing makes strategic cuts that improve the company's competitive position, and management addresses the problem of employees becoming demoralized.

Reducing Hours

Given the limitations of downsizing, many organizations are more carefully considering other avenues for eliminating a labour surplus (shown in Table 4.2). One alternative seen as a way to spread the burden more fairly is cutting work hours, generally with a corresponding reduction in pay. Besides the thought that this is a more equitable way to weather a slump in demand, companies choose a reduction in work hours because it is less costly than layoffs requiring severance pay, and it is easier to restore the work hours than to hire new employees after a downsizing effort. Window maker Pella, for example, put its employees on a four-day workweek, and Dell Computer offered its employees a chance to take extra (unpaid) days off at the end of the year.[9]

Early-Retirement Programs

Another popular way to reduce a labour surplus is with an early-retirement program. As we discussed in Chapter 1, the average age of the Canadian workforce is increasing. But even though many baby boomers are reaching traditional retirement age, indications are that this group has no intention of leaving the workforce soon.[10] Several forces fuel the drawing out of older workers' careers. First, the improved health of older people in general, combined with the decreased physical labour required by many jobs, has made working longer a viable option. Also, many workers fear their retirement savings and pension plans supplemented by the Canada/Quebec Pension Plan (CPP/QPP) and Old Age Security (OAS) pension will still not be enough to cover their expenses. Finally, protection from discrimination and eliminating mandatory retirement has limited organizations' ability to force older workers to retire. However, under the pressures associated with an aging labour force, many employers try to encourage older workers to leave voluntarily by offering a variety of early-retirement incentives. The more lucrative of these programs succeed by some measures. Research suggests that these programs encourage lower-performing older workers to retire.[11] Sometimes they work so well that too many workers retire.

Many organizations are moving from early-retirement programs to *phased-retirement programs*. In a phased-retirement program, the organization can continue to enjoy the experience of older workers while reducing the number of hours these employees work, as well as the cost of those employees. This option also can give older employees the psychological benefits of easing into retirement, rather than being thrust entirely into a new way of life.[12]

Employing Temporary and Contract Workers

While downsizing has been a popular way to reduce a labour surplus, the most widespread methods for eliminating a labour shortage are hiring temporary and contract workers and outsourcing work. Employers may arrange to hire a temporary worker through an agency that specializes in linking employers with people who have the necessary skills. The employer pays the agency, whom in turn pays the temporary worker. Employers may also contract directly with individuals, often professionals, to provide a particular service. Temporary and contract employment is popular with employers, because it gives them the flexibility they need to operate efficiently when demand for their products changes rapidly.

In addition to flexibility, temporary employment often offers lower costs. Using temporary workers frees the employer from many administrative tasks and financial burdens associated with being the "employer of record." The cost of employee benefits, including vacations, pension, life insurance, workers' compensation, and employment insurance, may account for 40 percent of payroll expenses for permanent employees. Assuming the agency pays for these benefits, a company using temporary workers may save money even if it pays the agency a higher rate for that worker than the usual wage paid to a permanent employee.

Agencies that provide temporary employees also may handle some of the tasks associated with hiring. Small companies that cannot afford their own testing programs often get employees who have been tested by the staffing agency. Many staffing agencies also train employees before sending them to employers. This reduces employers' training costs and eases the transition for the temporary worker and employer.

Finally, temporary workers may offer benefits not available from permanent employees. Because the temporary worker has little experience at the employer's organization, this person brings an objective point of view to the organization's problems and procedures. Also, a temporary worker may have a great deal of experience in other organizations that can be applied to the current assignment.

Besides using a staffing agency, a company can obtain workers for limited assignments by entering into contracts with them. If the person providing the services is an independent contractor, rather than an employee, the company does not pay employee benefits, such as health insurance and vacations. As with using temporary employees, the savings can be significant, even if the contractor works at a higher rate of pay.

As discussed in Chapter 1, this strategy carries risks, however. If the person providing the service is a contractor and not an employee, the company is not supposed to directly supervise the worker. The company can tell the contractor what criteria the finished assignment should meet, but not, for example, where or what hours to work. This distinction is significant, because if the company treats the contractor as an employee, the company has certain legal obligations, related to overtime pay and withholding income taxes.

When an organization wants to consider using independent contractors as a way to expand its labour force temporarily, human resources professionals can help by alerting the company to the need to verify that the arrangement will meet legal requirements. A good place to start is with the advice provided at the Canada Revenue Agency (www.cra.gc.ca) website. In addition, the organization may need to obtain legal or financial services advice.

Outsourcing

Instead of using a temporary employee to fill a single job, an organization might want a broader set of services. As discussed in Chapter 1, contracting with another organization to perform a broad set of services is called *outsourcing*. Organizations use outsourcing as a way to operate more efficiently and save money. They choose outsourcing firms that promise to deliver the same or better quality at a lower cost. One reason they can do this is that the outside company specializes in the services and can benefit from economies of scale (the economic principle that producing something in large volume tends to cost less for each additional unit than producing in small volume). This efficiency is often the attraction for outsourcing human resource functions such as payroll. Costs also are lower when the outsourcing firm is located in a part of the world where wages are relatively low. The labour forces of countries such as China, India, Jamaica, and those in Eastern Europe have been creating an abundant supply of labour.

The first uses of outsourcing emphasized manufacturing and routine tasks. However, technological advances in computer networks and transmission have speeded up the outsourcing process and have helped it spread beyond manufacturing areas and low-skilled jobs. For example, DuPont moved legal services associated with its $100 million asbestos case litigation to a team of lawyers working in the

Philippines. The work is a combination of routine document handling and legal judgments such as determining the relevance of a document to the case. Salaries for legal professionals in the Philippines are about one-fifth the cost of their North-American counterparts.[13]

Outsourcing may be a necessary way to operate as efficiently as competitors, but it does pose challenges. Quality-control problems, security violations, and poor customer service have sometimes wiped out the cost savings attributed to lower wages. To ensure success with an outsourcing strategy; companies should follow these guidelines:

- Learn about what the provider can do for the company, not just the costs. Make sure the company has the necessary skills, including an environment that can meet standards for clear communication, on-time shipping, contract enforcement, fair labour practices, and environmental protection.[14] Some companies are keeping outsourcing inside Canada in order to meet this full set of requirements.

- Do not offshore any work that is proprietary or requires tight security.[15]

- Start small and monitor the work closely, especially in the beginning, when problems are most likely. Boeing offers a cautionary tale with its ambitious plan to have a worldwide network of suppliers build all the components for its 787 Dreamliner. The project eventually fell three years behind schedule and went billions of dollars over budget as various subcontractors fell behind and failed to meet exacting quality standards. Along the way, Boeing went so far as to acquire some of the suppliers to gain more control over the production process.[16]

- Look for opportunities to outsource work in areas that promote growth, for example, by partnering with experts who can help the organization tap new markets.[17]

Overtime and Expanded Hours

Organizations facing a labour shortage may be reluctant to hire employees, even temporary workers, or to commit to an outsourcing arrangement. Especially if the organization expects the shortage to be temporary, it may prefer an arrangement that is simpler and less costly. Under some conditions, these organizations may try to garner more hours from the existing labour force, asking them to go from part-time to full-time or to work overtime.

A major downside of overtime is that the employer must pay nonmanagement employees additional pay above and beyond their normal wages for work done overtime. Even so, employers see overtime pay as preferable to the costs of hiring and training new employees. The preference is especially strong if the organization doubts that the current higher level of demand for its products will last long.

For a short time at least, many workers appreciate the added compensation for working overtime. Over extended periods, however, employees feel stress and frustration from working long hours. Overtime therefore is best suited for short-term labour shortages.

Implementing and Evaluating the Workforce Plan

For whatever HR strategies are selected, the final stage of workforce planning involves implementing the strategies and evaluating the outcomes. This stage is represented by the bottom part of Figure 4.1. When implementing the HR strategy, the organization must hold some individual accountable for achieving the goals. That person also must have the authority and resources needed to accomplish those goals. It is also important that this person issue regular progress reports, so the organization can be sure that all activities occur on schedule and that the early results are as expected.

Implementation that ties planning and recruiting to the organization's strategy and to its efforts to develop employees becomes a complete program of talent management. Today's computer systems have made talent management more practical. For example, companies can tap into databases and use analytic tools to keep track of which skills and knowledge they need, which needs have already been filled, which employees are developing experiences to help them meet future needs, and which sources of talent have met talent needs most efficiently.

In evaluating the results, the most obvious step is checking whether the organization has succeeded in avoiding labour shortages or surpluses. Along with measuring these numbers, the evaluation should identify which parts of the planning process contributed to success or failure. For example, consider a company where meeting human resource needs requires that employees continually learn new skills. If there is a gap between needed skills and current skill levels, the evaluation should consider whether the problem lies with failure to forecast the needed skills or with implementation. Are employees signing up for training, and is the right kind of training available?

Applying Workforce Planning to Employment Equity

As discussed in Chapter 2, many organizations have a human resource strategy that includes employment equity to support diversity goals or meet government requirements. Meeting diversity or employment equity goals requires that employers carry out an additional level of workforce planning aimed at those goals. In other words, besides looking at its overall workforce and needs, the organization looks at the representation of specific groups in its labour force—for example, the proportion of women and visible minorities.

Employment equity plans forecast and monitor the proportion of employees who are members of various protected groups (women, Aboriginal peoples, people with disabilities, and members of a visible minority group). The planning looks at the representation of these employees in the organization's job categories and career tracks. The planner can compare the proportion of employees who are in each group with the proportion each group represents in the labour market. For example, the organization might note that in a labour market that consists of 20 percent visible minorities, 60 percent of its customer service employees are members of a visible minority group. This type of comparison is called a **workforce utilization review**. The organization can use this process to determine whether there is any specific group whose proportion in the relevant labour market differs substantially from the proportion in the job category.

workforce utilization review
A comparison of the proportion of employees in protected groups with the proportion that each group represents in the relevant labour market.

If the workforce utilization review indicates that some group—for example, Aboriginal peoples—makes up 5 percent of the relevant labour market for a job category but that this same group constitutes only 2.5 percent of the employees actually in the job category at the organization, this is evidence of *underutilization*. That situation could result from problems in selection or from problems in internal movement (promotions or other movement along a career path). One way to diagnose the situation would be to use transitional matrices, such as that shown in Table 4.1 earlier in this chapter. Figure 4.2 compares participation of the employment equity groups with workforce availability for one of Canada's largest employers, the federal Public Service.

The steps in a workforce utilization review are identical to the steps in the workforce planning process shown in Figure 4.1. The organization must assess current utilization patterns, then forecast how these are likely to change in the near future. If these analyses suggest the organization is underutilizing certain groups and if forecasts suggest this pattern is likely to continue, the organization may need to set goals and timetables for changing. The planning process may identify new strategies for recruitment or selection. The organization carries out these HR strategies and evaluates their success.

FIGURE 4.2

Employment Equity in the Federal Public Service of Canada Compared to Workforce Availability

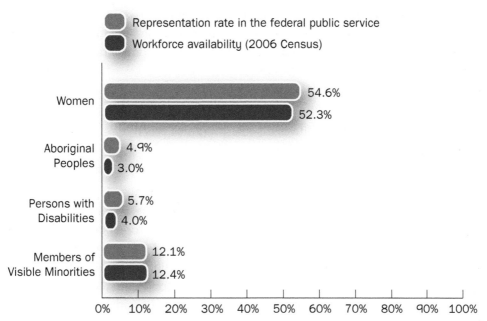

Source: "Employment Equity in The Federal Public Service: Staying Vigilant for Equality, Standing Senate Committee on Human Rights," December 2013, p. 16, www.parl.gc.ca/Content/SEN/Committee/412/ridr/rep/rep02dec13-e.pdf, retrieved February 1, 2015.

L○4 Identify the steps in the process of succession planning.

What Is Succession Planning?

HRC**1,4**

Organizations have always had to prepare for the retirement of their leaders, but the need is more intense than ever. The aging of the workforce means that a greater share of employees are reaching retirement age. Many organizations are fuelling the trend by downsizing through early-retirement programs. As positions at the top of organizations become vacant, many organizations have determined that their middle managers are fewer and often unprepared for top-level responsibility. In addition, other roles in the organization may also be particularly critical to organizational success. These situations has raised awareness of the need for a particular type of workforce planning, **succession planning**—the process of identifying and tracking high-potential employees who will be able to fill top management positions or other key positions when they become vacant.

succession planning
The process of identifying and tracking high-potential employees who will be able to fill top management positions or other key positions when they become vacant.

Succession planning offers several benefits.[18] It forces senior management to regularly and thoughtfully review the company's leadership talent. It assures that top-level management talent is available. It provides a set of development experiences that managers must complete to be considered for top management positions, so the organization does not promote managers before they are ready. Succession planning systems also help attract and retain ambitious employees by providing development opportunities.

Succession planning focuses on *high-potential employees,* that is, employees the organization believes can succeed in higher-level positions such as general manager of a business unit, director of a function (such as marketing or finance), or chief executive officer.[19] A typical approach to development of high-potential employees is to have them complete an individual development program including education, executive mentoring and coaching, and rotation through job assignments. Job assignments are based on the successful career paths of the managers whom the high-potential employees are preparing to replace. High-potential employees may also receive special assignments, such as making presentations and serving on committees and task forces.

Research shows that an effective program for developing high-potential employees has three stages:[20]

1. *Selection of high-potential employees*—Organizations may select outstanding performers and employees who have completed elite academic programs, such as earning a master's degree in business administration from a prestigious university. They may also use the results of psychological tests from assessment centres. For tips on selecting high-potential employees, see "HR How-To."

2. *Developmental experiences*—As employees participate in developmental experiences, the organization identifies those who succeed in the experiences. The organization looks for employees who continue to show qualities associated with success in top jobs, such as communication skills, leadership talent, and willingness to make sacrifices for the organization. In today's high-performance business environment, these assessments should measure whether participants in the program are demonstrating an ability to lead and delivering results that contribute to the company's success. Employees who display these qualities continue to be considered high-potential employees.

3. *Active involvement with the CEO*—High-potential employees seen by top management as fitting into the organization's culture and having personality characteristics necessary for representing the

HR How-To

Identifying High-Potential Employees

It makes sense to invest development dollars and time in the employees with the most potential to succeed when given greater responsibility. But how does an organization know which employees have high potential? Here are some tips for making the right choices:

- **Distinguish *potential* from *experience*.** Potential refers to a person's ability to grow into something more than he or she is today. A high-potential candidate is one who can grow into handling greater responsibilities—a larger budget, a bigger staff, and more complex activities. Success on a smaller scale is just one sign of potential. A high-potential candidate is also eager to assume greater responsibility, able to learn quickly, and willing to work hard to meet new challenges. In an assessment of potential, an employee's strong drive to learn from experience could outweigh a lack of experience in a particular area.

- **Seek nominations.** Organizations that are committed to succession planning give their managers responsibility for identifying employees with high potential. Waiting for employees to volunteer is less effective because people tend to overrate their own potential. But for managers' recommendations to be valid, the organization should also train managers in how to spot the qualities the organization is seeking.

- **Use several measures.** Performance appraisals may focus too much on specific experiences with a particular supervisor, and personality tests are sometimes easy for test takers to manipulate. Mix both measures with interviews, peer assessments, assessment centres, and intelligence testing for a fuller picture of the candidates for the program.

Sources: Len Karakowsky and Igor Kotlyar, "Do 'High-Potential' Leadership Programs Really Work?" *Globe and Mail (Toronto),* January 1, 2012, www.theglobeandmail.com; Claudio Fernández-Aráoz, Boris Groysberg, and Nitin Nohria, "How to Hang On to Your High Potentials," *Harvard Business Review,* October 2011, pp. 76–83; Tom Fox, "Developing the Leadership Skills of High-Potential Employees," *The Washington Post,* August 15, 2011, www.washingtonpost.com.

company become actively involved with the chief executive officer. The CEO exposes these employees to the organization's key people and gives them a greater understanding of the organization's culture. The development of high-potential employees may be a lengthy process.

Figure 4.3 breaks this process into eight steps. It begins with identifying the positions to be planned for and the employees to be included in the plan. Planning should also include establishing position requirements and deciding how to measure employees' potential for being able to fill those requirements. The organization also needs to develop a process for reviewing the existing talent. The next step is to link succession planning with other human resource systems. Then the organization needs a way to provide employees with feedback

FIGURE 4.3

Process for Developing a Succession Plan

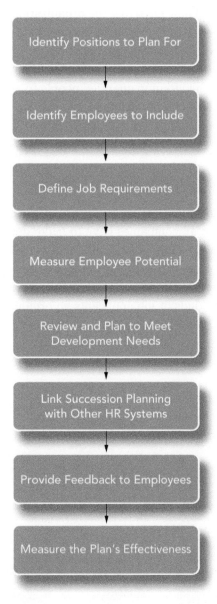

Sources: Based on B. Dowell, "Succession Planning," in *Implementing Organizational Interventions,* ed. J. Hedge and E. Pulakos (San Francisco: Jossey-Bass, 2002), pp. 78-109; R. Barnett and S. Davis, "Creating Greater Success in Succession Planning," *Advances in Developing Human Resources* 10 (2008): 721-39.

about career paths available to them and how well they are progressing toward their goals. Finally, measuring the plan's effectiveness provides information for continuing or adjusting future succession plans.

L○5 Discuss aspects of recruiting including employment branding and other recruitment policies organizations use to make job vacancies more attractive.

Recruiting Human Resources

HRC**1,4**

As the first part of this chapter shows, it is difficult to always predict exactly how many (if any) new employees the organization will have to hire in a given year in a given job category. The role of recruitment is to build a supply of potential new hires that the organization can draw on as the need arises. In human resource management, **recruiting** consists of any practice or activity carried on by the organization with the primary purpose of identifying and attracting potential employees.[21] It thus creates a buffer between workforce planning and the actual selection of new employees (the topic of the next chapter). The goals of recruiting (encouraging qualified people to apply for jobs) and selection (deciding which candidates would be the best fit) are different enough that they are most effective when performed separately, rather than combined as in a job interview that also involves selling candidates on the company.[22]

> **recruiting**
> Any activity carried on by the organization with the primary purpose of identifying and attracting potential employees.

Because of differences in companies' strategies, they may assign different degrees of importance to recruiting.[23] In general, however, all companies have to make decisions in three areas of recruiting: human resource policies, recruitment sources, and the characteristics and behaviour of the recruiter. As shown in Figure 4.4, these aspects of recruiting have different effects on whom the organization ultimately hires. Human resource policies influence the characteristics of the positions to be filled. Recruitment sources influence the kinds of job applicants an organization reaches. And the nature and behaviour of the recruiter affect the characteristics of both the vacancies and the applicants. Ultimately,

---

FIGURE 4.4

Three Aspects of Recruiting

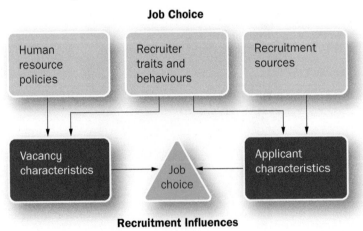

Recruitment Influences

an applicant's decision to accept a job offer—and the organization's decision to make the offer—depend on the *fit* between vacancy characteristics and applicant characteristics.

The remainder of this chapter explores these three aspects of recruiting: human resource policies, recruitment sources, and recruiter traits and behaviours.

Human Resource Policies

An organization's *human resource policies* are its decisions about how it will carry out human resource management, including how it will fill job openings. These policies influence the nature of the positions that are vacant. According to the research on recruitment, it is clear that characteristics of the vacancy are more important than recruiters or recruiting sources for predicting job choice. Several policies are especially relevant to recruitment:

- *Internal versus external recruiting*—Organizations with policies to "promote from within" try to fill vacancies by recruiting candidates internally—that is finding candidates who already work for the organization. Opportunities for advancement make a job more attractive to applicants and employees. Decisions about internal versus external recruiting affect the nature of jobs, recruitment sources, and the nature of applicants, as we will describe later in the chapter.

- *Lead-the-market pay strategies*—Pay is an important job characteristic for almost all applicants. Organizations have a recruiting advantage if their policy is to take a "lead the market" approach to pay—that is, pay more than the current market rate for a job. Higher pay can also make up for a job's less desirable features, such as working on a night shift or outdoors in extreme weather conditions. Organizations that compete for applicants based on pay may use bonuses, stock options, and other forms of pay besides wages and salaries. Chapter 8 will take a closer look at these and other decisions about pay.

- *Employer branding*—Besides advertising specific job openings, as discussed in the next section, organizations may promote themselves as a good place to work in general. **Employer branding,**

employer branding
A strategic approach of attaching a visual, emotional, or cultural brand to an organization.

Forestry student Shayna Mason is an example of an accomplished student who has provided a compelling testimonial about career opportunities in the forest products industry. These types of messages are likely to get the attention of young people and create a positive impression of the industry.

or *employment branding, or recruitment branding* is a strategic approach of attaching a visual, emotional, or cultural brand to an organization. Employer branding uses marketing techniques to attract, engage, and retain employees in the effort to become an *employer of choice.* For example, when an organization is recognized as one of "Canada's Top 100 Employers" the organization acquires the ability to use a well-known logo in various mediums—for example, print or a company website—to support and enhance their recruitment efforts.

An *employment brand* is the impression the company makes on employees and job seekers. Marketing it successfully is the same as marketing any other brand.[24] "The secret to an effective employment brand is differentiating an organization from the competition, targeting key benefits of the job to the right labour segments, and using multiple platforms to reach the right audiences."[25] This employment brand, the image an employer projects to potential hires, should be honest and paint a realistic picture of the company.[26] Just as marketers talk about the unique features of their products, employers need to first understand their own strengths and weaknesses and what they can offer top talent that their rivals cannot.[27] For example employers strive to be recognized not only as one of Canada's Top 100 Employers, but also to earn a spot in one of the other targeted categories, e.g., "Canada's Best Diversity Employers" or "Canada's Top Employers for Young People."

When an organization is recognized as a top employer, they are likely to experience a dramatic increase in the number of résumés they receive. Employer branding is not the exclusive domain of the private sector or even of individual organizations. "Savvy governments across the country are beginning to build and market a solid employment brand, creating catchy tag lines to grab the attention of jobseekers."[28] The tag line for Nova Scotia's public service is "Make a difference" and the Manitoba government's job opportunities site proclaims, 'Your search is over."[29] Entire industries are also using employment branding techniques to get the attention of prospective employees. To learn how Canada's Forest Products Association of Canada (www.fpac.ca) took a recruiting campaign online with a social media contest, see the "HR Best Practices" box.

L○6 List and compare sources of job applicants.

Recruitment Sources

Another critical element of an organization's recruitment strategy is its decisions about where to look for applicants. The total labour market is enormous and spread over the entire globe. As a practical matter, an organization will draw from a small fraction of that total market. The methods the organization chooses for communicating its labour needs and the audiences it targets will determine the size and nature of the labour market the organization taps to fill its vacant positions.[30] A person who responds to a job advertisement online is likely to be different from a person responding to a sign hanging outside a factory. The nearby "Did You Know?" box presents some data on sources of recruitment. Each of the major sources from which organizations draw recruits has advantages and disadvantages.

Internal Sources

As we discussed with regard to human resource policies, an organization may emphasize internal or external sources of job applicants. Internal sources are employees who currently hold other positions in the organization. Organizations recruit existing employees through **job posting**, or communicating

job posting
The process of communicating information about a job vacancy on company bulletin boards, in employee publications, on corporate intranets, and anywhere else the organization communicates with employees.

HR Best Practices

The Forest Products Industry's "Green Dream Contest"

The Forest Products Association of Canada (FPAC) recently launched an ambitious vision to "revitalize its brand as a modern, green industry based on renewable resource and one that needs brains as well as brawn." Goals include a 35 percent improvement in environmental performance, using innovation and market growth to generate economic activity by $20 billion, and hiring an additional 60,000 employees across Canada for jobs ranging from skilled trades to corporate roles, operations, and sciences.

In addition to launching a new website (www.thegreenestworkforce.ca), which showcases the sector's innovative, technology-focused, and environmental commitments, the FPAC introduced a social media competition called, "The Green Dream Contest," to capture the interest of young people and have them consider career opportunities in the forest products industry. "We know that we have to compete with other sectors for skilled workers and we see this online social media contest as a fun way to attract a next-generation workforce," says David Lindsay, president and CEO of FPAC. The first year of the contest was considered a significant success attracting university and college students to submit two-minute YouTube videos explaining "what would make them an ideal Green Dream intern." In 2013, eight paid, four-month summer internships were provided and the interns also received an iPad mini to blog about their work experience.

In 2014, the number of internships increased to 18 paid, four-month positions with nine leading forest products companies. Students submitted their applications online and solicited Facebook votes—individuals with the most votes received an interview. Students were hired in Alberta, British Columbia, Ontario, and New Brunswick into roles in human resources, engineering, communications, and forest management. Once again, the students received an iPad mini and were required to blog about their experiences. The blogs can be read at: http://thegreenestworkforce.ca/index.php/blog/. More than one million Canadians took part by applying, voting, or sharing information about careers in the forest products industry.

Sources: Monica Bailey, "Forest Products Industry Gets Out of The Woods," *Canadian HR Reporter*, July 14, 2014, p. 12-13; "Living the Green Dream: Eighteen Students Win Jobs Via Social Media," December 2013, www.fpac.ca/index.php/en/press-releases-full/living-the-green-dream-eighteen-students-win-jobs-via-social-media, retrieved February 6, 2015; "Job Blog," http://thegreenestworkforce.ca/index.php/blog/, retrieved February 6, 2015.

information about the vacancy on company bulletin boards, in employee publications, on corporate intranets, and anywhere else the organization communicates with employees. Managers also may identify candidates to recommend for vacancies. Policies that emphasize promotions and even lateral moves to achieve broader career experience can give applicants a favourable impression of the organization's jobs. The use of internal sources also affects what kinds of people the organization recruits.

For the employer, relying on internal sources offers several advantages.[31] First, it generates applicants who are well known to the organization. In addition, these applicants are relatively knowledgeable about the organization's vacancies, which minimizes the possibility they will have unrealistic expectations about the job. Finally, filling vacancies through internal recruiting is generally cheaper and faster than looking outside the organization.

One company that has benefited from a strong internal hiring system is Intercontinental Hotels Group. (www.ihgplc.com) Intercontinental has been opening about one new hotel every day. These expansion plans are driving a need for hundreds of thousands of new employees, but the company wants to fill as many positions as possible from inside the organization. Internal recruiting supports the organization's strategy of staffing with people who are so dedicated to the brand that this attitude shows up in exceptional customer service. People already working at the company are most likely to have developed the desired level of commitment. To match employees with open positions, the company runs a Careers Week twice a year. During Careers Week, Intercontinental encourages its employees to create a profile in the company's online talent management system. So far, 5,000 employees in 89 countries have created profiles that include preferences for the locations and functions in which they would like to work. When Intercontinental has an opening, it can easily search the profiles to find candidates who might be

Four in Ten Positions Are Filled with Insiders

In a survey of large, well-known businesses, respondents said over 40 percent of positions are filled with people who already work for the company and accept a promotion or transfer.

During the recent recession, hiring from within accounted for about half of all positions filled. As companies have begun to grow again, the greater demand for talent is requiring more external recruiting.

Sources of Hire

Question

1. Could a growing company fill more than half its open positions with internal recruiting? Why or why not?

Sources: Steven Rothberg, "Job Boards Are 2nd Largest Source of Hire: College Is 5th," *ResumeBear*, February 29, 2012, http://blog.resumebear.com; Tony Rosato, "What We Can Learn from the 2012 CareerXroads Sources of Hire Survey," Alstin Communications, February 24, 2012, http://blog.alstin.com; Gerry Crispin and Mark Mehler, "2012 Sources of Hire: Channels That Influence," CareerXroads, posted February 16, 2012, http://www.slideshare.net.

Note: "Internal movement" refers to jobs filled from employees currently in the company who are referred by managers or receive promotions or transfers; "all external sources" refers to employees found using sources outside the company such as electronic recruiting from company or job websites, employment agencies, colleges and universities, walk-in applicants, newspaper ads, and referrals.

interested and well qualified. Using the talent management system, Intercontinental is filling 84 percent of general manager positions and 26 percent of corporate jobs with current employees. The initiative has lowered recruiting costs, increased employee loyalty, and boosted productivity and profitability.[32]

External Sources

Despite the advantages of internal recruitment, organizations often have good reasons to recruit externally.[33] For entry-level positions and perhaps for specialized upper-level positions, the organization has no internal recruits from which to draw. Also, bringing in outsiders may expose the organization to new ideas or new ways of doing business. An organization that uses only internal recruitment can wind up with a workforce whose members all think alike and therefore may be poorly suited to innovation.[34] And finally, companies that are able to grow during a slow economy can gain a competitive edge when other organizations are forced to avoid hiring, freeze pay increases, or even lay off talented people.[35] So organizations often recruit through direct applicants and referrals, advertisements, employment agencies, schools, and websites.

Direct Applicants and Referrals

Even without a formal effort to reach job applicants, an organization may hear from candidates through direct applicants and referrals. **Direct applicants** are people who apply for a vacancy without prompting from the organization. **Referrals** are people who apply because someone in the organization prompted them to do so. According to the survey results shown in Figure 4.5, the largest share (close to one-fifth) of new employees hired by large companies came from referrals.[36] The target of an organization's recruitment efforts may also involve recruiter-initiated contacts including identifying and contacting **passive job seekers**—individuals who are not actively seeking a job, but represent a significant source of top talent. These sources of recruits share characteristics that make them excellent pools from which to draw.

direct applicants
People who apply for a vacancy without prompting from the organization.

referrals
People who apply for a vacancy because someone in the organization prompted them to do so.

passive job seekers
Individuals who are not actively seeking a job.

FIGURE 4.5

External Recruiting Sources

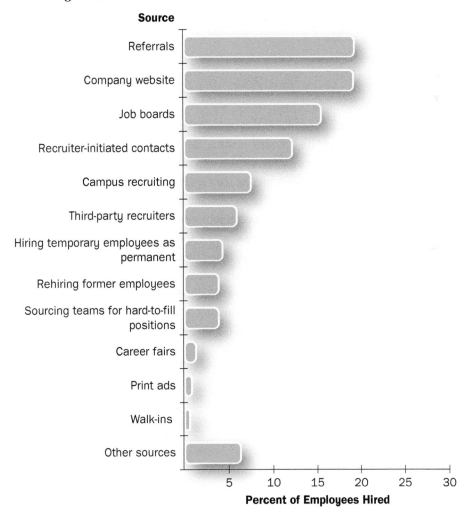

Note: Separate Source of Hire categories for mobile devices and social media have not been included because they are considered part of all categories.
Source: Gerry Crispin and Mark Mehler, "CareerXroads Source of Hire Report 2014, September 2014, www.careerxroads.com (data from 2013).

One advantage is that many direct applicants are to some extent already "sold" on the organization. Most have done some research and concluded there is enough fit between themselves and the vacant position to warrant submitting an application, a process called *self-selection*, which, when it works, eases the pressure on the organization's recruiting and selection systems. A form of aided self-selection occurs with referrals. Many job seekers look to friends, relatives, and acquaintances to help find employment. Using these personal networks not only helps the job seeker but also simplifies recruitment for employers.[37] Current employees (who are familiar with the vacancy as well as the person they are referring) decide that there is a fit between the person and the vacancy, so they suggest the person should apply for the job.

An additional benefit of using such sources is that it costs much less than formal recruiting efforts. Considering these combined benefits, referrals and direct applications are among the best sources of new hires. Some employers offer current employees financial incentives for referring applicants who are hired and perform acceptably on the job (e.g., if they stay 180 days). Other companies play off their good reputations in the labour market to generate direct applications.

The major downside of referrals is that they limit the likelihood of exposing the organization to fresh viewpoints. People tend to refer others who are like themselves. Furthermore, sometimes referrals contribute to hiring practices that are or that appear unfair, an example being **nepotism**, or the hiring of relatives. Employees may resent the hiring and rapid promotion of "the boss's son" or "the boss's daughter," or even the boss's friend.

nepotism
The practice of hiring relatives.

Online Recruiting

Few employers can fill all their vacant positions through direct applications and referrals, so most need to advertise openings. Most often today, that means posting information online. Online recruiting generally involves posting career information at company websites to address people who are interested in the particular company and posting paid advertisements at career sites to attract people who are searching for jobs. However, LinkedIn, Facebook, and Twitter "have fundamentally changed the way companies recruit by giving them a way to identify and connect with passive job seekers who they never had access to before."[38] For example, Nancy Moulday, manager of recruitment at TD Canada Trust, was unsuccessful attracting the right candidate for a senior account manager opening, using the corporate website and online job boards. So in the effort to be more proactive, Moulday turned to LinkedIn. She found three candidates who matched the specific qualifications, and ultimately hired one passive candidate who wasn't aware of the job or looking.[39] Canada is the one of the world's most active countries on LinkedIn. The site reports that 10 million Canadians use LinkedIn, representing half of working Canadians. Globally, LinkedIn has 300 million members.[40]

 E-HRM

Social networks can also be career networks.

Most large companies and many smaller ones make career information available at their websites. To make that information easier to find, they may register a link, e.g., http://jobs.bce.ca/ to access information about careers at Bell Canada. To be an effective recruiting tool, corporate career information should move beyond generalities, offering descriptions of open positions and an easy way to submit a résumé. One of the best features of this kind of online recruiting is the ability to target and attract job candidates whose values match the organization's values and whose skills match the job requirements.[41] Candidates

QR (Quick Response) codes have become powerful recruitment tools because they can take applicants directly to customized information such as a website, video, or to the company's social media such as Facebook, Twitter, YouTube, and LinkedIn without the need to type in a Web address.

also appreciate a response that the company has received their résumé—especially a response that gives a timetable about further communications from the company.

Accepting applications at the company website is not so successful for smaller and less well-known organizations, because fewer people are likely to visit the website. These organizations might get better results by going to the national job board websites, such as Monster and CareerBuilder, which attract a vast array of applicants. At these sites, job seekers submit standardized résumés. Employers can search the site's database for résumés that include specified key terms, and they can also submit information about their job opportunities, so that job seekers can search that information by key term. With both employers and job seekers submitting information to and conducting searches on them, these sites offer an efficient way to find matches between job seekers and job vacancies. However, a drawback is that the big job websites can provide too many leads of inferior quality, because they are so huge and serve all job seekers and employers, not a select segment.

Because of this limitation of the large websites, smaller, more tailored websites called "niche boards" focus on certain industries, occupations, or geographic areas. For example, Atlantic Canada-based Career Beacon (www.careerbeacon.com) is a job board particularly well-known by applicants from Atlantic Canada.

Ads in Newspapers and Magazines

Although computer search tools have made electronic job lists the most popular way to advertise a job opening, some recruiters still follow the traditional route and advertise open positions in newspapers or magazines. When the goal is to find people who know the local community, advertising in a local newspaper can reach that audience. Similarly, when the goal is to find people in a specialized field, advertising in a trade, professional, or industry publication can reach the right subset of job candidates.

Advertising can be expensive, so it is especially important that the ads be well-written. The person designing a job advertisement needs to answer two questions:

- What do we need to say?
- To whom do we need to say it?

With respect to the first question, an ad should give readers enough information to evaluate the job and its requirements, so they can make a well-informed judgment about their qualifications. Providing enough information may require long ads, which cost more. The employer should evaluate the additional costs against the costs of providing too little information: Vague ads generate a large number of applicants, including many who are not reasonably qualified. In practice, the people who write job ads tend to overstate the skills and experience required, perhaps generating too few qualified candidates.

Specifying whom to reach with the message helps the advertiser decide where to place the ad. Ads placed in the classified section of local newspapers are relatively inexpensive, yet reach many people in a specific geographic area who are currently looking for work. On the downside, this medium offers little ability to target skill levels. Typically, many of the people reading classified ads are either over- or under-qualified for the position. Also, people not looking for work rarely read the classifieds. For reaching a specific part of the labour market, including certain skill levels and more people who are employed, the organization may get better results from advertising in professional or industry journals.

Public Employment Agencies

Employers can register job vacancies at the federal government's Service Canada website, "Job Bank" (www.jobbank.gc.ca). In addition to posting job openings, employers can access information and links to government forms, services, and programs. Prospective employees can narrow their job search by province and are also provided access to a variety of resources and career navigation tools. Recent enhancements include added functionality such as *Job Match,* which allows employers and job seekers to be matched based on their respective needs and profiles as well as tools for jobseekers including job alerts.

Private Staffing Companies

In addition to providing temporary employees, private staffing companies provide assistance to employers in attracting temporary and permanent applicants. Job seekers apply to the private staffing company and are usually screened for suitability. These companies differ significantly in the types of services provided. It is important for both job seekers and employers to research and thoroughly assess private staffing firms so as to work with the company that will best meet their needs and expectations. These companies provide their services for a fee. Usually these fees are paid by the employer, for the service of receiving employee referrals.

For executives, managers, or professionals, an employer may use the services of a type of private staffing company called an *executive search firm* (ESF). People often call these agencies "headhunters" because, unlike other staffing companies, they find new jobs for people almost exclusively already employed. For job candidates, dealing with executive search firms can be sensitive. Typically, executives, managers, and professionals do not want to advertise their availability, because it might trigger a negative reaction from their current employers. ESFs serve as a buffer, providing confidentiality between the employer and the potential candidate. That benefit may give an employer access to candidates it cannot recruit in other, more direct ways.

Universities and Colleges

Most universities and colleges have placement services that seek to help their students and graduates obtain employment. On-campus interviewing is the most important source of recruits for entry-level professional and managerial vacancies.[42] Organizations tend to focus especially on universities and colleges that have strong reputations in areas for which they have critical needs—say petroleum engineering or accounting.[43]

Many employers have found that successfully competing for the best students requires more than just signing up prospective graduates for interview slots. One of the best ways to establish a stronger presence on a campus is with a cooperative education or internship program. These programs give an organization early access to potential applicants and let the organization assess their capabilities directly.

Another way of increasing the employer's presence on campus is to participate in university and college job fairs. In general, a job fair is an event where many employers gather for a short time to meet large numbers of potential job applicants. Although job fairs can be held anywhere (such as at a hotel or convention centre), campuses are ideal because of the many well-educated, not-yet-employed individuals there. Job fairs are an inexpensive means of generating an on-campus presence. They can provide one-on-one dialogue with students, however it is also important to "go mobile." For example, provide tablets and "apps that allow them to apply for jobs with as few clicks as possible." Embracing texting is another way for recruiters to demonstrate they are authentic and willing to answer students' questions as they come up.[44]

Evaluating the Quality of a Source

HRC 2, 9

In general, there are few rules that say what recruitment source is best for a given job vacancy. Therefore, it is wise for employers to monitor the quality of all their recruitment sources. One way to do this is to develop and compare **yield ratios** for each source.[45] A yield ratio expresses the percentage of applicants who successfully move from one stage of the recruitment and selection process to the next. For example, the organization might find the number of candidates interviewed as a percentage of the total number of résumés generated by a given source (i.e., number of interviews divided by number of résumés). A high

yield ratios
A ratio that expresses the percentage of applicants who successfully move from one stage of the recruitment and selection process to the next.

Capt. Jen Causey, an artillery officer with the 2nd Regiment, Royal Canadian Horse Artillery, based in Petawawa, Ontario, was staffing the booth at the Women in Leadership Career Fair at the University of Toronto. She is chatting with Cora Cheng, a second-year mechanical engineering student at U of T. How do career fairs benefit employers and the students at the same time?

TABLE 4.3

Results of a Hypothetical Recruiting Effort

	Recruiting Source					
	Local College/University	Renowned College/University	Employee Referrals	Newspaper Ad	Executive Search Firm	Company Website
Résumés generated	200	400	50	500	20	1,000
Interview offers accepted	150	100	45	400	20	80
Yield ratio	**75%**	**25%**	**90%**	**80%**	**100%**	**8%**
Applicants judged acceptable	100	95	40	50	19	40
Yield ratio	**67%**	**95%**	**89%**	**12.5%**	**95%**	**50%**
Accept employment offers	90	10	35	25	15	20
Yield ratio	**90%**	**10.5%**	**87.5%**	**50%**	**79%**	**50%**
Cumulative yield ratio	**90/200 45%**	**10/400 2.5%**	**35/50 70%**	**25/500 5%**	**15/20 75%**	**20/1,000 2%**
Cost	**$30,000**	**$50,000**	**$15,000**	**$20,000**	**$120,000**	**$500**
Cost per hire	**$333**	**$5,000**	**$429**	**$800**	**$8,000**	**$25**

yield ratio (large percentage) means the source is an effective way to find candidates to interview. By comparing the yield ratios of different recruitment sources, HR professionals can determine which is the best or most efficient for the type of vacancy.

Another measure of recruitment success is the *cost per hire*. To compute this amount, find the cost of using a particular recruitment source for a particular type of vacancy. Then divide that cost by the number of people hired to fill that type of vacancy. A low cost per hire means that the recruitment source is efficient; it delivers qualified candidates at minimal cost.

To see how HR professionals use these measures, look at the examples in Table 4.3. This table shows the results for a hypothetical organization that used six kinds of recruitment sources to fill a number of vacancies. For each recruitment source, the table shows four yield ratios and the cost per hire. To fill these jobs, the best two sources of recruits were local colleges/universities and employee referral programs. Company websites generated the largest number of recruits (1,000 résumés). However, only 40 were assessed acceptable, of which only half accepted employment offers, for a cumulative yield ratio of 20/1,000, or 2 percent. Recruiting at renowned colleges/universities generated highly qualified applicants, but relatively few of them ultimately accepted positions with the organization. Executive search firms produced the highest cumulative yield ratio. These generated only 20 applicants, but all of them accepted interview offers, most were assessed suitable, and 75 percent of these suitable candidates took jobs with the organization. However, notice the cost per hire. The executive search firms charged $120,000 for finding these 15 employees, resulting in the largest cost per hire. In contrast, local colleges and universities provided modest yield ratios at one of the lowest costs per hire. Employee referrals provided excellent yield ratios at a slightly higher cost.

As recruiting software and social sharing applications evolve, the distinction between use of the various recruiting sources is becoming increasingly blurred. However, Chris Gould, senior director of the talent acquisition solutions group for Aon Hewitt, anticipates "that we will see more 'social sharing' applications that will integrate with mobile, social media. These apps will make it easier to share jobs and will provide the ability to track click-throughs and sources."[46]

L○7 Describe the recruiter's role in the recruitment process, including limits and opportunities.

Recruiter Traits and Behaviours

HRC2

As we showed in Figure 4.4, the third influence on recruitment outcomes is the recruiter, including this person's characteristics and the way he or she behaves. The ideal recruiter is a *talent magnet*—top recruiters are able to attract talent. The recruiter affects the nature of both the job vacancy and the applicants generated. However, the recruiter often gets involved late in the recruitment process. In many cases, by the time a recruiter meets some applicants, they have already made up their minds about what they desire in a job, what the vacant job has to offer, and their likelihood of receiving a job offer.[47]

Many applicants approach the recruiter with some skepticism. Knowing it is the recruiter's job to sell them on a vacancy, some applicants discount what the recruiter says, in light of what they have heard from other sources, such as friends, published sources, and professors. When candidates are already familiar with the company through knowing about its products, the recruiter's impact is especially weak.[48] For these and other reasons, recruiters' characteristics and behaviours seem to have limited impact on applicants' job choices.

Characteristics of the Recruiter

Most organizations have to choose whether their recruiters are specialists in human resources or experts at particular jobs (i.e., those who currently hold the same kinds of jobs or supervise people who hold the jobs). According to some studies, applicants perceive HR specialists as less credible and are less attracted to jobs when recruiters are HR specialists.[49] The evidence does not completely discount a positive role for HR specialists in recruiting. It does indicate, however, that these specialists need to take extra steps to ensure that applicants perceive them as knowledgeable and credible.

In general, applicants respond positively to recruiters whom they perceive as warm and informative. "Warm" means the recruiter seems to care about the applicant and to be enthusiastic about the applicant's potential to contribute to the organization. "Informative" means the recruiter provides the kind of information the applicant is seeking. The evidence of impact of other characteristics of recruiters—including their age, sex, and race—is complex and inconsistent.[50]

Behaviour of the Recruiter

Recruiters affect results not only by providing plenty of information, but by providing the right kind of information. Perhaps the most-researched aspect of recruiting is the level of realism in the recruiter's message. Because the recruiter's job is to attract candidates, recruiters may feel pressure to exaggerate the positive qualities of the vacancy and to downplay its negative qualities. Applicants are highly sensitive to negative information. The highest-quality applicants may be less willing to pursue jobs when this type of information comes out.[51] But if the recruiter goes too far in a positive direction, the candidate can be misled and lured into taking a job that has been misrepresented. Then unmet expectations can contribute to a high turnover rate. When recruiters describe jobs unrealistically, people who take those jobs may come to believe that the employer is deceitful.[52]

Many studies have looked at how well **realistic job previews**—background information about jobs' positive and negative qualities—can get around this problem and help organizations minimize turnover among new employees. On the whole, the research suggests that realistic job previews have a weak and inconsistent effect on turnover.[53] Although recruiters can go overboard in selling applicants on the desirability of a job vacancy, there is little support for the belief that informing people about the negative characteristics of a job will "inoculate" them so that the negative features don't cause them to quit.[54]

realistic job previews
Background information about a job's positive and negative qualities.

Finally, for affecting whether people choose to take a job, but even more so, whether they stick with a job, the recruiter seems less important than an organization's human resource policies that directly affect the job's features (pay, security, advancement opportunities, and so on).

Enhancing the Recruiter's Impact

Nevertheless, although recruiters are probably not the most important influence on people's job choices, this does not mean recruiters cannot have an impact. Most recruiters receive little training.[55] If we were to determine what does matter to job candidates, perhaps recruiters could be trained in those areas.

Researchers have tried to find the conditions in which recruiters do make a difference. Such research suggests that an organization can take several steps to increase the positive impact that recruiters have on job candidates:

- *Recruiters should provide timely feedback.* Applicants dislike delays in feedback. They may draw negative conclusions about the organization (for starters, that the organization doesn't care about their application).

- *Recruiters should avoid offensive behaviour.* They should avoid behaving in ways that might convey the wrong impression about the organization.[56] Figure 4.6 quotes applicants who felt they had extremely bad experiences with recruiters. Their statements provide examples of behaviours to avoid.

- *The organization can recruit with teams rather than individual recruiters.* Applicants view job experts as more credible than HR specialists, and a team can include both kinds of recruiters. HR specialists on the team provide knowledge about company policies and procedures and ensure the integrity of the process, consistency, and compliance with human rights legislation.

Through such positive behaviour, recruiters can give organizations a better chance of competing for talented human resources. In the next chapter, we will describe how an organization selects the candidates who best meet its needs.

FIGURE 4.6

Recruits Who Were Offended by Recruiters

_____ has a management training program which the recruiter had gone through. She was talking about the great presentation skills that _____ teaches you, and the woman was barely literate. She was embarrassing. If that was the best they could do, I did not want any part of them. Also, _____ and _____ 's recruiters appeared to have real attitude problems. I also thought they were chauvinistic. (Arts undergraduate)

I had a very bad campus interview experience . . . the person who came was a last-minute fill-in. . . . I think he had a couple of "issues" and was very discourteous during the interview. He was one step away from yawning in my face. . . . The other thing he did was that he kept making these—nothing illegal, mind you—but he kept making these references to the fact that I had been out of my undergraduate and first graduate programs for more than ten years now. (MBA with ten years of experience)

One firm I didn't think of talking to initially, but they called me and asked me to talk with them. So I did, and then the recruiter was very, very rude. Yes, very rude, and I've run into that a couple of times. (Engineering graduate)

_____ had set a schedule for me which they deviated from regularly. Times overlapped, and one person kept me too long, which pushed the whole day back. They almost seemed to be saying that it was my fault that I was late for the next one! I guess a lot of what they did just wasn't very professional. Even at the point when I was done, where most companies would have a cab pick you up, I was in the middle of a snowstorm and they said, "You can get a cab downstairs." There weren't any cabs. I literally had to walk 12 or 14 blocks with my luggage, trying to find some way to get to the airport. They didn't book me a hotel for the night of the snowstorm so I had to sit in the airport for eight hours trying to get another flight. . . . They wouldn't even reimburse me for the additional plane fare. (Industrial relations graduate student)

The guy at the interview made a joke about how nice my nails were and how they were going to ruin them there due to all the tough work. (Engineering undergraduate)

Thinking ETHICALLY

Is Social Score Mixing Business and Pleasure?

Until recently, Facebook was mainly a place to keep up with the personal lives of family and friends. But after LinkedIn began to build a network of people focused on career development, Facebook wanted in on the career networking, too. It found a way in with an application called BranchOut, which offers a job board and job-hunting database. BranchOut users link to their Facebook account, and BranchOut pulls their information on education and work history from Facebook to create a BranchOut career profile. BranchOut also collects the user's connections to his or her Facebook friends.

To get people more engaged with the site, BranchOut came up with a quiz game called Social Score. The game displays pairs of randomly selected Facebook friends and asks the player to choose which of those friends he or she would rather work with. BranchOut keeps score, notifies the winners, and saves the data. It can then combine the scores with, say, job title to create rankings. For example, at least in theory, a recruiter could buy rankings of accountants or servers based on their ratings by their friends.

Some people see the Social Score game as a kind of middle-school-style popularity contest, not at all professional. Others can envision that the results would be a useful way to identify prospective hires with a strong social media presence, get along well with others, and would be a good cultural fit.

Questions

1. Does it seem ethical to you that a recruiter could evaluate a candidate based on his or her Social Score? Why or why not?

2. If you were to consider Social Score with random pairs of people in your own Facebook network (or in other social networks you belong to), how well do you think your scores would represent these people's actual performance of a job? Would the scores be more fair or less fair to them than what you would say if a recruiter directly asked you to evaluate them as a possible employee? Is it ethical to use the scores for hiring decisions? Why or why not?

Sources: Susan Berfield, "Dueling Your Facebook Friends for a New Job," *Bloomberg Businessweek,* March 3, 2011, www.businessweek.com; "LinkedIn Competitor Branches Out to 300 Million Users," *The Wall Street Journal,* February 8, 2012, http://blogs.wsj.com; BranchOut, "Branch-Out Wins 'Top HR Product' Award," news release, October 3, 2011, http://branchout.com.

SUMMARY

LO1 Discuss how to plan for the human resources needed to carry out the organization's strategy.

The first step in workforce planning is forecasting. Through trend analysis and good judgment, the planner tries to determine the supply of and demand for various human resources. Based on whether a surplus or a shortage is expected, the planner sets goals and creates a strategy for achieving those goals. The organization then implements its HR strategy and evaluates the results.

LO2 Determine the demand for and supply of workers in various job categories.

The planner can look at leading indicators, assuming trends will continue in the future. Multiple regression can convert several leading indicators into a single prediction of labour needs and supply available. Analysis of a transitional matrix can help the planner identify which job categories can be filled internally and where high turnover is likely.

L○3 Summarize the advantages and disadvantages of ways to eliminate a labour surplus and avoid a labour shortage.

To reduce a surplus, downsizing, pay reductions, and demotions deliver fast results but at a high cost in human suffering that may hurt surviving employees' motivation and future recruiting. Also, the organization may lose some of its best employees. Transferring employees, requiring them to share work, a hiring freeze, early-retirement packages, and retraining also have various advantages and disadvantages.

To avoid a labour shortage, requiring overtime is the easiest and fastest strategy, which can easily be changed if conditions change. However, overtime may exhaust workers and can hurt morale. Similarly, using temporary employees, outsourcing, transferring, retraining, hiring new employees, and using technology offer advantages and disadvantages requiring careful consideration.

L○4 Discuss the steps in the succession planning process.

Succession planning ensures that the organization identifies qualified employees to fill organizational roles that are anticipated to become available in the future. Succession planning focuses on high-potential employees.

L○5 Discuss aspects of recruiting including employment branding and other recruitment policies organizations use to make job vacancies more attractive.

Internal recruiting (hiring from within) generally makes job vacancies more attractive, because candidates see opportunities for growth and advancement. Lead-the-market pay strategies make jobs economically desirable. Employer branding projects an image of the organization, including its culture and key benefits.

L○6 List and compare sources of job applicants.

Internal sources, promoted through job postings, generate applicants who are familiar to the organization and motivate other employees by demonstrating opportunities for advancement. However, internal sources are usually insufficient for all of an organization's labour needs. Direct applicants and referrals, newspaper and magazine advertising, staffing agencies, and universities and colleges offer advantages and issues to be assessed.

Online recruiting gives organizations access to a global labour market, tends to be inexpensive, and allows convenient searching of databases; however, organizations may receive many applications from unqualified applicants. Online recruiting has become increasingly targeted, sophisticated, and likely to incorporate applications of social media.

L○7 Describe the recruiter's role in the recruitment process, including limits and opportunities.

Through their behaviour and other characteristics, recruiters influence the nature of the job vacancy and the kinds of applicants generated. Applicants tend to perceive job experts as more credible than recruiters who are HR specialists.

Recruiters can improve their impact by providing timely feedback, avoiding behaviour that contributes to a negative impression of the organization, and teaming up with job experts.

Critical Thinking Questions

1. Suppose an organization expects a labour shortage to develop in key job areas over the next few years. Recommend general responses the organization could make in each of the following areas:

   a. Recruitment

   b. Training, learning, and development

   c. Rewards (pay, employee benefits, and work environment)

2. Review the sample transitional matrix shown in Table 4.1. What jobs experience the greatest turnover (employees leaving the organization)? How might an organization with this combination of jobs reduce the turnover?

3. In the same transitional matrix, which jobs seem to rely the most on internal recruitment? Which seem to rely most on external recruitment? Why?

4. Why do organizations combine statistical and judgmental forecasts of labour demand, rather than relying on statistics or judgment alone? Give an example of a situation in which each type of forecast could be inaccurate.

5. Some organizations have detailed employment equity plans, complete with goals and timetables, for women, First Nations employees, people with disabilities, and members of visible minorities, yet have no formal workforce plan for the organization as a whole. Why might this be the case? What does this practice suggest about the role of human resource management in these organizations?

6. Is succession planning becoming more or less important? Explain your answer.

7. Give an example of a human resource policy that would help attract a larger pool of job candidates. Give an example of a human resource policy that would likely reduce the pool of candidates. Would you expect these policies to influence the quality as well as the number of applicants? Why or why not?

8. Discuss the relative merits of internal versus external recruitment. Give an example of a situation in which each of these approaches might be particularly effective.

9. List the jobs you have held. How were you recruited for each of these? From the organization's perspective, what were some pros and cons of recruiting you through these methods?

10. Recruiting people for jobs that require international assignments is increasingly important for many organizations. Where might an organization go to recruit people interested in such assignments?

11. What is your experience with the use of social media in the recruiting process, e.g., Facebook, Twitter, LinkedIn, and/or YouTube? What is your advice to managers and HR professionals in using these social channels?

Experiencing HR

To get a sense of what it feels like to undergo an assessment, prepare a basic assessment of your performance and potential as a college or university student. Identify four people who have some idea of your personality, study (or work) habits, and performance so far in school—for example, parents or other close family members, other students, a teacher, and a past or present supervisor. Ask each person to summarize what they see as your major strengths and areas for development as a student. Listen carefully and take notes. Focus on recording what they say, not on challenging their views.

Gather the notes from your interviews and your grade reports. If you have other performance feedback, such as graded essays or lab reports with comments, gather these as well. Review the assessment information, looking for themes and patterns in the feedback. Write a one- to two-page summary of what you learned, including answers to the following questions:

- What do other people see as your strengths and areas for development? How well do their views match what you consider to be your strengths and areas for development?
- How well do your accomplishments reflect your strengths? What would you need to do differently in order to put your strengths to work more fully?
- Are you a "high-potential" student? Why or why not?
- How did it feel to be assessed by others? How can you learn from the experience?

CASE STUDY 4.1:

Can Yahoo Still Attract Tech Workers?

In many fields, workers are practically begging employers to hire them, but in information technology, the demand for talent often outstrips the supply. Employers struggle to attract and keep software experts, always concerned about the risk that their best people will leave for a better offer somewhere else. For a high-tech worker, what often amounts to a better offer is a chance to be a part of the exciting new thing, whatever that is.

That presents a challenge for Yahoo. A couple of decades ago, the Web search company (now an advertising, news, and email company) was one of the hot businesses of the Internet age. Today Yahoo's sites attract 700 million visitors a month, and the company's 14,000 employees are well paid, but the excitement is no longer there. To the industry, Yahoo is part of the old Internet. The best and brightest want to be part of the new Internet, especially social media, cloud computing, and mobile apps.

In that environment, Yahoo is seeking pathways for growth even as some of its best talent is slipping out the doors. Greg Cohn, who worked his way up from business strategist to senior director responsible for new initiatives, admires Yahoo's management but left to start his own business. A vice-president of Yahoo's operations in Latin America also left, and so has the company's chief trust officer, who moved to a position at Google. In another sign of employee dissatisfaction, a recruiter told a reporter, "If you call nine people at Yahoo, you'll get nine calls back." In other words, leaving sounds like an option for just about everyone. Executives are preparing for a faster exodus as job growth heats up elsewhere in Silicon Valley.

Because of these trends, Yahoo forecasts that it will need to do intensive recruiting. But how do you get people to think about working for a company that many believe has passed its prime? Yahoo definitely has work to do. Software engineers who look up employee reviews on Glassdoor.com would notice that employees rate Yahoo just 3.6 on a scale of 1 to 5, trailing Facebook (4.4), Google (4.4), and Apple (3.9), and that only 69 percent of Yahoo employees would recommend their employer to a friend, trailing Google (93 percent), Facebook

(90 percent), and Apple (79 percent). Seeing that, an engineer probably wouldn't bother to look up a Yahoo careers page.

Observers note that Yahoo still earns most of its money by employing reporters to write stories and salespeople to sell ads, an old-media kind of operation that is hard to run at a profit. Yahoo outsourced Web search to Microsoft's Bing, and in spite of its leadership role in advertising, it has yet to offer much in the hot young market of mobile ads. Shifting from unprofitable, low-growth activities to activities with more potential could lead to significant staff cuts in some areas even as a hiring push continues in others. Still, one former employee sees hope. Geoff Ralston, who worked on Yahoo Mail, notes that EBay and Apple both survived periods when they seemed to be fading away. Ralston believes the solution is to buy or build "consumer experiences that are unbelievably great." That's a mission a tech worker would choose to accept.

Questions

1. What conclusions can you draw about the supply of and demand for labour at Yahoo?

2. What actions might Yahoo take to strengthen its recruiting efforts? How might these efforts support Yahoo's corporate strategy?

3. If you were responsible for college recruiting at Yahoo, where would you recruit, and what would you say? Why?

Sources: www.glassdoor.com/Reviews/Facebook-Reviews-E40772.htm, www.glassdoor.com/Overview/Working-at-Google-EI_IE9079.11,17.htm, www.glassdoor.com/Reviews/Apple-Reviews-EII38.htm, http://www.glassdoor.com/Reviews/Yahoo-Reviews-E5807.htm retrieved February 6, 2015; Kara Swisher, "Yahoo's New CEO Preps Major Restructuring, including Significant Layoffs," *All Things Digital*, March 5, 2012, http://allthingsd.com; Don Dodson, "Yahoo in Market for a Few Good Engineers," *America's Intelligence Wire*, December 15, 2011, Business & Company Resource Center, http://galenet.galegroup.com; Amir Efrati, "Yahoo Battles Brain Drain," *The Wall Street Journal*, December 5, 2011, http://online.wsj.com; Ladan Nikravan, "An Engine for Growth," *Chief Learning Officer*, September 2011, pp. 22-24; Peter Burrows, "The Web's Walking Dead," *Bloomberg Businessweek*, September 19, 2011, pp. 41-42.

CASE STUDY 4.2:

Recruiters Slip-Up Using Technology

Aileen Siu, an acting team leader in the Ontario cabinet office, learned a powerful lesson when she intended to forward an email to a colleague but actually sent the message back to the job applicant with one sentence: "This is the ghetto dude that I spoke to before." Evon Reid, an honours student at the University of Toronto had applied for a media analyst position at the cabinet office. "Ghetto dude? It means I'm black. It's very insulting. It's still pretty shocking to me." Reached on vacation, Craig Sumi, manager of the department, said Sui is "an unclassified, part-time employee. . . . low level." Reid told the Toronto Star: "She may be very low level to them but she was given a lot of responsibility. She was my only link into the cabinet office so she was very important to me."

Reid received apologies from both Craig Sumi and then Premier Dalton McGuinty who contacted Reid by phone. The premier told him, "he deserved an apology and there was no one better to deliver it than him," according to Reid. Sui said she was "multi-tasking" when she hit the wrong button and copied Reid. She also insisted the email didn't refer to anyone "outside my circle of friends." "It wasn't directed at Evon at all. That was internal. . . it didn't have anything to do with any of the applicants," said Siu, 26, a recent University of Toronto political science graduate.

Other recruiting blunders using technology may not result in media firestorms like the previous example but are still worthy of further reflection. As recruiters mine LinkedIn profiles in their industry or area, they spend a lot of time on the site, however, they sometimes neglect their own profiles. For example, recruiters that post "CONNECT WITH ME" in the name field of their own LinkedIn profile come across as desperate and unappealing to candidates. As organizations also turn to Twitter to announce job openings, some recruiters fail to interact with their followers. By focusing on pushing information out to followers rather than also engaging in two-way communication, they appear to lack sincerity and follow-through with prospective candidates.

Questions

1. In your opinion, what is the cause(s) of these inappropriate recruiter behaviours?
2. What important lessons can recruiters learn from these blunders?

Sources: "Mistakes Recruiters Make on LinkedIn," www.recruiter.com/recruiting-news/mistakes-recruiters-linkedin/, retrieved March 18, 2012; "What are Common Mistakes that Employers Make When Using Twitter as a Recruiting Tool?" www.focus.com/questions/what-are-common-mistakes-employers-make-when-using-twitter/, retrieved March 18, 2012; Lesley Young, "Careless Click Lands HR Staffer in Hot Water," *Canadian HR Reporter,* August 13, 2007, pp. 1–2; Linda Diebel, "'Ghetto Dude' Email Sent by Mistake: Province," July 21, 2007, p. A3; Linda Diebel, "McGuinty Apologies for 'Ghetto Dude' Email," *Toronto Star,* July 23, 2007, p. A2.

CHAPTER 5

Selecting Employees

WHAT DO I NEED TO KNOW?

After reading this chapter, you should be able to:

LO1	Identify the elements of the selection process.
LO2	Define ways to measure the success of a selection method.
LO3	Summarize the legal requirements for employee selection.
LO4	Compare the common methods used for selecting human resources.
LO5	Describe the major types of employment tests.
LO6	Discuss how to conduct effective interviews.
LO7	Explain how employers carry out the process of making a selection decision.

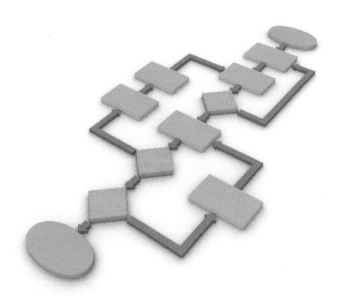

Companies are increasingly turning to data and algorithms to inform or even make hiring decisions.

Data-Driven Hiring

Ian Yates is the managing director of Toronto-based technology firm, Fitzii (www.fitzii.com). He likes to ask prospective clients, "Have you ever made a bad hire?" The answer is often an emphatic Yes! Finding the right person is perhaps the most important decision a manager can make and the risks and costs of a bad hire are high. What if there was a tool that promised to "make the employment cycle more efficient and cost-effective by doing everything from identifying the right candidates to detecting which employees are most likely to leave the company?"

More companies, of all sizes, are turning to data analysis and algorithms to make hiring decisions. For example, following a six-month trial, Xerox (www.xerox.com) uses software to make all hiring decisions for its 48,700 call centre jobs. The factors considered for hiring are often different from previous hiring criteria. Jobs formerly filled by considering work history and interviews "are left to personality tests and data analysis." "Some of the assumptions we had weren't valid," said Connie Harvey, Xerox's chief operating officer of commercial services.

Although hiring decisions have historically used personality tests, what's different is the scale—sophisticated software make it possible to assess more candidates, collect more data, and look more deeply into candidates' preferences and abilities. "Over time the algorithm learns," in a manner similar to how Google learns users' interests over time from their search history. At Xerox, applicants take a 30-minute test "that screens them for personality traits and puts them through scenarios they might encounter on the job." The program generates a score based on assessed potential—low potential (red); medium potential (yellow); and high potential (green).

Small firms are also using data-driven tools for hiring. SkinHealth Canada (www.skinhealthcanada.com), a small cosmetic medicine company, recently hired five of its ten employees using Fitzii's services. "I know it's working because we're going to achieve double-digit growth this year," says SkinHealth's managing director, David Potter. Because small firms do not typically have enough of their own information, they can benefit from using data aggregated from multiple companies or industries.

Hiring by algorithm has been described as the "self check-out of HR" and arguably is not perfect. One concern is that some qualified people may be screened out. However, according to Fitzel's Ian Yates, another outcome of data-driven hiring will be improved hiring diversity. "One of the biggest barriers to getting employed for a recent immigrant is the hiring process and the reliance on the résumé. By focusing on abilities and personality traits, Yates suggests, these candidates are more likely to be evaluated and hired.[1]

Introduction

Hiring decisions are about finding the people who will be a good fit with the job and the organization. Any organization that appreciates the competitive edge provided by good people must take the utmost care in choosing its members. The organization's decisions about selecting people are central to its ability to survive, adapt, and grow. Selection decisions become especially critical when organizations face tight labour markets or must compete for talent with other organizations in the same industry. If a competitor keeps getting the best applicants, the remaining companies have to make do with who is left.

This chapter will familiarize you with ways to increase the effectiveness of employee selection. The chapter starts by describing the selection process and how to evaluate possible methods for carrying out that process. It then takes an in-depth look at the most widely used methods: applications and résumés, employment tests, and interviews. The chapter ends by describing the process by which organizations arrive at a final selection decision.

L○1 Identify the elements of the selection process.

What Are the Steps in the Selection Process?

HRC2, 4

Through the process of selection, organizations make decisions about who will be chosen to fill job openings. Selection begins with the candidates identified through recruitment and attempts to reduce their number to the individuals who are most likely to be the best performers in the available jobs and fit with the culture of the organization. At the end of the process, the selected individuals are placed in jobs with the organization.

The process of selecting employees varies considerably from organization to organization and from job to job. At most organizations, however, selection includes the steps illustrated in Figure 5.1. First, a human resources professional reviews the applications received to see which meet the requirements of the job. For candidates who meet the requirements, the organization administers tests and reviews work samples to assess the candidates' competencies. Those with the best capabilities are invited to the organization for one or more interviews. Often, supervisors and team members are involved in this stage of the process. By this point, the decision makers are beginning to form conclusions about which candidates are likely to be the best performers. For the top few candidates, the organization should check references and conduct background checks to verify that the organization's information is correct. Then supervisors, teams, and other decision makers select a person to receive a job offer. In some cases, the candidate may negotiate with the organization regarding salary, benefits, and the like. If the candidate accepts the job, the organization places him or her in that job.

The ease of applying online has made this processing overwhelming for many recruiters. A simple job posting online could generate hundreds of responses in one day. Many employers are coping by automating much of the selection process with an applicant-tracking system. Typically, the system starts by receiving the data provided and matching it against the company's selection criteria. The system might find that half the applications and/or résumés lack necessary keywords, so it sends those applicants a polite "no thank you" message. The applications that survive the automated screening go to a hiring manager, often ranked by how well they meet preset criteria. The manager reviews these applications and selects candidates to contact for a telephone or face-to-face interview and/or testing.

FIGURE 5.1

Steps in the Selection Process

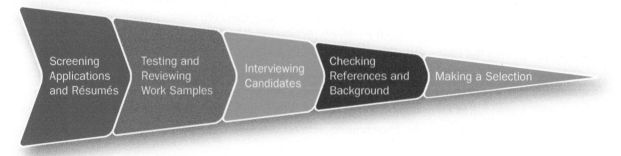

Critics point out that these automated systems may arbitrarily reject highly qualified people who submit a creatively worded application and/or résumé rather than simply mimicking the wording of the job posting. Moreover, a recent study by the Talent Board (www.thetalentboard.org) suggests that rejected job applicants have the potential to hurt a company's bottom line. More than 8 percent of the study's participants said that their job rejection would affect their relationship as customers with the company, the sentiment being "if I'm not good enough to work here I probably don't want to be a customer." Nevertheless, automated systems can make the application process more efficient by speeding up the steps and perhaps allowing applicants to check the status of their applications.[2]

How does an organization decide which of these elements to use, and in what order? Some organizations simply repeat a selection process that is familiar. If members of the organization underwent job interviews, they conduct job interviews, asking familiar questions. However, what organizations *should* do is to create a selection process in support of its job descriptions and specifications. In Chapter 3, we explained that job specifications identify the competencies required for successfully performing a job. The selection process should be set up in such a way that it lets the organization identify people who have the necessary competencies. The RCMP's hiring process is highly transparent—each step is identified and described in detail in the recruiting area of their website. See the "HR Best Practices" box.

HR Best Practices

How the RCMP Sources Talent

The Royal Canadian Mounted Police (RCMP, www.rcmp.gc.ca) provides policing services to eight provinces (except Ontario and Quebec), three territories, more than 150 municipalities, more than 600 Aboriginal communities, and three international airports. The RCMP provides careers that include over 150 specializations. And, for the first time in its history, the goal is to attract as many women and men into its training academy. The RCMP's hiring process is highly transparent, supported by extensive information and insight about expectations and requirements for each step in the hiring process. The RCMP website provides active links for each step of the selection process. Note: Candidates are screened in and screened out during Steps 2-9.

1. Attend a **Career Presentation.**

2. Register for and complete the **RCMP Entrance Exam** (RPAB—RCMP Police Aptitude Battery).

3. Complete a **Selection Package** that includes various documents.

4. Complete the **Regular Member Applicant Questionnaire** that examines suitability, reliability, and preparations for the security clearance assessment.

5. Participate in the **Physical Abilities Requirement Evaluation** (PARE), a critical incident simulation that includes "chasing, controlling, and apprehending a suspect."

6. **Regular Member Selection Interview** (RMSI) that screens for police officer competencies.

7. **Suitability/Reliability Interview** uses a polygraph examination to verify suitability and reliability.

8. **Field Investigation and Security Clearance,** i.e., a background investigation.

9. **Health Assessment** performed by RCMP designated physicians and includes a medical, dental, and psychological examination.

10. **Enrolment** as a Cadet (in a troop of 32) to start the 24-week training at the RCMP Academy in Regina, Saskatchewan.

Sources: "Careers," www.rcmp-grc.gc.ca/recruiting-recrutement/index-eng.htm, retrieved February 14, 2015; "About the RCMP," www.rcmp-grc.gc.ca/about-ausujet/index-eng.htm, retrieved February 14, 2015; Douglas Quan, "RCMP Sets an Ambitious New Goal: Recruit as Many Woman as Men," *National Post,* October 19, 2014, http://news.nationalpost.com/2014/10/19/rcmp-sets-an-ambitious-new-goal-recruit-as-many-women-as-men/, retrieved February 14, 2015; "How to Apply," www.rcmp-grc.gc.ca/recruiting-recrutement/rec/process-processus-eng.htm?gclid=CKLPpd7q4sMCFYY_aQodfyAAyw, retrieved February 14, 2015.

This kind of strategic approach to selection requires ways to measure the effectiveness of selection tools. From science, we have basic standards for this:

- The selection method provides *reliable* information.
- The method provides *valid* information.
- The information can be *generalized* to apply to the candidates.
- The method offers *high utility* (practical value).
- The selection criteria are *legal*.

L○2 Define ways to measure the success of a selection method.

What Are the Criteria for Evaluating Selection Methods?

Reliability

The **reliability** of a type of measurement indicates how free that measurement is from random error.[3] A reliable measurement therefore generates consistent results. Assuming that a person's intelligence is fairly stable over time, a reliable test of intelligence should generate consistent results if the same person takes the test several times. Organizations that construct intelligence tests therefore should be able to provide (and explain) information about the reliability of their tests.

> **reliability**
> The extent to which a measurement generates consistent results, i.e., is free from random error.

Usually, this information involves statistics such as *correlation coefficients*. These statistics measure the degree to which two sets of numbers are related. A higher correlation coefficient signifies a stronger relationship. At one extreme, a correlation coefficient of 1.0 means a perfect positive relationship—as one set of numbers goes up, so does the other. If you took the same vision test three days in a row, those scores would probably have nearly a perfect correlation. At the other extreme, a correlation of –1.0 means a perfect negative correlation—when one set of numbers goes up, the other goes down. In the middle, a correlation of 0 means there is no correlation at all. For example, the correlation between weather and intelligence would be at or near 0. A reliable test would be one for which scores by the same person (or people with similar attributes) have a correlation close to 1.0.

Validity

For a selection measure, **validity** describes the extent to which performance on the measure (such as a test score) is related to what the measure is designed to assess (such as job performance). Although we can reliably measure such characteristics as weight and height, these measurements do not provide much information about how a person will perform in a job. Thus, for most jobs, height and weight provide little validity as selection criteria. One way to determine whether a measure is valid is to compare many people's scores on that measure with their job performance. For example, suppose people who score above 60 words per minute on a keyboarding test consistently get high marks for their performance in data-entry jobs. This observation suggests the keyboarding test is valid for predicting success in that job.

validity
The extent to which performance on a measure (such as a test score) is related to what the measure is designed to assess (such as job performance).

As with reliability, information about the validity of selection methods often uses correlation coefficients. A strong positive (or negative) correlation between a measure and job performance means the measure should be a valid basis for selecting (or rejecting) a candidate. This information is important, not only because it helps organizations identify the best employees, but also because organizations can ensure that their selection process is fair and objective. Three ways of measuring validity are criterion-related, content, and construct validity.

Criterion-Related Validity

The first category, **criterion-related validity,** is a measure of validity based on showing a substantial correlation between test scores and job performance scores. In the example in Figure 5.2, a company compares two measures—an intelligence test and a university or college grade point average—with performance as sales representative. In the left graph, which shows the relationship between the intelligence test scores and job performance, the points for the 20 sales representatives fall near the 45-degree line.

HR Oops!

Hiring Clones

Entrepreneur Todd Morris made an all-too-common hiring mistake. As BrickHouse Security began to grow, he brought in individuals who pressed hard to get results and worked independently. Morris possesses the same qualities, and they enabled him to get his company off the ground. But as Morris hired more and more people, they needed to be able to collaborate. Instead, they were overly competitive and began complaining about one another.

Morris hired a consulting firm to help him figure out what was making the work environment so toxic. The consultants gave all the employees a personality test, which showed that Morris had been hiring people who tended to lack the kinds of human relations skills that are related to cooperating and listening. Morris now makes personality testing part of the selection process at BrickHouse, and he looks for people who are less like himself—the independent entrepreneur—and more like team players.

Morris's lesson is one that many companies could benefit from applying. A recent survey found that when an employee doesn't live up to expectations, the most common reason is that the employer failed to match the candidate's skills to the actual job requirements. Effective hiring decisions are not like making friends at a party. Instead of simply picking the individuals they feel most comfortable around, careful decision makers first establish the qualities they are seeking and then choose methods that consistently identify those qualities.

Questions

1. Morris felt he needed to be hard-driving and independent to get a business off the ground, so he looked for the same kinds of people to carry out the business. How would you rate the validity of his approach to choosing employees? How would you rate its reliability?

2. Besides the addition of personality tests, what other steps of Morris's hiring process might benefit from change?

Sources: April Joyner, "Are You a Narcissistic Boss?" *Inc.,* November 2011, www.inc.com; Robert Half Finance & Accounting, "Bad Match," news release, September 29, 2011, http://rhfa.mediaroom.com.

FIGURE 5.2

Criterion-Related Measurements of a Student's Aptitude

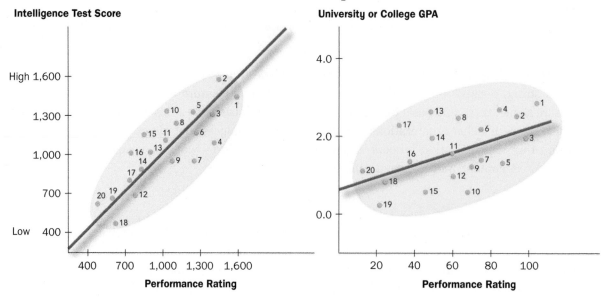

The correlation coefficient is near 0.90 (for a perfect 1.0, all the points would be on the 45-degree line). In the graph at the right, the points are scattered more widely. The correlation between university or college GPA and sales representatives' performance is much lower. In this hypothetical example, the intelligence test is more valid than GPA for predicting success at this job.

criterion-related validity
A measure of validity based on showing a substantial correlation between test scores and job performance scores.

Two kinds of research are possible for arriving at criterion-related validity:

1. **Predictive validation.** This research uses the test scores of all applicants and looks for a relationship between the scores and *future* performance. The researcher administers the tests, waits a set period of time, and then measures the performance of the applicants who were hired.

predictive validation
Research that uses the test scores of all applicants and looks for a relationship between the scores and future performance of the applicants who were hired.

2. **Concurrent validation.** This type of research administers a test to people who *currently* hold a job, then compares their scores to *existing* measures of job performance. If the people who score highest on the test also do better on the job, the test is assumed to be valid.

concurrent validation
Research that consists of administering a test to people who currently hold a job, then comparing their scores to existing measures of job performance.

Predictive validation is more time-consuming and difficult, but it is the best measure of validity. Job applicants tend to be more motivated to do well on the tests, and their performance on the tests is not influenced by their firsthand experience with the job. Also, the group studied is more likely to include people who perform poorly on the test—a necessary ingredient to accurately validate a test.[4]

Content and Construct Validity

Another way to show validity is to establish **content validity**—that is, consistency between the test items or problems and the kinds of situations or problems that occur on the job. A test that is "content-valid" exposes the job applicant to situations that are likely to occur on the job. It tests whether the applicant has the knowledge, skills, or ability, that is, competencies to handle such situations.

content validity
Consistency between the test items or problems and the kinds of situations or problems that occur on the job.

In the case of a company using tests for selecting a construction superintendent, tests with content validity included organizing a random list of subcontractors into the order they would appear at a construction site and entering a shed to identify construction errors that had intentionally been made for testing purposes.[5] More commonly today, employers use computer-role-playing games in which software is created to include situations that occur on the job. The game measures how the candidate reacts to the situations, and then it computes a score based on how closely the candidate's responses match those of an ideal employee.[6]

The usual basis for deciding that a test has content validity is through expert judgment. Experts can rate the test items according to whether they mirror essential functions of the job. Because establishing validity is based on the experts' subjective judgments, content validity is most suitable for measuring behaviour that is concrete and observable.

For tests that measure abstract qualities such as intelligence or leadership ability, establishment of validity may have to rely on **construct validity.** This involves establishing that tests really do measure intelligence, leadership ability, or other such "constructs," as well as showing that mastery of this construct is associated with successful performance of the job. For example, if you could show that a test measures something called "mechanical ability," and that people with superior mechanical ability perform well as assemblers, then the test has construct validity for the assembler job. Tests that measure a construct usually measure a combination of behaviours thought to be associated with the construct.

construct validity
Consistency between a high score on a test and a high level of a construct such as intelligence or leadership ability, as well as between mastery of this construct and successful performance on the job.

Ability to Generalize

Along with validity in general, we need to know whether a selection method is valid in the context in which the organization wants to use it. A **generalizable** method applies not only to the conditions in which the method was originally developed—job, organization, people, time period, and so on. It also applies to other organizations, jobs, applicants, and so on. In other words, is a selection method that was valid in one context also valid in other contexts?

generalizable
Valid in other contexts beyond the context in which the selection method was developed.

Researchers have studied whether tests of intelligence and thinking skills (called *cognitive ability*) can be generalized. The research has supported the idea that these tests are generalizable across many jobs. However, as jobs become more complex, the validity of many of these tests increases. In other words, they are most valid for complex jobs.[7]

Practical Value

Not only should selection methods such as tests and interview responses accurately predict how well individuals will perform, they should produce information that actually benefits the organization. Being valid, reliable, and generalizable adds value to a method. Another consideration is the cost of using the selection method. Selection procedures such as testing and interviewing cost money. They should cost significantly less than the benefits of hiring the new employees. Methods that provide economic value greater than the cost of using them are said to have **utility.**

> **utility**
> The extent to which the selection method provides economic value greater than its cost.

Football teams have been using cognitive tests to select players assuming that intelligence can be generalized to the job requirements, especially on teams that compete using complex offensive and defensive schemes. What other things, in addition to intelligence, would teams need to look for?

The choice of a selection method may differ according to the job being filled. If the job involves providing a product or service of high value to the organization, it is worthwhile to spend more to find a top performer. At a company where salespeople are responsible for closing million-dollar deals, the company will be willing to invest more in selection decisions. At a fast-food restaurant, such an investment will not be worthwhile; the employer will prefer faster, simpler ways to select workers who enter orders, prepare food, and keep the facility clean.

LO3 Summarize the legal requirements for employee selection.

What Are the Legal Standards for Selection?

HRC 2

Whether selecting a new employee or promoting an employee from within the organization, the selection process needs to be conducted in a way that meets human rights and privacy requirements.

Human rights legislation and privacy legislation described in Chapter 2 have implications for the selection process.

- The interview needs to be conducted in a way that candidates can be assessed without drawing out information that is not relevant to the job being filled. As summarized in Table 5.1, the organization may not ask questions on an application form or in an interview that gathers information about prohibited grounds of discrimination, even indirectly. For example, asking candidates for the dates they attended high school might indirectly gather information about applicants' age.

- Interview notes are made by interviewers to help distinguish among candidates. Even if these notes are only used by the interviewers, they cannot include references to prohibited grounds of discrimination (e.g., "white, female, 40-ish" would be inappropriate to include in interview notes).[8]

- Candidates must provide their consent before a background or reference check can be conducted. Because background and reference checks may unearth information about protected grounds such as age or religious affiliation, or other personal information, human rights commissions recommend that the applicant should first receive a conditional job offer. The employer's conditional job offer is offered subject to a successful background and reference check.

An important principle of selection is to combine several sources of information about candidates, rather than relying solely on interviews or a single type of testing. The sources should be chosen carefully to relate to the characteristics identified in the job description. When organizations do this, they are increasing the validity of the decision criteria. They are more likely to make hiring decisions that are fair and unbiased. They also are more likely to choose the best candidates.

L○4 Compare the common methods used for selecting human resources.

Job Applications and Résumés

HRC4

Nearly all employers gather background information on applicants at the beginning of the selection process. The usual ways of gathering background information are by asking applicants to fill out application forms and provide résumés. Organizations also verify the information by checking references and conducting background checks.

Asking job candidates to provide background information is inexpensive. The organization can get reasonably accurate information by combining applications and résumés with background checks and well-designed interviews.[9] A major challenge with applications and résumés is the sheer volume of work they generate for the organization. Especially considering how easy it is for candidates to submit applications or résumés online, human resource departments need to take steps to ensure they are not swamped with more than they can handle.

Applications

Asking each applicant to fill out an employment application is a low-cost way to gather basic data from many applicants. It also ensures that the organization has certain standard categories of information, such as mailing address and employment history, from each.

TABLE 5.1

Guidelines for Applications and Interviews

Subject	Avoid Asking	Preferred	Comments
Name	about name change: whether it was changed by court order, marriage, or other reason. for maiden name.		Ask after selection if needed to check on previously held jobs or educational credentials.
Address	for addresses outside Canada.	Ask place and duration of current or recent address.	
Age	for birth certificates, baptismal records, or about age in general.	Ask applicants whether they are eligible to work under Canadian laws regarding age restrictions.	If precise age is required for benefit plans or other legitimate purposes, it can be determined after selection.
Sex	about pregnancy, childbearing plans, or child care arrangements.	Ask applicant if the attendance requirements can be met.	During the interview or after selection, the applicant, for purposes of courtesy, may be asked which of Dr., Mr., Mrs., Miss, or Ms. is preferred.
Marital status	whether the applicant is single, married, divorced, engaged, separated, widowed, or living common-law. whether the applicant's spouse may be transferred. about the spouse's employment.	If transfer or travel is part of the job, the applicant can be asked whether he or she can meet these requirements. Ask whether there are any circumstances that might prevent completion of a minimum service commitment.	Information on dependants can be determined after selection if necessary.
Family status	about number of children or dependants. about child care arrangements.	Ask if the applicant would be able to work the required hours and, where applicable, overtime.	Contacts for emergencies and/ or details on dependants can be determined after selection.
National or ethnic origin	about birthplace, nationality of ancestors, spouse, or other relatives. whether born in Canada. for proof of citizenship.	Ask if the applicant is legally entitled to work in Canada.	Documentation of eligibility to work (papers, visas, etc.) can be requested after selection.
Photographs	for photo to be attached to applications or sent to interviewer before interview.		Photos for security passes or company files can be taken after selection.
Religion	about religious affiliation. for references from clergy or religious leader. whether the applicant will work a specific religious holiday.	Explain the required work shift, and ask whether such a schedule poses problems for the applicant.	Reasonable accommodation of an employee's religious beliefs is the employer's duty.
Disability	for a list of all disabilities, limitations, or health problems. whether the applicant drinks or uses drugs. whether the application has ever received psychiatric care or been hospitalized for emotional problems. whether the applicant has received workers' compensation.	Disclose any information on requirements or standards early in the process. Then ask whether the applicant has any condition that might affect ability to do the job.	A disability is only relevant to job ability if it: • threatens the safety or property of others. • prevents the applicant from safe and adequate job performance even when reasonable efforts are made to accommodate the disability.

Subject	Avoid Asking	Preferred	Comments
Pardoned conviction	whether an applicant has ever been convicted. whether the applicant has ever been arrested. whether the applicant has a criminal record.	If bonding is a job requirement, ask whether the applicant is eligible.	Inquiries about criminal record or convictions are discouraged unless related to job duties.
Sexual orientation	about the applicant's sexual orientation.		Contacts for emergencies and/or details on dependants can be determined after selection.

Note: This table provides examples and is not intended as a complete listing of all guidelines. The examples are based on federal human rights legislation; some provincial laws vary and may affect these examples.

Source: "Guide to Screening and Selection in Employment," Canadian Human Rights Commission, March 2007, pp. 6-10, www.chrc-ccdp.ca/eng/content/guide-screening-and-selection-employment. Reproduced with the permission of the Canadian Human Rights Commission.

Employment applications include areas for applicants to provide several types of information:

- *Contact information.* The employee's name, address, phone number, and email address.
- *Work experience.* Companies the applicant worked for, job titles, and dates of employment.
- *Educational background.* High school, college, or university attended and diploma(s) or degree(s) awarded.
- *Applicant's signature.* Signature or verification following a statement that the applicant has provided true and complete information.

The application form may include other areas for the applicant to provide additional information, such as specific work experiences, technical skills, certifications, or memberships in professional or trade associations. Also, including the date on an application is useful for keeping up-to-date records of job applicants. The application form should not request information that might violate human rights legislation. For example, questions about an applicant's birthplace, marital status, or number of children would be inappropriate.

By reviewing application forms, HR staff can identify which candidates meet minimum requirements for education and experience. They may be able to rank applicants—for example, giving applicants with five years' experience a higher ranking than applicants with two years of experience. In this way, the applications enable the organization to narrow the pool of candidates to a number it is prepared to test and interview.

Résumés

The usual way applicants introduce themselves to a potential employer is by submitting a résumé. An obvious drawback of this information source is that applicants control the content of the information, as well as the way it is presented. This type of information is therefore biased in favour of the applicant and may not even be accurate (although this is unethical). The Statistic Brain Research Institute claims that 53 percent of résumés contain falsifications, 33 percent include inaccurate job descriptions, and 21 percent list a fraudulent degree.[10] Some employers today see social media as an alternative source of information that is more relevant or more accurate, as described in "E-HRM." However, this inexpensive way to gather information does provide employers with a starting point. Organizations typically use résumés as a basis for deciding which candidates to investigate further.

E-HRM

Is LinkedIn making the résumé obsolete?

As with employment applications, an HR staff member reviews the résumés to identify candidates meeting such requirements including competencies, educational background, related work performed, and types of equipment the person has used. Because résumés are created by the job applicants (or the applicants have at least approved résumés created by someone they hire), they also may provide some insight into how candidates communicate and present themselves. Employers tend to decide against applicants whose résumés are unclear, messy, or contain mistakes. On the positive side, résumés may enable applicants to highlight accomplishments that might not show up in the format of an employment application. Review of résumés is most valid when the content of the résumé is assessed in terms of the elements of a job description and job specifications.

Organizations are increasingly turning to applicant tracking systems to centralize the handling of résumés and job applications from both internal and external applicants. Typically this involves completing an online application form on the employer's website and uploading a résumé. In many cases, information is electronically extracted from the résumé and inserted into the application form. Before submitting the application, the applicant verifies the information and performs any necessary edits.

An **applicant tracking system (ATS)** is a software application that streamlines the flow of information between job seekers, HR staff, and hiring managers. As organizations expand their corporate websites into interactive career centres, applicant tracking systems provide capabilities including multilingual support for global locations, generating applicant confirmation letters, pre-screening applications and résumés for education, specific competencies, and experience. Applicant tracking systems also support various data handling and report generation requirements associated with hiring employees, for example, storing résumés, tracking candidate sources, and connecting applications to specific hiring managers or job openings. By automating the process to match available talent with current job opportunities, the efficiency and speed of the overall hiring process is improved. Organizations can streamline the process, build relationships with candidates, cut hiring cycle-time, and increase the probability of hiring an available and interested candidate.[11]

applicant tracking system (ATS)
A software application that streamlines the flow of information between job seekers, HR staff, and hiring managers.

References

Application forms often ask that applicants provide the names of several references. Applicants provide the names and contact information of former employers or others who can vouch for their abilities and past job performance. In some situations, the applicant may provide letters of reference written by those people. It is then up to the organization to have someone contact the references to gather information or verify the accuracy of the information provided by the applicant.

As you might expect, references are not an unbiased source of information. Most applicants are careful to choose references who will say something positive. In addition, former employers and others may be afraid that if they express negative opinions, they will be sued. Their fear is understandable. In a former case, an employee sued his former supervisor for comments about how the employee had succeeded in overcoming attendance problems related to a struggle with multiple sclerosis. The employee felt that the disclosure of his prior attendance problems was defamatory.[12] (Disclosing his medical condition also would have posed problems for the potential future employer's ability to comply with human rights legislation.) This case shows that even well-intentioned remarks can cause problems.

Usually the organization checks references after it has determined that the applicant is a finalist for the job. Questions asked in reference checks need to adhere to the same requirements as applications and interviews (see Table 5.1).[13] Employers also have a duty to protect workers and the public from harassment or violence arising from placing an unfit or dangerous person in the workplace. **Negligent hiring** refers to a situation where an employer may be found liable for harm an employee causes to others if references and background checks were not performed adequately at the time of hiring. In these cases, the employer may be found to "have known or should have known" that an employee might cause harm to others in the workplace.

negligent hiring
A situation where an employer may be found liable for harm an employee causes to others if references and background checks were not performed adequately at the time of hiring.

Contacting references for all applicants would be time-consuming, and it does put a burden on the people contacted. Part of that burden is the risk of giving information seen as too negative or too positive. If the person who is a reference gives negative information, there is a chance the candidate will claim *defamation,* meaning the person damaged the applicant's reputation by making statements that cannot be proved truthful.[14] At the other extreme, if the person gives a glowing statement about a candidate, and the new employer later learns of misdeeds such as sexual misconduct or workplace violence, the new employer might sue the former employer for *misrepresentation.*[15]

Because such situations occasionally arise, often with much publicity, people who give references tend to give as little information as possible. Most organizations have policies that the human resource department will handle all requests for references and that they will only verify employment dates and sometimes the employee's final salary. In organizations without such a policy, HR professionals should be careful—and train managers to be careful—to stick to observable, job-related behaviours and to avoid broad opinions that may be misinterpreted. An irony with respect to policies about the content and handling of references, is that managers and colleagues in these organizations may well be actively providing highly visible and public references in the form of skills endorsements and recommendations in LinkedIn. "Human nature makes it difficult for a person, when asked, to deny the request to recommend someone. Therefore, a 'no recommending employees on LinkedIn' clause in a social media policy is helpful. It provides an ideal excuse when denying an employee that request and, hopefully, avoids causing offence."[16]

In spite of these drawbacks of references, the risks of not learning about significant problems in a candidate's past outweigh the possibility of getting only a little information. "An HR manager may be in the interesting position of declining to give an elaborate reference for any employee who intends to leave her organization, yet demand one for a person she wishes to hire. And applicants may find themselves to be essentially unemployable, as they discover they can't be hired without a satisfactory reference from their former employer."[17]

Background Checks

A background check is a way to verify that applicants are as they represent themselves to be. Unfortunately, not all candidates are open and honest. About eight out of ten large companies and over two-thirds of smaller organizations say they conduct criminal record background checks.[18]

Companies like BackCheck™ (www.backcheck.ca) specialize in pre-employment background checks such as criminal record checks, credit inquiries, education verifications, employment verifications, driving records, identity cross-checks, and reference checks. For example, Scotiabank ([www.scotiabank](www.scotiabank.com) [.com](www.scotiabank.com)) expanded their range of pre-employment screening with BackCheck to include criminal reference checks and identity verifications in addition to reference checking, employment and educational verifications, explains Stephen White, senior manager, global employment strategies, Scotiabank Group.[19]

Angus Stewart, vice-president of forensics and leader of corporate intelligence at KPMG LLP (www.kpmg.com) in Toronto, says that knowing what to look for is key to a successful search. "Education fraud is the most common," he says, adding that people lie about the degree they received or the institutions they attend. There is also the "diploma mill issue": people state degrees they ordered online from phoney institutions. "There's quite a bit of that."[20]

Also fuelling this growing use of background checks are applicants using complex and high-tech means to fraudulently impress employers. For example, a counterfeiting ring operating out of a house in Markham, Ontario may have supplied thousands of people with forged university degrees and transcripts as well as forged immigration documents, according to York Regional Police. The police confiscated forged degrees from the University of Toronto, the University of Western Ontario, Cape Breton University, and many others. Even university officials were hard pressed to detect the fakes. "These were of such high quality that our university people had to do a double take," said Detective Fred Kerr. "From an employer point of view, you're not going to catch what's wrong with them."[21]

Before performing a background check, employers need to keep in mind they need to get consent from the candidate. As discussed earlier in the chapter, conducting a background check after extending a contingent job offer can help to protect the potential employer from a discrimination claim if the applicant is not hired. Consent is also needed to comply with privacy legislation. Employers also need to "tread carefully" when it comes to social media checks or random background checks using search engines and/or social media. This growing trend of conducting these types of random social media background checks prompted Offices of the Privacy Commissioners of both Alberta and British Columbia to release "Guidelines for Social Media Background Checks" to help protect individual privacy. Employers are cautioned to follow the guidelines when using social media or search engines like Google to seek out information about potential employees. Even so, job seekers need to be aware that sites such as Twitter and Facebook may still be making them look good or bad to potential employers. According to Louise Fox, director of Toronto's Protocol Solutions: "Don't put anything online that you wouldn't want your mom to read or have published in the newspaper."[22]

LO5 Describe the major types of employment tests.

Employment Tests and Work Samples

When the organization has identified candidates whose applications or résumés indicate they meet basic requirements, the organization continues the selection process with this narrower pool of candidates. Often, the next step is to gather objective data through one or more employment tests. These tests fall into two broad categories:

1. **Aptitude tests** assess how well a person can learn or acquire skills and abilities. In the realm of employment testing, the best-known aptitude test is the General Aptitude Test Battery (GATB). The Public Service Commission of Canada (www.psc-cfp.gc.ca) also provides other employment-related tests such as the Administrative Support: The Office Skills Test (OST), which assesses the individual's aptitude for following directions, filing, arithmetic, checking, and vocabulary.[23]

Checking out employees is a growth industry as more organizations such as BackCheck™ conduct background checks on potential employees. Technology has helped reduce costs and streamline the process.

aptitude tests
Tests that assess how well a person can learn or acquire skills and abilities.

2. **Achievement tests** measure a person's existing knowledge and skills. For example, some organizations use interactive tests to assess applicants' skills using software such as Outlook, Excel, and PowerPoint.

achievement tests
Tests that measure a person's existing knowledge and skills.

Before using any test, organizations should investigate the test's validity and reliability. Besides asking the testing service to provide this information, it is wise to consult more impartial sources of information, such as the ones described in Table 5.2. The nearby "HR How-To" box discusses some types of employment tests used to screen job applicants.

Physical Ability Tests

Physical strength and endurance play less of a role in the modern workplace than in the past, thanks to the use of automation and current technology. Even so, many jobs still require certain physical abilities or psychomotor abilities (those connecting brain and body, as in the case of eye–hand coordination). When these abilities are essential to job performance or avoidance of injury, the organization may use physical ability tests. These evaluate one or more of the following areas of physical ability: muscular tension, muscular power, muscular endurance, cardiovascular endurance, flexibility, balance, and coordination.[24] Although these tests can accurately predict success at certain kinds of jobs, they also tend to exclude women and people with disabilities. As a result, use of physical ability tests can make the organization vulnerable to human rights complaints. It is therefore important to be certain that the abilities tested for really are essential to job performance or that the absence of these abilities really does create a safety hazard.

Sources of Information About Employment Tests

Mental Measurements Yearbook	Descriptions and reviews of tests that are commercially available
Principles for the Validation and Use of Personnel Selection Procedures (Society for Industrial and Organizational Psychology)	Guide to help organizations evaluate tests
Standards for Educational and Psychological Tests (American Psychological Association)	Description of standards for testing programs
Tests: A Comprehensive Reference for Assessments in Psychology, Education, and Business	Descriptions of thousands of tests
Test Critiques	Reviews of tests, written by professionals in the field

The RCMP have invested significant effort to develop an effective test to assess candidates' physical abilities—Physical Abilities Requirement Evaluation (PARE). The PARE is a job-related physical ability test developed as a result of extensive research and simulates a critical incident in which a police officer chases, controls, and apprehends a suspect.[25]

Cognitive Ability Tests

Although fewer jobs require muscle power today, brainpower is essential for most jobs. Organizations therefore benefit from people who have strong mental abilities. **Cognitive ability tests**—sometimes called "intelligence tests"—are designed to measure such mental abilities as verbal skills (skill in using written and spoken language), quantitative skills (skill in working with numbers), and reasoning ability (skill in thinking through the answer to a problem). Many jobs require all of these cognitive skills, so employers often get valid information from general tests. The Public Service Commission of Canada uses the General Competency Test Level 1 (GCT1) to measure thinking skills (understanding written material, solving numerical problems, and drawing logical conclusions) for administrative support position selection decisions. See nearby Figure 5.3 for a sample question and answer from the General Competency Test Level 1 (GCT1). The GCT2 is used to assess general cognitive abilities required for officer-level positions.[26] Many reliable tests are commercially available. The tests are especially valid for complex jobs and for those requiring adaptability in changing circumstances.[27]

cognitive ability tests
Tests designed to measure such mental abilities as verbal skills, quantitative skills, and reasoning ability.

Job Performance Tests and Work Samples

Many kinds of jobs require candidates who excel at performing specialized tasks, such as operating a certain machine, handling calls from customers, or designing advertising materials. To evaluate candidates for such jobs, the organization may administer tests of the necessary skills. Sometimes the candidates take tests that involve a sample of work, or they may show existing samples of their work. Testing may involve a simulated work environment, a difficult team project, or a complex computer programming puzzle.[28] Examples of job performance tests include tests of keyboarding speed and *in-basket tests*. An in-basket test measures the ability to juggle a variety of demands, as in a manager's job. The candidate is

HR How-To

Testing 101

Cognitive Ability

The Wonderlic Class Cognitive Ability Test (formerly the Wonderlic Personnel Test) is one of the most widely used employment tests to measure specific cognitive abilities. It is a 12-minute timed test with 50 questions.

Sample question: Three individuals form a partnership and agree to divide the profits equally. X invests $9,000, Y invests $7,000, and Z invests $4,000. If the profits are $4,800, how much less does X receive than if the profits were divided in proportion to the amount invested. [Answer: $560]

What it demonstrates: Cognitive ability tests measure an individual's ability to learn, adapt, solve problems, and understand instructions and are considered an important predictor of job success.

Emotional Intelligence

Based on research by psychologist Dr. Daniel Goleman, who claims a combination of self-awareness, empathy, and social skills is as important as factual knowledge in achieving success.

Sample question: You are a college student who had hoped to get an A in a course that was important for your future career aspirations. You have just found out you got a C– on the midterm. What do you do?

a) Sketch out a specific plan for ways to improve your grade and resolve to follow through.

b) Decide you do not have what it takes to make it in that career.

c) Tell yourself it really doesn't matter how much you do in the course, concentrate instead on other classes where your grades are higher.

d) Go see the professor and try to talk her into giving you a better grade.

[Answer: The most emotionally intelligent answer is 'a'—10 points; 'b'—0 points; 'c'—5 points; 'd'—0 points.]

What it shows: Proponents claim the combination of self-awareness, empathy, and social skills these tests measure are essential to success and effective leadership.

Personality

Many tests are available that ask questions about behavioural traits and tendencies. The usual approach is for the applicant to select their level of agreement or disagreement to each of a series of statements that assesses his/her approach to life and relationships.

Sample questions: Rate yourself on a five-point scale from strongly disagree to strongly agree: "I enjoy meeting new people," "I sometimes make mistakes," "I'm easily disappointed."

What it measures: Traits—for example, extroversion; agreeableness, and conscientiousness.

Sources: "Wonderlic Cognitive Ability Test Family," Wonderlic website, www.wonderlic.com/assessments/ability/cognitive-ability-tests, retrieved June 18, 2012; "EI quiz," HayGroup website, www.haygroup.com/leadershipandtalentondemand/demos/ei_quiz.aspx, retrieved June 18, 2012; Personality questionnaire examples," www.shldirect.com/personality_questionnaire_examples.html; retrieved June 18, 2012; and Wallace Immen, "Testing 101," *The Globe and Mail,* January 26, 2005, p. C2.

presented with simulated emails and messages describing the kinds of problems that confront a person in the job. The candidate has to decide how to respond to these messages, and in what order. Examples of jobs for which candidates provide work samples include graphic designers and writers.

Tests for selecting managers may take the form of an **assessment centre**—a wide variety of specific selection programs that use multiple selection methods to rate applicants or job incumbents on

FIGURE 5.3

Sample Question from the Public Service Commission of Canada's General Competency Test: Level 1 (GCT1)

Government of Canada MEMORANDUM	Gouvernement du Canada NOTE DE SERVICE

TO: All employees
FROM: Manager

We are pleased to announce that our Ministry's budget has been increased and consequently we will experience an increase in staff size. Because new positions will become available, we will be holding interviews within the next few weeks.

The main focus of this memo is to indicate a change concerning:

1. better ministerial policy.
2. better budget publicity.
3. more human resources.
4. more office space.

Source: General Competency Test Level I (GCTI)—Instructions and Sample Questions, www.psc-cfp.gc.ca/ppc-cpp/test-examen/gctl-ecgl/index-eng.htm. Public Service Commission 2011. Reproduced with the permission of the Public Service Commission of Canada.

their management potential. An assessment centre typically includes in-basket tests, tests of more general abilities, and personality tests. Combining several assessment methods increases the validity of this approach. For example, the Public Service Commission of Canada uses the *Human Resources Consultant Simulation Exercise,* which "simulates important aspects of a human resource consultant's job." The candidate receives exercise items including memoranda, letters, and reports and is given three hours to review the items and complete a written action plan, and prepare for an oral presentation. The next step is to make an oral presentation (30 minutes maximum) to the selection panel followed by questions from the panel. The final phase requires the candidate to provide assistance and advice to a manager as part of an interactive exercise.[29]

assessment centre
A wide variety of specific selection programs that use multiple selection methods to rate applicants or job incumbents on their management potential.

Job performance tests have the advantage of giving applicants a chance to show what they can do, which leads them to feel that the evaluation was fair.[30] The tests also are job-specific—that is, tailored to the kind of work done in a specific job. So they have a high level of validity, especially when combined with cognitive ability tests and a highly structured interview.[31] This advantage can become a disadvantage, however, if the organization wants to generalize the results of a test for one job to candidates for other jobs. The tests are more appropriate for identifying candidates who are generally able to solve the problems associated with a job, rather than for identifying which specific skills or traits the individual possesses.[32] Developing different tests for different jobs can become expensive. One way to save money is to prepare computerized tests that can be delivered online to various locations.

Personality Inventories

In some situations, employers may also want to know about candidates' personalities. For example, one way psychologists think of personality is in terms of the "Big Five" traits: extroversion, adjustment, agreeableness, conscientiousness, and inquisitiveness (explained in Table 5.3). There is evidence that people who score high on conscientiousness tend to excel at work, especially when they also have high cognitive ability.[33] For people-related jobs like sales and management, extroversion and agreeableness also seem to be associated with success.[34] Strong social skills help conscientious people ensure that they get positive recognition for their hard work.[35]

The usual way to identify a candidate's personality traits is to administer one of the personality tests that are commercially available. The employer pays for the use of the test, and the organization that owns the test then scores the responses and provides a report about the test taker's personality. An organization that provides such tests should be able to discuss the test's validity and reliability. Assuming the tests are valid for the organization's jobs, they have advantages. Administering commercially available personality tests is simple, and these tests should be able to demonstrate they do not violate human rights requirements. On the downside, compared with intelligence tests, people are better at "faking" their answers to a personality test to score higher on desirable traits.[36] For example, people tend to score higher on conscientiousness when filling out job-related personality tests than when participating in research projects.[37] Ways to address this problem include using trained interviewers rather than surveys, collecting information about the applicant from several sources, and letting applicants know that several sources will be used.[38]

A recent study found that 35 percent of organizations use personality tests when selecting personnel.[39] One reason is organizations' greater use of teamwork, where personality conflicts can be a significant problem. Traits such as agreeableness and conscientiousness have been associated with effective teamwork.[40] In addition, an organization might try to select team members with similar traits and values in order to promote a strong culture where people work together harmoniously, or they instead might look for a diversity of personalities and values as a way to promote debate and creativity.[41]

Honesty, Alcohol, and Drug Tests

No matter what employees' personalities may be like, organizations want employees to be honest and to behave safely. Some organizations are satisfied to assess these qualities on the basis of judgments from reference checks and interviews. Others investigate these characteristics more directly through the use of tests.

The most famous kind of honesty test is the polygraph, the so-called "lie detector" test. As a result of controversies associated with the use of polygraph tests, testing services have developed paper-and-pencil honesty (or integrity) tests. Generally these tests ask applicants directly about their attitudes toward honesty and integrity and their own experiences in situations inside and outside work. Most of

TABLE 5.3

Five Major Personality Dimensions Measured by Personality Inventories

1. Extroversion	Sociable, gregarious, assertive, talkative, expressive
2. Adjustment	Emotionally stable, non-depressed, secure, content
3. Agreeableness	Courteous, trusting, good-natured, tolerant, cooperative, forgiving
4. Conscientiousness	Dependable, organized, persevering, thorough, achievement-oriented
5. Inquisitiveness	Curious, imaginative, artistically sensitive, broadminded, playful

the research into the validity of these tests has been conducted by the testing companies, but evidence suggests they do have some ability to predict such behaviour as theft of the employer's property.[42]

As concerns about substance abuse and the harmful impacts of alcohol and drugs on employee safety and performance have grown, so has the use of alcohol and drug testing. As a measure of a person's past exposure to drugs, chemical testing has high reliability and validity. However, these tests are controversial for several reasons. Some people are concerned that they invade individuals' privacy. Others object from a legal perspective. Taking urine, saliva, and/or blood samples involves invasive procedures, and accusing someone of drug use is a serious matter. And, although breathalyzer tests can measure how much alcohol has been consumed and the person's level of impairment, current drug tests cannot measure impairment or assess if an employee is capable of performing the job.[43]

Employers considering the use of drug or alcohol tests should ensure that their testing programs conform to the drug and alcohol testing policy outlined in their relevant human rights legislation. As discussed in Chapter 2, the Canadian Human Rights Act prohibits discrimination related to a disability, and dependence on drugs or alcohol is considered a disability that must be accommodated to the point of undue hardship. For example, the Canadian Human Rights Commission's Policy on Alcohol and Drug Testing describes "testing for alcohol or drugs as a form of medical examination" and "pre-employment drug or alcohol testing is permitted only in limited circumstances."[44]

The approach to drug testing in Western Canada has tended to emphasize safety and has directly conflicted with Ontario Court of Appeal decisions. For example, the Alberta Court of Appeal upheld the employer's right to immediately terminate a new employee who failed a pre-employment drug screening test that was part of the hiring process for Kellogg Brown & Root (KBR), a subsidiary of Houston-based oil-and-gas giant, Haliburton. The employee had started work and been on the job for nine days when his marijuana-positive test results came back. The Alberta Court of Appeal ruled that the terminated employee was not an addict, but rather a recreational drug user, therefore he was not disabled and did not require accommodation. The Court ruled that there was no discrimination because the employer's drug testing policy was connected to workplace safety.[45]

To test tech workers' programming and problem-solving skills, Google sponsors contests called Code Jams at locations around the world. The winners gain fame as well as visibility with Google recruiters. The Code Jams also reinforce Google's reputation for hiring the best thinkers and offering them exciting challenges.

Medical Examinations

Especially for physically demanding jobs, organizations may wish to conduct medical examinations to see that the applicant can meet the job's requirements. Employers may also wish to establish an employee's physical condition at the beginning of employment, so that there is a basis for measuring whether the employee has suffered a work-related disability later on. At the same time, as described in Chapter 2, organizations may not discriminate against individuals with disabilities who could perform a job with reasonable accommodations. Likewise, they may not use a measure of physical ability that discriminates against women, older workers, etc., unless those requirements are valid in predicting the ability to perform a job. Medical exams must be related to job requirements and may not be given until the candidate has received a conditional job offer. Therefore, organizations must be careful in how they use medical examinations. Many organizations make selection decisions first, then conduct the exams to confirm that the employee can handle the job, with any reasonable accommodations required. Limiting the use of medical exams in this way also holds down the cost of what tends to be an expensive process.

L○6 Discuss how to conduct effective interviews.

Interviews

Supervisors and team members most often get involved in the selection process at the stage of employment interviews. These interviews bring together job applicants and representatives of the employer to obtain information and evaluate the applicant's qualifications and organizational fit. While the applicant is providing information, he or she is also forming opinions about what it is like to work for the organization. Most organizations use interviewing as part of the selection process. In fact, this method is used more than any other.

Interviewing Techniques

Interview techniques include choices about the type of questions to ask and the number of people who conduct the interview. Several question types are possible:

- In a **nondirective interview,** the interviewer has great discretion in choosing questions. The candidate's reply to one question may suggest other questions to ask. Non-directive interviews typically include open-ended questions about the candidate's strengths, weaknesses, career goals, and work experience. Because these interviews give the interviewer wide latitude, their reliability is not great and some interviewers ask questions that are not valid or even legal.

nondirective interview
A selection interview in which the interviewer has great discretion in choosing questions to ask each candidate.

- A **structured interview** establishes a set of questions for the interviewer to ask. Ideally, the questions are related to job requirements and cover relevant knowledge, skills, and experiences. The interviewer is supposed to avoid asking questions that are not on the list. Although interviewers may object to being restricted, the results may be more valid and reliable than with a nondirective interview.

structured interview
A selection interview that consists of a predetermined set of questions for the interviewer to ask.

- A **situational interview** is a structured interview in which the interviewer describes a situation likely to arise on the job and asks the candidate what he or she would do in that situation. This type of interview may have high validity in predicting job performance.[46]

situational interview

A structured interview in which the interviewer describes a situation likely to arise on the job, then asks the candidate what he or she would do in that situation.

- A **behavioural interview** is a situational interview in which the interviewer asks the candidate to describe how he or she handled a type of situation in the past. Questions about the candidates' actual experiences tend to have the highest validity.[47]

behavioural interview

A structured interview in which the interviewer asks the candidate to describe how he or she handled a type of situation in the past.

BMO Financial Group has been using behavioural interviews since the early 1990s for almost every position it fills. BMO even offers prospective employees advice about what a good answer includes—see Table 5.4. BMO Financial Group views behavioural interviews as most effective for external candidates because internal candidates have existing performance reviews and have been through the process at some point.[48]

The common setup for either a nondirective or structured interview is for an individual (an HR professional or the supervisor for the vacant position) to interview each candidate face to face. However,

Did You KNOW?

Hiring Decisions: Algorithms Are Better Than Instinct

In research conducted with Brian S. Connelly of the University of Toronto, it was found that although people "are very good at specifying what's needed for a position and eliciting information from candidates," hiring decisions made with an equation "outperforms human decisions by at least 25 percent." This effect is relevant to any situation where there are many candidates, e.g., front-line jobs, middle management, or even for executive positions. Below are bars that show the percentages of "above average employees" selected with hiring algorithms vs. human judgment.

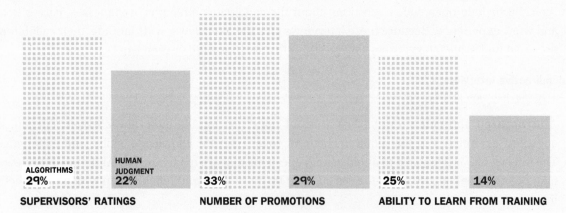

Source: Nathan R. Kuncel, David M. Klieger, and Deniz S. Ones, "In Hiring, Algorithms Beat Instinct," *Harvard Business Review*, May 2014, p. 32.

variations on this approach are possible. In a **panel interview,** several members of the organization meet to interview each candidate. A panel interview gives the candidate a chance to meet more people and see how people interact in that organization. It provides the organization with the judgments of more than one person, to reduce the effect of personal biases in selection decisions. Panel interviews can be especially appropriate in organizations that use teamwork. At the other extreme, some organizations conduct interviews without any interviewers; they use a computerized interviewing process. The candidate enters replies to the questions interactively and results are submitted electronically. Such a format eliminates a lot of personal bias—along with the opportunity to see how people interact. Therefore, electronic interviews are useful for gathering objective data, rather than assessing people skills.

panel interview
Selection interview in which several members of the organization meet to interview each candidate.

Advantages and Disadvantages of Interviewing

The wide use of interviewing is not surprising. People naturally want to see prospective employees first-hand. As we noted in Chapter 1, the top qualities that employers seek in new hires include communication skills and interpersonal skills. Talking face to face can provide evidence of these skills. Interviews can give insights into candidates' personalities and interpersonal styles. They are more valid, however, when they focus on job knowledge and skill. Interviews also provide a means to check the accuracy of information on the applicant's résumé or job application. Asking applicants to elaborate about their experiences and offer details reduces the likelihood of a candidate being able to invent a work history.[49]

Despite these benefits, interviewing is not necessarily the most accurate basis for making a selection decision. Research has shown that interviews can be unreliable, low in validity,[50] and biased against a number of different groups.[51] Interviews are also costly. They require that at least one person devote time to interviewing each candidate, and the applicants typically have to be brought to one geographic location. Interviews are also subjective, so they place the organization at greater risk of discrimination complaints by applicants who were not hired, especially if those individuals were asked questions not entirely related to the job.

Organizations can avoid some of these pitfalls.[52] Human resources staff should keep the interviews focused, structured, and standardized. The interview should focus on accomplishing a few goals, so

TABLE 5.4

BMO's (www.bmo.com) Advice to Job Seekers about Behavioural Interviews

YOUR BMO INTERVIEW

Behavioural-focused questions are used to understand and draw on your past work experience as being the best predictor of how in a similar situation you would behave in the future. When answering these types of questions a good answer includes:
- A description of the situation where the behaviour took place.
- An account of the actions you took to handle the situation or resolve the problem. Be specific and concise.
- An explanation of the results. Demonstrate to the interviewer that you understand how your actions impacted the results, what the outcomes were, and what you learned.

Don't ignore failures. An interviewer will want to hear about situations that didn't turn out as hoped. We all have experiences we wish we could "do over." What an interviewer will want to know is how would you do it over?

Spend some time anticipating questions you may encounter and think of ways you might answer them. This way you will feel more confident and prepared. Good luck!

Source: "Interviewing at BMO: Your BMO Interview," www.bmo.com/home/about/banking/careers/tools-and-resources/interviewing-at-bmo, retrieved April 2, 2012.

When interviewing candidates, it's valid to ask about willingness to travel if that is a requirement of the job. Interviewers might ask questions about previous business travel experiences and/or how interviewees handled situations requiring flexibility and self-motivation (qualities that would be an asset in someone who is travelling alone and solving business problems remotely).

that at the end of the interview, the organization has ratings on several observable measures, such as ability to express ideas. The interview should not try to measure abilities and skills—for example, intelligence—that tests can measure better. As noted earlier, situational and behavioural interviews are especially effective for doing this. Organizations can prevent problems related to subjectivity by training interviewers and using more than one person to conduct interviews. Training typically includes focusing on the recording of observable facts, rather than on making subjective judgments, as well as developing interviewers' awareness of their biases.[53] Finally, to address costs of interviewing, some organizations videotape interviews or use applications with video chat capabilities e.g., Skype.

Preparing to Interview

Organizations get the greatest benefits from interviewing if they prepare carefully. A well-planned interview should be standardized, comfortable for the participants, and focused on the job and the organization. The interviewer should have a quiet place in which to conduct interviews without interruption. This person should be trained in how to ask objective questions, what subject matter to avoid, and how to detect and handle his or her own personal biases or other distractions in order to fairly evaluate candidates.

The interviewer should have enough documents to conduct a complete interview. These should include a list of the questions to be asked in a structured interview, with plenty of space for recording the responses. When the questions are prepared, it is also helpful to determine how the answers will be assessed. For example, if questions are asked about how interviewees have handled certain situations, consider what responses are best in terms of meeting job requirements. If the job requires someone who develops new and creative solutions to problems, then a response that shows innovative behaviour would receive a higher score. The interviewer also should have a copy of the interviewee's employment application and résumé, to review before the interview and refer to during the interview. If possible, the interviewer should also have information on-hand about the organization and the job. Near the beginning of the interview, it is a good idea to go over the job specifications, organizational policies, and so on, so that the interviewee has a clearer understanding of the organization's needs and expectations.

The interviewer should schedule enough time to review the job requirements, discuss the interview questions, and give the interviewee a chance to ask questions. To close, the interviewer should thank the candidate for coming and provide information about what to expect—for example, that the organization will contact a few finalists within the next week or that a decision will be made by the end of the week.

LO7 Explain how employers carry out the process of making a selection decision.

Selection Decisions

HRC 2, 4

After reviewing applications, scoring tests, conducting interviews, and checking references, the organization needs to make decisions about which candidates will be provided a job offer. In practice, most organizations find more than one qualified candidate to fill an open position. The selection decision typically combines ranking based on objective criteria along with subjective judgments about which candidate will likely be the highest performer.

How Organizations Select Employees

The selection decision should not be a simple matter of whom the supervisor likes best or which candidate will take the lowest offer. Rather, the people making the selection decision should look for the best fit between candidate and position. In general, the person's performance will result from a combination of ability and motivation. Often, the selection is a choice among a few people who possess the basic qualifications. The decision makers therefore have to decide which of those people have the best combination of ability and motivation to fit in the position and in the organization as a whole.

The usual process for arriving at a selection decision is to gradually narrow the pool of candidates for each job. This approach, called the **multiple-hurdle model,** is based on a process such as the one shown earlier in Figure 5.1. Each stage of the process is a hurdle, and candidates who overcome a hurdle continue to the next stage of the process. For example, the organization reviews applications and/or résumés of all candidates, conducts some tests on those who meet minimum requirements, conducts initial interviews with those who had the highest test scores, follows up with additional interviews or testing, and then selects a candidate from the few who survived this process. Another, more expensive alternative is to take most applicants through all steps of the process and then to review all the scores to find the most desirable candidates. With this alternative, decision makers may use a **compensatory model,** in which a very high score on one type of assessment can make up for a low score on another.

> **multiple-hurdle model**
> Process of arriving at a selection decision by eliminating some candidates at each stage of the selection process.

> **compensatory model**
> Process of arriving at a selection decision in which a very high score on one type of assessment can make up for a low score on another.

Whether the organization uses a multiple-hurdle model or conducts the same assessments on all candidates, the decision maker or makers need criteria for choosing among qualified candidates. An obvious strategy is to select the candidates who score highest on tests and interviews. However, employee performance depends on motivation as well as ability. It is possible that a candidate who

Thinking ETHICALLY

Checking Out a Candidate's Social Profiles

Ninety-three percent of Canadian Internet users between the ages of 18–34 are on Facebook and more than half are on Twitter. So, it's not surprising that social sites have become the first stop for many recruiters and hiring managers to determine if a potential candidate is a good fit. Many job seekers are not aware of these instant background checks. In an Adecco Workplace Insights survey, 66 percent of Generation Y respondents were unaware that seemingly private photos, comments, and statements were audited by potential employers.

"It's a lot more common than I think the prospective employees realize," says Lynne Perry-Reid, a Calgary recruiter and co-founder of Corporate Connections. "Especially now that a lot of recruiters tend to be younger, maybe in their 30s, everyone is really involved in things [like] Facebook," she says, "so you can easily just type in someone's name to find out about them because you're already hooked into that network."

In a formal job interview, employers are not legally permitted to ask questions about a candidate's age, marital status, sexual orientation, or ethnicity but the individual's social profile on sites such as Facebook, Instagram, and Twitter can reveal all of these things to a prospective employer. Amber MacArthur, social media author and strategist cautions that all it takes is one click from a rogue contact to make details posted to a relatively secure profile—public information.

Controversy has also recently surrounded the practice of some companies to ask candidates to turn over Facebook login information as part of the hiring process. Facebook's chief privacy officer, Erin Egan offered this advice: "If you are a Facebook user, you should never have to share your password." Facebook has also warned employers not to demand the passwords of job applicants.

Questions

1. Are employers crossing the line when they look up job candidates on social sites such as Facebook, Instagram, and Twitter?

2. What do you do to ensure your own online profiles present a positive image to potential employers? What would you do if you were asked by a prospective employer to provide your Facebook password?

3. Suppose you are a recruiter and have identified an applicant who possesses excellent knowledge, skills, ability, and experience required for a position in your organization. Then you discover an awkward image of the prospective employee on a social media site. What would you do? What if you found that the applicant had recently tweeted: "omg i hate my job and my boss is a jerk."

Sources: Ryan Holmes, "Millenials Need Some Brushing Up; Their Social Media Skills Need Updating," *National* Post, May 12, 2014, p. FP 6; Michelle McQuigge, "Company Wants Your Facebook Password? Just Say No," *Globe and Mail,* March 28, 2012, B19; "Your Profile on Social Sites Can Make or Break Your Job Opportunities," *Financial Post,* September 19, 2007, www.canada.com/nationalpost/news/working/story, retrieved September 21, 2007; Derek Sankey, "Facebook Background Checks," *Calgary Herald,* 2007, http://working.canada.com/calgary/resources/story, retrieved April 4, 2008; Kristin Gissaro, "The Invasion of Recruiters on Social Networking Sites," www.ere.net.blogs/generational_recruiting, retrieved April 4, 2008.

scores very high on an ability test might be "overqualified," that is, the employee might be bored by the job the organization needs to fill, and a less-able employee might actually be a better fit. Similarly, a highly motivated person might learn some kinds of jobs very quickly, potentially outperforming someone who has the necessary skills. Furthermore, some organizations have policies of developing employees for career paths in the organization. Such organizations might put less emphasis on the skills needed for a particular job and more emphasis on hiring candidates who share the organization's values, show that they have the people skills to work with others in the organization, and are able to learn the skills needed for advancement.

Finally, organizations have choices about who will make the decision. Sometimes the immediate supervisor or manager makes the final decision, often alone. This person may couple knowledge of the job with a judgment about who will fit in best with others in the department. The decision could also be made by a human resources professional using standardized, objective criteria. Especially in organizations that value teamwork, selection decisions may be made by a work team or other panel of decision makers. As noted in the chapter opening and the Did You Know? feature, organizations are turning to data-driven methods to inform and/or make hiring decisions. This approach is an application of human capital analytics (see Chapter 1) to make evidence-based hiring decisions. A **hiring algorithm** is a mathematical model that predicts which job candidates are most likely to be high-performers after being hired. The use of this type of predictive model is intended to improve the quality of hiring decisions by reducing the human errors associated with biases and other perceptual distortions.

hiring algorithm
Mathematical model that predicts which job candidates are most likely to be high-performers after being hired.

Timing of the decision is also important. "Hiring managers are busy but the best candidates don't stay on the market long. And often the best candidate is lost in the process if the hiring manager takes too long to make a decision or if there's too much back-and-forth between the hiring manager and HR," explains Ken Graham, director of training and professional services at Adecco (www.adecco.ca) in Toronto.[54]

Communicating the Decision

The human resource department is often responsible for notifying applicants about the results of the selection process. When a candidate has been selected, the organization should communicate the offer to the candidate. The offer should include the job responsibilities, work schedule, rate of pay, starting date, and other relevant details. If placement in a job requires that the applicant complete a medical examination, the offer should state that contingency. The person communicating the offer should also indicate a date by which the candidate should reply with an acceptance or rejection of the offer. For some jobs, such as management and professional positions, the candidate and organization may negotiate pay, benefits, and work arrangements before they arrive at a final employment agreement.

The person who communicates this decision should keep accurate records of who was contacted, when, and for which position, as well as of the candidate's reply. The HR department and the immediate supervisor also should be in close communication about the job offer. When an applicant accepts a job offer, the HR department must notify the supervisor, so that he or she can be prepared for the new employee's arrival.

SUMMARY

LO1 Identify the elements of the selection process.

Selection typically begins with a review of candidates' employment applications and résumés. The organization administers tests to candidates who meet requirements, and qualified candidates undergo one or more interviews. Organizations check references and conduct background checks to verify the accuracy of information provided by candidates. A candidate is selected to fill each vacant position. Candidates who accept offers are placed in the positions for which they were selected.

L○2 Define ways to measure the success of a selection method.

One criterion is reliability, which indicates the method is free from random error, so that measurements are consistent. A selection method should also be valid, meaning that performance on the measure (such as a test score) is related to what the measure is designed to assess (such as job performance). A selection method also should be generalizable, so that it applies to more than one specific situation. Each selection method should have utility, meaning it provides economic value greater than its cost. Finally, selection methods should meet the legal requirements for employment decisions.

L○3 Summarize the legal requirements for employee selection.

The selection process must comply with human rights and privacy legislation and be conducted in a fair and consistent manner. Selection methods must be valid for job performance. Questions may not gather information about prohibited grounds. Employers must respect employees' privacy rights and obtain consent before conducting background checks.

L○4 Compare the common methods used for selecting human resources.

Nearly all organizations gather information through employment applications and résumés. These methods are inexpensive, and job applications standardize basic information received from all applicants. The information is not necessarily reliable, because each applicant provides the information. References and background checks help to verify the accuracy of the information. Employment tests and work samples are more objective. To be legal, any test must measure abilities that actually are associated with successful job performance. Tests should be selected to be related to successful job performance and avoid human rights violations.

Interviews are widely used to obtain information about a candidate's interpersonal and communication skills and to gather more detailed information about a candidate's background. Structured interviews are more valid than unstructured ones. Situational and behavioural interviews provide greater validity than general questions. Interviews are costly and may introduce bias into the selection process. Organizations can minimize the drawbacks through preparation and training.

L○5 Describe the major types of employment tests.

Physical ability tests measure strength, endurance, psychomotor abilities, and other physical abilities. They can be accurate but can discriminate and are not always job-related. Cognitive ability tests, or intelligence tests, tend to be valid, especially for complex jobs and those requiring adaptability. Job performance tests tend to be valid but are not always generalizable.

Personality tests measure personality traits such as extroversion and adjustment. Organizations may use honesty tests as well as pre-employment drug tests in some circumstances, e.g., for safety-sensitive jobs. A medical examination may be a condition of employment, but to avoid discrimination against persons with disabilities, organizations usually administer a medical exam only after making a conditional job offer.

L○6 Discuss how to conduct effective interviews.

Interviews should be focused, structured, and standardized. Interviewers should identify job requirements and create a list of questions related to the requirements. Interviewers should be trained to recognize their own personal biases and conduct objective interviews. Panel interviews can reduce problems related to interviewer bias. Interviewers also should be prepared to provide information about the job and the organization.

L○7 Explain how employers carry out the process of making a selection decision.

The organization should focus on the objective of finding the person who will be the best fit with the job and organization. Decision makers may use a multiple-hurdle model, in which each stage of the selection process eliminates some of the candidates from consideration at the following stages. An alternative is a compensatory model, in which all candidates are evaluated with all methods. A candidate who scores poorly with one method may be selected if he or she scores very high on another measure.

Critical Thinking Questions

1. What activities are involved in the selection process? Think of the last time you were hired for a job. Which of those activities were used in selecting you? Should the organization that hired you have used other methods as well? How could this organization improve its selection process?

2. Why should the selection process be designed to align with the organization's job descriptions and specifications?

3. Choose two of the selection methods identified in this chapter. Describe how you can compare them in terms of reliability, validity, ability to generalize, utility, and compliance with human rights legislation.

4. Why does predictive validation provide better information than concurrent validation? Why is this type of validation more difficult?

5. Do you think privacy guidelines influence organizations' use of social media background checks? Why or why?

6. Suppose your organization needs to hire several computer programmers, and you are reviewing résumés you obtained from an online service. What kinds of information will you want to gather from the "work experience" portion of these résumés? What kinds of information will you want to gather from the "education" portion of these résumés? What methods would you use for verifying or exploring this information? Why would you use those methods?

7. For each of the following jobs, select two kinds of tests you think would be most important to include in the selection process. Explain why you chose those tests.

    a. City bus driver

    b. Pharmaceutical sales representative

    c. Member of a team that sells complex high-tech equipment to manufacturers

    d. Member of a team that makes a component of the equipment in (c)

8. Suppose you are a human resources professional at a large retail chain. You want to improve the company's hiring process by standardizing interviews, so that every time someone is interviewed for a particular job category, that person answers the same questions. You also want to make sure the questions asked are relevant to the job and comply with human rights legislation. Think of three questions to include in interviews for each of the following jobs. For each question, state why you think it should be included.

   a. Cashier at one of the company's stores

   b. Store manager

   c. Accounts payable clerk at company headquarters

9. How can organizations improve the quality of their interviewing so that interviews provide valid information?

10. The following questions are favourites of three seasoned hiring managers. For each of the following questions provide your opinion of:

   i. What you think the interviewer is after

   ii. The best answer

   iii. The worst answer

      a. Del Rollo, director of hospitality, Jackson-Triggs Niagara Estate, Niagara-on-the-Lake asks: "*What is the greatest service experience you've had?*"

      b. Gary Hellard, manager of recruiting, WestJet Airlines, Calgary asks: "*Tell us what began as your most frustrating or tough day, and what you did so that it ended up being your most productive day.*"

      c. Nancy Blair, office leader, Egon Zehnder International Inc., Calgary asks: "*What do you hope this job is not?*"

Source: Tony Martin, "Why Are They Asking Me This?" Report on Business, *The Globe and Mail,* September 26, 2007, www.theglobeandmail.com, retrieved September 27, 2007.

11. Some organizations set up a selection process that is long and complex. In some people's opinion, this kind of selection process not only is more valid but also has symbolic value. What can the use of a long, complex selection process symbolize to job seekers? How do you think this would affect the organization's ability to attract the best employees?

Experiencing HR

Print out a copy of your résumé and LinkedIn profile. If you don't already have a résumé or LinkedIn profile, create one summarizing your education, work history, and accomplishments.

Find a job posting for a position and company that interests you. Compare your résumé and profile with the details in the job posting. What qualities on your résumé and profile match what the company is looking for? What words and phrases does the company use in its job posting and on its website that you could use (truthfully) to show you are a good fit with the company? What additional experiences and skills do you need before you would likely be considered for a job at this company?

Write a one-page paper summarizing your comparison. Attach your résumé and profile, and turn it in for credit on the assignment. Keep a copy of your summary to refer to later when planning the next step in your career.

CASE STUDY 5.1:

How Google Searches for Talent

Since 2003, Goggle's has been hosting an annual international programming competition that attracts around 10,000 participants who "race to solve a series of complex algorithms within a limited amount of time." Participants compete for cash prizes ranging from $250 for 76th–100th place to $10,000 for first place and possibly a job offer with Google. Google has also hosted country-specific Code Jams—Code Jam Africa and Code Jam India.

Here is a glimpse into Code Jam India:

It is the first day of spring in India, a day celebrated with riotous colour and revelry. But in one corner of Bangalore, India's info tech hub, the sunny Saturday is heavy with tension. At an Internet café, a group of engineers and math majors, all in their 20s, hunch over terminals, ready to write some killer code—and with luck, launch careers with one of the world's premier tech companies, Google Inc.

It's the Google India Code Jam, a contest to find the most brilliant coder in South and Southeast Asia. The fastest will win $6,900—and more importantly, the offer of a coveted job at one of Google's research and development centres. At the stroke of 10:30 a.m., the contestants begin, emerging exhausted three hours later. "It's been incredibly difficult and awesome," says Nirin Gupta, a computer science undergrad at the Indian Institute of Technology at Bombay.

Some 14,000 aspirants registered from all over South and Southeast Asia for the first round in February. The top 50 were selected for the finals in Bangalore: 39 from India, 8 from Singapore, and 3 from Indonesia. "It's a dog-eat-dog world," says Robert Hughes, president of TopCoder Inc., the testing company that runs the Code Jams. "Wherever the best talent is, Google wants them."

And the winner is . . . one of these clever IIT grads from India, right? Surprisingly, no. Ardian Poernomo, a third-year undergrad computer engineering student at Singapore's Nanyang Technological University, lands in first place. The number two finisher, Pascal Alfadian, a second-year student at the Universitas Katolik Para-hyangan in West Java, is Indonesian, too. Poernomo didn't commit to taking a job with Google, however. He may go for a doctorate degree in computer science in the United States.

Still, Google now has a new pool of Asian talent to choose from. According to Krishna Bharat, head of Google's India research and development centre, all the finalists will be offered jobs. And Google needs them. The search company has been frustrated by its inability to find top-notch engineers for its centre in India, according to industry insiders.

Google's frustrations in India stem from two factors. One is the red-hot job market in Indian tech. Engineering students are assured of a job a year before they graduate. And Google makes things hard for itself by having some of the most exacting hiring standards going. The contest is an example. Participants are tested on aptitude in problem solving, on designing and writing code, and on testing peer-written work. Finalists are asked to create and test software for unique

Web searches and to get from point A to B in a city with a minimum number of turns. The final challenge is programming a war-based board game, a task so complex that only winner Poernomo completed it.

For Google, the Code Jam will serve as a shortcut through its hiring regime. Candidates normally go through a seven-stage process that can last months—and at the end of it, they're more likely to be rejected than hired. Much of that screening can be set aside for Code Jam winners.

Questions

1. Why do you think Google uses a competition (Code Jam) as one of its selection methods? What are some benefits of this method?

2. What knowledge, skills, abilities, or other characteristics of computer programmers would the Code Jam *not* evaluate?

3. Would you predict that the Code Jam is a valid and reliable selection method for Google programmers? Would you advise Google to use similar methods for other positions in the company? Explain.

Sources: "Google Code Jam 2012," http://code.google.com/codejam, retrieved April 4, 2012; Allie Townsend, "Google Code Jam," *TimeSpecials:* Top 10 Nerdy Competitions," October 4, 2010, www.time.com/time/specials/packages/article/0,28804,2023019_2023018_2023034,00.html, retrieved April 4, 2012; and Josey Puliyenthuruthel, "How Google Searches—for Talent," *BusinessWeek,* April 11, 2005, http://web6.infotrac.galegroup.com.

CASE STUDY 5.2:

Speed Interviewing

Metzti Bryan stood along with about 100 other graphic communications management students in the school cafeteria at Toronto's Ryerson University waiting for the sound of a gong. When the gong sounded, the students charged into the cafeteria in frantic search of their first interview. After ten minutes, the gong sounded again to signal the next interview at this "speed-interviewing" event. Over a total of 120 minutes each student would speak with 12 potential employers. "It's like a race," said Ms. Bryan, describing the experience as both nerve-wracking and energizing. Ms. Bryan got the job she wanted and now conducts speed interviews for her employer.

Employers who recently took part in "CGA Speed Interview Nights" shared some insights about what they were looking for. Neil Focht, accounting manager at Enterprise Holdings Inc. says that little things, like a good handshake count. Neil adds: "It's good to give specific examples of past situations without giving too much detail."

McMaster University, Canada's third-largest medical school has been using a similar type of screening method—applicants rotate through 12 mini-interviews that are exactly eight minutes long. They are given the chance to discuss one scenario or answer one question before having to move quickly to the next interview when a bell sounds. The mini-interviews focus on both ethical issues and realistic medical scenarios.

Questions

1. In your opinion, does "speed interviewing" increase the validity of a selection process? Why or why not?

2. What additional selection methods might be appropriate for the initial screening of job applicants (i.e., prior to the speed interviewing process)?

3. Would you prefer this interview process to a traditional panel interview? Why or why not?

Sources: Zosia Bielski, "On Your Marks, Get Set. . . Hire!" *Globe and Mail,* December 1, 2009, L.1; "Speed Interviewing: What Employers Want," *CGA CareerView,* January 3, 2012, http://cgacareerview.wordpress.com/2012/01/03/speed-interviewing-what-employers-want/, retrieved March 28, 2012; and Anne Marie Owens, "Medical School's Novel Entrance Test–12 Eight Minute Interviews," *National Post,* April 5, 2004, pp. A1, A5.

VIDEO CASES PART 2

Video Case: 3 Steps to Recruiting on Facebook (www.hrreporter.com/videodisplay/402-3-steps-to-recruiting-on-facebook)

Based in Edmonton Alberta, Shahid Wazed is a social media recruitment thought leader who recently spoke at the 2015 HRPA Annual Conference in Toronto. Shahid suggests that talent leaders are expressing concerns that job boards are not attracting enough candidates to their career sites and they need to turn to less conventional methods to attract passive talent. He describes Facebook as an attractive platform for recruiting and shares an example of a recent City of Edmonton recruitment initiative to attract heavy duty mechanics. Although the City of Edmonton (www.edmonton.ca) had only been able to attract a few heavy duty mechanics to come to their career site, a Facebook advertising campaign attracted 99 qualified applicants within three days at a minimal cost—less than $2. The City of Edmonton also hosts a weekly one-half hour "live" session on Facebook that connects recruiters and job seekers who have questions or are seeking advice.

Shahid also cites statistics suggesting that 72 percent of job seekers look to Facebook for employment information; and that he expects Canadian job seekers' time on Facebook and LinkedIn to be similar to U.S. respondents—Facebook at 40 minutes a day vs. LinkedIn at 17 minutes a month. The importance of passive recruiting is also discussed including Shahid's assertion that Canadian companies are not nearly as active in recruiting passive talent as companies in China and the U.S.

Questions

1. What is "passive talent"? Why is passive talent so important to a company's recruitment efforts?

2. Do you agree with Shahid's assertion that the future of recruitment is "social, mobile, and in-bound." Why or why not?

Source: Based on "3 Steps to Recruiting on Facebook," *Canadian HR Reporter TV,* January 27, 2015. Reprinted by permission of Canadian HR Reporter. © Copyright Thomson Reuters Canada Ltd., January 27, 2015, Toronto, Ontario 1-800-387-5164. Web: www.hrreporter.com

Video Case: You're Hiring the Wrong People (www.hrreporter.com/videodisplay/404-youre-hiring-the-wrong-people)

Cameron Laker is the CEO and founder of Mindfield (www.mindfieldgroup.com), a Vancouver-based talent solutions provider. Cameron recently led a session at the 2015 HRPA Annual Conference and Tradeshow. He discusses how companies can improve the quality and performance of their hourly workforce by using data and technology to make great hires of front-line staff. Laker explains that data has become a critical part of making great hires and that companies need processes to support data-driven hiring strategies. He suggests that organizations can make better hiring decisions by going beyond pre-hire data, e.g., résumé information such as employment background and education and look at key behaviours and skill sets that actually translate to success in the job. How did employees perform? Were they engaged? Laker describes how linking performance and engagement results back to hiring decisions will result in continuous improvement in the quality of hiring decisions.

Questions

1. How does the use of data and technology in making hiring decisions change the role and demands on HR professionals and line managers in the hiring and selection process?

2. Do you think this type of "data-driven hiring strategy" will work when hiring professional or managerial level employees?

Source: Based on "You're Hiring the Wrong Person," *Canadian HR Reporter TV*, February 1, 2015. Reprinted by permission of Canadian HR Reporter. © Copyright Thomson Reuters Canada Ltd., February 1, 2015, Toronto, Ontario 1-800-387-5164. Web: www.hrreporter.com

Managing Talent

CHAPTER 6

Training, Learning, and Development

WHAT DO I NEED TO KNOW?

After reading this chapter, you should be able to:

LO1	Discuss how to link training, learning, and development to organizational needs and strategy.
LO2	Explain how to assess training needs and determine employees' readiness.
LO3	Describe how to plan and design an effective training program.
LO4	Summarize how to implement and evaluate a successful training program.
LO5	Describe methods for employee orientation and diversity management.
LO6	Discuss the approaches organizations use for employee development.
LO7	Explain how managers and peers develop employees through mentoring and coaching.
LO8	Identify the steps in the career management process and how managers are dealing with some critical development-related challenges.

Facebook uses its own social media tools as online learning resources.

Learning at Facebook

"This journey is 1% finished." If that proclamation gets your creative juices flowing, then you can appreciate why Facebook (www.facebook.com) thinks of employee training, learning, and development as more than a matter of acquiring competencies. As a fast-growing, innovative organization, Facebook needs its people to come to work not only prepared to complete tasks but also excited about finding new ways to help members build and use social connections. Stuart Crabb, Facebook's head of learning and development, defines his goal as fostering performance improvement by uncovering employees' strengths and giving them opportunities to build on those strengths. At Facebook, there is no mandated training or learning other than things required by law. "Everything is open, so anyone can participate in management and leadership training, for example." Facebook runs peer-to-peer programs that connect learners to teachers in topics that range from very technical and job specific to cappuccino art to organizational design.

In practice, this means learning opportunities for people who are busy, highly engaged in their work, and looking for active involvement. Challenging jobs are at the heart of learning at Facebook, and these are supplemented with online materials and discussion-oriented group experiences. Employees who want to learn about a topic can start at their computers, following links to fact sheets and webcasts. Not surprisingly, Facebook's own social media tools are one of its online learning resources: employees can join a Facebook group in which they share and review one another's ideas as well as receive and react to training content. Crabb also set up more than two dozen coaching circles in which participants meet regularly to work on issues they want help with. Facebook's most formal learning program is its orientation of new employees. This two-day program focuses on the organization's culture, with the aim of motivating and inspiring the new hires. In the hundred days that follow, new employees are given access to learning tools related to job skills.[1]

L○1 Discuss how to link training, learning, and development to organizational needs and strategy.

Introduction

Learning refers to "an activity or process of gaining knowledge or skills by studying, practising, being taught, or experiencing something"[2] and is enabled through an organization's training and development efforts. *Training* consists of an organization's planned efforts to help employees acquire job-related knowledge, skills, abilities, and behaviours, with the goal of applying these on the job. A training program may range from formal classes to one-on-one mentoring, and it may take place on the job or at remote locations. No matter what its form, training can benefit the organization when it is linked to organizational needs and when it motivates employees.

> **learning**
> An activity or process of gaining knowledge or skills by studying, practising, being taught, or experiencing something.

As we noted in Chapter 1, employees' commitment to their organization depends on how their managers treat them. To "win the war for talent" managers must be able to identify high-potential employees, make sure the organization uses the talents of these people, and reassure them of their value, so they remain satisfied and stay with the organization. Managers also must be able to listen. Although new employees need direction, they expect to be able to think independently and be treated with respect.

In all these ways, managers provide for **employee development**—the combination of formal education, job experiences, relationships, and assessment of personality and abilities to help employees prepare for the future of their careers. Human resource management establishes a process for employee development that prepares employees to help the organization meet its goals. Table 6.1 summarizes the traditional differences between training and development.

> **employee development**
> The combination of formal education, job experiences, relationships, and assessment of personality and abilities to help employees prepare for the future of their careers.

This chapter describes how to plan and carry out an effective training program and explores the purpose and activities of employee development. We begin by discussing how to develop effective training in the context of the organization's strategy. Next, we discuss how organizations assess employees' training needs. We then review training methods and the process of evaluating a training program, and discuss some special applications of training: orientation of new employees and the management of diversity. We also examine the relationships among development, training, and career management and look at development approaches, including formal education, assessment, job experiences, and interpersonal relationships. The chapter emphasizes the types of competencies that are strengthened by each development method, so employees and their managers can choose appropriate methods when planning for development. The steps of the career management process, emphasizing the responsibilities of employee and employer at each step of the process are discussed. The chapter concludes with a discussion of special challenges related to employee development, e.g., the so-called glass ceiling and dysfunctional managers.

Training, Learning, and Development Linked to Organizational Needs and Strategy

HRC 1, 7

Workplace training and employee development are key ingredients in the competitiveness of firms and ultimately of national competitiveness.[3] Rapid change, especially in the area of technology, requires that employees continually learn new skills. The new psychological contract, described in Chapter 1, has created the expectation that employees invest in their own career development, which requires learning opportunities. Growing reliance on teamwork creates a demand for the ability to solve problems in teams, an ability that often requires formal training. Finally, the diversity of the

TABLE 6.1

Training versus Development

	Training	Development
Focus	Current	Future
Use of work experiences	Low	High
Goal	Preparation for current job	Preparation for changes
Participation	Required	Voluntary

Canadian population, coupled with the globalization of business, requires that employees be able to work well with people who are different from them. Successful organizations often take the lead in developing this ability.

Some organizations are developing their employer brand and reputation for talent development. These organizations emphasize training, career, and developmental opportunities as a means of gaining competitive advantage.[4] How are Canadian firms investing in and supporting learning? How does Canada compare with other countries? The Conference Board of Canada explores these and other questions in its *Learning and Development Outlook, 12th Edition: Strong Learning Organizations, Strong Leadership (2014)*. The report reveals that "Canadian organizations are not doing enough to ensure that they have the strong learning cultures required to compete with the nations that are currently leaders in performance." Specifically, Canadian organizations are lagging other nations with respect to the consistency and importance placed on employee learning and skill development.[5]

This survey of employers suggests that the decline in spending on learning and development appears to have plateaued and there was actually a slight increase (less than 3 percent) in spending compared to 2010. The average per employee direct expenditure on training and development across all industries in Canada was $705 (up from $688 in 2010) and the average Canadian employee received 28 hours of training in 2013 (up from 25 hours in 2010).[6]

One way for organizations to remain competitive, even in the face of challenging economic conditions is to ensure they have a strong learning culture. However, the International Institute for Management Development (IMD) reports that Canada has slipped by various measures of importance placed on workforce training. The IMD recently ranked Canada as 28th place (out of 59 countries ranked)—slipping considerably from 19th place in 2012. That leaves Canada well behind China (which rose from 46th place in 2008 to 18th place in 2013) as well as Japan, Switzerland, and Denmark, which have all remained among the top four countries in the rankings.[7]

With learning so essential in modern organizations, it is important to provide training that is effective. An effective training program actually teaches what it is designed to teach, and participants learn skills and behaviours that will help the organization achieve its goals. Training programs may increase employees' competence and performance, enable the organization to respond to change, reduce turnover, enhance worker safety, improve customer service and product design, and meet many other goals. To achieve those goals, HR professionals approach training through **instructional design**—a process of systematically developing training to meet specified needs.[8]

instructional design
A process of systematically developing training to meet specified needs.

A complete instructional design process includes the steps shown in Figure 6.1. It begins with an assessment of the needs for training—what the organization requires that its people learn. Next, the organization ensures that employees are ready for training in terms of their attitudes, motivation, basic skills, and work environment. The third step is to plan the training program, including the program's objectives, instructors, and methods. The organization then implements the program. Finally, evaluating the results of the training provides feedback for planning future training programs. For an example of a company that effectively uses this process, see the nearby "HR Best Practices" box.

To carry out this process more efficiently and effectively, a growing number of organizations are using a **learning management system (LMS)**, a computer application that automates the administration,

learning management system (LMS)
A computer application that automates the administration, development, and delivery of training and development programs.

FIGURE 6.1

Stages of Instructional Design

HR Best Practices

Training Is a Well-Oiled Machine for Jiffy Lube

Most car owners know that regular oil changes are an essential part of their vehicle's maintenance, but if they aren't do-it-yourselfers, where should they take the car? Jiffy Lube (www.jiffylube.ca) tries to be the top choice by combining convenient locations with a reputation for professional service. Jiffy Lube has 20,000 employees and 2,000 service centres in Canada and the United States owned exclusively by franchisees, so Jiffy Lube could leave the employees' qualifications up to the service centre owners. Instead, the company has developed a training program aimed at ensuring that all its technicians are skilled in preventive maintenance. Franchise owners must ensure that all their technicians complete the training.

Jiffy Lube employs a staff of training experts in what it calls Jiffy Lube University (JLU). JLU provides Web-based in-store training and offers 60 courses on subjects such as customer service, technical procedures, and service standards. It also offers training in management skills such as leading, setting goals, and managing time, finances, and people. Together, these courses lead to ten different certifications. Each employee, depending on his or her position, is assigned to a training path requiring the completion of certain certifications within a specified time frame. For example, every new technician has 30 days to complete orientation and earn certifications in safety and product knowledge. Ken Barber, manager of learning and development for Jiffy Lube, describes these courses as "designed with our audience of 18- to 25-year-olds in mind." "So it's very interactive, there's a great deal of visuals involved [and] a lot of video. You can see as well as hear how to perform a service." Each training path defines the competencies the employee is supposed to learn, so that employees and their supervisors can readily see whether the employees are meeting expectations.

To develop the content of the training program, the JLU staff works with a Franchise Training Committee, which includes eight franchise managers. The committee reviews what the franchises are doing, identifies areas where changes are needed, and sets priorities for what training should emphasize. JLU also had the National Institute for Automotive Service Excellence (ASE) audit the training program to certify that the training materials and methods meet its quality standards.

Jiffy Lube's framework for learning is a four-part blended model. Most of the training material is delivered to employees online. Employees view the presentations on a computer and then take an online test to show they have learned the material. Their supervisors supplement the training by observing and coaching the employees on the job and noting their progress in guides created for that purpose. In addition, six full-time trainers travel around North America to deliver face-to-face management training. New supervisors receive a combination of computer-based and classroom training.

Franchise owners welcome the training program because it helps them succeed in meeting real-world challenges such as customer satisfaction and employee turnover. The technical training itself also helps to retain technicians. Seeing the training as part of a career path gives them a reason to stay and improve their earnings and status in the organization.

Although the program has so much going for it—employee satisfaction and ASE certification—the training team is serious about evaluation. It recently conducted an extensive evaluation of the entire program, updated the materials, and asked ASE to recertify the program. The company also surveyed franchise owners to make sure they remain satisfied that the program ensures they have qualified people. Jiffy Lube was recently awarded the No. 1 spot on the "2014 Training Top 125" awarded by the publication, *Training Magazine,* citing achievements including "a 900 percent increase in the number of stores at 100 percent certification, a reduction in turnover, a 93 percent approval rating by franchisees, and eight consecutive years of increased average revenue per customer and improved customer service scores."

Sources: Jiffy Lube, "About Jiffy Lube," www.jiffylube.com, accessed March 6, 2015; Lorri Freifeld, "Jiffy Lube Revs Up to No. 1," *Training Magazine,*" www.trainingmag.com/trgmag-article/jiffy-lube-revs-no-l retrieved March 6, 2015; Frank Kalman, "Jiffy Lube: Running Full Speed," *Chief Learning Officer,* May 20, 2013 www.clomedia.com/articles/jiffy-lube-running-full-speed, retrieved March 6, 2015; Jennifer J. Salopek, "Keeping Learning Well-Oiled," *T+D,* October 2011, pp. 32-35; "Best Practices and Outstanding Initiatives," *Training,* January/February 2011, EBSCOhost, http://web.ebscohost.com.

development, and delivery of a company's training programs.[9] Managers and employees can use the LMS to identify training and development needs and enrol in courses. LMSs can make learning programs more widely available and help companies reduce travel and other costs by providing online training. Administrative tools let managers track course enrolments and program completion. The system can be linked to the organization's performance management system, competency models, and other talent development resources in order to plan for and manage training needs, training outcomes, and associated rewards.

L○2 Explain how to assess training needs and determine employees' readiness.

What Is Needs Assessment?

HRC7

Instructional design logically should begin with a **needs assessment**, the process of evaluating the organization, individual employees, and employees' tasks to determine what kinds of training, if any, are necessary. As this definition indicates, the needs assessment answers questions in the three broad areas:[10]

needs assessment
The process of evaluating the organization, individual employees, and employees' tasks to determine what kinds of training, if any, are necessary.

1. *Organization*—What is the context in which training will occur?
2. *Person*—Who needs training?
3. *Task*—What topics should the training cover?

The answers to these questions provide the basis for planning an effective training program.

A variety of conditions may prompt an organization to conduct a needs assessment. Management may observe that some employees lack basic skills or are performing below expectations. Decisions to produce new products, apply new technology, or design new jobs should prompt a needs assessment because these changes tend to require new skills. The decision to conduct a needs assessment also may be prompted by outside forces, such as customer requests or legal requirements.

The outcome of the needs assessment is a set of decisions about how to address the issues that prompted the needs assessment. These decisions do not necessarily include a training program, because some issues should be resolved through methods other than training—for example, plans for better rewards to improve motivation, better hiring decisions, and better safety precautions.

Organization Analysis

Usually, the needs assessment begins with the **organization analysis**. This is a process for determining the appropriateness of training by evaluating the characteristics of the organization. The organization analysis looks at training needs in light of the organization's strategy, resources available for training, and management's support for training activities.

> **organization analysis**
> A process for determining the appropriateness of training by evaluating the characteristics of the organization.

Training needs will vary depending on whether the organization's strategy is based on growing or shrinking its workforce, whether it is seeking to serve a broad customer base or focusing on the specific needs of a narrow market segment, and various other strategic scenarios. An organization that concentrates on serving a niche market may need to continually update its workforce on a specialized skills set. A company cutting costs with a downsizing strategy may need to train employees in job search skills. The employees who remain following a downsizing may need cross-training so they can handle a wider variety of responsibilities.

Anyone planning a training program must consider whether the organization has the budget, time, and expertise for training. Even if training fits the organization's strategy, it can be viable only if the organization is willing to support the investment. Managers increase the success of training when they support it through such actions as helping trainees see how they can use their newly learned knowledge, skills, and behaviours on the job.[11] Conversely, the managers will be most likely to support training if the people planning it can show that it will solve a significant problem or result in a significant improvement, relative to its cost. Managers appreciate training proposals with specific goals, timetables, budgets, and methods for measuring success.

Person Analysis

Following the organizational assessment, needs assessment turns to the remaining areas of analysis: person and task. The **person analysis** is a process for determining individuals' needs and readiness for learning. It involves answering several questions:

> **person analysis**
> A process for determining individuals' needs and readiness for learning.

- Do performance deficiencies result from a lack of knowledge, skill, or ability? (If so, training is appropriate; if not, other solutions are more relevant.)
- Who needs training?
- Are these employees ready?

The answers to these questions help the manager identify whether training is appropriate and which employees need training. In certain situations, such as the introduction of a new technology or service, all employees may need training. However, when needs assessment is conducted in response to a performance issue, training is not always the best solution.

The person analysis is therefore critical when training is considered in response to a performance issue. In assessing the need for training, the manager should identify all the variables that can influence performance. The primary variables are the person's ability and skills, his or her mindset and motivation, the organization's input (including clear directions, necessary resources, and freedom from interference and distractions), performance feedback, and positive consequences to motivate good performance. Of these variables, only ability and skills can be affected by training. Therefore, before planning a training program, it is important to be sure that any performance issue results from a deficiency in knowledge and skills. Otherwise, training dollars will be wasted, because the training is unlikely to have much effect on performance.

The person analysis also should determine whether employees are ready to undergo training. In other words, the employees to receive training not only should require additional knowledge and skill, but must be willing and able to learn. (After our discussion of the needs assessment, we will explore the topic of employee readiness in greater detail.)

Task Analysis

The third area of needs assessment is **task analysis**, the process of identifying the tasks, knowledge, skills, and behaviours that training should emphasize. Usually, task analysis is conducted along with person analysis. Understanding shortcomings in performance usually requires knowledge about the tasks and work environment as well as the employee.

task analysis
The process of identifying the tasks, knowledge, skills, and behaviours that training should emphasize.

To carry out the task analysis, the HR professional looks at the conditions in which tasks are performed. These conditions include the equipment and environment of the job, time constraints (e.g., deadlines), safety considerations, and performance standards. These observations form the basis for a description of work activities, or the tasks required by the person's job. For a selected job, the analyst interviews employees and their supervisors to prepare a list of tasks performed in that job. Then the analyst validates the list by showing it to employees, supervisors, and other subject-matter experts and asking them to complete a questionnaire about the *importance, frequency,* and *difficulty* of the tasks. The information from these questionnaires is the basis for determining which tasks will be the focus of the training.

Readiness for Learning

Effective training requires not only a program that addresses real needs, but also a condition of employee readiness. **Readiness for learning** is a combination of employee characteristics and positive work environment that permit learning. It exists when employees are able and eager to learn and their organizations encourage learning.

readiness for learning
A combination of employee characteristics and positive work environment that permit learning.

Employee Readiness Characteristics

To be ready to learn, employees need basic learning skills, especially *cognitive ability,* which includes being able to use written and spoken language, solve math problems, and use logic to solve problems. However, recent forecasts of the skill levels of the workforce indicate that many companies will have to work with employees who lack basic skills.[12] For example, they may need to provide literacy training before some employees will be ready to participate in job-related training.

Employees learn more from training programs when they are highly motivated to learn—that is, when they really want to learn the content of the training program.[13] Employees tend to feel this way if they believe they are able to learn, see potential benefits from the training program, are aware of their need to learn, see a fit between the training and their career goals, and have the basic skills needed for participating in the program. Managers can influence a ready attitude in a variety of ways. For example, they can provide feedback that encourages employees, establish rewards for learning, and communicate with employees about the organization's career paths and future needs.

Work Environment

Readiness also depends on two broad characteristics of the work environment: situational constraints and social support.[14] *Situational constraints* are the limits on training's effectiveness that arise from the situation or the conditions within the organization. Constraints can include a lack of money for training, lack of time for training or practising, and failure to provide proper tools and materials for learning or applying the lessons of training.

Social support refers to the ways the organization's people encourage training, including giving trainees positive feedback and encouragement, sharing information about participating in training programs, and expressing positive attitudes toward the organization's training programs. Support can come from employees' peers. Readiness for learning is greater in an organization where employees share knowledge, encourage one another to learn, and have a positive attitude about carrying the extra load when co-workers are attending classes. The organization can also formally provide peer support by establishing **communities of practice**—groups of employees who work together, learn from each other, and develop a common understanding of how to get work accomplished. For example, group members can share how they coped with challenges related to what they learned. Schlumberger, which provides oil field services, sets up online communities of practice, where geologists, physicists, managers, engineers, and other employees around the world can trade knowledge to solve problems.[15] Organizations can also assign experienced employees as mentors to trainees, providing advice and support.

communities of practice
Groups of employees who work together, learn from each other, and develop a common understanding of how to get work accomplished.

LO3   Describe how to plan and design an effective training program.

How to Plan and Design the Training Program

Planning begins with establishing objectives for the training program. Based on those objectives, the planner (usually a specialist in the HR department) decides who will provide the training, what topics the training will cover, what training methods to use, and how to evaluate the training.

Objectives of the Program

Formally establishing objectives for the training program has several benefits. First, a training program based on clear objectives will be more focused and more likely to succeed. Employees learn best when they know what the training is supposed to accomplish. Finally, down the road, establishing objectives provides a basis for measuring whether the program succeeded, as we will discuss later in this chapter.

Effective training objectives have three components:

● They include a statement of what the employee is expected to do, the quality or level of performance that is acceptable, and the conditions under which the employee is to apply what he or she learned (for instance, physical conditions, mental stresses, or equipment failure).[16]

● They include performance standards that are measurable.

● They identify the resources needed to carry out the desired performance or outcome. Successful training requires employees to learn and also employers to provide the necessary resources.

A related issue at the outset is who will participate in the training program. Some training programs are developed for all employees of the organization or all members of a team. Other training programs identify individuals who lack required skills or have potential to be promoted, then provide training in the areas of need that are identified for the particular employees. When deciding whom to include in training, the organization has to avoid illegal discrimination. The organization must not—intentionally or unintentionally—exclude anyone due to a prohibited ground of discrimination, for example, sex, race, or age. During the training, all participants should receive equal treatment, such as equal opportunities for practise. In addition, the training program should provide accommodation for trainees with disabilities.

In-House or Contracted Out?

An organization can provide an effective training program, even if it lacks expertise in training. Many companies and consultants provide training services to organizations. Colleges, universities, technical institutes, and polytechnics often work with employers to train employees in a variety of skills.

To select a training service, an organization can send several vendors a *request for proposal (RFP)*, a document outlining the type of service needed, the type and number of references needed, the number of employees to be trained, the date by which the training is to be completed, and the date by which proposals should be received. A complete RFP also indicates funding for the project and the process by which the organization will determine its level of satisfaction. Putting together a request for proposal is time-consuming, but worthwhile because it helps the organization clarify its objectives, compare vendors, and measure results.

Vendors that believe they are able to provide the services outlined in the RFP submit proposals that provide the types of information requested. The organization reviews the proposals to eliminate any vendors that do not meet requirements and to compare the vendors that do qualify. They check references and select a candidate, based on the proposal and the vendor's answers to questions about its experience, work samples, and evidence that its training programs meet objectives.

The cost of purchasing training from a contractor can vary substantially. In general, it is much costlier to purchase specialized training tailored to the organization's requirements than to participate in a seminar or training course that teaches general skills or knowledge. Even in organizations that send employees to outside training programs, someone in the organization may be responsible for coordinating the overall training program. Called *training administration*, this is typically the responsibility of a human resources professional. Training administration includes activities before, during, and after training sessions.

What Training Methods Are Available?

Whether the organization prepares its own training programs or buys training from other organizations, it is important to verify that the content of the training relates directly to the training objectives. Relevance to the organization's needs and objectives ensures that training money is well spent. Tying training content closely to objectives also improves trainees' learning, because it increases the likelihood that the training will be meaningful and helpful.

After deciding on the goals and content of the training program, planners must decide how the training will be conducted. As we will describe in the next section, a wide variety of methods are available. Training methods fall into the broad categories described in Table 6.2: presentation, hands-on, and group-building methods.

Training programs may use these methods alone or in combination. In general, the methods used should be suitable for the course content and the learning abilities of the participants. The following sections explore the options in greater detail.

Figure 6.2 shows the percentages of companies using various broad categories of training methods. Although instructor-led classroom training continues to be the most dominantly used delivery method,

TABLE 6.2

Categories of Training Methods

Method	Techniques	Applications
Presentation methods: learners receive information provided by others	Lectures, workbooks, video clips, podcasts, websites	Conveying facts or comparing alternatives
Hands-on methods: learners are actively involved in trying out skills	On-the-job training, simulations, role-plays, computer games	Teaching specific skills; showing how skills are related to job or how to handle interpersonal issues
Group-building methods: learners share ideas and experiences, build group identities, learn about interpersonal relationships and the group	Group discussions, experiential programs, team training	Establishing teams or work groups; managing performance of teams or work groups

FIGURE 6.2

Delivery Methods as Percentage of Overall Learning Time, 2010 to 2012–2013

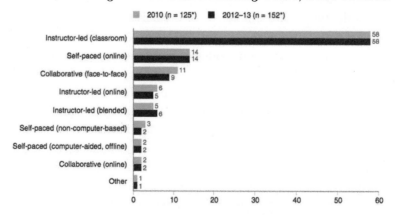

*organizations providing learning delivery methods summing to 100 per cent

Source: Colin Hall, *Learning and Development Outlook, 12th Edition: Strong Learning Organizations, Strong Leadership* (Ottawa: The Conference Board of Canada, February 2014), p. 41.

it has gradually lost ground to other methods. "In 2000, 80 percent of all learning delivery was done in the classroom, but by 2010, classroom learning represented just 58 percent of learning delivery, and it remained at this level for 2012–2013."[17]

Classroom Instruction

At school, we tend to associate learning with classroom instruction, and that type of training is most widely used in the workplace, too. Classroom instruction typically involves an instructor leading a group. Instructors often use slides, discussions, case studies, question-and-answer sessions, and role playing. Actively involving trainees enhances learning.

When the course objectives call for presenting information on a specific topic to many trainees, classroom instruction is one of the least expensive and least time-consuming ways to accomplish that goal. Learning will be more effective if trainers enhance lectures with job-related examples and opportunities for hands-on learning.

Technology has expanded the notion of the classroom to classes of trainees scattered in various locations. With *distance learning*, learners at different locations attend programs online, using their computers to view lectures, participate in discussions, and share documents. Technology applications in distance learning may include videoconferencing, email, instant messaging, document-sharing software, and web cameras. Distance learning provides many of the benefits of classroom training without the cost and time of travel to a shared location. The major disadvantage of distance learning is that interaction between the instructor and audience may be limited.

Audiovisual Training

Presentation methods need not require learners to attend a class. Learners can also work independently, using course material in workbooks, on DVDs, or on the Internet. Audiovisual techniques such as PowerPoint, Prezi, or other presentation software, and video or audio clips can also supplement classroom instruction.

Mobile technology is useful not only for entertainment, but can also be used for employees who are mobile and need to be in touch with the office. Smartphones, tablets, and laptop computers give employees additional flexibility for how and when they participate in training programs.

With modern technology, audiovisual material can easily be made available on a variety of devices, from desktop computers to the smaller screen of smartphones and tablets. Today's mobile devices can display charts, play audio podcasts, and link to video clips. The "HR How-To" box offers ideas for effectively delivering training on mobile devices.

Users of audiovisual training often have some control over the presentation. They can review material and may be able to slow down or speed up the lesson. Videos can show situations and equipment that cannot be easily demonstrated in a classroom. Another advantage of audiovisual presentations is that they give learners a consistent presentation, not affected by an individual trainer's goals and skills. The problems associated with these methods may include trying to present too much material, poorly written dialogue, overuse of features such as humour or music, and drama that distracts the key points. A well-written and carefully produced video can overcome such problems.

Computer-based Training

Although almost all organizations use classroom training, new technologies are gaining in popularity as technology improves and becomes less expensive. With computer-based training, participants receive course materials and instruction distributed over the Internet or on a storage device such as a USB

HR How-To

Developing Training Content for Mobile Devices

Workers are already using—or would like to use—a variety of mobile devices. Many carry a smartphone or other devices for listening to music and watching videos. Some download books and magazines onto e-readers; others have a tablet or a laptop computer. All of these devices have the potential to deliver effective training. The following tips can help trainers ensure that m-learning (mobile learning) and the associated apps are well developed and tailored to users' needs and the company's objectives:

- Keep the content brief and engaging. Text should get right to the point and consider combining both audio and visual cues to enable recall and recognition. For example, the mobile app, CPR Tempo, provides both audio and visual cues to assist with the timing of chest compressions in learning cardiopulmonary resuscitation techniques.

- Deliver "chunks" of content and make it easy to find that topic again, in case the learner wants to review it later. For example, the project manager professional certification, PMP ExamPrep, chunks learning by providing questions using mobile flashcards.

- Design screen displays to be as simple as possible so they download quickly and are easy to read. Use minimal graphics; avoid background images altogether.

- Include controls to pause, restart, and stop content. This enables users to cope with interruptions so they can give the training their full attention while it is in progress.

- Think about what kinds of content employees will want to access when they are on the go. A salesperson might welcome background information about clients or product specifications. Lessons that ask the learner to ponder a complex problem would be less effective.

- Be sure the content designers know about all the mobile devices that will be used. The design should use only programs that run on every device that is delivering the content. The Flash media player, for example, does not work as well on some devices. Also, different devices will lend themselves to different kinds of feedback and assessment. Many have touch screens or microphones; on others, typing is relatively easy.

Sources: Margaret Driscoll and Angela van Barneveld, "Applying Learning Theory to Mobile Learning," *TD at Work*, January 2015; Marissa Garff, "Implementing M-Learning: Make the Dream a Reality," *T+D*, January 2012, p. 16; Naomi Norman, "Mobile Learning Made Easy," *T+D*, December 2011, pp. 52–55; Julie Brink, "M-Learning: The Future of Training Technology," *T+D*, February 2011, pp. 27–29.

memory stick. Often, these materials are interactive, so participants can answer questions and try out techniques, with course materials adjusted according to participants' responses. Online training programs may allow trainees to submit questions and to participate in online discussions. Multimedia capabilities enable computers to provide sounds, images, and video presentations, along with text. Computer-based training is generally less expensive than putting an instructor in a classroom of trainees.

Current applications of computer-based training can extend its benefits:

- **E-learning** involves receiving training via the Internet or the organization's intranet, typically through some combination of web-based training modules, distance learning, and virtual classrooms. E-learning uses electronic networks for delivering and sharing information, and it offers tools and information for helping learners improve performance. Training programs may include links to other online information resources and to participants and experts for collaboration on problem solving. The e-learning system may also process enrolments, test and evaluate participants, and monitor progress.

e-learning
Receiving training via the Internet or the organization's intranet.

- **Electronic performance support systems (EPSSs)** are computer applications that provide access to skills training, information, and expert advice when a problem occurs on the job.[18] Employees needing guidance can use the EPSS to look up the particular information they need, such as detailed instructions on how to perform an unfamiliar task. Using an EPSS is faster and more relevant than attending classes, even classes offered online.

electronic performance support systems (EPSSs)
Computer application that provides access to skills training, information, and expert advice as needed.

The best e-learning combines the advantages of the Internet with the principles of a good learning environment. It takes advantage of the Web's dynamic nature and ability to use many positive learning features, including hyperlinks to other training sites and content, control by the learner, and ability for learners to collaborate.

On-The-Job Training

Although people often associate training with classrooms, much learning occurs while employees are performing their jobs. **On-the-job training (OJT)** refers to training methods in which a person with job experience and skill guides trainees in practising job skills at the workplace. This type of training takes various forms, including apprenticeships and internships.

on-the-job training (OJT)
Training methods in which a person with job experience and skill guides trainees in practising job skills at the workplace.

An **apprenticeship** is a work-study training method that teaches job skills through a combination of on-the-job training and classroom training. The OJT component of an apprenticeship involves the apprentice assisting a certified journeyperson in the work place. Typically, the technical training is provided by polytechnics, local trade schools, high schools, community colleges, or other technical institutes. On average, 85 percent of the apprentice's two-to-five-year training is spent in the workplace, the rest is spent at a training institution.[19] Some apprenticeship programs are sponsored by individual

apprenticeship
A work-study training method that teaches job skills through a combination of on-the-job training and classroom training.

companies, others by employee unions. Apprenticeship programs are usually administered by provincial and territorial government departments with support from advisory bodies such as apprenticeship and certification boards. To provide greater mobility across Canada for skilled workers, apprentices who have completed their training and certified journeypersons are able to obtain a "Red Seal" endorsement after completing an interprovincial standards exam that allows them to practise their trade anywhere in Canada.[20] For trainees, a major advantage of apprenticeship is the ability to earn an income while learning a trade, that is, "earning while learning." In addition, training through an apprenticeship is usually effective because it involves hands-on learning and extensive practice.

An **internship** is on-the-job learning sponsored by an educational institution as a component of an academic program. The sponsoring school works with local employers to place students in positions where they can gain experience related to their area of study. For example, summer internships are an integral component of the University of British Columbia's MBA program.[21]

internship
On-the-job learning sponsored by an educational institution as a component of an academic program.

Cooperative education is a plan of higher education that incorporates paid work experience as an important component of academic studies. Cooperative education is being readily accepted by government, business, and industry in Canada and throughout the world. Universities, colleges, polytechnics, other technical schools, and high schools are offering co-op programs to thousands of students in a growing number of disciplines.[22]

cooperative education
A plan of higher education that incorporates paid work experience as an integral part of academic studies.

To be effective, OJT programs should include several characteristics:

- The organization should issue a policy statement describing the purpose of OJT and emphasizing the organization's support for it.
- The organization should specify who is accountable for conducting OJT. This accountability should be included in the relevant job descriptions.
- The organization should review OJT practices at companies in similar industries.
- Managers and peers should be trained in OJT principles.
- Employees who conduct OJT should have access to lesson plans, checklists, procedure manuals, training manuals, learning contracts, and progress report forms.
- Before conducting OJT with an employee, the organization should assess the employees' level of basic skills.[23]

The OJT program at Canadian Air Transport Security Authority (CATSA, www.catsa.gc.ca) has many of these characteristics. After completing extensive classroom training including role-plays, and hands-on practise in a training lab, screening officers participate in "live-line-on-the-job training." Point leaders pay careful attention to the screening officers while they conduct various searches and investigations of passengers and their belongings. One class of trainees intercepted an item that looked like a rocket propelled grenade on the X-ray machine. After the police responded and searched the bag, it turned out to be cologne. Ten minutes later, on the same screening line, the search of a passenger's carry-on bag yielded over $30,000 in U.S. currency. Local police and Canadian Border Services Agency officers attended the checkpoint and conducted their investigations. Through this live-line OJT, trainees received invaluable first-hand experience of how to deal with the discovery of contraband at the screening checkpoint and work with stakeholders such as police, airport security, air carriers, and airport authorities.[24]

Simulations

A **simulation** is a training method that represents a real-life situation, with learners making decisions resulting in outcomes that mirror what would happen on the job. Simulations enable learners to see the impact of their decisions in an artificial, risk-free environment. They are used for teaching production and process skills as well as management and interpersonal skills. Airlines purchasing Boeing's (www.boeing.com) latest-model passenger jet, the 787 Dreamliner, use simulators to train the pilots who will fly it. Although the 787 flight deck is designed with the same layout as the familiar 777, it has a new feature called the head-up display (HUD). When flying conditions are poor, this small see-through screen drops down in pilots' line of vision to provide information to help them navigate. Pilots need to practise with the simulator until they are accustomed to landing the jet while using the HUD.[25]

simulation
A training method that represents a real-life situation, with learners making decisions resulting in outcomes that mirror what would happen on the job.

Simulators must have elements identical to those found in the work environment. The simulator needs to respond exactly as equipment would under the conditions and response given by the learner. For this reason, simulators are expensive to develop and need constant updating as new information about the work environment becomes available. Still, they are an excellent training method when the risks of a mistake on the job are great. Learners do not have to be afraid of the impact of bad decisions when using the simulator, as they would be with on-the-job training. Learners tend to be enthusiastic about this type of training and to learn quickly because the lessons are generally related very closely to job performance.

When simulations are conducted online, trainees often participate by creating **avatars**, or computer depictions of themselves, which they manipulate onscreen to play roles as workers or other participants in a job-related situation. One example is BP's (www.bp.com) use of Second Life to train new gas station employees in the safety features of gasoline storage tanks and piping systems. In Second Life, BP built three-dimensional renderings of the tank and pipe systems at a typical gas station. Trainees can "see" underground and observe the effect of using safety devices to control the flow of gasoline in a way they could never have done in real life.[26]

avatars
Computer depictions of trainees, which the trainees manipulate in an online role-play.

Another way to enhance the simulation experience is to use **virtual reality**, a computer-based technology that provides an interactive, three-dimensional learning experience. Using specialized equipment or viewing the virtual model on a computer screen, learners move through the simulated environment and interact with its components. Devices relay information from the environment to the participants' senses. For example, audio interfaces, gloves that provide a sense of touch, treadmills, or motion platforms create a realistic but artificial environment. Devices also communicate information about the trainee's movements to a computer. Virtual reality applications are as diverse as surgery and welding.[27]

virtual reality
A computer-based technology that provides an interactive, three-dimensional learning experience.

Business Games and Case Studies

Training programs use business games and case studies to develop employees' management skills. A case study is a detailed description of a situation that trainees study and discuss. Cases are designed to develop higher-order thinking skills, such as the ability to analyze and evaluate information. They also can be a safe way to encourage learners to take appropriate risks, by giving them practise in weighing and acting on uncertain outcomes. There are many sources of case studies, including the Richard Ivey School of Business (www.ivey.uwo.ca), Wilfrid Laurier University (www.wlu.ca), Harvard Business School (www.hbs.edu), and McGraw-Hill (www.mcgrawhill.com). One dilemma associated with the use of case studies is that they often require more time than the audience has available time (or attention span) for. The *mini case study* is intended to be delivered with less time e.g., 30 minutes, but still offers a powerful and engaging learning tool, albeit with less detail.[28]

With business games, learners gather information, analyze it, and make decisions that influence the outcome of the game. For instance, Markstrat integrated into a marketing course, requires participants to use strategic thinking (such as analyzing competitors) to increase their share of the market.[29] Games stimulate learning because they actively involve participants and mirror the competitive nature of business. A realistic game may be more meaningful to trainees than techniques such as classroom instruction.

Learning with case studies and games requires that participants come together to discuss the cases or the progress of the game. This requires face-to-face or virtual meetings. Also, participants must be willing to be actively involved in analyzing the situation and defending their decisions.

Behaviour Modelling

Research suggests that one of the most effective ways to teach interpersonal skills is through behaviour modelling.[30] This involves training sessions in which participants observe other people demonstrating the desired behaviour, then have opportunities to practise the behaviour themselves. For example, a training program could involve several days of four-hour sessions, each focusing on one interpersonal skill, such as communicating or coaching. At the beginning of each session, participants hear the reasons for using the key behaviours, then they watch a video of an expert performing the key behaviours. They practise through role-playing and receive feedback about their performance. In addition, they evaluate the performance of the expert in the video and discuss how they can apply the behaviour on the job.

Experiential Programs

To develop teamwork and leadership skills, some organizations enrol their employees in a form of training called **experiential programs**. In experiential programs, participants learn concepts and then apply them by simulating the behaviours involved and analyzing the activity, connecting it with real-life situations.[31]

experiential programs
Training programs in which participants learn concepts and apply them by simulating behaviours involved and analyzing the activity, connecting it with real-life situations.

Experiential training programs should follow several guidelines. A program should be related to a specific business problem. Participants should feel challenged and move outside their comfort zones but within limits that keep their motivation strong and help them understand the purpose of the program.

One form of experiential program, called **adventure learning**, uses challenging, structured physical activities, which may include difficult sports such as dogsledding or mountain-climbing. Other activities may be structured tasks like climbing walls, completing rope courses, climbing ladders, or making "trust falls" (in which each trainee falls backward into the arms of other group members).

adventure learning
A teamwork and leadership training program based on the use of challenging, structured physical activities.

The impact of adventure learning programs has not been rigorously tested, but participants report they gained a greater understanding of themselves and the ways that the organization insist that entire work groups participate together. This encourages people to see, discuss, and change the kinds of behaviour that keep the group from performing well.

Before requiring employees to participate in experiential programs, the organization should consider the possible drawbacks. Because these programs are usually physically demanding and often require participants to touch each other, companies face certain risks. Some employees may be injured or may feel that they were sexually harassed or that their privacy was invaded. Also, human rights and employment equity legislation (discussed in Chapter 2) raises questions about requiring employees with disabilities to participate in physically demanding training experiences.

Team Training

A possible alternative to experiential programs is team training, which coordinates the performance of individuals who work together to achieve a common goal. An organization may benefit from providing such training to groups when group members must share information and group performance depends on the performance of the individual group members. Success depends on individuals coordinating their activities to make decisions, perhaps in dangerous work situations performed in crews or teams—for example, the airline industry or in the military.

Ways to conduct team training include cross-training and coordination training.[32] In **cross-training**, team members understand and practise each other's skills so they are prepared to step in and take another member's place.

cross-training
Team training in which team members understand and practise each other's skills so that they are prepared to step in and take another member's place.

For example, Toronto Hydro (www.torontohydro.com) cross-trains supervisors so they can work across specializations. Jodi Engle, manager of organizational development and performance at Toronto Hydro says, "This enhances their skills. It's a great retention strategy, it gives them more variety and makes their job more meaningful."[33]

Coordination training trains the team in how to share information and decisions to obtain the best team performance. This type of training is especially important for commercial aviation and surgical teams. Both of these kinds of teams must monitor different aspects of equipment and the environment at the same time sharing information to make the most effective decisions regarding patient care or aircraft safety and performance.

Training may also target the skills needed by the teams' leaders. **Team leader training** refers to training people in the skills necessary for team leadership. For example, the training may be aimed at helping team leaders learn to resolve conflicts or coordinate activities.

coordination training
Team training that teaches the team how to share information and make decisions to obtain the best team performance.

team leader training
Training in the skills necessary for effectively leading the organization's teams.

One of the most important features of organizations today is teamwork. Experiential programs, including team-building exercises like wall-climbing and rafting, help build trust and cooperation among employees.

Action Learning

Another form of group building is **action learning**. In this type of training, teams or work groups get an actual problem, work on solving it, commit to an action plan, and are accountable for carrying out the plan. Ideally, the project is one for which the efforts and results will be visible not only to participants but also to others in the organization. The visibility and impact of the task are intended to make participation exciting, relevant, and engaging. To heighten the learning, organizations can get their best leaders involved as mentors and coaches to the participants.

> **action learning**
> Training in which teams get an actual problem, work on solving it, commit to an action plan, and are accountable for carrying it out.

The effectiveness of action learning has not been formally evaluated. This type of training seems to result in a great deal of learning, however; and employees are able to apply what they learn, because it involves actual problems the organization is facing. The group approach also helps teams identify behaviours that interfere with problem solving.

L○4 Summarize how to implement and evaluate a successful training program.

Implementing and Evaluating the Training Program

Learning permanently changes behaviour. For employees to acquire knowledge and skills in the training program and apply what they have learned in their jobs, the training program must be implemented in a way that applies what we know about how people learn.

Principles of Learning

Researchers have identified a number of ways employees learn best.[34] Table 6.3 summarizes ways training can best encourage learning. In general, effective training communicates learning objectives clearly,

TABLE 6.3

Ways That Training Helps Employees Learn

Training Activity	Ways to Provide Training Activity
Communicate the learning objective.	Demonstrate the performance to be expected. Give examples of questions to be answered.
Use distinctive, attention-getting messages.	Emphasize key points. Use pictures, not just words.
Limit the content of training.	Group lengthy material into chunks. Provide a visual image of the course material. Provide opportunities to repeat and practise material.
Guide trainees as they learn.	Use words as reminders about sequence of activities. Use words and pictures to relate concepts to one another and to their context. Prompt trainees to evaluate whether they understand and are using effective tactics to learn the material.
Elaborate on the subject.	Present the material in different contexts and settings. Relate new ideas to previously learned concepts. Practise in a variety of contexts and settings.
Provide memory cues.	Suggest memory aids. Use familiar sounds or rhymes as memory cues.
Transfer course content to the workplace.	Design the learning environment so that it has elements in common with the workplace. Require learners to develop action plans that apply training content to their jobs. Use words that link the course to the workplace.
Provide feedback about performance.	Tell trainees how accurately and quickly they are performing their new skill. Show how trainees have met the objectives of the training.

Sources: Adapted from R. M. Gagne, "Learning Processes and Instruction," *Training Research Journal I* (1995/96), pp. 17–28; and Traci Sitzmann, "Self-Regulating Online Course Engagement," *T&D*, March 2010, Business & Company Resource Center, http://galenet.galegroup.com.

presents information in distinctive and memorable ways, and helps trainees link the subject matter to their jobs.

Employees are most likely to learn when training is linked to their current job experiences and tasks.[35] There are a number of ways trainers can make this link. Training sessions should present material using familiar concepts, terms, and examples. As far as possible, the training context—such as the physical setting or the images presented on a computer—should mirror the work environment. Along with physical elements, the context should include emotional elements.

To fully understand and remember the content of the training, employees need a chance to demonstrate and practise what they have learned. Trainers should provide ways to actively involve the trainees, have them practise repeatedly, and have them complete tasks within a time that is appropriate in light of the learning objectives. Practise requires physically carrying out the desired behaviours, not just describing them. People tend to benefit most from practise that occurs over several sessions, rather than one long practise session.[36]

Training sessions should offer feedback so that trainees understand whether or not they are succeeding. Effective feedback focuses on specific behaviours and is delivered as soon as possible after the learners practise or demonstrate what they have learned.[37]

Well-designed training helps people remember the content. Training programs need to break information into chunks that people can remember. Research suggests that people can attend to no more than four to five items at a time. If a concept or procedure involves more than five items, the training program should deliver information in shorter sessions or chunks.[38] Other ways to make information more memorable include presenting it with visual images and practising some tasks enough that they become automatic.

Written materials should have an appropriate reading level. A simple way to assess **readability**—the difficulty level of written materials—is to look at the words being used and at the length of sentences. If training materials are too difficult to understand, several adjustments can help. The basic approach is to re-write the material looking for ways to simplify it:

- Substitute simple, concrete words for unfamiliar or abstract words.
- Divide long sentences into two or more short sentences.
- Divide long paragraphs into two or more short paragraphs.
- Add checklists (like this one) and illustrations to clarify the text.

Another approach is to substitute video, hands-on learning, or other nonwritten methods for some of the written material. A longer-term solution is to use tests to identify employees who need training to improve their reading levels and to provide that training first.

readability
The difficulty level of written materials.

Measuring Results of Training

HRC 2, 7, 9

After a training program ends, or at intervals during an ongoing training program, organizations should ensure that the training is meeting objectives. The stage to prepare for evaluating a training program is when the program is being developed. Along with designing course objectives and content, the planner should identify how to measure achievement of objectives. Depending on the objectives, the evaluation can use one or more of Kirkpatrick's evaluation levels:[39]

- Level 1: Learner reactions
- Level 2: Demonstration of learning
- Level 3: Behaviour change
- Level 4: Business results
- Level 5: Cost-benefit analysis

The Conference Board of Canada reports that over 92 percent of organizations administer reaction-level training evaluations, and that an increasing number of organizations are conducting learning, behaviour, and business results-level training evaluations.[40]

The usual way to measure whether participants have acquired information is to administer tests on paper or electronically. Trainers or supervisors can observe whether participants demonstrate the desired skills and behaviours. Changes in company performance have a variety of measures, many of which organizations keep track of for preparing performance appraisals, annual reports, and other routine documents, in order to demonstrate the highest measure of success—business results and cost-benefit analysis.

Evaluation Methods

Ultimately, the goal of implementation is **transfer of learning**, or on-the-job use of knowledge, skills, and behaviours learned in training. Transfer of learning requires that employees actually learn the content of the training program. Then, for employees to apply what they learned, certain conditions must be in place: social support, technical support, and self-management.

transfer of learning
On-the-job use of knowledge, skills, and behaviours learned in training.

Social support, as we saw in the discussion of readiness for training, includes support from the organization and from learner' peers. Before, during, and after implementation, the organization's managers need to emphasize the importance of training, encourage their employees to attend training programs, and point out connections between training content and employees' job requirements.

Transfer of learning is greater when organizations also provide technical resources that help people acquire and share information. Technical support may come from an electronic performance support system (EPSS), described earlier as a type of computer-based training. Knowledge management system including online and database tools also make it easy for employees to look up information they want to review or consult later.

Organizations are beginning to provide a strong combination of social and technical support for transfer of learning by setting up social media applications that promote learning as discussed in the e-HRM feature: Social Learning.

 E-HRM

Social learning—applying social learning to promote informal learning aligned with organizational strategy.

Evaluation of training also should evaluate training *outcomes,* that is, what (if anything) has changed as a result of the training. The relevant training outcomes are the ones related to the organization's goals for the training and its overall performance. Possible outcomes include the following:

- Learner satisfaction with the training program (reaction)
- Information such as facts, techniques, and procedures that learners can recall after the training (learning)
- Skills that learners can demonstrate in tests or on the job (behaviour)
- Changes in behaviour related to the content of the training, for example, concern for safety or support of diversity (behaviour)
- Improvements in individual, group, or company performance, for example, higher customer satisfaction, more sales, fewer defects (business results)
- Calculation to determine if the monetary benefits of the training program outweigh the costs (cost-benefit analysis). Note: *Return on investment (ROI)* refers to the monetary benefits of the investment compared to the amount invested, expressed as a percentage.

Training is a significant part of many organizations' budgets. Businesses that invest in training want to achieve a high return on investment—the monetary benefits of the investment compared to the amount invested, expressed as a percentage. For example, IBM's e-learning program for new managers, Basic Blue, costs $8,708 per manager.[41] The company has measured an improvement in each new manager's performance worth $415,000. That gives IBM a benefit of $415,000 − $8,708 = $406,292 for each manager. This is an extremely large return on investment: $406,292/$8,708 = 46.65, or 4,665 percent! In other words, for every $1 that IBM invests in Basic Blue, it receives almost $47.

Did You KNOW?

Use of Training Evaluation Methods

Most learning activities are evaluated at a Level 1 (Learner reactions).

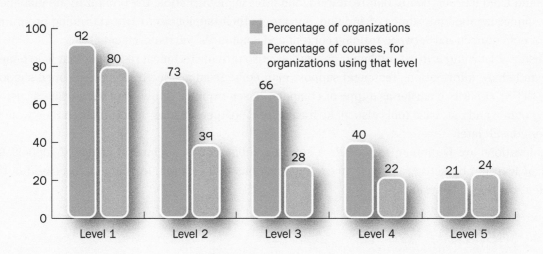

Legend:
- Percentage of organizations
- Percentage of courses, for organizations using that level

Data:
- Level 1: 92, 80
- Level 2: 73, 39
- Level 3: 66, 28
- Level 4: 40, 22
- Level 5: 21, 24

Source: Colin Hall, "Learning and Development Outlook, 12th Edition: Strong Learning Organizations, Strong Leadership" (Ottawa: The Conference Board of Canada, February 2014), p. 66.

For any of these methods, the most accurate but most costly way to evaluate the training program is to assess performance, knowledge, or behaviours among all employees before the training, then to train only some of the employees. After the training is complete, the performance, knowledge, or behaviour are again assessed, and the trained group is compared to the untrained group. A simpler but less accurate way to assess the training is to conduct a *pre-test* and *post-test* on all trainees, comparing their performance, knowledge, or behaviours before and after the training. This form of measurement does not rule out the possibility that change resulted from something other than training (e.g., a change in the rewards system). The simplest approach is to use only a post-test. Of course, this type of measurement does not enable accurate comparisons, but it may be sufficient, depending on the cost and purpose of the training.

The purpose of evaluating training is to help with future decisions about the organization's training programs. Using the evaluation, the organization may identify a need to modify the training and gain information about the kinds of changes needed. The organization may decide to expand on successful areas of training and cut back on training that has not delivered significant benefits.

LO5 Describe methods for employee orientation and diversity management.

Applications of Training

Two categories of training that have become widespread among North American companies are orientation of new employees (onboarding) and training in how to manage workforce diversity.

Orientation of New Employees—Onboarding

HRC 3, 4, 7

Many employees receive their first training during their first days on the job. This training is the organization's **orientation** program—its training designed to prepare employees to perform their jobs effectively, learn about the organization, and establish work relationships. Organizations provide for orientation because, no matter how realistic the information provided during employment interviews and site visits, people feel shock and surprise when they start a new job.[42] Also, employees need to become familiar with job tasks and learn the details of the organization's practices, policies, and procedures. Many HR professionals are rethinking traditional approaches to orientation due to pressures to maximize early productivity and engagement by creating a positive first impression. According to the Human Capital Institute (www.hci.org), 90 percent of newly hired employees decide whether they'll remain with the company during the first six months.[43] Increasingly, employee orientation is referred to as *onboarding*, reflecting the critical role these programs play.

> **orientation**
> Training designed to prepare employees to perform their jobs effectively, learn about their organization, and establish work relationships.

The objectives of orientation programs include making new employees familiar with the organization's rules, policies, and procedures. Such a program provides information about the overall company and about the department in which the new employee will be working. The topics include social as well as technical aspects of the job.

Orientation processes may combine various training methods such as printed and audiovisual materials, classroom instruction, on-the-job training, and e-learning. Decisions about how to conduct the orientation depend on the type of material to be covered and the number of new employees, among other factors. At I Love Rewards—now Achievers (www.achievers.com), the first five days on the job are spent in the "I Love Rewards University," where new recruits "sit in a room together and learn everything from dress code to how to make the organization's drink of choice, the RedPoint (part Sour Puss raspberry liqueur, part Crown Royal, and part Red Bull)."[44] At Bayer Inc. (www.bayer.ca) new employee orientation starts with making the new hires feel like they're already part of the company before their first day on the job. Bayer Inc.'s Toronto office uses an approach to onboarding new employees called "Hello Bayer," in which new hires log on to the internal onboarding website and take a virtual tour of the facility—"great for locating their cubicle's nearest washroom—or read up on workplace minutiae like parking spaces, security passes, and even company acronyms." Philip Blake, president and CEO of Bayer says, "It's all about feeling comfortable, fitting in and feeling wanted and welcome. This onboarding gives people the opportunity to see everything that they're coming to."[45]

Diversity Training

HRC 2, 7

In response to human rights and employment equity legislation and market forces, many organizations today are concerned about managing diversity—creating an inclusive environment that allows all employees to contribute to organizational goals and experience personal growth. This environment includes access to jobs as well as fair and positive treatment of all employees. Chapter 2 described how organizations manage diversity by anticipating employee needs and complying with legal requirements. Many organizations also provide training designed to teach employees attitudes and behaviours that support the management of diversity, such as appreciation of cultural differences and demonstrating behaviours that are respectful of employees with diverse values and backgrounds. Training designed to change employee attitudes about diversity and/or develop skills needed to work with a diverse workforce is called **diversity training**. These programs generally emphasize either attitude awareness and change or behaviour change.

> **diversity training**
> Training designed to change employee attitudes about diversity and/or develop skills needed to work with a diverse workforce.

Programs that focus on attitudes have objectives to increase participants' awareness of cultural and ethnic differences, as well as differences in personal characteristics and physical characteristics (such as disabilities). For example, at Air Canada (www.aircanada.com), employees receive training about the nuances of different cultures. "Cultures are very different and little gestures that you may experience from a customer, you may experience them differently than they're meant to be," says Louise McEvoy, former general manager of languages and diversity for Air Canada.[46]

Diversity training is more likely to get everyone onboard if it emphasizes respecting and valuing all the organization's employees in order to bring out the best work from everyone to open up the best opportunities for everyone. Programs that focus on behaviour aim at changing the organizational policies and individual behaviours that inhibit employees' personal growth and productivity. Sometimes these programs identify incidents that discourage employees from achieving their potential. The existing evidence regarding diversity training suggests that some characteristics make diversity training more effective.[47] Most important, the training should be tied to business objectives, such as understanding customers. The support and involvement of top management, and the involvement of managers at all levels, also are important. Diversity training should emphasize learning behaviours and skills, not blaming employees. Finally, the program should be well structured, connected to the organization's rewards for performance, and include a way to measure the success of the training.

L○6 Discuss the approaches organizations use for employee development.

Approaches to Employee Development

HRC7

The definition of employee development provided near the beginning of this chapter indicates that it is future-oriented. Development implies learning that is not necessarily related to the employee's current job.[48] Instead, it prepares employees for other positions in the organization and increases their ability to move into jobs that may not yet exist.[49] Development also may help employees prepare for changes in responsibilities and requirements in their current jobs, such as changes resulting from new technology, work designs, or customers.

Development for Careers

The concept of a career has changed in recent years. In the traditional view, a career consists of a sequence of positions within an occupation or organization.[50] For example, an engineer might start as a staff engineer, then with greater experience earn promotions to the positions of advisory engineer, senior engineer, and vice-president of engineering. In these examples, the career resembles a set of stairs from the entry to a profession or organization to the senior levels.

Recently, however, changes such as downsizing and restructuring have become the norm, so the concept of a career has become more fluid. Today's employees are more likely to have a **protean career**, one that frequently changes based on changes in the person's interests, abilities, and values and in the work environment. For example, an engineer might decide to take a sabbatical from her position to become a manager with Engineers without Borders (www.ewb.ca), so she can develop managerial skills and decide whether she likes being a manager. As in this example, employees in protean careers take responsibility for managing their careers. This concept is consistent with the modern *psychological contract* described in Chapter 1. Employees look for organizations to provide, not job security and a career ladder to climb, but instead development opportunities and flexible work arrangements.

protean career
A career that frequently changes based on changes in the person's interests, abilities, and values, and in the work environment.

To remain marketable, employees must continually develop new skills. Beyond knowing job requirements, employees need to understand the business in which they are working and be able to cultivate valuable relationships with co-workers, managers, suppliers, and customers. They also need to follow trends in their field and industry, so they can apply technology and knowledge that will match emerging priorities and needs. Learning such skills requires useful job experiences as well as effective training programs. More employees will follow a spiral career path in which they cross the boundaries between specialties and organizations. As organizations provide for employee development (and as employees take control of their own careers), they will need to (1) determine their interests, skills, and areas of needed development and (2) seek development experiences involving jobs, relationships, and formal courses. As discussed later in the chapter, organizations can meet these needs through a system for *career management* or *development planning*. Career management helps employees select development activities that prepare them to meet their career goals. It helps employers select development activities in line with their human resource needs.

The many approaches to employee development fall into four broad categories: formal education, assessment, job experiences, and interpersonal relationships.[51] Figure 6.3 summarizes these four methods. Many organizations combine these approaches.

Formal Education

Organizations may support employee development through a variety of formal educational programs, either at the workplace or off-site. These may include workshops designed specifically for the organization's employees, short courses offered by consultants, colleges, or universities, and MBA and executive MBA programs. As discussed earlier in this chapter, these programs may involve methods including lectures by business experts, business games and simulations, and experiential programs.

Many companies, including SaskTel (www.sasktel.com), PCL (www.pcl.com), and KPMG LLP (www.kpmg.com), operate training and development centres that offer in-house training. Universities including Queen's University (www.queensu.ca), the University of Western Ontario (www.uwo.ca), the University of Alberta (www.ualberta.ca), and UBC (www.ubc.ca) as well as colleges, e.g., George Brown College (www.georgebrown.ca), Humber College (www.humber.ca), Conestoga College (www.conestogac.on.ca), Durham College (www.durhamcollege.ca), and Seneca College (www.senecacollege.ca), offer management and professional development programs to organizations. A growing number of companies

FIGURE 6.3

Four Approaches to Employee Development

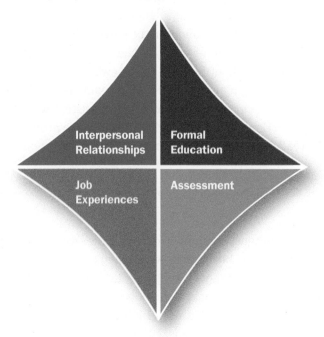

Assessment

Another way to provide for employee development is **assessment**—collecting information and providing feedback to employees about their behaviour, communication style, or skills.[52] Information for assessment may come from the employees, their peers, managers, and customers. The most frequent uses of assessment are to identify employees with managerial potential to measure current managers' strengths and weaknesses. Organizations also use assessment to identify managers with potential to move into higher-level executive positions. Organizations that assign work to teams may use assessment to identify the strengths and weaknesses of individual team members and the effects of the team members' decision-making and communication styles on the team's productivity.

> **assessment**
> Collecting information and providing feedback to employees about their behaviour, communication style, or skills.

For assessment to support development, the information must be shared with the employee being assessed. Along with that assessment information, the employee needs suggestions for correcting skill weaknesses and for using skills already learned. The suggestions might be to participate in training courses or develop skills through new job experiences. Based on the assessment information and available development opportunities, employees should develop action plans to guide their efforts at self-improvement.

It is increasingly recognized that excellent technical skills are not enough for individuals or organizations to be successful. "Strong people skills are equally important to attracting clients, building lasting relationships with both clients and colleagues, and expanding business."[53] As a result, organizations vary

HR Oops!

A Strong Middle, A Stronger Company

Research by Development Dimensions International (DDI www.ddiworld.com) finds that many of today's middle managers feel unprepared to handle their responsibilities. Middle managers are the layer of an organization's hierarchy that translates the top executives' vision into the projects and plans carried out by departments and teams. The middle managers oversee the supervisors and front-line managers who oversee those departments and teams. That means they have to be able to put a vision into practice, understand the financial impact of their performance, lead and motivate the people who report to them, and cultivate relationships throughout the organization with the people who can advance or interfere with their group's performance.

The middle managers surveyed by DDI said their most important challenges are leading change, executing strategic priorities, and making complex decisions. Asked about their preparation for handling those challenges, however, only 11 percent rated themselves well prepared.

Tacy M. Byham, DDI's vice-president of executive development, says the problem is that many organizations focus on preparing employees to be front-line supervisors and developing successful managers to move into top-level positions. That dual focus ignores the organization's needs for well-developed managers in the middle. Byham notes an additional consequence of ignoring development of middle managers: loss of talent. Managers tend to be more engaged in their work when they feel competent and valued. Lack of preparation translates into lack of trust in middle managers to make good decisions. Mid-level managers stuck in that situation indicate that they expect to move on to another employer before long.

Questions

1. Why do you think many organizations focus their development efforts primarily on top management and new (front-line) managers?

2. Imagine you are moving in your career from supervisor to middle manager. What changes would you hope for in your company's employee development program?

Sources: Development Dimensions International, "Reshaping the Middle of Organizations," news release, February 29, 2012, www.ddiworld.com; Roberta Matuson, "Leadership Starts in the Middle, Not at the Top," *Fast Company*, October 24, 2011, www.fastcompany.com; Ann Pace, "The Weary Middle," *T+D*, January 2011, p. 22.

in the methods and sources of information they use in developmental assessment. Many organizations appraise performance. Organizations with sophisticated development systems may use psychological tests to measure employees' skills, personality types, and communication styles. They may collect self, peer, and manager ratings of employees' behaviour and style of working with others. The tools used for these assessment methods include the *Myers-Briggs Type Indicator (MBTI)*, a popular psychological inventory, assessment centres, and 360-degree feedback. In addition, assessment of emotional intelligence (EQ) increases employees' self-awareness and facilitates their development with respect to intrapersonal and interpersonal skills, adaptability, and handling of stress.[54] Applying this kind of information about employees' preferences or tendencies helps organizations understand the communication, motivation, teamwork, work styles, and leadership of the people in their groups.

Myers-Briggs Type Indicator

The most popular psychological inventory for employee development is the **Myers-Briggs Type Indicator (MBTI)**. This assessment identifies individuals' preferences for source of energy, means of

Myers-Briggs Type Indicator (MBTI)
Psychological test that identifies individuals' preferences for source of energy, means of information gathering, way of decision making, and lifestyle, providing information for team building and leadership development.

information gathering, way of decision making, and lifestyle. The assessment consists of more than 100 questions about how the person feels or prefers to behave in different situations (such as "Are you usually a good 'mixer' or rather quiet and reserved?"). The assessment describes these individuals' preferences in the four areas:

1. The *energy* dichotomy indicates where individuals gain interpersonal strength and vitality, measured as their degree of introversion or extroversion. Extroverted types (E) gain energy through interpersonal relationships. Introverted types (I) gain energy by focusing on inner thoughts and feelings.

2. The *information-gathering* dichotomy relates to the preparations individuals make before making decisions. Individuals with a Sensing (S) preference tend to gather the facts and details to prepare for a decision. Intuitive types (N) tend to focus less on the facts and more on possibilities and relationships among them.

3. In *decision making,* individuals differ in the amount of consideration they give to their own and others' values and feelings, as opposed to the hard facts of a situation. Individuals with a Thinking (T) preference try always to be objective in making decisions. Individuals with a Feeling (F) preference tend to evaluate the impact of the alternatives on others, as well as their own feelings; they are more subjective.

4. The *lifestyle* dichotomy describes an individual's tendency to be either flexible or structured. Individuals with a Judging (J) preference focus on goals, establish deadlines, and prefer to be conclusive. Individuals with a Perceiving (P) preference enjoy surprises, are comfortable with changing a decision, and dislike deadlines.

The alternatives for each of the four dichotomies result in 16 possible combinations. Applying this kind of information about employees' preferences or tendencies helps organizations understand the communication, motivation, teamwork, work styles, and leadership of the people in their groups. For example, salespeople or executives who want to communicate better can apply what they learn about their own personality styles and the way other people perceive them. For team development, the MBTI can help teams match team members with assignments based on their preferences and thus improve problem solving.[55]

Research on the validity, reliability, and effectiveness of the MBTI is inconclusive.[56] People who take the MBTI find it a positive experience and say it helps them change their behaviour. However, MBTI scores are not necessarily stable over time. Studies in which the MBTI was administered at two different times found that as few as one-fourth of those who took the assessment were classified as exactly the same type the second time. Still, the MBTI is a valuable tool for understanding communication styles and the ways people prefer to interact with others. It is not appropriate for measuring job performance, however, or as the only means of evaluating promotion potential.

Assessment Centres

In addition to their use as a type of employment test to screen candidates as discussed in Chapter 5, assessment centres may engage multiple evaluators (assessors) to evaluate current employees' performance on a number of exercises.[57] Usually an off-site location such as a conference centre is used and 6 to 12 employees participate at one time. The primary use of assessment centres for development is to identify whether employees have the personality characteristics, administrative skills, and interpersonal skills needed for managerial jobs. Organizations also use them to determine whether employees have the skills needed for working in teams.

The types of exercises used in assessment centres include leaderless group discussions, interviews, in-baskets, and role-plays.[58] In a **leaderless group discussion**, a team of five to seven employees is assigned a problem and must work together to solve it within a certain time period. The problem may involve buying and selling supplies, nominating an employee for an award, or assembling a product. Interview questions typically cover each employee's work and personal experiences, skill strengths and weaknesses, and career plans. In-basket exercises, discussed as a selection method in Chapter 5, simulate the administrative tasks of a manager's job, using a pile of documents for the employee to handle. In role-plays, the participant takes the part of a manager or employee in a situation involving the skills to be assessed. For example, a participant might be given the role of a manager who must discuss performance problems with an employee, played by someone who works for the assessment centre. Other exercises in assessment centres might include interest and aptitude tests to evaluate an employee's vocabulary, general mental ability, and reasoning skills. Personality tests may be used to determine employees' ability to get along with others, tolerance for uncertainty, and other traits related to success as a manager or team member.

leaderless group discussion
An assessment centre exercise in which a team of five to seven employees is assigned a problem and must work together to solve it within a certain time period.

The assessors are usually managers who have been trained to look for employee behaviours that are related to the skills being assessed. Typically, each assessor observes and records one or two employees' behaviours in each exercise. The assessors review their notes and rate each employee's level of skills (for example, 5 = high level of leadership skills, 1 = low level of leadership skills). After all the employees have completed the exercises, the assessors discuss their observations of each employee. They compare their ratings and try to agree on each employee's rating for each of the skills.

As we mentioned in Chapter 5, research suggests that assessment centre ratings are valid for predicting performance, salary level, and career advancement.[59] Assessment centres may also be useful for development because of the feedback that participants receive about their attitudes and skill strengths.[60]

Benchmarks

A development method that focuses on measuring management skills is an instrument called **Benchmarks**. This measurement tool gathers ratings of a manager's use of skills associated with success in managing. The items measured by Benchmarks are based on research into the lessons that executives learn in critical events of their careers.[61] Items measure the 16 skills and perspectives listed in Table 6.4, including how well managers work with employees, acquire resources, and create a productive work climate. Research has found that managers who have these skills are more likely to receive positive performance evaluations, be considered promotable, and be promoted.[62]

To provide a complete picture of managers' skills, the managers' supervisors, their peers, and the managers themselves all complete the instrument. The results include a summary report, which the organization provides to the manager so he or she can see the self-ratings in comparison to the ratings by others. Also available with this method is a development guide containing examples of experiences that enhance each skill and ways successful managers use the skill.

Benchmarks
A measurement tool that gathers ratings of a manager's use of skills associated with success in managing.

360-Degree Feedback

As we will discuss in more detail in Chapter 7, a recent trend in performance appraisals, is *360-degree feedback*—performance measurement by the employee's supervisor, peers, direct reports, and customers. Often the feedback involves rating the individual in terms of skills, competencies, and work-related behaviours. For development purposes, the rater would identify an area of behaviour as a strength of

TABLE 6.4

Skills Related to Success as a Manager

Resourcefulness	Can think strategically, engage in flexible problem solving, and work effectively with higher management.
Doing whatever it takes	Has perseverance and focus in the face of obstacles.
Being a quick study	Quickly masters new technical and business knowledge.
Building and mending relationships	Knows how to build and maintain working relationships with co-workers and external parties.
Leading employees	Delegates to employees effectively, broadens their opportunities, and acts with fairness toward them.
Compassion and sensitivity	Shows genuine interest in others and sensitivity to employees' needs.
Straightforwardness and composure	Is honourable and steadfast.
Setting a developmental climate	Provides a challenging climate to encourage employees' development.
Confronting difficult employee situations	Acts decisively and fairly when dealing with difficult employee situations.
Team orientation	Accomplishes tasks through managing others.
Balance between personal life and work	Balances work priorities with personal life so that neither is neglected.
Decisiveness	Prefers quick and approximate actions to slow and precise ones in many management situations.
Self-awareness	Has an accurate picture of strengths and weaknesses and is willing to improve.
Hiring talented staff	Hires talented people for the team.
Putting people at ease	Displays warmth and a good sense of humour.
Acting with flexibility	Can behave in ways that are often seen as opposites.

Source: Adapted with permission from C. D. McCauley, M. M. Lombardo, and C. J. Usher, "Diagnosing Management Development Needs: An Instrument Based on How Managers Develop," *Journal of Management* 15 (1989), pp. 389–403. Reproduced with permission of Sage Publications, Inc. via Copyright Clearance Center.

that employee or an area requiring further development. The results presented to the employee show how he or she was rated on each item and how self-evaluations differ from other raters' evaluations. The individual reviews the results, seeks clarification from the raters, and sets specific development goals based on the strengths and weaknesses identified.[63]

There are several benefits of 360-degree feedback. Organizations collect multiple perspectives of performance, allowing employees to compare their own personal evaluations with the views of others. This method also establishes formal communications about behaviours and skill ratings between employees and their internal and external customers. Several studies have shown that performance improves and behaviour changes as a result of participating in upward feedback and 360-degree feedback systems.[64] Potential limitations of 360-degree feedback include the significant amount of time for raters to complete the evaluations. If raters, especially peers or direct reports, provide negative feedback, some managers might try to identify and punish them. A facilitator is needed to help interpret results. Finally, simply delivering ratings to a manager does not provide ways to act on the feedback (for example, development

One way to develop employees is to begin with an assessment, which may consist of assigning an activity to a team and seeing who brings what skills and strengths to the team. How can this assessment help employees?

planning, meeting with raters, or taking courses). As noted earlier, any form of assessment should be accompanied by suggestions for improvement and development of an action plan.

Job Experiences

Most employee development occurs through **job experiences**[65] the combination of relationships, problems, demands, tasks, and other features of an employee's job. Using job experiences for employee development assumes that development is most likely to occur when the employee's skills and experiences do not entirely match the skills required for the employee's current job. To succeed, employees must stretch their skills. In other words, they must learn new skills, apply their skills and knowledge in new ways, and master new experiences.[66] For example, companies that want to prepare employees to expand overseas markets are assigning them to a variety of international jobs.

job experiences
The combination of relationships, problems, demands, tasks, and other features of an employee's job.

The usefulness of job experiences for employee development varies depending on whether the employee views the experiences as positive or negative sources of stress. When employees view job experiences as positive stressors, the experiences challenge them and stimulate learning. When they view job experiences as negative stressors, employees may suffer from high levels of harmful stress. Of the job demands studied, managers were most likely to experience negative stress from creating change and overcoming obstacles (adverse business conditions, lack of management support, lack of personal support, or a difficult boss). Research suggests that all job demands except obstacles are related to learning.[67] Organizations should offer job experiences that are most likely to increase learning, and they should consider the consequences of situations that involve negative stress.

Although the research on development through job experiences has focused on managers, line employees also can learn through job experiences, e.g., use job experiences to develop skills needed for teamwork, including conflict resolution, data analysis, and customer service.

Various job assignments can provide for employee development. The organization may enlarge the employee's current job or move the employee to different jobs. Lateral moves include job rotation, transfer, or temporary assignment to another organization. The organization may also use downward moves or promotions as a source of job experience. Figure 6.4 summarizes these alternatives.

Job Enlargement

As Chapter 3 stated in the context of job design, *job enlargement* involves adding challenges or new responsibilities to employees' current jobs. Examples include completing a special project, switching roles within a work team, or researching new ways to serve customers. An accountant might join a task force developing new career paths for professional employees. The work on the project could give the accountant a leadership role through which he or she learns about the company's career development system while also practising leadership skills to help the task force reach its goals. In this way, job enlargement not only makes a job more interesting, but also creates an opportunity for employees to develop new skills.

Job Rotation

Another job design technique that can be applied to employee development is *job rotation*, moving employees through a series of job assignments in one or more functional areas. At Purdy's Chocolates (www.purdys.com) in British Columbia, employees are provided development opportunities. Plant workers are given the chance to run a shift to see if they have the potential to replace a lead hand or become a warehouse manager in the future.[68]

Job rotation helps employees gain an appreciation for the company's goals, increases their understanding of different company functions, develops a network of contacts, and improves problem-solving

FIGURE 6.4

How Job Experiences Are Used for Employee Development

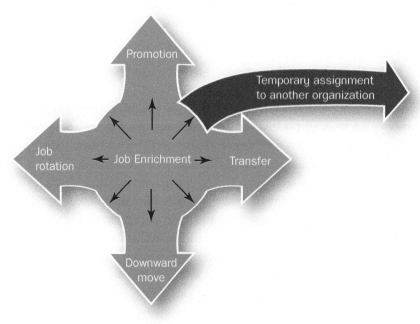

and decision-making skills.[69] However, the rotation of employees through a department may hurt productivity and increase the workload of those who remain after employees are rotated out. Job rotation is most likely to succeed when it meets certain conditions:[70]

- The organization establishes and communicates clear policies about which positions are eligible for job rotation. Job rotation for nonmanagement employees as well as managers can be beneficial, depending on the program's objectives.

- Employees and their managers understand and agree on the expectations for the job rotation, including which skills are to be developed.

- Goals for the program support business goals. These might including exposing high-potential employees to a variety of business units, customers, or geographic areas in preparation for management positions or rotating experienced, talented employees through several business units to mentor or coach them.

- The rotation schedule is realistic, taking into account how long employees will need to become familiar with their new position, as well as how much time is needed for employees to complete the assignments.

- Top management is committed to the program's success.

- Someone is responsible for measuring whether the program is meeting it goals.

Transfers, Promotions, and Downward Moves

Most companies use upward, downward, and lateral moves as an option for employee development. In a **transfer**, the organization assigns an employee to a position in a different area of the company. Transfers do not necessarily increase job responsibilities or compensation. They are usually lateral moves, that is, moves to a job with a similar level of responsibility. They may involve relocation to another department, location, or even to another country.

transfer
Assignment of an employee to a position in a different area of the company, usually in a lateral move.

Because transfers can provoke anxiety, many companies have difficulty getting employees to accept them. Employees most willing to accept transfers tend to be those with high career ambitions, a belief that the organization offers a promising future, and a belief that accepting the transfer will help the company succeed.[71]

A **downward move** occurs when an employee is given less responsibility and authority. The organization may demote an employee because of poor performance or move the employee to a lower-level position in another function so that the employee can develop different skills. The temporary cross-functional move is the most common way to use downward moves for employee development. For example, engineers who want to move into management often take lower-level positions, such as shift supervisor, to develop their management skills.

downward move
Assignment of an employee to a position with less responsibility and authority.

Many employees have difficulty associating transfers and downward moves with development; these changes may feel more like forms of punishment. Employees will be more likely to accept transfers and downward moves as development opportunities if the organization provides information about the

Working outside one's home country is the most important job experience that can develop an employee for a career in the global economy.

change and its possible benefits and involves the employee in planning the change. Employees are also more likely to be positive about such a recommendation if the organization provides clear performance objectives and frequent feedback.

A **promotion** involves moving an employee into a position with greater challenges, more responsibility, and more authority than in the previous job. Usually promotions include pay increases. Because promotions improve the person's pay, status, and feelings of accomplishment, employees are more willing to accept promotions than lateral or downward moves. Even so, employers can increase the likelihood that employees will accept promotions by providing the same kind of information and assistance that are used to support transfers and downward moves. Organizations can more easily offer promotions if they are profitable and growing. In other conditions, opportunities for promoting employees may be limited.

promotion
Assignment of an employee to a position with greater challenges, more responsibility, and more authority than in the previous job, usually accompanied by a pay increase.

Temporary Assignments with Other Organizations

In some cases, an employer may benefit from the skills an employee can learn at another organization. The employer may encourage the employee to participate in an **externship**—a full-time temporary position at another organization.

externship
Employee development through a full-time temporary position at another organization.

Temporary assignments can include a **sabbatical**—a leave of absence from an organization to renew or develop skills. Employees on sabbatical often receive full pay and benefits. Sabbaticals let employees get away from the day-to-day stresses of their jobs and acquire new skills and perspectives. Sabbaticals also allow employees more time for personal pursuits such as writing a book or spending more time with family members.

sabbatical
A leave of absence from an organization to renew or develop skills.

L○7 Explain how managers and peers develop employees through mentoring and coaching.

Interpersonal Relationships

Employees can also develop skills and increase their knowledge about the organization and its customers by interacting with a more experienced organization member. Two types of relationships used for employee development are *mentoring* and *coaching*.

Mentors

A **mentor** is an experienced, productive senior employee who helps develop a less experienced employee, called the *protégé* or *mentee*. Most mentoring relationships develop informally as a result of interests or values shared by the mentor and protégé. According to research, the employees most likely to seek and attract a mentor have certain personality characteristics: emotional stability, ability to adapt their behaviour to the situation, and high needs for power and achievement.[72] Mentoring relationships also can develop as part of the organization's planned effort to bring together successful senior employees with less experienced employees.

mentor
An experienced, productive senior employee who helps develop a less experienced employee (a protégé or mentee).

One major advantage of formal mentoring programs is that they ensure access to mentors for all employees, regardless of gender or other background. A mentoring program also can ensure that high-potential employees are matched with wise, experienced mentors in key areas—and that mentors are hearing the challenges facing employees who have less authority, work directly with customers, or hold positions in other parts of the organization.[73] However, in an artificially created relationship, mentors may have difficulty providing counselling and coaching.[74] One practical way employees can address this shortcoming is to look for more than one mentor, including informal relationships with interested people outside the organization. Employees also should accept the limits of mentoring relationships. Mentoring is not, for example, a substitute for therapy: a mentor might offer tips for navigating a business presentation, whereas a therapist is a better choice for someone who needs help with persistent anxiety.[75]

Mentoring programs tend to be most successful when they are voluntary and participants understand the details of the program. Rewarding managers for employee development is also important because it signals that mentoring and other development activities are worthwhile. In addition, the organization should carefully select mentors based on their interpersonal and technical skills, train them for the role, and evaluate whether the program has met its objectives.[76]

Mentors and mentees (protégés) can both benefit from a mentoring relationship. Table 6.5 summarizes the advantages of mentoring programs to both mentees (protégés) and mentors. Mentees (protégés) receive career support, including coaching, protection, sponsorship, challenging assignments, and visibility among the organization's managers. They also receive benefits of a positive relationship—a friend and role model who accepts them, has a positive opinion toward them, and gives them a chance to talk about their worries. Employees with mentors are also more likely to be promoted, earn higher salaries, and have more influence within their organization.[77] Acting as a mentor gives managers a chance to develop their interpersonal skills and increase their feelings that they are contributing something important to the organization. Working with a technically trained protégé on matters such as new research in the field may also increase the mentor's technical knowledge.

TABLE 6.5

Advantages of Mentoring Programs

For Protégés/Mentees	For Mentors
• Breaks down "silos" throughout the organization	• Maintains a pulse on the organization by keeping regular contact and communication with employees
• Increases communication	• Enhances interpersonal and leadership competencies
• Supports continuous learning throughout all levels of the organization	
• Enhances career development and growth	
• Improves employee satisfaction and engagement	
• Fosters a culture where employees support and help one another	

Source: Adapted from Conference Board of Canada, "Mentoring—Low Cost, Big Benefits," www.conferenceboard.ca/humanresource/mentoring-inside.htm, retrieved February 24, 2005.

So that more employees can benefit from mentoring, some organizations use *group mentoring programs,* which assign four to six protégés to a successful senior employee. A potential advantage of group mentoring is that protégés can learn from each other as well as from the mentor. The leader helps protégés understand the organization, guides them in analyzing their experiences, and helps them clarify career directions. Each member of the group may complete specific assignments, or the group may work together on a problem or issue.

A growing number of organizations have also implemented formal or informal **reverse mentoring** programs. Reverse mentoring "involves the pairing of a younger, junior employee acting as mentor to share expertise with an older, senior colleague."[78] The most obvious example may involve technology mentoring applications such as the use of social media, mobile computing, and the cloud. Like traditional mentoring, reverse mentoring benefits both mentors and mentees. For example, millennial employees acquire skills in guiding older employees, which contributes to their development as effective cross-generational leaders, while older employees acquire specific skills and insights in addition to building relationships across generations. A potential issue associated with reverse mentoring relates to the role-reversal implications, which can be challenging to both mentors and mentees. Careful time management and a shared commitment to building this type of non-traditional relationship is needed. For example, experienced executives will require a mindset that embraces learning and acknowledges the vulnerability associated with openly sharing their developmental need with a younger, less experienced employee.[79]

reverse mentoring
Pairing of a younger, junior employee acting as mentor to share expertise with an older senior colleague, the mentee.

Coaching

A **coach** is a peer or manager who works with an employee to provide a source of motivation, help him or her develop skills, and provide reinforcement and feedback. Coaches may play one or more of three roles:[80]

1. Working one-on-one with an employee, as when giving feedback.

2. Helping employees learn for themselves—for example, helping them find experts and teaching them to obtain feedback from others.

3. Providing resources such as mentors, courses, or job experiences.

coach
A peer or manager who works with an employee to provide a source of motivation, help him or her develop skills, and provide reinforcement and feedback.

William Gray, president of Mentoring Solutions Inc. (www.mentoring-solutions.com) and former UBC professor, draws a distinction between mentoring and coaching. Gray describes mentoring as developing the "whole person" and coaching involves developing a specific skill set.[81]

Coaches may be internal to the organization, external resources, or a combination. Internal coaches allow the organization to "start small" and may allow more people to access coaching resources. Use of internal coaching resources may also enhance affordability, availability, and provide the context for the use of specific workplace examples. However, external coaches because they are removed from the client's organization, may be less likely to hold any biases as they support their clients, may offer more experience and proficiency, as well as confidentiality, particularly if performance issues have prompted the coaching relationship.[82]

Research suggests that coaching helps managers improve by identifying areas for improvement and setting goals.[83] Getting results from a coaching relationship can take at least six months of weekly or monthly meetings. To be effective, a coach generally conducts an assessment, asks questions that challenge the employee to think deeply about his or her goals and motives, helps the employee create an action plan, and follows up regularly to help the employee stay on track. Employees contribute to the success of coaching when they persevere in practising the behaviours identified in the action plan.[84]

L○8 Identify the steps in the career management process and how managers are dealing with some critical development-related challenges.

Career Management Systems

Employee development is most likely to meet the organization's needs if it is part of a human resource system of career management. In practice, organizations' career management systems vary. Some rely heavily on informal relationships, while others are sophisticated programs. As shown in Figure 6.5, a basic career management system involves four steps: data gathering, feedback, goal setting, and action planning and follow-up. Ways to make this system more effective include gathering data in areas associated with success, keeping feedback confidential and specific, involving higher level management in planning and follow-up, and crafting action plans that are realistic and targeted to building expertise needed for the person's career path.[85] Human resources professionals can also contribute to the system's success by ensuring it is linked to other HR practices such as performance management, training, and recruiting.

Data Gathering

In discussing the methods of employee development, we highlighted several assessment tools. Such tools may be applied to the first stage of career development. **Self-assessment** refers to the use of information by employees to determine their career interests, values, aptitudes, and behavioural tendencies.

self-assessment
The use of information by employees to determine their career interests, values, aptitudes, behavioural tendencies, and development needs.

FIGURE 6.5

Steps in the Career Management Process

	Data gathering	Feedback	Goal setting	Action planning & Follow-up
Criteria for success	Focus on competencies needed for career success.	Maintain confidentiality.	Involve management and coaches/mentors.	Involve management and coaches/mentors.
	Include a variety of measures.	Focus on specific success factors, strengths, and improvement areas.	Specify competencies and knowledge to be developed.	Measure success and adjust plans as needed.
			Specify developmental methods.	Verify that pace of development is realistic.

Self-assessment tools often include psychological tests such as the Myers-Briggs Type Inventory (described earlier in the chapter), the Strong-Campbell Interest Inventory, and the Self-Directed Search. The Strong-Campbell Inventory helps employees identify their occupational and job interests. The Self-Directed Search identifies employees' preferences for working in different kinds of environments—sales, counselling, and so on. Tests may also help employees identify the relative value they place on work and leisure activities. Self-assessment tools can help an employee consider his or her current career status, future plans, and the fit between the career and current situation and resources. Some organizations provide counsellors to help employees in the self-assessment process and to interpret the results of psychological tests.

Completing a self-assessment can help employees identify a development need. This need can result from gaps between current skills or interests and the type of work or position the employee has or wants.

Feedback

In the next step of career management, **feedback**, employees receive information about their competencies and where these assets fit into the organization's plans. The employee's responsibility is to identify what skills she or he could realistically develop in light of the opportunities available. The organization's responsibility is to communicate the performance evaluation and the opportunities available to the employee, given the organization's long-range plans. Opportunities might include promotions and transfers. Some organizations develop and communicate **career paths**—the identified pattern or progression of jobs or roles within an organization to provide clarity about how an employee may progress into more senior positions. Career paths may include a wide variety of jobs or may provide specific information related to cumulative responsibilities for a managerial, technical, or professional career. Career-path information can also enhance the discussion of opportunities between employees and their managers by providing consistent language related to how jobs and roles are defined in the organization.[86]

Usually the employer supports the reality check as part of a performance appraisal or as the feedback stage of performance management. In well-developed career management systems, the manager may hold separate discussions for performance feedback and career development. Performance management will be discussed in Chapter 7.

feedback
Information employers give employees about their skills and knowledge and where these assets fit into the organization's plans.

career paths
The identified pattern or progression of jobs or roles within an organization.

Goal Setting

On the basis of the information from the self-assessment and feedback, the employee sets short- and long-term career objectives. These goals usually involve one or more of the following categories:

- Desired roles, such as becoming a team leader within three years.
- Level of competency—for example, to apply one's budgeting skills to improve the unit's cash flow problems.
- Work setting—for example, to move to corporate marketing within two years.
- Skill acquisition, such as learning how to use the company's human resource information system.

As in these examples, the goals should be specific, and they should include a date by which the goal is to be achieved. It is the employee's responsibility to identify the goal and the method of determining her or his progress toward each goal. Usually the employee discusses the goals with his or her manager. The organization's responsibilities are to ensure that the goal is specific, challenging, and achievable, and to help the employee reach the goal.

Action Planning and Follow-Up

In the final step, employees prepare an action plan for *how* they will achieve their short- and long-term career goals. The employee is responsible for identifying the steps and timetable to reach the goals. The employer should identify resources needed, including courses, work experiences, and relationships. The employee and the manager should meet in the future to discuss progress toward career goals.

Action plans may involve any one or a combination of the development methods discussed earlier in the chapter—training, assessment, job experiences, or the help of a mentor or coach. The approach used depends on the particular developmental needs and career objectives. For example, suppose the program manager in an information systems department uses feedback from clients to determine that greater knowledge of project management software is needed. The manager plans to increase that knowledge by reading articles (formal education), meeting with software vendors, and contacting the vendors' customers to ask them about the software they have used (job experiences). The manager and his supervisor agree that six months will be the target date for achieving the higher level of knowledge through these activities.

The outcome of action planning often takes the form of a *development plan*. Figure 6.6 is an example of a development plan for a project manager. Development plans usually include descriptions of strengths and areas for development, career goals, and development activities for reaching each goal.

Development-Related Challenges

HRC**2, 7**

A well-designed system for employee development can help organizations face widespread challenges: the glass ceiling and dysfunctional behaviour by managers.

FIGURE 6.6

Development Plan

Name: **Title:** Project Manager   **Immediate Manager:**

Competencies
Please identify your three greatest strengths and areas for development.
Strengths
- Strategic thinking and execution (confidence, command skills, action orientation).
- Results orientation (creating a motivating work environment, perseverance).
- Spirit for winning (building team spirit, customer focus, respect colleagues).

Areas for Development
- Written communications (ability to write clearly and succinctly).
- Concern for people (too much focus on successful completion of projects rather than developing relationships with individuals involved in the projects).

Career Goals
Please describe your overall career goals.
- *Long-term.* Accept positions of increased responsibility to a level of general manager (or beyond). The areas of specific interest include but are not limited to product and brand management, technology and development, strategic planning, and marketing.
- *Short-term.* Continue to improve my skills in marketing and brand management while utilizing my skills in product management, strategic planning, and global relations.

Next Assignments
Identify potential next assignments (including timing) that would help you develop toward your career goals.
- Manager or director level in planning, development, product, or brand management. Timing estimated to be Spring 2017.

Training, Learning, and Development Needs
List both training, learning, and development activities that will either help you develop in your current assignment or provide overall career development.
- Master's degree classes will allow me to practise and improve my written communications skills. The dynamics of my current position, teamwork, and reliance on other individuals allow me to practise patience and to focus on individual team members' needs along with the success of the project.

Employee _____   **Date** _____
Immediate Manager _____   **Date** _____
Mentor _____   **Date** _____

The Glass Ceiling

As we mentioned in Chapter 1, women and other members of the employment equity target groups are rare in the top level of Canadian corporations. Observers of this situation have noted that it looks as if an invisible barrier is keeping these individuals from reaching the top jobs, a barrier that has come to be known as the **glass ceiling**. For example, according to data from Catalyst, only 20.8 percent of board seats at Canada's Stock Index companies are held by women. By way of comparison, 19.2 percent of board seats at U.S. Stock Index companies are held by women, however, in European Stock Index Companies, 35.5 percent of board seats in Norway and 29.7 percent of board seats in France are held by women.[87]

Indra Nooyl, current chairperson and CEO of PepsiCo, joined PepsiCo in 1994 and became president and CFO back in 2001. Her success at the company gives her the distinction of being one of the women to break through the "glass ceiling."

glass ceiling
Circumstances resembling an invisible barrier that keep most women and other members of the employment equity groups from attaining the top jobs in organizations.

The glass ceiling is likely caused by a lack of access to training programs, appropriate developmental job experiences, and developmental relationships such as mentoring.[88] With regard to developmental relationships, women and other members of the employment equity groups often have trouble finding mentors. They may not participate in the organization's, profession's, or community's "old boys' network." Also, recent evidence finds differences in how women and men pursue advancement and in how executives perceive women's and men's qualifications and ambitions. Female managers tend to find more mentors who give advice; their male counterparts find, on average, mentors who are more senior and will sponsor them for key positions. Patterns of promotion suggest that companies are more willing to select men from outside the organization based on their potential, while women do better when they stay with the same company where they can demonstrate a track record of accomplishments. Consistent with this difference, women who actively promote their achievements tend to advance further in an organization, whereas broadcasting their achievements does not make much difference in their male colleagues' advancement.[89]

However, the glass ceiling metaphor has been criticized because it describes an absolute barrier at a specific high level in organizations and fails to incorporate the complex and varied challenges women and other members of the employment equity target groups face in their careers. A better metaphor may be a *labyrinth*, connoting a complex journey with many twists and turns and puzzles to solve along the way to the top jobs.[90] Organizations can use development systems to help break through the glass ceiling or "navigate the labyrinth." Managers making developmental assignments need to carefully consider whether stereotypes are influencing the types of assignments men and women receive. A formal process for regularly identifying development needs and creating action plans can make these decisions more objective.

Dysfunctional Managers

A manager who is otherwise competent may engage in some behaviours that make him or her ineffective or even "toxic"—someone who stifles good ideas and drives away employees. These dysfunctional

Thinking ETHICALLY

Can You Teach People to Be Ethical?

Ethical leadership is critical for employees in many settings. For example, in an industrial environment, ethical leadership of safety programs puts employees' well-being ahead of short-term cost savings. And in the accounting profession, high ethical standards are essential for preserving a firm's reputation. Therefore, organizations have an interest in developing ethical leaders who in turn foster ethical behaviour among all employees.

Jim Spigener, a safety consultant, recalls working with a chief executive whose son had recently become a civil engineer for a construction company. Spigener asked his client whether he hoped that the construction company's CEO placed the same value on his employees' safety that the client placed on his own employees' safety. The startled client replied that he hoped his son's CEO had higher standards. In this way, Spigener was coaching his CEO client to think about safety in a new, personal way—hoping that the client, in his role as a leader, would begin to express this new understanding to others at the company.

Many accounting firms use mentoring relationships to foster commitment to integrity and ethical decision making. Ernst & Young, for example, matches newly hired staff members with mentors and has set up a system where the staff can post comments about the mentoring and coaching behaviours they observe. One of the most important ways mentors can develop ethical behaviour is by modelling that behaviour themselves. Mentors also try to help employees sort out the nuances of how to behave ethically amidst the real-world challenges of time pressures and office politics.

Questions

1. Compare the example of the safety consultant coaching a CEO with the example of Ernst & Young mentoring accountants. How are these development approaches similar and different?

2. Besides coaches or mentors, what other resources could an organization provide to develop ethical employees? Which of these do you think would be most effective, and why?

3. Can an organization "develop" ethical employees, or is it just a matter of hiring people who are already ethical? How much effort should an organization put into developing strengths in the area of ethics?

Sources: Jim Spigener, "Leaders Who 'Get' Safety: Values and Personality Shape Personal Ethics," *Industrial Safety & Hygiene News*, October 2009, Business & Company Resource Center, http://galenet.galegroup.com; and Robert Giagnon, "More than a Legacy," *CA Magazine*, September 2009, Business & Company Resource Center, http://galenet.galegroup.com.

behaviours include insensitivity to others, inability to be a team player, arrogance, poor conflict-management skills, inability to meet business objectives, and inability to adapt to change.[91] For example, a manager who has strong technical knowledge but is abrasive and discourages employees from contributing their ideas is likely to have difficulty engaging employees and may alienate people inside and outside the organization.

When a manager is an otherwise valuable employee and is willing to improve, the organization may try to help him or her change the dysfunctional behaviour. The usual ways to provide this type of development include assessment, training, and counselling. Development programs for managers with dysfunctional behaviour may also include specialized programs such as one called Individual Coaching for Effectiveness (ICE). The ICE program includes diagnosis, coaching, and support activities tailored to each manager's needs.[92] Psychologists conduct the diagnosis, coach and counsel the manager, and develop action plans for implementing new skills on the job. Research suggests that managers who participate in programs like ICE improve their skills and are less likely to be terminated.[93] One possible conclusion is that organizations can benefit from offering development opportunities to all valuable employees, not just to top performers.

SUMMARY

L○1 Discuss how to link training, learning, and development to organizational needs and strategy.

Organizations need to establish training programs that are effective. Organizations create such programs through instructional design. This process begins with a needs assessment, then ensures readiness for training, plans a training program, implements the program, and evaluates the results.

L○2 Explain how to assess training needs and determine employees' readiness.

Needs assessment consists of an organization analysis, person analysis, and task analysis. The organization analysis determines the appropriateness of training by evaluating the characteristics of the organization, including its strategy, resources, and management support. The person analysis determines individuals' needs and readiness for learning. Task analysis identifies the tasks, knowledge, skills, and behaviours that training should emphasize.

Readiness for learning is a combination of employee characteristics and positive work environment that permit learning. Necessary employee characteristics include ability to learn the subject matter, favourable attitudes toward the training, and motivation to learn. In a positive work environment, both peers and management support training.

L○3 Describe how to plan and design an effective training program.

Planning begins with establishing objectives for the training program. These should define an expected performance or outcome, the desired level of performance, and the conditions under which the performance should occur. On the basis of the objectives, the planner decides who will provide the training, what topics the training will cover, what training methods to use, and how to evaluate the training.

Even when organizations purchase outside training, someone in the organization, usually a member of the HR department, often is responsible for training administration. The training methods selected should be related to the objectives and content of the training program. Methods may include presentation methods, hands-on methods, or group-building methods.

L○4 Summarize how to implement and evaluate a successful training program.

Implementation should apply principles of learning and seek transfer. In general, effective training communicates learning objectives, presents information in distinctive and memorable ways, and helps participants link the subject matter to their jobs. Consideration should also be given to ensuring employees have the required workplace literacy skills to succeed and perform well in their jobs.

Training can be evaluated at five levels—learner reactions, demonstration of learning, behaviour change, business results, and cost-benefit analysis. Evaluation should look for transfer by measuring whether employees are performing the tasks taught in the training program. Assessment of training also should evaluate training outcomes.

LO5 Describe methods for employee orientation and diversity management.

Employee orientation (onboarding) is designed to prepare new employees to perform their job effectively, learn about the organization, and establish work relationships. A typical orientation program includes information about the overall company and the department in which the new employee will be working, covering social as well as technical aspects of the job. Orientation programs may combine several training methods, from printed materials to on-the-job training to e-learning.

Diversity training is designed to change employee attitudes about diversity and/or develop skills needed to work with a diverse workforce. Diversity training is most effective when it is tied to business objectives, has management support, emphasizes behaviours and skills, and is tied to organizational policies and practices that value diversity, including a way to measure success.

LO6 Discuss the approaches organizations use for employee development.

Organizations may use formal educational programs at the workplace or offsite such as workshops, college and university programs, company-sponsored training, or programs offered by independent institutions. Organizations may use the assessment process to help employees identify strengths and areas requiring further development.

Job experiences contribute to development through a combination of relationships, problems, demands, tasks, and other features of an employee's job. Job experiences that support employee development may include job enlargement, job rotations, transfers, promotions, downward moves, and temporary assignments with other organizations.

Interpersonal relationships with a more experienced member of the organization—often in the role of mentor or coach can help employees develop their understanding of the organization and its customers.

LO7 Explain how managers and peers develop employees through mentoring and coaching.

A mentor is an experienced, productive senior employee who helps develop a less experienced employee. Although most mentoring relationships develop informally, organizations can link mentoring to development goals by establishing a formal mentoring program. Reverse mentoring pairs younger junior employees who share expertise with older, senior colleagues.

A coach is a peer or manager who works with an employee to motivate the employee, help him or her develop skills, and provide reinforcement and feedback. Coaches should be prepared to take on one or more of three roles: working one-on-one with an employee, helping employees learn for themselves, and providing resources, such as mentors, courses, or job experiences.

LO8 Identify the steps in the career management process and how managers are dealing with some critical development-related challenges.

In the first step of the career management process—data gathering, employees determine their career interests, values, aptitudes, and behavioural tendencies. The second step is feedback, during which the organization communicates information about the employee's skills and knowledge and how these fit into the organization's plans. The employee then sets goals and discusses them with his or her manager, who ensures that the goals are specific, challenging, and attainable. Finally, the employee works with his or her manager to create an action plan for development activities that will help the employee achieve the goals.

The "glass ceiling" is a barrier that has been observed preventing women and other members of the employment equity target groups from achieving top jobs in an organization. Development programs can ensure that these employees receive access to development resources. For dysfunctional managers who have the potential to contribute to the organization, the organization may offer development targeted at correcting the areas of dysfunction.

Critical Thinking Questions

1. "Melinda!" bellowed Toran to the company's HR specialist, "I've got a problem, and you've got to solve it. I can't get people in this plant to work together as a team. As if I don't have enough trouble with our competitors and our past-due accounts, now I have to put up with running a zoo. You're responsible for seeing that the staff gets along. I want a training proposal on my desk by Monday." Assume you are Melinda.

   a. Is training the solution to this problem? How can you determine the need for training?

   b. Summarize how you would conduct a needs assessment.

2. How should an organization assess readiness for learning? In Question 1, how do Toran's comments suggest readiness (or lack of readiness) for learning?

3. Many organizations turn to e-learning as a less expensive alternative to classroom training. What are some other advantages of substituting e-learning for classroom training? What are some disadvantages?

4. Consider your current job, or one you have held recently.

   a. How was orientation (onboarding) handled?

   b. What types of training did you receive for the job?

   c. How did orientation (onboarding) and training affect your performance on the job? Your commitment to the organization?

   d. Would it be appropriate to provide employee orientation (onboarding) purely online? Why or why not?

   e. Is there anything the organization could have done to make the orientation (onboarding) and/or training processes more effective?

5. Why do organizations provide diversity training? What kinds of goals are most suitable for such training?

6. What are the four broad categories of development methods? Why might it be beneficial to combine all of these methods into a formal development program?

7. Recommend a development method for each of the following situations, and explain why you chose that method.

   a. An employee recently promoted to the job of plant supervisor has been unsuccessful in sustaining employee performance quality standards.

   b. A sales manager annoys salespeople by directing every detail of their work.

   c. An employee has excellent leadership skills but lacks knowledge of the financial side of business.

   d. An organization is planning to organize its production workers into teams for the first time.

8. Many people feel that mentoring relationships should occur naturally, in situations where senior managers feel inclined to play that role. What are some advantages of setting up a formal mentoring program, rather than letting senior managers decide how and whom to help?

9. How is a coach different than a mentor? What are some advantages of using someone outside the organization as a coach? Any disadvantages?

10. Why should organizations be interested in helping employees plan their careers? What benefits can companies gain? What are the risks?

11. What metaphors were used to describe the barriers that women and other employment equity group members still face to advancement into senior executive positions? Can you think of any other relevant metaphors? Which metaphor do you feel is most relevant? Why?

12. Why might an organization benefit from giving employee development opportunities to a dysfunctional manager, rather than simply dismissing the manager? Do these reasons apply to nonmanagement employees as well?

Experiencing HR

Go online and visit eHow (www.ehow.com), YouTube (www.youtube.com), or another site recommended by your instructor. Use the site's search function to look up a lesson on how to do one of the following tasks:

● Conduct a job interview

● Dress business casual

● Give a presentation

● Cook chili

● Clean a laptop computer

● Handle an upset customer

View the presentation you selected, taking notes to help you recall its content and methods. Then write a one-page review of the presentation. Rate the presentation's content (was it relevant and understandable?) and methods (was it engaging and effective?). Also, note whether the presentation provided a means for assessing what was learned. Finally, suggest how the presentation could have been improved. What could make it more effective as part of an employer's training program?

CASE STUDY 6.1:

Growing the Next Gen

Busy senior HR professionals have a lot on their plates. With teams to lead, deliverables to meet and metrics to measure, it's not surprising that there isn't a lot of time to think about who will fill their shoes in the future, and how they will pass along a lifetime of accumulated industry knowledge to the next generation. Good, full-time HR jobs are hard to come by these days. People aren't retiring at age 65 as they used to, and the economy isn't generating many new jobs in the field. It can be difficult for recent graduates to get their careers rolling. That makes it a good time for those who have enjoyed successful careers in human resources to think about giving the next generation a hand.

"We have to figure out a way to fill the experience gap," explains Sandra Smith, chief HR officer at Southlake Regional Health Centre (www.southlakeregional.org) in Newmarket, Ontario. "We need to think differently about ways of involving new grads in the industry, even when they don't yet have a job." In her current role, Smith oversees policies that affect the hospital's 3,000 staff members, 600 physicians, and 1,000 volunteers. During her 15-year HR career, she has always tried to look at the big picture. She believes that applying creative talent management and workforce planning solutions to help the next generation can be relatively inexpensive.

"Most of the new grads are flexible; they're usually willing to do a few jobs at once," said Smith. "Full-time jobs would be best for them; but if they aren't available, what else can we create? Well, we can look at creating paid internships or project-specific jobs for new grads. Most departments have those foundational projects such as basic recruitment or job evaluations, or other projects for which new grads would have the theoretical foundation. It would give them really good experience, but it would also provide very good value for companies."

Stephanie Canito knows the value of practical on-the-job experience. While she was enrolled in the human resources program at George Brown College, she completed a co-op placement at Southlake Regional Health Centre in 2010. After graduation, she was offered a job at the hospital as an HR advisor. "My co-op was a wonderful learning experience. I was exposed to the different disciplines within Southlake's HR team, and I've had the privilege of continuing to learn and grow with them," said Canito. "To promote knowledge transfer, the industry should look at establishing HR models within organizations that promote mentorship and coaching, and allow for information sharing and practical exposure." "I think the one thing the next generation is eager for is the opportunity to apply their skills and knowledge."

"We need to be creating a strategy and work for our future," concluded Smith. "I have been very lucky in my career; I need to give back. Most of us want to do that, I think."

Questions

1. Which of the training and development methods described in this chapter are included in Southlake Regional Health Centre's approach to developing recent grads?

2. Are there any other training and development methods that would be effective for recent grads considering careers in HR?

3. What is your advice to Southlake Regional Health Centre in choosing mentors and/or coaches to work with recent graduates?

Source: Excerpted from Lisa Gordon, "Growing the Next Gen," *HR Professional,* March/April 2015, pp. 29–30. Reprinted by permission of Canadian HR Reporter. © Copyright Thomson Reuters Canada Ltd., March/April 2015, Toronto, Ontario 1-800-387-5164. Web: www.hrreporter.com

CASE STUDY 6.2:

Building Foundation Skills at Loewen

Loewen (www.loewan.com) is one of Canada's largest premium wood window and door manufacturers. Based in Steinbach, Manitoba, Loewen employs almost 1,700 people, however it comes from humble roots—starting as a small family-owned sawmill in the early 1900s.

As Loewen needed more employees for their expanding production needs in Manitoba, one of the workers in the plant approached the HR manager to let her know that there were several new families that had just arrived from Germany and needed work. In total, 15 people were extended job offers, however, Loewen faced several challenges associated with having a diverse workforce with varying English language skills. Due to communication issues, employees took longer than necessary to complete work tasks. Communication and cultural differences among employees impeded cross-training efforts and led to misunderstandings and internal conflict. Workers' safety was also affected because company safety training and work instructions were geared for an audience who spoke English as their first language and managers found it difficult to assess whether employees fully understood shop floor safety procedures.

Loewen's Foundation Skills program was introduced initially as a pilot project to allow employees to upgrade their "English as an additional language" and improve their literacy skills. Specific objectives for the program were created including being able to read and discuss safe work procedure documents; being able to communicate orally with their co-workers and supervisors; and being able to fully participate in Loewen Windows production, using English when following and giving instructions.

Most of the employees taking part in the program work on the shop floor—93 percent are plant labourers, however administrative staff and leaders have also participated in the program. Loewen partnered with community group, Southeast English Language and Literacy Services for Adults, an organization that focuses on working with local immigrants. Employees enrolled in the program attend four hours of class per week for 20 weeks. Loewen picks up 50 percent of the fees and the full cost of the books, and the other 50 percent is covered by government funding. Participants in the program attend class half on company time and half on their own time.

As a result of this program, Loewen has benefited through high employee retention rates—which has reduced hiring costs and improved efficiencies. Participants in the program also learn new jobs faster and operational flexibility has improved because workers are able to provide vacation and illness coverage for others in busy departments. Managers see employees' time away from their job tasks for training as an investment in safety, the community, and their employees.

Questions

1. Loewen's commitment to continuous learning emphasizes a belief that the organization benefits when employees learn and enhance their abilities. How should Loewen evaluate the effectiveness of its Foundation Skills program?

2. How do employees benefit from this investment in learning?

3. Do you think Loewen's Foundation Skills program is a good model for other organizations? Why or why not?

Sources: Alison Campbell, "A Clear View of Safety at Loewen Windows," Case Study: April 2010, The Conference Board of Canada; www.loewen.com/hr/CareerToolbox.html, retrieved April 9, 2012; and "Section 4.9 Loewen Windows Pilot Project: New Employees English Language Training Program," *Centre for Canadian Language Benchmarks*, www.language.ca/display_page.asp?page_id=850, retrieved April 9, 2012.

CHAPTER 7

Managing Employees' Performance

WHAT DO I NEED TO KNOW?

After reading this chapter, you should be able to:

LO1	Identify the relevance of performance management and the steps in the process.
LO2	Discuss the purposes of performance management systems.
LO3	Define five criteria for measuring the effectiveness of a performance management system.
LO4	Compare the major methods for measuring performance.
LO5	Describe major sources of performance information in terms of their advantages and disadvantages.
LO6	Define types of rating errors and explain how to minimize them.
LO7	Explain how to effectively provide performance feedback.
LO8	Summarize ways to achieve performance improvement.
LO9	Discuss legal and ethical issues that affect performance management.

Acklands-Grainger is Canada's largest distributor of industrial, safety, and fastener products and has been recognized by Waterstone Human Capital for its performance-oriented culture.

Performance Management at Acklands-Grainger

Acklands-Grainger (www.acklandsgrainger.com) is Canada's largest distributor of industrial, safety, and fastener products. Founded in Winnipeg, Manitoba in 1889, the company's early beginnings focused on the manufacture and sale of carriages, wagons, farm machinery, and a variety of other supplies and equipment. Today, Acklands-Grainger has more than 2,200 employees, 175 branches, and six distribution centres located coast-to-coast across Canada and sells over 350,000 products. Acklands-Grainger integrates drivers of performance in all of its human resource processes. Donna Pascal, vice-president of Human Resources explains the importance of clarifying employee performance expectations. "Starting with clear performance expectations—what we need from people to be successful—and linking that in terms of how we reward them and recognize them, has been key." The five performance drivers are wow the customer, have a winning attitude, drive for the best results, make the team better, and lead the way. "This is how our leadership team built the legacy and builds that culture for every team member, so they link it in their performance reviews, said Pascal. "Being very transparent on these expectations creates that culture and creates that trust in our leadership team."[1]

Introduction

Performance management is the process through which managers ensure that employees' activities and outputs contribute to the organization's goals. This process requires knowing what activities and outputs are desired, observing whether they occur, and providing feedback to help employees meet expectations. In the course of providing feedback, managers and employees may identify performance issues and establish ways to resolve those issues.

L○1 Identify the relevance of performance management and the steps in the process.

Relevance of Performance Management to Organizational Strategy and Performance

HRC1,4

In high-performing organizations, performance management is considered a "dynamic business process that enables performance and drives organizational and individual success—not as a static yearly process."[2] Relevance of this dynamic approach to the performance management process gains value through integration with other human resource management practices including workforce and succession planning, hiring and promotion decisions, learning, development planning, and rewards.[3]

In a survey of 164 chief financial officers (CFOs), performance management emerged as a top priority—73 percent said that, within their first 100 days on the job, "they were expected to come up with a new plan for performance management."[4] However, despite the importance placed on performance management and the widespread implementation—94 percent of organizations responding to a recent Conference Board of Canada survey have a performance management system, less than half of responding organizations (47 percent) say their performance management system is "effective" or "very effective."[5] See Figure 7.1.

FIGURE 7.1

Effectiveness of Performance Management System

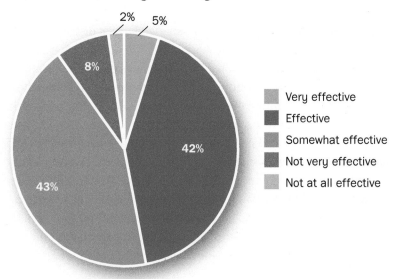

Legend:
- Very effective
- Effective
- Somewhat effective
- Not very effective
- Not at all effective

Slices: 2%, 5%, 8%, 42%, 43%

Source: "Compensation Planning Outlook 2014" (Ottawa: Conference Board of Canada, October 2013), p. 21.

In this chapter we examine a variety of approaches to performance management. We begin by describing the steps in the performance management process and then discuss the purpose of carrying out this process. Next, we discuss specific approaches to performance appraisal, including the strengths and weaknesses of each approach. We also look at various sources of performance information. The next section explores the kinds of errors that commonly occur during the assessment of performance, as well as ways to reduce those errors. Then we describe ways of giving performance feedback effectively and intervening when performance must improve. Finally, we summarize legal and ethical issues affecting performance management.

The Process of Performance Management

HRC 1, 3, 4

Although many employees have come to dread the annual "performance appraisal" meeting, at which a boss picks apart the employee's behaviours and apparent attitudes from the past year, performance management can potentially deliver many benefits. Effective performance management can tell top performers that they are valued, encourage communication between managers and their employees, establish uniform standards for evaluating employees, and help the organization identify its strongest performers. Performance appraisals, properly done, meet an "ethical obligation of leadership" by providing information that all members of an organization want to know so they can succeed: "What is it you expect of me? How am I doing at meeting your expectations?"[6] And, according to a recent SHRM Globoforce Employee Recognition Survey, 83 percent of employees who are satisfied with their reviews are also satisfied with their jobs overall (versus only 55 percent for those dissatisfied).[7]

Figure 7.2 shows the six steps in the performance management process. As shown in the model, feedback and formal performance evaluation are important parts of the process; however, they are not the

FIGURE 7.2

Steps in the Performance Management Process

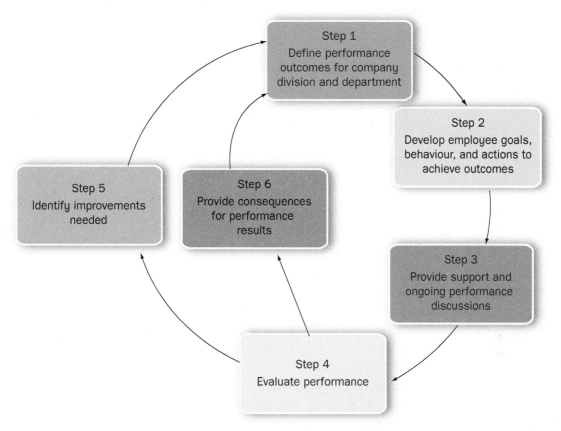

Sources: Based on E. Pulakos, *Performance Management* (Oxford, England: Wiley-Blackwell, 2009); H. Aguinis, "An Expanded View of Performance Management," in J. W. Smith and M. London (eds.), *Performance Management* (San Francisco: Jossey-Bass, 2009), pp. 1–43; and J. Russell and L. Russell, "Talk Me Through It: The Next Level of Performance Management," *T+D,* April 2010, pp. 42–48.

only critical components. An effective performance management process contributes to the company's overall competitive advantage and must be given visible support by the CEO and other senior managers. This support ensures that the process is consistently used across the company, appraisals are completed on time, and giving and receiving ongoing performance feedback is recognized as an accepted part of the company's culture.

The first two steps of the process involve identifying what the company is trying to accomplish (its goals or objectives) and developing employee goals and actions to achieve these outcomes. Typically the outcomes benefit customers, the employee's peers or team members, and the organization itself. The goals, behaviours, and activities should be measurable and become part of the employee's job description.

Step three in the process—organizational support—involves providing employees with training, necessary resources and tools, and ongoing feedback between the employee and manager, which focuses on accomplishments as well as issues and challenges that influence performance. For effective performance management, both the manager and the employee have to value feedback and exchange it on a regular basis—not just once or twice a year. Also, the manager needs to make time to provide ongoing feedback to the employee and learn how to give and receive it.

Step four involves evaluating performance; that is, when the manager and employee discuss and compare targeted goals and supporting behaviour with actual results. This step includes the formal performance appraisal(s).

The final steps of the performance management process involve both the employee and manager identifying what the employee can do to capitalize on performance strengths and address weaknesses (step 5) and providing consequences for achieving (or failing to achieve) performance outcomes (such as pay increases, bonuses, or action plans) (step 6). This includes identifying training needs; adjusting the type or frequency of feedback the manager provides to the employee; clarifying, adjusting, or modifying performance outcomes; and discussing behaviours or activities that need improvement.

L○2 Discuss the purposes of performance management systems.

What Are the Purposes of Performance Management?

Organizations establish performance management systems to meet three broad purposes: strategic, administrative, and developmental.

Strategic purpose means effective performance management helps the organization achieve its business objectives. It does this by helping to link employees' behaviour with the organization's goals. Performance management starts with defining what the organization expects from each employee. It measures each employee's performance to identify where those expectations are and are not being met. This enables the organization to take corrective action, such as training, incentives, or discipline. Performance management can achieve its strategic purpose only when measurements are truly aligned with the organization's goals and when the goals and feedback about performance are communicated to employees. For example, at Maple Leaf Foods (www.mapleleaffoods.com) employee performance is based on not only achieving specific outcomes, but also demonstrating behaviours that are consistent with the 21 corporate values developed by president and CEO Michael McCain. This focus on *how* results are achieved includes things like "Do What's Right" (act with integrity, behave responsibly, and treat people with respect) and "Dare to be Transparent" (have the courage to be candid and direct, and communicate openly). At Maple Leaf Foods, every employee's performance is ranked based on two key performance dimensions—results achieved and values consistency.[8]

The *administrative purpose* of a performance management system refers to how organizations use the system to provide information for day-to-day decisions about salary, benefits, and recognition programs. Performance management can also support decision making related to employee retention, termination for poor performance, and hiring or layoffs. Because performance management supports these administrative decisions, the information in a performance appraisal can have a great impact on the future of individual employees. Managers recognize this, which is the reason they may feel uncomfortable conducting performance appraisals when the appraisal information is negative and, therefore, likely to lead to a layoff, disappointing pay increase, or other negative outcome.

Finally, performance management has a *developmental purpose,* meaning that it serves as a basis for developing employees' knowledge and skills. Even employees who are meeting expectations can become more valuable and high-performing when they receive and discuss performance feedback. Effective performance feedback makes employees aware of their strengths and of the areas in which they can improve. Discussing areas in which employees fall short can help the employees and their manager uncover the source of problems and identify steps for improvement. Although discussing shortcomings may feel uncomfortable, it is necessary when performance management has a developmental purpose. As described in the "Did You Know?" box, millennial and Gen X employees tend to prefer positive feedback.

L○3 Define five criteria for measuring the effectiveness of a performance management system.

What Are the Criteria for Effective Performance Management?

HRC 1, 4, 9

In Chapter 5, we saw that there are many ways to predict performance of a job candidate. Similarly, there are many ways to measure the performance of an employee. For performance management to achieve its goals, its methods for measuring performance must be effective. Selecting these measures is a critical part of planning a performance management system. As summarized in Figure 7.3, several criteria determine the effectiveness of performance measures.

- *Fit with strategy*—A performance management system should aim at achieving employee behaviour and mindset that support the organization's strategy, goals, and culture. If a company emphasizes customer service, then its performance management system should define the kinds of

Did You KNOW?

Millennials & Gen X Prefer Praise to Corrective Feedback

Given the choice, both Millennials and Gen X are more than twice as likely to prefer feedback that focuses on work done well rather than work done poorly.

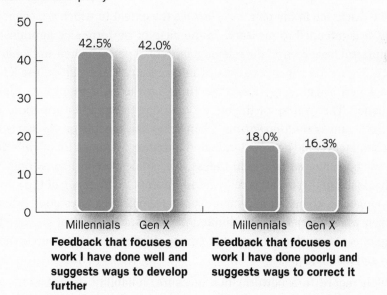

Source: Naoko Hawkins, Jane Vellone, and Ruth Wright, "Workplace Preferences of Millennials and Gen X: Attracting and Retaining the 2020 Workforce," Table 5: Type of Feedback on Job Performance Preferred by Millennials and Gen X, June 2014, *The Conference Board of Canada*, p. 25.

FIGURE 7.3

Criteria for Effective Performance Measures

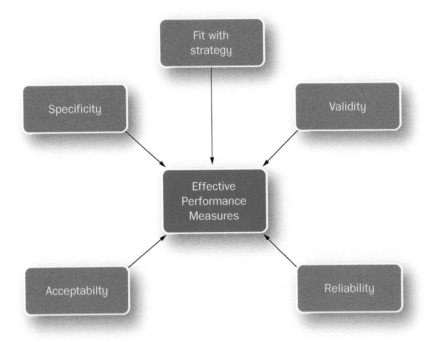

behaviour that contribute to excellent customer service. Performance appraisals should measure whether employees are engaging in those behaviours. Feedback should help employees enhance their performance in those areas. When an organization's strategy changes, human resources professionals should help managers assess how the performance management system should change to serve the new strategy.

- *Validity*—As we discussed in Chapter 5, *validity* is the extent to which a measurement tool actually measures what it is intended to measure. In the case of performance appraisal, validity refers to whether the appraisal measures all the relevant aspects of performance and omits irrelevant aspects of performance. Figure 7.4 shows two sets of information. The circle on the left represents all the information in a performance appraisal; the circle on the right represents all relevant measures of job performance. The overlap of the circles contains the valid information. Information that is gathered but irrelevant is *contamination*. Comparing salespeople on the basis of how many calls they make to customers could be a contaminated measure. Making a lot of calls does not necessarily improve sales or customer satisfaction, unless every salesperson makes only well-planned calls. Information that is not gathered but is relevant represents a *deficiency* of the performance measure. For example, suppose a company measures whether employees have good attendance records but not whether they work efficiently. This limited performance appraisal is unlikely to provide a full picture of employees' contribution to the company. Performance measures should minimize both contamination and deficiency.

- *Reliability*—With regard to a performance measure, reliability describes the consistency of the results that the performance measure will deliver. *Interrater reliability* is consistency of results when more than one person measures performance. Simply asking a supervisor to rate an employee's performance on a scale of 1 to 5 would likely have low interrater reliability; the rating will differ

FIGURE 7.4

Contamination and Deficiency of a Job Performance Measure

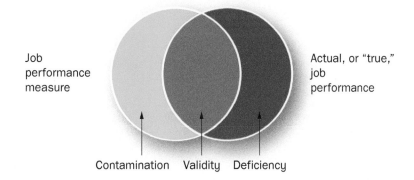

Job performance measure

Actual, or "true," job performance

Contamination   Validity   Deficiency

depending on who is assessing the employees. *Test-retest reliability* refers to consistency of results over time. If a performance measure lacks test-retest reliability, determining whether an employee's performance has truly changed over time will be impossible.

- *Acceptability*—Whether or not a measure is valid and reliable, it must meet the practical standard of being acceptable to the people who use it. For example, the people who use a performance measure must believe that it is not too time-consuming. Likewise, if employees believe the measure is unfair, they will not use the feedback as a basis for improving their performance.

- *Specificity*—A performance measure should specifically tell employees what is expected of them and how they can meet those expectations. Being specific helps performance management meet the goals of supporting strategy and developing employees. Being specific may also mean the performance measure can be defined in quantitative terms. If a measure does not specify what an employee must do to help the organization achieve its goals, it does not support the strategy. If the measure fails to point out performance gaps, employees will not know how to improve.

LO4 Compare the major methods for measuring performance.

How Is Performance Measured?

Organizations have developed a wide variety of methods for measuring performance. Some methods rank each employee to compare employees' performance. Other methods break down the evaluation into ratings of individual attributes, behaviours, or results. Many organizations use a measurement system that includes a variety of these measures. Table 7.1 compares these methods in terms of our criteria for effective performance management.

Making Comparisons

The performance appraisal method may require the rater to compare one individual's performance with that of others. This method involves some form of ranking, in which some employees are the highest performers, some are fully meeting expectations, and others are not. The usual techniques for making comparisons are simple ranking, forced distribution, and paired comparison.

TABLE 7.1

Basic Approaches to Performance Management

Approach	Fit With Strategy	Validity	Reliability	Acceptability	Specificity
			Criteria		
Comparative	Poor, unless manager takes time to make link	Can be high if ratings are done carefully	Depends on rater, but usually no measure of agreement used	Moderate; easy to develop and use but resistant to normative standard	Very low
Attribute	Usually low; requires manager to make link	Usually low; can be fine if developed carefully	Usually low; can be improved by specific definitions of attributes	High; easy to develop and use	Very low
Behavioural	Can be quite high	Usually high; minimizes contamination and deficiency	Usually high	Moderate; difficult to develop, but accepted well for use	Very high
Results	Very high	Usually high; can be both contaminated and deficient	High; main problem can be test-retest—depends on timing of measure	High; usually developed with input from those to be evaluated	High regarding results, but low regarding behaviours necessary to achieve them

Simple ranking requires managers to rank employees in their group from the highest performer to the lowest performer. In a variation on this approach, *alternation ranking*, the manager works from a list of employees. First, the manager decides which employee is the highest performer and crosses that person's name off the list. From the remaining names, the manager selects the lowest performing employee and crosses off that name. The process continues with the manager selecting the second-highest, second-lowest, third-highest, and so on until all the employees have been ranked. The major downside of ranking involves validity. To state a performance measure as broadly as "highest" or "lowest" doesn't define what exactly is effective or ineffective about the person's contribution to the organization. Ranking therefore raises questions about fairness.

Another way to compare employees' performance is with the **forced-distribution method.** This type of performance measurement assigns a certain percentage of employees to each category in a set of categories. For example, the organization might establish the following percentages and categories:

- Outstanding—5 percent
- Exceeds expectations—20 percent
- Meets expectations—55 percent
- Developmental—15 percent
- Below expectations—5 percent

simple ranking
Method of performance measurement that requires managers to rank employees in their group from the highest to the lowest performer.

forced-distribution method
Method of performance measurement that assigns a certain percentage of employees to each category in a set of categories.

The manager completing the performance appraisal would rate 5 percent of his or her employees as outstanding, 20 percent as exceeding expectations, and so on. A forced-distribution approach works best if the members of a group really do vary this much in terms of their performance. It overcomes the temptation to rate everyone high in order to avoid conflict. Research simulating some features of forced rankings found that they improved performance when combined with goals and rewards, especially in the first few years, when the system eliminated the lowest performers.[9] However, a manager who does very well at selecting, motivating, and training employees will have a group of high-performers. This manager would have difficulty assigning employees to the lower categories. In that situation, saying that some employees are "below expectations" or "developmental" may not only be inaccurate, but will hurt morale.

The Conference Board of Canada reports that although only 15 percent of surveyed organizations use a forced-distribution performance management system, an additional 40 percent of surveyed organizations have guidelines or recommendations to ensure a normal distribution of performance ratings.[10] Figure 7.5 illustrates these findings.

Another variation on rankings is the **paired-comparison method.** This approach involves comparing each employee with each other employee to establish rankings. Suppose a manager has five employees, Jaida, Ramat, Caitlin, Ming, and David. The manager compares Jaida's performance to Ramat's and assigns one point to whichever employer is the higher performer. Then the manager compares Jaida's performance to Caitlin's, then to Ming's, and finally to David's. The manager repeats this process with Ramat, comparing his performance to Caitlin's, Ming's, and David's. When the manager has compared every pair of employees, the manager counts the number of points for each employee. The employee with the most points is considered the top-ranked employee. Clearly, this method is time-consuming if a group has more than a handful of employees. For a group of 15, the manager must make 105 comparisons.

paired-comparison method
Method of performance measurement that compares each employee with each other employee to establish rankings.

In spite of the drawbacks, ranking employees offers some benefits. It counteracts the tendency to avoid controversy by rating everyone favourably or near the centre of the scale. Also, if some managers tend to

FIGURE 7.5

Forced Performance Distribution and Guidelines

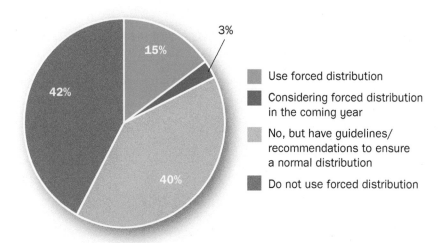

Source: "Compensation Planning Outlook 2014" (Ottawa: Conference Board of Canada), p. 22.

evaluate behaviour more strictly (or more leniently) than others, a ranking system can erase that tendency from performance scores. Therefore, ranking systems can be useful for supporting decisions about how to distribute pay raises or layoffs. Some ranking systems are easy to use, which makes them acceptable to the managers who use them. A major drawback of rankings is that often they are not linked to the organization's goals. Also, a simple ranking system leaves the basis for ranking open to interpretation. In that case, the rankings are not helpful for employee development and may hurt morale or result in legal challenges.

Rating Individuals

Instead of focusing on arranging a group of employees from highest to lowest performance, performance measurement can look at each employee's performance relative to a uniform set of standards. The measurement may evaluate employees in terms of attributes (characteristics, traits, or competencies) believed necessary for success in the job or in the organization. Or the measurements may identify whether employees have *behaved* in desirable ways, such as helping co-workers or working safely. The performance management system must identify the desired attributes or behaviours, then provide a form on which the manager can rate the employee in terms of those attributes or behaviours. Typically, the form includes a rating scale, such as a scale from 1 to 5, where 1 is the lowest level of performance and 5 is the highest.

Rating Attributes

The most widely used method for rating attributes is the **graphic rating scale.** This method lists attributes and provides a rating scale for each. The employer uses the scale to indicate the extent to which the employee being rated displays the attributes. The rating scale may provide points to circle (as on a scale going from 1 for "significantly below expectations" to 5 for "exceptional"), or it may provide a line representing a range of scores, with the manager marking a place along the line. Figure 7.6 shows an example of a graphic rating scale that uses a set of ratings from 1 to 5. A drawback of this approach is that it leaves to

FIGURE 7.6

Example of a Graphic Rating Scale

The following areas of performance are significant to most positions. Indicate your assessment of performance on each dimension by circling the appropriate rating.

PERFORMANCE DIMENSIONS	RATING				
	OUTSTANDING	EXCEEDS EXPECTATIONS	MEETS EXPECTATIONS	DEVELOPMENTAL	BELOW EXPECTATIONS
Client service	5	4	3	2	1
Communication	5	4	3	2	1
Leadership	5	4	3	2	1
Professionalism	5	4	3	2	1
Teamwork	5	4	3	2	1
Interpersonal skills	5	4	3	2	1
Initiative	5	4	3	2	1
Creativity	5	4	3	2	1
Problem solving	5	4	3	2	1

the particular manager the decisions about what is "outstanding teamwork" or "exceeds expectations" in problem solving. The result is low reliability, because managers are likely to arrive at different assessments.

graphic rating scale
Method of performance measurement that lists attributes and provides a rating scale for each attribute; the employer uses the scale to indicate the extent to which an employee displays each attribute.

To get around this problem, some organizations use **mixed-standard scales,** which use several statements describing each attribute to produce a final score for that attribute. The manager scores the employee in terms of how the employee compares to each statement. Consider the sample mixed-standard scale in Figure 7.7. To create this scale, the organization determined that the relevant attributes are initiative, client orientation, and relations with others. For each attribute, statements were written to describe a person having a high level of that attribute, a medium level, and a low level. The sentences for the attributes were rearranged so that the nine statements about the three attributes are mixed together. The manager who uses this scale reads each statement, then indicates whether the employee performs above (+), at (0), or below (−) the level described. The key in the middle section of Figure 7.7 tells how to use the pluses, zeros, and minuses to score performance. Someone who excels at every level of performance (pluses for high, medium, and low performance) receives a score of 7 for that attribute. Someone who fails to live up to every description of performance (minuses for high, medium, and low) receives a score of 1 for that attribute. The bottom of Figure 7.7 calculates the scores for the ratings used in this example.

mixed-standard scales
Method of performance measurement that uses several statements describing each attribute to produce a final score for that attribute.

Rating attributes is the most popular way to measure performance in organizations. In general, attribute-based performance methods are easy to develop and can be applied to a wide variety of jobs and organizations. If the organization is careful to identify which attributes are associated with high performance, and to define them carefully on the appraisal form, these methods can be reliable and valid. However, appraisal forms often fail to meet this standard. In addition, measurement of attributes may not be clearly linked to the organization's strategy. Furthermore, employees tend perhaps rightly to be defensive about receiving a mere numerical rating on some attribute. How would you feel if you were told you scored 2 on a 5-point scale of initiative or communication skill? The number might seem arbitrary, and it doesn't tell you how to improve.

Rating Behaviours

One way to overcome the drawbacks of rating attributes is to assess employees' behaviour. To rate behaviours, the organization begins by defining which behaviours are associated with success on the job. Which kinds of employee behaviour help the organization achieve its goals? The appraisal form asks the manager to rate an employee in terms of each of the identified behaviours.

One way to rate behaviours is with the **critical-incident method.** This approach requires managers to keep a record of specific examples of the employee behaving in ways that are either effective or ineffective. Here's an example of a critical incident in the performance evaluation of an appliance repair person:

critical-incident method
Method of performance measurement based on managers' records of specific examples of the employee behaving in ways that are either effective or ineffective.

FIGURE 7.7

Example of a Mixed-Standard Scale

Three competencies being assessed:	Levels of performance in statements:
Initiative (INTV)	High (H)
Client orientation (CLO)	Medium (M)
Relations with others (RWO)	Low (L)

Instructions. Please indicate next to each statement whether the employee's performance is above (+), equal to (0), or below (–) the statement.

INTV	H	1.	This employee is a real self-starter. The employee always takes the initiative and his/her supervisor never has to prod this individual.	+
CLO	M	2.	Although this employee has some difficulty anticipating client needs, s/he is usually friendly and approachable.	+
RWO	L	3.	This employee has a tendency to get into unnecessary conflicts with other people.	0
INTV	M	4.	While generally this employee shows initiative, occasionally his/her supervisor must prod him/her to complete work.	+
CLO	L	5.	This employee frequently needs assistance in handling customer requests.	+
RWO	H	6.	This employee is on good terms with everyone. S/he can get along with people even when s/he does not agree with them.	–
INTV	L	7.	This employee has a bit of a tendency to sit around and wait for directions.	+
CLO	H	8.	This employee creates and maintains long-term client relationships.	–
RWO	M	9.	This employee gets along with most people. Only very occasionally does s/he have conflicts with others on the job, and these are likely to be minor.	–

Scoring Key:

STATEMENTS			SCORE
HIGH	MEDIUM	LOW	
+	+	+	7
0	+	+	6
–	+	+	5
–	0	+	4
–	–	+	3
–	–	0	2
–	–	–	1

Example score from preceding ratings:

	STATEMENTS			SCORE
	HIGH	MEDIUM	LOW	
Initiative	+	+	+	7
Client orientation	0	+	+	6
Relations with others	–	–	0	2

A customer called in about a refrigerator that had stopped dispensing water. The technician prediagnosed the cause of the problem based on known issues with the particular make and model of refrigerator, and checked his truck for the necessary parts. When he found he did not have them, he checked the parts out from inventory so that the customer's refrigerator would be repaired on his first visit and the customer would be satisfied promptly.

This incident provides evidence of the employee's knowledge of refrigerator repair and concern for efficiency and customer satisfaction. Evaluating performance in this specific way gives employees feedback about what they do well and what requires improvement. The manager can also relate the incidents to how the employee is helping the company achieve its goals. Keeping a daily or weekly log of critical incidents requires significant effort, however, and managers may resist this requirement. Also, critical incidents may be unique, so they may not support comparisons among employees.

A **behaviourally anchored rating scale (BARS)** builds on the critical incident approach. The BARS method is intended to define performance dimensions specifically, using statements of behaviour that describe different levels of performance.[11] (The statements are "anchors" of the performance levels.) The scale in Figure 7.8 shows various performance levels for "listening, understanding, and responding." The statement at the top (rating 5) describes the highest level of listening, understanding, and responding. The statement at the bottom describes behaviour associated with ineffective or counterproductive performance. These statements are based on data about past performance. The organization gathers many critical incidents representing effective and ineffective performance, then classifies them from most to least effective. When experts about the job agree

behaviourally anchored rating scale (BARS)
Method of performance measurement that rates behaviour in terms of a scale showing specific statements of behaviour that describe different levels of performance.

An employee's performance measurement differs from job to job. For example, a salesperson's performance is measured by the dollar amount of sales, the number of new customers, and customer satisfaction surveys. How would the performance measurement of a vehicle sales associate differ from those of a service technician?

FIGURE 7.8

BARS Rating Dimension: Customer Service Representative

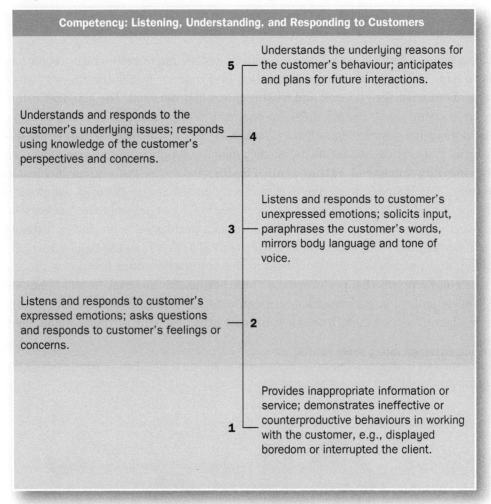

Source: Adapted from "Manager's HR Toolkit," BC Public Service Agency.

the statements clearly represent levels of performance, they are used as anchors to guide the rater. Although BARS can improve interrater reliability, this method can bias the manager's memory. The statements used as anchors can help managers remember similar behaviours, but at the expense of other critical incidents.[12]

A **behavioural observation scale (BOS)** is a variation of a BARS. Like a BARS, a BOS is developed from critical incidents.[13] However, while a BARS discards many examples in creating the rating scale, a BOS uses many of them to define all behaviours necessary for effective performance (or behaviours that signal ineffective performance). As a result, a BOS may use 15 behaviours to define levels of performance. Also, a BOS asks the manager to rate the frequency with which the employee has exhibited the behaviour during the rating period. These ratings are averaged to compute an overall performance rating. Figure 7.9 provides a simplified example of a BOS for assessing a supervisor's behaviour "overcoming resistance to change."

behavioural observation scale (BOS)
A variation of BARS, which uses all behaviours necessary for effective performance to rate performance at a task.

FIGURE 7.9

Example of a Behavioural Observation Scale

Overcoming Resistance to Change

Directions: Rate the frequency of each behaviour from 1 (Almost Never) to 5 (Almost Always).

1. Describes the details of the change to employees.
   Almost Never 1   2   3   4   5   Almost Always

2. Explains why the change is necessary.
   Almost Never 1   2   3   4   5   Almost Always

3. Discusses how the change will affect the employee.
   Almost Never 1   2   3   4   5   Almost Always

4. Listens to the employee's concerns.
   Almost Never 1   2   3   4   5   Almost Always

5. Asks the employee for help in making the change work.
   Almost Never 1   2   3   4   5   Almost Always

6. If necessary, specifies the date for a follow-up meeting
   to respond to the employee's concerns.
   Almost Never 1   2   3   4   5   Almost Always

Score: Total number of points = _____

Performance

Points	Performance Rating
6–10	Below expectations
11–15	Developmental
16–20	Meets expectations
21–25	Exceeds expectations
26–30	Outstanding

Scores are set by management.

A major drawback of this method is the amount of information required. A BOS can have 80 or more behaviours, and the manager must recall how often the employee exhibited each behaviour in a 6-to-12-month rating period. This is taxing enough for one employee, but managers often must assess ten or more employees. Even so, compared to BARS and graphic rating scales, managers and employees have said they prefer BOS for ease of use, providing feedback, maintaining objectivity, and suggesting training needs.[14]

Another approach to assessment builds directly on a branch of psychology called *behaviourism*, which holds that individuals' future behaviour is determined by their past experiences—specifically, the ways in which past behaviours have been reinforced. People tend to repeat behaviours that have been rewarded in the past. Providing feedback and reinforcement can therefore modify individuals' future behaviour. Applied to behaviour in organizations, **organizational behaviour modification (OBM)** is a plan for managing the behaviour of employees through a formal system of feedback and reinforcement. Specific OBM techniques vary, but most have four components:[15]

1. Define a set of key behaviours necessary for job performance.

2. Use a measurement system to assess whether the employee exhibits the key behaviours.

organizational behaviour modification (OBM)
A plan for managing the behaviour of employees through a formal system of feedback and reinforcement.

3. Inform employees of the key behaviours, perhaps in terms of goals for how often to exhibit the behaviours.

4. Provide feedback and reinforcement based on employees' behaviour.

OBM techniques have been used in a variety of settings. For example, a community health agency used OBM to increase the rates and timeliness of critical job behaviours by showing employees the connection between job behaviours and the agency's accomplishments.[16] This process identified job behaviours related to administration, record keeping, and service provided to clients. Feedback and reinforcement improved staff performance. OBM also increased the frequency of safety behaviours in a processing plant.[17]

Behavioural approaches such as organizational behaviour modification and rating scales can be very effective. These methods can link the company's goals to the specific behaviour required to achieve those goals. Behavioural methods also can generate specific feedback, along with guidance in areas requiring improvements. As a result, these methods tend to be valid. The people to be measured often help in developing the measures, so acceptance tends to be high as well. When raters are well trained, reliability also tends to be high. However, behavioural methods do not work as well for complex jobs in which it is difficult to see a link between behaviour and results or there is more than one good way to achieve success.[18]

Measuring Results

Performance measurement can focus on managing the objective, measurable results of a job or work group. Results might include sales, costs, or productivity (output per worker or per dollar spent on production), among many possible measures. Two of the most popular methods for measuring results are measurement of productivity and management by objectives.

Productivity is an important measure of success, because getting more done with a smaller amount of resources (money or people) increases the company's profits. Productivity usually refers to the output of production workers, but it can be used more generally as a performance measure. To do this, the organization identifies the outcomes it expects a group or individual to accomplish. At a repair shop, for instance, the desired outcome might be something like "quality of repair." The next step is to define how to measure quality of repair. The repair shop could track the percentage of items returned because they still do not work after a repair and the percentage of quality-control inspections passed. For each measure, the organization decides what level of performance is desired. Finally, the organization sets up a system for tracking these measures and giving employees feedback about their performance in terms of these measures. This type of performance measurement can be time-consuming to set up, but research suggests it can improve productivity and performance.[19]

Management by objectives (MBO) is a system in which people at each level of the organization set goals in a process that flows from top to bottom, so employees at all levels are contributing to the organization's overall goals. These goals become the standards for evaluating each employee's performance. An MBO system has three components:[20]

management by objectives (MBO)
A system in which people at each level of the organization set goals in a process that flows from top to bottom, so employees at all levels are contributing to the organization's overall goals; these goals become the standards for evaluating each employee's performance.

1. Goals are specific, difficult, and objective. The goals listed in the second column of Table 7.2 provide two examples for a bank.

2. Managers and their employees work together to set the goals.

3. The manager gives objective feedback through the rating period to monitor progress toward the goals. The two right-hand columns in Table 7.2 are examples of feedback given after one year.

MBO can have a very positive effect on an organization's performance. In 70 studies of MBO's performance, 68 showed that productivity improved.[21] The productivity gains tended to be greatest when top management was highly committed to MBO. Also, because staff members are involved in setting goals, it is likely that MBO systems effectively link individual employees' performance with the organization's overall goals.

In general, evaluation of results can be less subjective than other kinds of performance measurement. This makes measuring results highly acceptable to employees and managers alike. Results-oriented performance measurement is also relatively easy to link to the organization's goals. However, measuring results has problems with validity, because results may be affected by circumstances beyond each employee's performance. Also, if the organization measures only final results, it may fail to measure significant aspects of performance that are not directly related to those results. If individuals focus only on aspects of performance that are measured, they may neglect significant skills or behaviours. For example, if the organization measures only productivity, employees may not be concerned enough with customer service. The outcome may be high efficiency (costs are low) but low effectiveness (sales are low, too).[22] Finally, focusing strictly on results does not provide guidance on how to improve.

To increase the accuracy and amount of data and to obtain more frequent employee evaluations, mobile technology offers a promising application, referred to as *event capturing,* which would enable managers to make short descriptive entries (e.g., limit the number of characters) to capture behaviours, outcomes, or performance on an ongoing basis throughout the year. Alternatively, a less sophisticated variation would require managers to send themselves emails with employee observations they save for later retrieval. These frequent, technology-enabled observations not only increase the accuracy and amount of data but also reduce the effect of the recency emphasis error that will be discussed later in the chapter.[23]

Balanced Scorecard

The **balanced scorecard** is an organizational approach to performance management that integrates strategic perspectives including financial, customer, internal business processes, and learning and growth. Robert S. Kaplan and David P. Norton developed this widely adopted approach, illustrated in Figure 7.10. The basic idea is that managers are encouraged to go beyond meeting just traditional

balanced scorecard
An organizational approach to performance management that integrates strategic perspectives including financial, customer, internal business processes, and learning and growth.

TABLE 7.2

Management by Objectives: Two Objectives for a Bank

Key Result Area	Objective	% Complete	Actual Performance
Loan portfolio management	Increase portfolio value by 8% over the next 12 months	87.5	Increased portfolio value by 7% over the past 12 months
Sales	Generate fee income of $30,000 over the next 12 months	150	Generated fee income of $45,000 over the past 12 months

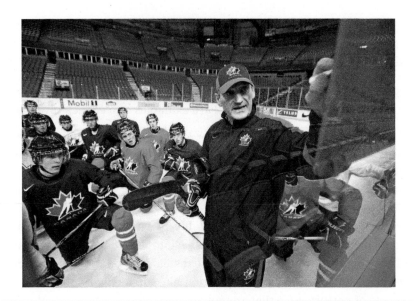

Coaches provide feedback to their team just as managers provide feedback to their employees. Feedback is important so that individuals know what they are doing well and what areas they may need to work on.

FIGURE 7.10

The Balanced Scorecard

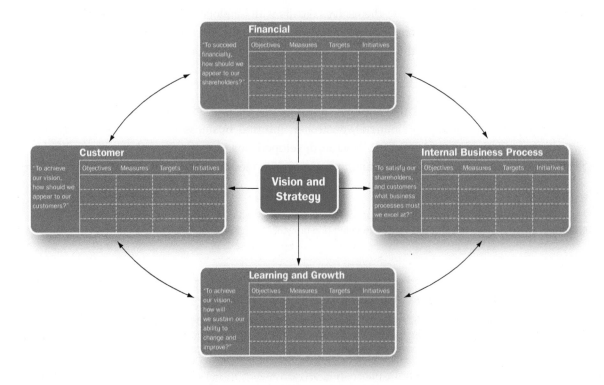

Source: Reprinted by permission of Harvard Business Review. Robert S. Kaplan and David P. Norton "Using the Balanced Scorecard as a Strategic Management System," July–August 2007 p. 153. Copyright © 2007 by the Harvard Business School Publishing Corporation; all rights reserved.

financial targets, and recognize and simultaneously monitor the progress of other important goals such as customer and employee satisfaction.[24] Use of a balanced scorecard provides the means to align strategy at all levels of the organization and serves as "an excellent guide to measure and manage the performance of all employees."[25] Balanced scorecards are widely used in both the public and private sector. A sampling of the organizations that use balanced scorecards as part of their strategic management and performance management systems include: J. D. Irving Ltd. (www.jdirving.com), Canadian Cancer Society (www.cancer.ca), Carleton University (www.carleton.ca), Nova Scotia Power Inc. (www.nspower.ca), The Cooperators (www.cooperators.ca), and Great-West Life Assurance Company (www.greatwestlife.com).

L○5 Describe major sources of performance information in terms of their advantages and disadvantages.

What Are the Sources of Performance Information?

All the methods of performance measurement require decisions about who will collect and analyze the performance information. To qualify for this task, a person should have an understanding of the job requirements and the opportunity to see the employee doing the job. The traditional approach is for managers to gather information about their employees' performance and arrive at performance ratings. However, many sources are possible. Possibilities of information sources include managers, peers, direct reports, self, and customers.

Using just one person as a source of information poses certain problems. People tend to like some people more than others, and those feelings can bias how an employee's efforts are perceived. Also, one person is likely to see an employee in a limited number of situations. A supervisor, for example, cannot see how an employee behaves when the supervisor is not there—for example, when a service technician is at the customer's facility. To get as complete an assessment as possible, some organizations combine information from most or all of the possible sources, in what is called a *multi-rater* or **360-degree performance appraisal.**

360-degree performance appraisal
Performance measurement that combines information from the employee's managers, peers, direct reports, self, and customers.

The John Molson School of Business at Montreal's Concordia University (www.concordia.ca) conducted a study to learn about the experiences of 101 large Canadian organizations with 360-degree programs. The study found that 43 percent of the organizations surveyed used 360-degree, that is, multi-rater approaches. Companies are using 360-degree performance reviews because of advantages including increased measurement accuracy and perceived fairness. Respondents also identified challenges such as resistance from individuals because of concerns about the process being time, cost-, and energy-consuming, trust issues including anonymity of feedback, and the need to ensure a clear purpose and link to organizational strategy are in place before implementing 360-degree performance appraisal.[26] Netflix (www.netflix.com) instituted informal 360-degree performance reviews when they stopped doing formal performance reviews. The 360-degree reviews were kept simple, people were asked to "identify things that colleagues should stop, start, or continue." Initially, an anonymous software system was used, but later that shifted to the use of signed feedback, and now many teams hold their 360-degree reviews face-to-face.[27]

Managers

The most-used source of performance information is the employee's manager. It is usually safe for organizations to assume that supervisors have extensive knowledge of the job requirements and that they have enough opportunity to observe their employees. In other words, managers possess the basic qualifications for this responsibility. Another advantage of using managers to evaluate performance is that they have an incentive to provide accurate and helpful feedback, because their own success depends so much on their employees' performance.[28] Finally, when managers try to observe employee behaviour or discuss performance issues in the feedback session, their feedback can improve performance, and employees tend to perceive the appraisal as accurate.[29]

Still, in some situations, problems can occur with using supervisors as the source of performance information. For employees in some jobs, the supervisor does not have enough opportunity to observe the employee performing job duties. A sales manager with many offsite sales associates cannot be with the sales associates on many visits to customers. Even if the sales manager does make a point of travelling with sales associates for a few days, they are likely to be on their best behaviour while the manager is there. The manager cannot observe how they perform at other times.

Peers

Another source of performance information is the employee's peers or coworkers. Peers are an excellent source of information about performance in a job where the supervisor does not often observe the employee. Examples include law enforcement and sales. For these and other jobs, peers may have the most opportunity to observe the employee in day-to-day activities. Peers have expert knowledge of job requirements. They also bring a different perspective to the evaluation and can provide extremely valid assessments of performance.[30]

Peer evaluations obviously have some potential disadvantages. Friendships (or rivalries) have the potential to bias ratings. Research, however, has provided little evidence that this is a problem.[31] Another disadvantage is that when the evaluations are done to support administrative decisions, peers are uncomfortable with rating employees for decisions that may affect themselves. Generally, peers are more willing to participate in reviews to be used for employee development.[32]

Direct Reports

For evaluating the performance of managers, direct reports are an especially valuable source of information. Direct reports—the people reporting to the manager—often have the best chance to see how well a manager treats employees. At HCL Technologies (www.hcltech.com), for example, managers not only receive reviews from their employees but are expected to publish the reports on the company's internal website to create a climate that values open communication and personal development. Sanjeev Nikore, a vice-president who did this, learned that his employees found him resistant to delegating. He acknowledged he needed to improve his people skills, made some changes, and earned a key promotion.[33]

Direct report evaluations have some potential problems because of the power relationships involved. Direct reports are reluctant to say negative things about the person to whom they report; they prefer to provide feedback anonymously. Managers, however, have a more positive reaction to this type of feedback when the employees are identified. When feedback requires that the direct reports identify themselves, they tend to give the manager higher ratings.[34] Another problem is that when managers receive ratings from direct reports, the employees have more power, so managers tend to emphasize employee satisfaction, even at the expense of productivity. This issue arises primarily when the evaluations are used for administrative decisions. Therefore, as with peer evaluations, direct report evaluations are most appropriate for developmental purposes. To protect employees, the process should be anonymous and use at least three employees to rate each manager.

Despite these challenges, direct report ratings of managers could become even more widespread for the simple reason that individuals are growing used to the experience of using social media to publish online ratings of everything from movies and restaurants to professors and doctors. For more on this phenomenon and how it might affect performance management, see the e-HRM feature: "Crowdsourcing: The Future of Appraisals?"

 E-HRM

Crowdsourcing: The future of appraisals?

Self

No one has a greater chance to observe the employee's behaviour on the job than does the employee himself or herself. Self-ratings are rarely used alone, but they can contribute valuable information. A common approach is to have employees evaluate their own performance before the feedback session. This activity gets employees thinking about their accomplishments and performance. Areas of disagreement between the self-appraisal and other evaluations can be fruitful topics for the feedback session. At an Australia-based software company called Atlassian (www.atlassian.com), self-appraisals are part of weekly performance feedback. Employees use an online app that displays performance-related questions such as, "How often have you stretched yourself?" and lets employees move a dot along a scale with a range of possible answers. The responses then serve as a catalyst for discussion in meetings between each employee and his or her supervisor.[35]

The obvious problem with self-ratings is that individuals have a tendency to inflate assessments of their performance. Especially if the ratings will be used for administrative decisions, exaggerating one's contributions has practical benefits. Also, social psychologists have found that, in general, people tend to blame outside circumstances for their failures while taking a large part of the credit for their successes. Supervisors can reduce this tendency by providing frequent feedback, but, because people tend to perceive situations this way, self-appraisals are not appropriate as the basis for administrative decisions.[36]

Customers

Services are often produced and consumed on the spot, so the customer is often the only person who directly observes the service performance and may be the best source of performance information. Many companies in service industries have introduced customer evaluations of employee performance. Marriott (www.marriott.com) provides a customer satisfaction card in every room and emails surveys to a random sample of its hotel customers. Whirlpool's (www.whirlpool.com) Consumer Services Division conducts both mail and telephone surveys of customers after factory technicians have serviced their appliances. These surveys allow the company to evaluate an individual technician's customer-service behaviours while in the customer's home.

Using customer evaluations of employee performance is appropriate in two situations.[37] The first is when an employee's job requires direct service to the customer or linking the customer to other services within the organization. Second, customer evaluations are appropriate when the organization is interested in gathering information to determine what products and services the customer wants. That is, customer evaluations contribute to the organization's goals by enabling HRM to support the organization's marketing activities. In this regard, customer evaluations are useful both for evaluating an employee's performance and for helping to determine whether the organization can improve customer service by making changes in HRM activities such as training or compensation.

The weakness of using customer feedback for performance measurement is their expense. The expenses of a traditional survey can add up to hundreds of dollars to evaluate one individual. Many organizations therefore limit the information gathering to short periods once a year.

L06 Define types of rating errors and explain how to minimize them.

Errors in Performance Measurement

As we noted in the previous section, one reason for gathering information from several sources is that performance measurements are not completely objective, and errors can occur. People observe behaviour, and they have no practical way of knowing all the circumstances, intentions, and outcomes related to that behaviour, so they interpret what they see. In doing so, observers make a number of judgment calls, and in some situations may even distort information on purpose. Therefore, fairness in rating performance and interpreting performance appraisals requires that managers understand the kinds of distortions that commonly occur.

Types of Rating Errors

Several kinds of errors and biases commonly influence performance measurements. Usually people make these errors unintentionally, especially when the criteria for measuring performance are not specific.

Similar to Me

A common human tendency is to give a higher evaluation to people we consider similar to ourselves. Most of us tend to think of ourselves as effective. If others seem to be like us in some way—physical characteristics, family or economic background, attitudes, or beliefs—we expect them to be effective as well. Research has demonstrated that this effect, called the **similar-to-me error,** is strong. One unfortunate result (besides inaccuracy) is that when similarity is based on characteristics such as race or sex, the decisions may be discriminatory.[38]

> **similar-to-me error**
> Rating error of giving a higher evaluation to people who seem similar to oneself.

Contrast

Sometimes, instead of comparing an individual's performance against an objective standard, the rater compares that individual with other employees. Suppose an employee is completely competent and does exactly what the job requires. But that employee has several co-workers who are outstanding; they keep breaking sales records or thinking up innovative ways to shave time off production processes. If the person rating the employee is contrasting the employee's performance with the exceptional co-workers and gives lower performance ratings than the employee deserves, this is **contrast error.** The reduced rating does not accurately reflect what the employee is accomplishing.

contrast error
Rating error caused by comparing employee's performance to co-workers rather than to an objective standard.

Errors in Distribution

Raters often tend to use only one part of a rating scale—the low scores, the high scores, or the middle of the range. Sometimes a group of employees really do perform equally well (or poorly). In many cases, however, similar ratings for all members of a group are not an accurate description of performance, but an error in distribution. When a rater inaccurately assigns high ratings to all employees, this is called a **leniency error.** When a rater incorrectly gives low ratings to all employees, holding them to unreasonably high standards, the resulting error is called a **strictness error.** Rating all employees as somehow "average" or in the middle of the scale is called the **central tendency.** This central tendency effect is reinforced through the prevalence of "odd-numbered" performance levels. The Conference Board of Canada's research notes that more than two-thirds of surveyed organizations use 3- or 5-level performance levels.[39]

leniency error
Rating error of assigning inaccurately high ratings to all employees.

strictness error
Rating error of giving low ratings to all employees, holding them to unreasonably high standards.

central tendency
Incorrectly rating all employees at or near the middle of a rating scale.

These errors pose two problems. First, they make it difficult to distinguish among employees rated by the same person. Decisions about promotions, job assignments, and so on are more difficult if employees all seem to be performing at the same level. Second, these errors create problems in comparing the performance of individuals rated by different raters. If one rater is lenient and the other is strict, employees of the strict rater will receive significantly fewer rewards than employees of the lenient rater. The rewards are not tied to actual performance but are to some degree erroneous.

Recency Emphasis

Raters sometimes base an annual rating only on the employee's most recent work. Raters may have difficulty remembering things that happened several months to a year ago versus work from a few weeks before the performance review. This **recency emphasis** error can also occur when the supervisor is rushing the evaluation process because of heavy workload or lack of time.[40]

recency emphasis
Rating error that occurs when an annual rating is based only on most recent work performed.

Focus on Activities

Rushing due to insufficient time or heavy workload may also contribute to a **focus on activities,** which happens when employees are assessed on how busy they appear rather than how effective they are in achieving results.[41]

focus on activities
Rating error when employees are assessed on how busy they appear rather than how effective they are in achieving results.

Halo and Horns

Another common problem is that raters often fail to distinguish among different aspects of performance. Consider a research lab that hires chemists. A chemist who expresses herself very well may appear to have greater knowledge of chemistry than a chemist with poor communication skills. In this example, a rater could easily fail to distinguish between communication skills and scientific skills.

This type of error can make a person look better, or worse, overall. When the rater reacts to one positive performance aspect by rating the employee positively in all areas of performance, the bias is called the **halo error.** As in the example of the chemist who communicates well, giving the impression of overall intelligence. In contrast, when the rater responds to one negative aspect by rating an employee low in other aspects, the bias is called the **horns error.** Suppose an employee sometimes arrives to work late. The rater takes this as a sign of lack of motivation, lack of ambition, and inability to follow through with responsibility—an example of the horns error.

halo error
Rating error that occurs when the rater reacts to one positive performance aspect by rating the employee positively in all areas of performance.

horns error
Rating error that occurs when the rater responds to one negative aspect by rating an employee low in other aspects.

When raters make halo and horns errors, the performance measurements cannot provide the specific information needed for useful feedback. Halo error signals that no aspects of an employee's performance need improvement, possibly missing opportunities for employee development. Horns error can cause the employees to feel defensive and frustrated, rather than motivated to improve.

What Can be Done to Reduce Errors?

Usually people make these errors unintentionally, especially when the criteria for measuring performance are not very specific. Raters can be trained how to avoid rating errors.[42] For example, prospective raters watch video segments with story lines designed to lead them to make specific rating errors. After rating the fictional employees in the videos, raters discuss their rating decisions and how errors affected their rating decisions. Training programs offer tips for avoiding the errors in the future. After the training sessions, it is helpful to use surveys to determine how confident managers are about their ability to apply the learning back on the job and what, if any barriers to implementation may exist. Training participants may also identity an "accountability partner," a peer to stay in touch with to share progress and challenges faced in applying the skills, and making behaviour changes.[43]

Another training method for raters focuses not on errors in rating, but on the complex nature of employee performance.[44] Raters learn to look at many aspects of performance that deserve their attention. Actual examples of performance are studied to bring out various performance dimensions and the standards for those dimensions. The objective of this training is to help raters evaluate employees' performance more thoroughly and accurately.

Political Behaviour in Performance Appraisals

Unintentional errors are not the only cause of inaccurate performance measurement. Sometimes the people rating performance distort an evaluation on purpose, to advance their personal goals. This kind of appraisal politics is unhealthy, especially because the resulting feedback does not focus on helping employees contribute to the organization's goals. High-performing employees who are rated unfairly will become frustrated, and low-performing employees who are overrated will be rewarded rather than encouraged to improve. Therefore, organizations try to identify and discourage appraisal politics.

Several characteristics of appraisal systems and company culture tend to encourage appraisal politics. Appraisal politics are most likely to occur when raters are accountable to the employee being rated, the goals of rating are not compatible with one another, performance appraisal is directly linked to highly desirable rewards, top executives tolerate or ignore distorted ratings, and senior employees tell newcomers company "folklore" that includes stories about distorted ratings.

Political behaviour occurs in every organization. Organizations can minimize appraisal politics by establishing an appraisal system that is fair. One technique is to hold a **calibration session,** a meeting at which managers discuss employee performance ratings and provide evidence supporting their ratings with the goal of eliminating the influence of rating errors. In a survey by the Society for Human Resource Management (SHRM), more than half of organizations conduct formal calibration sessions and 35 percent of organizations report "regularly" changing ratings as a result of these sessions.[45] As they discuss ratings and the ways they arrive at ratings, managers may identify undervalued employees, notice whether they are much harsher or more lenient than other managers, and help each other focus on how well ratings are associated with relevant performance outcomes.

calibration session
Meeting at which managers discuss employee performance ratings and provide evidence supporting their ratings with the goal of eliminating the influence of rating errors.

For example, when consultant Dick Grote leads calibration meetings for his clients, he often displays flip charts, one for each rating on a scale, and gives each manager a different coloured Post-it Note pad. On their Post-it Notes, the managers write the names of each employee they assess, and they attach a note for the rating they would provide that employee. The distribution of colours on the flip charts provide visually strong information about how the different managers assess their employees. A cluster of green notes on "outstanding" and yellow notes on "meets expectations" would suggest that one manager is a much tougher rater than others, and they could then discuss how they arrive at these different conclusions.[46] Calibrating talent is also discussed in the "HR Best Practices" box. The organization can also

HR Best Practices

Calibrating Talent

Effective performance management systems rate performance consistently. This foundation is the basis for reliability of performance management systems, and it is critical to creating fairness in how employees' performance is assessed. By definition, performance management systems assess how well an employee meets the expectations associated with the job and the organization's goals; but according to a study of 5,970 employees who each report to two managers, the majority of the employees received inconsistent performance ratings. "The study found that employees rated outstanding by one manager were rated lower by their other manager 62 percent of the time."

Many companies use a calibration process to make sure that performance appraisals are consistent across managers. This process is ideally led by an experienced facilitator such as a senior human resources professional, who brings together supervisors and managers to discuss each employee's rating and its rationale. Some organizations are taking this a step further, using these meetings not only to calibrate performance but also to have meaningful discussions about the organization's talent. These types of discussions reinforce succession planning.

A Toronto-based utility, Direct Energy (www.directenergy.com), also enhances the calibration process with technology that provides real-time access to performance ratings as they happen. Terry Fox, director of HR operations, describes how calibration works at Direct Energy: "The focus is on the high-value discussion about who the high-performers are and why, and finding ways to share the pool of high-performing employees with peers to help those people develop."

Sources: Joanne Sammer, "Calibrating Consistency," *HR Magazine,* January 2008, pp. 73–75; Christee Gabour Atwood, "Implementing Your Succession Plan," *T+D,* November 2007, p. 54; and David Brown, "Performance Management Systems Need Fixing," *Canadian HR Reporter,* April 11, 2005, p. 1.

help managers give accurate and fair appraisals by training them to use the appraisal process, encouraging them to recognize accomplishments that the employees themselves have not identified, and fostering a climate of openness in which employees feel they can be honest about their weaknesses.[47]

L○7 Explain how to effectively provide performance feedback.

Performance Feedback

HRC 3, 4, 6, 7

Once the manager and others have assessed an employee's performance, this information needs to be shared with the employee. Although the feedback stage of performance management is essential, it may be uncomfortable to managers and employees and may even undermine employee engagement and commitment if not handled effectively. In a productive and meaningful performance feedback session both parties need to feel heard, understood, and respected even if they don't necessarily agree on all of the points discussed.[48]

Scheduling Performance Feedback

Performance feedback should be a regular, expected management activity. The practice or policy at many organizations is to give formal performance feedback once a year. But annual feedback is not enough. One reason is that managers are responsible for dealing with performance gaps as soon as they occur. If the manager notices a problem with an employee's behaviour in June, but the annual appraisal is scheduled for November, the employee will miss months of opportunities for improvement.

Another reason for frequent performance feedback is that feedback is most effective when the information does not surprise the employee. If an employee has to wait for up to a year to learn what the manager thinks of their work, the employee will wonder whether they are meeting expectations. Employees should instead receive feedback so often that they know what the manager will say during their annual performance review. Generational differences in the workplace also contribute to different perspectives about what is timely feedback. Millennials may expect immediate feedback because their reference points are often built around short-time frames and accomplishments.[49] For example, Ernst and Young (www.ey.com) created an online "Feedback Zone," where employees can request or submit performance feedback at any time beyond the formal evaluations required twice a year. In a survey, the Conference Board of Canada found that almost half of both Gen X and Millennials indicated they preferred feedback "as needed," in contrast to less than 10 percent stating a preference for annual feedback. These results support existing research indicating that "Millennials expect leaders to be freely available to give frequent feedback."[50]

Preparing for a Feedback Session

Managers should be well prepared for each formal feedback session. The manager should create the right context for the meeting. The location should be neutral. If the manager's office is perceived to be distracting or too formal, a conference room may be more appropriate. In announcing the meeting to an employee, the manager should describe it as a chance to discuss the role of the employee, the role of the manager, and the relationship between them. Managers should also say (and believe) that they would like the meeting to be an open dialogue.

Managers should also enable the employee to be well prepared. The manager should ask the employee to complete a self-assessment ahead of time. The self-assessment requires employees to think

When giving performance feedback, do it in an appropriate meeting place. Meet in a setting that is neutral and free of distractions. What other factors are important for a feedback session?

about their performance over the past rating period and to be aware of their strengths and areas for improvement, so they can participate more fully in the discussion. Even though employees may tend to overstate their accomplishments, the self-assessment can help the manager and employee identify areas for discussion. When the purpose of the assessment is to define areas for development, employees may actually understate their performance. Also, differences between the manager's and the employee's rating may be fruitful areas for discussion. This approach to performance feedback is consistent with creating a coaching culture to manage, assess, and develop employees and requires managers to have well-developed coaching skills.[51] And employees apparently appreciate the importance of performance reviews. Results of a Ceridian Canada and Harris Decima survey stated that 71 percent of employees said their performance review made them feel valued and 91 percent said their performance reviews either met (79 percent) or exceeded (12 percent) their expectations.[52]

Conducting the Feedback Session

During the feedback session, managers can take any of three general approaches, however, some feedback techniques and approaches work better than others. In the "tell-and-sell" approach, managers tell the employees their ratings and then justify those ratings. In the "tell-and-listen" approach, managers tell employees their ratings and then let the employees explain their side of the story. In the "problem-solving" approach, managers and employees work together to solve performance problems in an atmosphere of respect and encouragement. Not surprisingly, research demonstrates that the problem-solving approach is superior. Perhaps surprisingly, most managers rely on the tell-and-sell approach.[53] Managers can improve employee satisfaction with the performance appraisal feedback process and improve performance by creating two-way communication, by letting employees voice their opinions and discuss performance goals.[54]

Applying some additional principles will also make performance feedback more effective. Feedback should include a balanced and accurate assessment of how the employee is doing. The discussion should include a specific discussion of areas in which the employee's performance met, exceeded, and fell short of expectations. Any areas of required improvement should lead to problem solving.

The content of the feedback should emphasize behaviour, not personalities. For example, "You did not meet the deadline" can open a conversation about what needs to change, but "You're not motivated" may make the employee feel defensive and angry. The feedback session should end with goal setting and a decision about when to follow up. When delivered and received well, most people perceive feedback as it is intended to be—constructive, useful, and helpful.[55] The "HR How-To" box provides additional guidance on delivering performance feedback.

HR How-To

Discussing Employee Performance

Employees and managers often dread feedback sessions, because they expect some level of criticism, and criticism feels uncomfortable. However, there are ways to structure communication about employee performance so that it is constructive. Here are some ideas for talking about employee performance in a way that is clear, honest, and fair:

- **Prevent surprises.** Employees should have clear job descriptions and receive clear directions. Supervisors should be communicating regularly with employees about expectations and how well they are performing. Then when the formal feedback is delivered to an employee, it should be consistent with what the employee has been hearing since the previous review.

- **Use specific, concrete examples.** Statements about "attitude" or "commitment" require some mind-reading, and employees may feel misunderstood. In contrast, references to specific accomplishments and examples of behaviour are more objective. Even if the supervisor is concerned about attitude, talking about behaviours can open a discussion of the real changes that might be needed: "Several customers commented that you seemed angry when you spoke to them. Let's talk about what's happening in those conversations so you can find a way to come across to customers as pleasant." Specific comments are especially important to back up negative feedback; employees will ask for examples if they don't hear any.

- **Focus on goals.** If in a prior review, the employee and supervisor planned for the employee to complete more projects on time, they should compare the previous on-time performance with the most recent measure to look for improvement.

- **Listen as well as talk.** Especially when the reviewer is nervous, the instinct is to fill up the interview time with comments. However, this interview is a valuable opportunity for the supervisor to learn about the employee's expectations and hopes for learning and advancement. Employees who feel heard are more likely to recognize that the review is fair and that their contributions are valued.

- **Be honest.** If performance is not acceptable, don't pretend that it is. Pretending is disrespectful of the employee and could get the organization in legal trouble if the employee is later let go and believes the company discriminated. If the employee asks a question and the supervisor is unsure of the answer, honesty is again the wisest course. Guessing at an answer related to an employee's future is another way to create problems for the organization, as well as for the supervisor's relationship with the employee.

- **Treat employees with respect.** Besides careful listening and honesty, ways to show respect include providing appreciation and looking for solutions rather than simply placing blame on employees when performance is less than desired. Treating mistakes as a chance to learn encourages employees to do their best and continue improving. In a respectful climate, conversations about performance can be, if not enjoyable, as least positive and productive.

Sources: Jeff Haden, "Nine Ways to Ruin a Performance Review," *Inc.*, January 10, 2012, www.inc.com; T. L. Stanley, "Creating a No-Blame Culture," *Supervision*, October 2011, pp. 3–6; C. Anne Pontius, "Addressing Management Issues: Performance-Evaluation Anxiety," *Medical Laboratory Observer*, February 2011, p. 6.

L○8 Summarize ways to achieve performance improvement.

Performance Improvement

When performance evaluation indicates that an employee's performance is below expectations, the feedback process should launch an effort to address the performance gap. Even when the employee is meeting current standards, the feedback session may identify areas in which the employee can improve in order to contribute more to the organization in a current or future job. In sum, the final feedback stage of performance management involves identifying areas for improvement and ways to improve performance in those areas.

As is shown in Figure 7.11, the most effective way to improve performance varies according to the employee's ability and motivation. In general, when employees have high levels of ability and motivation, they perform at or above expectations. But when they lack ability, motivation, or both, corrective action is needed. The type of action called for depends on what is missing:

- *Lack of ability*—When a motivated employee lacks knowledge, skills, or abilities in some area, the manager may offer training, and more detailed feedback. Sometimes it is appropriate to restructure the job so the employee can meet the job demands.

FIGURE 7.11

Diagnosing Performance

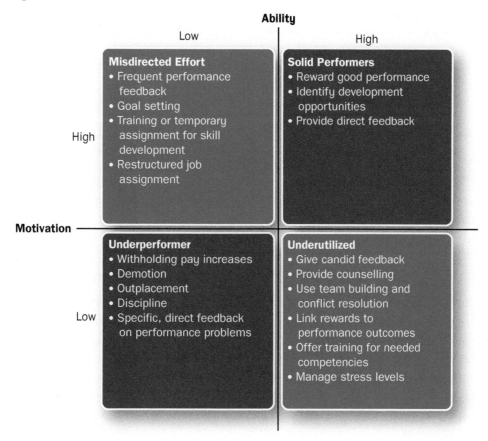

Source: Based on M. London, *Job Feedback* (Mahwah, NJ: Lawrence Erlbaum Associates, 1997), pp. 96, 97. Used by permission.

- *Lack of motivation*—Managers with an unmotivated employee can explore ways to demonstrate that the employee is being treated fairly and rewarded adequately. The solution may be as simple as delivering more positive feedback. Employees may also benefit from a referral for counselling or help with stress management.

- *Lack of both*— Employees whose performance is below expectations because they have neither the motivation nor the ability to perform the job may not be a good fit for the position. Performance may improve if the manager directs their attention to the significance of the problem by withholding rewards or by providing specific feedback. If the employee does not respond, the manager may have to demote or terminate the employee.

A documented performance improvement plan may be introduced by the supervisor as a means to discuss and reach agreement on next steps. A **performance improvement plan** is a summary of performance gaps and includes an action plan mutually agreed to by the employee and supervisor with specific dates to review progress. If employees do not respond by improving their performance, the organization may have to discipline or terminate these underperformers.

performance improvement plan
Summary of performance gaps and includes an action plan mutually agreed to by the employee and supervisor with specific dates to review progress.

As a rule, employees who combine high ability with high motivation are solid performers. As Figure 7.11 indicates, managers should by no means ignore these employees on the grounds of leaving well enough alone. Rather, such employees are likely to appreciate opportunities for further development. Rewards and direct feedback help to maintain these employees' high levels of motivation and performance.

L○9 Discuss legal and ethical issues that affect performance management.

What Are the Legal and Ethical Issues?

HRC2, 4

In developing and using performance management systems, human resources professionals need to ensure that these systems meet legal requirements, such as the avoidance of discrimination related to any of the prohibited grounds, avoiding psychological harassment, and protecting employees' privacy.

Legal Requirements for Performance Management

Because performance measures play a central role in decisions about pay, promotions, and discipline, employment-related legal challenges may be directed at an organization's performance management system. Legal challenges related to performance management usually involve charges of illegal discrimination, and unjust or constructive dismissal.

Claims often allege that the performance management system discriminated against employees on the basis of one of the protected grounds identified in human rights legislation such as age or sex. Many performance measures are subjective, and measurement errors, such as those described earlier in the chapter, can easily occur.

With regard to lawsuits filed on the grounds of unjust or constructive dismissal, the usual claim is that the person was dismissed for reasons besides the ones that the employer states. In this type of situation, courts generally focus on the employer's performance management system, looking to see whether the dismissal could have been based on poor performance. To defend itself, the employer would need a performance management system that provides evidence to support its employment decisions. The "HR Oops!" feature provides an illustrative example.

HR Oops!

Long-Term Worker Wins Constructive Dismissal

Dunstan Morgan, 56, was a dock supervisor at Vitran Express Canada, a freight transportation company based in Concord, Ontario. He joined Vitran's predecessor in 1984 and was promoted two years later to dock supervisor. Morgan enjoyed his work and received positive feedback from Vitran for several years. However, in 2003, a new shift manager, came in and problems began to surface between the two men.

In November 2006, Morgan was told he had made several errors that had cost the company money. Morgan felt intimidated but confirmed his commitment to the company. In January 2007, he received a negative performance appraisal in which the shift manager told him he wasn't doing his job properly and others didn't want to work with him. Morgan was warned that "substantial improvement" was needed and that he would be under review. Morgan felt the meeting was "bizarre" and the shift manager acted in a "confrontational, aggressive fashion." In June 2007, Morgan was told his job performance wasn't up to standards and there would be monthly meetings to review his progress, beginning in August. Morgan tried to ensure there were no errors and made suggestions for improvements. He was conscious of not appearing adversarial, but the monthly meetings didn't happen.

In December 2009, Morgan was called to a meeting with his direct superior and the HR manager where he was told his job performance was lacking. Numerous errors were listed over the previous five years, although Morgan was confused because many of them had not been brought to his attention at the time. He also felt that many of the errors were by dock workers and were common in the transportation industry. During the meeting, Morgan was told Vitran had certain expectations, but they were general and no definite solutions were given. He was also told his superior would shadow him on the job for a few hours each week to help him improve. However, the shadowing didn't happen the way it had been presented to him. Instead, Morgan's superior watched him from a distance and didn't offer any comments or suggestions for improvement. This went on for about one month and Morgan wasn't told when it was over, nor was he given feedback.

Morgan met with management again in April 2010 and was given a letter outlining other errors he had made. On more than one occasion, Morgan emailed management to address the errors he had been accused of and explain his side of things, but he received no response. In June 2010, Morgan injured his ankle on the dock. He continued to work but, after a couple of days, he was told by his doctor to take some time off work. When he returned one week later, management told him there was no evidence of his injury on the surveillance video.

Later that month, Morgan underwent skill and personality testing. When the results came in, management told him he did not meet the requirements to work in the fast-paced environment of the dock supervisor position. Morgan was flabbergasted, since he had done the job for 24 years. He also felt he had been set up because the volume of freight had increased while his staff had decreased. In September 2010, Morgan was told his performance was unsatisfactory and he wasn't suited for his job. A new position—freight analyst—with the same salary was created for him but there was little supervisory responsibility. Morgan felt embarrassed about the change and felt it was a demotion. He decided he couldn't return to work for Vitran as he would be humiliated having to face the workers he had trained. Morgan sued for constructive dismissal.

The court found Morgan did fine as a dock supervisor for many years before any problems were brought to his attention. And though he had to take responsibility for the workers under his supervision, many of the errors were routine and happened during other shifts as well. And, notably, the errors were not brought to Morgan's attention at the time they happened and he was not given an indication of performance issues until 2006. This seemed to indicate he was targeted at a certain point in time, said the Ontario Superior Court of Justice. The way Morgan was treated in the meetings was "disrespectful and unwarranted," found the court. The vagueness with which his job abilities were assessed and what he could do to meet expectations was unfair, said the court, as was Vitran's inability to explain

(continued)

why Morgan was unsuited for a job he had done for the past 24 years. Vitran was ordered to pay Morgan 18 months' notice for constructive dismissal, for a total of $80,911.88.

Questions

1. Based on the information provided, what shortcomings are in evidence with Vitran's approach to performance management? For example, consider criteria for effective performance management, giving performance feedback, and handling performance improvement.

2. What advice do you have for the HR manager at Vitran?

Source: Jeffrey Smith, "Long-Term Worker Wins Constructive Dismissal," *Canadian HR Reporter*, January 13, 2014, p. 5.

Thinking ETHICALLY

Are Forced Rankings Fair?

Emotions can run high when it comes to the performance management practice of using forced rankings to identify the top performers to retain and the bottom performers to let go. When Jack Welch was chief executive officer of General Electric (www.ge.com), he introduced and later championed this method. At GE, managers were ranked according to their performance against goals and sorted into the top 20 percent (who were richly rewarded), the middle 70 percent, and the bottom 10 percent (who often were asked to leave). Today LendingTree (www.lendingtree.com) follows a similar approach, ranking managers as 1s (the top 15 percent), 2s (the middle 75 percent), and 3s (the bottom 10 percent. The idea is that if the organization lays off the 3s, it can later replace them with people who have the potential to become 1s, improving the overall performance. American International Group (AIG) www.aig.com, recently began ranking employees on a scale of 1 to 5, with the biggest bonuses awarded to the top categories and no bonuses to the worst performers.

Critics deride the method, which they call "rank and yank," as ruthless and even demotivating. In their view, organizations should hire and develop good talent, so if the organization is well run, it shouldn't have any underperformers. In addition, they say, the practice tempts managers to compete against one another and perhaps undermine one another when they should be cooperating to help the organization attain its goals. If the organization wants teamwork but being a team player means you help your colleague meet more goals than you did and earn a higher ranking, would you want to be a team player?

Jack Welch insists that forced ranking is actually the fairest approach if done well. Assuming that the organization has made its goals clear, every manager knows where he or she stands. If the organization dismisses someone for being one of the lowest performers, the decision is fairly based on performance rather than personalities or other irrelevant criteria. People who have underperformed their colleagues know it and respect the reasons for the decisions. In addition, forced rankings can correct for any unfairness that results from the common error of a manager tending to be harsh or lenient compared with peers evaluating other employees. Nevertheless, surveys suggest that many organizations are uncomfortable with the method. A study by the Conference Board of Canada, for example, found that only 15 percent of organizations surveyed use a forced ranking system.

Questions

1. Based on the description of forced rankings here and in text of the chapter, how fair would you say this method is to employees being ranked? How relevant to the organization's strategy? How useful for employee development?

2. How fair are forced rankings relative to the other methods of measuring performance described in this chapter?

3. At an organization that wants to use forced rankings because it supports this strategy, what measures can it take to make sure the process is as ethical as possible?

Sources: Nicole Stewart and Elyse Lamontagne, "Compensation Planning Outlook 2014" (Ottawa: Conference Board of Canada), p. 22; Leslie Kwoh, "'Rank and Yank' Retains Vocal Fans," *The Wall Street Journal*, January 31, 2012, http://online.wsj.com; Liz Ryan, "Ten Management Practices to Throw Overboard in 2012," *Bloomberg Businessweek*, January 23, 2012, EBSCOhost, http://web.ebscohost.com; Jonathan A. Segal, "The Dirty Dozen Appraisal Errors," *Bloomberg Businessweek*, January 17, 2011, EBSCOhost, http://web.ebscohost.com.

To protect against both kinds of legal challenges, it is important to have a performance management system based on valid job analyses, as described in Chapter 3, with the requirements for job success clearly communicated to employees. Performance measurement should evaluate behaviours or results, on the basis of objective criteria. The organization should use multiple raters (including self-appraisals) and train raters in how to use the system. The organization should provide for a review of all performance ratings by upper-level managers and set up a system for employees to appeal when they believe they were evaluated unfairly. Along with feedback, the system should include a process for coaching or training employees to help them improve, rather than simply dismissing poor performers.

Supervisors must also be careful to ensure performance feedback does not go beyond "reasonable criticism." The Ontario Court of Appeal provided guidance to what a supervisor can and cannot do in the context of performance appraisal and performance improvement in the case of Viren Shah, a 12-year employee at Xerox Canada (www.xerox.ca) The court determined that Shah's manager passed beyond the "bounds of reasonableness" when Shah received critical performance reviews that were not based on any substantiated concerns and the manager's behaviour was described as "authoritarian, impatient, and intolerant."[56] As discussed in Chapter 2, provinces including Ontario, Saskatchewan, and Quebec have passed legislation that expands the definition of harassment, but employees in other provinces also have protection from employers who go too far in their criticism of employees.[57]

Employee Monitoring and Employee Privacy

Computer technology and other types of employee monitoring now support many performance management systems. Organizations often store records of employees' performance ratings, disciplinary actions, and work-rule violations in electronic databases. Many companies use personal computers or other technology-enabled devices to monitor productivity and other performance measures.

Although electronic monitoring can improve productivity, it also generates privacy concerns. Critics point out that an employer should not monitor employees when it has no reason to believe that anything is wrong. They complain that monitoring systems threaten to make the workplace an electronic sweatshop in which employees are treated as robots, robbing them of dignity. Some note that employees' performance should be measured by accomplishments, not just time spent at a desk or workbench. Electronic systems should not be a substitute for careful management. Monitoring may be used more positively to gather information for coaching employees and helping them develop their skills.

When monitoring is necessary, managers should communicate the reasons for using it. For example, companies argue that global positioning systems (GPS) are used to improve the efficiency of locating, dispatching, and routing employees to job sites. However, GPS systems may be used to create a *geofence*—an invisible boundary based on GPS tracking software that alerts the boss by email or instant messaging if any employee strays outside his or her designated work area.[58] Employers are cautioned to consider the privacy rights of workers before they install GPS in their vehicle fleets and to clearly explain to employees how GPS will be used.[59] As discussed in Chapter 2, the federal Personal Information Protection and Electronic Documents Act (PIPEDA) has additional implications for performance management. For example, organizations are required to ensure that personal information including an employee's performance review is securely protected, retained only for a specified time, and accessible to the employee.

SUMMARY

L○1 Identify the relevance of performance management and the steps in the process.

In high-performing organizations, performance management is a dynamic process that enables performance and drives organizational and individual success and is integrated with other human resources functions. Performance management is the process through which managers ensure that employees' activities and outputs contribute to the organization's goals. The organization begins by specifying which aspects of performance are relevant; the relevant aspects of performance are measured through performance appraisal; and finally, in performance feedback sessions, managers provide employees with information about their performance so they can modify their behaviour to meet the organization's goals.

L○2 Discuss the purposes of performance management systems.

Organizations establish performance management systems to meet three broad purposes. Effective performance management helps the organization with strategic purposes, that is, meeting business objectives. It does this by helping to link employees' behaviour with the organization's goals. The administrative purpose of performance management is to provide information for day-to-day decisions about salary, benefits, recognition, and retention or termination. The developmental purpose of performance management is using the system as a basis for developing employees' knowledge and skills.

L○3 Define five criteria for measuring the effectiveness of a performance management system.

Performance measures should fit with the organization's strategy by supporting its goals and culture. Performance measures should be valid, that is, measure all the relevant aspects of performance and do not measure irrelevant aspects of performance. These measures should also provide interrater and test-retest reliability, so that appraisals are consistent among raters and over time. Performance measurement systems should be acceptable to the people who use them or receive feedback from them. Finally, a performance measure should specifically tell employees what is expected of them and how they can meet those expectations.

L○4 Compare the major methods for measuring performance.

Performance measurement may use ranking systems such as simple ranking, forced distribution, or paired comparisons to compare one individual's performance with that of other employees. Although time-consuming, and may be seen as unfair under some circumstances, ranking counteracts some forms of rater bias and helps distinguish employees for administrative decisions. Other approaches involve rating employees' attributes, behaviours, or outcomes. Rating attributes is relatively simple but not always valid and requires a great deal of information, but these methods can be very effective. Rating results, such as productivity or achievement of objectives, tends to be less subjective than other kinds of rating; however, validity may be a problem because of factors outside the employee's control. A balanced scorecard is a widely used strategic approach.

L○5 Describe major sources of performance information in terms of their advantages and disadvantages.

Performance information may come from an employee's self-appraisal and from appraisals by the employee's manager, employees, peers, and customers. Organizations may combine many sources into a 360-degree performance appraisal. Employees' supervisors may produce accurate information, and peers are an excellent source of information about performance in a job where the supervisor does not often observe the employee. Disadvantages are that friendships (or rivalries) may bias ratings and peers may be uncomfortable with the role of rating a friend. Direct reports often have the best chance to see how a manager treats employees; however, employees may be reluctant to contribute candid opinions about a supervisor unless they can provide information anonymously.

Self-appraisals may be biased, but they do come from the person with the most knowledge of the employee's behaviour on the job, and they provide a basis for discussion in feedback sessions, opening up fruitful comparisons and areas of disagreement between the self-appraisal and other appraisals. Customers may be an excellent source of performance information, although obtaining customer feedback tends to be expensive.

L○6 Define types of rating errors and explain how to minimize them.

A common tendency is to give higher evaluations to people we consider similar to ourselves. Other errors involve using only part of the rating scale or contrasting an employee unfavourably with very high performers. Giving all employees ratings at the high end of the scale is called leniency error. Rating everyone at the low end of the scale is called strictness error. Rating at or near the middle is called central tendency. Basing an employee's rating only on the most recent work performed is called recency emphasis; and focusing on activities—for example, how busy the employee looks, rather than results—is also problematic. Halo/horns error refers to rating employees positively/negatively in all areas because of strong/weak performance observed in one area.

Ways to reduce rater error are training raters to be aware of their tendencies to make rating errors and training them to be sensitive to the complex nature of employee performance so they will consider many aspects of performance in greater depth. Politics also may influence ratings. Organizations can minimize appraisal politics by establishing a fair appraisal system, and bringing managers together to discuss ratings in calibration sessions.

L○7 Explain how to effectively provide performance feedback.

Performance feedback should be a regular, scheduled management activity, carried out in a way that both parties feel heard, understood, and respected. Managers should prepare by establishing a neutral location, emphasizing that the feedback session will be a chance for discussion and asking the employee to prepare a self-assessment. During the feedback session, managers should strive for a problem-solving approach and encourage employees to voice their opinions and discuss performance goals. The manager should look for opportunities to reinforce desired behaviour and should limit criticism. The discussion should focus on behaviour and results rather than on personalities.

L○8 Summarize ways to achieve performance improvement.

If an employee is motivated but lacks ability, provide training, give detailed feedback about performance, and consider restructuring the job. For an employee with ability but lacking motivation, investigate whether outside problems are a distraction, and if so refer the employee for help. If the problem has to do with the employee not feeling appreciated or rewarded, try to meet the employee's needs and evaluate whether additional rewards are appropriate. For an employee lacking both ability and motivation, consider whether the employee is a good fit for the position. Specific feedback or withholding rewards may spur improvement, or the employee may have to be demoted or terminated. Solid employees who are high in ability and motivation will continue so and may be able to contribute even more if the manager provides appropriate direct feedback, rewards, and opportunities for development.

L○9 Discuss legal and ethical issues that affect performance management.

Lawsuits related to performance management usually involve charges of discrimination, psychological harassment, and constructive or unjust dismissal. Managers must make sure that performance management systems and decisions treat employees properly, without regard to their age, sex, or other protected grounds. A system is more likely to be legally defensible if it is based on behaviours and results, and if multiple raters evaluate each person's performance. The system should also include a process for coaching and training employees. An ethical issue of performance management is the use of employee monitoring. This type of performance measurement provides detailed, accurate information, but employees may find it unwelcome.

Critical Thinking Questions

1. How does a complete performance management system differ from the use of annual performance appraisals only?

2. Give two examples of an administrative decision that would be based on performance management information. Give two examples of developmental decisions based on this type of information.

3. Consider how you might rate the performance of three instructors from whom you are currently taking a course. (If you are currently taking only one or two courses, consider this course and two you recently completed.)

   a. Would it be harder to *rate* the instructors' performance or to *rank* their performance? Why?

   b. Write three items to use in rating the instructors—one each to rate them in terms of a competency, a behaviour, and an outcome.

   c. Which measure in *(b)* do you think is most valid? Most reliable? Why?

   d. Many educational institutions use surveys or questionnaires to gather data from students about their instructors' performance. Would it be appropriate to use the data for administrative decisions? Developmental decisions? Other decisions? Why or why not?

4. Imagine that a pet supply store is establishing a new performance management system to help employees provide better customer service. Management needs to decide who should participate in measuring the performance of each of the store's salespeople. From what sources should the store gather information? Why?

5. Would the same sources be appropriate if the store in Question 4 will use the performance appraisals to support decisions about which employees to promote? Explain.

6. Suppose you were recently promoted to a supervisory job in a company where you have worked for two years. You genuinely like almost all your co-workers, who now report to you. The only exception is one employee, who dresses more formally than the others, frequently interrupts others during team meetings, and is much older than you. Given your pre-existing feelings for the employees, how can you measure this employee's performance fairly and effectively?

7. Continuing the example in Question 6, imagine that you are preparing for your first performance feedback session. You want the feedback to be effective—that is, you want the feedback to result in improved performance. List five or six steps you can take to achieve your goal.

8. Besides giving employees feedback, what steps can a manager take to improve employees' performance?

9. Suppose you are a human resources professional helping to improve the performance management system of a company that sells and services office equipment. The company operates a call centre that takes calls from customers having problems with their equipment. Call centre employees are supposed to verify that the problem is not one the customer can easily handle (e.g., equipment that will not operate because it has come unplugged). Then, if the problem is not resolved over the phone, the employees arrange for service technicians to visit the customer. The company can charge the customer only if a service technician visits, so performance management of the call centre employees focuses on productivity—how quickly they can complete a call and move on to the next caller. To measure this performance efficiently and accurately, the company uses employee monitoring.

    a. How would you expect the employees to react to the monitoring? How might the organization address the employees' concerns?

    b. Besides productivity in terms of number of calls, what other performance measures should the performance management system include?

    c. How should the organization gather information about the other performance measures?

10. Based on your understanding of effective performance management as discussed in this chapter, identify specific practices that would likely enhance the motivation, ability, and performance of younger employees?

Experiencing HR

If your school publishes student reviews of instructors, look up and read some of these reviews, taking notes on the kinds of comments students make. If your school does not publish reviews, do the same at a public website such as Rate My Professors (www.ratemyprofessors.com).

Consider how, if at all, a professor and school might make use of reviews such as these. Review the criteria for effective performance management, and consider the following questions: Do the reviews suggest relevant areas of improvement? Do they address the qualities or behaviour that could enable a school to accomplish its mission? Do the ratings seem thoughtful or just a place for students to complain if they struggle in a class?

Imagine you are a consultant invited to a small college or university that has a mission to provide excellent teaching. You have been asked to advise the school on how it might use student appraisals as part of a 360-degree review process to support the development of professors' teaching skills. Based on what you have learned about performance management and seen of your school's or online reviews, write a one- or two-page recommendation to the school. Consider possible uses of student reviews as well as any steps the school should take to keep the process fair and legal.

CASE STUDY 7.1:

Performance Measurement for School Teachers

Schools have a major responsibility to their communities: preparing children to become responsible citizens, productive employees, and smart consumers. Unfortunately, trends such as test scores, dropout rates, readiness for work and higher education, and persistent differences between ethnic and economic groups suggest that schools sometimes fail to deliver.

Meeting the goals requires talented, motivated teachers who understand what behaviours are associated with successful instruction and have the necessary resources. A basic tool for achieving this should be a school's performance management system. However, efforts to design measures for teacher performance suggest that it is complicated. Certainly, politics plays a role, but performance measurement for schools is challenging even from a strictly HR point of view.

The traditional approach has been to identify the teachers with the longest tenure and greatest education, then to reward these teachers with job retention and pay. The rationale is that the measures are objective (a teacher has a master's degree or doesn't and has clearly worked for some number of years), so they can be applied equitably. In addition, an experienced, highly educated teacher logically would have skills that a recent graduate has yet to learn. Still, former students would say the teachers who inspired them most are not always the oldest ones.

An approach to measuring performance that has recently been emphasized is students' performance on standardized tests. This measure focuses on results, but test scores have their drawbacks. First, they raise the question of how much control a teacher has over scores. If a teacher's class contains many students with behavioural or learning issues, or poor preparation in previous grades, should the teacher's evaluation take that into account—and if so, how? Standardized tests also need to measure the outcomes that matter most. Should the school only be preparing students to recall facts on a multiple-choice test—or also to express their reasoning in writing? Daniel Laitsch, associate professor of education at Simon Fraser University says these tests are meant to measure "too many things, e.g., teachers, schools, curriculum and entire jurisdictions (in addition to student achievement), and this stretches their validity in appraising any of them." Professor Laitsch describes testing students as "an atrocious way to evaluate teacher effectiveness, without any research to support the theory."

The Canadian Council of Chief Executives (CCCE) recently commissioned a report, "Effective Management of Human Capital in Schools," authored by Sachin Maharaj an education researcher, writer and teacher in Toronto. The report notes that Canadian teachers are not subject to regular performance reviews, for example, Ontario teachers undergo a limited evaluation every five years, and Alberta does not require any evaluation. The report advances various recommendations of the author including:

- "School administrators should receive ongoing, rigorous training that equips them to render fair, accurate, and consistent assessment of teacher performance."

- "Teacher appraisals should occur every two years at a minimum and should include multiple classroom observations, some of which are not prearranged."

- "Teacher evaluations should incorporate feedback from students."

- "The results of teacher appraisals should help drive decisions dealing with hiring, promotion, compensation, dismissals, and layoffs."

Bill Gates, Microsoft's founder, suggests that researchers investigate why some teachers get better outcomes than others. He proposes observing teachers with practical skills such as bringing order to a classroom and engaging a student who is lagging behind, to identify exactly what these teachers are doing. Then those behaviours could be measured in other teachers and taught to those who lack the skills. Teachers can be trained to give peer reviews based on this type of model. The Bill & Melinda Gates Foundation funded a survey of teachers, to get their perspective on what would help them perform better. According to that survey, teachers want to receive more evaluations, from more sources. Most agree that the best measure of their success should be the progress students make during the school year.

Questions

1. How well do the performance management ideas described in this case meet the three purposes of performance management (strategic, administrative, and developmental)?

2. How well do the ideas meet the five criteria for effective performance management?

3. From a human resource management perspective, what additional principles do you think school systems should apply to managing teachers' performance?

Sources: "Performance Reviews of Teachers Would Improve K-12 Education, Report Says," Canadian Council of Chief Executives, January 23, 2014, www.ceocouncil.ca, retrieved March 12, 2015; Sachin Maharaj, "Effective Management of Human Capital in Schools: Recommendations to Strengthen the Teaching Profession," January 2014, pp. 1–27; Rachel Giese and Caroline Alphonso, "The Debate Over Standardized Testing in Schools is as Divisive as Ever," *The Globe and Mail,* May 31, 2013; Harold McNeil, "Superintendent Describes Difficulty in Implementing Teacher Evaluations," *Buffalo (NY) News,* March 21, 2012, Business & Company Resource Center, http://galenet.galegroup.com; Amanda Paulson, "Surprise: Teachers Crave Evaluation," *Christian Science Monitor,* March 16, 2012, www.csmonitor.com; Stephanie Banchero, "Teacher Evaluations Pose Test for States," *The Wall Street Journal,* March 8, 2012, http://online.wsj.com; Mary Stegmeir, "Iowa Officials Rework Plan on Teacher Reviews," *Des Moines Register,* February 29, 2012, www.desmoinesregister.com; Alan Hughes, "Can Bill Gates Save Our Schools?" *Black Enterprise,* October 2011, EBSCOhost, http://web.ebscohost.com.

Case Study 7.2:

How Google Searches for Performance Measures

If there's one thing Google knows, it's how to use software to wade through massive amounts of data and find what is most relevant. So it should come as no surprise that when the information technology powerhouse wanted to develop better managers, it started by looking at the data. As it turns out, Google found plenty to learn.

Like most businesses, Google had files of data about managers—results of performance reviews, surveys measuring employee attitudes, and nominations for management awards. Unlike most businesses, Google figured out how to analyze all that data to come up with a profile of the kind of manager whose team is most successful. The company's people analytics group (which brings together psychologists, MBAs, and data-mining experts) analyzed 10,000 observations about managers in terms of more than 100 variables, looking for patterns. The initial finding was a surprise to some at a company that had once operated without managers: teams with good managers outperform teams with bad managers. But what makes a good manager? Under the leadership of Google's senior vice-president People Operations, Laszlo Bock, the company distilled its findings into a list of the behaviours that get results:

1. Be a good coach.
2. Empower your team, and don't micromanage.
3. Express interest in team members' success and personal well-being.
4. Be productive and results-oriented.
5. Be a good communicator, and listen to your team.
6. Help your employees with career development.
7. Have a clear vision and strategy for the team.
8. Have key technical skills so you can help advise the team.

Perhaps those points sound obvious. But keep in mind that someone hired as a programming or analytic whiz and later promoted to a managerial role might not have given much thought to, say, cultivating the ability to express interest in team members' success, which ranks far above technical skills. Seeing this on a list identifies the behaviour as something statistically related to superior performance not just in general, but at Google specifically. Furthermore, this is a behaviour that can be measured (for example, by asking employees if their supervisor expresses interest in them), and it can be learned by managers who want to improve.

By building performance measures in the eight key areas, Google was able to evaluate its managers' performance and identify those who needed to improve in particular areas. It developed training programs in the eight types of desired behaviour. Before and after providing performance appraisals, training, and coaching, Google conducted surveys to gauge managers' performance. It measured a significant improvement in manager quality for 75 percent of its lowest-performing managers. But Bock isn't resting on that success. Google intends to keep crunching the data, in case the criteria for a successful Google manager change at some point in the future. One thing is for sure: Google will continue to follow the data.

Questions

1. How well does Google's approach to performance management meet the five criteria for effectiveness of a performance management system? How well does it fit with the company's mission to organize information and make it universally accessible and useful?

2. What errors could arise in the way Google collects performance data on managers? How could it minimize these errors?

3. Suppose you are responsible for delivering performance feedback to managers at Google. How would you present the information so as to promote the managers' success at the company?

Sources: Adam Bryant, "Google's Quest to Build a Better Boss," *The New York Times,* March 12, 2011, www.nytimes.com; Clara Byrne, "People Analytics: How Google Does HR by the Numbers," *VentureBeat,* September 20, 2011, http://venturebeat.com; Pat Galagan, "Measure for Measure," *T+D,* May 2011, pp. 28–30.

VIDEO CASES PART 3

Video Case: Benefits of Mentorship Programs (www.hrreporter.com/videodisplay/327-benefits-of-mentorship-programs)

Christian Codrington, senior manager with the British Columbia Human Resources Management Association (B.C. HRMA, www.hrma.ca), discusses the organization's mentorship program. The mentorship program matches young mentees (protégés) looking for guidance in their career and assistance in next occupational challenges with mentors looking to give back on a volunteer basis. The B.C. HRMA facilitates the intake process to match the needs, wants, and geographies of the mentees and mentors.

Christian describes some of the benefits for mentors including a reason to reach out to their own networks to help identify other people to assist their mentees, find out what's going on in the minds of the younger leaders, and also to reflect on their earlier career experiences as they provide guidance. Although the duration of the B.C. HRMA's program is only a few months, many of the relationships become long-lasting, continuing on outside the program. At the start of the mentorship, mentees come up with the goals they would like to achieve and achievement of those goals is one measure of success of the mentoring program. In addition, questions are asked of all participants in order to learn and make changes to the program.

Questions

1. Based on the video, what are the benefits of the mentorship program to both the mentees (protégés) and mentors?

2. What are the potential benefits of having employees matched with mentors outside (rather than inside) the organization? Any potential risks?

Source: Based on "Benefits of Mentorship Programs," *Canadian HR Reporter TV,* July 30, 2013. Reprinted by permission of Canadian HR Reporter. © Copyright Thomson Reuters Canada Ltd., July 30, 2013, Toronto, Ontario 1-800-387-5164. Web: www.hrreporter.com.

Video Case: Increasing Talent Comprehension of Business Objectives (www.hrreporter.com/videodisplay/325-increasing-talent-comprehension-of-business-objectives)

Karen McKay, vice-president of HR for Eli Lilly Canada, Inc. (www.lilly.ca), discusses HR's role in getting talent to understand the firm's business purpose, culture, and how that fits together to ensure the intended customer experience is achieved. She describes how HR plays a critical role in developing the communication as well as aligning the HR strategies, structures and systems to meet the business purposes of the pharmaceutical firm.

McKay describes how Eli Lilly Canada re-vamped their feedback processes and reward systems to become more spontaneous and visible and connect rewards and behaviours that led to those rewards. She explains that although this real-time provision of feedback and rewards was undertaken with the younger generation in mind, it has become a core part of their business. She also explores the need to strike the right balance between accountability, structure, and process so that employees have autonomy as well as the boundaries and guidance they need to produce better results.

Questions

1. What aspects of effective performance management are discussed in the video?

2. How does Eli Lilly Canada's emphasis on spontaneous feedback and rewards contribute to creating a customer-focused, high-performing culture?

Source: Based on "Increasing Talent Comprehension of Business Objectives," *Canadian HR Reporter TV*, July 16, 2013. Reprinted by permission of Canadian HR Reporter. © Copyright Thomson Reuters Canada Ltd., July 16, 2013, Toronto, Ontario 1-800-387-5164. Web: www.hrreporter.com

PART 4

Compensating and
Rewarding Human Resources

Total Rewards

WHAT DO I NEED TO KNOW?

After reading this chapter, you should be able to:

LO1 Discuss how organizations implement a "total rewards" approach to compensating and rewarding employees.

LO2 Identify the kinds of decisions and influences involved in providing base pay to employees.

LO3 Describe alternatives to job-based pay.

LO4 Describe how organizations recognize individual, team, and organizational performance through the use of incentives.

LO5 Discuss the role of benefits as part of employee total rewards.

LO6 Summarize the types of employee benefits offered by employers.

LO7 Discuss the importance of effectively communicating the organization's approach to total rewards.

LO8 Discuss issues related to compensating and rewarding executives.

Food retailer Longo's has a total rewards approach to compensating and rewarding employees.

Total Rewards at Longo's

Family-owned grocery retailer Longo's (www.longos.com), in business since 1956 and based in Vaughan, Ontario, has more than doubled its number of employees during the past six years—from 1,800 to 4,400. "When we did our engagement surveys, we weren't getting credit for some of the great things we had in place and there were some clearly identified gaps that needed to be addressed within our total rewards offering," says Liz Volk, vice-president of HR.

Longo's enhanced total rewards approach, which received the *Innovation in Total Rewards Award* from a HR Summit Conference consists of five parts:

- *Compensation*, e.g., market-competitive wages and bonus program;
- *Benefits*, e.g., flexible health and dental plan, group retirement savings plan, and team member discounts;
- *Growth and Opportunity*, e.g., tuition reimbursement and internal career opportunities;
- *Recognition and Performance*, e.g., service and special recognition awards;
- *Work/Life Balance*, e.g., sports team sponsorship program.

Longo's is focusing on increasing "visibility and transparency around total rewards." For example, each Longo's employee receives an individualized rewards statement, which outlines compensation, benefits, and retirement savings plan, and also includes information about wellness programs, corporate social responsibility, training and development, and other opportunities, says Volk. Longo's also put up total rewards communication boards in each of its 27 stores and managers are encouraged to discuss total rewards in daily team member huddles and direct employees to the total rewards boards to see what's new.[1]

L○1 Discuss how organizations implement a "total rewards" approach to compensating and rewarding employees.

Introduction

HRC 1, 2, 6

Many organizations are recognizing the strategic value of adopting a comprehensive approach to compensating and rewarding employees, frequently referred to as **total rewards**. Figure 8.1 shows how a total rewards strategy reflecting the organization's culture, business, and HR strategy is a powerful tool to attract, motivate, and retain satisfied employees while achieving desired business results.

total rewards
A comprehensive approach to compensating and rewarding employees.

Organizations such as Longo's and RBC (www.rbcroyalbank.com) define their approach to employee compensation and benefits to take into account the "overall work experience provided to employees."[2] Organizations with this total rewards approach create a *value proposition* for current and prospective employees that considers the total value they receive for contributing their time and energy to the company. Because compensation, benefits, and the work experience have a major impact on employee attitudes and behaviours, total rewards influence what kinds of employees are attracted to (and remain with) the organization. A survey on strategic rewards and pay practices reported that Canadian companies cited the primary reason for developing a total rewards strategy was to align rewards with the business strategy.[3] As shown in Figure 8.2, the Conference Board of Canada's Compensation Planning Outlook 2015 identified the top rewards activities and priorities for the next 12 to 18 months as: maintaining

FIGURE 8.1

Total Rewards Model

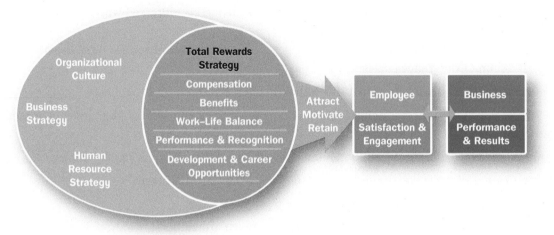

Total Rewards Model
Strategies to Attract, Motivate, and Retain Employees

Sources: Courtesy of WorldatWork Canada.

FIGURE 8.2

Top Rewards Activities and Priorities

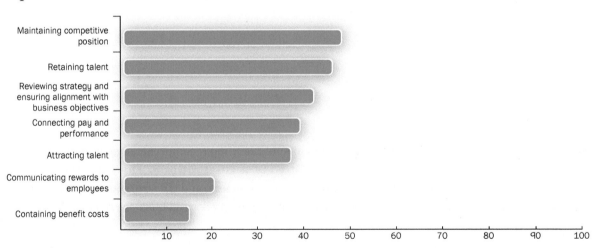

Source: Katie Fleming and Nicole Stewart, "Compensation Planning Outlook 2015" (Ottawa: Conference Board of Canada, October 2014), p. 15. Reprinted with permission by the Conference Board of Canada.

competitive position; retaining talent; reviewing strategy and ensuring alignment with business objectives; connecting pay and performance; and attracting talent.[4]

Employees care about policies affecting their compensation, benefits, and the work experience itself because the policies affect the employee's income, well-being, and security. Also, employees consider these elements a sign of status and success. They attach great importance to compensation and rewards when they evaluate their relationship and satisfaction with their employers. As the workforce becomes increasingly diverse, the definition of what employees expect in exchange for their work will become increasingly complex. For example, Table 8.1 provides some generational total rewards preferences for consideration. This chapter addresses total rewards, however, the primary emphasis will be on forms

TABLE 8.1

Generational Emphasis Within Total Rewards

Traditionalist (1922–1945)	Incentives and stocks, promotions, health benefits (life/disability), pensions, stability, formal recognition, community involvement
Baby Boomers (1946–1964)	High-visibility projects, promotions, support around work/life issues, personal learning and development, onsite facilities, industry recognition
Gen-X (1965–1980)	Training, learning, and development, challenging tasks/stretch assignments, independent work environment, project variety, work/life balance, flexible work arrangements, variable pay
Gen-Y (1981–2000)	Meaningfulness of work/projects, manager feedback, casual work environment, daily work/life balance, access to senior leaders, mentoring, social activities, community involvement, flextime

Source: Adapted from Adwoa K. Buahene and Giselle Kovary, "The Great Divide," *HR Professional,* October/November 2007, p. 27.

of **total compensation**, that is, direct and indirect compensation including base pay, incentives, and benefits received in exchange for the employee's contribution of time, talent, effort, and results.[5] In addition, Chapter 1 discussed (and Chapter 11 will discuss) attributes of work environments where employees are more likely to experience satisfaction and engagement, Chapter 6 explored training, learning, and development opportunities provided employees, and Chapter 7 examined performance processes. A comprehensive "Total Rewards Inventory" checklist outlining elements that could be included in an organization's value proposition is provided in Figure 8.3.

total compensation
All types of financial rewards and tangible benefits and services employees receive as part of their employment.

This chapter opens by describing the role of **direct compensation**, all types of financial rewards employees receive as part of their employment, and defines the kinds of influences on managers making pay level decisions. We describe methods of evaluating jobs and market data to develop effective pay structures. Next, we look at the elements of incentive pay systems. The many kinds of incentive pay fall into three broad categories: incentives linked to individual, team, or organizational performance. Choices from these categories should consider not only their strengths and weaknesses, but also their fit with the organization's goals. This chapter also looks at **indirect compensation**, the benefits and services employees receive in exchange for their work, including the important role benefits play. The chapter also covers why and how organizations should effectively communicate with employees about their total rewards. Finally, this chapter looks at an issue also linked to organizational performance—executive compensation.

direct compensation
Financial rewards employees receive in exchange for their work.

indirect compensation
The benefits and services employees receive in exchange for their work.

LO2 Identify the kinds of decisions and influences involved in providing base pay to employees.

Decisions About Base Pay

HRC3,6

Because pay is important both in its effect on employees and on account of its cost, organizations need to plan what they will pay employees in each job. An unplanned approach, in which each

FIGURE 8.3

Total Rewards Inventory

To get a comprehensive view of your organization's value proposition, simply check off the rewards your organization currently provides.

Compensation	Benefits	Work/Life		Performance & Recognition	Development & Career Opportunities

Base Wages
☐ Salary Pay
☐ Hourly Pay
☐ Piece Rate Pay
 	
Premium Pay
☐ Shift Differential Pay
☐ Weekend/Holiday Pay
☐ On-Call Pay
☐ Call-In Pay
☐ Hazard Pay
☐ Bilingual Pay
☐ Skill-Based Pay
 	
Variable Pay
☐ Commissions
☐ Team-Based Pay
☐ Bonus Programs
  ☐ Referral Bonus
  ☐ Hiring Bonus
  ☐ Retention Bonus
  ☐ Project Completion Bonus
☐ Incentive Pay
  Short-Term:
  ☐ Profit Sharing
  ☐ Individual Performance–Based Incentives
  ☐ Performance-Sharing Incentives
  Long-Term:
  ☐ Restricted Stock
  ☐ Performance Shares
  ☐ Performance Units
  ☐ Stock Options/Grants
	Legally Required/Mandated
	☐ Employment Insurance
	☐ Workers' Compensation Insurance
	☐ Canada Pension Plan/Quebec Pension Plan
	
	Health & Welfare
	☐ Medical Plan
	☐ Dental Plan
	☐ Vision Plan
	☐ Prescription Drug Plan
	☐ Flexible Spending Accounts (FSAs)
	☐ Health Reimbursement Accounts (HRAs)
	☐ Health Savings Accounts (HSAs)
	☐ Life Insurance
	☐ Spouse/Dependent Life Insurance
	☐ AD&D Insurance
	☐ Short-Term/Long-Term Disability Insurance
	
	Retirement
	☐ Defined Benefit Plan
	☐ Defined Contribution Plan
	☐ Profit-Sharing Plan
	☐ Hybrid Plan
	
	Pay for Time Not Worked
	☐ Vacation
	☐ Holiday
	☐ Sick Leave
	☐ Bereavement Leave
	☐ Leaves of Absence (personal, medical, family)
		Workplace Flexibility/ Alternative Work Arrangements
		☐ Flextime
		☐ Flexible Schedules
		☐ Telecommuting
		☐ Alternative Work Sites
		☐ Compressed Workweek
		☐ Job Sharing
		☐ Part-Time Employment
		☐ Seasonal Schedules
		
		Paid and Unpaid Time Off
		☐ Maternity/Family Leave
		☐ Sabbaticals
		
		Health and Wellness
		☐ Employee Assistance Programs
		☐ On-Site Fitness Facilities
		☐ Discounted Fitness Club Rates
		☐ Preventive Care Programs
		☐ Weight Management Programs
		☐ Smoking Cessation Assistance
		☐ On-Site Massages
		☐ Stress Management Programs
		☐ Voluntary Immunization Clinics
		☐ Wellness Initiatives
		☐ Health Screenings
		☐ Nutritional Counselling
		☐ On-Site Nurse
		☐ Business Travel Health Services
		☐ Occupational Health Programs
		☐ Disability Management
		☐ Return-to-Work Programs
		☐ Reproductive Health/Pregnancy Programs
		
		Community Involvement
		☐ Community Volunteer Programs
		☐ Matching Gift Programs
		☐ Shared Leave Programs
		☐ Disaster Relief Funds
		☐ Sponsorships/Grants
		☐ In-Kind Donations
			Caring for Dependants
			☐ Dependant Care Reimbursement Accounts
			☐ Dependant Care Travel-Related Expense Reimbursement
			☐ Dependant Care Referral and Resource Services
			☐ Dependant Care Discount Programs or Vouchers
			☐ Emergency Dependant Care Services
			☐ Childcare Subsidies
			☐ On-Site Caregiver Support Groups
			☐ On-Site Dependant Care
			☐ Adoption Assistance Services
			☐ After-School Care Programs
			☐ University and college/Scholarship Information
			☐ Scholarships
			☐ Mother's Privacy Rooms
			☐ Summer Camps and Activities
			
			Financial Support
			☐ Financial Planning Services and Education
			☐ Adoption Reimbursement
			☐ Transit Subsidies
			☐ Savings Bonds
			
			Voluntary Benefits
			☐ Long-Term Care
			☐ Auto/Home Insurance
			☐ Pet Insurance
			☐ Legal Insurance
			☐ Identity Theft Insurance
			☐ Employee Discounts
			☐ Concierge Services
			☐ Transit Passes
			☐ Parking
			
			Culture Change Initiatives
			☐ Work Redesign
			☐ Team Effectiveness
			☐ Diversity/Inclusion Initiatives
			☐ Work Environment Initiatives
				Performance
				☐ Manager/Employee 1:1 Meetings
				☐ Performance Reviews
				☐ Project Completion/Team Evaluations
				☐ Performance Planning/Goal-Setting Sessions
				
				Recognition
				☐ Service Awards
				☐ Retirement Awards
				☐ Peer Recognition Awards
				☐ Spot Awards
				☐ Managerial Recognition Programs
				☐ Organization-Wide Recognition Programs
				☐ Exceeding Performance Awards
				☐ Employee of the Month/Year Awards
				☐ Appreciation Luncheons, Outings, Formal Events
				☐ Goal-Specific Awards (quality, efficiency, cost savings, productivity, safety)
				☐ Employee Suggestion Programs
					Learning Opportunities
					☐ Tuition Reimbursement
					☐ Tuition Discounts
					☐ Corporate Universities
					☐ New Technology Training
					☐ On-the-Job Learning
					☐ Attendance at Outside Seminars and Conferences
					☐ Access to Virtual Learning, Podcasts, Webinars
					☐ Self-Development Tools
					
					Coaching/Mentoring
					☐ Leadership Training
					☐ Exposure to Resident Experts
					☐ Access to Information Networks
					☐ Formal or Informal Mentoring Programs
					
					Advancement Opportunities
					☐ Internships
					☐ Apprenticeships
					☐ Overseas Assignments
					☐ Internal Job Postings
					☐ Job Advancement/Promotion
					☐ Career Ladders and Pathways
					☐ Succession Planning
					☐ On/Off Ramps Through Career Lifecycle
					☐ Job Rotations

Source: Based on WorldatWork "Your Total Rewards Inventory," p. 4, retrieved May 5, 2008.

employee's pay is independently negotiated, will likely result in unfairness, dissatisfaction, and rates that are either overly expensive or so low that positions are hard to fill. Organizations therefore make decisions about two aspects of pay structure: job structure and pay level. **Job structure** consists of the relative pay for different jobs within the organization. It establishes relative pay among different functions and different levels of responsibility. For example, job structure defines the difference in pay between an entry-level accountant and an entry-level assembler, as well as the difference between an entry-level accountant, a senior accountant, and the director of accounting. **Pay level** is the average amount (including wages, salaries, and incentives) the organization pays for a particular job. Together, job structure and pay levels establish a **pay structure** that helps the organization achieve goals related to employee motivation, cost control, and the ability to attract and retain talented human resources.

job structure
The relative pay for different jobs within the organization.

pay level
The average amount (including wages, salaries, and bonuses) the organization pays for a particular job.

pay structure
The pay policy resulting from job structure and pay-level decisions.

The organization's job structure and pay levels are policies of the organization. Establishing a pay structure simplifies the process of making decisions about individual employees' pay by grouping together employees with similar jobs. As shown, in Figure 8.4, human resources professionals develop this pay structure based on legal requirements, market forces, and the organization's goals, such as attracting a high-quality workforce and meeting principles of fairness.

FIGURE 8.4

Issues in Developing a Pay Structure

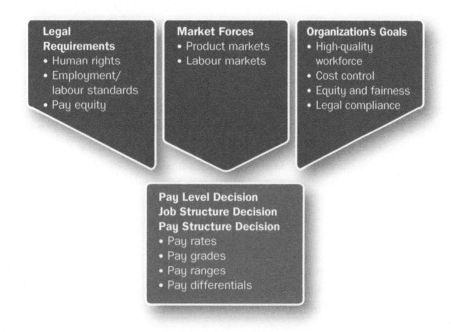

What Are the Legal Requirements?

HRC 2, 6

All of an organization's decisions about compensation and rewards need to at least *comply* with the applicable laws. As discussed in Chapter 2, although these laws differ across federal, provincial, and territorial jurisdictions, a common core of legal requirements exists.

- *Human rights legislation*—Employers may not base differences in rewards on an employee's age, sex, race, or other prohibited grounds of discrimination. Any differences in pay must instead be tied to such business-related considerations as job responsibilities or performance.

- *Employment/labour standards acts*—The Canada Labour Code and the relevant provincial and territorial laws include minimum requirements for wages, hours of work, overtime pay, vacation, statutory holidays, as well as other specific provisions. Executives, professionals, administrative, and outside sales employees are usually considered "exempt" employees and are not eligible for certain provisions such as overtime pay that "non-exempt" employees receive.

- *Pay equity legislation*—Pay equity legislation is in place federally and in several provincial jurisdictions, and attempts to address the wage gap between female and male-dominated jobs to ensure that jobs of equal value within the organization receive similar rates of pay. Organizations use job evaluation (described later in the chapter) to establish the worth of an organization's jobs in terms of such criteria as their difficulty and their importance to the organization. The employer then compares the evaluation points awarded to each job with the pay for each job. If jobs have the same number of evaluation points, they should be paid equally.

Economic Influences on Pay

An organization cannot make spending decisions independently of the economy. Organizations must keep costs low enough that they can sell their products profitably, yet they must be able to attract workers in a competitive labour market. Decisions about how to respond to the economic forces of product markets and labour markets limit an organization's choices about pay structure.

Product and Labour Markets

The organization's *product market* includes organizations that offer competing goods and services—competing to serve the same customers. Organizations under pressure to cut labour costs may respond by reducing staff levels, freezing pay levels, postponing hiring decisions, or requiring employees to bear more of the cost of benefits such as insurance premiums. However, organizations also compete to obtain human resources in *labour markets*—competing with other firms to hire the same skilled employees.

Pay Level: Deciding What to Pay

Although legal requirements and economic influences limit organizations' choices about pay levels, there is a range within which organizations can make decisions.[6] The size of this range depends on the details of the organization's competitive environment. If many workers are competing for a few jobs, employers will have more choice, however, in tight labour markets workers will have more choice.

Two employees who do the same job cannot be paid different wages because of gender, race, age, or other prohibited grounds of discrimination. It would be illegal to pay these two employees differently because one is male and the other is female. Only if there are differences in their experience, skills, seniority, or job performance are there legal reasons why their pay might be different.

When organizations have a broad range in which to make decisions about pay, they can choose to pay *at, above,* or *below* the rate set by market forces. Economic theory holds that the most profitable level, all things being equal, would be at the market rate. Often, however, all things are *not* equal from one employer to another. For instance, an organization may gain an advantage by paying above the market rate if it uses the higher pay as one means to attract top talent and then uses these excellent employees' knowledge to be more innovative, produce higher quality, or work more efficiently.

This approach is based on the view of employees as resources. Higher pay may be an investment in superior human resources. Having higher labour costs than your competitors is not necessarily bad if you also have the best and most effective workforce, which produces more products of better quality. Pay policies are one of the most important human resource tools for encouraging desired employee behaviours and discouraging undesired behaviours. Therefore, organizations must evaluate pay as more than a cost—but also as an investment that can generate returns in attracting, retaining, and motivating a high-quality workforce. Of course, employers do not always have this much flexibility. Some companies are under intense pressure to charge low prices for their products, and some companies are trying to draw workers from a pool that is too small to satisfy all employers' needs.

Gathering Information About Market Pay

To compete for talent, organizations use **benchmarking**, a procedure in which an organization compares its own practices against those of successful competitors. In terms of compensation, benchmarking involves the use of pay surveys. These provide information about the going rates of pay at competitors in the organization's product and labour markets. An organization can conduct its own surveys, but the federal government and other organizations make a great deal of data available already.

benchmarking
A procedure in which an organization compares its own practices against those of successful competitors.

For example, the federal government's Job Bank site (www.jobbank.gc.ca) provides earnings data by city or postal code, for occupations listed in the National Occupational Classification (NOC). Many industry, trade, and professional groups also collect wage and salary data. Employers should check with the relevant groups to see what surveys are available. Consulting firms also will provide data, including the results of international surveys, and can tailor data to an organization's particular needs. Human resources professionals need to determine whether to gather data focusing on particular industries, regions, or on job categories.

How Do Employees Judge Pay Fairness?

HRC3,6

In developing a pay structure, it is important to keep in mind employees' perceptions about fairness. If employees perceive their pay as unfair they may experience pay dissatisfaction and be less motivated to achieve organizational goals. Employees evaluate their pay relative to the pay of other employees. Social scientists have studied this kind of comparison and developed *equity theory* to describe how people make judgments about fairness.[7] According to equity theory, people measure outcomes such as pay in terms of their inputs. For example, an employee might think of her pay in terms of her degree, her three years of experience, and her 45+ hour workweeks. To decide whether a certain level of pay is equitable, the person compares her ratio of outcomes and inputs with other people's outcome/input ratios. The person in the previous example might notice that an employee with less education or experience is earning more than she is (unfair) or that an employee who works 55 hours a week is earning more (fair). In general, employees compare their pay and contributions using several considerations:

- What they think employees in other organizations earn for doing the same job.
- What they think other employees holding different jobs within the organization earn for doing work at the same or different levels.
- What they think other employees in the organization earn for doing the same job as theirs.

How employees respond to their impressions about equity can have a great impact on the organization. Typically, if employees see their pay as equitable, their attitudes and behaviour continue unchanged. If employees see themselves as receiving an advantage, they usually rethink the situation to see it as merely equitable. But if employees conclude that they are under rewarded, they are likely to make up the difference in one of three ways. They might put forth less effort (reducing their inputs), find a way to increase their outcomes (e.g., asking for a raise), or withdraw by leaving the organization or refusing to cooperate.

Job Structure: Relative Value of Jobs

HRC1,6

Along with market forces and principles of fairness, organizations consider the relative contribution each job should make to the organization's overall performance. One typical way of doing this is with a **job evaluation**, an administrative procedure for measuring the relative internal worth of the organization's jobs. Usually, the organization does this by assembling and training a job evaluation committee,

job evaluation
An administrative procedure for measuring the relative internal worth of the organization's jobs.

consisting of people familiar with the jobs to be evaluated. The committee often includes a human resources specialist and, if its budget permits, may hire an outside consultant.

To conduct a job evaluation, the committee identifies each job's *compensable factors,* meaning the characteristics of a job that the organization values and chooses to pay for. As shown in Table 8.2, an organization might consider the effort required and skill requirements of people performing information technology-related jobs. Other compensable factors might include working conditions and responsibility. Based on the job attributes defined by job analysis (discussed in Chapter 3), the jobs are rated for each factor. The rater assigns each factor a certain number of points, giving more points to factors when they are considered more important and when the job requires a high level of that factor. Often the number of points comes from one of the *point manuals* published by trade groups and management consultants. If necessary, the organization can adapt the scores in the point manual to the organization's situation or even develop its own point manual. As in the example in Table 8.2, the scores for each factor are totalled to arrive at an overall evaluation for each job.

Job evaluations provide the basis for decisions about *relative internal worth*—value of the job within the organization, necessary to meet pay equity requirements as discussed in Chapter 2. According to the sample assessments in Table 8.2, the job of systems analyst is worth more to this organization than the job of data entry clerk. Therefore, the organization would be willing to pay significantly more for the work of a systems analyst than it would for the work of a data entry clerk.

The organization may limit its pay survey to jobs evaluated as *key jobs.* These are jobs that have relatively stable content and are common among many organizations, so it is possible to obtain survey data about what people earn in these jobs. Organizations can make the process of creating a pay structure more practical by defining key jobs. Research for creating the pay structure is limited to the key jobs that play a significant role in the organization. Pay for the key jobs can be based on survey data, and pay for the organization's other jobs can be based on the organization's job structure. A job with a higher evaluation score than a particular key job would receive higher pay than that key job.

Pay Structure: Putting It All Together

HRC 1, 6

The pay structure reflects decisions about how much to pay (pay level) and the relative value of each job (job structure). The organization's pay structure should reflect what the organization knows about market forces, as well as its own unique goals and the relative contribution of each job to achieving the goals. By balancing this external and internal information, the organization's goal is to set levels of pay that employees will consider equitable and motivating. Organizations typically apply the information by establishing

TABLE 8.2

Job Evaluation of Three Jobs

JOB TITLE	Compensable Factors				
	SKILL	EFFORT	RESPONSIBILITY	WORKING CONDITIONS	TOTAL
Data entry clerk	20	40	20	30	110
Computer programmer	80	60	50	20	210
Systems analyst	110	70	70	20	270

some combination of pay rates, pay grades, and pay ranges. Within this structure, they may state the pay in terms of a rate per hour, commonly called an **hourly wage**, a rate of pay for each unit produced, known as a **piecework rate**, or a rate of pay per week, month, or year worked, called a **salary**.

hourly wage
Rate of pay for each hour worked.

piecework rate
Rate of pay for each unit produced.

salary
Rate of pay for each week, month, or year worked.

Pay Rates

If the organization's main concern is to match what people are earning in comparable jobs, the organization can base pay directly on market research into as many of its key jobs as possible. To do this, the organization looks for survey data for each job title. If it finds data from more than one survey, it must weight the results according to their quality and relevance. In light of that knowledge, the organization decides what it will pay for the job.

The next step is to determine salaries for the non-key jobs, for which the organization has no survey data. Instead, the person developing the pay structure creates a graph like the one in Figure 8.5. The vertical axis shows a range of possible pay rates, and the horizontal axis measures the points from the job evaluation. The analyst plots points according to the job evaluation and pay rate for each key job. Finally, the analyst fits a line, called a **pay policy line**, to the points plotted. (This can be done statistically, using a procedure called regression analysis.) Mathematically, this line shows the relationship between job evaluation and rate of pay. Using this line, the analyst can estimate the market pay level for a given job evaluation. Looking at the graph gives approximate numbers, or the regression analysis will provide an equation for calculating the rate of pay. For example, using the pay policy line in Figure 8.5, a job with 315 evaluation points would have a predicted salary of $7,783 per month.

pay policy line
A graphed line showing the mathematical relationship between job evaluation points and pay rate.

The pay policy line reflects the pay structure in the market, which does not always match rates in the organization (see key job F in Figure 8.5). Survey data may show that people in certain jobs are actually earning significantly more or less than the amount shown on the pay policy line. For example, some kinds of expertise are in short supply. People with that expertise can command higher pay, because they can easily leave one employer to get higher pay somewhere else. Suppose, in contrast, that local businesses have laid off many warehouse employees. Because so many of these workers are looking for jobs, organizations may be able to pay them less than the rate that job evaluation points would suggest.

When job structure and market data conflict in these ways, organizations have to decide on a way to resolve the two. One approach is to stick to the job evaluations and pay according to the employees' worth to the organization. Organizations that do so will be paying more or less than they have to, so they will likely have more difficulty competing for customers or employees. A way to moderate this approach is to consider the importance of each position to the organization's goals.[8] If a position is critical for meeting the organization's goals, paying more than competitors pay may be worthwhile.

At the other extreme, the organization could base pay entirely on market forces. However, this approach also has some practical drawbacks. One is that employees may conclude that pay rates are

FIGURE 8.5

Pay Policy Lines

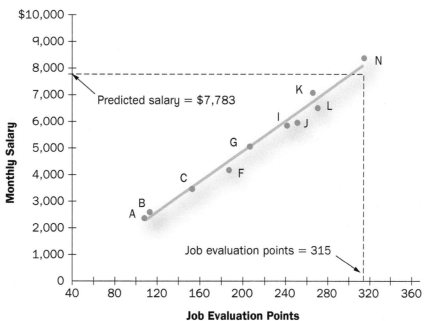

unfair. Two vice-presidents or two supervisors will expect to receive similar pay because their responsibilities are similar. If the differences between their pay are large, because of different market rates, the lower-paid employee will likely be dissatisfied. Also, if the organization's development plans include rotating managers through different assignments, the managers will be reluctant to participate if managers in some departments receive lower pay. Organizations therefore must weigh all the objectives of their pay structure to arrive at suitable rates.

Pay Grades

A large organization could have hundreds or even thousands of different jobs. Setting a pay rate for each job would be extremely complex. Therefore, many organizations group jobs into **pay grades**—sets of jobs having similar worth or content, grouped together to establish rates of pay. For example, the organization could establish five pay grades, with the same pay available to employees holding any job within the same grade.

pay grades
Sets of jobs having similar worth or content, grouped together to establish rates of pay.

A drawback of pay grades is that grouping jobs will result in rates of pay for individual jobs that do not precisely match the levels specified by the market and the organization's job structure. Suppose, for example, that the organization groups together its senior accountants (with a job evaluation of 255 points) and its senior systems analysts (with a job evaluation of 270 points). Surveys might show that the market rate of pay for systems analysts is higher than that for accountants. In addition, the job evaluations give more points to systems analysts. Even so, for simplicity's sake, the organization pays the same rate for the two jobs, because they are in the same pay grade. The organization would have to pay more than the market requires for accountants or pay less than the market rate for systems analysts (so it would probably have difficulty recruiting and retaining them).

Pay Ranges

Usually, organizations want some flexibility in setting pay for individual jobs. They want to be able to pay the most valuable employees the highest amounts and to give rewards for performance. Flexibility also helps the organization balance conflicting information from market surveys and job evaluations. Therefore, pay structure usually includes a **pay range** for each job or pay grade. In other words, the organization establishes a *minimum, maximum,* and *midpoint* of pay for employees holding a particular job or a job within a particular pay grade or band. Employees holding the same job may receive somewhat different pay, depending on where their pay falls within the range.

> **pay range**
> A set of possible pay rates defined by a minimum, maximum, and midpoint of pay for employees holding a particular job or a job within a particular pay grade or band.

A typical approach is to use the market rate or the pay policy line as the midpoint of a range for the job or pay grade. The minimum and maximum values for the range may also be based on market surveys of those amounts. Pay ranges are most common for professional and administrative jobs and for jobs not covered by a union contract. Figure 8.6 shows an example of pay ranges based on the pay policy line in Figure 8.5. Notice that the jobs are grouped into five pay grades, each with its own pay range. In this example, the range is widest for employees who are at higher levels in terms of their job evaluation

FIGURE 8.6

Sample Pay Grade Structure

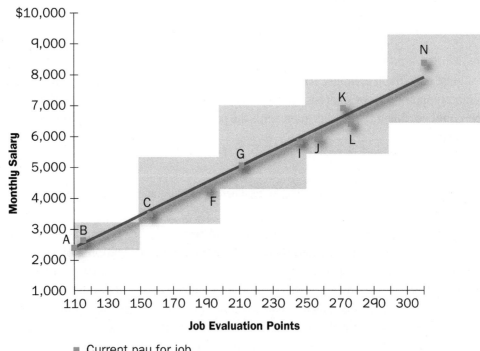

■ Current pay for job
━ Pay policy line

points. That is because the performance of these higher-level employees will likely have more effect on the organization's performance, so the organization needs more latitude to reward them. For instance, as discussed earlier, the organization may want to select a higher point in the range to attract an employee who is more critical to achieving the organization's goals.

Usually pay ranges overlap somewhat, so that the highest pay in one grade is somewhat higher than the lowest pay in the next grade. Overlapping ranges gives the organization more flexibility in transferring employees among jobs, because transfers need not always involve a change in pay. On the other hand, the less overlap, the more important it is to earn promotions in order to keep getting raises. Assuming the organization wants to motivate employees through promotions (and assuming enough opportunities for promotion are available), the organization will want to limit the overlap from one level to the next.

LO3 Describe alternatives to job-based pay.

Alternatives to Job-Based Pay

The traditional and most widely used approach to developing a pay structure focuses on setting pay for jobs or groups of jobs.[9] This emphasis on jobs has some limitations. The precise definition of a job's responsibilities can contribute to a mindset that some activities "are not in my job description," at the expense of flexibility, innovation, quality, and customer service. Organizations may avoid change because it requires repeating the time-consuming process of creating job descriptions and related paperwork. Another change-related problem is that when the organization needs a new set of competencies, the existing pay structure may be rewarding the wrong behaviours. Finally, a pay structure that rewards employees for winning promotions may discourage them from gaining valuable experience through lateral career moves.

Organizations have responded to these problems with a number of alternatives to job-based pay structures. Some organizations have found greater flexibility by **broadbanding**, a pay structure that consolidates pay grades into a few "broad bands," thereby reducing the number of pay ranges in the organization's pay structure. For example, in the 1990s IBM changed from a pay structure with 5,000 job titles and 24 salary grades to one with 1,200 jobs and 10 bands. Broadbanding reduces the opportunities for promoting employees, but this type of pay structure tends to encourage and provide administrative flexibility for employees to make lateral career moves.

broadbanding
A pay structure that consolidates pay grades into a few "broad bands."

Another way organizations have responded to the limitations of job-based pay has been to move away from the link to jobs and toward pay structures that reward employees based on their knowledge and skills (competencies).[10] **Competency-based pay systems** (also known as *skill-based pay systems*) are pay structures that set pay according to the employees' level of skill or knowledge and what they are capable of doing. Paying for competencies makes sense at organizations where changing technology requires employees to continually widen and deepen their knowledge. Competency-based pay also supports efforts to involve employees and enrich jobs because it encourages employees to add to their knowledge so they can make decisions in many areas. In this way, competency-based pay helps organizations become more

competency-based pay systems
Pay structures that set pay according to the employees' levels of skill or knowledge and what they are capable of doing.

flexible and innovative. More generally, competency-based pay can encourage a climate of learning and adaptability and give employees a broader view of how the organization functions.

A disadvantage associated with this type of pay system is that it rewards employees for acquiring skills but does not provide a way to ensure that employees actually use their new skills.[11] The result may be that the organization is paying employees more for learning skills that the employer is not benefiting from. The challenge for HRM is to design work so that the work design and pay structure support one another.

Pay Structure and Actual Pay

Usually, the human resource department is responsible for establishing the organization's pay structure. But building the structure is not the end of the organization's decisions about pay structure. The structure represents the organization's policy, but what the organization actually does may be different. As part of its management responsibility, the HR department therefore should compare actual pay to the pay structure, making sure that policies and practices match.

A common way to do this is to measure a *compa-ratio,* the ratio of average pay to the midpoint of the pay range. Figure 8.7 shows an example. Assuming the organization has pay grades, the organization would find a compa-ratio for each pay grade: the average paid to all employees in the pay grade divided by the midpoint for the pay grade. If the average equals the midpoint, the compa-ratio is 1. More often the compa-ratio is somewhat above 1 (meaning the average pay is above the midpoint for the pay grade) or below 1 (meaning the average pay is below the midpoint).

Assuming that the pay structure is well planned to support the organization's goals, the compa-ratios should be close to 1. A compa-ratio greater than 1 suggests that the organization is paying employees more than planned and may have difficulty keeping costs under control. A compa-ratio less than 1 suggests that the organization may be underpaying employees and may have difficulty attracting and retaining qualified employees.

LO4 Describe how organizations recognize individual, team, and organizational performance through the use of incentives.

Incentive (Variable) Pay

The first part of this chapter discussed the framework for total rewards and setting pay for jobs. Now we focus on using pay to recognize and reward employees' contributions to the organization's success.

FIGURE 8.7

Finding a Compa-Ratio

Pay Grade: 1
Midpoint of Range: $4,675 per month

Salaries of Employees in Pay Grade
Employee 1	$5,306
Employee 2	$4,426
Employee 3	$5,223
Employee 4	$5,114

Compa-Ratio

$$\frac{\text{Average}}{\text{Midpoint}} = \frac{\$5,017.25}{\$4,675.00} = 1.07$$

Average Salary of Employees
$5,306 + $4,426 + $5,523 + $5,114 = $20,069
$20,069 ÷ 4 = $5,017.25

In contrast to decisions about pay structure, organizations have wide discretion in setting performance-related pay, called **incentive pay** or *pay for performance*. Organizations can tie incentive pay to individual performance, profits, or many other measures of success. They select incentives based on their costs, expected influence on performance, and fit with the organization's broader HR and company policies and goals. These decisions are significant. A study of 150 organizations found that the way organizations paid employees was strongly associated with their level of profitability.[12]

incentive pay
Forms of pay linked to an employee's performance as an individual, group member, or organization member.

Many organizations offer incentive pay in the effort to energize, direct, or influence employees' behaviour. According to the Conference Board of Canada, 83 percent of Canadian organizations have at least one incentive pay plan. These plans are particularly popular in the private sector—92 percent of companies reported having one or more plans while 56 percent of public sector organizations also have one or more incentive plans.[13] Incentive pay is influential because the amount paid is linked to certain predefined behaviours or outcomes. For example, an organization can pay a salesperson a *commission* for closing a sale, or the members of a production department can earn a *bonus* for meeting a monthly production goal. Knowing they can earn extra money for closing sales or meeting departmental goals, the employees often try harder or get more creative than they might without the incentive pay. In addition, the policy of offering higher pay for higher performance may make an organization attractive to high performers when it is trying to recruit and retain these valuable employees.[14]

For incentive pay to motivate employees to contribute to the organization's success, the plans must be well designed. In particular, effective plans meet the following requirements:

- Performance measures are linked to the organization's goals.
- Employees believe they can meet performance standards.
- The organization gives employees the resources they need to meet their goals.
- Employees value the rewards given.
- Employees believe the reward system is fair.
- The plan takes into account that employees may ignore any goals that are not rewarded.

The "HR How-To" box provides some additional ideas for creating and implementing an effective incentive-pay plan that aligns with a company's strategy. Since incentive pay is linked to particular outcomes or behaviours, the organization is encouraging them to demonstrate those desired outcomes and behaviours. As obvious as that may sound, the implications are more complicated. If incentive pay is extremely rewarding, employees may focus on only the performance measures rewarded under the plan and ignore measures that are not rewarded. Many call centres pay employees based on how many calls they handle, as an incentive to work quickly and efficiently. However, speedy call handling does not necessarily foster good customer relationships. Organizations may combine a number of incentives so employees do not focus on one measure to the exclusion of others.

Another criticism is the concern that individual pay for performance can "foster an individualistic culture or a culture of entitlement."[15] Employees must also believe they have the ability and resources to meet the performance standards and that the performance standards are under their control. As we will discuss in the section on rewards for organizational performance, this is a challenge in the

HR How-To

Aligning Incentive Programs with Company Strategy

Here are some measures organizations can take to enhance the link between incentive pay and the organization's strategy:

- Identify the top performers who contribute to the organization's success. That requires knowing what kinds of accomplishments actually translate into sustainable profitability, as well as measuring who is responsible for those achievements. These people need to know that incentive pay is available and know what they must accomplish to earn it.

- Customize incentive plans rather than copy the competition. Salary surveys provide important baseline data, but incentive pay should reflect the company's own values, performance criteria, and employee characteristics.

- When the organization has a set budget to use for performance-related pay, consider all the measures of past and future performance that are relevant for allocating the budget. For example, an organization could direct pay increases to people who have specific skills it will need in the future or who have skills and attitudes that suggest they may contribute a great deal to the organization over the long term. In other situations, a history of consistently meeting goals, such as sales targets, may be most relevant to the company's success.

- Acknowledge that when incentives are linked to performance, low performers will not receive the incentives. It can feel uncomfortable to tell employees that they will not get a raise or their team will not get a bonus this quarter. However, assuming the organization provides employees with the training and resources they need to meet performance targets, the consequences of failure can either spur employees to try harder or create an environment where unmotivated employees leave and make room for motivated ones.

- Recognize the limits of pay as a reward. If the company already compensates its most valuable employees at above-market rates, then that employee, at least in theory, is not likely to leave for a higher-paying job (the labor market is actually paying less). In that situation, more money will not likely improve employee retention; the company should look for other ways to show the employee that he or she is appreciated. The employee might appreciate more time off, a more flexible schedule, or a chance to mentor others.

Sources: Lori Wisper and Ken Abosch, "Does Merit Pay Still Have Merit in the New Economic Reality?" WorldatWork, www.worldatwork.org, accessed April 19, 2012; "Aligning Incentive Pay Programs with Business Goals," Report on Salary Surveys, February 2012, pp. 9–10; Stephen Miller, "Pay for Performance: Make It More than a Catchphrase," SHRM Online Compensation Discipline, May 30, 2011, www.shrm.org.

case of incentives based on an organization's profits or stock price. Employees at lower levels of the organization may doubt that they have much influence over these performance measures. Therefore, these incentives likely will not have much effect on these employees' behaviour, at least in large companies.

Other attitudes that influence the success of incentive pay include whether employees value the rewards and think the pay plan is fair. Most, if not all, employees value pay, but it is important to remember that earning money is not the only reason people try to do a good job. As discussed in other chapters (see Chapters 1, 6, and 11), people also want interesting work, appreciation for their efforts, flexibility, and a sense of belonging to the work group—not to mention the inner satisfaction of work well done. Therefore, a complete plan for compensating and rewarding employees has many components, from pay to work design to developing managers so they can exercise positive leadership.

We will now identify elements of incentive pay systems. We consider each option's strengths and limitations with regard to these principles. The many kinds of incentive pay fall into three broad categories: incentives linked to individual, team, or organizational performance. Choices from these categories should consider not only their strengths and weaknesses, but also their fit with the organization's goals.

The choice of incentive pay may affect not only the level of motivation, but also the kinds of employees who are attracted to and stay with the organization. For example, there is some evidence that organizations with team-based rewards will tend to attract employees who are more team-oriented.[16]

See the "Did You Know?" on the use of spot bonuses.

Pay for Individual Performance

Organizations may reward individual performance with a variety of incentives.

- *Piecework rate*—As an incentive to work efficiently, some organizations pay production workers a piecework rate, a wage based on the amount they produce. The amount paid per unit is set at a level that rewards employees for above-average production volume. An obvious advantage of piece rates is the direct link between how much work the employee does and the amount the employee earns. However, for complex jobs or jobs with hard-to-measure outputs, piecework plans do not apply very well. Also, unless a plan is well-designed to include performance standards, it may not reward employees for focusing on quality or customer satisfaction if it interferes with the day's output. In Figure 8.8, the employees quickly realize they can earn huge bonuses by writing software "bugs" and then fixing them, while writing bug-free software affords no chance to earn bonuses.

- *Standard hour plans*—Another quantity-oriented incentive for production workers is the **standard hour plan**, an incentive plan that pays workers extra for work done in less than a preset "standard

standard hour plan
An incentive plan that pays workers extra for work done in less than a preset "standard time."

Did You Know?

Awarding Spot Bonuses

In 2014, a majority of companies (60 percent) paid *spot bonuses*—bonuses delivered on the spot for special recognition—most frequently to reward performance above and beyond expectations or upon the completion of a project. This represents a significant increase from 2010 when only 43 percent of organizations reported paying spot bonuses. In organizations that award these bonuses, maximum payouts to managers, supervisors, and professionals are typically in the range of $2,500 to $5,000.

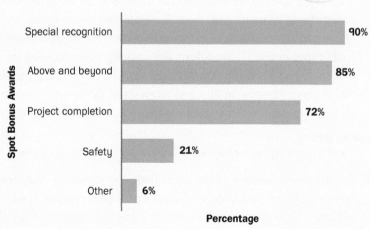

Question

1. From the perspective of an employer, how could you determine whether the increase in the use of spot bonuses makes good business sense?

Source: "Bonus Programs and Practices," June 2014, pp. 6, 9, and 19, www.worldatwork.org.

FIGURE 8.8

How Incentives Sometimes "Work"

Source: DILBERT, reprinted by permission of United Features Syndicate, Inc.

time." The organization determines a standard time to complete a task, such as tuning up a car engine. If the mechanic completes the work in less than the standard time, the mechanic receives an amount of pay equal to the wage for the full standard time. Suppose the standard time for tuning up an engine is 2 hours. If the mechanic finishes the tune-up in 1.5 hours, the mechanic receives 2 hours of pay for 1.5 hours worked. Working that fast over the course of a week could add significantly to the mechanic's pay. In terms of pros and cons, standard hour plans are much like piecework plans. They encourage employees to work as fast as they can, but not necessarily to care about quality or customer service.

- *Merit pay*—Almost all organizations have established some program of **merit pay**—a system of linking pay increases to ratings on performance appraisals. An advantage of merit pay is that it provides a method for rewarding performance in all of the dimensions measured in the organization's performance management system. If that system is appropriately designed to measure all the important job behaviours, then the merit pay is linked to the behaviours the organization desires. This link seems logical, although so far there is little research showing the effectiveness of merit pay.[17] A drawback of merit pay, from the employer's standpoint, is that it can quickly become expensive. Managers at a majority of organizations rate most employees' performance in the top two categories (out of four or five).[18] Therefore, the majority of employees are eligible for the biggest merit increases, and their pay rises rapidly. Another drawback of merit pay is that it assumes that performance is based on employees' ability and motivation, however, performance may be enhanced or reduced by factors beyond the employees' control, e.g., economic conditions or a manager's rating bias.

merit pay
A system of linking pay increases to ratings on performance appraisals.

- *Performance bonuses*—Like merit pay, performance bonuses reward individual performance, but bonuses are not rolled into base pay. The employee must re-earn them during each performance period. In some cases, the bonus is a one-time reward. Bonuses may also be linked to objective performance measures rather than potentially subjective ratings. Bonuses for individual performance can be extremely effective and give the organization great flexibility in deciding what kinds of behaviour to reward.

- *Commissions*—A variation on piece rates and bonuses is the payment of **commissions**, or pay calculated as a percentage of sales. For instance, a flooring sales consultant might earn commissions

commissions
Incentive pay calculated as a percentage of sales.

Many sales associates in the auto industry earn a straight commission, meaning that 100 percent of their pay comes from commission instead of a salary. What type of individual might enjoy a job like this?

equalling 6 percent of the price of the flooring the person sells during the period. In a growth-oriented organization, sales commissions need not be limited to salespeople.

 E-HRM

Broadcasting bonuses—using social media and sales incentives technologies.

Pay for Team Performance

Employers may address the drawbacks of individual incentives by including team incentives in the organization's compensation plan. To earn team incentives, employees must cooperate and share knowledge so that the entire team can meet its performance targets. Widely used team incentives include gainsharing, bonuses, and team awards.

Gainsharing

Organizations that want employees to focus on efficiency may adopt a **gainsharing** program, which measures increases in productivity and effectiveness and distributes a portion of each gain to employees. For example, if a factory enjoys a productivity gain worth $30,000, half the gain might be the company's share. The other $15,000 would be distributed among the employees in the factory. Knowing that they can enjoy a financial benefit from helping the company be more productive, employees supposedly will look for ways to work more efficiently and improve the way the factory operates.

gainsharing
Team incentive program that measures improvements in productivity and effectiveness and distributes a portion of each gain to employees.

Gainsharing addresses the challenge of identifying appropriate performance measures for complex jobs. Even for simpler jobs, setting acceptable standards and measuring performance can be complicated.

Gainsharing frees employees to determine how to improve their own and their team's performance. It also broadens employees' focus beyond their individual interests. But in contrast to profit sharing, discussed later, it keeps the performance measures within a range of activity that most employees believe they can influence. Organizations can enhance the likelihood of a gain by providing a means for employees to share knowledge and make suggestions, as we will discuss later in this chapter.

Gainsharing is most likely to succeed when organizations provide the right conditions. Among the conditions identified, the following are among the most common:[19]

- Management commitment.
- Need for change or strong commitment to continuous improvement.
- Management acceptance and encouragement of employee input.
- High levels of cooperation and interaction.
- Employment security.
- Information sharing on productivity and costs.
- Goal setting.
- Commitment of all involved parties to the process of change and improvement.
- Performance standards and calculations that employees understand and consider fair and that is closely related to managerial objectives.
- Employees who value working in teams.

Team Bonuses and Awards

In contrast to gainsharing plans, which typically reward the performance of all employees at a facility, bonuses for team performance tend to be for smaller work groups.[20] These bonuses reward the members

Team members that meet a sales goal or a product development team that meets a deadline or successfully launches a product may be rewarded with a bonus for team performance. What are some advantages and disadvantages of team bonuses?

of a group for attaining a specific goal, usually measured in terms of physical output. Team awards are similar to team bonuses, but they are more likely to use a broad range of performance measures, such as cost savings, successful completion of a project, or even meeting deadlines.

Both types of incentives have the advantage that they encourage group or team members to cooperate so that they can achieve their goal. However, depending on the reward system, competition among individuals may be replaced by competition among teams. Competition may be healthy in some situations, as when teams try to outdo one another in satisfying customers. On the downside, competition may also prevent necessary cooperation among teams. To avoid this, the organization should carefully set the performance goals for these incentives so that concern for costs or sales does not obscure other objectives, such as quality, customer service, and ethical behaviour.

Pay for Organizational Performance

Two important ways organizations measure their performance are in terms of their profits and their stock price. In a competitive marketplace, profits result when an organization is efficiently providing products that customers want at a price they are willing to pay. Stock is the owners' investment in a corporation; when the stock price is rising, the value of that investment is growing. Rather than trying to figure out what performance measures will motivate employees to do the things that generate high profits and a rising stock price, many organizations offer incentive pay tied to those organizational performance measures. The expectation is that employees will focus on what is best for the organization.

These organization-level incentives can motivate employees to align their activities with the organization's goals. At the same time, linking incentives to the organization's profits or stock price exposes employees to a high degree of risk. Profits and stock price can soar very high very fast, but they can also fall. The result is a great deal of uncertainty about the amount of incentive pay each employee will receive in each period. Therefore, these kinds of incentive pay are likely to be most effective in organizations that emphasize growth and innovation, which tend to need employees who thrive in a risk-taking environment.[21]

Profit Sharing

Under **profit sharing**, payments are a percentage of the organization's profits and do not become part of the employees' base salary. Organizations use profit sharing for a number of reasons. It may encourage employees to think more like owners, taking a broad view of what they need to do in order to make the organization more effective. They are more likely to cooperate and less likely to focus on narrow self-interest. Also, profit sharing has the practical advantage of costing less when the organization is experiencing financial difficulties. If the organization has little or no profit, this incentive pay is small or nonexistent, so employers may not need to rely as much on layoffs to reduce costs.[22]

profit sharing
Incentive pay in which payments are a percentage of the organization's profits and do not become part of the employees' base salary.

An organization setting up a profit-sharing plan should consider what to do if profits fall. If the economy slows and profit-sharing payments disappear along with profits, employees may become discouraged or dissatisfied. If profit sharing is offered to all employees but most employees think only management decisions about products, price, and marketing have much impact on profits, they will conclude that there is little connection between their actions and their rewards. In that case, profit sharing will have little impact on employee behaviours. This problem is even greater when employees have to wait months before profits are distributed. The time lag between high performance, behaviour, and financial rewards is sometimes simply too long to be motivating.

Given the limitations of profit-sharing plans, one strategy is to use them as a component of a pay system that includes other kinds of pay more directly linked to individual behaviour. This increases employees' commitment to organizational goals while addressing concerns about fairness.

Stock Ownership

While profit-sharing plans are intended to encourage employees to "think like owners," a stock ownership plan actually makes employees part owners of the organization. Like profit sharing, employee ownership is intended as a way to encourage employees to focus on the success of the organization as a whole. The drawbacks of stock ownership as a form of incentive pay are similar to those of profit sharing. Specifically, it may not have a strong effect on individuals' motivation. Employees may not see a strong link between their actions and the company's stock price, especially in larger organizations. The link between pay and performance is even harder to appreciate because the financial benefits mostly come when the stock is sold—typically when the employee leaves the organization. Ownership programs usually take the form of *stock options* or *employee stock ownership plans*. These are illustrated in Figure 8.9.

Stock Options

One way to distribute stock to employees is to grant **stock options**—the right to buy a certain number of shares of stock at a specified price. (Purchasing the stock is called *exercising* the option.) Suppose that in 2013 a company's employees received options to purchase the company's stock at $10 per share. The employees will benefit if the stock price rises above $10 per share, because they can pay $10 for something (a share of stock) that is worth more than $10. If in 2016 the stock is worth $18, they can exercise their options and buy stock for $10 a share. If they want to, they can sell their stock for the market price of $18, receiving a gain of $8 for each share of stock. Of course, stock prices can also fall. If the 2016 stock price is only $8, the employees would not exercise the options.

stock options
Rights to buy a certain number of shares of stock at a specified price.

Traditionally, organizations have granted stock options to their executives. In recent years, many organizations pushed eligibility for options further down in the organization's structure. Some studies suggest that organizations perform better when a large percentage of top and middle managers are eligible for long-term incentives such as stock options. This evidence is consistent with the idea of encouraging employees to think like owners.[23]

FIGURE 8.9

Types of Pay for Organizational Performance

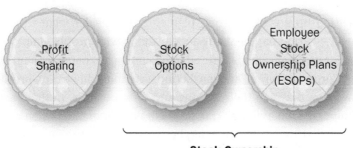

Stock Ownership

Corporate scandals have drawn attention to another challenge of using stock options as incentive pay. As with other performance measures, employees may focus so much on stock price that they lose sight of other goals, including ethical behaviour. Ideally, managers would bring about an increase in stock price by adding value in terms of efficiency, innovation, and customer satisfaction. But there are other, unethical ways to increase stock price by tricking investors into thinking the organization is more valuable and more profitable than it actually is. Hiding losses and inflating the recorded value of revenues are just two ways some companies have boosted stock prices, enriching managers until these misdeeds come to light.

Employee Stock Ownership Plans

While stock options are most often used with top management, a broader arrangement is the **employee stock ownership plan (ESOP)**. In an ESOP, the organization distributes shares of stock to its employees by placing the stock into a trust managed on the employees' behalf. Employees receive regular reports on the value of their stock, and when they leave the organization, they may sell the stock to the organization or (if it is a publicly traded company) on the open market. For example, WestJet's Share Purchase Program enables WestJetters to receive up to 20 percent of their salaries in WestJet shares. Shares can be purchased as common shares or can be directed into RRSPs with WestJet matching the employee's contributions.[24]

employee stock ownership plan (ESOP)
An arrangement in which the organization distributes shares of stock to all its employees by placing it in a trust.

Although ESOPs are the most common form of employee ownership they raise a number of issues. On the negative side, they carry a significant risk for employees. Problems with the company's performance therefore can take away significant value from the ESOP. Many companies set up ESOPs to hold retirement funds, so these risks directly affect employees' retirement income.

Still, ESOPs can be attractive to employers. Along with tax and financing advantages, ESOPs give employers a way to build pride in and commitment to the organization. Employees have a right to participate in votes by shareholders (if the stock is registered on a national exchange, such as the TSX).[25] This means employees participate somewhat in corporate-level decision making. Refer to Table 8.3 for a summary of the advantages and disadvantages of individual, team, and organizational incentives.

TABLE 8.3

An Overview of Incentive Pay

Criterion	Incentives	Advantages	Disadvantages
Individual performance	Piecework rates, sales commissions	Exert most powerful impact on productivity.	Do not promote teamwork or ensure a corresponding increase in product quality. May be difficult to measure.
Team performance	Gainsharing, team-based incentive plans	Encourage teamwork.	Yield a moderate impact on productivity.
Organizational performance	Profit sharing and stock sharing, including stock ownership, stock options, and employee stock ownership plan	Increase shareholder returns and company profit.	Generate only a small increase in productivity.

Source: "Implementing Total Rewards Strategies," *SHRM Foundation*, p. 12, www.shrm.org/about/foundation/research/Documents/07RewardsStratReport.pdf, retrieved August 16, 2012.

L○5 Discuss the role of benefits as part of employee total rewards.

What Is the Role of Employee Benefits?

HRC6

Employees at almost every organization receive more than cash in exchange for their efforts. They also receive a package of **employee benefits**—compensation in forms other than cash (indirect compensation). Examples include paid vacation time, employer-paid health insurance, and pension plans, among a wide range of possibilities.

> **employee benefits**
> Compensation in forms other than cash.

As part of the total compensation provided to employees, benefits serve functions similar to pay. Benefits contribute to attracting, retaining, and motivating employees. The variety of possible benefits also helps employers tailor their offerings to the kinds of employees they need. Employers need to examine their benefits package regularly to see whether they still meet employees' needs and expectations. Even if employers spend large sums on benefits and services, if employees do not understand how to use them or why they are valuable, the cost of the benefits will be largely wasted.[26] Employers need to communicate effectively so that the benefits succeed in motivating employees.

Employees have come to expect that benefits will help them maintain economic security. Canada Pension Plan/Quebec Pension Plan, company pension plans, and retirement savings plans help employees prepare for their retirement. Insurance plans help to protect employees from unexpected costs such as prescription drugs. This important role of benefits is one reason that some benefits are required by law, e.g., Employment Insurance.

Even though many kinds of benefits are not required by law, they have become so common that today's employees expect them. Many employers find that attracting qualified workers requires them to provide health and retirement benefits of some sort. A large employer without such benefits would be highly unusual and would have difficulty competing in the labour market. A national survey conducted by Ipsos-Reid found that Canadian employees value their health benefits. As reported by Benefits Canada, 91 percent of survey respondents said that other than salary, a "good job" was defined as having a good benefits package—"benefits are serving as a proxy or a marker for a good workplace."[27] The 2014 Sanofi Canada Healthcare Survey reveals that "millennial employees are more likely than their older co-workers to see benefits as a right—while 63 percent of baby boomers see health benefits as a perk or privilege, this sentiment falls to 50 percent among generation Y employees."[28]

Like other forms of compensation and rewards, benefits impose significant costs. On average, out of every dollar spent on compensation, 30 cents or more go to benefits and this share has grown over the past decades.[29] An organization managing its labour costs must pay careful attention to the cost of its employee benefits.

Overall, employers are concerned about balancing various issues related to benefits provided to employees. Several forces have made benefits and services a significant part of compensation packages. One is that laws require employers to provide certain benefits, such as contributions to Canada Pension Plan and Employment Insurance. Also, tax laws can make benefits favourable. For example, employees do not pay income taxes on most benefits they receive, but they pay income taxes on cash compensation. Therefore, an employee who receives a $1,000 raise "takes home" less than the full $1,000, but an employee who receives an additional $1,000 worth of non-taxable benefits receives the full benefits. Another cost advantage of paying benefits is that employers, especially large ones, often can get a better deal on insurance or other programs than employees can obtain on their own.

Finally, some employers assemble creative benefits packages to set them apart in the competition for talent. For example, Netflix (www.netflix.com) lets people take off as much time as they want and doesn't keep track. This policy is in keeping with its HR strategy of "hiring adults"—experts who already have a history of success, love movies, and can manage their time. Since the company's success comes from people driven by a passion for what they do and what they can accomplish, offering freedom as a benefit contributes to attracting and keeping the right talent.[30] Apple (www.apple.com) and Facebook (www.facebook.com) recently attracted attention by offering female employees $20,000 toward "egg freezing" as part of its comprehensive benefits package (the same benefit is offered to men by covering the cost of sperm freezing.[31]

L○6 Summarize the types of employee benefits offered by employers.

What Benefits Are Required by Law?

HRC 2, 6

Governments require various forms of security to protect workers from financial hardships of being off work. Because these benefits are required by law, employers cannot gain an advantage in the labour market by offering them, nor can they design the nature of these benefits.

- **Canada Pension Plan (CPP)/Quebec Pension Plan (QPP)**. These plans, established in 1966, cover all workers in Canada who are age 18 and older and have annual income exceeding $3,500. CPP/QPP is a mandatory **contributory plan** that provides retirement pensions, disability benefits, and survivor benefits. Workers who meet eligibility requirements receive benefits according to their age and earnings history.[32]

Canada Pension Plan (CPP)/Quebec Pension Plan (QPP)
A contributory, mandatory plan that provides retirement pensions, disability benefits, and survivor benefits.

contributory plan
All costs of the plan are funded by employees, employers, and the plan's own investments.

- **Employment Insurance (EI)**. This federally mandated program provides temporary financial assistance to non-working Canadians who have lost their jobs through no fault of their own, while they look for another job or upgrade their skills. Coverage is also extended to also include eligible workers who are sick, are pregnant, or are caring for a newborn or adopted child, providing compassionate care to a gravely ill family member or for parents caring for a critically ill child.[33]

Employment Insurance (EI)
A federally mandated program to provide temporary financial assistance to non-working Canadians.

- **Workers' Compensation Acts**. Provincial programs that provide benefits to workers who suffer work-related injuries or illnesses. Workers' compensation operates under a principle of *no-fault liability*, meaning that an employee does not need to show that the employer was grossly negligent in order to receive compensation, and the employer is protected from lawsuits. The benefits fall into three major categories: wage-loss benefits, medical services, and rehabilitative services. Workers' compensation is entirely funded by employers—neither workers nor the government contribute. The amount employers pay depends on the industry and kinds of occupations involved as well as the size of the employer's payroll. Organizations can minimize the cost of this benefit by keeping workplaces safe and making employees and their managers conscious of safety issues, as discussed in Chapter 2.

Workers' Compensation Acts
Provincial programs that provide benefits to workers who suffer work-related injuries or illnesses.

What Optional Benefits Do Some Employers Provide?

Other types of benefits are optional. These include various kinds of insurance, retirement plans, and paid leave. Part-time workers often receive fewer benefits than full-time employees. The most widely offered benefits are paid leave for vacations and holidays (that exceed the legally required minimums specified in employment/labour standards legislation), life and medical insurance, and retirement plans. The extent to which the employer pays for the benefit varies widely among organizations. Some organizations require employees to pay a significant percentage of the premiums for insurance plans such as dental coverage. Other organizations pick up 100 percent of the premiums.

Benefits such as health insurance usually extend to employees' dependents. To ensure an employer does not face a charge of discrimination related to sexual orientation and/or marital status as a protected ground of discrimination, employers cover different-sex as well as same-sex partners.

Paid Leave

Employment/labour standards legislation outlines minimum vacation entitlements and paid holidays. Many employers provide vacation and holidays in addition to the minimum legislated requirements. Some organizations also offer additional days off for personal reasons or to contribute their time to a charitable organization.

Sick leave programs pay employees for days not worked because of illness. The amount of sick leave is often based on length of service, so that it accumulates over time—for example, one day added to sick leave for each month of service. Employers have to decide how many sick days to grant and whether to let them continue accumulating year after year. As reported by the Conference Board of Canada, the overall absenteeism rate has increased from an average of 6.0 days per employee in 2006–2007 to 7.0 days in 2013–2014. Absenteeism in the public sector averages 8.7 days per employee in contrast to 6.1 days in the private sector.[34]

An organization's policies for time off may include other forms of paid and unpaid leave. For a workforce that values flexibility, the organization may offer paid *personal days*, days off employees may schedule according to their personal needs, with the supervisor's approval. Typically, organizations offer a few personal days in addition to sick leave. *Floating holidays* are paid holidays that vary from year to year. The organization may schedule floating holidays so that they extend a Tuesday or Thursday holiday into a long weekend. Organizations may also give employees discretion over the scheduling of floating holidays. Employers should establish policies for leaves without pay—for example, leaves of absence to pursue nonwork goals or to meet family needs. Unpaid leave is also considered an employee benefit because the employee usually retains seniority and benefits during the leave.

Group Insurance and Benefits

HRC6, 8

As we noted earlier, rates for group insurance are typically lower than for individual policies. Also, insurance benefits are not subject to income tax, as wages and salaries are. When employees receive insurance as a benefit, rather than higher pay so they can buy their own insurance, employees can get more for their money. Because of this, most employees value group insurance. The most common types of insurance and benefits offered as employee benefits are medical, life insurance, and disability insurance.

- *Medical insurance.* The policies typically cover medical expenses that are incurred over and above provincially funded medical coverage. Some employers offer additional coverage, such as dental care, vision care, and prescription drug programs. Employers must also make choices about coverage of so-called "lifestyle drugs," that is, drugs considered "cosmetic" or "discretionary." Examples are medical treatments for obesity, infertility, erectile dysfunction, male pattern baldness, and smoking cessation.[35] An alternative to traditional employer-provided medical insurance is a **health spending account**, in which an employer puts aside a specific amount of money per employee to cover health-related costs. Employees decide what health care services they will purchase with their allocation. Major insurers, such as Great-West Life (www.greatwestlife.com), administer the health spending account, usually for a fixed percentage fee. Health spending accounts are particularly attractive to small companies because the cost to the employer for employee benefits and administration is capped.[36]

health spending account
A specific amount of money set aside per employee by the employer to cover health-related costs.

- *Employee wellness program.* One way to lower the cost of health insurance is to reduce employees' need for health care services. Employers may try to do this by offering an employee wellness program, a set of communications, activities, and facilities designed to change health-related behaviours in ways that reduce health risks discussed in Chapter 2. Typically, wellness programs aim at specific health risks, such as high blood pressure, high cholesterol levels, smoking, and obesity, by encouraging preventive measures such as exercise and good nutrition. However, many organizations are adopting an integrated strategic approach to wellness that promotes a corporate culture to support employees in taking responsibility for their health and overall wellness.

According to recent research by the International Foundation of Employee Benefit Plans, the prevalence of wellness programs has grown significantly over the last ten years, with more than 40 percent of Canadian employers implementing new programs since 2008. And 60 percent of the Canadian organizations surveyed said they provide program incentives such as fitness discounts (29 percent), gift cards and gift certificates (27 percent), and non-cash incentives such as prizes and raffles (27 percent) to boost employee participation.[37] "Incentives create more interest in the program and inspire people who aren't usually active to get involved," explains Kathleen Jones, business solutions manager at Fraser & Hoyt Incentives (www.fh-incentives.ca) in Halifax.[38] The "HR Best Practices" box describes how companies are using wellness programs and other methods to slow the increases in their cost for health insurance benefits.

- *Employee assistance program (EAP).* As discussed in Chapter 2 an employee assistance program (EAP) provides confidential counselling services to employees experiencing personal problems. Many organizations also extend these services to family members. Left untreated, personal problems may cause an employee to lose their ability to cope and work performance will suffer. Employees must be able to feel confident the program respects their confidentiality. Other considerations include the range of offerings provided (some EAP providers offer a very broad range of services

HR Best Practices

Reining in Rising Health Care Costs

In a recent study, researchers reported that effective wellness programs result in cost savings due to improved employee health. Organizations including Canada Life (www.canadalife.com), Dupont (www.dupont.ca), Prudential Insurance (www.prudential.ca), and Citibank (www.citi.com) reported positive ROI (return on investment) in the range of $2 to $6.85 savings for each dollar of investment in employee wellness. When employees take better care of themselves, they don't need as much care from their doctors and other health care professionals. Current research suggests that to achieve an ROI from a wellness program, at least 60 percent employee participation is needed. With results like that, it is no surprise that some companies want to spread out the returns to employees' families covered by health insurance benefits. For example, at Dell (www.dell.ca), when employees' partners participate in wellness programs, the company applies a discount to employees' health benefits premiums. The anticipated "hockey stick" growth of mobile health apps and wearable technologies with health tracking capabilities is also anticipated to be encouraged by employers as another way to engage employees in taking an active role in maintaining a healthy and active lifestyle.

Other companies are saving money by limiting who is covered. In two-career couples, a company could be paying for a family plan when an employee's partner already has a full health care plan through his or her own employer. In such cases, the employer could be paying a great deal of money for benefits that have little practical value to the employees receiving the coverage. Therefore, some employers are establishing policies that either exclude partners with their own insurance or else require the employee to pay a surcharge for covering a partner who has insurance already through his or her employer. Other employers are letting prices, rather than rules, guide employees to cost-effective choices. These employers charge higher premiums for a partner's coverage than for an employee's coverage. This gives employees an incentive to get coverage for their partner from the partner's employer. Xerox Corporation (www.xerox.ca) is one of the companies using a surcharge; it expects to cut the cost of health benefits by 2 percent—a substantial sum at a large organization.

In an effort that exemplifies the company's culture of relying on data and analytics, Google is approaching health care costs by finding ways to nudge employees into healthy behaviour—and measuring to make sure that those nudges are actually delivering results. For example, Google moved its cafeteria salad bar to a spot just inside the entrance and shifted the dessert selection to an out-of-the-way location because it found that whatever employees see first is most likely to go on their plates. And by the plates, the company posted a sign saying that people who use bigger dishes tend to eat more. After the sign went up, the use of small plates rose by 50 percent. Measuring plate usage is a lot less intrusive than tracking employees' weight, and the company hopes such efforts will result in trimmer, healthier workers, who presumably will cost less to insure.

Sources: Armina Ligaya and April Fong, "Health App Hints at Apple Wearables," *National Post*, June 2014, p. FP2; Lydia Makrides, "A Measure of Success," *Benefits Canada*, March 2013, p. 17; Cliff Kuang, "In the Cafeteria, Google Gets Healthy," *Fast Company*, March 2, 2012, www.fastcompany.com; David Tobenkin, "Spousal Exclusions on the Rise," *HR Magazine*, November 2011, pp. 55–58; Michelle Conlin, "Health Care: Human Resources Targets Your Family," *Bloomberg Businessweek*, January 21, 2010, www.businessweek.com.

that may overlap with health, wellness and lifestyle-related services), proximity to counsellors, client references, and availability of effectiveness reporting measures.[39]

- *Life insurance.* Employers may provide life insurance to employees or offer the opportunity to buy coverage at low group rates. With a *term life insurance* policy, if the employee dies during the term of the policy, the employee's beneficiaries receive a payment called a death benefit. In policies purchased as an employee benefit, the usual death benefit is a multiple of the employee's yearly pay. The policies may provide additional benefits for accidental death. Along with a basic policy, the employer may give employees the option of purchasing additional coverage, usually at a nominal cost.

- *Disability insurance.* Employees risk losing their incomes if a disability makes them unable to work. Disability insurance provides protection against this loss of income. Typically, **short-term disability insurance** provides benefits for six months or less. **Long-term disability insurance** provides benefits after that initial period, potentially for the rest of the disabled employee's life. Disability payments are a percentage of the employee's salary—typically 50 to 70 percent. Payments under short-term plans may be higher. Often the policy sets a maximum amount that may be paid each month. Because its limits make it more affordable, short-term disability coverage is offered by more employers.

short-term disability insurance
Insurance that pays a percentage of a disabled employee's salary as benefits to the employee for six months or less.

long-term disability insurance
Insurance that pays a percentage of a disabled employee's salary after an initial period and potentially for the rest of the employee's life.

Retirement Plans

HRC 1, 2, 6

Employers have no obligation to offer retirement plans beyond the protection of CPP/QPP security, but many offer some form of pension or retirement savings plan. Almost 6.2 million employees in Canada are members of registered pension plans (RPPs).[40] Figure 8.10 provides a breakdown of registered pension plans and members by type of plan.

An additional issue facing employers' approaches to retirement plans is a growing interest in **phased retirement**, a gradual transition into full retirement by reducing hours or job responsibility.[41] Employers are facing an increasing demand for phased retirement programs from employees who are healthier, living longer, and have personal or financial reasons to continue working in some capacity. Employers also benefit from retaining older workers with valued skills and experience who wish to retire gradually. Phased retirement also provides the employer with more time to transfer knowledge and skills to younger employees[42]; however, many employers are worried about the implications and costs of providing benefits coverage to older employees.

phased retirement
A gradual transition into full retirement by reducing hours or job responsibility.

Employers have a choice of using defined benefit plans or defined contribution plans. Both are described below:

- *Defined benefit plans.* Employers have a choice of using registered retirement plans (RPPs) that define the amount to be paid out after retirement or plans that define the amount the employer will invest each year. A **defined benefit plan** defines the benefits to be paid according to a formula stipulated in the plan.[43] Usually the amount of this defined benefit is calculated for each employee based on the employee's years of service, age, and earnings level (e.g., a percentage of the average of the employee's five highest-earnings years). These calculations typically result in pension payments that may provide 70 percent of pre-retirement income for a long-service employee. Using years of service as part of the basis for calculating benefits gives employees an incentive to stay with the organization as long as they can, so it can help to reduce voluntary turnover. Overall, 71.5 percent

defined benefit plan
A pension plan that defines the benefits to be paid according to a formula stipulated in the plan.

of employees in Canada with an RPP, were in a defined benefit pension plan, however, participation in this type of plan has declined from more than 85 percent just over a decade earlier,[44] largely due to the migration of new and existing private sector employees to defined contribution plans. For example, in 2012, RBC stopped offering new Canadian hires access to its defined benefit plan.

FIGURE 8.10

Membership in Registered Pension Plans by Type of Plan and Sector

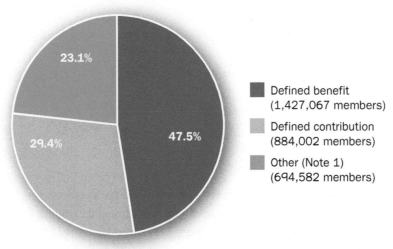

Private Sector (2012)

Defined benefit
(1,427,067 members)

Defined contribution
(884,002 members)

Other (Note 1)
(694,582 members)

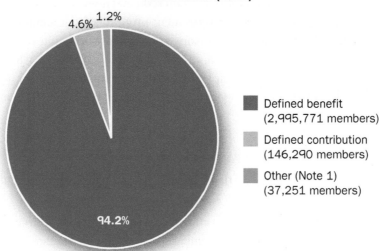

Public Sector (2012)

Defined benefit
(2,995,771 members)

Defined contribution
(146,290 members)

Other (Note 1)
(37,251 members)

Note 1: Other plans include having a hybrid, composite, defined benefit/defined contribution, and other component.
Source: Statistics Canada, "Table 1: Registered pension plan membership, by sector and type of plan," *The Daily*, August 28, 2014, www.statcan.gc.ca/daily-quotidien/140828/t140828d001-eng.htm, retrieved May 21, 2015.

Existing employees can remain in RBC's defined benefits plan or switch to the defined contribution plan, which was made attractive through features such as higher employer contributions.[45]

● *Defined contribution plans.* An alternative to defined benefits is a **defined contribution plan**, specifies the contributions made by the employer, as well as the employee. Pension benefits paid are based upon the accumulated contributions and investment returns achieved.[46] These plans free employers from the risks that investments will not perform as well as expected. They put the responsibility for wise investing squarely on the shoulders of each employee. A defined contribution plan is also easier to administer. Considering the advantages to employers, it is not surprising that a growing share of retirement plans in the private sector are defined contribution plans. Defined contribution plans also offer an advantage to employees in today's highly mobile workforce. They do not penalize employees for changing jobs. With these plans, retirement earnings are less related to the number of years an employee stays with any particular company.

defined contribution plan
A retirement plan that specifies the contributions made by the employer as well as the employee and pension benefits are based upon the accumulated contributions and investment returns achieved.

Family-Friendly Benefits and Services

HRC 1, 3, 6

As employers have recognized the importance of employees' need to balance their work and outside commitments including the care of family members, pursuit of education, personal development, and volunteer activities, many have implemented "family-friendly" HR practices. Options such as flextime and telework were discussed in Chapter 1. In addition, some organizations provide benefits and services including child and/or elder care, parental leave top-up, and adoption assistance. For example, the Ontario Public Service (www.ontario.ca) supports employees who are new mothers with maternity leave top-up payments (up to 93 percent of salary for 32 weeks) as well as parental top-up for new fathers and adoptive parents (up to 93 percent of salary for 17 weeks). Georgian College (www.georgiancollege.ca) also offers maternity and parental top-ups as well as a variety of alternative working options from telecommuting to reduced hours in the summer.[47]

Companies including Netflix and Virgin America have implemented "unlimited vacation" policies described as "Take what you want, take what you need." What type of organizational culture and employees are likely to be the best fit to adopt this approach? Do you think this will be a successful "HR experiment" for these organizations?"

According to Statistics Canada, approximately 2.7 million Canadians provide unpaid care to people 65 years and older. Many of these people have been referred to as the *sandwich generation*—with dual responsibility of raising children and providing care for aging parents or relatives. Due to the aging of the baby boomers this segment is expected to grow, resulting in increased stress and demands on employees.[48] Some employers have responded by providing benefits and services including access to counselling, flexible schedules, referral services, and access to information and other resources available in the community or region.

The value of these family-friendly benefits accrue to not only employees but to employers as well in the form of increased productivity, enhanced commitment, and reduced stress.[49]

Other Benefits

The scope of possible employee benefits is limited only by the imagination of the organization's decision makers. Organizations have developed a wide variety of benefits to meet the needs of employees and to attract and keep the kinds of workers who will be of value to the organization. Traditional extras include subsidized cafeterias, onsite health care for minor injuries or illnesses, and moving expenses for newly hired or relocating employees. Stores and manufacturers may offer employee discounts on their products. See the "HR Oops!" box.

To encourage learning and attract the kinds of employees who wish to develop their knowledge and skills, many organizations offer *tuition reimbursement* programs. A typical program covers tuition and related expenses for courses that are relevant to the employee's current job or future career at the organization. Employees are reimbursed for these expenses after they demonstrate they have completed an approved course. Tuition reimbursement is an important perk at many organizations on top employer lists.

Especially for demanding, high-stress jobs, organizations may look for benefits that help employees put in the necessary long hours and alleviate stress. Recreational activities such as onsite

HR Oops!

Underestimating the Importance of Employee Discounts

Part of knowing what employees value is knowing what they don't want to lose. Brian Dunn learned that the hard way as an executive of Best Buy.

Dunn hoped to improve profitability by cutting costs, and he thought employees would accept a smaller employee discount. To be certain, the company monitored comments on its employee social-networking site, the Watercooler. The results were soon in: employees flooded the site with 54 pages of comments, most of them furious.

Just five days later, Dunn reviewed the reaction with senior management. The decision was easy: Best Buy backed down and restored the employee discount to its original level.

Questions

1. Are you surprised that employee discounts are a highly valued benefit at Best Buy? Why or why not? What kinds of employees would this benefit attract?

2. Suggest a way that Best Buy could have reduced the costs of benefits without sparking employee anger.

Source: Based on Matthew Boyle, "Look Before You Chop Employee Perks," *BusinessWeek*, February 20, 2009, www.businessweek.com.

basketball courts or company-sponsored softball teams provide for social interaction as well as physical activity.

Selecting Employee Benefits

Although the government requires certain benefits, employers have wide latitude in creating the total benefits package they offer employees.[50] Decisions about which benefits to include should take into account the organization's goals, its budget, and the expectations of the organization's current employees and those it wishes to recruit in the future. Employees have come to expect certain things from employers. An organization that does not offer the expected benefits will have more difficulty attracting and keeping talented workers. Also, if employees believe their employer feels no commitment to their welfare, they are less likely to feel committed to their employer.

An Organization's Objectives

A logical place to begin selecting employee benefits is to establish objectives for the benefits package. This helps an organization select the most effective benefits and monitor whether the benefits are doing what they should. Unfortunately, research suggests that most organizations do not have written objectives for benefits.

Among companies that do set goals, the most common objectives include controlling the cost of health care benefits and retaining employees.[51] The first goal explains the growing use of wellness programs and employee-directed health plans. For the second goal, employers need to learn what employees care about. In some cases, the approach may be indirect, helping the company distinguish itself as an employer that certain kinds of employees will be attracted and committed to. For example, a company that establishes itself as committed to the environment could offer benefits in line with that goal—say bicycle storage for commuters and vouchers for taking the bus to work.[52] Employees with a passion for the environment would be especially engaged by such offerings.

Hill + Knowlton Strategies (www.hkstrategies.ca) has received recognition as a great place to work and for its travelling refreshment cart to celebrate the end of the week.

Employees' Expectations and Values

Employees expect to receive benefits that are legally required and widely available, and they value benefits they are likely to use. For example, the "HR Oops!" box illustrates the value employees place on product discounts. To meet employee expectations about benefits, it can be helpful to see what other organizations offer. Employers should also consider that the value employees place on various benefits is likely to differ from one employee to another. As outlined earlier in the chapter, a basic demographic factor such as age can influence the kinds of benefits employees want. However, these were only general observations; organizations should check which considerations apply to their own employees and identify more specific needs and differences.

The choice of benefits may influence current employees' satisfaction and may also affect the organization's recruiting, in terms of both the ease of recruiting and the kinds of employees attracted to the organization.

Flexible Benefits

Organizations can address differences in employees' needs and engage their employees by offering **flexible benefits plans** in place of a single benefits package for all employees. These plans, often called flexible benefits or *flex benefits*, offer employees a set of alternatives from which they can choose the types and amounts of benefits they want. The plans vary. Some impose minimum levels for certain benefits, such as health care coverage; some allow employees to receive money in exchange for choosing a "light" package; and some let employees pay extra for the privilege of receiving more benefits. For example, some plans let employees give up vacation days for more pay or to purchase extra vacation days in exchange for a reduction in pay.

> **flexible benefits plans**
> Benefits plans that offer employees a set of alternatives from which they can choose the types and amounts of benefits they want.

Flexible benefits plans have a number of advantages.[53] The selection process can make employees more aware of the value of the benefits, particularly when the plan assigns each employee a sum of money to allocate to benefits. Also, the individual choice in a flexible benefits plan enables each employee to match his or her needs to the company's benefits, increasing the plan's actual value to the employee. Superior Propane (www.superiorpropane.com), a Calgary-based Canadian marketer of propane and appliances, switched to a flex benefits plan for its 1,800 employees. Terry Gill, vice-president of human resources, says that Superior Propane changed to flex benefits to "attract a more diverse group of employees to fit in with our new performance-based culture. We realized that most employees wanted opportunity and choice—a 'one-size-fits-all' plan wouldn't work."[54]

A drawback of flexible benefits plans is that they have a higher administrative cost, especially in the design and startup stages. Organizations can avoid some of the higher cost, however, by using software packages and standardized plans that have been developed for employers wishing to offer flexible benefits. Another possible drawback is that employee selection of benefits will increase rather than decrease costs, because employees will select the kinds of benefits they expect to need the most. For example, an employee expecting to need a lot of dental work is more likely to sign up for a dental plan. The heavy use of the dental coverage would then drive up the employer's premiums for that coverage. Costs can also be difficult to estimate when employees select their benefits. Organizations frequently respond by requiring employees to share in the costs of benefits.

L○7 Discuss the importance of effectively communicating the organization's approach to total rewards.

Communicating Total Rewards to Employees

"Communication is often a weak link. An average program well-communicated will do better than an outstanding program poorly communicated."[55] A comprehensive communications strategy is required to help employees understand the total value the organization is investing in its approach to compensating and rewarding employees. This is essential so that total rewards can achieve their objectives including focusing employees on organizational goals, attracting and retaining employees, and creating a motivating environment.

Because they interact with their employees each day, managers play a significant role in communication. The HR department should prepare them to explain to their employees why the organization's approach to compensating and rewarding employees is designed as it is, and to determine whether employee concerns indicate a need for change. Employees are interested in their compensation and rewards and they need a great deal of detailed information. It follows that technology and supporting databases can play a significant role. More employers are using technology to provide employees with tools and information related to both communication and administration of employee compensation and rewards.

Employees and job applicants often lack a clear sense of the market value of total rewards that an organization offers. For example, research asking employees about their benefits has shown that employees significantly underestimate the cost and value of their benefits.[56] Probably a major reason for their lack of knowledge is a lack of communication from employers. When New Brunswick Power (www.nbpower.com) teamed up with its union to communicate the benefits of the move to a flexible benefits plan, the objective was to "get the message out to workers that this was their plan, they owned it, and they needed to get an understanding of how it worked." The company provided training sessions, and provided every employee with items to take home to discuss with their families.[57]

Employers have many options for communicating information about benefits. Research from Sun-Life (www.sunlife.ca) showed that different generational groups have different preferences for receiving information from their employers about rewards—baby-boomers are most likely to prefer paper-based communications, Gen-X appreciates online communication, and Gen-Y prefers online communication to anything else.[58] To increase the likelihood that employees will receive and understand the messages, employers can combine several media, such as videos, brochures, question-and-answer meetings, online total rewards statements, intranet pages, memos, presentations, and email.

Communication efforts are also moving beyond ensuring employees receive and understand the messages to "driving action, enabling employees to make the best possible use of the programs available to them," according to Diane McElroy, a senior vice-president with Aon Hewitt in Toronto. McElroy adds that some employers are even developing total rewards statements for *prospective* employees as part of the job offer. "Some organizations are providing these statements when they make offers to job candidates. That way, if the potential new hire receives another offer—especially one with a higher base salary—he or she can make an informed comparison and determine whether a bigger paycheque really does mean great compensation. This can be a smart approach in a tight labour market."[59] In summary, an investment of creativity in employee communication can reap great returns in the form of committed, satisfied employees, and the achievement of organizational objectives including employee attraction and retention.

L○8 Discuss issues related to compensating and rewarding executives.

Executive Compensation and Rewards

HRC 1, 6, 9

The media have drawn public attention to the issue of executive compensation and rewards. The issue attracts notice because of the very high pay that the top executives of major North American companies have received in recent years. A significant part of executive compensation comes in the form of performance-based pay such as bonuses and stock. For example, in 2013, Gerald Schwartz, CEO of Onex Corporation (www.onex.com; #1 on the Top Paid CEO Listing) received a base salary of $1,339,611, a bonus of $25,178,068, and stock options of $61,399,347 for total compensation of $87,917,026. In 2013, RBC's CEO, Gordon Nixon (#6 on the Top Paid CEO Listing) received a base salary of $1,500,000, bonus of $2,932,000, $6,600,000 in company shares, $1,6500,000 in stock options, pension value increase of $1,312,000, and other benefits of $44,877 for a total of $14,038,877.[60]

Although high amounts like this apply to only a small proportion of the total workforce, the issue of executive pay is relevant to pay structure in terms of equity theory. As we discussed earlier in the chapter, employees draw conclusions about the fairness of pay by making comparisons among employees' inputs and outcomes. By many comparisons, CEO pay is high. In 2013, Canada's 100 highest paid CEOs of companies listed on the TSX Index received $9.2 million on average, an increase of 25 percent since 2008.[61] The Conference Board Task Force on Executive Compensation and Pay Governance endorses ensuring strong links between an organization's financial performance and executive compensation, referred to as *value leverage* i.e., "pay percentile equals performance percentile"—a percentage change in executive compensation should directly relate to a percentage change in their organization's performance.[62] To help make sense of all the numbers, the Financial Post publishes its CEO Scorecard, which provides *Bang for Buck* ratings for Canadian executives. For example, an executive scoring "around $1 is getting what they should be getting, according to a proprietary algorithm which takes into account a CEO's comparative compensation and company revenue as well as their performance" in their industry-related TSX index. The CEO Scorecard provides a helpful snapshot to see what companies likely overspent on executive compensation and what companies are likely getting a bargain.[63]

Overall, executive compensation and rewards are complicated due to the number of items included, for example, base salary, bonuses, stock ownership, stock options, and benefits. Top executives help to set the tone or culture of the organization, and employees at all levels are affected by behaviour at the top. As a result, the equity of executive compensation and rewards can affect more employees than, say, the compensation and rewards received by warehouse workers or clerical staff. Another way to think about the equity of CEO pay is to compare it with the pay of other employees in the organization. Again, equity theory would consider not only the size of the executive pay relative to pay for other employees but also the amount the CEOs contribute. In 2013, Canada's 100 highest paid CEOs received 195 times the average Canadian worker's wage, up from 105 times the average Canadian worker's wage in 1998. In 2013, Canadian workers earned an average wage of $47,358.[64] "By 11:41 a.m. on January 2, 2013, the second paid day and first working day of the year, the average top CEO had earned as much as the average Canadian worker would make all year.[65]

Executive Incentives and Benefits

Because executives have a much stronger influence over the organization's performance than other employees do, incentive pay for executives warrants special attention. Assuming that incentives influence performance, decisions about incentives for executives should have a great impact on how well the executives and the organization perform. Along with overall pay levels for executives, organizations need to create incentive plans for this small but important group of employees.

To encourage executives to develop a commitment to the organization's long-term success, executive compensation often combines short-term and long-term incentives. *Short-term incentives* include bonuses based on the year's profits, return on investment, or other measures related to the organization's goals. Sometimes, to gain tax advantages, the actual payment of the bonus is deferred (e.g., by making it part of a retirement plan). *Long-term incentives* include stock options and stock purchase plans. The rationale for these long-term incentives is that executives will want to do what is best for the organization because that will cause the value of their stock to grow. A corporation's shareholders—its owners—want the corporation to encourage managers to act in the owners' best interests. They want managers to care about the company's profits and stock price, and incentive pay can encourage this interest. One study has found that relying on such long-term incentives is associated with greater profitability.[66]

As well as legally required benefits and the benefits extended to other employees in the organization, executives often receive extra benefits and services. These executive benefits and services may include such far-reaching benefits as use of corporate aircraft, company-provided or subsidized homes, memberships and tickets to sporting and cultural events, in addition to benefits such as company cars, sabbaticals, and extended vacations.

Performance Measures for Executives

The balanced scorecard approach discussed in Chapter 7 is useful in designing executive pay. Whirlpool, for example, has used a balanced scorecard that combines measures of whether the organization is delivering value to shareholders, customers, and employees. These measures are listed in Table 8.4. Rewarding achievement of a variety of goals in a balanced scorecard reduces the temptation to win bonuses by manipulating financial data.

TABLE 8.4

Balanced Scorecard for Whirlpool (www.whirlpool.com) Executives

Type of Measures	Value Creation
Shareholder value	Economic value added Earnings per share Cash flow Total cost productivity
Customer value	Quality Market share Customer satisfaction
Employee value	High-performance culture index High-performance culture deployment Training and development diversity

Source: E. L. Gubman, *The Talent Solution* (New York: McGraw-Hill, 1998).

Thinking ETHICALLY

The Ethics of Sick Leave

Ethical issues arise with paid time off for illness, from both the employer's and employee's perspectives. On the employer's side, decisions about sick leave are generally influenced by costs. The employer is paying the employee while the employee is not working. In a large corporation, it may be relatively simple for the many well employees to keep projects moving ahead while some employees are ill. But in a small organization, the absence of a few employees—or even just one or two—can create significant backlogs, especially if some of those employees have no colleagues qualified to do their work. In a controversial effort to reduce absenteeism, the Toronto Transit Commission (TTC, www.ttc.com) negotiated a policy with workers that requires a doctor's note after just one sick day and the note must be submitted within 72 hours of the absence.

From the employees' perspective, ethical questions involve their impact on others at work and their needs for time to take care of themselves and their dependants. Going to work when sick takes a personal toll and can spread the illness to one's co-workers and customers. Staying home can leave co-workers without support they need to carry out their work. In cases where the company does not pay for sick time, staying home to rest also may create a financial hardship. Low-wage workers are the least likely to have jobs that pay for sick leave.

These decisions are complicated for employees who have dependants. Typically, sick leave is meant for a worker's own illness, but as a practical matter, parents with sick children use this time when a child is ill. This may be seen as an abuse of the policy—or as the employee's only recourse for fulfilling personal duties when a policy does not recognize the realities of family life. But even employees without dependants feel tempted sometimes to take a "mental health" day when they are not actually sick but are mentally or physically worn out.

Questions

1. For an employee, what is the ethical choice to make about going to work when he or she is ill? How does your answer depend on whether the employee is paid for the time off? How does your answer change, if at all, when the sick person is the employee's young child?

2. For an employer, does ethical conduct require providing employees with paid time off for illness? Why or why not?

Sources: Sarah Dobson, "Doctors Call in Sick on Notes," *Canadian HR Reporter*, February 24, 2014, pp. 1, 10; Sarah E. Needleman, "Sick-Time Rules Re-emerge," *The Wall Street Journal*, February 29, 2012, http://online.wsj.com; and Madeleine Gecht, "Should Every Worker Have Paid Sick Leave? The Ethics of Employee Benefits and Rights," *Ethical Inquiry* (International Center for Ethics, Justice, and Public Life, Brandeis University), August 2011, www/brandeis.edu.

Ethical Issues

HRC 1, 2, 6

Incentive pay for executives lays the groundwork for significant ethical issues. When an organization links pay to its stock performance, executives need the ethical backbone to be honest about their company's performance even when dishonesty or clever shading of the truth offers the tempting potential for large earnings. As scandals involving WorldCom, Enron, Nortel Networks, and other companies have shown, the results can be disastrous when unethical behaviour is implicated.

Among these issues is one we have already touched on in this chapter: the difficulty of setting performance measures that encourage precisely the behaviour desired. In the case of incentives tied to stock performance, executives may be tempted to inflate the stock price in order to enjoy bonuses and valuable stock options. The intent is for the executive to boost stock value through efficient operations, technological innovation, effective leadership, and so on. Unfortunately, individuals at some companies determined that they could obtain faster results through accounting practices that stretched the norms in order to present the company's performance in the best light. When such practices are discovered to be misleading, stock prices plunge and the company's reputation is damaged, sometimes beyond repair.

A related issue when executive pay includes stock or stock options is insider trading. When executives are stockholders, they have a dual role as owners and managers. This places them at an advantage over others who want to invest in the company. An individual, a pension fund, or other investors have less information about the company than its managers do—for example, whether product development is proceeding on schedule, whether a financing deal is in the works, and so on. An executive who knows about these activities could therefore reap a windfall in the stock market by buying or selling stock based on his or her knowledge about the company's future. Although regulators place strict limits on this "insider trading," some executives have violated these limits. In the worst cases, executives have sold stock, secretly knowing their company was failing, before the stock price collapsed. The losers are the employees, retirees, and other investors who hold the now-worthless stock.

As news stories have reminded us, linking pay to stock price can reward unethical behaviour, at least in the short term and at least in the minds of a handful of executives. Yet, given the motivational power of incentive pay, organizations cannot afford to abandon incentives for their executives. These temptations are among the reasons that executive positions demand individuals who maintain the highest ethical standards.

SUMMARY

L○1 Discuss how organizations implement a "total rewards" approach to compensating and rewarding employees.

Many organizations are recognizing the strategic value of taking a comprehensive approach to compensating and rewarding employees. This "total rewards" approach frequently involves creating a value proposition for current and prospective employees that clearly identifies all of the aspects that are valued by employees in exchange for their time and expertise. Canadian companies take a total rewards approach to attract and retain valued employees and improve capacity to meet organizational goals.

L○2 Identify the kinds of decisions and influences involved in providing base pay to employees.

Organizations make decisions to define a job structure, or relative pay for different jobs within the organization. They establish relative pay for different functions and different levels of responsibility for each function. Organizations must also establish pay levels, or the average paid for the different jobs. These decisions are based on the organization's goals, market data, legal requirements, and principles of fairness. Together job structure and pay level establish a pay structure policy. Organizations typically begin with a job evaluation to measure the relative worth of their jobs. The organization then creates a pay structure that includes pay grades or pay ranges for each job in the organization.

L○3 Describe alternatives to job-based pay.

To obtain more flexibility, organizations may reduce the levels in the organization's job structure. This process of delayering or broadbanding involves creating broad bands of jobs within pay ranges. Other organizations reward employees according to their competencies. They establish competency-based pay systems, or structures that set pay according to the employees' level of knowledge and what they are capable of doing.

L○4 Describe how organizations recognize individual, team, and organizational performance through the use of incentives.

Organizations may recognize individual performance through such incentives as piece-work rates, standard hours plans, merit pay, sales commissions, and bonuses for meeting individual performance objectives. Common team incentives include gainsharing, bonuses, and team awards. Incentives for meeting organizational objectives include profit sharing and stock ownership.

L○5 Discuss the role of benefits as part of employee total rewards.

Like pay, benefits and services help employers attract, retain, and provide a source of motivation for employees. Employees expect at least a minimum level of benefits, and providing more than the minimum helps an organization compete in the labour market. Benefits and services are also a significant expense, but employers provide benefits and services because employees value them and many are required by law.

L○6 Summarize the types of employee benefits offered by employers.

Employers must contribute to the Canada Pension Plan/Quebec Pension Plan, Employment Insurance, and Workers' Compensation. In addition, employers offer various kinds of insurance, retirement plans, and paid leave. Due to the increasing costs of providing employee benefits, many Canadian organizations are seeking ways to hold back the costs. Many employers have responded to work/life role conflicts by offering family-friendly benefits. Organizations need to establish objectives and select benefits that support those objectives. Flexible benefits are a means to give employees control over the benefits they receive.

L○7 Discuss the importance of effectively communicating the organization's approach to total rewards.

A comprehensive communications strategy is needed to help employees understand and value all the components in an organization's approach to total rewards. Managers and the human resource department share responsibility for this important requirement. Technology can provide employees access to information and other tools associated with administration of compensation and rewards. Employers have many options for communicating information about total rewards. Using a combination of media increases employees' understanding.

L○8 Discuss issues related to compensating and rewarding executives.

Executive compensation has drawn public scrutiny because top executive compensation is much higher than the average worker's pay. Chief executive officers have an extremely large impact on the organization's performance, but critics complain that when performance falters, executive pay does not decline as fast as the organization's profits or stock price. Performance measures should encourage behaviour that is in the organization's best interests, including ethical behaviour.

Critical Thinking Questions

1. Some individuals evaluate prospective employers' job offers based only on direct pay considerations. What additional factors should be considered when evaluating job offers from employers?

2. Why might an organization choose to pay employees more than the market rate? Why might it choose to pay less? What are the consequences of paying more or less than the market rate?

3. What are the advantages of establishing pay ranges, rather than specific pay levels, for each job? What are the drawbacks of this approach?

4. Suppose a small startup business wants to establish a competency-based pay structure. What would be some advantages of this approach? List the issues the company should be prepared to address in setting up this system. Consider the kinds of information you will need and the ways employees may react to the new pay structure.

5. With some organizations and jobs, pay is primarily wages or salaries, and with others, incentive pay is more important. For each of the following jobs, state whether you think the pay should emphasize base pay (wages and salaries) or incentive pay (bonuses, profit sharing, and so on). Give a reason for each.

    a. An accountant at a manufacturing company

    b. A salesperson for a software company

    c. A mechanic for a major airline

    d. A marketing manager for a telecommunications company

    e. A recruitment specialist for the federal government

6. Why do some organizations link incentive pay to the organization's overall performance? Is it appropriate to use stock performance as an incentive for employees at all levels? Why or why not?

7. Why do employers provide employee benefits, rather than providing all compensation in the form of pay and letting employees buy the benefits and services they want?

8. Of the benefits discussed in this chapter, list the ones you consider essential—those benefits you would require in any job offer. Why are these benefits important to you?

9. Why is it important to communicate information about total rewards? Suppose you work in the HR department of a company that has decided to add new elements to its total rewards—onsite massage plus an increased budget to support learning and development opportunities for all employees. How would you recommend communicating this change? What information should your messages include? How would you know if your communication strategy was successful?

10. Do you think executive total compensation is too high? Why or why not?

Experiencing HR

Divide into groups of four or five. (Or, if your instructor directs, students may complete the research independently and then discuss their results in class.) You have been asked by your manager to be part of a workplace task force that will examine millennial employees' needs, preferences, and expectations of benefits plans.

- Look up articles from the publication, *Benefits Canada*, from your college or university's e-library that specifically refer to millennial (Gen Y) employees.
- Review "reasons for selection" for organizations recognized as *Canada's Top Employers for Young People* (www.canadastop100.com/young_people).

Discuss the results you found and come up with advice for your organization, e.g., What benefits may be the most important to millennial employees? What communication strategies and channels should you use when communicating with millennial employees about their benefits? What types of administrative procedures and processes should the organization have in place, e.g., for submitting reimbursement claims?

Write a one-page report or make a brief class presentation summarizing your findings.

CASE STUDY 8.1:

How Fog Creek Software Pays Developers

When Joel Spolsky and Michael Pryor founded Fog Creek Software (www.fogcreek.com) their vision was of a company run by people whose technical backgrounds meant they understood what really motivates programmers. The company would hire the best, make them comfortable, pay them well, and then get out of the way so they could create great products.

Early on, Spolsky and Pryor set out to develop a pay structure that would be consistent with the company's mission. They decided that the system should be so objective that there would be no questioning or judgment calls about which employee earns how much. And the results would be so objective and fair that there would be no incentive to be secretive about what any employee earns.

Like any computer pro, Spolsky went online for ideas. He discovered that Construx (www.construx.com), a software consulting firm, had posted online an outline for measuring levels of the software profession. Using this as a starting point, Spolsky created a job structure for Fog Creek. The structure is straightforward: every employee is assigned to a level between 8 (summer interns) and 16 (chief executive officer). Assignment to a level is not a judgment call but is based on a formula incorporating the employee's experience, skills, and scope of responsibility.

- Experience is measured as the number of years of full-time experience in the field of the employee's job at Fog Creek, counting only years after the employee finished school. At any given level, every employee earns the same salary.
- Skills are defined with descriptive statements along a continuum. For example, at the lowest level is a programmer "learning the basic principles of software engineering" who needs close supervision. At the other extreme would be someone who makes a unique contribution—a programmer who "has consistently had major success during participation in all aspects of small and large projects."
- Scope of responsibility ranges from primarily supporting another employee to running multiple projects.

Based on this job structure, Spolsky created a chart that is used for assigning each employee to a level.

Spolsky also created a chart that indicates the base salary for each level, based on market salaries obtained from sources such as Salary.com and Glassdoor.com. Each employee earns the amount specified by the chart. Every year, the company's managers review each employee's work to see if the employee should be assigned to a new level. Every employee who is reassigned then earns the amount associated with the new level. Employees also earn a bonus based on the company's profits for the year.

Fog Creek's system has been challenged by the stiff competition for programmer talent. If the company paid extra to lure in new employees at a higher rate, the existing employees would demand a raise or see their treatment as unfair. Rather than expect employees to accept the "salary inversion" of newer employees earning more than their more-experienced colleagues, Fog Creek has responded to talent crunches by raising the salaries of all employees at a given level to make them as high as the going market rate for that level. Spolsky believes that the solution is expensive but essential for maintaining equity and keeping talent.

Questions

1. How well does Fog Creek Software's pay structure meet (a) legal requirements; (b) the conditions of product markets; and (c) the conditions of labour markets?

2. Joel Spolsky set out to create a pay structure that's objective. Based on the information given, how objective would you say Fog Creek's system is? What other qualities besides objectivity do you think Fog Creek employees might care about?

3. Fog Creek is a small company with a few dozen technical employees. How might its pay structure need to change (if at all), if the company grows to hundreds of employees? Would these changes likely appeal to the employees?

Sources: Joel Spolsky, "Why I Never Let Employees Negotiate a Raise," *Inc.,* April 2009, www.inc.com; and Fog Creek Software, "Careers," and "About the Company," corporate website, www.fogcreek.com, accessed April 21, 2010.

CASE STUDY 8.2:

Airbus Benefits Aim for Topflight Performance

"We aspire to be top in class for everything we do," Stephen Dumbleton told a reporter. The rewards manager at Airbus (www.airbus.com) UK was explaining the company's benefits package, and he was explaining how it is intended to support the company's strategy. Airbus is one of the world's largest aircraft makers, and making jetliners and military aircraft requires excellence in product design, manufacturing, sales, and service. To support efforts at recruiting and keeping employees who will deliver on the company's exacting standards, Airbus wants to provide benefits that make the company an attractive employer.

Adding a further layer of complexity to this challenge, Airbus has operations in several countries and customers around the world. Most workers are located at the headquarters in France and in the United Kingdom, Germany, and Spain, so benefits packages must meet European requirements for employers. And even just in the United Kingdom, Airbus UK's 10,000 employees represent

60 nationalities. The average age is 41, and most employees are men, although the company is striving to attract more female employees, especially in engineering.

Airbus UK compared its total compensation with that of other companies and determined that other employers offered better compensation packages for management-level employees. In contrast, for nonmanagement employees, Airbus was at an acceptable level. But addressing dissatisfaction with compensation packages in Britain by boosting pay was impractical, because pay would be compared across geographic regions, and the company would have to raise pay levels worldwide. Instead, Airbus addressed the weak management compensation package with a flexible approach to benefits.

To design a benefits package for this diverse workforce, Airbus conducted focus groups of high-performing managers in Britain. The groups generated a variety of ideas suggesting a desire for a flexible benefits package. The greatest desire was for private medical insurance (individuals in Britain can use the public health care system but also have the option to purchase coverage from private insurers). Working from a budget starting at 150 British pounds (about $285) per manager per month, the benefits team selected a menu of benefits that started with private medical insurance and added choices from a set of other benefits, which included the choice to opt out of the medical insurance. A company called Vebnet (www.vebnet.com) contracted with Airbus to set up an interactive Web portal where managers select the benefits they wish to receive within the budgeted amount for their position. The portal presents the choices in three categories: health, security, and lifestyle. Some of the choices are unusual, including a will-writing service and discounts on wine.

One advantage of offering this attractive benefits package to managers is that it creates an additional incentive for employees to develop their careers at Airbus and move into the management ranks. The company identifies high-potential employees and communicates with them to be sure they know a generous benefits package awaits them when they are promoted into their first management position. Dumbleton explains, "We try to make it clear that even though it may be a while before someone is promoted to the next grade, it will be worth the wait."

Still, some of Airbus's creative benefits are available to nonmanagement employees, too. In Britain, for example, one of the most popular benefits is participation in the bikes for work program, which helps people pay for bicycles they can ride to work. Employee participation has risen year after year as employees have signed up to cut their transportation costs, stay fit, and reduce their carbon footprint.

Airbus uses multiple channels to communicate about its benefits. Some messages go out through traditional media such as email and notices on bulletin boards. Television screens in the company play Airbus's corporate channel, including news and background information about various benefits. The company occasionally mails information about the flexible benefits scheme to employees at their homes—but not often, to avoid intrusiveness. The company also prepares total reward statements so that employees can readily review the value of their benefits package. Since it introduced My Flex to managers, company surveys indicate that their satisfaction with their total compensation has improved, and enrolment levels in the various options provide confirmation that the employees do indeed desire the choices made available to them. Dumbleton hopes that the success of this effort at the management level will lead to an expansion of similar benefits packages tailored to other levels of the organization.

Questions

1. How does the My Flex benefits package support Airbus's strategy?

2. Why do you think Airbus first offered flexible benefits just to managers in Britain? What would have been the pros and cons of launching it to all employees worldwide instead?

3. Airbus UK says it wants to attract more female employees, especially female engineers. How could it use its benefits package to help meet the goal of attracting and retaining female engineers?

Sources: Vebnet, "Vebnet Working in Partnership with Airbus Operations Ltd.," Research and Insight: Case Studies, January 2012, www.vebnet.com; Tynan Barton, "Reach for the Sky," *Employee Benefits,* February 2011, pp. 40–44; "Interview with Stephen Dumbleton, Reward Manager at Airbus Operations," *Employee Benefits,* November 1, 2010, www.emplyeebenefits.co.uk.

VIDEO CASE PART 4

Video Case: Changing Employee Benefits at Longo's (www.hrreporter.com/videodisplay/ 193-changing-employee-benefits-at-longos)

Liz Volk, vice-president of Human Resources at food retailer Longo's, discusses how changes were made to their employee benefits plan and how they communicated with employees. The organization had doubled its size in the previous 3½ years and it was recognized that the traditional benefits plan in place for the previous 25 years needed to change to be sustainable as well as relevant for employees. With different stages of generations and needs within the business it was viewed to be critical to provide a total rewards approach.

Challenges encountered included the diverse employee population; working different hours; being able to bring all team members together; and dealing with language issues. It was also recognized that employees had limited knowledge of their current benefits. During the design stage, HR went out and did "sneak peeks" with employees at the stores. Explanation of current benefits was provided and employees were able to provide input that led to subsequent plan design changes.

Face-to-face enrolment sessions were conducted a few months later. The new employee benefits program was branded, "Fresh Journey to a Whole New You." To help ensure employees know what they have, a variety of communication methods are being used—communication boards on total rewards, newsletters, huddles for messages around wellness, and "lunch and learns" with benefits vendors.

Questions

1. How is Longo's redesigned approach to employee benefits rewarding to employees? To the organization overall?

2. Compare and contrast Longo's approach to communication with recommendations provided in Chapter 8 for communicating total rewards to employees. Is there anything else that Longo's should do to ensure that employees receive and fully understand their benefits?

Source: Based on "Changing Employee Benefits at Longo's," *Canadian HR Reporter TV,* October 25, 2011. Reprinted by permission of Canadian HR Reporter. © Copyright Thomson Reuters Canada Ltd., October 25, 2011, Toronto, Ontario 1-800-387-5164. Web: www.hrreporter.com

PART 5

Meeting
Other HR Goals

CHAPTER 9

Collective Bargaining and Labour Relations

WHAT DO I NEED TO KNOW?

After reading this chapter, you should be able to:

LO1   Define unions and labour relations and their role in organizations.

LO2   Identify the labour relations goals of management, labour unions, and society.

LO3   Summarize laws and regulations that affect labour relations.

LO4   Describe the union organizing process.

LO5   Explain how management and unions negotiate collective agreements.

LO6   Summarize the practice of collective agreement administration.

LO7   Describe more cooperative approaches to labour-management relations.

Air Canada and its pilots' union have a collective labour agreement that may signal ten years of labour peace.

Labour Peace for Air Canada?

Air Canada (www.aircanada.com) and its pilots have agreed to a long-term collective agreement that extends to September 2024. The ten year agreement was reached a year and a half before the previous contract expired and was Air Canada's first deal with pilots since 1996 negotiated without arbitration or a strike. Air Canada calls the agreement a "landmark deal that is tangible evidence of a culture shift" and "provides stability to support growth." Air Canada pilots get a $10,000 signing bonus, more than a 20 percent wage increase over the duration of the agreement, two percent cash bonuses in 2016 and 2017, as well as an enhanced profit-sharing formula—similar to upper management's. Although the agreement provides for negotiation of specific items every three years, pilots have agreed to give up the right to strike and send disagreements to mediation or arbitration as long as the airline achieves its growth targets. Union president Craig Blandford describes the deal as "an investment in the airline's future." "We've just come up with this deal without any outside pressure or help so we're hoping we can carry that through in the next 10 years—that kind of relationship of mutual respect for each other when we sit down and talk." Jazz Aviation and its pilots have also agreed to a new contract and extended its agreement with Air Canada to the end of 2025. Can Air Canada be as successful in its negotiations with the unions that represent mechanics, flight attendants, call centre, and airport workers?[1]

Introduction

The presence of unions in a government agency or business changes some aspects of human resource management by directing more attention to the interests of employees as a group. In general, employees and employers share the same interests. They both benefit when the organization is strong and growing, providing employees with jobs and employers with profits. But although the interests of employers and employees overlap, they obviously are not identical. In the case of pay, workers benefit from higher pay, but high pay cuts into the organization's profits, unless pay increases are associated with higher productivity or better customer service. Workers may negotiate differences with their employers individually, or they may form unions to negotiate on their behalf. This chapter explores human resource activities in organizations where employees belong to unions or where employees are seeking to organize unions or engage in collective bargaining.

We begin by formally defining unions and labour relations, then describe the history, scope, and impact of union activity. We next summarize government laws and regulations affecting unions and labour relations. The following three sections detail types of activities involving unions: union organizing, collective agreement negotiation, and collective agreement administration. Finally, we identify ways in which unions and management are working together in arrangements that are more cooperative than the traditional labour–management relationship.

LO1 Define unions and labour relations and their role in organizations.

Role of Unions and Labour Relations

HRC 1,2,5

In Canada today, most workers act as individuals to select jobs that are acceptable to them and to negotiate pay, benefits, flexible hours, and other work conditions. Especially when there is competition for labour and employees have hard-to-find skills, this arrangement produces satisfactory results for most employees. At times, however, workers have believed their needs and interests do not receive enough consideration from management. One response by workers is to act collectively by forming and joining labour **unions**, organizations formed for the purpose of representing their members' interests and resolving conflicts with employers.

Unions have a role because some degree of conflict is inevitable between workers and management.[2] For example, managers can increase profits by lowering workers' pay, but workers benefit in the short term if lower profits result because their pay is higher. Still, this type of conflict is more complex than a simple tradeoff, such as wages versus profits. Rising profits can help employees by driving up profit sharing or other benefits, and falling profits can result in layoffs and a lack of investment. Although employers can use programs like profit sharing to help align employee interests with their own, some remaining divergence of interests is inevitable. Labour unions represent worker interests and the collective bargaining process provides a way to manage the conflict. In other words, through systems for hearing complaints and negotiating agreements, unions and managers resolve conflicts between employers and employees.

unions
Organizations formed for the purpose of representing their members' interests in dealing with employers.

As unionization of workers became more common, universities and colleges developed training in how to manage union–management interactions. This specialty, called **labour relations**, emphasizes skills that managers and union leaders can use to foster effective labour–management cooperation, minimize costly forms of conflict (such as strikes), and seek win-win solutions to disagreements. Labour relations involve three levels of decisions:[3]

labour relations
A field that emphasizes skills managers and union leaders can use to minimize costly forms of conflict (such as strikes) and seek win-win solutions to disagreements.

1. *Labour relations strategy.* For management, the decision involves how the organization will work with unions or develop (or maintain) nonunion operations. This decision is influenced by outside forces such as public opinion and competition. For unions, the decision involves whether to resist changes in how unions relate to the organization or accept new kinds of labour–management relationships.

2. *Negotiating contracts.* As we will describe later in the chapter, collective agreement negotiations in a union setting involve decisions about pay structure, job security, work rules, workplace safety, and many other issues. These decisions affect workers' and the employer's situation for the term of the contract.

3. *Administering collective agreements.* These decisions involve day-to-day activities in which union members and the organization's managers may have disagreements. Issues include complaints of work rules being violated or workers being treated unfairly in particular situations. A formal grievance procedure is typically used to resolve these issues.

Later sections in this chapter describe how managers and unions carry out the activities connected with these levels of decisions, as well as the goals and legal constraints affecting these activities.

Types of Unions and Affiliations

Most union members belong to a national or international union. Figure 9.1 shows the number of workers covered by Canada's ten largest unions.

Traditionally, unions were characterized by being either *craft* or *industrial* unions. Members of a craft union all had a particular skill or occupation, e.g., International Brotherhood of Electrical Workers representing electricians (IBEW, www.ibew.org); whereas industrial unions consisted of members who are linked by their work in a particular industry, e.g., the former Canadian Auto Workers. These distinctions between types of unions are less clear today. For example, some "locals" of the IBEW now represent a variety of types of employees in the electrical industry and UNIFOR (www.unifor.org), Canada's largest private sector union (created in 2013 with the merger of the Canadian Auto Workers and the Communications, Energy, and Paperworkers Union of Canada) has members who work in every major sector of the Canadian economy.[4] In addition, *public sector unions* represent employees who work in the public sector. For example, the Public Service Alliance of Canada (PSAC, http://psacunion.ca) represents more than 170,000 members from every province and territory in Canada who work diverse roles in federal government departments, airports, universities, First Nations communities, and the security industry, among others.[5]

Unions affiliate with labour congresses for assistance at national and international levels. Among the labour congresses in Canada, the **Canadian Labour Congress (CLC)** (www.canadianlabour.ca) has the largest coverage affiliation. The CLC is the umbrella organization for dozens of affiliated Canadian and international unions, as well as provincial federations of labour and regional labour councils. In 2013, the CLC covered more than 3 million workers—69.2 percent of workers covered by collective agreements.[6] An important responsibility of the CLC is to represent labour's interests in issues such as wages and benefits, ensuring safe and healthy workplaces, environmental sustainability, and respect for human rights in Canada and throughout the world.[7] The organization also provides information, support, and analysis that member unions can use in their activities.

Canadian Labour Congress (CLC)
The umbrella organization for dozens of affiliated Canadian and international unions, as well as provincial federations of labour and regional labour councils.

Hassan Yussuff, president of the Canadian Labour Congress (CLC).

FIGURE 9.1

Canada's Top-Ten Labour Organizations (2013)

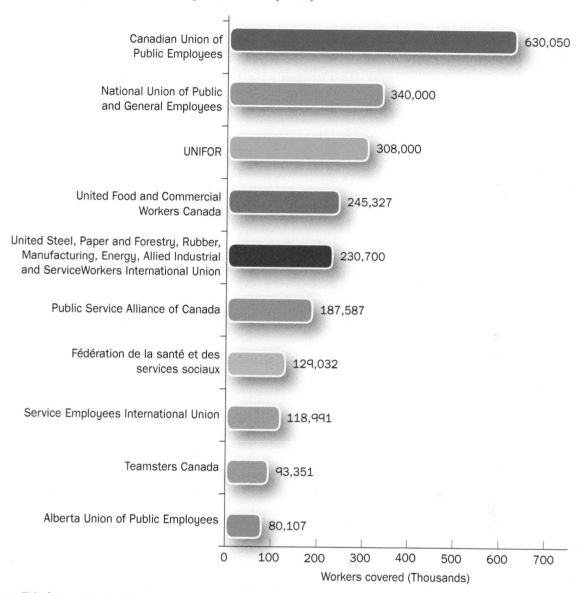

Source: "Union Coverage in Canada, 2013, Appendix 2—Labour Organizations with 30,000 or More Covered Workers, 2013," June 11, 2014, *Government of Canada,* www.labour.gc.ca/eng/resources/info/publications/union_coverage/union_coverage.shtml, retrieved April 8, 2015.

Local Unions

Most national unions consist of multiple local units. Even when a national union plays the most critical role in negotiating the terms of a collective bargaining agreement, negotiation occurs at the local level for work rules and other issues that are locally determined. In addition, administration of the agreement largely takes place at the local union level. As a result, most day-to-day interaction between labour and management involves the local union.

Typically, the local union elects officers, such as president, vice-president, and treasurer. The officers may be responsible for contract negotiation, or the local may form a bargaining committee for that purpose. When the union is engaged in bargaining, the national union provides help, including background data about other settlements, technical advice, and the leadership of a representative from the national office.

Individual members participate in local unions in various ways. At meetings of the local union, they elect officials and vote on resolutions. Most of workers' contact is with the **union steward**, an employee elected by union members to represent them in ensuring that the terms of the agreement are enforced. The union steward helps to investigate complaints and represents employees to supervisors and other managers when employees file grievances alleging contract violations.[8] Because of union stewards' close involvement with employees, it is to management's advantage to cultivate positive working relationships with them.

union steward
An employee elected by union members to represent them in ensuring that the terms of the collective agreement are enforced.

History and Trends in Union Membership

Labour unions have existed in Canada as early as 1812. Unionism in Canada had early ties to Britain, as tradesmen active in the British trade union movement immigrated to Canada and settled in Atlantic Canada. The first national labour organization, a forerunner of the Canadian Labour Congress, was formed in 1873. During the early 1900s labour activities escalated as workers demanded better wages, shorter workdays, and improved working conditions. Strikes involving large numbers of workers were frequent, with the Winnipeg General Strike in 1919 being perhaps the most well-known. As labour politics developed, unionization was supported by the Co-operative Commonwealth Federation (CCF), which later became the New Democratic Party (NDP). Collective bargaining was first recognized in 1937. Post–World War II, U.S. unions began to spread into Canada and influenced Canada's labour legislation. In 1967, the federal government passed legislation that extended collective bargaining rights to government workers and today, the majority of government workers have the right to unionize.[9] Exceptions included the military and the Royal Canadian Mounted Police (RCMP, www.rcmp-grc.gc.ca), however as discussed in the nearby "HR Oops!," the Supreme Court of Canada recently made a game-changing ruling that impacts the RCMP.[10]

Unionization levels continued to grow in both the private and public sectors until the mid-1990s despite pressures on unions that labour costs had not kept pace with productivity.[11] Union membership in Canada peaked in 1994, reaching 36.1 percent of employees.[12] In 2013, labour organizations reported that 4,735,367 workers in Canada were covered by collective agreements.[13] The overall unionization rate or *union density* has remained stable over the past six years.[14]

In Canada, unionization is much higher in the public sector than the private sector—71.4 percent for the public sector, in contrast to 16.4 percent for the private sector.[15] As illustrated in Figure 9.2, union membership is concentrated in public administration; utilities, education; health care and social services. Among the least unionized sectors are agriculture, entertainment and hospitality, finance and professional services, as well as wholesale and retail trade.

Figure 9.3 illustrates the significant variation in rates of union membership among the provinces. Newfoundland and Labrador (39.8 percent) and Quebec (39.5 percent) have the highest rates of unionization. Alberta (22.8 percent) and Ontario (28.0 percent) have the lowest rates of union density. Unionization also varies by firm size. Unionization is most common in large organizations.

HR Oops!

RCMP Forbidden No Longer

Although more than 250 police forces in Canada are unionized, the Royal Canadian Mounted Police's employer, the Canadian Government, has had a "century-long preoccupation" to keep Mounties out of unions. Until 1974, "Mounties were subject to immediate dismissal if they tried to join together to raise workplace issues." More recently, RCMP members were allowed to form voluntary associations funded by members to work with management to establish pay and benefits—however, top leadership ultimately controlled the final result. The grievance process, was described as "just a big round circle" by Rip Mills, a retired Mountie and spokesperson for the Mounted Police Association of Ontario. "Right now, there are thousands of grievances in the RCMP that go nowhere." But the federal government was recently given notice that it has a year to come up with a new system for RCMP bargaining, when the Supreme Court ruled on a case launched back in 2006. Canada's top court ruled that RCMP members have the right to engage in meaningful collective bargaining with its management, however, it did not go so far as to explicitly state they have a right to form a union.

Questions

1. Do you think the RCMP should be able to unionize? Why or why not?

2. Does this Supreme Court decision establish an "adversarial model of labour relations?" Explain.

Sources: Sean Fine, "Supreme Court Backs Mounties' Right to Unionize," *The Globe and Mail,* January 16, 2015, www.theglobeandmail.com/news/national/supreme-court-backs-mounties-right-to-collective-bargaining/article22486356/, retrieved April 12, 2015; Canadian Press, "RCMP Have Right to Collective Bargaining, Supreme Court Rules," *The National Post,* January 16, 2015, http://news.nationalpost.com/news/canada/rcmp-have-right-to-collective-bargaining-supreme-court-rules, retrieved April 12, 2015; and James Fiz-Morris, RCMP Officers Have Right to Collective Bargaining, Supreme Court Rules, *CBC News,* www.cbc.ca/news/politics/rcmp-officers-have-right-to-collective-bargaining-supreme-court-rules-1.2912340, retrieved April 12, 2015.

FIGURE 9.2

Union Density in Canada by Industry, 2013

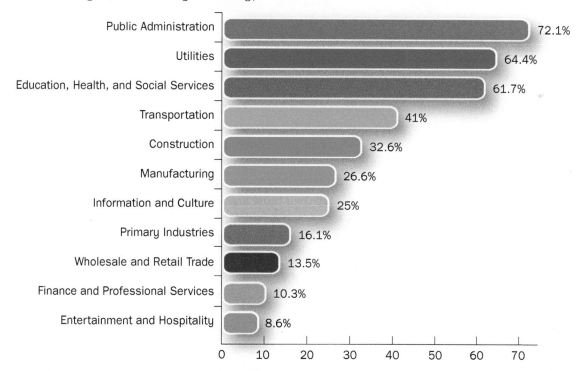

Source: "Overview of Collective Bargaining in Canada, 2013, Chart 13 Union Density, by Industry, 2012 and 2013," Government of Canada Labour Program, www.labour.gc.ca/eng/resources/info/publications/collective_bargaining/collective_bargaining.shtml, retrieved April 12, 2015. The Labour Program-ESDC uses an industrial grouping of the North American Industry Classification System (NAICS) that is different from other departments. Employees in the Arts, Entertainment and Recreational Services sector [71] are usually included under Entertainment and Hospitality, but have been grouped under the Information and Culture industry in keeping with the information as provided by Statistics Canada. NAICS sectors for these discrepancies are provided in square brackets.

FIGURE 9.3

Unionization Rate by Province, 2013

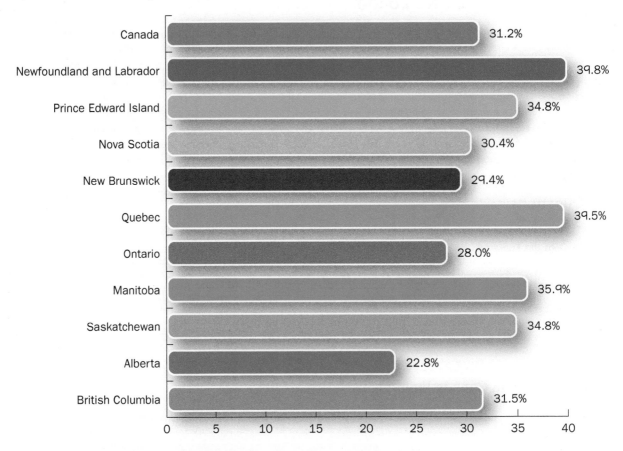

Source: "Overview of Collective Bargaining in Canada, 2013, Table I—Union Coverage by Province, 2012–2013," Government of Canada Labour Program, www.labour.gc.ca/eng/resources/info/publications/collective_bargaining/collective_bargaining.shtml, retrieved April 12, 2015, Statistics Canada, Labour Force Survey (CANSIM, table 282-0078).

The overall decline in union membership has been attributed to several factors.[16] The factor cited most often seems to be change in the structure of the economy. Much recent job growth has occurred among women and youth in the service sector of the economy, while union strength has traditionally been among urban blue-collar workers, especially middle-aged workers.

Another force working against union membership is management efforts against union organizing. In a survey, almost half of large employers said their most important labour goal was to be union-free. Efforts to control costs have contributed to employer resistance to unions.[17] On average, unionized workers receive higher pay than their nonunionized counterparts, and the pressure is greater because of international competition. In the past, union membership across an industry such as automobiles or steel resulted in similar wages and work requirements for all competitors. Today, North American producers have to compete with companies that have entirely different pay scales and work rules, often putting the North American companies at a disadvantage.

Another way management may be contributing to the decline in union membership is by adopting human resource practices that increase employees' commitment to their job and employer. Competition for scarce human resources can lead employers to offer much of what employees traditionally sought through union membership. Government regulations, too, can make unions seem less important. Stricter regulation in such areas as workplace safety and human rights leaves fewer areas in which unions can show an advantage over what employers already have to offer. Despite the declining level of overall unionization in Canada, total union dues are significant. According to the Ministry of Finance, about $860-million worth of union dues were deducted from tax returns in 2012,[18] however, it was recently reported in a *"Special to the Financial Post"* publication that union dues paid are actually much higher: "total union dues in Canada come to about $2.5 billion" and that "Canadian unions are the most privileged in the world."[19]

Unions have made strategic decisions in recent years to organize the growing private-service sector. This sector includes workers employed in hotels, home care agencies, and offices. Often, these employees are women. This extension of union activity into the service sector has been one reason for the most significant transformation in union membership, that is, the mix of men and women. As reported by Statistics Canada, in 2012, 31.3 percent of women were members of unions in contrast to 28.5 percent of men.[20] The percentage of women who are members of unions has remained relatively stable over the past three decades (31.4% in 1981 to 31.3% in 2012), whereas the percentage of men who are members of unions has declined (42.1% in 1981 to 28.5% in 2012). See the "Did You Know?" box. The overall increase in women membership in unions have been attributed to the increasing:

- Number of women in the paid workforce
- Number of women in the highly unionized public sector
- Unionization of part-time employees (many of whom are women)
- Number of women employed in nontraditional male-dominated occupations and industries[21]

The mindset with respect to collective action and unionization is also an important consideration of union leaders. Union density among employees aged 17 to 24 years of age is only 14.8 percent—a significant decline from 26.4 percent in 1981.[22] Former CLC president Georgetti emphasized the group-minded nature of millennials: "We have noted that Generation Y travels in packs" and "this bodes well for selling this group of workers on the notion of collective action."[23] However, Prem Benimadhu with the Conference Board of Canada, suggests that younger workers are less likely to want or need union representation— "Once workers figure out that they can negotiate successfully on their own behalf, it will be hard for unions to convince them to join up and pay dues for the same service," he concluded.[24]

Did You KNOW?

Differences Among the Sexes—Unionization Rate

The gap between the unionization rate between men and women continues to widen.

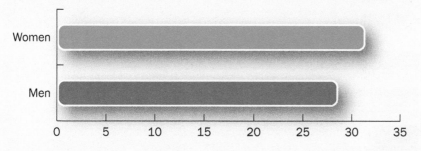

Source: Diane Galarneau and Thao Sohn, "Long Term Trends in Unionization; Table I Unionization Rates by Sex and Age, Employed Individuals Aged 17-64," *Statistics Canada,* November 2013, p. 4, www.statcan.gc.ca/pub/75-006-x/2013001/article/11878-eng.pdf, retrieved April 8, 2015.

As Figure 9.4 indicates, the percentage of Canadian workers who belong to unions, although much higher than in the United States, is lower than some other countries. More dramatic is the difference in "coverage"—the percentage of employees whose terms and conditions of employment are governed by a union contract, whether or not the employees are technically union members. In Western Europe, it is common to have coverage rates of 80 to 90 percent, so the influence of labour unions far outstrips what membership levels would imply.[25] Also, employees in western Europe tend to have a larger formal role

The Canadian Union of Public Employees' (CUPE's www.cupe.ca) National Young Workers Committee is made up of activists under the age of 30. The goal of the committee is "to develop and maintain an active, educated young worker membership."[26]

FIGURE 9.4

Union Membership Rates in Selected Countries

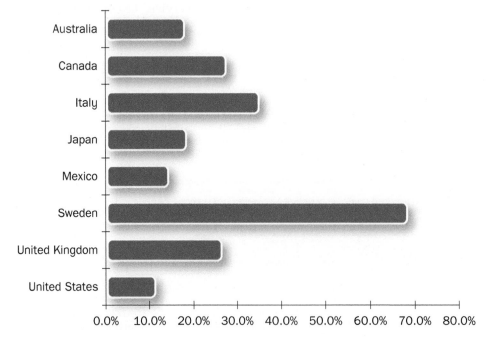

Note: Data for 2007, except U.S. coverage rate for 2005.

Source: Organisation for Economic Co-operation and Development, StatExtracts, http://stats.oecd.org, accessed May 3, 2012.

in decision making than in Canada. This role, including worker representatives on boards of directors, is often mandated by the government. But as markets become more and more global, pressure to cut labour costs and increase productivity is likely to be stronger in every country. Unless unions can help companies improve productivity or organize new production facilities opened in lower-wage countries, union influence may decline in countries where it is now strong.

What Is the Impact of Unions on Company Performance?

HRC 1, 2, 5, 9

Organizations are concerned about whether union organizing and bargaining will hurt their performance, in particular unions' impact on productivity, profits, and stock performance. Researchers have studied the general relationship between unionization and these performance measures. Through skillful labour relations, organizations can positively influence outcomes.

There has been much debate regarding the effects of unions on productivity.[27] The view that unions decrease productivity is based on work rules and limits on workloads set by union contracts and production lost to such union actions as strikes and work slowdowns. At the same time, unions can have positive effects on productivity.[28] They can reduce turnover by giving employees a route for resolving problems.[29] Unions emphasize pay systems based on seniority, which remove incentives for employees to compete rather than cooperate. The introduction of a union also may force an employer to improve its management practices and pay greater attention to employee ideas.

Although there is evidence that unions have both positive and negative effects on productivity, most studies have found that union workers are more productive than nonunion workers. Still, questions remain. Are highly productive workers more likely to form unions, or does a union make workers more productive? The answer is unclear. In theory, if unions caused greater productivity, we would expect union membership to be rising.[30]

Even if unions do raise productivity, a company's profits and stock performance may still suffer if unions raise wage and benefits costs by more than the productivity gain. On average, union members receive higher wages and more generous benefits than nonunion workers, and evidence shows that unions have a large negative effect on profits. Also, union coverage tends to decline faster in companies with a lower return to shareholders.[31] In summary, companies wishing to become more competitive must continually monitor their labor relations strategy.

These studies look at the average effects of unions, not at individual companies or innovative labour relations. Some organizations excel at labour relations, and some have worked with unions to meet business needs. Many companies depend on unions to recruit and train new workers through apprenticeship programs. For example, in the organized construction industry, apprenticeships are administered through labour unions and employer partnerships, financed by industry training trust funds that own and operate training facilities. Building trades unions, along with their employer partners, have created Joint Apprenticeship & Training Committees (JATCs) in most provinces and territories.[32]

L○2 Identify the labour relations goals of management, labour unions, and society.

What Are the Goals of Each Group?

Resolving conflicts in a positive way is usually easiest when the parties involved understand each other's goals. Although individual cases vary, we can draw some general conclusions about the goals of labour unions and management. Table 9.1 provides a summary of current negotiation issues from the

TABLE 9.1

Current Negotiation Issues

Management Issues	Union Issues
1. Wages	1. Wages
2. Productivity	2. Employment security
3. Business competitiveness	3. Health benefits
4. Flexible work practices	4. Pensions
5. Organizational change	5. Outsourcing and contracting out
6. Health benefits	6. Employment and pay equity
7. Pensions	7. Flexible work practices
8. Outsourcing and contracting out	8. Organizational change
9. Employment and pay equity	9. Training and skills development
10. Employment security	10. Variable pay
11. Training and skills development	11. Technological change
12. Variable pay	12. Productivity
13. Technological change	13. Business competitiveness
14. Other (e.g., vacation, type of work, etc.)	14. Other (e.g., vacation, type of work, etc.)

Note: Respondents were given a list of 14 possible choices and asked to indicate the top three negotiation issues for both management and union.

Source: Katie Fleming and Nicole Stewart, "Compensation Planning Outlook 2015, Table 24 Current Negotiation Issues," October 2014, The Conference Board of Canada, p. 26.

perspective of management and unions. Society, too, has goals for labour and business, given form in the laws regulating labour relations.

Goals of Management

Management goals are to increase the organization's profits and/or increase productivity. Managers tend to prefer options that lower costs and raise output. A concern is that a union will create higher costs in wages and benefits, as well as raise the risk of work stoppages. Managers may also fear that a union will make managers and workers into adversaries or limit management's discretion in making business and employment decisions.

When an employer has recognized a union, management's goals continue to emphasize restraining costs and improving output. Managers continue to prefer to keep the organization's operations flexible, so they can adjust activities to meet competitive challenges and customer demands. Therefore, in their labour relations, managers prefer to limit increases in wages and benefits and to retain as much control as they can over work rules and schedules.

Goals of Unions

In general, unions have the goals of obtaining pay, job security, and working conditions that satisfy their members and of giving members a voice in decisions that affect them. Traditionally, they obtain these goals by gaining power in numbers. The more workers who belong to a union, the greater the union's power. More members translates into greater ability to halt or disrupt operations. Larger unions also have greater financial resources for continuing a strike; the union can help to make up for the wages the workers lose during a strike. The threat of a long strike—stated or implied—can make an employer more willing to meet the union's demands.

As mentioned earlier, union membership is indeed linked to better compensation. Statistics Canada reports that in February 2015 the average hourly wage of employees with union coverage earned $28.51 per hour, almost 22 percent more than the $23.38 per hour earned by employees without union coverage.[33]

Unions typically want to influence the *way* pay and promotions are determined. Unlike management, which tries to consider employees as individuals so that pay and promotion decisions relate to performance differences, unions try to build group solidarity and avoid possible arbitrary treatment of employees. To do so, unions try to have any pay differences based on seniority, on the grounds that this measure is more objective than performance evaluations. As a result, where workers are represented by a union, it is common for all employees in a particular job classification to be paid at the same rate. As well as working to advance the interests of members, unions often engage in **social unionism**, that is, activities intended to influence social and economic policies of government. For example, CUPE (the Canadian Union of Public Employees) is actively supporting far-ranging issues including advocating urgent action on climate change, opposition to Bill C-51—the *Anti-Terrorism Act*, rethinking child care, and lessening the negative health impacts of shift work.[34]

social unionism
A type of unionism that attempts to influence social and economic policies of government.

However, the survival and security of a union ultimately depends on its ability to ensure a regular flow of new members and member dues to support the services it provides. In 1946, Supreme Court of Canada Justice Ivan Rand brought down a significant decision that affected union financial security in Canada. The case came about as part of an arbitrated settlement of a labour dispute between the Ford Motor Company and the United Auto Workers. The **Rand Formula** is a union security provision that makes the payment of labour union dues mandatory even if the worker is not a member of the union. The rationale for the principle was that every employee benefits from union representation.[35] Unions typically place high priority on negotiating two types of contract provisions with an employer that are critical to a union's security and viability: checkoff provisions and provisions relating to union membership or contribution.

Rand Formula
A union security provision that makes payment of labour union dues mandatory even if the worker is not a member of the union.

Under a **checkoff provision**, the employer, on behalf of the union, automatically deducts union dues from employees' paycheques.

checkoff provision
A requirement that the employer, on behalf of the union, automatically deducts union dues from employees' paycheques.

The strongest union security arrangement is a **closed shop**, under which a person must be a union member before being hired or the **union shop**, an arrangement that requires an employee to join the union within a certain time after beginning employment.

closed shop
A union security arrangement under which a person must be a union member before being hired.

union shop
A union security arrangement that requires employees to join the union within a certain amount of time after beginning employment.

These provisions are ways to address unions' concern about "free riders"—employees who benefit from union activities without belonging to a union. By law, all members of a bargaining unit, whether union members or not, must be represented by the union. If the union is required to offer services to all bargaining unit members even though some of them do not pay dues, it may not have enough financial resources to operate successfully.

Goals of Society

The activities of unions and management take place within the context of society, with society's values driving the laws and regulations that affect labour relations. As long ago as the late 1800s and early 1900s, industrial relations scholars saw unions as a way to make up for individual employees' limited bargaining power.[36] At that time, clashes between workers and management could be violent, and many people hoped that unions would replace the violence with negotiation. Since then, observers have expressed concern that unions in certain industries have become too strong, achieving their goals at the expense of employers' ability to compete or meet other objectives. Overall, however, societal goals for government include ensuring that neutral rules exist to ensure balance is maintained between the powers of unions and employers.

Rather than being left to the activities of unions and management, many societal goals are also enforced through laws and regulations. As discussed in Chapter 2, human rights, pay equity, employment equity, privacy and other types of legislation determine how workers are treated by their employers. In addition, as we will see in the next section, a set of laws and regulations also exists to give workers the right to choose to join unions.

L○3 Summarize laws and regulations that affect labour relations.

Laws and Regulations Affecting Labour Relations

HRC**2,5**

The laws and regulations pertaining to labour relations affect unions' size and bargaining power, so they significantly affect the degree to which unions, management, and society achieve their varied goals. These laws and regulations set limits on union structure and administration and the ways in which unions and management interact.

Canada's overall labour relations legal framework is decentralized and relatively complex. Since a ruling of the Supreme Court of Canada in 1925, responsibility for labour relations is primarily a provincial/territorial responsibility. Which organizations fall under federal versus provincial/territorial legislation was discussed in Chapter 2. Federally regulated private-sector employees are regulated by the Canada Labour Code (Part 1—Industrial Relations). Each province and territory has its own distinct labour laws. Each jurisdiction—federal, provincial, and territorial—also has laws governing public-sector employees. There are additional labour statutes that apply to specific occupations determined to be essential services, for example, teachers, law enforcement officers, firefighters, and health care employees.

A recent decision by the Supreme Court of Canada affirming the right of public sector employees' right to strike is considered a historic ruling that has implications for public service unions. The Supreme Court decision struck down Saskatchewan labour legislation, the *Public Service Essential Services Act*, which restricted the public sector workers who could strike. Justice Rosalie Abela wrote in the Supreme Court ruling: "The right to strike is not merely derivative of collective bargaining; it is an indispensable component of that right."[37]

In recent years, governments have become been particularly active in intervening to end labour disputes. For example, the Conference Board of Canada reported that during the first seven months of 2011 the federal government had intervened in more than 80 work stoppages involving more than 500 workers. This represented more federal government interventions than the cumulative total for the previous 30 years (1980–2010). This trend has continued including the recent threat of legislation that prompted CP Rail and the Teamsters to reach a deal to end a one-day strike of more than 3,000 locomotive engineers and other train workers.[38]

Although some differences exist among jurisdictions, the main features of labour legislation in Canada can be summarized as follows:

- Methods to certify a union that will represent a group of employees
- Requirement of the employer to recognize the union chosen by the majority of its employees and to accept the union as the employees' exclusive representative for bargaining purposes
- Responsibility to bargain in good faith with the intention to reach an agreement
- Requirement of the employer to deduct union dues from employees
- Minimum length of a collective agreement (at least one year)
- Regulation of strike and lockout activities
- Creation of a labour relations board (or specialized tribunal) to interpret and enforce the labour laws in their jurisdiction
- Prohibition of identified **unfair labour practices** by management and labour (see the "HR How-To" box)

unfair labour practices
Prohibited conduct of an employer, union, or individual under the relevant labour legislation.

There is a **Labour Relations Board (LRB)** (or similar structure) in each jurisdiction that serves as a specialized quasi-judicial tribunal with authority to interpret and enforce the labour laws in their jurisdiction.

Labour Relations Board (LRB)
A specialized tribunal with authority to interpret and enforce the labour laws in their jurisdiction.

Prevention of Unfair Labour Practices

When someone believes that an unfair labour practice has taken place, he or she may file a complaint with the appropriate Labour Relations Board for the jurisdiction. All parties are provided a copy of the complaint and the process usually involves the Labour Relations Board conducting a preliminary investigation to determine if the complaint has merit and if it may be possible for the parties to resolve the complaint themselves. If the Labour Relations Board finds the complaint has merit and determines the complaint cannot be resolved through the parties, the Labour Relations Board will conduct a formal hearing with the parties present. Either the case can be dismissed at this point or the Labour Relations Board has the authority to issue orders to halt unfair labour practices. If the union or employer does not comply with the Labour Relations Board order, the order can be referred to the courts for enforcement.[39]

HR How-To

Avoiding Unfair Labour Practices

A common core of labour legislation prohibits employers, unions, and individuals from engaging in unfair labour practices. Each jurisdiction in Canada has specific provisions dealing with unfair labour practices by management and unions. Some of the most common examples of unfair labour practices that management must not engage in:

1. Interfering in the formation of a union or contributing to it financially (although, there have been allowances for the providing of an office for the union to conduct business and for paid leave for union officials conducting union business)

2. Discriminating against an employee because the individual is or is not a member of a union

3. Discriminating against an employee because the individual chooses to exercise rights granted by labour relations law

4. Intimidating or coercing an employee to become or not become a member of a union

Activities that a union is not permitted to engage in include:

1. Seeking to compel an employer to bargain collectively with the union if the union is not the certified bargaining agent

2. Attempting at the workplace and during working hours to persuade an employee to become or not become a union member

3. Intimidating, coercing, or penalizing an individual because he or she has filed a complaint or testified in any proceeding pursuant to the relevant labour law

4. Engaging in, encouraging, or threatening illegal strikes

5. Failing to represent employees fairly

Source: Hermann Schwind, Hari Das, and Terry Wagar, *Canadian Human Resource Management*, 9th ed. (Toronto: McGraw-Hill Ryerson, 2010), p. 507.

LO4 Describe the union organizing process.

What Is the Union Organizing Process?

Unions begin their involvement with an organization's employees by conducting an organizing campaign. To meet its objectives, a union needs to convince a majority of workers that they should receive better pay or other employment conditions and that the union will help them do so. The employer's objectives will depend on its strategy—whether it seeks to work with a union or convince employees that they are better off without union representation.

The Process of Organizing

The organization process begins with a membership application such as the one shown in Figure 9.5. Union representatives contact employees, present their message about the union, and invite them to sign an application for membership. By signing the application and paying a nominal fee in some jurisdictions, the employee indicates they want the union to represent them.

When the necessary number of employees have signed membership applications, the union will apply to the appropriate Labour Relations Board for certification. Requirements differ among jurisdictions. For example, if the employer is in the private sector and falls under federal jurisdiction, the local can be certified without holding a representation vote if more than 50 percent of employees provide their support. If there is less than 35 percent employee support, the application can be dismissed but if the union has obtained between 35 and 50 percent of employee support, a representation vote must be conducted.[40]

FIGURE 9.5

Example of an Application for Membership

APPLICATION FOR MEMBERSHIP

Ontario Public Service Employees Union, 100 Lesmill Road, Toronto, ON M3B 3P8

I hereby apply for and accept membership in, and authorize OPSEU, its agents or representatives, to act for me as my exclusive representative in collective bargaining, in respect to all the terms and conditions of my employment and to negotiate contracts with my employer covering all such matters.

X _____ Date _____
(Signature of applicant)

On behalf of the above organization, I hereby accept this application.

X _____ Date _____
(Signature of recruiter)

Last name (please print) _____

First name (please print) _____

Address _____ Apt. # _____

City _____ Prov. _____ Postal code _____

Phone (home) _____ Phone (work) _____

Employed by (name of college) _____

Campus _____ Department _____

First name (please print) _____

☐ Faculty: Part-time ☐ Faculty: Sessional ☐ Support: Part-time ☐ Support: Non-recurring project

Home or secure e-mail address _____

Source: Ontario Public Service Employees Union.

Management Strategies

Sometimes an employer will recognize a union after a majority of employees have signed membership applications. More often, there is a hotly contested election campaign. During the campaign, unions try to persuade employees that their wages, benefits, treatment by employers, and chances to influence workplace decisions are too poor or small and that the union will be able to obtain improvements in these areas. Management typically responds with its own messages providing an opposite point of view. Management messages say the organization has provided a valuable package of wages and benefits and has treated employees well. Management also argues that the union will not be able to keep its promises but will instead create costs for employees, such as union dues and lost income during strikes. Employers use a variety of methods to avoid unionization in organizing campaigns.[41] Their efforts range from hiring consultants to distributing leaflets and letters to presenting the company's viewpoint at meetings of employees. Some management efforts go beyond what the law permits, especially in the eyes of union organizers.

Supervisors have the most direct contact with employees. Thus, as Table 9.2 indicates, it is critical that they establish good relationships with employees even before there is any attempt at union organizing.

TABLE 9.2

What Supervisors Should and Should Not Do to Reduce the Likelihood of Unionization

What To Do
Report any direct or indirect signs of union activity to a core management group.
Deal with employees by carefully stating the company's response to pro-union arguments. These responses should be coordinated by the company to maintain consistency and to avoid threats or promises. Take away union issues by following effective management practices all the time:
• Deliver recognition and appreciation.
• Solve employee problems.
• Protect employees from harassment or humiliation.
• Provide business-related information.
• Be consistent in treatment of employees.
• Accommodate special circumstances where appropriate.
• Ensure due process in performance management.
• Treat all employees with dignity and respect.

What To Avoid
Threatening employees with harsher terms and conditions of employment or employment loss if they engage in union activity.
Interrogating employees about pro-union or anti-union sentiments that they or others may have or reviewing union authorization cards or pro-union petitions.
Promising employees that they will receive favourable terms or conditions of employment if they forgo union activity.
Spying on employees known to be, or suspected of being, engaged in pro-union activities.

Source: Excerpted from "Unshackle Your Supervisors to Stay Union Free," by J. A. Segal in *HR Magazine,* June 1998. Copyright 1998 by Society for Human Resource Management, Alexandria, VA. Used with permission. All rights reserved.

Supervisors also must know what *not* to do if a union drive takes place. They should be trained in the legal principles discussed earlier in this chapter.

Can a Union be Dercertified?

Union members' right to be represented by unions of their own choosing also includes the right to vote out an existing union. The action is called *decertifying* the union. Decertification follows the same process as a representation election. An application to decertify a union may not be acted upon during a legal strike or lockout. In some jurisdictions when a collective agreement is in place, decertification applications may only be filed during specified "open periods." Laws in some jurisdictions require the employer to post and annually circulate information related to union decertification.

L○5 Explain how management and unions negotiate collective agreements.

Collective Bargaining

HRC 1, 2, 5

When a union has been certified, that union represents employees during contract negotiations. In **collective bargaining**, a union negotiates on behalf of its members with management representatives to arrive at a contract defining conditions of employment for the term of the contract and to resolve

collective bargaining

Negotiation between union representatives and management representatives to arrive at an agreement defining conditions of employment for the term of the agreement and to administer that agreement.

differences in the way they interpret the contract. Typical collective agreements include provisions for pay, benefits, work rules, and resolution of workers' grievances. Table 9.3 shows typical provisions negotiated in collective agreements. The nearby "HR Best Practices" feature identifies several innovative provisions recently negotiated that respond to various diverse interests of employers and union members.

TABLE 9.3

Typical Provisions in Collective Agreements

Rights of Parties	*Recognition of Union Security*
	• Union membership
	• Union security
	• Leave for union business
	• Restrictions on contracting out
	Management Rights to Test
	• Drug and alcohol testing
	• Intelligence and aptitude testing
	• Electronic surveillance
	• Internet/telephone monitoring
	• Medical examinations
	• Other tests
	Employee Rights/Security
	• Harassment
	• Employment Equity Program
	• Assistance programs, e.g., substance abuse
Organization of Work	*Technological Change*
	• Advance notice
	• Obligation to provide training, instruction, or retraining
	• Layoff protection
	• Wage protection
	• Special leaves, severance pay, and/or retirement offers
	Distribution of Work
	• Flexibility in work assignment
	• Job rotation
	• Semi-autonomous work groups or teams
	• Job sharing
Labour Relations	*Labour Relations*
	• Grievance procedures
	• Bargaining method or approach
	• Application of the agreement
	• Job evaluation (position evaluation)
	• Joint committees
	• Participation (other than committees)
Education, Training, and Development	*Education, Training, and Employee Development*
	• Leave
	• Reimbursement for tuition fees and books
	• Multiskilling, i.e., flexibility for the employee
	• Contribution to a training fund
	• Apprenticeship programs

(continued on next page)

Conditions of Work	*Work Schedule*
	• Normal hours of work
	• Type of work schedules
	• Special provisions
	Overtime
	• Clause limiting the use of overtime
	• Compensatory days in lieu of pay (banking)
	• Overtime pay
	• Meal allowance (overtime)
	Job Security and Termination
	• No layoffs while the agreement is in effect
	• Layoffs by seniority
	• Bumping rights
	• Retention of seniority
	• Work sharing (reduction in hours to avoid layoffs)
	• Education/training with pay
	• Supplementary employment insurance benefit
	Pay
	• Cost-of-living allowance
	• Wage guarantees
	Leaves and Vacations
	• Paid holidays
	• Annual vacation
	• Family leave
	• Paid sick leave plan
	Benefits
	• Private group insurance plans
	• Pension plans (funding, administration)
	Provisions Relating to Part-Time Workers
	• Maximum hours of work normally allowed
	• Ratio of part-time to full-time workers
	• Holidays, vacations, sick leave, benefits, pension plan, seniority

Source: "Collective Agreement Provisions," General Overview, The Labour Program—Working For You, www.hrsdc.gc.ca/eng/labour/overview.shtml. Human Resources and Skills Development website, www.hrsdc.gc.ca. Retrieved: November 2, 2004. Reproduced with the permission of the Minister of Public Works and Government Services, 2012.

Collective bargaining differs from one situation to another in terms of *bargaining structure*—that is, the range of employees and employers covered by the contract. An agreement may involve a narrow group of employees in a craft union or a broad group in an industrial union. Agreements may cover one or several facilities of the same employer, or the bargaining structure may involve several employers. Many more interests must be considered in collective bargaining for an industrial union with a bargaining structure that includes several employers than in collective bargaining for a craft union in a single facility.

The majority of collective agreement negotiations take place between unions and employers that have been through the process before. In the typical situation, management has come to accept the union as an organization it must work with. The situation can be very different when a union has just been certified and is negotiating its first collective agreement. For example, the Labour Relations Code of the Province of British Columbia recognizes that negotiation of the first collective agreement is more difficult for unions and employers and specifies a process for settlement that could include the use of arbitration,[42] a process discussed later in this chapter.

Unifor members and allies from across Ontario rallied at the Toronto Pearson International Airport to protest proposed outsourcing of services for seniors and other passengers requiring wheelchair assistance.

Bargaining Over New Collective Agreements

Clearly, the outcome of collective agreement negotiations can have important consequences for labour costs, productivity, and the organization's ability to compete. Therefore, unions and management need to prepare carefully for collective bargaining. Preparation includes establishing objectives for the agreement, reviewing the old agreement, gathering data (such as compensation paid by competitors and the company's ability to survive a strike), predicting the likely demands to be made, and establishing the cost of meeting the demands.[43] This preparation can help negotiators develop a plan for how to negotiate. Different situations and goals call for different approaches to bargaining, such as the following alternatives proposed by Richard Walton and Robert McKersie:[44]

- *Distributive bargaining* divides an economic "pie" between two sides—for example, a wage increase means giving the union a larger share of the pie.

- *Integrative (mutual-gains) bargaining* looks for win-win solutions, or outcomes in which both sides benefit. If the organization's labour costs hurt its performance, integrative bargaining might seek to avoid layoffs in exchange for work rules that improve productivity.

- *Attitudinal structuring* focuses on establishing a relationship of trust. The parties are concerned about ensuring that the other side will keep its part of any bargain.

- *Intraorganizational bargaining* addresses conflicts within union or management groups or objectives, such as between new employees and workers with high seniority or between cost control and reduction of turnover.

The collective bargaining process may involve any combination of these alternatives.

Negotiations go through various stages.[45] In the earliest stages, many more people are often present than in later stages. On the union side, this may give all the various internal interest groups a chance to participate and voice their goals. Their input helps communicate to management what will satisfy union members and may help the union achieve greater solidarity. At this stage, union negotiators often present a long list of proposals, partly to satisfy members and partly to introduce enough issues that they will have flexibility later in the process. Management may or may not present proposals of its own. Sometimes management prefers to react to the union's proposals.

During the middle stages of the process, each side must make a series of decisions, even though the outcome is uncertain. How important is each issue to the other side? How likely is it that disagreement on particular issues will result in a strike? When and to what extent should one side signal its willingness to compromise?

In the final stage of negotiations, pressure for an agreement increases. Public negotiations may be only part of the process. Negotiators from each side may hold one-on-one meetings or small-group meetings where they escape some public relations pressures. A neutral third party may act as a go-between or facilitator. In some cases, bargaining breaks down as the two sides find they cannot reach a mutually acceptable agreement. The outcome depends partly on the relative bargaining power of each party. That power, in turn, depends on each party's ability to withstand a strike, which costs the workers their pay during the strike and costs the employer lost production and possibly lost customers. Refer to the "HR Best Practices" box.

HR Best Practices

Innovative Clauses in Collective Agreements

Bargaining parties sometimes negotiate innovative clauses in an effort to alter working conditions or to address economic challenges. Following are a few examples of such clauses that employers and unions recently negotiated.

Contingent Wage Adjustments

The Health Employers Association of B.C. and the Health Science Professionals Bargaining Association of BC negotiated a new "Economic Stability Dividend." For every 1 percent that provincial real GDP exceeds the government forecast, employees will receive an additional 0.5 percent wage increase. The dividend will be calculated annually for each year of the collective agreement.

Transfer Between Employees

Yukon College and the Public Service Alliance of Canada negotiated a new provision that allows workers to confidentially transfer unused vacation time to other employees on compassionate grounds.

Alternative Dispute Resolution

In Chapel Island, Nova Scotia, Aboriginal fishermen represented by the UFCW negotiated a clause that introduces a new conflict resolution approach. The fishermen, who are citizens of the Potlotek First Nation, will have the option of resolving contract disputes through a process called the Kisikuewey Wantaqo'suti Procedure, which permits mediation by Band Elders.

Language and Diversity

Canada Safeway Limited and the UFCW have committed to work together in the implementation of ethnic model stores, which will target specific demographic niches. Employees with the appropriate linguistic profile may be transferred to stores where they can effectively communicate with a store's target customer base. Both parties have recognized that the stores selected for this implementation are essential to overall growth and job security. A joint union/employer process will be implemented to manage the transition for employees in impacted stores.

Source: "Overview of Collective Bargaining in Canada, 2013," *Government of Canada Labour Program*, www.labour.gc.ca/eng/resources/info/publications/collective_bargaining/collective_bargaining.shtml, pp. 7-8, retrieved April 12, 2015.

What Happens When Bargaining Breaks Down?

The intended outcome of collective bargaining is an agreement with terms acceptable to both parties. If one or both sides determine that negotiation alone will not produce such an agreement, bargaining breaks down. To bring this impasse to an end, the union may strike, the employer may lockout employees, or the parties may bring in outside help to resolve their differences.

Strikes and Lockouts

A **strike** is a collective decision of the union members not to work or to slow down until certain demands or conditions are met. The union members vote, and if the majority favours a strike, they all go on strike at that time or when union leaders believe the time is right. Strikes are typically accompanied by *picketing*—the union stations members near the work site with signs indicating the union is on strike. During the strike, the union members do not receive pay from their employer, but the union may be able to make up for some of the lost pay. The employer loses production unless it can hire replacement workers, and even then, productivity may be reduced. Often, other unions support striking workers by refusing to cross their picket line—for example, refusing to make deliveries to a company during a strike. A **lockout** on the other hand, is initiated by the employer. A lockout is a closure of a place of employment or refusal of the employer to provide work as a way to compel employees to agree to certain demands or conditions.

strike
A collective decision by union members not to work or to slow down until certain demands or conditions are met.

lockout
A closure of a place of employment or refusal of the employer to provide work as a way to compel employees to agree to certain demands or conditions.

The vast majority of labour–management negotiations do not result in a work stoppage, i.e., strike or lockout. Figure 9.6 shows a chronological perspective of work stoppages in Canada for 1980–2013. In 2013, the number of workers involved in work stoppages was the highest since 2004, however, this was largely due to a two-week construction strike in Quebec involving 175,000 workers and a dispute between the Canadian Red Cross Society and 4,500 union members.[46] The estimated number of person-days lost through work stoppages has fluctuated significantly ranging from more than 4.1 million in 2005 to 0.9 million in 2008, 2.2 million in 2009, 1.2 million in 2010, and 1.5 million in 2013.[47] Not only do workers lose wages and employers lose production, but the negative experience of a strike or lockout can make future interactions more difficult. When strikes or lockouts do occur, the conduct of each party during the strike can do lasting harm to labour–management relations. Violence by either side or threats of job loss or actual job loss because jobs went to replacement workers can make future relations difficult.

What Are the Alternatives to Strikes and Lockouts?

Because strikes and lockouts are so costly and disruptive, unions and employers generally prefer other methods for resolving conflicts. Three of the most common alternatives are mediation, conciliation, and arbitration. All of these rely on a neutral third party, who usually is appointed by the federal or provincial Minister of Labour.

The least formal and most widely used of these procedures is **mediation**, in which a third party or *mediator* hears the views of both sides and facilitates the negotiation process. He or she has

mediation
Conflict resolution procedure in which a mediator hears the views of both sides and facilitates the negotiation process but has no formal authority to dictate a resolution.

FIGURE 9.6

Number of Work Stoppages and Workers Involved (000s), 1980–2013

Sources: "Overview of Collective Bargaining in Canada, 2013, Chart 9—Number of Work Stoppages and Workers Involved, 2004–2013," *Government of Canada Labour Program,* www.labour.gc.ca/eng/resources/info/publications/collective_bargaining/collective_bargaining.shtml, retrieved April 12, 2015; and Sharanjit Uppal, "Unionization 2011," Statistics Canada, Table 4, "Major Wage Settlements, Inflation and Labour Disputes," www.statcan.gc.ca/pub/75-001-x/2011004/tables-tableaux/11579/tbl04-eng.htm, retrieved May 21, 2012.

no formal authority to impose a resolution, so a strike remains a possibility. In a survey studying negotiations between unions and large businesses, mediation was used in almost four out of ten negotiation efforts.[48]

Conciliation, most often used for negotiations with government bodies, typically reports on the reasons for the dispute, the views and arguments of both sides, and (sometimes) a recommended settlement, which the parties may decline. The public nature of these recommendations may pressure the parties to reach a settlement. Even if they do not accept the conciliator's recommended settlement, the hope of this process is that the conciliator will identify or frame issues in a way that makes agreement easier. Sometimes merely devoting time to this process gives the parties a chance to reach an agreement. In most jurisdictions in Canada, conciliation is mandatory before a strike or lockout can be called. Again, however, there is no guarantee that a strike or lockout will be avoided.

> **conciliation**
> Conflict resolution procedure in which a third party to collective bargaining reports the reasons for a dispute, the views and arguments of both sides, and possibly a recommended settlement, which the parties may decline.

The most formal type of outside intervention is **arbitration,** under which an arbitrator or arbitration board determines a settlement that is *binding,* meaning the parties have to accept it. There is wide acceptance of "rights arbitration," which focuses on enforcing or interpreting agreement terms, but arbitration in the writing of collective agreements or setting of agreement terms has traditionally been reserved for special circumstances such as negotiations between unions and government agencies, where strikes may be illegal or especially costly. Occasionally, arbitration has also been used with businesses in situations where strikes have been extremely damaging. For example, when back-to-work legislation is imposed by the Minister of Labour, a provision to impose a settlement if the two sides can't reach an agreement is likely to be included.

arbitration
Conflict resolution procedure in which an arbitrator or arbitration board determines a binding settlement.

It may be suggested that the general opinion that union and management representatives are in the best position to resolve conflicts themselves because they are closer to the situation than an arbitrator is being tested as evidenced by the significant number of recent government interventions in labour disputes.

L○6 Summarize the practice of collective agreement administration.

Administration of the Collective Agreement

HRC 5

Although the process of negotiating a collective agreement (including the occasional strike) receives the most publicity, other union–management activities occur far more often. Bargaining over a new contract typically occurs only about every three years, but administering labour agreements goes on day after day, year after year. The two activities are linked, of course. Vague or inconsistent language in the agreement can make administering the agreement more difficult. The difficulties can create conflict that spills over into the next round of negotiations.[49] Events during negotiations—strikes, the use of replacement workers, or violence by either side—also can lead to difficulties in working successfully under a conflict.

Collective agreement administration includes carrying out the terms of the agreement and resolving conflicts over interpretation or violation of the agreement. Under a collective agreement, the process for resolving these conflicts is called a **grievance procedure**. This procedure has a key influence on

grievance procedure
The process for resolving union–management conflicts over interpretation or violation of a collective agreement.

Canada Post locked out workers following a series of rotating strikes.

success in collective agreement administration. A grievance procedure may be started by an employee or discharged employee who believes the employer violated the agreement or by a union representative on behalf of a group of workers or union representatives.

For grievances launched by an employee, a typical grievance procedure follows the steps shown in Figure 9.7. The grievance may be settled during any of the four steps. In *Step 1*, the employee talks to his or her supervisor about the problem. If this conversation is unsatisfactory, the employee may involve the union steward in further discussion. The union steward and employee decide whether the problem has been resolved and, if not, whether it is a violation of the collective agreement. If the problem was not resolved and does seem to be an agreement violation, the union moves to *Step 2,* putting the grievance in writing and submitting it to a manager. The union steward meets with a management representative to try to resolve the problem. Management consults with the labour relations staff and puts its response in writing too at this second stage. If Step 2 fails to resolve the problem, the union appeals the grievance to top management and representatives of the labour relations staff. The union may involve more local

---

FIGURE 9.7

Steps in an Employee-Initiated Grievance Procedure

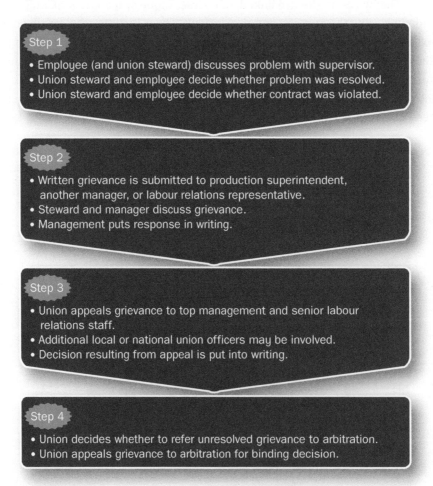

Step 1
- Employee (and union steward) discusses problem with supervisor.
- Union steward and employee decide whether problem was resolved.
- Union steward and employee decide whether contract was violated.

Step 2
- Written grievance is submitted to production superintendent, another manager, or labour relations representative.
- Steward and manager discuss grievance.
- Management puts response in writing.

Step 3
- Union appeals grievance to top management and senior labour relations staff.
- Additional local or national union officers may be involved.
- Decision resulting from appeal is put into writing.

Step 4
- Union decides whether to refer unresolved grievance to arbitration.
- Union appeals grievance to arbitration for binding decision.

Sources: Adapted from T. A. Kochan, *Collective Bargaining and Industrial Relations* (Homewood, IL: Richard D. Irwin, 1980), p. 395; and J. A. Fossum, *Labour Relations* (Boston: McGraw-Hill/Irwin, 2002), pp. 448-52.

or national officers in discussions at this stage (see *Step 3* in Figure 9.7). The decision resulting from the appeal is put into writing. If the grievance is still not resolved, the union may decide (*Step 4*) to appeal the grievance to an arbitrator. If the grievance involves a discharged employee, the process may begin at Step 2 or 3 however, and the time limits between steps may be shorter. Grievances filed by the union on behalf of a group may begin at Step 1 or Step 2.

 E-HRM

#justcausetermination: Arbitrators agree with employers in recent cases.

The majority of grievances are settled during the earlier steps of the process. This reduces delays and avoids the costs of arbitration. If a grievance does reach arbitration, the arbitrator makes the final ruling in the matter.

Employers can assess the grievance procedure in terms of various criteria.[50] One consideration is effectiveness: how well the procedure resolves day-to-day questions about the collective agreement. A second basic consideration is efficiency: whether it resolves issues at a reasonable cost and without major delays. The company also should consider how well the grievance procedure adapts to changing circumstances. For example, if sales drop off and the company needs to cut costs, how clear are the provisions related to layoffs and subcontracting of work? In the case of contracts covering multiple business units, the procedure should allow for resolving local contract issues, such as work rules at a particular facility. Companies should also consider whether the grievance procedure is fair—whether it treats employees equitably and gives them a voice in the process.

From the point of view of employees, the grievance procedure is an important means of getting fair treatment in the workplace. Its success depends on whether it provides for all the kinds of issues that are likely to arise (such as how to handle a business slowdown), whether employees feel they can file a grievance without being punished for it, and whether employees believe their union representatives will follow through. Too many grievances may indicate a problem—for example, the union members or managers do not understand how to uphold the collective agreement or have no desire to do so. At the same time, a very small number of grievances may also signal a problem. A very low grievance rate may suggest a fear of filing a grievance, a belief that the system does not work, or a belief that employees are poorly represented by their union.

L07 Describe more cooperative approaches to labour–management relations.

Labour–Management Cooperation

HRC**1,5**

The traditional understanding of union–management relations is that the two parties are adversaries, meaning each side is competing to win at the expense of the other. There have always been exceptions to this approach. And since at least the 1980s, there seems to be wider acceptance of the view that greater cooperation can increase employee commitment and motivation while making the workplace more flexible.[51] Also, evidence suggests that employees who worked under traditional labour relations systems and then under the new, more cooperative systems prefer the cooperative approach.[52]

Cooperation between labour and management may feature employee involvement in decision making, self-managing employee teams, joint labour–management committees, broadly defined jobs, and sharing of financial gains and business information with employees.[53] The search for a win-win solution requires that unions and their members understand the limits on what an employer can afford in a competitive marketplace.

Without the union's support, efforts at employee empowerment are less likely to survive and less likely to be effective if they do survive.[54] Unions have often resisted employee empowerment programs, precisely because the programs try to change workplace relations and the role that unions play. Union leaders have often feared that such programs will weaken unions' role as independent representatives of employee interests.

An effective day-to-day relationship between labour and management is critical to achieving cooperation. In an adversarial type of environment, union–management communication consists of dealing with grievances; however, a cooperative model requires effective communication, trust, and mutual respect as the foundation for the day-to-day relationship. Many management and union leaders recognize that new approaches are needed to handle mutual concerns—"A sense of shared purpose is required to increase the effectiveness of the organization."[55]

Labour–management committees provide a relatively flexible approach to labour–management cooperation in the workplace. Over the past two decades, the use of *joint labour–management committees* has been growing. More than 80 percent of labour and management respondents to a Conference Board of Canada study reported that they have experience in using joint labour–management committees. The most common issues that such committees deal with are summarized in Table 9.4.

Employers build cooperative relationships by the way they treat employees—with respect and fairness, in the knowledge that attracting talent and minimizing turnover are in the employer's best interests. "In the end we must look for opportunities to create a more collaborative culture in Canadian workplaces to ensure the long-term sustainability of our businesses."[56]

TABLE 9.4

Most Common Joint Labour–Management Committees

1. Pay, benefits, pensions

2. Business issues/updates

3. General labour relations

4. Training/apprenticeships

5. Job evaluation/classifications/postings

6. Operations/technology

7. Hours of work/scheduling

Source: Judith Lendvay-Zwicki, "The Canadian Industrial Relations System: Current Challenges and Future Options," Conference Board Document, April 2004, p. 17, www.conferenceboard.ca, retrieved April 19, 2004.

Thinking ETHICALLY

Is the Seniority System Fair?

Traditionally, union contracts have called for pay and promotion systems that reward employees with higher pay and advancement as they achieve greater seniority, that is, more years on the job. In a company, with a unionized workforce, employees with comparable amounts of experience would have comparable earnings. Employees with greater seniority would earn more than newer employees and employees with the most seniority would be promoted if they met the minimum requirements of the job opportunity.

Some people have questioned whether tying pay and advancement to seniority is effective or even fair. For example, a top-performing, recently hired employee with educational qualifications that exceed the requirements of a desired job may become frustrated when he/she is not even selected for an interview because many employees with greater seniority applied. However, union leaders view the seniority clause as the means to ensure fairness in how employees are rewarded in an organization.

In a survey of Canadian organizations, consulting firm Watson Wyatt found that one of the top five reasons that employees quit their jobs is dissatisfaction with promotional opportunities.

Source: Virginia Galt, "Stress, Not Money, Main Cause of Turnover," *The Globe and Mail,* December 15, 2007, p. B10.

Questions

1. Why do you think unions have traditionally favoured a system of linking pay and advancement to seniority? Who benefits? Why do you think management might favour a system of linking pay and advancement to performance? Who benefits?

2. What employee rights does seniority-based pay fulfill? What standards for ethical behaviour does it meet? (See Chapter 1 to review a description of employee rights and ethical standards.)

3. What employee rights does a performance-based pay and promotion system fulfill? What standards for ethical behaviour does it meet?

SUMMARY

LO1 Define unions and labour relations and their role in organizations.

A union is an organization formed for the purpose of representing its members in resolving conflicts with employers. Labour relations is the management specialty emphasizing skills that managers and union leaders can use to minimize costly forms of conflict and to seek win-win solutions to disagreements.

In Canada, union membership has declined marginally from a peak in 1994. Unionization is associated with more generous compensation and higher productivity but lower profits. Unions may reduce a business's flexibility and economic performance.

LO2 Identify the labour relations goals of management, labour unions, and society.

Management goals are to increase the organization's profits and/or productivity. Managers generally expect that unions will make these goals harder to achieve. Unions have the goal of obtaining pay and working conditions that satisfy their members. Society's values have included the hope that the existence of unions will replace conflict or violence between workers and employers with fruitful negotiation.

LO3 Summarize laws and regulations that affect labour relations.

Laws and regulations affect the degree to which management, unions, and society achieve their varied goals. Canada's overall labour relations legal framework is decentralized with responsibility for labour relations shared among the federal, provincial, and territorial governments.

A common core of labour legislation exists that includes prohibiting unfair labour practices by management and labour. Labour Relations Boards or similar quasi-judicial tribunals exist within each jurisdiction to administer and enforce labour laws.

LO4 Describe the union organizing process.

Organizing begins when union representatives contact employees and invite them to sign a membership application. When the required numbers of employees have signed membership applications, the union will apply to their appropriate Labour Relations Board for certification. Requirements for certification differ among federal, provincial, and territorial jurisdictions.

LO5 Explain how management and unions negotiate collective agreements.

Negotiations take place between representatives of the union and the management bargaining unit. The process begins with preparation, including research into the other side's strengths and demands. The union presents its demands, and management sometimes presents demands as well. Then the sides evaluate the demands and the likelihood of a strike.

In the final stages, pressure for an agreement increases, and a neutral third party may be called on to help reach a resolution. If bargaining breaks down, the impasse may be broken with a strike, lockout, mediation, conciliation, or arbitration.

LO6 Summarize the practice of collective agreement administration.

Collective agreement administration is a daily activity under the collective agreement. It includes carrying out the terms of the agreement and resolving conflicts over interpretation or violation of the agreement.

Conflicts are resolved through a grievance procedure that begins with an employee talking to his or her supervisor about the problem and possibly involving the union steward. If this does not resolve the conflict, the union files a written grievance and union and management representatives meet to discuss the problem. If this effort fails, the union appeals the grievance to top management and ultimately the use of an arbitrator may be required for final resolution.

LO7 Describe more cooperative approaches to labour–management relations.

In contrast to the traditional view that labour and management are adversaries, some organizations and unions work more cooperatively. Cooperation may feature employee involvement in decision making, self-managing employee teams, joint labour–management committees, broadly defined jobs, and sharing of financial gains and business information with employees. Cooperative labour relations seem to contribute to an organization's success.

Critical Thinking Questions

1. Why do employees join unions? Did you ever belong to a union? If you did, do you think union membership benefited you? If you did not, do you think a union would have benefited you? Why or why not?

2. Why do managers at most companies prefer that unions not represent their employees? Can unions provide benefits to an employer? Explain.

3. Can highly effective human resource management practices make unions unnecessary? Explain.

4. How has union membership in Canada changed over the past few decades? How does union membership in Canada compare with union membership in other countries? How might these patterns in union membership affect the HR decisions of an international company?

5. What legal responsibilities do employers have regarding unions? What are the legal requirements affecting unions?

6. "Management gets the kind of union it deserves." Discuss.

7. If the parties negotiating a collective agreement are unable to reach a settlement, what actions can resolve the situation?

8. Why are most negotiations settled without a strike or lockout? Under what conditions might management choose to accept a strike?

9. What are the usual steps in a grievance procedure? What are the advantages of resolving a grievance in the first step? What skills would a supervisor need so grievances can be resolved in the first step?

10. The "HR Best Practices" box in this chapter gives examples of innovative negotiated provisions in collective agreements. What interests of workers and management may be met by each of these provisions?

Experiencing HR

Divide into groups of six students each. List your names in order of your birthdates (month and day). The first half of the students on the list will be the management team in this exercise, and the second half of the students will be the union team. (If the class size results in a group with an odd number of members, the last person on the list in that group can choose which team to join.)

Imagine that you work for a manufacturing company whose machinists belong to a union. As international competition for your products has increased, management is concerned that it needs to reduce costs and is considering changes to employees' benefits such as insurance and pension plans. Management has been proud of what it sees as the company's history of innovation and a positive working environment. The union has been proud of what it sees as its role in promoting fair and safe working conditions, as well as job opportunities that have built a strong community. The machinists' collective agreement is set to expire next year, so management and union representatives have agreed to meet and begin discussing the issue of costs of employee benefits.

Spend five minutes in your separate teams deciding what positions you want to take. Then spend 15 minutes together, trying to find a way forward that takes into account the interests of labour and management. After this discussion, work independently to write your own assessment: Do you think your company and union can arrive at an agreement that is fair to both sides? Why or why not?

CASE STUDY 9.1:

Walmart Reacts to Unionization

2005: Walmart Canada (www.walmart.ca) dealt a decisive blow to union forces, announcing it would shut down the first Walmart store to successfully certify in North America in almost a decade. "We honestly were hoping we could avoid this—it's a sad day for us," Walmart spokesperson Andrew Pelletier said of the decision to shutter the four-year-old outlet in Jonquière, Quebec, which the retailer says was losing money. "Despite nine days of meeting with the union over more than a three-month period, we have been unsuccessful in reaching an agreement that would allow the store to operate efficiently and, ultimately, profitably."

"We're all in shock," said one employee reached the next day at the Jonquière store. Michael Fraser, the United Food and Commercial Workers Union president, was not available for comment. The store's 190 workers will be offered "generous" severance packages and career counselling," Mr. Pelletier said.

While the big-box giant had never before closed a store in this country for economic reasons, the news did not come as a surprise. The announcement of the closure of the Jonquière store was the latest event in a longstanding fight between the world's biggest retailer and unions determined to organize the corporation's workers throughout North America. Walmart insists it does not promote an anti-union agenda. "We bargained in good faith," Mr. Pelletier said.

However, union organizers and some industry analysts say otherwise. "Walmart, like a lot of other companies with a nonunionized workforce, is scared to death of unions," said David Abella, an analyst at New-York based Rochdale Investment Management. Even if they could manage that store with the union, it could lead to a domino effect across Canada and the United States. The UFCW scored a minor victory recently when a Saskatchewan appeal overturned a decision barring the province's labour board from accessing internal Walmart documents, among them one titled "Walmart: A Manager's Tool Box to Remaining Union-Free." Jonquière's certification was viewed as a big win for the UFCW, one that has not been realized since 1996, when the Ontario Labour Relations Board unionized a Walmart in Windsor, Ontario. The store was later decertified after a high-profile campaign by anti-union employees, which included allegations of union misconduct.

"Shutting down the Jonquière store for any reason is completely legal," said Anil Verna, a professor of industrial relations at the University of Toronto. "Any business can open or close as they see fit. Most of the time it is about whether the operations are profitable or not. In this case, the timing kind of looks suspicious, but not knowing the numbers for the store, it's difficult to make a conclusive inference that [unionization] had anything to do with it."

Source: Hollie Shaw, "Walmart Closes First Union Store in Quebec," *Financial Post*, February 10, 2005, pp. A1, A9. Material reprinted with permission of The National Post Company, a Can West Partnership.

What's Happened Since?

2008–2012: Walmart closed a tire-and-lube garage in Gatineau, Quebec (just across the river from Ottawa) after an arbitrator imposed the first-ever collective agreement on a Walmart operation in North America. The five mechanics and manager were offered jobs at other (non-unionized) Walmart locations. The approximately 150 workers at the Gatineau Walmart were also certified in 2008, however were unable to negotiate a collective agreement. In the summer of 2010, a collective agreement was also arbitrator-imposed, but just over one year later, employees at the Walmart Gatineau voted to decertify the union. "This follows an application made by our Hull associates earlier this year to decertify the union at their store," said Andrew Pelletier, Walmart's vice president of corporate affairs and sustainability. "Walmart respects the decision of our Hull associates. They have made their views clear in this matter." The United Food and Commercial Workers Canada union declined to comment.

2014–2015: In June 2014, Canada's top court ruled that Walmart violated Quebec Labour law when it closed the Jonquière store back in 2005. According to Derek Johnstone, Ontario's Regional Director for the UFCW, "there have been 24 different groups of Walmart workers across Canada since the company came here who have tried to join the UFCW. In every one of these cases, Walmart has done whatever it can to convince them otherwise." Not counting the Jonquière store, 3 other Walmart stores successfully unionized, however at all three, workers later voted for decertification of the union. "Currently, there are no unionized Walmart stories in Canada."

In early 2015, Walmart Canada announced plans to complete another 29 supercentre projects in the coming year. This expansion follows Target's closure in Canada and will bring Walmart Canada's store count to 396 by the end of January 2016.

Questions

1. Do you believe that Walmart is "anti-union"? Explain your response.

2. What impact could a unionized Walmart have on other unionized workers in Canada?

3. Would you be willing to pay more for products from a unionized Walmart? Explain.

Sources: The Canadian Press, " Walmart Canada Plans Major Expansion: $340 Million for 29 New Supercentres," *Huffington Post*, www.huffingtonpost.ca/2015/02/11/walmart-canada-expansion_n_6659430.html, February 11, 2015, retrieved April 13, 2015; Hollie Shaw, "Quebec Ruling Against Walmart Canada Closing Unionized Store Hollow Victory for Labour," *Financial Post*, June 27, 2014, http://business.financialpost.com/news/retail-marketing/Walmart-violated-quebecs-labour-code-by-closing-store-after-worker-unionization-attempt-court-rules, retrieved April 13, 2015; "Quebec Wal-Mart Workers Leave Union," *CBC News*, October 31, 2011, www.cbc.ca/news/canada/ottawa/story/2011/10/31/ottawa-gatineau-walmart-workers.html, retrieved May 24, 2012 and "Wal-Mart Closes Shop Where Union Contract Imposed," *CBC News*, October 16, 2008, www.cbc.ca/news/canada/ottawa/story/2008/10/16/walmart-garage.html, retrieved May 24, 2012.

CASE STUDY 9.2:

Class-Action Litigation—New Tool for Unions?

A Denny's (www.dennys.ca) case in B.C. may signal the beginning of a different union organizing strategy. On March 5, 2012, the Supreme Court of British Columbia certified a class action brought on behalf of temporary foreign workers recruited to work at a Denny's Restaurant franchise in Vancouver—*Domínguez v. Northland Properties Corp* (COB Denny's Restaurants).

The lawsuit alleged recruiting companies engaged by the Denny's franchisee charged agency fees contrary to the Employment Standards Act. It also claimed damages, aggravated damages, and punitive damages against the franchisee for breach of contract in failing to pay overtime and provide 40 hours of work per week as promised, as well as breach of fiduciary duty, a duty of good faith and fair dealing, and unjust enrichment. The decision is significant because it is one of very few class actions certified in B.C. arising in an employment context. Moreover, it may signal the beginning of a new organizing strategy by unions in difficult-to-organize sectors.

This case involved about 75 temporary foreign workers who were recruited from the Philippines to work at the franchisee's restaurant. A Labour Market Opinion had been obtained from Human Resources and Skills Development Canada (HRSDC) for each of the workers in essentially the same terms. Although the employment contracts differed somewhat, they were in a form similar to the HRSDC sample contract that provided for 40 hours of work per week, with overtime at time-and-one-half. Prior to the litigation, complaints had been made to the director of employment standards who had determined there was an overtime violation in the case of one worker and a violation of section 10 of the Employment Standards Act when the recruiting firms used by the franchisee charged a recruitment fee.

The court certified the action as a class action under the Class Proceedings Act because the causes of action alleged in the claim were common to the group. Even though there were some differences in the employment contracts, the court found there was sufficient commonality, in both the facts and causes of action, to make certification as a class action appropriate. The court further held that common issues of alleged systemic effects (failure to record hours worked) and a claim for an aggregate assessment of damages and punitive damages were appropriate for certification. The United Food and Commercial Workers union (UFCW) and National Union of Public and General Employees (NUPGE) have thrown their support behind this action, as seen on NUPGE's website: "(NUPGE) has signed a protocol with UFCW Canada to assist in organizing exploited groups of workers, such as migrates and employees of Walmart."

The Denny's case may be the first instance of unions using class-action litigation as an organizing strategy. In doing so, they have taken a page out of the playbook of unions in the United States that have, for years, used wage and hour claims, both in collective actions and class actions, to gain the support of non-union workers. Working with class-action plaintiffs' attorneys, unions in the U.S. have obtained multimillion-dollar settlements from employers anxious to avoid the significant cost of litigation and adverse publicity. By supporting the class-action suit, unions are able to generate support within groups of employees that would have difficulty advancing their claims individually.

The U.S. has had a long history with class-action employment litigation, with the courts now taking steps to tighten the requirements for certification. By contrast, the phenomenon of such litigation is relatively new in Canada and Denny's demonstrates our courts will take a liberal approach to certification. Plaintiffs' class-action attorneys in the U.S. stepped into the void left by unions unable to organize in the retail and service industries. Unions then saw the opportunity to use class-action litigation to garner worker support from those who would benefit by being a member of the class. The Denny's case indicates this strategy may be just beginning in B.C.

Questions

1. Do you think using class-action litigation is an effective organizing strategy for the UFCW?
2. What types of provisions typically found in collective agreements would likely be of highest priority for Denny's employees if they became unionized?
3. What advice would you give Denny's management if employees form a union at this franchise operation?

Source: Tom Roper, "Class-Action Litigation—New Tool for Unions?" *Canadian HR Reporter*, February 25, 2013, pp. 23–24.

CHAPTER 10

Managing Human Resources Globally

WHAT DO I NEED TO KNOW?

After reading this chapter, you should be able to:

LO1	Summarize how the growth in international business activity affects human resource management.
LO2	Identify the factors that most strongly influence HRM in international markets.
LO3	Discuss how differences among countries affect workforce planning at organizations with international operations.
LO4	Describe how companies select and train human resources in a global labour market.
LO5	Discuss challenges related to managing performance and rewarding employees globally.
LO6	Explain how employers prepare employees for international assignments and for their return home.

Iconic Canadian brand, Tim Hortons has its sights set on global expansion.

Tim Hortons Poised for Global Growth

Tim Hortons (www.timhortons.com) took the No.1 spot—again—on the annual survey of favourite Canadian brands conducted by New York-based Reputation Institute. In addition, Tims cracked the Top 10 list of Canadians' "favourite brands in the world"—a list that includes Apple (www.apple.com/ca), Disney (www.disney.com), and Nestlé (www.nestle.ca). Although Tims has 850 locations in the U.S., the brand has "had trouble gaining traction" and is making changes to adapt flavours, portion sizes, and recipes to the American consumer, rather than treat the U.S. as an extension of Canada. Tim Hortons also has locations in the United Arab Emirates (UAE) and Kuwait and "plans to expand its partnership in the Middle East to 120 multi-format restaurants in the UAE, Qatar, Bahrain, Kuwait and Oman over five years."

This global growth strategy has been energized with new ownership—in 2014, 3G Capital (www.3g-capital.com), a Brazil-based global investment company became the majority owner of Restaurant Brands International, a merger of Burger King (www.burgerking.ca) and Tim Hortons. According to Josh Kobza, Restaurant Brands International's head of finance, "the goal is to get the expansion ball rolling more quickly, and pursue the model 3G forged at Burger King of signing 'master' franchise agreements with domestic operators who have the local know-how to succeed." Burger King presently operates 13,000 restaurants globally. It is expected that Tim Hortons will soon be following Burger King's lead by opening franchises in China. Burger King presently operates hundreds of restaurants in China, and Starbucks (www.starbucks.ca) will soon have 2,000 locations, however, this nation of 1.3 billion still does not have access to the iconic double-double or the Tim Hortons French vanilla missed by Ontario-Jiangsu exchange student, Deng Yongning Nui, who is now back in China after studying for one year at the University of Waterloo (www.uwaterloo.ca). "One more thing that I want to mention is that the coffee and doughnuts of Tim Hortons are amazing. I miss the Tom Hortons French vanilla so much now."[1]

Introduction

This chapter discusses the HR issues that organizations must address in a world of global competition. We begin by describing how the global nature of business is affecting human resource management in organizations. Next, we identify how global differences among countries affect organizations' decisions about human resources. In the following sections we explore workforce planning, selection, training, and reward practices in international settings. Finally, we examine guidelines for managing employees on international assignments.

LO1 Summarize how the growth in international business activity affects human resource management.

HRM in a Global Environment

HRC 1, 2

The environment in which organizations operate is rapidly becoming a global one. More and more companies are entering international markets by exporting their products, building facilities in other countries, and entering into alliances with foreign companies. At the same time, companies based in other countries are investing in setting up operations in Canada. Indeed, most organizations now function in the global economy. The HRM function needs to continuously reexamine its role in supporting this expanding pace of business globalization. This requires HRM to:

- Align HRM processes and functions with global requirements.

- Adopt a *global mindset* including a thorough understanding of the global environment and the impact on managing people worldwide.

- Enhance its own capabilities and competencies to become a business partner in acting on global business opportunities.[2]

What is behind the trend toward expansion into global markets? Foreign countries can provide a business with new markets in which there are millions or billions of new customers; developing countries often provide such markets, but developed countries do so as well. In addition, companies set up operations overseas because they can operate with lower labour costs—for example, video game developers that pay $12,000 to $15,000 per month for North American employees can hire workers in India at monthly pay scales in the range of $4,000 to $5,000.[3]

As discussed in Chapter 1, outsourcing jobs to lower-cost nations will continue to increase. For example, countries such as the "BRICs" (Brazil, Russia, India, and China) have been particularly attractive, because they have offered both low-cost labour and fast-growing economies. Recently, Russia's economy has been threatened in part due to sanctions imposed by Canada and many other countries driven by the crisis in Ukraine.[4]

Finally, thanks to advances in telecommunications and information technology, companies can more easily spread work around the globe, wherever they find the right mix of labour costs and abilities. Teams with members in different time zones can keep projects moving around the clock, or projects can be assigned according to regions with particular areas of expertise. Once organizations have taken advantage of these opportunities, they sometimes find themselves locked into overseas arrangements. In the consumer electronics industry, for example, so much of the manufacturing has shifted to China and other low-wage countries that North American companies no longer would have suppliers nearby if they tried to build a factory in the United States or Canada.[5]

Global activities are simplified and encouraged by trade agreements among nations; for example, most countries in Western Europe belong to the European Union (EU) and share a common currency, the euro. Canada, Mexico, and the United States have encouraged trade among themselves with the North American Free Trade Agreement (NAFTA) and more recently, Canada and Korea established the "Canada-Korea Free Trade Agreement" (CKFTA).[6] The World Trade Organization (WTO) resolves trade disputes among more than 100 participating nations.

As these trends and arrangements encourage international trade, they increase and change the demands on human resource management. Organizations with customers or suppliers in other countries need employees who understand those customers or suppliers. Organizations that operate facilities in foreign countries need to understand the laws and customs that apply to employees in those countries. They may have to prepare managers and other employees to take international assignments. They have to adapt their human resource plans and policies to different settings. Even if some practices are the same worldwide, the company now has to communicate them to its international workforce. A variety of international activities require managers to understand HRM principles and practices prevalent in global markets.

Vancouver-based Lululemon (www.lululemon.com), designer and seller of yoga and fitness-inspired apparel, continues its aggressive plans for global growth. Lululemon currently has stores in Canada, the United States, the U.K., Australia, and New Zealand and plans to open approximately 20 stores in both Europe and Asia by the end of 2017.[7]

To meet these complex and challenging requirements of global mobility, the Canadian Employee Relocation Council (CERC, www.cerc.ca) recently introduced the Canadian Global Mobility Professional (CGMP) designation. "Global mobility is one the fastest growing areas in HR," says Charlene Kiszazak, global mobility process improvement specialist at Calgary-based Talisman Energy. The new program consists of three levels of study and each level has its own specific designation. In level three, the focus is on international relocation policy development and program administration.[8]

Employees in an International Workforce

HRC1

When organizations operate globally, their employees are very likely to be citizens of more than one country. Employees may come from the employer's home country, a host country, or a third country. The **home country** is the country in which the organization's headquarters is located. For example, Canada is the home country of Fairmont Hotels & Resorts (www.fairmont.com), because Fairmont's

home country
The country in which an organization's headquarters is located.

headquarters are in Toronto. A Fairmont employee who is a Canadian citizen and works at Fairmont's headquarters or one of its Canadian properties is therefore a *home-country national.*

A **host country** is a country (other than the home country) in which an organization operates a facility. Barbados is a host country of Fairmont because Fairmont has operations there. Any Barbadian workers hired to work at Fairmont's Barbados property would be *host-country nationals,* that is, employees who are citizens of the host country.

host country
A country (other than the home country) in which an organization operates a facility.

A **third country** refers to a country that is neither the home country nor the host country. (The organization may or may not have a facility in the third country.) In the example of Fairmont's operations in Barbados, the company could hire an Australian manager to work there. The Australian manager would be a *third-country national,* because the manager is neither from the home country (Canada) nor from the host country (Barbados).

third country
A country that is neither the home country nor the host country of an employer.

When organizations operate globally, they need to decide whether to hire home-country nationals, host-country nationals, or third-country nationals for the overseas operations. Usually, they hire a combination of these. In general, employees who take assignments in other countries are called *expatriates.* In the Fairmont example, the Canadian and Australian managers working in Barbados would be expatriates during those assignments.

The extent to which organizations use home-country, host-country, or third-country nationals varies. Until recently, Western companies tended to use home-country nationals to manage operations in China, where employers found a shortage of management skills. Today, however, those skills are more widely available, and at multinational companies, three-fourths of senior executives are now host country nationals. Employers prefer these leaders because they understand the culture of their customers, governments, and business partners. Competition is stiffest for hiring Asian managers who lived in the host country but were educated in North America or Europe.[9]

Employers in the Global Marketplace

Just as there are different ways for employees to participate in international business—as home-country, host-country, or third-county nationals—so there are different ways for employers to do business globally, ranging from simply shipping products to customers in other countries to transforming the organization into a truly global one, with operations, employees, and customers in many countries. Figure 10.1 shows the major levels of global participation.

Most organizations begin by serving customers and clients within a domestic marketplace. Typically, a company's founder has an idea for serving a local, regional, or national market. The business must recruit, hire, train, and compensate employees to produce the product, and these people usually come from the business owner's local labour market. Selection and training focus on employees' technical abilities and, to some extent, on interpersonal skills. Pay levels reflect local labour conditions. If the product succeeds, the company might expand operations to other domestic locations, and HRM decisions become more complex as the organization draws from a larger labour market and needs systems for training and engaging employees in several locations. As the employer's workforce grows, it is also likely to become more diverse. Even in small domestic organizations, a significant share of workers may be immigrants. In this way, even domestic companies are affected by issues related to the global economy.

FIGURE 10.1

Levels of Global Participation

As organizations grow, they often begin to meet demand from customers in other countries. The usual way that a company begins to enter foreign markets is by *exporting*, or shipping domestically produced items to other countries to be sold there. For example, Loewen (www.loewen.com), the Steinbach, Manitoba-based manufacturer of premium wood doors and windows, produces all of its products in its 587,000 square-foot plant in Steinbach but sells products to countries including the United States, Japan, and Mexico.[10] Eventually, it may become economically desirable to set up operations in one or more foreign countries. An organization that does so becomes an **international organization**. The decision to participate in international activities raises a host of HR issues, including the basic question of whether a particular location provides an environment where the organization can successfully acquire and manage human resources.

international organization
An organization that sets up one or a few facilities in one or a few foreign countries.

While international companies build one or a few facilities in another country, **multinational companies** expand on a broader scale. They build facilities in a number of different countries as a way to keep production and distribution costs to a minimum. In general, when organizations become multinationals, they move production facilities from relatively high-cost locations to lower-cost locations. The lower-cost locations may have lower average wage rates, or they may reduce distribution costs by being nearer to customers. The HRM challenges faced by a multinational company are similar but larger than those of an international organization, because more countries are involved. More than ever, the organization needs to hire people who can function in a variety of settings, give them necessary training, and provide flexible compensation systems that take into account the different pay rates, tax systems, and costs of living from one country to another.

multinational company
An organization that builds facilities in a number of different countries in an effort to minimize production and distribution costs.

At the highest level of involvement in the global marketplace are **global organizations**. These flexible organizations compete by offering top products tailored to segments of the market while keeping costs as low as possible. A global organization locates each facility based on the ability to effectively, efficiently,

global organizations
Organizations that choose to locate a facility based on the ability to effectively, efficiently, and flexibly produce a product or service, using cultural differences as an advantage.

and flexibly produce a product or service, using cultural differences as an advantage. Rather than treating differences in other countries as a challenge to overcome, a global organization treats different cultures as a source of competitive advantage. It may have multiple headquarters spread across the globe, so decisions are more decentralized. This type of organization needs HRM practices that encourage flexibility and are based on an in-depth knowledge of differences among countries. Global organizations must be able to recruit, develop, retain, and fully utilize employees who can get results across national boundaries.

 E-HRM

Inviting job hunters to virtual career fairs to reach workers anywhere in the world.

A global organization needs a **transnational HRM system**[11] that features decision making from a global perspective, managers from many countries, and ideas contributed by people from a variety of cultures. Decisions that are the outcome of a transnational HRM system balance uniformity (for fairness) with flexibility (to account for cultural and legal differences). This balance and the variety of perspectives should work together to improve the quality of decision making. The participants from various countries and cultures contribute ideas from a position of equality, rather than the home country's culture dominating

transnational HRM system
Type of HRM system that makes decisions from a global perspective, includes managers from many countries, and is based on ideas contributed by people representing a variety of cultures.

L○2 Identify the factors that most strongly influence HRM in international markets.

What Factors Affect HRM in International Markets?

HRC**3, 4, 7**

Whatever their level of global participation, organizations that operate in more than one country must recognize that the countries are not identical and differ in terms of many factors (see Figure 10.2):

- culture
- education and skill levels
- economic system
- political-legal system

Culture

By far the most important influence on international HRM is the culture of the country in which a facility is located. *Culture* is a community's set of shared assumptions about how the world works and what ideals are worth striving for.[12] Cultural influences may be expressed through customs, languages, religions, and so on.

In Taiwan, a country that is high in collectivism, co-workers consider themselves more as group members instead of individuals.

Culture is important to HRM for two reasons. First, it often determines the other three international influences. Culture can greatly affect a country's laws, because laws often are based on the culture's definitions of right and wrong. Culture also influences what people value, so it affects people's economic systems and efforts to invest in education.

Even more important for understanding human resource management, culture often determines the effectiveness of various HRM practices. Practices that are effective in Canada, for example, may fail or even backfire in a country with different beliefs and values.[13] Consider the six dimensions of culture that Geert Hofstede identified in his study of culture:[14]

1. *Individualism/collectivism* describes the strength of the relation between an individual and other individuals in the society. In cultures that are high in individualism, such as Canada, the United States, the Netherlands, and Singapore, people tend to think and act as individuals rather than as members of a group. People in these countries are expected to stand on their own two feet, rather than be protected by the group. In cultures that are high in collectivism, such as China, Chile, and

FIGURE 10.2

Factors Affecting Human Resource Management in International Markets

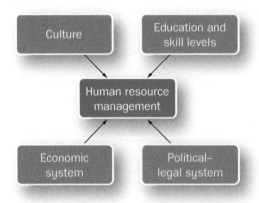

Bangledesh, people think of themselves mainly as group members. They are expected to devote themselves to the interests of the community, and the community is expected to protect them when they are in trouble.

2. *Power distance* concerns the way the culture deals with unequal distribution of power and defines the amount of inequality that is normal. In countries with large power distances, including India and the Philippines, the culture defines it as normal to maintain large differences in power. In countries with small power distances, such as Denmark and Israel, people try to eliminate inequalities. One way to see differences in power distance is in the way people talk to one another. In the high power distance country of Mexico, people address one another with a title (e.g., Señor Smith). At the other extreme, in Canada, in most situations people use one another's first names—behaviour that would be disrespectful in some other cultures.

3. *Uncertainty avoidance* describes how cultures handle the fact that the future is unpredictable. High uncertainty avoidance refers to a strong cultural preference for structured situations. In countries such as Greece and Portugal, people tend to rely heavily on religion, law, and technology to give them a degree of security and clear rules about how to behave. In countries with low uncertainty avoidance, including Singapore and Jamaica, people seem to take each day as it comes.

4. *Masculinity/femininity* is the emphasis a culture places on practices or qualities that have traditionally been considered masculine or feminine. A "masculine" culture is a culture that values achievement, money making, assertiveness, and competition. A "feminine" culture is one that places a high value on relationships, service, care for the weak, and preserving the environment. In this model, Germany and Japan are examples of masculine cultures, and Sweden and Norway are examples of feminine cultures.

5. *Long-term/short-term orientation* suggests whether the focus of cultural values is on the future (long term) or the past and present (short term). Cultures with a long-term orientation value saving and persistence—which tend to pay off in the future. Many Asian countries, including Japan and China, have a long-term orientation. Short-term orientations, as in the cultures of Canada, the United States, and Nigeria, promote respect for past tradition, and for fulfilling social obligations in the present.

6. *Indulgence/restraint* describes whether the culture encourages satisfying or suppressing gratification of human drives. A culture with an indulgent orientation encourages having fun and enjoying life. Restraint-orientation cultures use strict social norms to suppress gratification. In this dimension, Australia, Canada, and the United States have cultures characterized as indulgent, whereas, India and China promote restraint.

Such cultural characteristics as these influence the ways members of an organization behave toward one another, as well as their attitudes toward various HRM practices. For instance, cultures differ strongly in their opinions about how managers should lead, how decisions should be handled, and what motivates employees. In Germany, managers achieve their status by demonstrating technical skills, and employees look to managers to assign tasks and resolve technical problems. In the Netherlands, managers focus on seeking agreement, exchanging views, and balancing the interests of the people affected by a decision.[15] Clearly, differences like these would affect how an organization selects and trains its managers and measures their performance.

Cultures strongly influence the appropriateness of HRM practices. For example, the extent to which a culture is individualistic or collectivist will affect the success of a total rewards. Compensation tied to individual performance may be seen as fairer and more motivating by members of an individualistic culture; a culture favouring individualism will be more accepting of great differences in pay between the organization's highest- and lowest-paid employees. Collectivist cultures tend to have much flatter pay structures.

The success of HRM decisions related to job design, benefits, performance management, and other systems related to employee motivation also will be shaped by culture. In an interesting study comparing call centre workers in India (a collectivist culture) and the United States (an individualistic culture), researchers found that in the United States, employee turnover depended more on person-job fit than on person-organization fit. In the United States, employees were less likely to quit if they felt that they had the right skills, resources, and personality to succeed on the job. In India, what mattered more was for employees to feel they fit in well with the organization and were well connected to the organization and the community.[16]

Despite cultural differences, the factors that engage workers are relatively similar across cultures. Table 10.1 provides a look at what engages employees in four countries. Finally, cultural differences can affect how people communicate and how they coordinate their activities. In collectivist cultures, people tend to value group decision making, as in the previous example. When a person raised in an individualistic culture works closely with people from a collectivist culture, communication problems and conflicts often occur. People from the collectivist culture tend to collaborate heavily and may evaluate the individualistic person as unwilling to cooperate and share information with them. Cultural differences in communication affected the way an agricultural company embarked on employee involvement at its facilities in North America and Brazil.[17] Employee involvement requires information sharing, but in Brazil, high power

TABLE 10.1

What Keeps Foreign Workers Engaged

United States	China
• Confidence they can achieve career objectives	• Sense of personal accomplishment
• Sense of personal accomplishment	• Fair pay, given performance
• Confidence organization will be successful	• Comparable benefits to industry
• Quality is a high priority	• Confidence in senior management
• Opportunity for growth and development	• IT systems support business needs
• Information and assistance to manage career	• Opportunities for training
United Kingdom	**Brazil**
• Sense of personal accomplishment	• Sense of personal accomplishment
• Confidence in senior management	• Confidence in senior management
• Opportunities for training	• Opportunities for training
• Fair pay, given performance	• Fair pay, given performance
• Good reputation for customer service	• Good reputation for customer service
• Regular feedback on performance	• Comparable benefits to industry

Source: Mercer HR Consulting, *Engaging Employees to Drive Global Business Success: Insight from Mercer's What's Working Research,* www.mercer.com/referencecontent .htm?idContent=1288115, retrieved September 14, 2008, quoted in Lesley Young, "Attracting, Keeping Employees Overseas," *Canadian HR Reporter,* April 7, 2008, www.hrreporter.com, retrieved May 26, 2008.

distance leads employees to expect managers to make decisions, so they do not desire information that is appropriately held by managers. Involving the Brazilian employees required engaging managers directly in giving and sharing information to show that this practice was in keeping with the traditional chain of command. Also, because uncertainty avoidance is another aspect of Brazilian culture, managers explained that greater information sharing would reduce uncertainty about their work. At the same time, greater collectivism in Brazil made employees comfortable with the day-to-day communication of teamwork. The individualistic North American employees needed to be sold more on this aspect of employee involvement.

Because of these challenges, organizations must prepare both managers and employees to recognize and handle cultural differences. They may recruit managers with knowledge of other cultures or provide training, as described later in the chapter. For expatriate assignments, organizations may need to conduct an extensive selection process to identify individuals who can adapt to new environments. At the same time, it is important to be wary of stereotypes and avoid exaggerating the importance of cultural differences. Recent research that examined Hofstede's model of cultural differences found that differences among organizations within a particular culture were sometimes larger than differences from country to country.[18] This finding suggests that it is important for an organization to match its HR practices to its values; individuals who share those values are likely to be interested in working for the organization.

HR Best Practices

Developing Talent in India

India represents a massive marketplace, and its businesses have been expanding at breakneck speed. Companies in the West are eager to hire Indian workers with computer skills and the ability to communicate in English. India's educational system is trying to keep pace with the demand; in engineering alone, 770,000 new graduates join the workforce each year.

As companies try to keep up with the demand for employees, they are finding that many of these new graduates are not really prepared to work. By one estimate, only about one-fourth of new engineering graduates have all the skills they need to handle an engineering job, and another one-fourth can do so with training. The others will have to fill less-skilled positions.

Infosys (www.infosys.com), a $6 billion provider of outsourced services, tackles the challenge with extensive training. The company aggressively recruits the best candidates from universities and then sends them to an eight-month training program. Infosys is not alone; research into Indian management practices found that India's leading businesses are deeply committed to employee development. Top executives named talent development, not cost cutting, as their company's highest priority for human resource management. In information technology, companies provide new hires with an average of 60 days of formal training. Even in industries with low-skill jobs, companies invest in training. At call centres, for example, new employees receive about 30 days of training. In contrast, the Conference Board of Canada recently reported that Canadian companies provide an average of 13 *hours* of training annually to employees in non-technical jobs.

In visits to India to explore the commitment to training, university researchers learned how Indian companies are making a talented workforce out of inconsistently educated professionals. These employers are treating their training programs as an essential driver of success. They have studied the Western companies that outsourced functions to India, and they selected and improved management and training practices that would be relevant. They started with basic skills and employee orientation then moved on to create management development programs. The companies built training centres and hired trainers—sometimes hundreds of them. Infosys operates its Global Education Centre in the city of Mysore; the centre has the capacity to train 13,500 employees in technical, communications, and management skills.

Sources: Colin Hall, "Learning and Development Outlook 2014," *Conference Board of Canada,* p. 23; Raju Gopalakrishnan, "Bangalore Software Industry Trying to Avoid an Ironic Fate," *Chicago Tribune,* April 17, 2012, sec. 2, p. 3; Peter Cappelli, "India's Management Mind-Set," *HR Magazine,* August 2011, pp. 59—62; Vivek Wadhwa, "Why America Needs to Start Educating Its Workforce Again," *TechCrunch,* March 27, 2010, http://techcrunch.com.

Education and Skill Levels

Countries also differ in the degree to which their labour markets include people with education and skills of value to employers. As discussed in Chapter 1, Canada suffers from a shortage of skilled workers in many occupations, and the problem is expected to increase. On the other hand, the labour markets in many countries are very attractive because they offer high skills and low wages.

Educational opportunities also vary from one country to another. In general, spending on education is greater per student in high-income countries than in poorer countries.[19] Poverty, diseases such as ebola and AIDS, and political turmoil keep children away from school in some areas. A concerted international effort to provide universal access to primary education has dramatically reduced the number and proportion of children without access to schooling, especially in South Asia. However, the problem persists in sub-Saharan Africa.[20] The "BRICs and Emerging Economies Rankings 2015" provides a *Top 100* ranking of higher education institutions in the BRICs and countries classified as "emerging economies." China dominates the list with more than one-quarter of the top 100, including top ranked, Peking University and #2 ranked, Tsinghua University. Taiwan is the next most dominant in the rankings with 19 institutions in the top 100; India has 11; and Russia has 7 (including #5 ranked Loonosov Moscow State University), up from only 2 universities in 2014, and Turkey has 3 of the top 10 ranked institutions.[21]

Companies with foreign operations locate in countries where they can find suitable employees. The education and skill levels of a country's labour force affect how and the extent to which companies want to operate there. In countries with a poorly educated population, companies will limit their activities to low-skill, low-wage jobs. In contrast, India's large pool of well-trained technical workers is one reason the country has become a popular location for outsourcing computer programming jobs. But even there, companies are finding they need to invest heavily in training and development, as described in the nearby "HR Best Practices" box.

Economic System

A country's economic system whether capitalist or socialist, as well as the government's involvement in the economy through taxes or compensation, price controls, and other activities, influences human resource management practices in a number of ways.

As with all aspects of a region's or country's life, the economic system and culture are likely to be closely tied, providing many of the incentives or disincentives for developing the value of the labour force. Socialist economic systems provide ample opportunities for educational development because the education system is free to students. At the same time, socialism may not provide economic rewards (higher pay) for increasing one's education. In capitalist systems, students bear more of the cost of their education, but employers reward those who invest in education.

The health of an economic system affects human resource management. In developed countries with great wealth, labour costs are relatively high. Such differences show up in compensation systems and in recruiting and selection decisions.

In general, socialist systems take a higher percentage of each worker's income as the worker's income increases. Capitalist systems tend to let workers keep more of their earnings. In this way, socialism redistributes wealth from high earners to the poor, while capitalism apparently rewards individual accomplishments. In any case, since the amount of take-home pay a worker receives after taxes may thus differ from country to country, in an organization that pays two employees in two countries $100,000 each, the employee in one country might take home more than the employee in the other country. Such differences make pay structures more complicated when they cross national boundaries, and they can affect recruiting of candidates from more than one country.

Political-Legal System

A country's political-legal system—its government, laws, and regulations—strongly impinges on human resource management. The country's laws often dictate the requirements for certain HRM practices, such as training, compensation, selection, and labour relations. As we noted in the discussion of culture, the political-legal system arises to a large degree from the culture in which it exists, so laws and regulations reflect cultural values.

For example, Canada has been a leader in eliminating discrimination in the workplace. Because the value of diversity is important in Canadian culture, legal safeguards such as human rights laws discussed in Chapter 2 exist, which affect hiring and other HRM decisions. As a society, Canada also has strong beliefs regarding the fairness of pay systems. Thus, pay equity legislation (discussed in Chapter 2), provides for equal pay for work of equal value. Other laws and regulations dictate much of the process of negotiation between unions and management. All these are examples of laws and regulations that affect the practice of HRM in Canada. When Canadian companies employ workers in other countries, the workers are usually covered by the employment laws in their own countries. Employment laws in many countries offer workers less protection than Canadian legislation provides.

Similarly, laws and regulations in other countries reflect the norms of their cultures. In Western Europe, where many countries have had strong socialist parties, some laws have been aimed at protecting the rights and benefits of workers. The European Union has agreed that employers in member nations must respect certain rights of workers, including workplace health and safety; equal opportunities for men and women; protection against discrimination based on sex, race, religion, age, disability, and sexual orientation; and labour laws that set standards for work hours and other conditions of work. Concerning work hours, the EU expects employers in member nations to schedule no more than 48 hours of work each week, 11 hours of rest in each 24-hour period, at least one day off each week, and at least four weeks of paid vacation each year, subject to the nation's practices and laws.[22]

Students at the University of Warsaw in Poland are provided with a government-supported education. In general, former Soviet countries tend to be generous in funding education, so they tend to have highly educated and skilled labour forces. Countries such as Canada and the United States generally leave higher education up to individual students to pay for, but the labour market rewards students who earn a college diploma or university degree.

An organization that expands internationally must gain expertise in the host country's legal requirements and ways of dealing with its legal system, often leading organizations to engage an international relocation consulting firm or hire one or more host-country nationals to help in the process. Some countries have laws requiring that a certain percentage of the employees of any foreign-owned subsidiary be host-country nationals, and in the context of our discussion here, this legal challenge to an organization's HRM may hold an advantage if handled creatively.

LO3 Discuss how differences among countries affect workforce planning at organizations with international operations.

Workforce Planning in a Global Economy
HRC4

As economic and technological change creates a global environment for organizations, workforce planning is involved in decisions about participating as an exporter or as an international, multinational, or global company. Even purely domestic companies may draw talent from the international labour market. For example, officials from Saskatchewan's five health regions and the provincial health recruitment agency actively recruited and hired hundreds of registered nurses from the Philippines to help cope with identified shortages of nurses in the province.[23] As organizations consider decisions about their level of international activity, HR professionals should provide information about the relevant human resource issues, such as local market pay rates and labour laws. When organizations decide to operate internationally or globally, workforce planning involves decisions about where and how many employees are needed for each international facility.

Decisions about where to locate include HR considerations such as the cost and availability of qualified workers. In addition, HR specialists need to work with other members of the organization to weigh these considerations against financial and operational requirements. As discussed earlier, India and China have been popular locations because of low labour costs. But as the job creation has driven up living standards and demand for labour, it has driven up the price of labour in those countries. Cost-oriented call centres are looking to locations such as the Philippines and Eastern Europe. In response, Indian contractors have started up companies that offer more specialized skills, such as engineering, biotechnology, and computer animation. In China, where pay for factory workers has risen 69 percent over the past few years, the main advantage of continuing to operate there may become the greater buying power of the Chinese consumer.[24]

Other location decisions involve outsourcing, described in Chapter 1. Many companies have boosted efficiency by arranging to have specific functions performed by outside contractors. Many—but not all—of these arrangements involve workers outside North America in lower-wage countries.

In Chapter 3, we saw that workforce planning includes decisions to hire and lay off workers to prepare for the organization's expected needs. Compared with other countries, Canada allows employers wide latitude in reducing their workforce, giving Canadian employers the option of hiring for peak needs, then laying off employees if needs decline. Other governments put more emphasis on protecting workers' jobs. European countries, and France in particular, tend to be very strict in this regard.

Canadian Global
Mobility Professional

Developed in partnership with Centennial College, the Canadian Employee Relocation Council recently introduced a program leading to the Canadian Global Mobility Professional designation. This level of certification provides knowledge and tools needed to handle the complexities of global mobility issues including environmental assessment, policy development, financial management, immigration, compensation, and repatriation.

L○4 Describe how companies select and train human resources in a global labour market.

Selecting Employees in a Global Labour Market

Many companies such as Fairmont have headquarters in Canada plus operations around the world. To be effective, employees in Fairmont's Mexico operations need to understand that region's business and social culture. Organizations often meet this need by hiring host-country nationals to fill most of their foreign positions. A key reason is that a host-country national can more easily understand the values and customs of the local workforce than someone from another part of the world can. Also, training for and transporting families to foreign assignments is more expensive than hiring people in the foreign country. Employees may be reluctant to take a foreign assignment because of the difficulty of relocating internationally. Sometimes the move requires the employee's partner to quit a job, and some countries will not allow the employee's partner to seek work, even if jobs might be available.

Even so, organizations fill many key foreign positions with home-country employees. Sometimes a person's technical and human relations skills outweigh the advantages of hiring locally.

In other situations, Canada's local labour market simply does not offer enough qualified people to fill available jobs in Canada. At organizations located where needed skills are in short supply, hiring immigrant employees may be part of an effective recruitment and selection strategy.[25] Canada's *Temporary Foreign Worker Program (TFWP)*, permits Canadian employers to "hire foreign nationals to fill temporary labour and skill shortages when qualified Canadian citizens or permanent residents are not available."[26] Workers are classified as "higher-skilled," e.g., registered nurse or "lower-skilled," e.g., housekeeper. Some industries and operations have come to rely heavily on foreign temporary workers—for example, 75 of 157 employees at North Nova Seafoods (www.nnseafoods.ca) in Nova Scotia were temporary foreign workers in 2014, however, due to recent changes to the program, temporary foreign workers can now only represent 30 percent of a company's workforce, leading to concerns there may not be enough capacity to process the catch.[27]

Whether the organization is hiring immigrants or selecting home-country or third-country nationals for international assignments, some basic principles of selection apply. Selection of employees for international assignments should reflect criteria that have been associated with success in working globally:

● Competency in the employee's area of expertise.

● Ability to communicate verbally and nonverbally in the foreign country.

● Flexibility, tolerance of ambiguity, and sensitivity to cultural differences.

● Motivation to succeed and enjoyment of challenges.

● Willingness to learn about the foreign country's culture, language, and customs.

● Support from family members.[28]

Respondents to the Global Mobility Policy & Practice: 2014 survey, listed "*inability of the family to adjust* (61 percent) as the number-two reason assignments fail. It is eclipsed only by *changing business conditions* (63 percent) as a reason for assignment failure. The importance of family is reinforced by the fact that 76 percent of respondents rated *family or personal circumstances* as the number one reason why employees turn down assignments."[29]

Providing "trailing partner" career transition services may make the difference whether or not an international assignment will be accepted. Personality may also be important. Research has found successful completion of international assignments to be most likely among employees who are extroverted (outgoing), agreeable (cooperative and tolerant), and conscientious (dependable and achievement-oriented).[30]

Qualities of flexibility, motivation, agreeableness, and conscientiousness are so important because of the challenges involved in entering another culture. The emotions that accompany an international assignment tend to follow a cycle like that in Figure 10.3.[31] For a month or so after arriving, the foreign worker enjoys a "honeymoon" of fascination and euphoria as the employee enjoys the novelty of the new culture and compares its interesting similarities to or differences from the employee's own culture. Before long, the employee's mood declines as he or she notices more unpleasant differences and experiences feelings of isolation, criticism, stereotyping, and even hostility. As the mood reaches bottom, the employee is experiencing **culture shock**, the disillusionment and discomfort that occur during the process of adjusting to a new culture and its norms, values, and perspectives. Eventually, if employees persist and continue learning about their host country's culture, they develop a greater understanding and a support network. As the

culture shock
Disillusionment and discomfort that occur during the process of adjusting to a new culture.

Qualities associated with success in foreign assignments are the ability to communicate in the foreign country, flexibility, enjoying a challenging situation, and support from family members. What would persuade you to take a global assignment?

FIGURE 10.3

Emotional Stages Associated with a Foreign Assignment

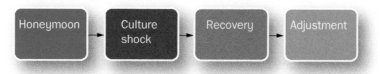

Source: Adapted from Delia Flanja, "Culture Shock in Intercultural Communication," *Studia Europaea* (October 2009), Business & Company Resource Center, http://galenet.galegroup.com.

employee's language skills and comfort increase, the employee's mood should improve as well. Eventually, the employee reaches a stage of adjustment in which he or she accepts and enjoys the host country's culture.

Employers often have difficulty persuading candidates to accept foreign assignments. Not only do the employee and employee's family have to contend with culture shock, but the employee's partner commonly loses a job when an employee makes an international move. Some organizations solve this problem with a compromise: the use of **virtual expatriates**, or employees who manage an operation abroad without locating permanently in that country.[32] They take frequent trips to the foreign country, and when they are home, they use technologies such as videoconferencing and electronic collaboration tools to stay in touch. An assignment as a virtual expatriate may be less inconvenient to family members and less costly to the employer. The arrangement, sometimes referred to as a *commuter assignment* does have disadvantages. Most notably, by limiting personal contact to sporadic trips, the virtual expatriate will likely have a harder time building relationships. Short-term assignments are also growing in popularity. According to a study involving more than 200 multinational organizations, 100 percent of these North American companies reported using short-term assignments.[33] The assignments generally last six to 12 months, and help companies react in a more nimble way to global opportunities. Often these assignments involve a specific project.[34] As illustrated in Figure 10.4, the percentage of family members who said they were "always allowed" to relocate the globally assigned employees was down by 14 percentage points from 2012 to 2014.

virtual expatriates
Employees who manage an operation abroad without permanently locating in the country.

Selection practices widely accepted in Canada may pose challenges for Canadian employers who are hiring host country or third-country nationals. For example, background checking is widely accepted in many parts of Europe and Australia, and has recently become more accepted as a best practice in India. However, in Japan and the United States, cultural and legal differences influence how the request will be perceived and what information is accessible.[35]

Training and Developing a Global Workforce

HRC7

In an organization whose employees come from more than one country, some special challenges arise with regard to training and development:

1. Training and development programs should be effective for all participating employees, regardless of their country of origin;

2. When organizations hire employees to work in a foreign country or transfer them to another country, the employer needs to provide training in how to handle the challenges of working in the foreign country.

FIGURE 10.4

Families Less Likely to be "Always Allowed" to Relocate for Global Assignments

Source: "Global Mobility Policy & Practice: 2014 Survey Executive Summary Report," p. 5, http://guidance.cartusrelocation.com/rs/cartus/images/2014_Global_Mobility_Policy_Practices_Survey_Exec_Summary.pdf, retrieved April 19, 2015.

Training Programs for an International Workforce

Developers of effective training programs for an international workforce must ask certain questions.[36] The first is to establish the objectives for the training and its content. Decisions about the training should support those objectives. The developers should next ask what training techniques, strategies, and media to use. Some will be more effective than others, depending on the learners' language and culture, as well as the content of the training. For example, in preparation for training, Canadian employees might expect to discuss and ask questions about the training content, whereas employees from other cultures might consider this level of participation to be disrespectful, so for them some additional support might be called for. Language differences will require translations and perhaps an interpreter at training activities. Next, the developers should identify any other interventions and conditions that must be in place for the training to meet its objectives. For example, training is more likely to meet its objectives if it is linked to performance management and has the full support of management. Finally, the developers of a training program should identify who in the organization should be involved in reviewing and approving the training program.

The plan for the training program must consider international differences among trainees. For example, economic and educational differences might influence employees' access to and ability to access web-based training. Cultural differences may influence whether they will consider it appropriate to ask questions and whether they expect the trainer to spend time becoming acquainted with employees or to get down to business immediately. Table 10.2 provides examples of how cultural characteristics can affect training design.

Cross-Cultural Preparation

When an organization selects an employee for a position in a foreign country, it must prepare the employee for the foreign assignment. This kind of training is called **cross-cultural preparation**, preparing employees to work across national and cultural boundaries, and it often includes family members

cross-cultural preparation
Training to prepare employees and their family members for an assignment in a foreign country.

Effects of Culture on Training Design

Cultural Dimension	Impact on Training
Individualism	Culture high in individualism expects participation in exercises and questioning to be determined by status in the company or culture.
Uncertainty avoidance	Culture high in uncertainty avoidance expects formal instructional environments. Less tolerance for more casual facilitative style.
Masculinity	Culture low in masculinity values relationships with fellow trainees. Female trainers less likely to be resisted in low-masculinity cultures.
Power distance	Culture high in power distance expects trainer to be expert. Trainers expected to be an authority and in careful control of session.
Time orientation	Culture with a long-term orientation will have trainees who are likely to accept development plans and assignments.

Source: Based on B. Filipczak, "Think Locally, Act Globally," *Training*, January 1997, pp. 41–48.

who will accompany the employee on the assignment. The training is necessary for all three phases of an international assignment:

1. Preparation for *departure*—language instruction and an orientation to the foreign country's culture.

2. The *assignment* itself—some combination of a formal program and mentoring relationship to provide ongoing further information about the foreign country's culture.

3. Preparation for the *return* home—providing information about the employee's community and home-country workplace (from company newsletters, local newspapers, and so on).

Methods for providing this training may range from lectures for employees and their families to visits to culturally diverse communities.[37] Employees and their families may also spend time visiting a local family from the country where they will be working. In many organizations, cross-cultural training is mandatory. In the later section on managing expatriates, we provide more detail about such preparation. Canadian-based companies sometimes need to be reminded that foreign-born employees who come to Canada—need cross-cultural preparation as much as Canadian employees sent on foreign assignments.[38] In spite of the many benefits of living in Canada, relocation can be challenging. As with expatriates, organizations can prepare foreign-born employees by providing information about getting the resources they need to live and work safely and comfortably in their new surroundings. For example, when Maple Leaf Foods (www.mapleleaffoods.com) hired 40 new foreign workers form El Salvador and Honduras for their operations in Brandon, Manitoba, employees' needs were actively considered to help make an effective transition to Canada. Morgan Curran-Blaney, plant manager, described the process to help the new recruits. "We have . . . basic living training, so living in Canada, this is what you can expect. We help them set up bank accounts here in town; we give them sort of a welcome package, the necessities that you would need to start out in Canada." Maple Leaf also arranges housing including furnishing the houses and apartments.[39]

Global Employee Development

At global organizations, international assignments are a part of many career paths. The organization benefits most if it applies the principles of employee development in deciding which employees should be offered jobs in other countries. Career development helps employees make the transitions to and from their assignments and helps the organization apply the knowledge the employees obtain from these assignments.

LO5   Discuss challenges related to managing performance and rewarding employees globally.

Performance Management Across National Boundaries

HRC4

The general principles of performance management may apply in most countries, but the specific methods that work in one country may not work well in another. Therefore, organizations have to consider legal requirements, local business practices, and national cultures when they establish performance management methods in other countries. Differences may include which behaviours are rated, how and the extent to which performance is measured, who performs the rating, and how feedback is provided.[40]

For example, National Rental Car (www.nationalcar.ca) uses a behaviourally based rating scale for customer service representatives. To measure the extent to which customer service representatives' behaviours contribute to the company's goal of improving customer service, the scale measures behaviours such as smiling, making eye contact, greeting customers, and solving customer problems. Depending on the country, different behaviours may be appropriate. In Japan, culturally defined standards for polite behaviour include the angle of bowing as well as proper back alignment and eye contact. In Ghana and many other African nations, appropriate measures would include behaviours that reflect loyalty and repaying of obligations as well as behaviours related to following regulations and procedures.

The extent to which managers measure performance may also vary from one country to another. In rapidly changing regions, such as Southeast Asia, the organization may have to update its performance plans more often than once a year.

Feedback is another area in which differences can occur. Employees around the world appreciate positive feedback, but Canadian employees are much more used to receiving direct feedback than are employees in other countries. In Mexico, managers are expected to provide positive feedback before focusing the discussion on behaviours the employee needs to improve.[41] At the Thai office of Singapore Airlines (www.singaporeair.com), managers resisted giving negative feedback to employees because they feared this would cause them to have bad karma, contributing to their reincarnation at a lower level in their next life.[42] The airlines therefore allowed the managers to adapt their feedback process to fit local cultures.

Compensating and Rewarding an International Workforce

HRC6

Chapter 8 explained that *total rewards* includes decisions about pay structure, incentive pay, employee benefits and services and even development and career opportunities and other characteristics of the work environment such as work/life balance. All these decisions become more complex when an organization has an international workforce. Johnson & Johnson (www.jnjcanada.com) meets the challenge by creating a global compensation strategy for its 250 pharmaceutical, consumer, and medical-device businesses with employees in 70 countries. J&J developed the strategy at its U.S. headquarters because compensation expertise at the company varied from one region to another. However, it had representatives from each region serve on the project teams so the company would be familiar with local issues, such as the need for frequent salary reviews in Venezuela and Argentina, where high inflation rates take a toll on buying power.[43]

Pay Structure

As Figure 10.5 shows, market pay structures can differ substantially across countries in terms of both pay level and the relative worth of jobs. For example, compared with the labour market in Germany, the market in Mexico provides much lower pay levels overall. In Germany, bus drivers average higher pay than kindergarten teachers, while the relative pay of teachers is greater in Mexico and South Korea. For all the types of jobs shown, the pay difference between jobs are much less dramatic in Germany than in the other two countries. In Brazil, for example, companies have trouble finding enough managers with technical expertise, because big construction projects and oil drilling are driving heavy demand for those positions. In addition, the fast-growing Brazilian economy has drawn many multinationals to locate facilities in Brazil, further increasing the demand for managers there. Finally, Brazilian managers tend to be loyal employees, so recruiters need to offer especially tempting compensation packages to lure them away.[44]

FIGURE 10.5

Earnings in Selected Occupations in Three Countries

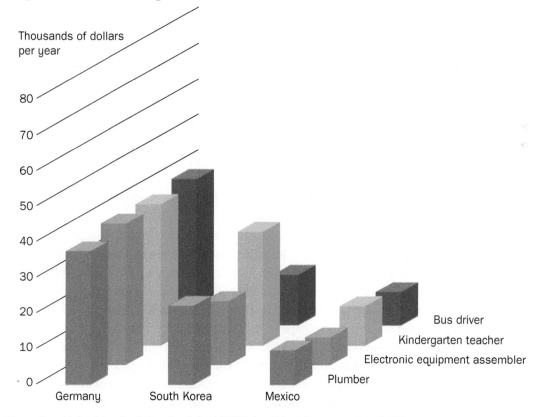

Source: Wage and hour data from International Labour Organization, LABORSTA, http://laborsta.ilo.org, accessed May 10, 2012.

Differences such as these create a dilemma for global companies: Should pay levels and differences reflect what workers are used to in their own countries? Or should they reflect the earnings of colleagues in the country of the facility, or earnings at the company headquarters? For example, should a German engineer posted to Mumbai be paid according to the standard in Germany or the standard in Mumbai? If the standard is Germany, the engineers in Mumbai will likely see the German engineer's pay as unfair. If the standard is Mumbai, the company will likely find it impossible to persuade a German engineer to take an assignment in Mumbai. Dilemmas such as these make a global compensation strategy important as a way to show employees that the pay structure is designed to be fair and related to the value that employees bring to the organization.

These decisions affect a company's costs and ability to compete. The average hourly labour costs in industrialized countries such as Canada, the United States, Germany, and Japan are far higher than these costs in newly industrialized countries such as Mexico, Brazil, and the Philippines.[45] As a result, we often hear that Canadian labour costs are too high to allow Canadian companies to compete effectively unless the companies shift operations to low-cost foreign subsidiaries. That conclusion oversimplifies the situation for many companies. Merely comparing wages ignores differences in education, skills, and productivity.[46] If an organization gets more or higher-quality output from a higher-wage workforce, the higher wages may be worth the cost. Besides this, if the organization has many positions requiring highly skilled workers, it may need to operate in (or hire immigrants from) a country with a strong educational system, regardless of labour costs. Finally, labour costs may be outweighed by other factors, such as transportation costs or access to resources or customers. When a production process is highly automated, differences in labour costs may not be significant.

Cultural and legal differences also can affect pay structure. Some countries, including Colombia, Greece, and Malaysia, require that companies provide salary increases to employees earning minimum wage. In Venezuela, employers must provide employees with a meal allowance. In Mexico and Puerto Rico, employers must pay holiday bonuses. Organizations with a global pay strategy must adjust the strategy to account for local requirements and determine how pay decisions for optional practices will affect their competitive standing in local labour markets.[47]

Incentive Pay

Besides setting a pay structure, the organization must make decisions with regard to incentive pay, such as bonuses and stock options. Although stock options became a common form of incentive pay in North America during the 1990s, European businesses did not begin to embrace this type of compensation until the end of that decade. However, Canada and Europe differ in the way they award stock options. European companies usually link the options to specific performance goals, such as the increase in a company's share price compared with that of its competitors.

Employers are adding incentives to compensate employees working in high-risk parts of the world. The list of global hot spots in the world is long—"Iraq, Somalia, Afghanistan, Sudan, Chad, and Lebanon are just a few of the countries where employees can encounter a myriad of problems including disease, a higher incidence of crime, civil unrest, and war."[48] A study conducted by Watson Wyatt, found that many companies are offering added incentives to reward staff for working in high-risk areas.[49] For example, a "major U.S. engineering and construction company with federal contracts to rebuild Iraq compensates for the hazardous duty by offering each typical $130,000-a-year expatriate an extra $75,000 tax-free a year in foreign service, hardship, and danger allowance."[50] Oil and gas companies, have adopted a "total security" approach to keep employees safe from harm that includes keeping employees "informed and isolated from the general population and surrounding them with security when they venture beyond their secure, well-protected enclaves. This approach is effective—and expensive."[51]

Employee Benefits and Services

As in Canada, compensation packages in other countries include benefits and services. Decisions about benefits and services must take into account the laws of each country involved, as well as employees' expectations and values in those countries (see "HR How-To"). Some countries require paid parental leave, and some countries, in addition to Canada, have nationalized health care systems, which would affect the value of private health insurance in a reward package. Availability of partner relocation assistance is a differentiator

HR How-To

Tailoring Benefits to an International Workforce

As we saw in Chapter 8, to be motivating, employee benefits need to be valued. Therefore, organizations may need to tailor their benefits to the differences in values that may occur in one location or another.

One way to achieve this is to think of the organization's worldwide employees as a highly diverse workforce and offer flexible benefits. Informa (www.informacanada.com) is a media company with employees in 40 countries. Its benefits package is shaped by the needs of each group of employees. In the U.K., for example, the employees are relatively young, so pension plans are hard for many of those employees to appreciate. So the company offers a set of short-term, medium-term, and long-term savings plans for employees to choose from. It increases their value by providing financial education to help employees appreciate the value of saving when they are young and when compound interest will have the greatest impact on their eventual wealth. Benefits choices such as these are communicated on the company website, in total-reward statements, and in a booklet sent to employees' homes.

Companies can balance the focus on diversity with savings from pooling their purchases on a global scale. This can enable benefits budgets to deliver the greatest value. Businesses such as MetLife (www.metlife.com) and Zurich Employee Benefits Network (www.zurich.com) serve many countries and can set up insurance and other financial benefits that meet local governments' requirements. Life and health insurance plans may be priced more attractively if the employer purchases them from one company for all its employees worldwide.

Sources: MetLife, "Multination: Solutions for a Global Workforce," http://metlife.com, accessed May 11, 2012; MAXIS Global Benefits Network, "Employee Benefits Solutions for Multinational Companies," www.maxisnetowrk.com, accessed May 11, 2012; "Multinational Pooling," *Employee Benefits*, March 2012, Business & Company Resource Center, http://galenet.galegroup.com; "Informed Choice," *Employee Benefits*, December 2011, Business & Company Resource Center, http://galenet.galegroup.com; Steve Minter, "Respect Underpins Success of Mexican Plant," *Industry Week*, September 2011, p. 14.

A large number of journalists found shelter in the old building of the French nongovernmental organization in Afghanistan. Taking an overseas assignment, especially in a harsh or potentially dangerous climate, requires the challenge of adjusting to life in a new country, so many companies pay employees higher salaries to compensate for this hardship.

for many organizations in attracting employees to global assignments. For example, some organizations provide the "trailing partner" with educational and career assistance. Pension plans are more widespread in parts of Western Europe than in Canada, the United States, or Japan. Over 90 percent of workers in Switzerland have pension plans, as do all workers in France. Among workers with pension plans, Canadian workers are significantly less likely to have defined benefit plans than workers in Japan or Germany.

Paid vacation, also discussed in Chapter 8, tends to be more generous in Western Europe than in North America. Figure 10.6 compares the number of hours the average employee works in various countries. Of these countries, workers in Mexico, Chile, the United States, and Japan States put in more hours than Canadian workers. In the other countries, the norm is to work fewer hours than a Canadian worker over the course of a year.

International Labour Relations

HRC**5**

Companies that operate across national boundaries will increasingly need to work with unions in more than one country. Organizations establish policies and goals for labour relations, overseeing labour agreements, and monitoring labour performance (e.g., output and productivity).[52] The day-to-day decisions

FIGURE 10.6

Average Hours Worked in Selected Countries

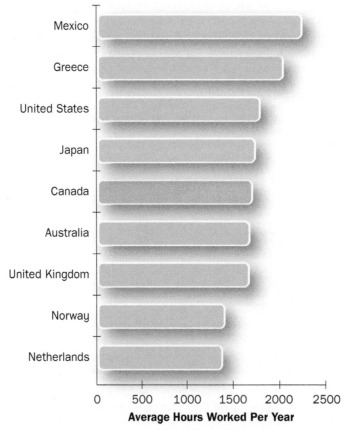

Source: Organisation for Economic Co-operation and Development, "Average Annual Hours Actually Worked per Worker," OECD StatExtracts, http://stats.oecd.org, accessed April 20, 2015.

about labour relations are usually handled by each foreign subsidiary. The reason is that labour relations on an international scale involve differences in laws, attitudes, and economic systems, as well as differences in negotiation styles.

At least in comparison with European organizations, North American organizations exert more centralized control over labour relations in the various countries where they operate. Management therefore must recognize differences in how various countries understand and regulate employees.[53] Legal differences range from who may form a union to how much latitude an organization is allowed in laying off workers. General Motors, in trying to pare back its Opel operations in Europe, ran into union requirements that forbade plant closings. In an effort to demonstrate that the union workers were not expected to make all the sacrifices, GM eliminated bonuses for salaried workers, but the gesture was poorly received in the relatively labour-friendly environment of Europe.[54] In some situations, governments get involved to protect workers who immigrate to other countries. Many workers from Indonesia and the Philippines, for example, travel to the Middle East to find work and have complained about poor working conditions. The Philippines negotiated an agreement with Saudi Arabia setting minimum pay, and the Indonesian government negotiated with Malaysia to protect the rights of Indonesian maids, including the right to hold their own passports.[55]

International labour relations must also take into account that negotiations between labour and management take place in a different social context, not just different economic and legal contexts. Cultural differences that affect other interactions come into play in labor negotiations as well. Negotiators will approach the process differently depending on whether the culture views the process as primarily cooperative or competitive and whether it is local practice to negotiate a deal by starting with the specifics or agreeing on overall principles.[56] Working with host-country nationals can help organizations navigate such differences in negotiation style.

Managing Expatriates

At some point, most international and global organizations assign employees to foreign posts. According to Statistics Canada, there are "about 68,000 Canadians working abroad at any given time and, with more companies active in the global marketplace, this number is expected to increase."[57] In addition, "North American companies are relying on more women to pursue international business opportunities—about four times as many as in 2001."[58] These assignments give rise to significant human resource challenges, from selecting employees for these assignments to preparing them, compensating them, helping them adjust, remain safe, providing support, and preparing for return home. The same kinds of HRM principles that apply to domestic positions can help organizations avoid mistakes in managing expatriates: planning and goal setting, selection aimed at achieving the HR goals, and performance management that includes evaluation of whether the overseas assignment delivered value relative to the costs involved.[59] See what category of mistakes you think triggered the problem described in the "HR Oops!" box.

Selecting Expatriates

The challenge of managing expatriates begins with determining which individuals in the organization are most capable of handling an assignment in another country. Expatriates need technical competence in the area of operations, in part to help them earn the respect of employees. Of course, many other skills are also necessary for success in any new job, especially one that involves working overseas. Depending on the nature of the assignment and the culture where it is located, the organization should consider each candidate's skills, learning style, and approach to problem solving. Each of these should be related to

HR Oops!

How to Recruit a Public Outcry

British Prime Minister David Cameron learned the hard way that sometimes only a local candidate will do. The British police had been rocked by scandal and scathing criticism. The department had responded ineffectively to rioting in London in the summer of 2011, and the police department was mixed up in the scandal in which News Corporation reporters arranged to hack into the phones of public figures. Looking for someone to lead an overhaul of the police department, Cameron looked across the Atlantic and saw someone with major accomplishments: Bill Bratton.

Bratton headed the police departments in Boston, Los Angeles, and New York City. His accomplishments included leading those organizations as they restored morale and reduced crime in each city. Based on those successes, Cameron believed Bratton could help the department rein in gang violence and soothe racially based tensions as commissioner of the London Metropolitan Police. So praising Bratton's experience and knowledge, he invited the retired commissioner, now a security consultant, to come work for the British government.

Bratton was intrigued by the offer, but the British public was appalled, as were the British police unions. One detective was quoted calling the choice "a sad indictment of what the government thinks of our senior officers in this country." Britain's Home Secretary pointed out that the London police commissioner is also responsible for national security and there should be a British citizen in the position. Prime Minister Cameron opted to work with Bratton as a consultant instead.

Questions

1. Should recruiting always aim to find the person whose talents and experience are the best match for a position, or should some jobs be reserved for locals? Why?

2. How could Prime Minister Cameron have avoided the embarrassment of reversing his recruiting decision while considering the best options to fill the commissioner's position?

Sources: Kroll, "William J. Bratton," www.kroll.com, accessed May 11, 2012; "When Talent Stops at the Border," *Bloomberg Businessweek*, August 29, 2011, EBSCOhost, http://web.ebscohost.com; Alyssa Newcomb, "Bill Bratton: 'I Never Close Any Door Before It's Opened,'" *ABC News*, August 13, 2011, http://abcnews.go.com; Janet Stobart, "Bratton as Advisor Doesn't Sit Well with Some British Police," *Los Angeles Times*, August 14, 2011, http://articles.latimes.com.

achievement of the organization's goals, such as solving a particular problem, transferring knowledge to host-country employees, or developing future leaders for the organization.[60]

A successful expatriate must have a high level of *cross-cultural competence*—be sensitive to the host country's cultural norms, flexible enough to adapt to those norms, and strong enough to survive the culture shock of living in another culture. In addition, if the expatriate has a family, the family members must be able to adapt to a new culture. Adaptation requires three kinds of skills:[61]

1. Ability to maintain a positive self-image and feeling of well-being.

2. Ability to foster relationships with the host-country nationals.

3. Ability to perceive and evaluate the host country's environment accurately.

In a study that drew on the experience of people holding international assignments, expatriates told researchers that the most important qualities for an expatriate are, in order of importance, family situation, flexibility and adaptability, job knowledge and motivation, relational skills, and openness to other cultures.[62] To assess candidates' ability to adapt to a new environment, interviews should address topics such as the ones listed in Table 10.3. The interviewer should be certain to give candidates a clear and complete preview of the assignment and the host-country culture. This helps the candidate evaluate the assignment and consider it in terms of his or her family situation, so the employer does not violate the employee's privacy.[63]

L○6 Explain how employers prepare employees for international assignments and for their return home.

Preparing Expatriates

Once the organization has selected an employee for an overseas assignment, it is necessary to prepare that person through training and development. Because expatriate success depends so much on the entire family's adjustment, the employee's partner should be included in the preparation activities. Employees selected for expatriate assignments already have job-related skills, so preparation for expatriate assignments often focuses on cross-cultural training—that is, training in what to expect from the host country's culture. The general purpose of cross-cultural training is to create an appreciation of the host country's culture so expatriates can behave appropriately.[64] Paradoxically, this requires developing a greater awareness of one's own culture, so that the expatriate can recognize differences and similarities between the cultures and, perhaps, home-culture biases.

On a more specific level, cross-cultural training for foreign assignments includes the details of how to behave in business settings in another country—the ways people behave in meetings, how employees expect managers to treat them, and so on. As an example, Germans value promptness for meetings to a much greater extent than do Latin Americans—and so on. How should one behave when first meeting one's business counterparts in another culture? The "outgoing" personality style so valued in North America may seem quite rude in other parts of the world.[65]

Employees preparing for a foreign assignment also need information about such practical matters as housing, schools, recreation, shopping, and health care facilities in the country where they will be living. This is a crucial part of the preparation.

Communication in another country often requires a determined attempt to learn a new language. Some employers try to select employees who speak the language of the host country, and a few provide language training. Most companies assume that employees in the host country will be able to speak the host country's language. Even if this is true, host country nationals are not necessarily fluent in the home country's language, so language barriers often remain. This is true even when employees move to a country that nominally speaks the same language. For example, a Canadian employee working in England might be surprised to discover that when a project suddenly goes awry, it has "hit the buffers," while if it is proceeding smoothly, it is "on cam." And a client who says, "Give me a bell," isn't requesting an unusual sort of gift, but rather a phone call.[66]

Along with cross-cultural training, preparation of the expatriate should include career development activities. Before leaving for a foreign assignment, expatriates should discuss with their managers how the foreign assignment fits into their career plans and what types of positions they can expect upon their return. This prepares the expatriate to develop valuable skills during the overseas assignment and eases the return home when the assignment is complete.

When the employee leaves for the assignment, the preparation process should continue. Expatriate colleagues, coaches, and mentors can help the employee learn to navigate challenges as they arise. For example, workers in a new culture sometimes experience internal conflict when the culture where they are working expects them to behave in a way that conflicts with values they learned from their own culture. For example, an Italian manager had difficulty motivating the workforce in India because the employees were used to authoritarian leadership, and the manager felt as if that style was harsh and disempowering. By talking over the problem with experienced expatriates, the manager came to understand why the situation was so awkward and frustrating. He identified specific ways in which he could be more assertive without losing his temper, so that his employees in India would better understand what was expected of them. Practising a new style of leadership became more satisfying as the manager realized that the employees valued his style and that he was becoming a more capable cross-cultural leader.[67]

TABLE 10.3

Topics for Assessing Candidates for Global Assignments

Motivation

- Investigate reasons and degree of interest in wanting to be considered.
- Determine desire to work abroad, verified by previous concerns such as personal travel, language training, reading, and association with foreign employees or students.
- Determine whether the candidate has a realistic understanding of what working and living abroad requires.
- Determine the basic attitudes of the spouse/partner toward an overseas assignment.

Health

- Determine whether any medical problems of the candidate might be critical to the success of the assignment.
- Determine whether the candidate is in good physical and mental health.

Language Ability

- Determine potential for learning a new language.
- Determine any previous language(s) studied or oral ability (judge against language needed on the overseas assignment).
- Determine the ability of the spouse/partner to meet the language requirements.

Resourcefulness and Initiative

- Can the candidate make and stand by decisions and judgments?
- Does the candidate have the intellectual capacity to deal with several dimensions simultaneously?
- Is the candidate able to reach objectives and produce results with whatever people and facilities are available, regardless of the limitations and barriers that might arise?
- Is the candidate able to operate without a clear definition of responsibility and authority on a foreign assignment?
- Will the candidate be able to explain the aims and company philosophy to the local managers and workers?
- Does the candidate possess sufficient self-discipline and self-confidence to overcome difficulties or handle complex problems?
- Can the candidate work without supervision?
- Can the candidate operate effectively in a foreign environment without normal communications and supporting services?

Adaptability

- Is the candidate sensitive to others, open to the opinions of others, cooperative, and able to compromise?
- What are the candidate's reactions to new situations, and efforts to understand and appreciate differences?
- Is the candidate culturally sensitive, aware, and able to relate across the culture?
- Does the candidate understand his or her own culturally derived values?
- How does the candidate react to criticism?
- What is the candidate's understanding of the government system?

- Will the candidate be able to make and develop contacts with peers in the foreign country?

- Does the candidate have patience when dealing with problems?

- Is the candidate resilient; can he or she bounce back after setbacks?

Career Planning

- Does the candidate consider the assignment more than a temporary overseas trip?

- Is the move consistent with the candidate's career goals and aspirations?

- Is the employee's career planning realistic?

- What is the candidate's basic attitude toward the company?

- Is there any history or indication of interpersonal problems with this employee?

Financial

- Are there any current financial and/or legal considerations that might affect the assignment?

- Are financial considerations negative factors? Will undue pressures be brought to bear on the employee as a result of the assignment?

Source: Excerpted with permission pages 55–57, *"Multinational People Management: A Guide for Organizations and Employees,"* by David M. Noer. Copyright © 1975 by the Bureau of National Affairs, Inc., Washington, DC, 20037. Published by the Bureau of National Affairs, Inc. Washington, DC 20037. For copies of BNA Books publications call toll free 1-800-960-1220.

Managing Expatriates' Performance

HRC 4

Performance management of expatriates requires clear goals for the international assignment and frequent evaluation of whether the expatriate employee is on track to meet those goals. Communication technology including email, teleconferencing, and video conferencing provide a variety of ways for expats' managers to keep in touch with these employees to discuss and diagnose issues before they can interfere with performance. In addition, before employees leave for a global assignment, HR should work with managers to develop criteria for measuring the success of the assignment.[68] Measures such as productivity should take into account any local factors that could make expected performance different in the host country than in the company's home country. For example, a country's labour laws or the reliability of the electrical supply could affect the facility's output and efficiency.

Compensating and Rewarding Expatriates

HRC 6

One of the greatest challenges of managing expatriates is determining the compensation package. Most organizations use a *balance sheet approach* to determine the total amount of the package. This approach adjusts the employee's compensation so that it gives the employee the same standard of living as in the home country plus extra pay for any hardships of locating globally. As is shown in Figure 10.7, the balance sheet approach begins by determining the purchasing power of compensation for the same type of

FIGURE 10.7

The Balance Sheet for Determining Expatriate Compensation

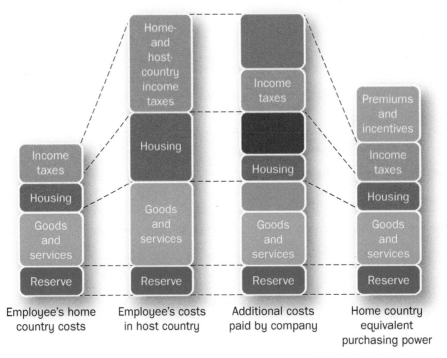

Employee's home country costs   Employee's costs in host country   Additional costs paid by company   Home country equivalent purchasing power

Source: C. Reynolds, "Compensation of Overseas Personnel," in J. J. Famularo, ed., *Handbook of Human Resource Administration,* 2nd ed. (New York: McGraw-Hill, 1986), p. 51. Reprinted with permission. Copyright © 1986 by The McGraw-Hill Companies.

job in the employee's own country—that is, how much a person can buy, after taxes, in terms of housing, goods and services, and a reserve for savings. Next, this amount is compared with the cost (in dollars, for a Canadian company) of these same expenses in the foreign country.

In Figure 10.7, the greater size of the second column means the costs for a similar standard of living in the foreign country are much higher in every category except the reserve amount. For the expatriate in this situation, the employer would pay the additional costs, as shown by the third column. Finally, the expatriate receives additional purchasing power from premiums and incentives. Because of these added incentives, the expatriate's purchasing power is more than what the employee could buy at home with the salary for an equivalent job. (Compare the fourth column with the first.) Expatriates sent to expensive destinations such as Singapore and Hong Kong can receive $200,000 a year in subsidies to cover the expenses of housing, transportation, and schools for their children—plus an additional $100,000 to cover the cost of taxes on these benefits. Adding in the costs to relocate the employee and his or her family can send the total bill for the assignment up to $1 million.[69] That high cost is one of the reasons employers are investing more in recruiting and training local talent. In addition, many companies are expecting their employees, particularly those on a "leadership track" to be mobile globally, so are examining their global rewards policies in the effort to contain costs.[70]

After setting the total pay, the organization divides this amount into the four components of a *total compensation* package:

1. *Base* salary—determining the base salary is complex because different countries use different currencies (dollars, yen, euros, and so on). The exchange rate—the rate at which one currency may be exchanged for another—constantly shifts in response to a host of economic forces, so the

Germany Tops Priciest Countries

According to report results from KMPG, Germany tops the list as the country with the highest business costs. Rankings are based on business costs with the highest cost country ranking 10 and the lowest cost country ranking 1.

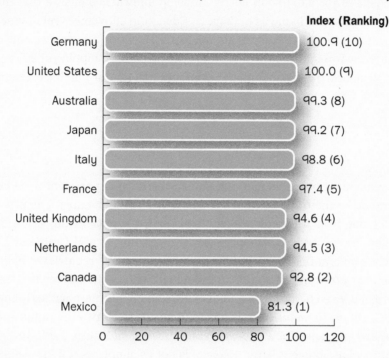

Index (Ranking)

Country	Index (Ranking)
Germany	100.9 (10)
United States	100.0 (9)
Australia	99.3 (8)
Japan	99.2 (7)
Italy	98.8 (6)
France	97.4 (5)
United Kingdom	94.6 (4)
Netherlands	94.5 (3)
Canada	92.8 (2)
Mexico	81.3 (1)

Sources: Based on "KPMG's Guide to International Location Costs 2012 Edition," Exhibit 2.I, p. 7; "Competitive Alternatives: KPMG's Guide to International Location Costs 2014 Edition," p. I2.

real value of a salary in terms of dollars is constantly changing. Also, as discussed earlier, the base salary may be comparable to the pay of other employees in the home country or comparable to other employees at the foreign subsidiary. Because many organizations pay a salary premium as an incentive to accept an overseas assignment, expatriates' salaries are often higher than pay for staying in the home country.

2. *Tax equalization allowance*—"Tax equalization holds that the worker neither gains nor loses with regards to tax liability as a result of an international assignment."[71] Countries have different systems for taxing income, and in some countries, tax rates are higher than in Canada. Usually, the employer of an expatriate withholds the amount of tax to be paid in the home country, then pays all of the taxes due in the country where the expatriate is working.

3. *Benefits and services*—Most of these issues have to do with whether an employee can use the same benefits in the foreign country. For example, if an expatriate has been contributing to a pension plan in Canada, does this person have a new pension plan in the foreign country? Or can the expatriate continue to contribute to the Canadian pension plan? Similarly, health benefits may involve receiving care at certain health facilities. While the person is abroad, does the same health plan cover services received in the foreign country? In one case, flying an employee back to Canada

for certain procedures actually would have cost less than having the procedures done in the country where the person was working. But the company's health plans did not permit this alternative. An employer may offer expatriates additional benefits to address the problem of uprooting a partner when assigning an employee overseas.

4. *Allowance to make a foreign assignment more attractive*—Cost of living allowances make up the differences in expenses for day-to-day needs. Housing allowances ensure that the expatriate can maintain the same standard of living as in Canada. Education allowances reimburse expatriates who pay tuition for their children to attend private schools. Relocation allowances cover the expenses of making the move to the foreign country, including transportation, shipping or storage of possessions, and expenses for temporary housing until the employee can rent or purchase a home.

Helping Expatriates Return and Minimizing Turnover

HRC 3

As the expatriate's assignment nears its end, the human resource department faces a final challenge: helping the expatriate make the transition back to his or her home country. The process of preparing expatriates to return home from a foreign assignment is called **repatriation**. According to a study by a partnership between PricewaterhouseCoopers (www.pwc.com/ca) and Cranfield University School of Management (www.som.cranfield.ac.uk) more than 25 percent of repatriated employees leave the company within one year after an international assignment ends.[72] Often, repatriation issues are discussed, at least informally, even before the candidate accepts an international assignment. The use of a well-written *international assignment letter* is a helpful means to clarify the rights and responsibilities of both the employer and employee for a relocation and subsequent return. Table 10.4 describes what to include in an international assignment letter. Reentry is not as simple as it might sound. Culture shock takes place in reverse. The experience has changed the expatriate, and the company's and expatriate's home culture may have changed as well. Also, because of differences in economies and compensation levels, a returning expatriate may experience a decline in living standards. The standard of living for an expatriate in many countries includes household help, a car and driver, private schools, and club memberships.

repatriation
The process of preparing expatriates to return home from a foreign assignment.

Companies are increasingly making efforts to help expatriates through this transition and take steps to ensure expatriates stay with the company after their return. Expatriates are more likely to stay with a company that provides them opportunities to use their international experience.[73] Two activities help the process along: *communication* and *validation*.[74] Communication refers to the expatriate receiving information and recognizing changes while abroad. The more the organization keeps in contact with the expatriate, the more effective and satisfied the person is likely to be upon return. The expatriate plays a role in this process as well. Expatriates should work at maintaining important contacts in the company and industry. Communication related to performance and career development before and during the international assignment also should help the employee return to a choice of positions that are challenging and interesting. Validation means giving the expatriate recognition for the international service when this person returns home. Expatriates who receive family repatriation support and recognition from colleagues and top managers for their international service and future contribution have fewer troubles with reentry than those whose contributions are disregarded. Validation should also include planning

TABLE 10.4

What to Include in an International Assignment Letter

Assignment	• Location
	• Duration of assignment
Remuneration	• Base salary
	• Incentives and benefits
	• Pension plans
	• Currency of payment
Tax Issues	• Tax equalization
	• Tax advice
	• Tax reporting
Host Country	• Housing
Relocation Program	• Home and automobile sale
	• Family allowances (if family doesn't relocate)
	• House hunting
	• Moving
	• Schooling
	• Elder care
	• Language training
	• Cultural acclimatization programs
Vacation and Home Leave	• Number of trips
	• Emergency and compassionate travel provisions
Repatriation	• Timing (e.g., to coincide with family needs such as school terms)
	• Employment opportunities upon the employee's return
	• Assignment debriefing
	• Financial counselling
	• Dealing with dismissal or resignation

Sources: Joyce Head, "How Paper Can Protect International Relocations," *Canadian HR Reporter,* March 13, 2006, p. 14; and Margaret Sim and Liam Dixon, "Unraveling Comp, Benefits for Expatriates," *Canadian HR Reporter,* December 3, 2007, p. 23.

for how the returning employee will contribute to the organization. What skills will this person bring back? What position will he or she fill? The new skills may be much more than knowledge of a particular culture. For example, the person may have learned how to lead or negotiate with a diverse group of people.[75]

Thinking ETHICALLY

A Sustainable Advantage

Most growing companies have to contend with stiff industry competition, cash-flow troubles, and difficulties opening new sales channels. Not many have to dodge landmines, operate in isolated third world locations, and train foreign workers who seriously distrust outsiders—all while introducing untested technology to industry skeptics.

Welcome to Frederick Davidson's everyday reality. The president and CEO of Vancouver-based contract mineral drilling company Energold Drilling Corp. (www.energold.com) has overcome all of these hurdles, to operate in 22 countries (most of them developing nations chosen for their high mineral-drilling potential and scarcity of direct competition) with a contingent of about 1,100 employees.

As Davidson explains, Energold's success came when it found a solution to a common drilling industry problem—the massive environmental damage left behind by rigs and crews. Five years after the company's launch, it shifted its focus from mineral exploration to contract drilling. While less risky, contract drilling remains highly competitive. Demand shifts constantly, rigs are difficult to relocate, and firms essentially rely on their own research to predict the next big market opportunity. To succeed, Energold would have to stand out. How? As is so often the case, inspiration came from an unexpected place: a remote mining site in the Dominican Republic.

To reach a proposed drilling location situated across a small town on the Caribbean island, Energold would have to drag a 10-ton drill across a river and farmers' fields, destroying the landscape in the process. Typical industry practice was for drilling companies simply to compensate farmers for the damaged land. Davidson felt there had to be a better way. "I thought, 'Exploration is a high-risk business and the likelihood of finding something is very nominal, so why desecrate the landscape?'" he recalls. Besides, sustainability was becoming a key plan in corporate social responsibility mandates being adopted by most major mining companies.

Davidson and his team started researching options for less cumbersome drilling technologies and processes that would do less damage to surrounding ecosystems. That's when one of Energold's geologists came forward and explained that he'd once used a smaller, lighter underground drilling rig that could be disassembled and carried to a drilling site on foot. Intrigued, Davidson investigated and learned that no other firms in his field were using the equipment to green their drilling practices. He approached the manufacturer of the component drills, Delta, B.C.-based Hydracore Drills Ltd., and in short order was able to strike a supply deal, albeit a non-exclusive one.

With that, Energold had a clear competitive advantage. By incorporating component drilling rigs into its business model, the firm could move into frontier locations that its rivals had long ignored to drill for minerals—safely, cheaply, and without damaging the often fragile social and environmental fabrics. And by training locals and paying them competitively, Energold provided income to poor communities. All this gave its customers, including mining giant Rio Tinto PLC, a valuable chance to twin the public relations battle on the corporate social responsibility front.

Energold's focus on frontier markets has meant contending with many challenges, one of the largest being oppressive or corrupt regulatory regimes in Third World nations. Never once, Davidson stresses, has Energold bribed an official to circumvent often obtuse local rules. "We don't pay people off," he says. "We've had occasion in which we've shipped a rig in and it has sat in customs for a year until [bribe-seeking officials] finally gave up and released it." Energold typically budgets about $200,000 per year to cover delays or equipment losses, yet Davidson is quick to point out that his firm has yet to lose a rig on-site or in transit. Energold also enlists on-the-ground expertise. In Mexico, for instance, the firm recruited skilled, multilingual locals to its on-site management teams to help overcome regulatory hurdles. Davidson says Energold's ethical stance appeals to sophisticated customers, even when they are very anxious to start drilling.

Source: Chris Atchison, "A Sustainable Advantage," *Canadian Business*, June 1, 2011, www.canadianbusiness.com/article/47511-a-sustainable-advantage, retrieved May 28, 2012. Chris Atchison is the founder of Shockwave Strategic Communications, a Toronto-based marketing-communications agency.

Questions

1. Can a company remain profitable over the long term when it adopts a higher ethical standard than exists in the countries in which it operates?

2. Suppose you work in the HR department of Energold. How can your department support the principles behind these ethics-based decisions?

3. How is HRM affected when a company such as Energold takes an ethics-based position to refuse to offer bribes despite this practice being accepted as standard business practice in some countries? Will it be easier or harder to find and keep talented people? Why?

SUMMARY

LO1 Summarize how the growth in international business activity affects human resource management.

More and more companies are entering international markets by exporting and operating foreign facilities. Organizations therefore need employees who understand customers and suppliers in other countries. They need to understand local laws and customs and be able to adapt their plans to local situations. To do this, organizations may hire a combination of home-country, host-country, and third-country nationals. They may operate on the scale of an exporter or an international, global, or multinational organization. A global organization needs a transnational HRM system, which makes decisions from a global perspective, includes employees from many countries, and is based on ideas contributed by people representing a variety of cultures.

LO2 Identify the factors that most strongly influence HRM in international markets.

By far the most important influence is the culture of each market—its set of shared assumptions about how the world works and what ideals are worth striving for. A culture has the dimensions of individualism/collectivism, high or low power distance, high or low uncertainty avoidance, masculinity/femininity, long-term or short-term orientation, and indulgence/restraint. Countries also differ in the degree to which their labour markets include people with education and skills of value to employers. Another influence on international HRM is the foreign country's political-legal system—its government, laws, and regulations. Finally, a country's economic system, capitalist or socialist, as well as the government's involvement in the country's economy, such as through taxes and price controls, is a strong factor determining HRM practices.

LO3 Discuss how differences among countries affect workforce planning at organizations with international operations.

As organizations consider decisions about their level of international activity, HR professionals should provide information about the relevant human resource issues. When organizations decide to operate internationally or globally, workforce planning involves decisions about where and how many employees are needed for each international facility. Some countries limit employers' ability to lay off workers, so organizations would be less likely to staff for peak periods. Other countries allow employers more flexibility in meeting human resource needs. HRM professionals need to be conversant with such differences.

L○4 Describe how companies select and train human resources in a global labour market.

Many organizations with international operations fill most positions with host-country nationals. These employees can more easily understand the values and customs of the local workforce, and hiring locally tends to be less expensive than moving employees to new locations. Organizations also fill foreign positions with home-country and third-country nationals who have human relations skills associated with success in international assignments. When sending employees on global assignment, organizations prepare the employees (and often their families) through cross-cultural training. During the assignment, there is communication with the home country and mentoring. For the return home the employer provides further training.

L○5 Discuss challenges related to managing performance and rewarding employees globally.

The general principles of performance management may apply in most countries, but the specific methods that work in one country may not work well in another. Pay structures can differ substantially among countries in terms of pay level and the relative worth of jobs. Organizations have to decide whether to set pay levels and differences in terms of what workers are used to in their own countries or in terms of what employees' colleagues earn at headquarters. Typically, companies have resolved this dilemma by linking pay and benefits more closely to those of the employee's home country, but this practice may be weakening so that it depends more on the nature and length of the global assignment.

These decisions affect the organization's costs and ability to compete, so organizations consider local labour costs in their location decisions. Along with the basic pay structure, organizations must make decisions regarding incentive pay, such as bonuses and stock options. Laws may dictate differences in benefit packages, and the value of benefits will differ if a country requires them or makes them a government service.

L○6 Explain how employers prepare employees for international assignments and for their return home.

When an organization has selected an employee for an international assignment, it must prepare the person for the experience. In cross-cultural training, the soon-to-be-expatriate learns about the foreign culture he or she is heading to, and studies her or his own home-country culture as well for insight. Preparation of the expatriate should also include career development activities to help the individual acquire valuable career skills during the international assignment and at the end of the assignment to handle repatriation successfully. Communication of changes at home and validation of a job well done abroad help the expatriate through the repatriation process.

Critical Thinking Questions

1. Identify the home country, host country(ies), and third country(ies) in the following example: A global soft-drink company called Cold Cola has headquarters in Halifax,

Nova Scotia. It operates production facilities in the United States, and in Jakarta, Indonesia. The company has assigned a manager from Moncton, New Brunswick, to head the U.S. facility and a manager from Hong Kong to manage the Jakarta facility.

2. What are some HRM challenges that arise when a Canadian company expands from domestic markets by exporting? When it changes from simply exporting to operating as an international company? When an international company becomes a global company?

3. In recent years, many North American companies have invested in Russia and sent Canadian managers there in an attempt to transplant North American-style management. According to Hofstede, Canadian culture has low power distance, moderate uncertainty avoidance, short-term orientation, high individualism, moderate masculinity, and high indulgence. Russia's culture has high power distance, high uncertainty avoidance, long-term orientation, low individualism, low masculinity, and low indulgence. In light of what you know about cultural differences, how well do you think Canadian managers can succeed using each of the following HRM practices? (Explain your reasons.)

   a. Selection decisions based on extensive assessment of individual abilities

   b. Appraisals based on individual performance

   c. Systems for gathering suggestions from workers

   d. Self-managing work teams

   e. Unlimited vacation time

4. Besides cultural differences, what other factors affect human resource management in an organization with international operations?

5. Suppose you work in the HR department of a company that is expanding into a country where the law and culture make it difficult to lay off employees. How should your knowledge of that requirement affect workforce planning for the overseas operations?

6. Why do multinational organizations hire host-country nationals to fill most of their foreign positions, rather than sending expatriates for most jobs?

7. What types of factors would you consider to be "hardships" in accepting a global assignment? What monetary premium or incentive would you expect to receive from your employer for each of the hardships identified?

8. For an organization with operations in three different countries, what are some advantages and disadvantages of setting compensation according to the labour markets in the countries where the employees live and work? What are some advantages and disadvantages of setting compensation according to the labour market in the company's headquarters? Would the best arrangement be different for the company's top executives and its production workers? Explain.

9. What abilities make a candidate more likely to succeed in an assignment as an expatriate? Which of these abilities do you have? How might a person acquire these abilities?

10. In the past, a large share of expatriate managers from Canada have returned home before successfully completing their international assignments. Suggest some possible reasons for the high "failure" rate. What can HR departments do to increase the success of expatriates?

Experiencing HR

Imagine that you work in the human resource department of a small but growing company that runs a chain of clothing stores. The top managers believe that by next year, the company will be able to get financing to expand overseas, where consumer demand is growing. They are researching whether the next step should involve opening a few stores in Brazil or in China. Other members of your company are investigating the marketing and financial aspects of the expansion. You have been asked to learn more about the human resources issues the company would face in each country.

Review this chapter and do some research online or in your library to identify HR issues that are likely to be important in each country. Write a one- or two-page summary of what you learned about each country, what your company should investigate further before moving into either country, and which of the two countries you would recommend from a human resources perspective.

Some good places to get started with basic information about the countries include *The World Factbook* (www.cia.gov/library/publications/the-world-factbook/); the *International Labor Comparisons: Country at a Glance* (www.bls.gov/fls/country.htm); and the topics and statistics pages of the International Labor Organization (www.ilo.org). You could also use an Internet search to look for links to information about each country's culture.

CASE STUDY 10.1:

"Designed by Apple In California—Assembled in China"

Although Apple built computers in the U.S. for most of its corporate history it has joined other electronics companies in moving its assembly lines to China to achieve the cost advantages of less expensive labour. In recent years, working conditions at these factories have come under intense scrutiny, particularly after at least ten workers committed suicide at factories owned by Foxconn (www.foxconn.com), the Taiwanese electronics manufacturer. Foxconn manufactures more than 40 percent of the world's electronics—the sheer scale and volume of its operations make it China's single biggest exporter. In addition to assembling iPhones, iPads, and other devices for Apple, Foxconn also manufactures products for many other companies including Dell (www.dell.ca), Hewlett-Packard (www.hp.com), and Intel (www.intel.ca).

In 2012, Apple became the first technology company to join the Fair Labor Association (FLA, www.fairlabor.org), a nonprofit global monitoring group. Timothy Cook, Apple's chief executive invited the FLA to conduct inspections of its suppliers' factories in China and elsewhere. Cook also personally visited one of the factories where Apple products are made. "Our team has been working for years to educate workers, improve conditions and make Apple's supply chain a model for the industry, which is why we asked the FLA to conduct these audits."

The Fair Labor Association conducted an audit of three large Chinese factories owned by Foxconn: Guanlan (assembles iPhones and iPods); Longhua (assembles iPads and Macs), and Chengdu (assembles iPads and components). The resulting audit criticized the long hours and dangerous working conditions—inspectors found at least 50 breaches of Chinese regulations as well as the code of conduct Apple signed when it joined the Fair Labor Association in

January 2012. Assessors found cases of employees working longer hours and more consecutive days than allowed by FLA standards and Chinese law. For example, FLA's audit found that the average weekly working hours were 56.1 hours per week (49.1 hours permitted by Chinese law); average maximum weekly hours was 61.1 hours, and longest consecutive period without a rest break was 11.6 days. The FLA auditors found no issues related to child or forced labour, according to the report—the average age of workers was 23 years. And it was reported that Foxconn employees received higher wages than required under Chinese law—starting at 1,800 yuan ($285) a month with the average pay reported as 2,687 yuan in one plant, 2,872 in another (the minimum set by government in China is 1,500 yuan). The FLA also interviewed more than 35,000 Foxconn employees—48 percent responded that how much they worked was "reasonable," 18 percent said "too long," and 34 percent "want to work more to earn more money." Although there was some variation among factories, 43 percent of workers overall said they had seen or experienced an accident at work and 65 percent said they felt pain after a full day of work.

Foxconn has agreed to bring hours in line with legal limits by July 2013 and compensate its more than 1.2 million employees for overtime lost due to the shorter workweek. "We are committed to work with Apple to carry out the remediation program, developed by both our companies," Foxconn said in an emailed statement. "Our success will be judged by future FLA audits and the monitoring of the implementation of the remediation program, by reviews carried out by Apple and other customers and by future employee surveys." Foxconn has also pledged that workers will not see a pay decline because of corresponding wage increases. "The eyes of the world are on them and there's just no way they can't deliver," FLA president Auret van Heerden says. "It's a real showstopper."

Questions

1. What effect do you think Apple's efforts to improve pay and working conditions for employees will have on other organizations that manufacture or assemble products in China?

2. What advice would you offer Apple's CEO and senior HR managers regarding their role in Foxconn's HR practices at its factories?

3. Would you be willing to pay more for Apple products assembled in factories with improved pay, safety, and working conditions for workers?

Sources: "Foxconn Technology," *The New York Times,* May 28, 2012, retrieved May 28, 2012; "Foxconn to Set Up $210 Million Apple Production Line in China," *The Economic Times,* May 21, 2012, retrieved May 28, 2012; Nick Wingfield, "Fixing Apple's Supply Lines," *The New York Times,* April 2, 2012; Stanley James, "Foxconn Auditor Finds 'Serious' Violations of Chinese Law," *BusinessWeek,* March 30, 2012; and "A List of Labor Concerns at Foxconn," *The New York Times,* March 29, 2012.

CASE STUDY 10.2:

Global Company IAMGOLD Strengthens Its Talent Acquisition Capabilities

Having most of your workers spread around the world can make recruitment even more challenging than usual. But one Toronto-based mining company simplified its efforts with help from a talent acquisition software provider. IAMGOLD (www.iamgold.com) is a mid-tier mining company with four operating gold mines (including current joint ventures) on three continents. It employs a team of more than 5,000 workers globally, primarily at operations in Canada, West Africa, and South America.

Prior to 2013, IAMGOLD managed candidates and recruitment processes manually, with local HR staff in various countries doing their best to facilitate the talent acquisition needs of their operation, and head office HR staff working primarily with search firms to fill expatriate positions. But in 2012, the company determined it needed to strengthen its talent acquisition capabilities globally and it established four business goals:

- Implement a standardized global talent acquisition framework to support talent policies, global mobility and enable real-time reporting. As a publicly held company, this was very important: Human resources had previously found it difficult to provide management with reporting on its efforts.

- Establish a strong global sourcing strategy that leverages multiple sources, including social media and commercial job boards, via a single platform.

- Develop a global talent database that enables sharing of talent information across both continents and operations.

- Trim talent acquisition costs by reducing the need to engage external recruitment firms.

IAMGOLD did a review of talent acquisition software suppliers and selected Lumesse's (www .lumesse.com) TalentLink, a SaaS-based on-demand global talent acquisition solution. The product was available in 30 languages—including French, English, and Dutch—which the company needed, and Lumesse also understood the challenges and complexities of having a decentralized HR function and having users in several countries. The TalentLink team also offered a rapid deployment with an implementation phase of 12 weeks and its solution was easy to implement, configure, and use. The latter was crucial because IAMGOLD doesn't have a large professional talent acquisition team—most of the HR team members involved in recruiting are HR generalists with many different responsibilities.

While IAMGOLD handles most system change requests itself, it also engaged Lumesse as system administrator to handle more complex system enhancements and to continue to define best practices and optimize the tool. The company is now able to source talent by leveraging multiple channels, including LinkedIn and specialized mining job boards such as InfoMine and Jobs4Mining. IAMGOLD also implemented the ability for candidates to apply directly with their LinkedIn profiles. TalentLink uses Burning Glass's parsing technology to read profile data and places the information into TalentLink's online application data fields. It also uses a job board aggregator function so job postings can be easily managed from a single place in the system, saving time by eliminating the additional step of manually creating job postings on boards. There's also robust tracking of the sources used to attract candidates—last year, more than 150 positions were filled via this means.

Results

With the new systems, IAMGOLD's four business goals for its talent acquisition strategy were met.

The company now has a global talent position dashboard that reports to the executive management team on a quarterly basis. Reported metrics include the number of positions open, the number filled, how long they have been open, at what level they are open and new positions versus replacement positions. In the future, this information will support strategic talent decisions and inform IAMGOLD's sourcing strategy. The company also has robust governance around the hiring approval process. In the past, department heads and executives may not have known about individual open positions; now, senior leaders have a clear line of sight into all hiring activities.

The mining firm grew its global database to more than 10,000 mining professionals in less than one year via a variety of social media and job board sources, exceeding expectations.

IAMGOLD can now measure the return on investment on efforts to promote its employee value proposition globally. Engaged prospects can be converted to active candidates who are now captured in the new system. Talent pools are created and managed by recruiters in the system, which enables re-engagement and marketing to candidates for future opportunities. IAMGOLD also has a tool to facilitate internal mobility across its operations. For example, a highly skilled expatriate employee living in West Africa discovered an open position in South America on TalentLink and submitted an internal application, resulting in a successful transfer.

By creating one centralized system to manage candidates, IAMGOLD has greatly reduced its need to use outside recruiters. Using a conservative formula, the new platform contributed to cost savings of close to $1 million in the first year of operation.

Going Forward

Some local recruiting efforts at operations outside of Canada are still not supported by technology and employment applications continue to be received and managed on paper. Ultimately, the goal is to manage all talent acquisition activity using the new system. Ongoing change management and education of hiring managers and its human resources community will continue to be a focus in the near future. And metrics from the system will start to play a key role in realizing IAMGOLD's talent strategy.

Questions

1. What are some of the staffing challenges experienced by organizations operating in multiple global locations?

2. Does IAMGOLD's new approach to staffing described in the case align with the description of a transnational HRM system provided in this chapter? Explain.

Source: Charles Doucot, "Mining for Talent," *HR Reporter,* pp. 9, 11, February 9, 2015, www.hrreporter.com, retrieved April 21, 2015.

CHAPTER 11

Creating and Sustaining High-Performance Organizations

WHAT DO I NEED TO KNOW?

After reading this chapter, you should be able to:

Lo1	Define high-performance work systems and identify the elements, outcomes, and conditions associated with such a system.
Lo2	Describe how organizations assess employee satisfaction and engagement.
Lo3	Explain how human resource management can contribute to high performance.
Lo4	Discuss the role of HRM technology in high-performance work systems.
Lo5	Summarize ways to measure the effectiveness of human resource management.

TELUS's Work Styles program, which encourages employees to work where and when they are the most productive, has reported results including increased levels of employee engagement, enhanced environmental sustainability, and lower organizational costs.

Measuring Results of TELUS's Work Styles Program

TELUS (www.telus.com) is Canada's second largest telecommunications company with 13.9 million customer connections, and more than $12 billion in annual revenues. TELUS offers a program called *Work Styles* that provides employees the ability to work in the office, at a mobile site, or at home. Sandy McIntosh, VP Human Resources for TELUS Customer Solutions explains the "goal is to have 40 percent of our team members working on a mobile basis, 30 percent working within TELUS buildings, and another 30 percent working from home full time." Benefits of the Work Styles program include increased engagement, productivity, and business results as well as significant cost savings for the company. Andrea Goertz, Chief Communications & Sustainability Officer, explains that at TELUS, employee engagement has gone from 53 percent in 2007 to 83 per cent in 2014—the highest score worldwide for a company of its size and workforce mix—according to global HR organization Aon Hewitt (www.aon.com/canada/). TELUS also reports that the Work Styles program has significant environmental sustainability and organizational benefits including a reduction of more than 5.6 million kg of carbon emissions since the program was implemented in 2010; projected net cash flow savings of $63.5 million over the next 13 years for travel related expenses; as well as projected 20-year net cash flow savings of $166 million for corporate real estate.[1]

Introduction

This chapter summarizes the role of human resource management in creating an organization that achieves a high level of performance, measured in such terms as long-term profits, quality, and customer satisfaction. We begin with a definition of *high-performance work systems* and a description of these systems' elements and outcomes. Next, we identify the conditions that contribute to high performance and how to assess employee satisfaction and engagement. We explain how the various HRM functions can contribute to high performance and discuss the role of HRM technology. Finally, we introduce ways to measure the effectiveness of human resource management.

L○1 Define high-performance work systems and identify the elements, outcomes, and conditions associated with such a system.

What Is a High-Performance Work System?

HRC**1,2**

The challenge facing managers today is how to make their organizations into *high-performance work systems* with the right combination of people, technology, and organizational structure to make full use of resources and opportunities in achieving their organizations' goals. To function as a high-performance work system, each of these elements must fit well with the others in a smoothly functioning whole. Many manufacturers use the latest in processes including flexible manufacturing technology and just-in-time inventory control (meaning parts and supplies are automatically restocked as needed), but, of course, these processes do not work on their own; they must be run by skilled people. Organizations have to determine what kinds of people fit their needs, and then locate, train, and motivate those special people.[2] According to research, organizations that introduce integrated high-performance work practices usually experience increases in productivity and long-term financial performance.[3]

Creating a high-performance work system contrasts with traditional management practices. In the past, decisions about technology, organizational structure, and human resources were treated as if they were unrelated. An organization might acquire a new information system, restructure jobs, or add an office in another country without considering the impact on its people. More recently, managers have realized that success depends on how well all the elements work together. For instance, based on his experience at global customer contact centre Vixicom (www.vixicom.com), Luis Echevarria determined that managing a call centre where agents reliably meet customers' needs is more than a matter of hiring experienced agents with positive attitudes. Rather, Echevarria says, the call centre needs to keep abreast of the latest technology, which routes calls efficiently to minimize customer wait times. Managers need to learn how to select employees who not only speak cheerfully on the phone but also can quickly assess a situation and make decisions that go beyond what is on a script. For the agents to apply that skill requires job designs that empower the agents to some degree. Finally, the centre needs a compensation plan with at least half of total compensation linked to desired behaviour and goal achievement because incentive pay creates a motivating atmosphere for employees who excel at this type of work.[4]

Elements of a High-Performance Work System

As shown in Figure 11.1, in a high-performance work system, the elements that must work together include organizational structure, task design, people (the selection, training, and development of employees), reward systems, and information systems, and human resource management plays an important role in establishing all these.

Organizational structure is the way the organization groups its people into useful divisions, departments, and reporting relationships. The organization's top management makes most decisions about structure, for instance, how many employees report to each supervisor, and whether employees are

FIGURE 11.1

Elements of a High-Performance Work System

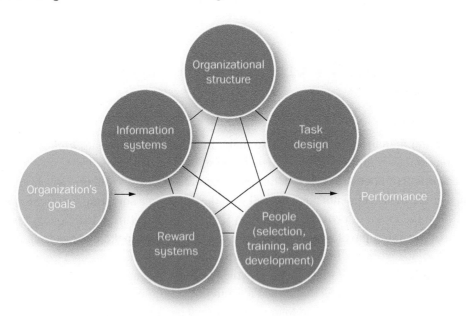

grouped according to the functions they carry out or the customers they serve. Such decisions affect how well employees coordinate their activities and respond to change. In a high-performance work system, organizational structure promotes cooperation, learning, and continuous improvement.

Task design determines how the details of the organization's necessary activities will be grouped, whether into jobs or team responsibilities. In a high-performance work system, task design makes jobs efficient while encouraging high-quality results. In Chapter 3, we discussed how to carry out this HRM function through job analysis and job design.

The right *people* are a key element of high-performance work systems. HRM has a significant role in providing people who are well suited and well prepared for their jobs. Human resources professionals help the organization recruit and select people with the needed qualifications. Training, learning, development, and career management ensure that these people are able to perform their current and future jobs and fit with the culture of the organization.

Reward systems contribute to high performance by encouraging people to strive for objectives that support the organization's overall goals. Reward systems consider the performance measures by which employees are assessed, the methods of measuring performance, and the incentive pay and other rewards linked to success. Human resource management plays an important role in developing and administering reward systems, as we saw in Chapter 8.

The final element of high-performance work systems is the organization's *information systems*. Managers make decisions about the types of information to gather and the sources of information. They also must decide who in the organization should have access to the information and how they will make the information available. Modern information systems, including the Internet, have enabled organizations to share information widely. HR departments take advantage of this technology to give employees access to information about benefits, training opportunities, job openings, and more, as we will describe later in this chapter.

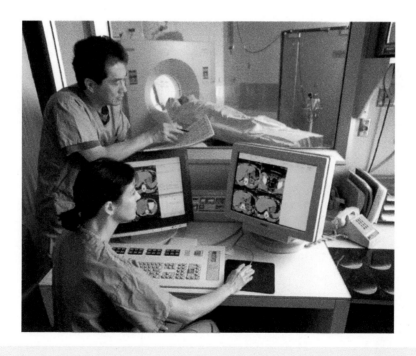

In a high-performance work system, all the elements—people, technology, and organizational structure—work together for success.

Outcomes of a High-Performance Work System

HRC 2

Consider the practices of steel minimills (which produce steel to make a limited quantity of products for the construction industry). Some minimills have strategies based on keeping their costs below competitors' costs; low costs let them operate at a profit while winning customers with low prices. Other steel minimills focus on "differentiation," meaning they set themselves apart in some way other than low price—for example, by offering higher quality or unique product lines. Research has found that the minimills with cost-related goals tend to have highly centralized structures, so managers can focus on controlling through a tight line of command. These organizations have low employee participation in decisions, relatively low wages and benefits, and pay highly contingent on performance.[5] At minimills that focus on differentiation, structures are more complex and decentralized, so authority is more spread out. These minimills encourage employee participation and have higher wages and more generous benefits. They are high-performance work systems. In general, these differentiator mills enjoy higher productivity, lower scrap rates, and lower employee turnover than the mills that focus on low costs.

Outcomes of a high-performance work system thus include higher productivity and efficiency. These outcomes contribute to higher profits. A high-performance work system may have other outcomes, including high product quality, great customer satisfaction, and low employee turnover. Some of these outcomes meet intermediate goals that lead to higher profits (see Figure 11.2). For example, high quality contributes to customer satisfaction, and customer satisfaction contributes to growth of the business. Likewise, improving productivity lets the organization do more with less, which satisfies price-conscious customers and may help the organization win over customers from its competitors. Other ways to lower

FIGURE 11.2

Outcomes of a High-Performance Work System

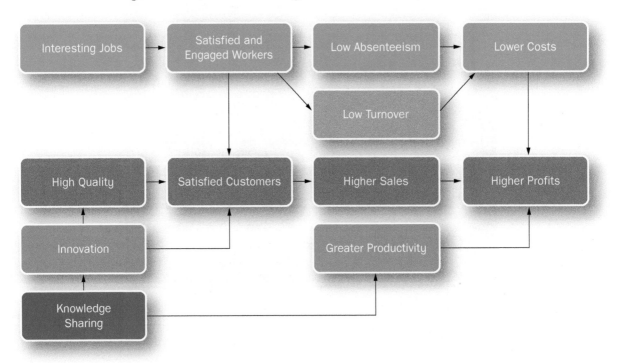

cost and improve quality are to reduce absenteeism and turnover, providing the organization with a steady supply of experienced workers. In the previous example of minimills, some employers keep turnover and scrap rates low. Meeting those goals helps the minimills improve productivity, which helps them earn more profits.

In a high-performance work system, the outcomes of each employee and work group contribute to the system's overall high performance. The organization's individuals and groups work efficiently, provide high-quality goods and services, and so on, and in this way, they contribute to meeting the organization's goals. When the organization adds or changes goals, people are flexible and make changes as needed to meet the new goals.

Conditions That Contribute to High Performance

Certain conditions underlie the formation of a high-performance work system:[6]

- Teams perform work.
- Employees participate in selection.
- Employees receive formal performance feedback and are actively involved in the performance improvement process.
- Ongoing training is emphasized and rewarded.
- Employees' rewards and compensation relate to the company's financial performance.
- Equipment and work processes are structured and technology is used to encourage maximum flexibility and interaction among employees.
- Employees participate in planning changes in equipment, layout, and work methods.
- Work design allows employees to use a variety of skills.
- Employees understand how their jobs contribute to the finished product or service.
- Ethical behaviour is encouraged.

Practices involving rewards, employee empowerment, and jobs with variety, contribute to high performance by giving employees skills, incentives, knowledge, autonomy—as well as satisfaction and engagement—conditions associated with high performance. Ethical behaviour is a necessary condition of high performance because it contributes to good long-term relationships with employees, customers, and the public.

Teamwork and Empowerment

HRC3

Today's organizations empower employees. **Employee empowerment** means giving employees responsibility and authority to make decisions regarding all aspects of product development or customer service.[7] They expect employees to make more decisions about how they perform their jobs. One of the most popular

employee empowerment
Giving employees responsibility and authority to make decisions regarding all aspects of product development or customer service.

It's important for companies to capture and share the knowledge of workers who have had years to learn their specialty.

ways to empower employees is to design work so that it is performed by teams. On a work team, employees bring together various skills and experiences to produce goods or provide services. The organization may charge the team with making decisions traditionally made by managers, such as hiring team members and planning work schedules. Teamwork and empowerment contribute to high performance when they improve employee satisfaction and engagement and give the organization fuller use of employees' ideas and expertise.

For empowerment to succeed, managers must serve in linking and coordinating roles[8] and providing the team with the resources it needs to carry out its work. The manager should help the team and its members interact with employees from other departments or teams and should make sure communication flows in both directions—the manager keeps the team updated on important issues and ensures that the team shares information and resources with others who need them.

Knowledge Sharing

HRC7

For more than two decades, managers have been interested in creating a **learning organization**, that is, an organization in which the culture values and supports lifelong learning by enabling all employees to continually acquire and share knowledge. The people in a learning organization have resources for training and development, and they are encouraged to share their knowledge with colleagues. Managers take an active role in identifying training needs and encouraging the sharing of ideas.[9] An organization's information systems, discussed later in this chapter, have an important role in making this learning activity possible. Information systems capture knowledge and make it available even after individual employees who provided the knowledge have left the organization. Ultimately, people are the essential

learning organization
An organization that supports lifelong learning by enabling all employees to acquire and share knowledge.

ingredients in a learning organization. They must be committed to learning and willing to share what they have learned. A learning organization has several key features:[10]

- It engages in **continuous learning**, each employee's and each group's ongoing efforts to gather information and apply the information to their decisions. In many organizations, the process of continuous learning is aimed at improving quality. To engage in continuous learning, employees must understand the entire work system they participate in, the relationships among jobs, their work units, and the organization as a whole. Employees who continuously learn about their work system are adding to their ability to improve performance.

---

continuous learning
Each employee's and each group's ongoing efforts to gather information and apply the information to their decisions in a learning organization.

- Knowledge is *shared.* Therefore, to create a learning organization, one challenge is to shift the focus of training away from merely teaching skills and toward a broader focus on generating and sharing knowledge.[11] In this view, training is an investment in the organization's human resources; it increases employees' value to the organization. Also, training content should be related to the organization's goals. Human resource departments can support the creation of a learning organization by planning training programs that meet these criteria, and they can help to create both face-to-face and electronic systems for employee collaboration to create, capture, and share knowledge.

- *Critical, systemic thinking is widespread.* This occurs when organizations encourage employees to see relationships among ideas and to test assumptions and observe the results of their actions. Reward systems can be set up to encourage employees and teams to think in new ways.

- The organization has a *learning culture*—a culture in which learning is rewarded, promoted, and supported by managers and organizational objectives. This culture may be reflected in performance management systems and pay structures that reward employees for gathering and sharing more knowledge. A learning culture creates the conditions in which managers encourage *flexibility* and *experimentation.* The organization should encourage employees to take risks and innovate, which means it cannot be quick to punish ideas that do not work out as intended.

- *Employees are valued.* The organization recognizes that employees are the source of its knowledge. It therefore focuses on ensuring the development and well-being of each employee.

Continuous learning and knowledge sharing can support an environment of employee empowerment. For example, some organizations are giving employees access to software that monitors their productivity on the assumption that if they know data about their performance, they can use the data to improve their own productivity. Software called RescueTime (www.rescuetime.com) measures how long computer users spend on each website and application, as well as their time away from the computer; TallyZoo lets users enter data—say, time spent on activities and amount of work completed—and create interactive graphs for measuring progress and spotting trends and other patterns. One employee who used tools such as these discovered that he was most productive when he switched tasks periodically, so he set up the software to remind him every 20 minutes to do something different. A programmer who assumed that chatting online was making him less productive tested that assumption and found that time chatting was associated with writing *more* lines of code. Armed with that information, the programmer gave a higher priority to networking with co-workers and customers. Notice in these examples that the workers had latitude to discover how they work best and to control how they applied what they learned.[12]

Job Satisfaction

HRC3

A condition underpinning any high-performance organization is that employees experience *job satisfaction*—they experience their jobs as fulfilling or allows them to fulfill one's important job values.[13] Several aspects of job satisfaction are:

- Job satisfaction is related to a person's *values*, defined as "what a person consciously or unconsciously desires to obtain."

- Different employees have different views of which values are *important,* so the same circumstances can produce different levels of job satisfaction.

- Job satisfaction is based on *perception*, not always on an objective and complete measurement of the situation. Each person compares the job situation to his or her values, and people are likely to differ in what they perceive.

Research supports the idea that employees' job satisfaction and job performance are related.[14] Higher performance at the individual level should contribute to higher performance for the organization as a whole. In sum, values, perceptions, and ideas of what is important are the three components of job satisfaction. People will be satisfied with their jobs as long as they perceive that their jobs meet their important values. As shown in Figure 11.3 organizations can contribute to job satisfaction in several ways.

Employee Engagement

A condition underpinning any high-performance organization is that employees are fully engaged with their work. As discussed in Chapter 1, *employee engagement* refers to the extent that an employee experiences full involvement in one's work and commitment to one's job and organization. Engagement has

FIGURE 11.3

Increasing Job Satisfaction

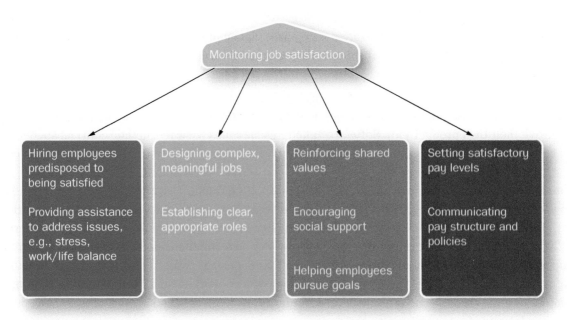

both an emotional and cognitive component and is evidenced through employee behaviours. For example, employees are engaged when they:[15]

- Speak positively about the organization to co-workers, potential employees, and customers,

- Have an intense desire to be a member of the organization, and

- Exert extra effort and are dedicated to doing the very best job possible to contribute to the organization's business success.

Employees who are engaged in their work and committed to the company they work for provide a clear competitive advantage to that firm, including higher productivity, better customer service, and lower turnover.[16] Companies that sustain and improve engagement levels systematically gather feedback from employees, analyze their responses, and implement changes. In these companies, engagement measures are considered as important as customer service or financial data. Employee engagement tends to require job satisfaction.

Consultants at Towers Watson (www.towerswatson.com) have found that employee engagement is associated with greater profitability, especially when engagement is coupled with employee well-being and access to the necessary resources.[17] Aon Hewitt (www.aon.com/canada) has measured an association between employee engagement and companies' stock market performance. At companies studied by Aon Hewitt, those with the highest levels of employee engagement also experience lower turnover, better employee retention, and greater productivity.[18] And as the nearby "Did You Know?" box suggests, many employees agree with the idea that the way they are treated at work affects their attitudes and effort on the job.

Globally, Aon Hewitt has found that the practices that do the most to promote employee engagement are opportunities for career progress, recognition for accomplishments, and brand alignment. **Brand alignment** is the process of ensuring that HR policies, practices, and programs support or are congruent with an organization's overall culture or brand, including its products and services. One way to ensure HR policies align with a company's strategic vision is to educate employees about the company's brand and their role in bringing that brand to life as part of everyday work activities. Some companies discuss brand alignment as part of employee orientation programs while others develop in-depth training programs about the company's brand and how each employee is an important contributor to the company's overall success. In North America, employers have the most impact on brand alignment by providing career opportunities, using effective performance management systems, and maintaining a positive reputation.[19]

brand alignment
The process of ensuring that HR policies, practices, and programs support or are congruent with an organization's overall culture (or brand), products, and services.

Some organizations also foster employees' *passion* for their work. Passionate people are fully engaged with something so that it becomes part of their sense of who they are. Feeling this way about one's work has been called *occupational intimacy*.[20] People experience occupational intimacy when they love their work, when they and their co-workers care about one another, and when they find their work meaningful. Human resources managers have a significant role in creating these conditions. For example, they can select people who care about their work and customers, provide methods for sharing knowledge, design work to make jobs interesting, and establish policies and programs that show concern for employees' needs. Such efforts may become increasingly important as the business world increasingly uses employee empowerment, teamwork, and knowledge sharing to build flexible organizations.[21]

Disengaged and Overwhelmed Employees

Organizations need employees who are fully engaged and committed to their work, however, according to the Deloitte 2014 Human Capital Trends Study, "companies are struggling to engage our modern, 21st century workforce."[22] Gallup research "shows that only 13% of employees around the world are actively engaged at work, and more than twice that number are so disengaged they are likely to spread negativity to others."[23] It was also recently reported that "two-thirds of today's employees feel overwhelmed." For example, workers say they "would like to work fewer hours, they are too distracted (mobile device users check their phones 150 times per day), and they are flooded with too many emails, conference calls, meetings, and other distractions."[24]

The organization needs to prevent a broader negative condition, called **job withdrawal**—or a set of behaviours with which employees try to avoid the work situation physically, mentally, or emotionally. Job withdrawal results when circumstances such as the nature of the job, supervisors and co-workers, pay levels, or the employee's own disposition cause the employee to become dissatisfied with the job. As shown in Figure 11.4, this job dissatisfaction produces job withdrawal. Job withdrawal may take the form of behaviour change, physical job withdrawal, or psychological withdrawal. Some researchers believe employees engage in the three forms of withdrawal behaviour in that order, while others think they select from these behaviours to address the particular sources of job dissatisfaction they experience.[25] Although the specifics of these models vary, the consensus is that withdrawal behaviours are related to one another and are at least partially caused by job dissatisfaction.[26]

job withdrawal
A set of behaviours with which employees try to avoid the work situation physically, mentally, or emotionally.

L○2 Describe how organizations assess employee satisfaction and engagement.

How Are Employee Satisfaction and Engagement Assessed?

The usual way to assess satisfaction and engagement is with some kind of survey. A systematic, ongoing program of employee surveys should be part of the organization's human resource strategy. This allows the organization to monitor trends. Although the types of questions asked in employee job satisfaction

FIGURE 11.4

Job Withdrawal Process

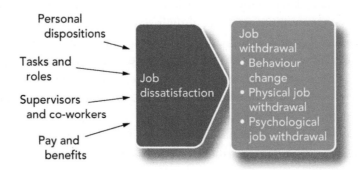

Did You KNOW?

Appreciation Drives Effort

In a recent survey, only about half of employees said they love their job and that their company cares about them. Almost 4 in 10 said they intended to look for a new job. But whether or not they intend to stay, solid majorities said they would work harder if their employer better recognized and appreciated their efforts.

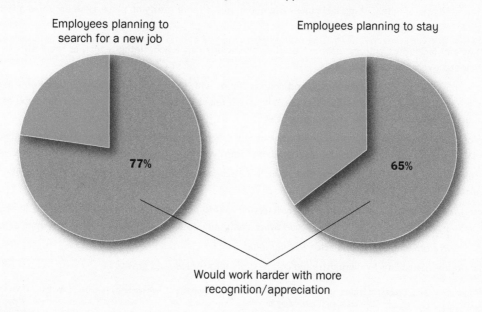

Employees planning to search for a new job

77%

Employees planning to stay

65%

Would work harder with more recognition/appreciation

Question

1. How can employers demonstrate to employees that the organization values them and appreciates their efforts?

Sources: Globoforce, "Globoforce Workforce Mood Tracker: The Impact of Recognition on Employee Retention," September 2011, www.globoforce.com; Globoforce, "Thirty-Eight Percent of Workers Seek New Jobs, according to Globoforce Workforce Mood Tracker."

and engagement surveys may vary, some of the common themes generally measured include pride and satisfaction with employer; opportunity to perform challenging work; recognition and positive feedback for contributions; personal support from supervisor; and understanding of the link between one's job and the company's overall mission. For example, if satisfaction with promotion opportunities has been falling over several years, the trend may signal a need for better career management (a topic of Chapter 6). An organizational change, such as a merger, also might have important consequences for employee job satisfaction and engagement. In addition, ongoing surveys give the organization a way to measure whether practices adopted to enhance employee satisfaction and engagement are working. Organizations can also compare results from different departments to identify groups with successful practices that may apply elsewhere in the organization. Another benefit is that some scales provide data that organizations can use to compare themselves to others in the same industry. This information will be valuable for creating and reviewing human resource policies that enable organizations to attract and retain employees in a competitive job market.

To obtain a survey instrument, an excellent place to begin is with one of the many established scales. For example, the validity and reliability of many satisfaction scales have been tested, so it is possible to

HR Best Practices

Creating a Positive Work Environment

The relatively new fields of positive psychology and positive organizational behaviour have contributed to the idea that individuals and organizations not only can work on problems but also can take steps that favour the creation of a happy outlook and upbeat workplace. Critics suspect that these kinds of approaches merely sugarcoat miserable situations, but used appropriately, some techniques can make work a more satisfying place. Here are some approaches that HR professionals might want to consider:

- Coaches and facilitators with expertise in positive psychology can teach methods such as meditation and the practice and expression of gratitude.

- When confronted with news, dilemmas, and changes, start with the assumption that the situation is not necessarily bad (or good). Define setbacks as learning experiences. Keeping an open mind can help you and your team identify more alternatives and opportunities.

- Look for positive employee behaviours and outcomes and coach managers to do the same. Use performance feedback to identify task strengths and character strengths employees can build on, not just weaknesses to correct.

- Use selection and development tools that match employees' talents to positions and career paths in the organization.

- Structure work so employees can see why it matters and so they have enough control over their time to engage in activities they care about. Define how the organization contributes to society, and express that mission to employees.

- Ask for ideas from employees, and listen to their ideas.

- Model positive behaviour by demonstrating compassion, forgiveness, and gratitude.

Sources: Michael Lee Stallard, "Connect to Engage," *T+D*, April 2015, pp. 48–55; Sue Shellenbarger, "Thinking Happy Thoughts at Work," *Wall Street Journal*, January 27, 2010, http//online.wsj.com; Chet Taranowski, "Advocating for a Positive Workplace," *Journal of Employee Assistance*, January 2009, Business & Company Resource Center, http://galenet.galegroup.com; Ann Pace, "Unleashing Positivity in the Workplace," *T+D*, January 2010, Business & Company Resource Center, http://galenet.galegroup.com; and Stacey Burling, "Psychologists Converge on Philadelphia to Study Happiness," *Philadelphia Inquirer*, June 21, 2009, Business & Company Resource Center, http://galenet.galegroup.com.

Co-worker relationships can contribute to satisfaction and engagement, and organizations therefore try to provide opportunities to build positive relationships. Would a strong sense of teamwork and friendship help you enjoy your work more? Enhance your performance?

compare the instruments. The main reason for an organization to create its own scale would be that it wants to measure aspects of work specific to the organization (such as satisfaction with a particular benefits plan).

A widely used measure of job satisfaction is the Job Descriptive Index (JDI). The JDI emphasizes specific aspects of satisfaction—pay, the work itself, supervision, co-workers and promotions. Figure 11.5 shows several items from the JDI scale. Other scales measure general satisfaction using broad questions such as "All in all, how satisfied are you with your job?"[27] Some scales avoid language altogether, relying on pictures. The faces scale in Figure 11.6 is an example of this type of measure. Other scales exist for measuring more specific aspects of satisfaction. For example, the Pay Satisfaction Questionnaire (PSQ) measures satisfaction with specific aspects of pay, such as pay levels, structure, and raises.[28]

However, critics describe the traditional employee satisfaction feedback process as: "The individual has his or her moment of self-expression, a fleeting participation in the great collective search for truth, then silence, nada, frustration as the status quo prevails."[29] With this in mind, the Gallup Organization (www.gallup.com) set about to create a better employee feedback process that linked the elements of employee engagement to improved business outcomes, for example, sales growth, productivity, customer loyalty, and the generation of value.[30] Table 11.1 identifies Gallup's questions for measuring employee engagement.

In spite of surveys and other efforts to retain employees, some employees inevitably will leave the organization. This presents another opportunity to gather information for retaining employees: the **exit interview**—a meeting of the departing employee with the employee's supervisor and/or a human resources specialist to discuss the employee's reasons for leaving. A well-conducted exit interview can uncover reasons why employees leave and perhaps set the stage for some of them to return. HR professionals can help make exit interviews more successful by arranging for the employee to talk to someone from the HR department (rather than the departing employee's supervisor) in a neutral location or over the phone.[31] Questions should start out open-ended and general, to give the employee a chance to name the source of the dissatisfaction or explain why leaving is attractive.

exit interview
A meeting of a departing employee with the employee's supervisor and/or human resources specialist to discuss the employee's reasons for leaving.

FIGURE 11.5

Example of a Job Descriptive Index (JDI)

Instructions: Think of your present work. What is it like most of time? In the blank beside each word given below, write

_____Y_____ for "Yes" if it describes your work
_____N_____ for "No" if it does NOT describe your work
_____?_____ if you cannot decide

Work Itself	Pay	Promotion Opportunities
_____ Routine	_____ Less than I deserve	_____ Dead-end job
_____ Satisfying	_____ Highly paid	_____ Unfair policies
_____ Good	_____ Insecure	_____ Based on ablility

Supervision	Co-workers
_____ Impolite	_____ Intelligent
_____ Praises good work	_____ Responsible
_____ Doesn't supervise enough	_____ Boring

Source: W. K. Balzar, D. C. Smith, D. E. Kravitz, S. E. Lovell, K. B. Paul, B. A. Reilly, and C. E. Reilly, *User's Manual for the Job Descriptive Index (JDI)* (Bowling Green, OH: Bowling Green State University, 1990).

FIGURE 11.6

Example of a Simplified, Nonverbal Measure of Job Satisfaction

Job Satisfaction from the Faces Scale
Consider all aspects of your job. Circle the face that
best describes your feelings about your job in general.

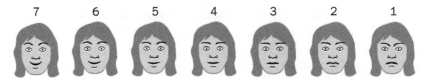

Source: R. B. Dunham and J. B. Herman and published in the *Journal of Applied Psychology* (1975), pp. 629-31. Reprinted with permission.

A recruiter armed with information about what caused a specific person to leave may be able to negotiate a return when the situation changes. And when several exiting employees give similar reasons for leaving, management should consider whether this indicates a need for change. A recent twist on the exit interview is a **stay interview**—a meeting with an employee to explore his or her thoughts and feelings about the job and to uncover issues in the effort to prevent that employee from becoming disgruntled.[32]

stay interview
A meeting with an employee to explore his or her thoughts and feelings about the job and to uncover issues in the effort to prevent that employee from becoming disgruntled.

TABLE 11.1

Measuring Employee Engagement: Gallup's Twelve Questions

To identify the elements of worker engagement, Gallup conducted hundreds of focus groups and many thousands of worker interviews in all kinds of organizations, and at all levels, in most industries, and in many countries. The result was 12 key employee expectations that, when satisfied, form the foundation of strong feelings of engagement.

1. Do you know what is expected of you at work?

2. Do you have the materials and equipment you need to do your work right?

3. At work, do you have the opportunity to do what you do best every day?

4. In the last seven days, have you received recognition or praise for doing good work?

5. Does your supervisor, or someone at work, seem to care about you as a person?

6. Is there someone at work who encourages your development?

7. At work, do your opinions seem to count?

8. Does the mission/purpose of your company make you feel your job is important?

9. Are your associates (fellow employees) committed to doing quality work?

10. Do you have a best friend at work?

11. In the last six months, has someone at work talked to you about your progress?

12. In the last year, have you had opportunities at work to learn and grow?

Source: John Thackeray "Feedback for Real," March 15, 2001, http://gmj.gallup.com/content/default.asp?ci=811.

In the long run, a high-performance organization fosters the kind of work culture that encourages high levels of motivation, satisfaction, commitment, and engagement. The newer generations in the workforce are much more likely to speak up, saying: "I'm not a happy camper and you need to do more to keep me here, or I am going to pick up my skill set and go somewhere else."[33]

 E-HRM

Staying connected to former employees via social media.

L○3 Explain how human resource management can contribute to high performance.

HRM's Contribution to High Performance

HRC 1,2

Management of human resources plays a critical role in determining companies' success in meeting the challenges of a rapidly changing, highly competitive environment.[34] Total rewards, staffing, training and development, performance management, and other HRM practices are investments that directly affect employees' motivation and ability to provide products and services that are valued by customers. Table 11.2 lists examples of HRM practices that contribute to high performance.

Research suggests that it is more effective to improve HRM practices as a whole than to focus on one or two isolated practices, such as the organization's pay structure or selection system.[35] Also, to have the intended influence on performance, the HRM practices must fit well with one another and the organization as a whole.[36] For ideas on how HR professionals can strengthen the connection to the organization's mission, see "HR How-To."

TABLE 11.2

HRM Practices That Can Help Organizations Achieve High Performance

• HRM practices match organization's goals.	• Performance management system measures customer satisfaction and quality.
• Individuals and groups share knowledge.	• Organization monitors employees' satisfaction and engagement.
• Work is performed by teams.	• Discipline system is progressive.
• Organization encourages continuous learning.	• Reward systems reward skills and accomplishments.
• Work design permits flexibility in where and when tasks are performed.	• Skills and values of a diverse workforce are valued and used.
• Selection system is job-related and legal.	• Technology reduces time and costs of tasks while preserving quality.

HR How-To

Supporting Line Management

Human resource management contributes most to building high-performance organizations when HR professionals understand the goals of the business and clearly demonstrate how they can help achieve those goals. Here are some ways that HR professionals can collaborate better with line managers and top executives:

- Learn about the organization's business. Whether the organization is a manufacturing corporation or a not-for-profit agency, it creates products or services and makes them available to customers or clients. HR professionals should have a basic understanding of the organization's production processes, markets, competitors, and technologies, as well as the major opportunities and threats facing the organization. Generally, this understanding will require some knowledge about finance, accounting, and other tools of business measurement.

- Follow and analyze the trends affecting the business. Anticipate where human resource management can equip the organization to ride or drive the trends rather than merely react to laws, technology change, or market forces.

- Avoid using HRM jargon when talking to the organization's leaders. Especially at the highest levels, managers are likely to be annoyed by jargon such as *proactive, synergy,* and *value added.* At any level, managers will appreciate communication that avoids or defines technical terms and abbreviations of the HRM profession.

- If HR professionals have not been included in strategy or planning meetings, identify specific contributions the profession can make to achieving strategic goals. Then visit the person organizing the meeting, and ask to be included in order to present the idea. Be ready to make a brief statement of how the idea will benefit the organization in terms of its business goals. Communicate honestly and respectfully. When line managers offer their perspectives, listen carefully. If their attitudes or viewpoints are different from the HR perspective, take time to consider that the different viewpoint also might be important.

- Be assertive in expressing the value of effective human resource management. Know the research showing relationships between effective HR practices and organizational performance, and be ready to tell how HR programs support high performance. For example, in recent years, executives have been keenly aware of the need for talent management and succession planning.

Sources: Human Resources Professionals Association and Knightsbridge Human Capital Solutions, "The Role and Future of HR: The CEO's Perspective," 2011 Research Highlight, www.hrpa.ca, accessed May 21, 2012; Bureau of National Affairs, "Attorney Urges HR Professionals to Think Like the CEO," *HR Focus,* April 2012, p. 10; Sage (UK) Ltd., "Top 10 Tips for HR to Build Effective Relationships with Line Managers," *Sage Blog,* January 20, 2011, www.sage.com.

Job Design

HRC4

For the organization to benefit from teamwork and employee empowerment, jobs must be designed appropriately. Often, a high-performance work system places employees in work teams where employees collaborate to make decisions and solve problems. Individual employees also may be empowered to serve on teams that design jobs and work processes.

Job design aimed at empowerment includes access to resources such as information technology. The Lowe's (www.lowes.ca) chain of home improvement stores wanted to empower its salespeople with more information they need to close sales. So it equipped the salespeople with iPhones that have apps for price scanning, locating items in the store, checking inventory, and looking up competitors' prices. Eventually, the phones also will be able to scan customers' credit cards to complete sales transactions.[37] Lowe's hopes this much access to information will enable its salespeople to initiate conversations with shoppers and walk them through the entire decision process to the closing of a sale.

Recruitment and Selection

At a high-performance organization, recruitment and selection aim at obtaining the kinds of employees who can thrive in this type of setting. These employees are enthusiastic about and able to contribute to teamwork, empowerment, and knowledge sharing. Qualities such as creativity and ability to cooperate as part of a team may play a large role in selection decisions. High-performance organizations need selection methods that identify more than technical skills like ability to perform accounting and engineering tasks. Employers may use group interviews, open-ended questions, and psychological tests to find employees who innovate, share ideas, and take initiative. For example, at Imaginet (www.imaginet.com), the Winnipeg-based software application firm recognized by Queen's School of Business (www.business.queensu.ca) as "Best Small to Medium Employer in Canada," employees actively contribute to the hiring process to attract like-minded top talent.[38]

Training, Learning, and Development

HRC**7**

When organizations base hiring decisions on qualities like decision making and teamwork skills, training may be required to help employees learn the specific skills they need to perform the duties of their job. Extensive training and development also are part of a learning organization, described earlier in this chapter. And when organizations delegate many decisions to work teams, the members of those teams likely will benefit from participating in team development activities that prepare them for their roles as team members.

Business Development Bank of Canada (BDC, www.bdc.ca) demonstrates its commitment to training and development by annually investing approximately 5 percent of payroll in learning. The federal Crown corporation offers financing, business loans, consulting, and venture capital to businesses and is participating in a project sponsored by the federal government to substantiate the return on investment of training. "We know there's a declining investment in training overall in Canada. And we know that has a big impact on growth productivity, so it's sort of a win-win type of project to learn ourselves what a return-on-investment (ROI) project is all about," said Jacinthe Higgs, director of learning strategies at BDC.[39]

Performance Management

HRC**4**

In a high-performance organization, employees know the organization's goals and what they must do to help achieve those goals. HR departments can contribute to this ideal through the design of the organization's performance management system. As we discussed in Chapter 7, performance management should be related to the organization's goals. For example, banks today want tellers to do more than merely process transactions, much of which can be handled electronically. Tellers are now expected to identify customer needs and offer products, as well as to maintain positive relationships between customers and the bank. This calls for sophisticated goal setting and performance measurement—not merely numbers of transactions processed, for example, but numbers of customers retained by the branch, scores in customer satisfaction surveys, or value of certificates of deposit or other services sold.[40]

To set up a performance management system that supports the organization's goals, managers need to understand the process of employee performance. As is shown in Figure 11.7, individual employees

FIGURE 11.7

Employee Performance as a Process

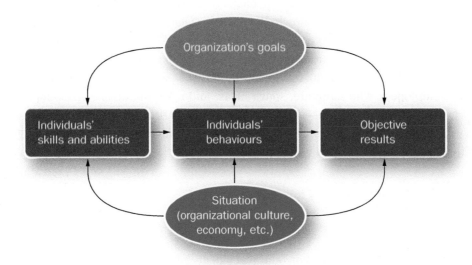

bring a set of skills and abilities to the job, and by applying a set of behaviours, they use those skills to achieve certain results. But success is more than the product of individual efforts. The organization's goals should influence each step of the process. The organization's culture and other factors influence the employees' abilities, behaviours, and results. It must not be forgotten that sometimes uncontrollable forces such as economic conditions enter the picture.

This model suggests some guidelines for performance management. First, every aspect of performance management should be related to the organization's goals. Business goals should influence the kinds of employees selected and their training, the requirements of each job, and the measures used for evaluating results. Generally, this means the organization identifies what each department needs to do to achieve the desired results, then defines how individual employees should contribute to their department's goals. More specifically, the following guidelines describe how to make the performance management system support organizational goals:[41]

- *Define and measure performance in precise terms*—Focus on outcomes that can be defined in terms of how frequently certain behaviours occur. Include criteria that describe ways employees can add value to a product or service (such as through quantity, quality, or timeliness). Include behaviours that go beyond the minimum required to perform a job (such as helping co-workers).

- *Link performance measures to meeting customer needs*—"Customers" may be the organization's external customers, or they may be internal customers (employees receiving services from a co-worker). Service goals for internal customers should be related to satisfying external customers.

- *Measure and correct for the effect of situational constraints*—Monitor economic conditions, the organization's culture, and other influences on performance. Measures of employees' performance should take these influences into account.

This approach gives employees the information they need to behave in ways that contribute to high performance. In addition, organizations should help employees identify and obtain the abilities they need to meet their performance goals.

Compensation and Rewards

HRC**6**

Organizations can reinforce the impact of this kind of performance management by linking employee compensation and rewards in part to performance measures. Chapter 8 described a number of methods for doing this, including merit pay, gainsharing, and profit sharing. At Intel (www.intel.ca), part of employees' variable pay (individual bonus and profit sharing) is tied to the achievement of corporate objectives, including specific objectives for operating sustainably—for example, reducing greenhouse gas emissions per chip manufactured, increasing the energy efficiency of notebook computers, and reducing the amount of chemical waste sent to landfills down to zero. The percentage of the bonus tied to meeting objectives is greater for employees near the top of the organization, where they have more control over whether the targets are met.[42] Compensation and rewards systems also can help to create the conditions that contribute to high performance, including teamwork, involvement, and employee satisfaction and engagement. For example, compensation and rewards can be linked to achievement of team objectives.

Organizations can increase employee empowerment, satisfaction, and engagement by including employees in decisions about rewards and by communicating the basis for decisions about pay. When the organization designs a pay structure, it can set up a task force that includes employees with direct experience in various types of jobs. Some organizations share financial information with their employees and invite them to recommend pay increases for themselves, on the basis of their contributions. Employees may also participate in setting individual or group goals for which they can receive bonuses. Research has found that employee participation in decisions about pay policies is linked to greater satisfaction with the pay and the job.[43] And as we discussed in Chapter 8, when organizations explain their reward structures to employees, the communication can enhance employees' satisfaction and belief that the system is fair.

Managing Voluntary and Involuntary Turnover

HRC**3, 4, 5**

Along with administering job satisfaction and engagement surveys, more organizations are analyzing basic HR data to look for patterns in employee retention and turnover. Organizations must try to ensure that good performers want to stay with the organization and that employees whose performance is chronically low are encouraged—or forced—to leave. Both of these challenges involve *employee turnover*, that is, employees leaving the organization. When the organization initiates the turnover (often with employees who would prefer to stay), the result is **involuntary turnover**. Examples include terminating an employee for under-performance or laying off employees during a downturn. Most organizations use the word *termination* to refer only to a discharge related to a discipline problem, but some organizations call any involuntary turnover a termination. When the employees initiate the turnover (often when the organization would prefer to keep them), it is **voluntary turnover**. For example, employees may leave to go back to school, travel, take a job with a different organization, or start their own business.

---

involuntary turnover
Turnover initiated by an employer (often with employees who would prefer to stay).

voluntary turnover
Turnover initiated by employees (often when the organization would prefer to keep them).

In general, organizations try to avoid the need for involuntary turnover and to minimize voluntary turnover, especially among top performers, however employers are not always aware of the reasons employees would change jobs. Table 11.3 identifies the five key reasons top performers in Canadian organizations would change jobs, however, these reasons contrast with the five key reasons employers *think* their top performers would change jobs.

Figure 11.8 shows how voluntary turnover has stabilized in recent years, at a level well below the rate for some past years (e.g., 9.7 percent for 2007–08). Both kinds of turnover are costly, as

TABLE 11.3

Employers Are Not Always Aware of the Reasons Top Performers Would Change Jobs

| | Why Would Top Performers Leave? | |
Rank	Employers Say	Employees Say
1	Career development opportunities	Work-related stress
2	Promotion opportunities	Promotion opportunities
3	Relationship with supervisor	Base pay
4	Base pay	Trust/confidence in management
5	Work-related stress	Job security

Note: Rank represents the frequency the item was selected as one of the most important reasons (from a list of 23 items) top performers would leave an organization; Top performers are those whose performance was rated "far exceeds expectations" (i.e., in the top 10 percent) by their supervisors in their most recent performance review.

Source: "Leading Through Uncertain Times, The 2011/2012 Talent Management and Rewards Study: North America," Towers Watson, p. 8, www.towerswatson.com. Reprinted with the permission of Towers Watson.

FIGURE 11.8

Voluntary Turnover Rates (average percentage of employees)

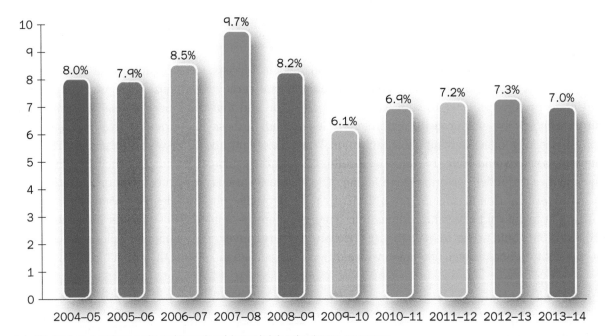

Note: Voluntary turnover applies to regular employees only, and does not include early retirements or severances.

Source: Katie Fleming and Nicole Stewart, "Compensation Planning Outlook 2015," *The Conference Board of Canada*, October 2014, p. 20.

summarized in Table 11.4. Replacing workers is expensive, and new employees need time to learn their jobs and build teamwork skills.[44] Although estimates of the cost of turnover fluctuate widely, Hay Group (www.haygroup.com/ca) vice-president, David Sissons, cites the cost of turnover as 1.5 times the annual salary for a manager or professional, 0.5 times the annual salary for an hourly worker, and as much as 2.0 times annual salary for a top sales or senior-level person.[45] In addition, people today are more likely to take legal action against a former employer if they feel they were unfairly dismissed. The prospect of workplace violence also raises the risk associated with discharging employees. Effective human resource management can help the organization minimize both kinds of turnover, as well as carry it out effectively when necessary. Despite a company's best efforts at selection, training, and compensation, some employees will fail to meet expectations, be uncoachable, or will violate company policies. When this happens, organizations need to apply a discipline program that might ultimately lead to discharging the individual.

For a number of reasons, discharging employees can be a very difficult but potentially important way to maintain a high-performance and engaging work culture. The decision also has legal aspects that can affect the organization. Historically, if the organization and employee do not have a specific employment contract, the employer or employee may end the employment relationship at any time. This is the *employment-at-will doctrine.* This doctrine has eroded significantly, however. Employees who have been terminated sometimes sue their employers for wrongful dismissal, and in such cases the courts may award employees significant financial settlements. Publicity associated with the proceedings may also be embarrassing or harmful to the employer's reputation. Along with the financial risks of dismissing an employee, there are issues of personal safety. Distressing as it is that some former employees go to the courts, far worse are the employees who react to a termination decision with violence. Although any number of organizational actions or decisions may incite violence among employees, the "nothing else to lose" aspect of an employee's dismissal makes the situation dangerous, especially when the nature of the work adds other risk factors.[46]

Retaining top performers is not always easy either, and recent trends have made this more difficult than ever. Today's psychological contract, in which workers feel responsibility for their own careers rather than loyalty to a particular employer, makes voluntary turnover more likely. Also, competing organizations are constantly looking at each other's top performers. For high-demand positions, such as software engineers, "poaching talent" from other companies has become the norm.

Employment/labour standards laws in each of the federal, provincial, and territorial jurisdictions set out the minimum requirements employers must follow when terminating or laying off employees. For example, no notice or compensation is legally needed if the employee quit or retired, the employee had been employed for less than the required minimum (usually three months), the employee was employed on an "on-call" basis, or the employee was terminated for *just cause.* Examples of "just cause" for dismissal that are considered serious violations of the employment relationship are dishonesty; willful

TABLE 11.4

Costs Associated with Turnover

Involuntary Turnover	Voluntary Turnover
Recruiting, selecting, and training replacements	Recruiting, selecting, and training replacements
Lost productivity	Lost productivity
Lawsuits	Loss of talented employees
Workplace violence	

disobedience to a supervisor; and failure to comply with known policies or procedures or meet performance requirements.[47]

Because of the critical financial and personal risks associated with employee dismissal, it is easy to see why organizations must develop a standardized, systematic approach to discipline and discharge. These decisions should not be left solely to the discretion of individual managers or supervisors. The precedent-setting Supreme Court case of *Wallace v. United Grain Growers* (1997) sent a clear message that employers must act fairly and respectfully when handling an employee termination. The *Wallace* case gave judges a legal precedent to award employees additional notice or damages if the employer treats an employee callously or unfairly during termination. In summary, policies that can lead to employee separation should be based on not only the legal requirements but also on principles of justice to ensure the system is seen as fair. Figure 11.9 summarizes these principles of justice. For example, in support of these principles, many organizations provide **outplacement counselling**, which tries to help dismissed employees manage the transition from one job to another. Some organizations have their own staff for conducting outplacement counselling. Other organizations have contracts with outside providers to help with individual cases. Either way, the goals for outplacement programs are to help the former employee address the psychological issues associated with losing a job—grief, depression, and fear in a respectful manner—while at the same time helping the person find a new job.

outplacement counselling
A service in which professionals try to help dismissed employees manage the transition from one job to another.

Handling Employee Discipline Appropriately

In order to maintain a positive, motivating, and high-performance work environment for all employees, organizations look for methods of handling problem behaviour that are fair, legal, and effective.

The principles of justice suggest that the organization prepare for problems by establishing a formal discipline process in which the consequences become more serious if the employee repeats the offence.

FIGURE 11.9

Principles of Justice

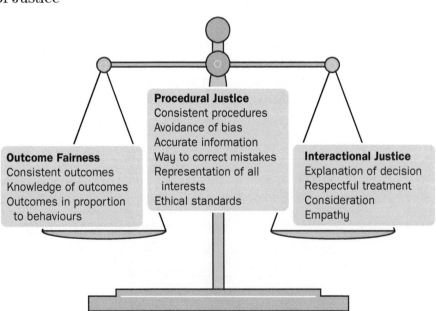

Outcome Fairness
Consistent outcomes
Knowledge of outcomes
Outcomes in proportion
   to behaviours

Procedural Justice
Consistent procedures
Avoidance of bias
Accurate information
Way to correct mistakes
Representation of all
   interests
Ethical standards

Interactional Justice
Explanation of decision
Respectful treatment
Consideration
Empathy

Such a system is called **progressive discipline**. A typical progressive discipline system identifies and communicates inappropriate behaviours and responds to a series of offences with the actions shown in Figure 11.10—spoken and then written warnings, temporary suspension, and finally, termination. This process fulfills the purpose of discipline by teaching employees what is expected of them and creating a situation in which employees must try to do what is expected. It seeks to prevent inappropriate behaviour (by publishing rules) and to correct, rather than merely punish, inappropriate behaviour.

progressive discipline
A formal discipline process in which the consequences become more serious if the employee repeats the offence.

Such procedures may seem exasperatingly slow, especially when the employee's misdeeds hurt the team's performance. In the end, however, if an employee must be discharged, careful use of the procedure increases other employees' belief that the organization is fair and reduces the likelihood that the employee will take legal action (or at least that the employee will win in court). For situations in which inappropriate behaviour is dangerous, the organization may establish a stricter policy, even terminating an employee for the first offence. In that case, it is especially important to communicate the procedure—not only to ensure fairness, but also to prevent the inappropriate or even dangerous behaviour.

Creating a formal discipline process is a primary responsibility of the human resource department. The HR professional should consult with supervisors and managers to identify inappropriate behaviours and establish rules and consequences for violating the rules. The rules should cover disciplinary problems such as the following behaviours encountered in many organizations:

- Absenteeism
- Lateness
- Unsafe work practices
- Poor quantity or quality of work
- Harassment of co-workers or customers
- Theft or misuse of company property
- Cyberslacking (conducting personal business online during work hours)

For each infraction, the HR professional would identify a series of responses, such as those in Figure 11.10. In addition, the organization must communicate these rules and consequences to every

FIGURE 11.10

Progressive Discipline Responses

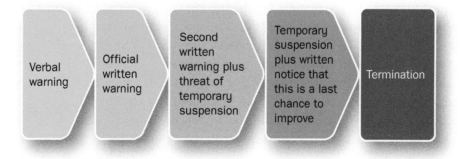

employee. Ways of publishing rules include presenting them in an employee handbook, posting them on the company's intranet, and displaying them on a bulletin board. Supervisors should be familiar with the rules, so that they can discuss them with employees and apply them consistently.

Along with rules and a progression of consequences for violating the rules, a progressive discipline system should have requirements for documenting the rules, offences, and responses. To ensure fairness, the discipline system should provide an opportunity to hear every point of view and to correct errors. Before discussing and filing records of misbehaviour, it is important for the supervisor to investigate the incident. The employee should be made aware of what he or she is said to have done wrong and should have an opportunity to present his or her version of events. A method of gathering objective performance data should be used to support the fairness and objectivity of the discipline system.

For example, BFI Canada (www.bficanada.com), a waste management company in Edmonton, demonstrated the use of progressive discipline that ultimately led to dismissing an employee. The employee was disciplined four times for various infractions—he received a verbal warning for damaging a trailer during loading, a written warning for damaging a structure while backing up a loader, a one-day suspension for neglecting to perform a pre-trip inspection of his vehicle, and a three-day suspension for insubordination. Following these incidents, he was dismissed when a dashboard camera detected he was using a cellphone while driving, a violation of company policy and a violation of Alberta legislation.[48]

Besides developing these policies, HR professionals have a role in carrying out progressive discipline.[49] In meetings to communicate disciplinary actions, it is wise to have an HR representative there to support the employee's supervisor. When an employee is suspended or terminated, the organization should designate a person to escort the employee from the building to protect the organization's people and property.

Finally, the issue of off-the-job behaviour is also of concern to employers. Employers are frequently concerned if an employee's off-the-job behaviour, including social media activity, might affect the organization's business or reputation in some way.

Corporate Social Responsibility

HRC 1,2

Corporate social responsibility (CSR) is an evolving concept integrating social, environmental, and economic concerns into an organization's values, culture, decision making, strategy, and operations in a way that creates wealth and improves society.[50] CSR may also be referred to as *corporate responsibility, corporate citizenship, responsible business,* or *triple bottom line* (social, environmental, and economic performance) just to name a few frequently used alternative terms. Canada is recognized as a leader in social responsibility and "CSR remains a concept that is openly embraced by a strong majority of Canadians."[51] For example, research firm GlobeScan (www.globescan.com) found that 92 percent of Canadians said that "the more socially and environmentally responsible a company is, the more likely they are to purchase its products or services." Additionally, "91 percent of Canadians surveyed prefer to work for a company that is socially and environmentally responsible." The more socially and environmentally responsible a company is, the more attractive it becomes as an employer.[52]

Vancity, Canada's largest credit union, built its head office on Vancouver's SkyTrain line to encourage employees to commute to work.

Demonstrating corporate social responsibility such as sustainability, promoting volunteerism, providing meaningful work, and having high ethical standards are important factors to retain and engage employees. These factors may be particularly important among young employees.

Sustainability and Environmental Stewardship

There is a growing trend among young, intelligent employees leaving lucrative private sector jobs to integrate their personal values with their professional goals. Monica Da Ponte, manager of marketing alliances for WWF (World Wide Fund for Nature, www.wwf.org), spent seven years with a leading consumer packaged-goods company after finishing her undergraduate degree. "After some travelling and a better understanding of what was happening globally, I realized I was doing all this great work for something I did not believe in. That's when I started volunteering at WWF–Canada and pursuing my MBA with a focus on sustainability and nonprofit management," says Da Ponte. Now Da Ponte has struck a balance where she gets to 'walk her talk' with respect to her values, while fully utilizing her business knowledge and skills.[53] According to Ron Dembo, CEO of Zerofootprint (www.zerofootprintsoftware.com), a Toronto-based consultancy focusing on sustainable commerce: "Two years ago, if you went to a company's corporate responsibility person, you would have found that environmental issues did not rank high." The cultural change has been so sudden that a lot of corporations haven't caught up to the fact that this issue can have an impact on employee morale, loyalty, and engagement, he said.[54] For example, a poll on green employment by MonsterTRAK.com, a job website for students and entry-level hires, found that

HR Oops!

Starbucks Brews Up Controversy with "Race Together" Campaign

"Here's a venti caramel macchiato for Jake — and has anyone told you about our 'Race Together' initiative? Uh huh. Uh huh. No, I'm sorry sir. No, it's not because you're bl — No, I just have to give out 30 of these today and —No, you're right, it's stupid and I'm sorry. Oh, your drink is the wrong size? Sorry, I'm just so nervous. . . ." The following is a scenario of an awkward barista-customer exchange during Starbucks' (www.starbucks.ca) controversial 'Race Together' campaign.

Starbucks is well known for its commitment to social responsibility according to Manda Cuthbertson, director of operations and delivery at employer branding firm Blu Ivy Group (www.bluivygroup.com) in Toronto, however, the social campaign that had baristas writing the words, 'Race Together' on customers' cups, was met with skepticism and criticism, particularly on social media. CEO Howard Schultz said the intent of the campaign was to "stimulate conversation, compassion, and actions around race." However, in the wake of the response, senior vice-president for global communication, Corey duBrowa, even temporarily deleted his personal Twitter account. "I felt personally attacked in a cascade of negativity. I got overwhelmed by the volume and tenor of the discussion."

Asking employees to start conversations around core values invited scrutiny around Starbucks own track record of limited diversity of senior leadership and racial diversity. In addition, questions were raised about how baristas were trained and prepared for the conversations. A spokesperson for Starbucks said the CEO "delivered a video through a retail portal to all the company's employees on the initiative, but no formal training" was provided.

Questions

1. Why do you think Starbucks received such harsh criticism for its 'Race Together' campaign?

2. What advice do you have for CEO Howard Schultz about engaging and supporting employees in interactions with customers that extend beyond the usual duties and expectations of their jobs?

Sources: Liz Bernier, "Brewing Up Controversy," *Canadian HR Reporter*, April 20, 2015, p. I, II; Nancy Wartik, "Readers Respond to Starbucks 'Race Together' Initiative," *New York Times*, www.nytimes.com/2015/03/21/business/readers-respond-to-starbucks-race-together-initiative.html?_r=0, March 21, 2015, retrieved May 12, 2015; and Sydney Ember, "What Was Starbucks Thinking? 'Race Together' Campaign Generates Hostile Responses," *The National Post*, March 19, 2015, http://news.nationalpost.com/news/what-was-starbucks-thinking-race-together-campaign-generates-hostile-responses, retrieved May 12, 2015.

"92 percent would be more inclined to work for an environmentally friendly company and 80 percent of young professionals are interested in securing a job that has a positive impact on the environment."[55]

Almost a decade ago, Vancity (www.vancity.com) became the first carbon neutral financial institution in North America. Vancity met this goal with the help of experts including the University of British Columbia (www.ubc.ca), Ecotrust Canada (www.ecotrust.ca), and the David Suzuki Foundation (www.davidsuzuki.org).[56] Vancity has been committed to the environment since at least the early 1990s. The company makes it easier for employees to commute to work—back in the mid-1990s Vancity built its corporate head office on the SkyTrain line and encourages alternative transportation. For example, Vancity has a pool of Smart Cars and cruiser bikes at its Vancouver head office for employees to use to get to meetings and appointments (so they can leave their cars at home). Vancity appears to be attracting and retaining employees with similar values—63 percent of Vancity employees commute to work using alternative transportation compared to 33 percent in metro Vancouver overall.[57]

Volunteerism

Charitable initiatives—whether ongoing fundraisers or annual events—foster a sense of community within an organization, thereby increasing employees' satisfaction, engagement, and retention. For example, one of Deloitte's (www.deloitte.com) company values is "commitment to each other." Deloitte "believes that supporting the communities in which we do business makes good business sense and is an important part of our corporate responsibility." In one year, Deloitte staff raised $2 million for United Way (www.unitedway.org) across Canada, and it sponsors a nationwide Impact Day on which employees are encouraged to spend one paid workday together involved in local community projects. Beth Tyndall, senior manager of human resources at Deloitte, says, "By supporting people through their community activities, Deloitte generates employee engagement and commitment. Local charities benefit as well."[58]

A similar sense of volunteerism is fostered at TD Bank Group (www.td.com) where employees are provided time off to work as volunteers for a charitable organization of their choice. If they put in more than 40 hours of volunteering, they can even apply for a $500 grant that goes directly to their charity. Says Teri Currie, a member of the senior executive team, "Pride in an organization is best described as what employees are doing when no one is looking: Are they engaged with customers? With fellow employees? With the larger community?"[59] And at TELUS, team members and retirees have contributed $350 million to charitable organizations across Canada and volunteered 5.4 million hours of service in local communities.[60]

Meaningful Work

Another way organizations foster engagement is to match employees with on-the-job roles and projects that are connected to their values and create a sense of meaning and purpose for the employee. For example, when John Hancock joined Microsoft Canada (www.microsoft.com) in Toronto as a consultant, he went to work on an 18-month project with law enforcement agencies to develop a Child Exploitation Tracking System (CETS) to battle online sexual abuse. Five years later, Microsoft assigned him to be in charge of helping police forces around the world get CETS up and running. He says he's proud that the resources of Microsoft could be put toward developing such an important social tool. "Knowing that Microsoft Canada was the driving force behind the initiative is part of the attraction of coming into work every day."[61] Fostering pride and engagement through the opportunity to make a difference is also being promoted by governments across the country. For example the Nova Scotia government promotes pride in the public sector through the slogan "Make a Difference" as part of its strategy to attract, engage, and retain employees.[62]

Ethics

In the long-run, a high-performance organization meets high ethical standards. Ethics, defined in Chapter 1, establishes fundamental principles for behaviour, such as honesty and fairness. Organizations and their employees must meet these standards if they are to maintain positive long-term relationships with their employees, customers, and community. For example, Gerlinde Herrmann, president of The Herrmann Group (www.herrmanngroup.com), an HR management consulting firm in Ontario, cautions employers not to make empty promises about being an environmentally friendly organization to attract candidates—a practice experts call *greenwashing*. Herrmann, who serves on SHRM's Corporate Social Responsibility and Sustainability Special Expertise Panel, notes that potential employees check organizations' backgrounds and talk with employees to find out whether organizations deliver.[63]

Ethical behaviour is most likely to result from values held by the organization's leaders combined with systems that promote ethical behaviour. A number of organizational systems can promote ethical behaviour.[64] These include a written code of ethics that the organization distributes to employees and requires them to use in decision making. Publishing a list of ethical standards is not enough, however. The organization should reinforce ethical behaviour. For example, performance measures should include ethical standards. The organization should provide channels employees can use to ask questions about ethical behaviour or to seek help if they are expected to do something they believe is wrong.

Organizations also can provide training in ethical decision making, including training for supervisors in how to handle employees' concerns about ethical matters.

As these examples suggest, ethical behaviour is a human resource management concern. The systems that promote ethical behaviour include such HRM functions as training, performance management, and discipline policies. In today's business climate, ethical behaviour can also help a company attract workers—and customers—who share those high standards.

For example, Express Scripts Canada (ESC, www.express-scripts.ca), based in Mississauga, Ontario, was recently recognized as a "World's Most Ethical Company" by the Ethisphere Institute (www.ethisphere.com) for its best practices in corporate ethics. ESC drives its ethics-based culture through clearly communicated values called "Express Way," a code of conduct to guide employees' behaviours that provides both clear rules as well as the requirement to successfully complete annual training; monitoring various information and compliance audits that are provided directly to a committee of the board of directors.[65]

Taking a Key Role in Mergers and Acquisitions

Mergers and acquisitions dominate the business landscape. But the risks are high. It is estimated that 80 percent of mergers and acquisitions actually reduce shareholder value due to a combination of business and people issues. Reasons for these failures include:

- Combining strategic weaknesses rather than strategic strengths
- Top management conflict
- Failure to win employee support
- Loss of competitive position due to extended time to complete the deal.[66]

"In the past, HR issues might have been an afterthought in mergers and acquisitions (M&As), with the HR department only stepping in and playing a role once the deal was done. But there is growing recognition HR can and should contribute right from the start."[67] According to a survey conducted by the Society for Human Resource Management Foundation, "there is a direct correlation between involvement by human resources and successful mergers and acquisitions."[68]

Josée Dykun, vice-president of HR at Montreal-headquartered Yellow Pages Group (www.ypg.com), says that she gets involved "right at the start of the process, when the company decides to purchase another business." At this early stage, often referred to as *due diligence,* her work involves "identifying potential risks and liabilities and any potential integration issues in terms of alignment of things like working conditions, benefits, and pensions."[69] Sandra Munteanu, TELUS Senior Advisor, describes the importance of HR work during this due diligence phase. "We have a very comprehensive list of questions. We assess market culture, management team skills, key employees and potential cultural gaps. We collect data on everything," said Munteanu.[70]

The change and upheaval that accompanies a merger or acquisition is a key opportunity for HR to demonstrate its expertise to executives and serve as a trusted advisor. The key areas of HR due diligence are outlined in Table 11.5.

LO4 Discuss the role of HRM technology in high-performance work systems.

What Is the Role of HRM Technology?

Human resource departments can improve their own and their organization's performance by appropriately using new technology. New technology usually involves *automation and collaboration*—that is, using equipment and information processing to perform activities that had been performed by people

TABLE 11.5

Key Areas of HR Due Diligence in Mergers and Acquisitions

Key M&A Considerations	HR'S Role
Culture	• Assess the similarities and differences between the two companies with respect to issues such as where authority lies and how decisions are made. • Assess the emotional element of how employees feel about the company, leaders, and their openness to the change. • Map out differences between the acquiring company and the target company including how to bridge the gaps. • Create and execute a comprehensive communication plan to share a vision of the future and engage employees.
Analysis and retention of talent	• Ensure leadership talent is in place to lead and implement the transition. • Assess each key individual relative to competencies aligned to the needs of the new group. • Identify key people and take steps to retain them. • Put people in the right roles during the merger/acquisition. • Discuss individual job and career options.
Rewards structure	• Examine rewards and work environment factors.
Legal issues, e.g., outstanding human rights challenges	• Assess all outstanding legal issues including timetable for resolution and stakeholders involved.
Union issues, e.g., collective agreements	• Identify key stakeholders including history of relationship, and develop an integration timetable.

Sources: Adapted from Ruth N. Bramson, "HR's Role in Mergers and Acquisitions—Human Resource Management," http://findarticles.com, retrieved June 10, 2008; and Uyen Vu, "HR's Role in Mergers, Acquisitions," *Canadian HR Reporter*, December 4, 2006, pp. 17, 21.

and facilitating electronic communication between people. Over the last few decades, automation has improved HRM efficiency by reducing the number of people needed to perform routine tasks. Using automation can free HRM experts to concentrate on ways to determine how human resource management can help the organization meet its goals, so technology also can make this function more valuable.[71] For example, information technology provides ways to build and improve systems for knowledge generation and sharing, as part of a learning organization. Among the applications are databases or networking sites where employees can store and share their knowledge, online directories of employee skills and experiences, and online libraries of learning resources, such as technical manuals and employees' reports from seminars and training programs.

HRM Applications

HRC9

New technologies continue to be introduced. In fact, so many HRM applications are developed that publications serving the profession (such as *HR Magazine* and *Workforce*) devote annual issues to reviewing this topic. Some of the technologies that have been widely adopted are transaction processing, decision support systems, and expert systems.[72]

Transaction processing refers to computations and calculations involved in reviewing and documenting HRM decisions and practices. It includes documenting decisions and actions associated with employee relocation, training expenses, and enrolments in courses and benefit plans. Transaction processing also includes the activities required to meet government reporting requirements, such as filling out employment equity reports on which employers report information about employment equity group participation rates. Computers enable companies to perform these tasks more efficiently. Employers can fill out computerized forms and store HRM information in databases, so that it is easier to find, sort, and report.

transaction processing
Computations and calculations involved in reviewing and documenting HRM decisions and practices.

Decision support systems are computer software systems designed to help managers solve problems. They usually include a "what if?" feature that managers can use to enter different assumptions or data and see how the likely outcomes will change. This type of system can help managers make decisions for workforce planning. The manager can, for example, try out different assumptions about turnover rates to see how those assumptions affect the number of new employees needed. Or the manager can test a range of assumptions about the availability of a certain skill in the labour market, looking at the impact of the assumptions on the success of different recruiting plans. Possible applications for a decision support system include forecasting (discussed in Chapter 3) and succession planning (discussed in Chapter 4).

decision support systems
Computer software systems designed to help managers solve problems by showing how results vary when the manager alters assumptions or data.

Expert systems are computer systems that incorporate the decision rules used by people who are considered to have expertise in a certain area. The systems help users make decisions by recommending actions based on the decision rules and the information provided by the users. An expert system is designed to recommend the same actions that a human expert would in a similar situation. For example, an expert system could guide an interviewer during the selection process. Some organizations use expert systems to help employees decide how to allocate their money for benefits (as in a flexible plan) and help managers schedule the labour needed to complete projects. Expert systems can deliver both high quality and lower costs. By using the decision processes of experts, an expert system helps many people to arrive at decisions that reflect the expert's knowledge. It helps avoid the errors that can result from fatigue and decision-making biases, such as biases in appraising employee performance, described in Chapter 7; and it can increase efficiency by enabling fewer or less-skilled employees to do work that otherwise would require many highly skilled employees.

expert systems
Computer systems that support decision making by incorporating the decision rules used by people who are considered to have expertise in a certain area.

In proactive HR departments, transaction processing, decision support systems, and expert systems are often part of a human resource information system. Also, these technologies may be linked to employees through a network such as an intranet. Information systems and networks have been evolving rapidly; the following descriptions provide a basic introduction.

Human Resource Information Systems

A standard feature of a modern HRIS is the use of *relational databases*, which store data in separate files that can be linked by common elements. These common elements are fields identifying the type of data. Commonly used fields for an HR database include name, social insurance number, job status (full- or part-time), hiring date, position, title, rate of pay, job history, job location, mailing address, birth date, and emergency contacts. A relational database lets a user sort the data by any of the fields. For example, depending on how the database is set up, the user might be able to look up tables listing employees by location, rate of pay for various jobs, or training courses employees have completed, or languages spoken. This system is far more sophisticated than the old-fashioned method of filing employee data by name, with one file per employee.

The ability to locate and combine many categories of data has a multitude of uses in human resource management. Databases have been developed to track employee benefit costs, training courses, and compensation. The system can meet the needs of managers as well as the HR department. On an oil rig, for example, management might look up data listing employee names along with safety equipment issued and appropriate skill certification. HR managers at headquarters might look up data on the same employees to gather information about wage rates or training programs needed. Another popular use of an HRIS is applicant tracking, or maintaining and retrieving records of job applicants. This is much faster and easier than trying to deal with printed résumés. With relational databases, HR staff can retrieve information about specific applicants or obtain lists of applicants with specific skills, career goals, work history, and employment background. Such information is useful for workforce planning, recruitment, succession planning, and career development. Taking the process a step further, the system could store information related to hiring and terminations. By analyzing such data, the HR department could measure the long-term success of its recruiting and selection processes.

One of the most creative developments in HRIS technology is the **HR dashboard**, a display of a series of HR-related indicators, or measures, showing human resource goals and objectives and the progress toward meeting them. Managers with access to the HRIS can look at the HR dashboard for an easy-to-scan review of HR performance.

HR dashboard

A display of a series of HR measures, showing human resource goals and objectives and progress toward meeting them.

Human Resource Management Online: E-HRM

During the last decade or so, organizations have seen the advantages of sharing information in computer networks. At the same time, the widespread adoption of the Internet has linked people around the globe. As we discussed in Chapter 1, more and more organizations are engaging in E-HRM, providing HR-related information over the Internet. Because much human resource information is confidential, organizations may do this with an intranet, which uses Internet technology but allows access only to authorized users (such as the organization's employees). For HR professionals, Internet access also offers a way to research new developments, post job openings, trade ideas with colleagues in other organizations, and obtain government documents. In this way, E-HRM combines company-specific information on a secure intranet with links to the resources on the broader Internet.

As Internet use has increasingly taken the form of social-media applications, E-HRM has moved in this direction as well. Generally speaking, social media bring networks of people together to collaborate on projects, solve problems, or socialize. Social-media applications for human resource management include YouTube access to instructional videos, Facebook-style networking sites where employees can share project updates and ideas for improvement, Web pages where employees can identify peers' accomplishments and deliver rewards, and crowdsourcing tools for performance appraisals. In terms of job design, social media can promote teamwork by providing an easy means of collaboration, and for recruiting over great distances social media can allow virtual job fairs and/or selection interviews. As the use of social media continues to expand, creative minds will devise many other applications that forward-thinking HR professionals can introduce as ways to get employees more fully engaged with the organization and one another.

A benefit of E-HRM is that employees can help themselves to the information they need when they need it, instead of contacting an HR staff person. For example, employees can go online to enrol in or select benefits, submit insurance claims, or fill out employee satisfaction surveys. This can be more convenient for the employees, as well as more economical for the HR department. Adding another kind of convenience, some companies are offering access to online coaching. Employees can look up answers to common problems in databases, post questions for colleagues to answer, or contact a professional online. Thanks to the versatility and efficiency of this kind of coaching, employers can offer it to employees at all levels, not just executives or high-potential managers targeted for development.[73]

Most administrative and information-gathering activities in human resource management can be part of E-HRM. For example, online recruiting has become a significant part of the total recruiting effort, as candidates submit résumés online. Employers go online to retrieve suitable résumés from job search sites or retrieve information from forms they post at their own websites. For selection decisions, the organization may have candidates use one of the online testing services available; these services conduct the tests, process the results, and submit reports to employers. Companies can automate aspects of job design, such as schedules, delivery routes, and production layouts. Online appraisal or talent management systems provide data that can help managers spot high performers to reward or types of skills where additional training is a priority. After Comcast (www.comcast.com) installed a computerized talent management system, supervisors caught up with a backlog of performance appraisals, and management became able to find the best employees to groom for promotions.[74] Many types of training can be conducted online, as we discussed in Chapter 6. Herman Miller (www.hermanmiller.com), which makes office furniture, set up a performance support system that lets its salespeople use their mobile devices to learn about new product features whether they are in the office or out with clients.[75] Online surveys of employee satisfaction or engagement can be quick and easy to fill out. Besides providing a way to administer the survey, an intranet is an effective vehicle for communicating the results of the survey and management's planned response.

Not only does E-HRM provide efficient ways to carry out human resource functions, it also poses new challenges to employees and new issues for HR managers to address. The Internet's ability to link people anytime, anywhere has accelerated such trends as globalization, the importance of knowledge sharing, the need for flexibility, and cloud computing. As discussed in Chapter 1, cloud computing is another recent advance in technology that has several implications for HR practices. Cloud computing involves using a network of remote servers hosted on the Internet to store, manage, and process data. These services are offered by data centres around the world (and not within an organization's offices) and are collectively called "the cloud." These services offer the ability to access information that's delivered on demand from any device, anywhere, at any time. Global giant Siemens (www.siemens.com) is said to have the largest cloud computing system in the world for its more than 400,000 employees across 190 countries. In an effort to become more efficient, the company standardized its global recruitment and personal development processes into a single system via the cloud.[76]

L○5 Summarize ways to measure the effectiveness of human resource management.

Effectiveness of Human Resource Management

HRC 1, 2, 9

In recent years, human resource management at many organizations has been taking a customer-oriented approach. For an organization's human resource division, "customers" are the organization as a whole and its other divisions. They are customers of HRM because they depend on HRM to provide a variety of services that result in a supply of talented, motivated employees. Taking this customer-oriented approach, human resource management defines its customer groups, customer needs, and the activities required to meet those needs, as shown in Table 11.6. These definitions give an organization a basis for defining goals and measures of success.

Depending on the situation, a number of techniques are available for measuring HRM's effectiveness in meeting its customers' needs. These techniques include reviewing a set of key indicators, measuring the outcomes of specific HRM activity, and measuring the economic value or ROI (return on investment) of HRM programs.

Human Resource Management Audits

An **HRM audit** is a formal review of the outcomes of HRM functions. To conduct the audit, the HR department identifies key functions and the key measures of organizational performance and customer satisfaction that would indicate each function is succeeding. Table 11.7 lists examples of these measures for a variety of HRM functions: staffing, rewards, benefits, training, appraisal and development, and overall effectiveness. The audit may also look at any other measure associated with successful management of human resources—for instance, compliance with employment-related legislation, succession planning, maintaining a safe workplace, and positive labour relations. An HRM audit using customer satisfaction measures supports the customer-oriented approach to human resource management. When HR functions are outsourced, these audits need to look at both HR functions performed internally and those that are outsourced.

HRM audit

A formal review of the outcomes of HRM functions, based on identifying key HRM functions and measures of organizational performance.

After identifying performance measures for the HRM audit, the staff carries out the audit by gathering information. The information for the key business indicators is usually available in the organization's documents. Sometimes the HR department has to create new documents for gathering specific types of data. The usual way to measure customer satisfaction is to conduct surveys. Employee surveys provide information about the satisfaction of these internal customers. Many organizations conduct surveys of top executives to get a better view of how HRM practices affect the organization's business success. To benefit from the HR profession's best practices, companies also may invite external auditing teams to audit specific HR functions. Of course, the benefits of the audit are only as great as the company's response to what it learns and applies to enhance existing processes and tools.

TABLE 11.6

Customer-Oriented Perspective of Human Resource Management

Who Are Our Customers?	What Do Our Customers Need?	How Do We Meet Customer Needs?
• Managers and supervisors	• Committed employees	• Qualified staffing
• Strategic planners	• Competent employees	• Performance management
• Employees		• Rewards
		• Training, learning, and development

TABLE 11.7

Key Measures of Success for an HRM Audit

Business Indicators	Customer Satisfaction Measures
Staffing	
Average days taken to fill open requisitions	Anticipation of human resource needs
Ratio of acceptances to offers made	Timeliness of referring qualified workers to line supervisors
Ratio of employment equity target group applicant representation in local labour market	Treatment of applicants
Per capita requirement costs	Skill in handling terminations
Average years of experience/education of hires	Adaptability to changing labour market conditions
Compensation	
Per capita (average) merit increases	Fairness of existing job evaluation system
Ratio of recommendations for reclassification to number of employees	Competitiveness in local labour market
Percentage of overtime hours to regular time	Relationship between pay and performance
Ratio of average salary offers to average salary in community	Employee satisfaction with pay
Benefits	
Average workers' compensation payments	Promptness in handling claims
Benefit cost per payroll dollar	Fairness and consistency in the application of benefit policies
Percentage of sick leave to total pay	Communication of benefits to employees
	Assistance provided to managers in reducing potential for unnecessary claims
Training	
Percentage of employees participating in training programs	Extent to which training programs meet the needs of employees and the company
Percentage of employees receiving tuition reimbursement	Communication to employees about available training opportunities
Training dollars/days per employee	Quality of orientation/onboarding programs
Employee Appraisal and Development	
Distribution of performance appraisal ratings	Assistance in identifying management potential
Appropriate psychometric properties of appraisal forms	Organizational development activities provided by HRM department
Overall Effectiveness	
Ratio of human resources staff to employee population	Accuracy and clarity of information provided to managers and employees
Turnover rate	Competence and expertise of staff
Absenteeism rate	Working relationship between organizations and HRM department
Ratio of per capita revenues to per capita cost	
Net income per employee	

Source: Reprinted with permission, excerpts from Chapter 1.5, "Evaluating Human Resource Effectiveness," pp. 187–227, by Anne S. Tsui and Luis R. Gomez-Mejia, from *Human Resource Management: Evolving Roles and Responsibilities*, ed. Lee Dyer. © 1988 by The Bureau of National Affairs, Inc., Washington, DC 20037.

Analyzing the Effect of HRM Programs

Another way to measure HRM effectiveness is the use of **HR analytics**. This process involves measuring a program's success in terms of whether it achieved its objectives and whether it delivered value in an economic sense. For example, if the organization sets up a training program it should set up goals for that program, such as the training's effect on learning, behaviour, and performance improvement (results). The analysis would then measure whether the training program achieved the preset goals. Increasingly HR is being called on to measure its impact. The Conference Board of Canada identifies "measurement" as an important HR issue and indicates that HR measures must be meaningful due to the importance of HR's role in building organizational capabilities.[77]

> **HR analytics**
> Type of assessment of HRM effectiveness that involves determining the impact of, or the financial cost and benefits of, a program or practice.

Senior management and other organizational stakeholders are asking for metrics or measures that relate to the value of the firm's human capital and the return on investment in that human capital. A report from CFO Research Services (www.cfo.com) and Mercer Human Resource Consulting (www.mercer.com) revealed that chief financial officers' opinions of HR are improving—most of the 180 CFOs surveyed see human capital as a value driver rather than a cost. However, the survey also showed that just 16 percent of CFOs said they knew to a "considerable" or "great" extent the return on investments in human capital.[78]

"Traditional financial numbers are an indicator of past performance, but reliable measures of human capital are much better indicators of future performance, and therefore growth, and therefore shareholder value," says Curt Coffman of the Gallup Organization.[79] However, caution about calculating the value of human capital is needed. "Accounting deals principally with fixed assets. Once you buy them all they do is depreciate over time," says Jac Fitz-enz, the founder of Human Capital Source (www.humancapitalsource.com). "But humans are just the opposite: they appreciate over time as they grow and develop."[80] Furthermore, the return on investment of specific, isolated HR initiatives is needed. When individual HR initiatives are evaluated in isolation on strictly quantitative terms, there may be a tendency to focus on cost containment only with a failure to consider qualitative considerations and indirect benefits. For example, if an investment in human capital, such as a training program, yields tangible results, such as an increase in product quality and a decrease in product returns, this only quantifies part of the return on investment. The ROI calculation may not fully capture the improved employee and/or customer satisfaction achieved as a result of the training. Figure 11.11 provides the math for calculating the return on investment of an investment in human capital including both direct and indirect costs and benefits.

In general, HR departments should be able to improve their performance through some combination of greater efficiency and greater effectiveness. Greater efficiency means the HR department uses fewer and less-costly resources to perform its functions. Greater effectiveness means that what the HR department does—for example, selecting employees or setting up a performance management system—has a more beneficial effect on employees' and the organization's performance. The computing power

FIGURE 11.11

ROI Math

$$\text{ROI \%} = \frac{\text{Realized direct/indirect benefits} - \text{Total direct/indirect costs} \times 100}{\text{Total direct/indirect costs}}$$

SOURCE: Adapted from "ROI Math," *Canadian HR Reporter,* February 28, 2005, p. 15.

Thinking ETHICALLY

How Can HRM Help Maintain an Ethical Culture?

On some level, the choice to behave ethically is always a personal choice. However, there are some measures that organizations can take to promote ethical conduct. And many of those efforts can start or be supported by human resources professionals.

One approach, for example, is to create a climate of trust. Businesspeople can readily see that trust provides a strong foundation for all kinds of business relationships, including purchase contracts, labour-management agreements, and employees' confidence in the fairness of supervisors' decisions. People are more likely to trust an organization, manager, or employee when they see evidence of competence, openness and honesty, concern for stakeholders including employees and the community, reliability in keeping commitments, and identification with the organization in the sense that an individual's values match up with the values expressed by the organization. HR professionals can provide performance feedback, training, coaching, and rewards to foster the development of many of these drivers of trust. Job design in which employees are empowered to deliver excellent customer care, make well-crafted products, or deliver other valued outcomes helps to align individual practices with an organization's highest values.

Another way to maintain an ethical culture is to define ethical conduct and ethical abuses and to respond appropriately when these are detected. Ethical conduct should be rewarded. Employee development programs should include goals for the trust-building ethical practices of leaders, and developmental work assignments should include opportunities to try out those kinds of behaviour. Ethical abuses should be punished, not ignored or hidden. When ethical violations are tolerated, employees take away the message that the organization is not actually serious about ethics. HR professionals can support these objectives with performance measures and pay policies that reward ethical conduct, never ethical lapses.

Questions

1. Imagine that you work in the human resource department of a company that sells medical equipment. One of the salespeople, who has an enormous amount of student loans, is tempted to misrepresent the uses of the equipment in order to increase his sales and therefore the commissions he earns. As an HR professional, how much can you do to shape a salesperson's conduct so that it remains ethical (and legal)?

2. Would you prefer to work at a company where the human resource department has developed and established policies to promote ethical conduct, such as the ones described here? Why or why not?

Sources: Pamela Shockley-Zalabak, "A Matter of Trust," *Communication World*, May–June 2011, pp. 17–21; Ross Tartell, "Can Leadership Ethics Be Learned?" *Training*, May/June 2011, EBSCOhost, http://web.ebscohost.com; Christiane Krieger-Boden, "Ethics, Trust and Altruism in Society, Politics and Business," background paper to Global Economic Symposium 2011, August 8, 2011, accessed at www.global-economic-symposium.org.

available to today's organizations, coupled with people who have skills in HR analytics, enables companies to find more ways than ever to identify practices associated with greater efficiency and effectiveness. For example, organizations can measure patterns in employees' social networks—who is talking to whom, how often—and combine that with performance data. One lesson from such research is that a recruiter's closest friends and colleagues are less useful as a source of leads to qualified job candidates than are people the recruiter communicates with only occasionally. These less-close associates are likelier to have acquaintances who aren't already familiar to the recruiter.[81]

HRM's potential to affect employees' well-being and the organization's performance makes human resource management an exciting and rewarding field. As we have shown throughout the book, every HRM function calls for decisions that have the potential to help individuals and organizations achieve their goals. For HR professionals to fulfill that potential, they must ensure that their decisions are well grounded. The field of human resource management provides tremendous opportunity to future researchers and managers who want to make a difference in many people's lives and contribute to the success of organizations.

SUMMARY

LO1 Define high-performance work systems and identify the elements, outcomes, and conditions associated with such a system.

A high-performance work system is the right combination of people, technology, and organizational structure that makes full use of the organization's resources and opportunities in achieving its goals. The elements of a high-performance work system are organizational structure, task design, people, reward systems, and information systems. These elements must work together in a smoothly functioning whole.

A high-performance work system achieves the organization's goals, typically including growth, productivity, and high profits. On the way to achieving these overall goals, the high-performance work system meets such intermediate goals as high quality, innovation, customer satisfaction, job satisfaction, employee engagement, and reduced absenteeism and turnover. Many conditions contribute to high-performance work systems by providing employees with skills, incentives, knowledge, and autonomy.

LO2 Describe how organizations assess employee satisfaction and engagement.

Employee satisfaction and employee engagement is usually assessed with a survey. Having a systematic ongoing program of surveys allows the organization to monitor trends and should be part of the HR strategy. Conducting surveys should be taken seriously because they raise employee expectations. Exit interviews may be used to uncover reasons employees leave. Stay interviews may uncover issues that if addressed effectively, support employee retention.

LO3 Explain how human resource management can contribute to high performance.

Jobs should be designed to foster teamwork and employee empowerment. Recruitment and selection should focus on obtaining employees who have the qualities necessary for teamwork and knowledge sharing. Training also is important, because of its role in creating a learning organization. The performance management system should be related to the organization's goals, with a focus on meeting internal and external customers' needs. Total compensation and rewards should include links to performance, and employees should be included in decisions about compensation.

Generally, organizations try to avoid the need for involuntary turnover and minimize voluntary turnover. Organizations also need to handle employee discipline effectively in order to foster fairness and meet legal requirements. Although HR has historically been excluded from playing an early and strategic role in a merger or acquisition, there is growing evidence that when HR is involved early, the merger or acquisition is more likely to be successful.

LO4 Discuss the role of HRM technology in high-performance work systems.

Technology can improve the efficiency of the human resource management functions and support knowledge sharing. HRM applications involve transaction processing, decision support systems, and expert systems, often as part of a human resource information system using relational databases, which can improve the efficiency of routine tasks and the quality of decisions. With Internet technology, organizations can use E-HRM to let all the organization's employees help themselves to the HR information they need whenever they need it.

LO5 Summarize ways to measure the effectiveness of human resource management.

Taking a customer-oriented approach, HRM can improve quality by defining the internal customers who use its services and determining whether it is meeting those customers' needs. One way to do this is with an HRM audit, a formal review of the outcomes of HRM functions. The audit may look at any measure associated with successful management of human resources. Audit information may come from the organization's documents and surveys of customer satisfaction. Another way to measure HRM effectiveness is the use of HR analytics. Analysis can measure success in terms of whether a program met its objectives, and whether it delivered value in an economic sense, such as by leading to productivity improvements and generating a return on investment.

Critical Thinking Questions

1. What is a high-performance work system? What are its elements? Which of these elements involve human resource management?

2. How does your workplace compare to the conditions for high performance identified near the beginning of this chapter? Discuss.

3. As it has become clear that HRM can help create and maintain high-performance work systems, it appears that organizations will need two kinds of human resources professionals: one focuses on identifying how HRM can contribute to high performance; the other develops expertise in particular HRM functions, such as how to administer a benefits program that complies with legal requirements. Which is more interesting to you? Why?

4. Consider your current job or a job you recently held. Overall, were you satisfied or dissatisfied? How would you describe your level of engagement? How did your level of satisfaction and engagement affect your behaviour and performance on the job?

5. Why are exit interviews important? Should an organization care about the opinions of people who are leaving? How are those opinions relevant to employee retention?

6. How can an organization promote ethical behaviour among its employees?

7. Summarize how each of the following HR functions can contribute to high performance.

   a. Job design

   b. Recruitment and selection

   c. Training, learning, and development

   d. Performance management

   e. Compensation and rewards

8. Why do you think that a merger or acquisition is more likely to be successful when HR is involved from the start of the process?

9. How can HRM technology make a human resource department more productive? How can technology improve the quality of HRM decisions?

10. Why should human resource departments measure their effectiveness? What are some ways they can go about measuring effectiveness?

Experiencing HR

Divide into groups of about six students each. Visit the website for *Canada's Top 100 Employers* (www.canadastop100.com/national/). Scan the complete list of companies, and then choose a company that interests your group. Click the link for the company information. Read the reasons for selecting this company as one of the best, and take notes on what you learn. Next, visit the Glassdoor website (www.glassdoor.ca) and use its search function to look up company information for the company you selected. On the company page, use the Reviews link to read the information employees have posted about what it is like to work at this company. Look for patterns, and take notes on what you learn.

As a group, discuss what these two sources tell you about employee engagement and job satisfaction at the company you selected. What criteria does the Top 100 Employers list use for selecting organizations? What criteria do the reviewers on Glassdoor use for reporting their satisfaction or dissatisfaction? What criteria from this chapter are not mentioned? Imagine you work in HR at the company you evaluated. What would you do to address any dissatisfaction you observe in the Glassdoor reviews? Be prepared to summarize your discussion in class (or, if your instructor directs, write a one-page summary of your discussion).

CASE STUDY 11.1:

The Keg: Maintaining the Sizzle

Employees at the Keg stay for years—an eternity in the food-service business and a testament to its work culture. The stately dining room at the Keg Mansion in downtown Toronto is empty—for now. It's 4 o'clock on a Friday afternoon, and Stephanie Brownridge is setting up her section for the night. Like all the other Fridays, it's going to be a busy one. The 29-year-old is doing the usual: rolling up the silverware, setting down the wineglasses, dimming the lights way down low. In her head, she's going over the "sizzle." That's Keg-speak for the exhausting features spiel servers have to memorize and recite for each table. She's got three, maybe four, different versions in her arsenal. This month, it's all about the pistachio-crusted salmon. Her first guests arrive at 5 o'clock. They sit. She sizzles: "If you're not feeling the steak tonight, the salmon is my favourite," she says. "It's so yummy; it has maple butter on it." They look impressed.

First one down. That night, Brownridge will say her sizzle at least 15 more times as the restaurant fills up with suits, tourists, and giddy young couples who saved up all week for a fancy night out. And that's not even the most repetitive part. "It's the ghost stories," she says. The Keg Mansion is housed in a Toronto heritage building once occupied by the prominent Massey family and, according to lore, a servant hung herself in the front foyer. "Every other table will ask if I've seen the ghost," Brownridge says. "Am I tired of telling the story? Absolutely. But it's part of the job."

Sizzling, storytelling, serving: Brownridge does it until her last guests leave, often in the wee hours of the morning—all for $9.50 an hour, plus tips. Evenings and weekends might be the rest of the world's playtime, but it's her nine-to-five. "The long hours are not my favourite," she admits. Yet despite the stressful nature of the job, Brownridge has been doing it for seven years—an eternity in the food-service industry. And she doesn't plan to quit any time soon. "Even if I got a better-paying job somewhere else, I'd probably keep this job a couple days a week because I actually really love it," she says, her gaze becoming fixed. "Seriously, I'm not lying."

Her love of the job isn't just thanks to a great team or a great boss—it starts with her boss's boss's boss. Keg Restaurants Ltd. CEO David Aisenstat is one of the executives who not only understands why it's important to engage employees—he knows how to do it. Aisenstat may now oversee a successful chain of 107 restaurants in Canada and the U.S., but boyhood memories of making milkshakes and bussing tables are still painfully entrenched in his brain; he understands how gruelling the business can be. It's one reason why the Vancouver-based company has placed such strong focus on engaging its workforce. The Keg has made the list of the 50 Best Employers in Canada for 13 straight years; this year, some 85 percent of its front-line workers reported high satisfaction with their job, and turnover rates are well below industry average. Tenure like Brownridge's is not rare. The Keg's secret is deceptively simple: people at the Keg aren't just told that they matter, they are shown exactly why, and that is a serious driver of engagement. Every employee, from the greeter to the griller, is made to understand how integral their work is to the success of the company. "There are no second-class citizens here. You can't serve a dish without a dishwasher and you can't seat a customer without a busboy," says Aisenstat. "Our people are the most important factor if we want to succeed. I'd say they're even more important than our steaks."

It sounds nice to equate good staff with good sales—it's what a CEO is supposed to say. But pleasant platitudes don't create an army of merry journeymen. Action does. And that's where the Keg excels.

Cocktail hour is over and the medium-rares start coming out of the kitchen. The pace is frenetic, but Brownridge's energy is still as high and her sizzles as peppy as they were earlier in the shift. It's all that "Kegger" blood, the moniker given to the 6,900 people who work at the company in Canada. Brownridge is what you'd call an exemplary Kegger. She's pretty, talkative—the kind of girl who was probably popular in high school but nice to the nerds, too. In fact, a lot of the Keg's employees are like that, even the guy who preps salads in the back, thanks to a hiring process that prefers personality over experience. The firm's favoured recruiting tactic is to ask current staff to recommend their like-minded, extroverted friends. "Keggers are people people," the Keg's HR director, Dean Sockett, says. "They've got a sense of humour and they're lots of fun to be around."

Making things fun—getting employees to truly engage—is tricky to do even for "cushy" jobs. Just try doing it in hospitality, where employees tend to defect—or, perhaps worse, go on autopilot—much more often than the norm. Working in a restaurant or hotel often means dealing with unpredictable schedules, long hours, low pay, and lousy customers. And it's work that attracts the young and green, which naturally fuels turnover.

Engaging employees is too often seen as a simple matter that can be fixed with perks and pay, which is why so many bosses in low-paying, unglamourous industries think it's a futile effort. But at its core, engagement is about a strong foundation of management practices that empower workers and inspire them to excel, says Neil Crawford, a partner at consulting firm Aon Hewitt, which measures engagement levels among firms to compile its annual Best Employers in Canada rankings. Any employer can offer that kind of engagement. "You need to have an environment where people feel like there are more opportunities to improve, that they're constantly getting feedback and feeling valued," says Crawford. His research underscores why this matters: Companies with highly engaged employees regularly achieve higher-than-average levels of productivity, customer satisfaction, and revenue growth.

That's why the Keg cultivates camaraderie from the very moment a Kegger gets hired. The company employs a unique approach to training, in which every new recruit is paired with an employee who teaches them how to bartend, bus, expedite, host—pretty much every role short of manning the grill. It's sort of like a booze-shilling buddy system. After the pair has spent four or five training shifts together, the company gives them snacks and drinks on the house so they can, essentially, hang out. Ta-da, one new friendship.

It's a smart way to address one of the job's inherent drawbacks: the hours. "Restaurants aren't like a normal, nine-to-five business," says Kelowna-based employee-engagement expert Linda Edgecombe (who, coincidentally, worked at the Keg in the '80s, and recalls quaffing B-52 shooters with her workplace pals after-hours). "Evening shifts are hard on your employees' social life and relationships. If you want to reduce turnover, you have to create an environment that they want to hang out in." Cultivating on-the-job friendships also takes the edge off the grind and underscores that employee experience matters. If it all sounds a bit like a Barney song, it's worth noting that besties are actually good for business. "If you can have a friend at work, you're going to be much more engaged and perform better," says David Zinger, a Winnipeg-based employee-engagement consultant. It's why Brownridge can't bring herself to leave. "I've left and come back twice because the people make this an awesome place to work," she says. "I've made all my best friends here."

Kegger friendships are buttressed by a strong element of mutual respect; there's little of the toxic interpersonal resentments that fester in many high-stress workplaces. (According to the Keg's Best Employers survey, 84 percent of its front-line employees have good feelings about their co-workers.) And that's all by design. The fact that every employee has to learn how to do the job of everyone else helps each one understand—and appreciate—the unique pressures of each role. When the waitress knows not to toss dirty forks in the rinse pit, the dishwasher feels more respected and valued; when the bar-back understands why letting Polar Ice stores run low might anger thirsty patrons, the bartender feels more supported. It's a virtuous cycle that makes everyone feel important.

This doesn't stop with co-workers. A full 80 percent of managers are hired from within, meaning they know what it's like to work in the trenches. Moreover, Keg managers don't hide out in the office; they are trained to pick up a scrub brush or a martini shaker if it will de-stress the staff and lead to a better customer experience. This policy is about more than getting the job done; it's a highly visual way to stress that no Kegger is above doing the work of any other. "This helps everyone see that the hierarchy is limited here," says Sockett. (Some 83 percent of Keggers consider their managers to be effective leaders.)

There's a wine spill in the dining room. There's always a wine spill somewhere at the Keg. They're the bane of the restaurant business: an instant killer of customer experience, and a huge embarrassment for the staff.

Lucky for Brownridge, the spill didn't happen in her section. She's been spill-free her last couple of shifts; the last really bad one was when a ramekin of ketchup flew off a plate she was carrying and hit the floor. It splattered on her guest's suit. He was miffed. She was mortified—but she also knew it wouldn't ruin her shift.

The Keg has a budget for incidents like this. Whatever the damage, the restaurant, not the staff, will foot the bill, and offer up an apology letter and cheque for dry-cleaning to the guest. (In one recent incident, a server spilled melted butter on a guest's $2,000 Gucci purse. The manager cut a cheque on the spot, calming both the stressed staffer and the irked customer in one fell swoop.) "There's nothing more frustrating on a busy night when you're scrambling around and you screw up," says the Mansion's general manager, Robert Duncan. "We don't believe in making them pay for their mistakes." The fund also covers the bills of people who've dined and dashed—which many foodservice employers dock from employee paycheques—along with comped extras for customers whom the staff deem worthy. It all tells employees that the company has their interests at heart. "If we're able to enhance the guest experience, then there's a much better chance that the staff will get a better tip as a result," Duncan adds.

As for difficult customers, staff are encouraged to page a manager if things get out of hand, and managers are trained to side with their staff in defusing the situation. According to Alexandria McKinney, who, as one of the Keg's lead hostesses, is usually the first one to face the impatient and expletive-inclined, this is a huge plus. "It's a very fearless environment in that way," she says, "because managers will always have our back." Even if that means losing a bill. Aisenstat himself once kicked out a belligerent guest overheard calling a server "a . . . idiot." Gestures like these not only make employees feel supported, they also neatly reverse the "customer is king" mantra that wears down so many front-line workers.

The Keg lends that extra bit of empowerment and control back to the staff in other ways: in allowing last-minute schedule changes (something appreciated by the students on staff during exam time), in encouraging open dialogue practices (employees fill out anonymous surveys of management twice a year), and in promising consistency (if you've always worked Mondays, then you can expect to work Mondays). Brownridge found out just how unique these policies are in her dalliances working at other establishments—once in fine dining, the other time at another steak-house. It only took a few shifts at each to reveal that not every restaurant is so supportive. "Here, it's more flexible," she says.

The restaurant starts to clear out, which means two or three Keggers will clock out every half hour until close. At around 11 p.m., it's Brownridge's turn. She cashes out, changes clothes, and goes upstairs to the bar to join a couple other Keggers who are done for the night. They drink beer, order something to eat off the menu, complain about a customer or two, decompress. As the night progresses, more Keggers join the table. The empty glasses pile up. "We always joke that we give the Keg back all the money we make," says Brownridge.

It's that friendship factor again, and it's fostered in ways that don't involve rounds of Keg-sized Caesars, too. There are annual two-day staffer-only ski trips, which cost the firm a cool $140,000 each year. There are softball tournaments, baseball outings, and summer barbeques. And there's the annual Keg Oscars and Kitchen Emmys, a prom-like soiree that celebrates the work of exceptional performers. This year, the Mansion staff all went together, renting a limo and wearing matching red boutonnieres and corsages.

It all transfers into a culture of inclusion, empowerment, and support in which everyone is made to feel like a someone. A closer inspection of the restaurant's Best Employers data shows that culture-related factors are the main reasons workers wrap on an apron and happily clock in for the night—they even trump pay. It's something that all employers, especially those who struggle to fill physically demanding, repetitive, customer-facing jobs, should take note of before dismissing employee engagement as a useless buzzword. The Keg's management say its people-friendly policies facilitate better customer experiences, which lead to stronger sales, which lead to happier shareholders. In this context, it's hard to argue that making the effort to get employees excited about prepping steaks, bussing tables, and telling a ghost story about a long-dead maid for the 283rd time isn't worth the energy.

Source: Mai Nguyen, "How to Make Any Job Sizzle," *Canadian Business*, December 2014, pp. 64–69.

Questions

1. On the basis of the information provided in the case, how does the Keg encourage teamwork and empowerment?

2. What does the Keg do to keep employees like Stephanie Brownridge satisfied, engaged, and willing to stay with the organization?

3. On the basis of the information provided in the case, identify how the Keg's HR practices contribute to high performance. What advice do you have to enhance HR practices at the Keg?

CASE STUDY 11.2:

Fairmont Hotels & Resorts: Growing Environmental Stewardship

While the health of the world's ecosystem is a hot topic, it has been a priority at Fairmont Hotels & Resorts (www.fairmont.com), one of "Canada's Greenest Employers" since 1990. With the debut of its "Green Partnership Program," the Toronto-based company initiated a chain-wide environmental program, and literally wrote the book in its industry on how to build a greener business—entitled the "Green Partnership Guide," now in its third edition. The program has expanded to 50 locations around the world, garnered several international awards, and been an inspiration for others in the hospitality industry and beyond. The move to greener pastures was prompted by the company's locations (then known as Canadian Pacific Hotels) in sensitive environments, such as national parks, biosphere reserves, and coastal zones or wetlands. "We realized we had to mitigate our operation impacts on the environment, because if you take care of the environment, you take care of the very resource that brings your guests to explore in the first place," said Michelle White, director of environmental affairs at Fairmont.

Looking to have a gentler environmental footprint, the company first focused on waste management (recycling, organics diversion, and food and goods redistribution), energy conservation (lighting retrofits, HVAC upgrades, alternative technology, and sustainability), and water conservation (tap aerators, low-flow shower heads, low-flush toilets, and wastewater recycling).

The rise of responsible tourism has also meant Fairmont is sharing the benefits of business with the community, particularly in emerging markets where economic development is a challenge. A Fairmont property in Mexico is selling local tours, and giving part of the proceeds back to the community and the rest to a conservation fund for the biosphere. "Over time, we realized you couldn't be a really green hotel and good corporate citizen unless you also look at your community involvement," said White.

Beyond helping the environment, Fairmont has seen gains in areas such as guest loyalty, brand identity, and media interest, while developing a reputation as an environmental leader and demonstrating corporate social responsibility. There have also been cost efficiencies, such as lighting or retrofits that reduce utilities consumption, though White admits costs can vary, depending on the supporting infrastructure.

Fairmont has garnered award-praise for its efforts. For example Fairmont received the global tourism business award for the best corporate social responsibility program at MKG's Worldwide Hospitality Awards, the global tourism business award from the World Travel and Tourism Council, and is recognized as one of Canada's Greenest Employers. But behind it all is the commitment and enthusiasm of its 26,000 employees around the world, including 10,500 in Canada. "Before implementing a program of this scale, you want to make sure you have a lot of employee buy-in," she said. "If they care about those things at home, they like to see that brought over to their workplace as well."

"The biggest challenge in any environmental program is making sure your employees are engaged, and that often comes with making sure employees are informed," White adds. For every new hotel or new market, the green program has been heartily embraced, said Mike Taylor, manager of media relations for Fairmont. "It's definitely something new employees latch on to and feel passionate about and are very connected to from day one," said Taylor. "At every single hotel, that's the predominant program that really resonates with employees." For example, Toronto's Royal York has an organic rooftop garden and Vancouver's Fairmont Pacific Rim established a partnership with the Stanley Park Ecology Society in support of their efforts as stewards of the city's landmark park.

While the program is administered corporately, volunteer "green teams" at each property meet monthly to discuss and review ways to improve the operational performance in various departments. Fairmont also runs an environmental incentive program that recognizes the green team that has performed the best on a quarterly basis, and rewards two hotels that have had the best overall environmental performance each year. The green focus is definitely used as a retention tool and makes employees feel empowered. "They have an ownership or a management group that supports that approach to sustainable tourism," said Taylor. "And at the end of the day, it's the right thing to do and it's the right thing for the planet."

Michael Adams, president of The Environics Group of research and communications consulting companies in Toronto, says he sees people increasingly concerned about whether they work for environmentally responsible companies. "They don't want to go home and have to apologize to their children about where they work and what they do. They want to feel proud of what they do." said Adams.

Questions

1. On the basis of the information provided in the case, what costs and benefits has Fairmont experienced by implementing its Green Partnership program?

2. Would you be more likely to be satisfied, engaged, and/or loyal, and/or remain with a company that shows evidence of corporate social responsibility such as being committed to the environment? Explain your response.

Sources: "Employer Review: Fairmont Hotels & Resorts (2012)," www.eluta.ca/green-at-fairmont, retrieved June 14, 2012; "Green Partnership Program," www.fairmont .com/EN_FA/AboutFairmont/environment/GreenPartnershipProgram/, retrieved June 14, 2012; Sarah Dobson, "Fairmont Finds It's Easy Being Green," *Canadian HR Reporter*, March 26, 2007, p. 14; Uyen Vu, "Climate Change Sparks Attitude Shift," *Canadian HR Reporter*, March 26, 2007, p. 11; and Adine Mees and Jamie Bonham, "Corporate Social Responsibility Belongs with HR," *Canadian HR Reporter*, April 4, 2004.

VIDEO CASES PART 5

Video Case: HR Key to Positive Labour Relations (www.hrreporter.com/ videodisplay/376-hr-key-to-positive-labour-relations)

Buzz Hargrove, director of the Centre for Labour Management Relations at Ryerson University (www.ryerson.ca), explains how a positive labour-management relationship benefits a company. Hargrove says HR plays a vital role because they are the people in the organization that deal with the union on a day-to-day basis. Positive labour relations are described as an investment in the workforce that result in productivity, quality, and delivery as well as cost savings. HR's role supports the relationship with the union and therefore with the employees. Hargrove suggests that HR should start by spending the appropriate amount of time building relationships with the union's elected representatives. Hargrove suggests that HR best practices in building positive labour relations include open and honest communications; knowing the people you're dealing with—knowing why someone feels so strongly about a particular issue; a sense of humour to build relationships; and having integrity.

Questions

1. In the video, Hargrove suggests that the organization's managers should not deal with employees directly because that is "going over the heads" of labour representatives. Do you think a company's managers would agree with this advice? Why or why not?

2. What effect will adopting the HR best practices described in the video, likely have on the company's labour relations outcomes and processes, e.g., collective bargaining?

Source: Based on "HR Key to Positive Labour Relations," *Canadian HR Reporter TV*, March 10, 2015. Reprinted by permission of Canadian HR Reporter. © Copyright Thomson Reuters Canada Ltd., March 10, 2015, Toronto, Ontario 1-800-387-5164. Web: www.hrreporter.com

Video Case: Fostering Employee Engagement (www.hrreporter.com/executive-series/videodisplay/191-fostering-employee-engagement)

Senior vice-president of Strategy and Stakeholder Relations at the Healthcare of Ontario Pension Plan (HOOPP, www.hoopp.com), Victoria Hubbell discusses how the organization significantly enhanced its employee engagement scores—from 52 percent to 91 percent. Hubbell describes how the organization, in a very methodical way, started focusing on employees and their needs. Overall, HOOPP's approach to enhancing employee engagement was to identify the business practices; incorporate better development, training, and learning opportunities; foster increased empowerment; and create decision making where it should be.

Four specific elements identified as the biggest driers of engagement at HOOPP are:

1. *Culture*—Hubbell describes HOOPP as having a culture of profound respect and collaboration and that people look forward to coming to work.

2. *Work/life balance*—Although it's not always the perfect balance, work is regarded in a healthy way in order to avoid a toxic, frenzied approach.

3. *Resilience training*—To help people focus, make better decisions, and improve clarity and creativity during times of change, a corporate-wide program was launched starting with the CEO and his team.

4. *Opportunities for interesting work*—HOOPP recognizes the importance of having work that is valued and that taps into employees' intellect and creativity.

Questions

1. What elements of a high-performance work system are discussed in the video?

2. What effect will this high level of employee engagement likely have on HOOPP employees' behaviour and performance on the job?

Source: Based on "Fostering Employee Engagement," *Canadian HR Reporter TV*, October 11, 2011. Reprinted by permission of Canadian HR Reporter. © Copyright Thomson Reuters Canada Ltd., October 11, 2011, Toronto, Ontario 1-800-387-5164. Web: www.hrreporter.com

NOTES

CHAPTER 1

1. "Canada's Top 100 Employers: National Competition," www.canadastop100.com/about.html, retrieved January 5, 2015; *Fortune: Best Companies 2014,*" fortune.com/best-companies/google-1/, retrieved January 5, 2015; www.google.ca/about/careers/, retrieved January 5, 2015; Jillian D'Onfro and Kevin Smith, "Google Employees Reveal Their Favorite Perks About Working for the Company," *Business Insider,* July 14, 2014, www.businessinsider.com/google-employees-favorite-perks-2014-7?op=1, retrieved January 5, 2015; www.jobvine.co.za/content/files/ig/jobvine-infographic.pdf, retrieved, January 5, 2015.

2. Janice Cooney and Allison Cowan, "Training and Development Outlook 2003: Canadian Organizations Continue to Under-Invest" (Ottawa: Conference Board of Canada, 2003), p. 1.

3. Ruth Wright, "The Strategic Value of People: Human Resource Trends and Metrics" (Ottawa: Conference Board of Canada, July 2006), p. i.

4. A. S. Tsui and L. R. Gomez-Mejia, "Evaluating Human Resource Effectiveness," in *Human Resource Management: Evolving Rules and Responsibilities,* ed. L. Dyer (Washington, DC: BNA Books, 1988), pp. 1187–227; M. A. Hitt, B. W. Keats, and S. M. DeMarie, "Navigating in the New Competitive Landscape: Building Strategic Flexibility and Competitive Advantage in the 21st Century," *Academy of Management Executive* 12, no. 4 (1998), pp. 22–42; J. T. Delaney and M. A. Huselid, "The Impact of Human Resource Management Practices on Perceptions of Organizational Performance," *Academy of Management Journal* 39 (1996), pp. 949–69.

5. Owen Parker, "It's the Journey That Matters: 2005 Strategic HR Transformation Study Tour Report 2006" (Ottawa: Conference Board of Canada, 2006), p. 1.

6. Ibid.

7. S. A. Snell and J. W. Dean, "Integrated Manufacturing and Human Resource Management: A Human Capital Perspective," *Academy of Management Journal* 35 (1992), pp. 467–504; M. A. Youndt, S. Snell, J. W. Dean Jr., and D. P. Lepak, "Human Resource Management, Manufacturing Strategy, and Firm Performance," *Academy of Management Journal* 39 (1996), pp. 836–66.

8. Charles Greer, *Strategic Human Resource Management,* 2nd ed. (New Jersey: Prentice-Hall, 2001), p. 1.

9. Steve Wexler, "How Many HR Employees Do You Have—and Should You Have—In Your Organization?" Institute for Corporate Productivity, May 21, 2010, www.i4cp.com.

10. E. E. Lawler, "From Human Resource Management to Organizational Effectiveness," *Human Resource Management,* 44 (2005), pp. 165–169.

11. Joanne Sammer, "A Marriage of Necessity," *HR Magazine,* October 2011, pp. 58–62.

12. Wendy S. Becker, "Are You Leading a Socially Responsible and Sustainable Human Resource Function?" *People & Strategy,* March 2011, pp. 18–23.

13. Brad Power, "IBM Focuses HR on Change," *Bloomberg Businessweek,* January 10, 2012, www.businessweek.com.

14. A. Arcand and M. Lefebvre, "Canada's Lagging Productivity: What If We Had Matched the U.S. Performance?" (Ottawa: Conference Board of Canada, November 2011), p. 1.

15. M. Wei, "East Meets West at Hamburger University," *Bloomberg Businessweek,* January 31–February 6, 2011, pp. 22–23.

16. "Immigration and Ethnocultural Diversity in Canada," Statistics Canada, www12.statcan.gc.ca/nhs-enm/2011/as-sa/99-010-x/99-010-x2011001-eng.cfm, retrieved January 7, 2015.

17. Ibid.

18. www.statcan.gc.ca/daily-quotidien/100309/dq100309a-eng.htm, retrieved March 2, 2012.

19. "Saskatchewan Jobs Mission: Premier Brad Wall to Ireland Amid Skilled Labour Shortage," www.huggingtonpost.ca, retrieved March 2, 2012.

20. Jeff Hale, "Ask What Another Country Can Do for You," *The Globe and Mail,* February 22, 2007, p. B11.

21. Jean-Francois Potvin, "HR Outsourcing is Gaining Ground," *Benefits Canada,* November 23, 2012, www.benefitscanada.com/news/hr-outsourcing-is-gaining-ground-570, retrieved January 21, 2012.

22. Ibid.

23. Jeffrey M. Jones, "Record 64% Rate Honesty, Ethics of Members of Congress Low," Gallup, December 12, 2011, www.gallup.com; Corruption Currents, "Survey Sees Less Misconduct But More Reporting and Retaliation," *The Wall Street Journal,* January 5, 2012, blogs.wsj.com.

24. G.F. Cavanaugh, D. Moberg, and M. Velasquez, "The Ethics of Organizational Politics," *Academy of Management Review* 6, (1981), pp. 363–374.

25. Uyen Vu, "Climate Change Sparks Attitude Shift," *Canadian HR Reporter,* March 26, 2007, p. 11.

26. "Communication—Response to HRPAs Announcement of Three New Provincial Designations," November 5, 2014, www.chrp.ca/news/201275/Communication-Response-to-HRPAs-announcement-of-three-new-provincial-designations.htm, retrieved January 8, 2015; "Certified Human Resources Professional Competency Framework," c.ymcdn.com/sites/www.chrp.ca/resource/resmgr/Recertification/CHRP_Competency_FrameworkPV_.pdf, retrieved January 10, 2015; "Overview of HRPA's CHRL Designation Process," www.hrpa.ca/REGULATIONANDHRDESIGNATIONS/Pages/CHRP.aspx, retrieved January 8, 2015, "HRPA—About HRPA," www.hrpa.ca/AboutHRPA/Pages/Default.aspx, retrieved January 8, 2015.

27. "The 2013 Market Value of CHRP Certification," PayScale, resources.payscale.com/rs/payscale/images/research_PayScale-CHRP-market-value.pdf, retrieved January 10, 2015.

28. A. Fox, "Mixing It Up," *HR Magazine,* May 2011, pp. 22–27; B. Hite, "Employers Rethink How They Give Feedback," *The Wall Street Journal,* October 13, 2008, p. B5; E. White, "Age is as Age Does: Making the

Generation Gap Work for You," *The Wall Street Journal*, June 30, 2008, p. B3.

29. Marian Scott, "Study Shows High Workplace Diversity Encourages Tolerance," *Leader-Post*, January 21, 2012, p. B5.

30. Piali Roy, "Steam Whistle's Commitment to Hiring New Immigrants," *YongeStreet*, September 1, 2010, www.yongestreetmedia.ca/features/steamwhistle 0901.aspx, retrieved January 24, 2012.

31. "Aboriginal Peoples in Canada: First Nations People, Metis and Inuit," Statistics Canada, www12.statcan.gc.ca/nhs-enm/2011/as-sa/99-011-x/99-011-x2011001-eng.cfm, retrieved January 7, 2015.

32. www.chrc-ccdp.ca/discrimination/barrier_freeen .asp, retrieved April 3, 2004.

33. "How Canada Performs: A Report Card on Canada" (Ottawa: Conference Board of Canada, June 2007), p. 82.

34. "Industry Report 2000," *Training*, October 2000, p. 48.

35. J.A. Neal and C.L. Tromley, "From Incremental Change to Retrofit: Creating High-Performance Work Systems," *Academy of Management Executive* 9 (1995), pp. 42–54.

36. Evan Rosen, "Every Worker Is a Knowledge Worker," *Bloomberg Businessweek*, January 11, 2011, www.businessweek.com; Joe McKendrick, "These Days, Who Is Not a 'Knowledge Worker'?" *SmartPlanet*, April 12, 2010, www.smartplanet.com.

37. R. Vance, *Employee Engagement and Commitment* (Alexandria, VA: Society for Human Resource Management, 2006); M. Huselid, "The Impact of Human Resource Management Practices on Turnover, Productivity, and Corporate Financial Performance," *Academy of Management Journal* 38 (1995), pp. 635–72; S. Payne and S. Webber, "Effects of Service Provider Attitudes and Employment Status on Citizenship Behaviors and Customers' Attitudes and Loyalty Behavior," *Journal of Applied Psychology* 91 (2006), pp. 365–68; and J. Hartner, F. Schmidt, and T. Hayes, "Business-Unit Level Relationship between Employee Satisfaction, Employee Engagement, and Business Outcomes: A Meta-analysis," *Journal of Applied Psychology* 87 (2002), pp. 268–79.

38. "Learning—Educational Attainment/Indicators of Well-being in Canada," Employment and Social Development Canada, www4.hrsdc.gc.ca/.3ndic.1t.4r@-eng.jsp?iid=29#M_1, retrieved January 9, 2015.

39. Ray Turchansky, "Proof Education Is Smart Investment," *Financial Post*, March 22, 2004, p. FP13.

40. M. J. Kavanaugh, H. G. Guetal, and S. I. Tannenbaum, *Human Resource Information Systems: Development and Application* (Boston: PWS-Kent, 1990).

41. Dave Zielinski, "HRIS Features Get More Strategic," *HR Magazine*, December 2011, p. 15.

42. Dan Lyons, "Is Workday Silicon Valley's Next Big IPO?" *Newsweek*, February 6, 2012, www.thedailybeast.com/newsweek.

43. N. Lockwood, *Maximizing Human Capital: Demonstrating HR Value with Key Performance Indicators* (Alexandria, VA: SHRM Research Quarterly, 2006).

44. "Social Technologies on the Front Line: The Management 2.0 M-Prize Winners," *McKinsey Quarterly*, September 2011, www.mckinseyquarterly.com.

45. J. O'Toole and E. Lawler III, *The New American Workplace* (New York: Palgrave Macmillan, 2006).

46. D. M. Rousseau, "Psychological and Implied Contracts in Organizations," *Employee Rights and Responsibilities Journal* 2 (1989), pp. 121–29.

47. Vanessa Wong, "How Great is Unlimited Vacation Time, Really?" September 24, 2014, www.businessweek.com/articles/2014-09-25/why-a-tiny-number-of-companies-offer-unlimited-vacation-time, retrieved January 10, 2015 and "Why We're Letting Virgin Staff Take as Much Holiday as They Want," www.virgin.com/richard-branson/why-were-letting-virgin-staff-take-as-much-holiday-as-they-want, retrieved January 10, 2015.

CHAPTER 2

1. "People with Disabilities," *Sodexo website*, www.sodexo.com, retrieved March 27, 2015; "Sodexo Canada Recognized as a Best Diversity Employer," *Canada NewsWire*, February 10, 2014, www.newswire.ca/en/story/1303223/sodexo-canada-recognized-as-a-best-diversity-employer, retrieved March 28, 2015; Liz Bernier, "Breaking Down Barriers—1 Cup at a Time," *Canadian HR Reporter*, November 4, 2013, pp. 18, 20; "Creating Confidence Through Coffee," *Vancouver Coastal Health*, www.vch.ca/about-us/news/archive/2013-news/willow-bean-café, retrieved March 28, 2015; "New Café Aims to Brew Up Awareness About Mental Health," *British Columbia Newsroom*, www.newsroom.gov.bc.ca/2013/03/new-caf-aims-to-brew-up-awareness-about-mental-health.html, March 27, 2013, retrieved March 27, 2015; "Canada's Best Diversity Employers," www.canadastop100.com/diversity/, retrieved March 24, 2015.

2. "Canada's Best Diversity Employers," www.canadastop100.com/diversity/, retrieved March 24, 2015.

3. Shannon Klie, "Lots of Talk, Not Much Action on Diversity," *Canadian HR Reporter*, January 15, 2008, p. 1.

4. "2003 Employment Equity Annual Report," p. 24, www.hrsdc.gc.ca/en, retrieved July 13, 2004.

5. "HR Leaders Talk," *Canadian HR Reporter*, January 28, 2008, pp. 11–12.

6. "Business Results Through Health and Safety," Ontario Workplace Safety and Insurance Board website, www.wsib.on.ca/wsib/website.nsf, retrieved April 19, 2004.

7. www.ccohs.ca/oshanswers/legisl/ire.htm, retrieved February 25, 2004.

8. "Anti-Discriminatory Casebook," www.chrcccdp.ca/Legis&Poli/AntiDiscriminationCasebook_Recueil Decisions, retrieved February 18, 2004.

9. Ran LeClair, "The Evolution of Accommodation," *Canadian HR Reporter*, February 24, 2003, p. 7.

10. "Bona Fide Occupational Requirements and Bona Fide Justifications Under the Canadian Human Rights Act," pp. 4, 5, www.chrc-ccdp.ca/publications/BFOR, retrieved February 18, 2004.

11. "Mandatory Retirement in Canada," www.hrsdc.gc.ca/en/lp/spila/clli/eslc/19Mandatory_Retirement.shtml, retrieved October 20, 2008; "Retiring Mandatory Retirement," February 21, 2008, www.cbc.ca/news/background/retirement/mandatory_retirement.html, retrieved October 20, 2008.

12. www.chrc-ccdp.ca/discrimination/apfa_uppt/page4-eng.aspx, retrieved March 23, 2012.

13. Canadian Human Rights Commission, "Fact Sheet: Duty to Accommodate," January 2006, p. 2.

14. Andrew Duffy, "Steven Fletcher's Line in the Sand," *Leader-Post*, November 28, 2014, p. D8; www.thestevenfletcherstory.ca/about_steven.php, retrieved March 23, 2012; Paul Samyn, "Tearing Down Barriers Big Job," *Winnipeg Free Press*, July 16, 2004, p. A3;

Paul Egan, "He's Breaking Barriers," *Winnipeg Free Press,* July 4, 2004, pp. A1, A2; Parliament of Canada website, www2.parl.gc.ca, retrieved April 13, 2008.

15. Liz Bernier, "Diversity Not Just About Compliance," *Canadian HR Reporter,* March 10, 2014, pp. 1, 6.

16. Andrew Duffy, "Steven Fletcher's Line in the Sand," *Leader-Post,* November 28, 2014, p. D8; www.thestevenfletcherstory.ca/about_steven.php, retrieved March 23, 2012; Paul Samyn, "Tearing Down Barriers Big Job," *Winnipeg Free Press,* July 16, 2004, p. A3; Paul Egan, "He's Breaking Barriers," *Winnipeg Free Press,* July 4, 2004, pp. A1, A2; Parliament of Canada website, www2.parl.gc.ca, retrieved April 13, 2008.

17. "What is Harassment?" *Canadian Human Rights Commission website,* www.chrc-ccdp.ca/eng/content/what-harassment, retrieved April 1, 2015.

18. "Study Reveals Slight Decline in Workplace Harassment, *OHS Canada,* July 2, 2014, www.ohscanada.com/health-safety/study-reveals-slight-decline-in-workplace-harassment/1003140322/, retrieved April 1, 2015.

19. "Seneca Discrimination and Harassment Policy Statement," www.senecacollege.ca/policies/dh.html, retrieved March 24, 2015.

20. "Identifying Sexual Harassment," *Ontario Human Rights Commission,* www.ohrc.on.ca/en/policy-preventing-sexual-and-gender-based-harassment/2-identifying-sexual-harassment, retrieved March 25, 2015.

21. Reference to Colvin v. Gillies 2004 HRTO3 from "Identifying sexual harassment," *Ontario Human Rights Commission,* www.ohrc.on.ca/en/policy-preventing-sexual-and-gender-based-harassment/2-identifying-sexual-harassment, retrieved March 25, 2015.

22. Kathryn May, "Public Servants Face Harassment," *The Leader-Post,* February 7, 2015, p. B5.

23. Ibid.

24. "Employment Equity Designated Groups," *Government of Canada,* http://jobs-emplois.gc.ca/centres/inside-ausein/ee-eng.php, retrieved March 25, 2015.

25. Ibid.

26. Ibid.

27. "Employment Equity Act: Annual Report 2013, Chart 1: Progress in Representation over Time in the Federally Regulated Private Sector," *Employment and Social Development Canada,* December 11, 2014, p. 2.

28. www.priv.gc.ca/fs-fi/02_05_d_15_e.cfm#contenttop, retrieved March 23, 2012.

29. "A Guide for Canadians: What Is the Personal Information Protection and Electronic Documents Act?," www.privcom.gc.ca/information.

30. "Nova Scotia Heritage Day," http://novascotia.ca/lae/employmentrights/NovaScotiaHeritageDay.asp, retrieved March 25, 2015; "New Leaves of Absence," Ontario Ministry of Labour, www.labour.on.ca/english/es/newleaves.php, retrieved March 25, 2015; www.labour.gov.on.ca/english/es/pubs/guide/organdonor.php, retrieved March 23, 2012; Lesley Young, "Job-Protected Leave for Organ Donations Possible," *Canadian HR Reporter,* October 8, 2007, p. 1.

31. Zane Schwartz, "Unpaid Internships Are Just Wrong," *The Globe and Mail,* May 3, 2013, www.theglobeandmail.com, retrieved March 26, 2015.

32. Todd Humber, "Hefty Bill on Unpaid Overtime," *Canadian HR Reporter,* September 8, 2014, p. 26; Tim Kiladze, "Scotiabank Settles Class Action on Overtime Pay," *The Globe and Mail,* July 24, 2014, www.globeandmail.com, retrieved March 29, 2015; Jacquie McNish and Tara Perkins, CIBC Overtime Lawsuit Dismissed, *The Globe*

and Mail, June 19, 2009, www.theglobeandmail.com/report-on-business/cibc-overtime-lawsuit-dismissed/article1188529/, retrieved March 24, 2012; "CN Faces $250M Class Action Lawsuit," www.cbc.ca/money/story/2008/03/25/en.html, retrieved April 14, 2008; "CN Hit with Class-Action Lawsuit on Unpaid Overtime," *Canadian HR Reporter,* www.hrreporter.com, March 25, 2008; Gary Norris, "KPMG Faces Employee Class Action Lawsuit in Ontario for Overtime Pay," www.cbc.ca/cp/business/070904/b0904111A.html, retrieved October 4, 2007; Virginia Galt and Janet McFarland, "CIBC Faces Massive Overtime Lawsuit," *The Globe and Mail,* June 5, 2007, www.theglobeandmail.com, retrieved March 18, 2008; "CIBC Faces $600-Million Suit over Unpaid Overtime," *CanWest News Service,* June 5, 2007, www.canada.com/components, retrieved March 18, 2008.

33. "CHL Class Action," *Charney Lawyers website,* www.charneylawyers.com/Charney/chlclassaction.php, retrieved March 29, 2015 and Bob Duff, "Lawsuit Threatens to Change CHL Dynamic," *The Leader-Post,* October 21, 2014, p. C4.

34. "How Canada Performs: Gender Income Gap," *Conference Board of Canada,* www.conferenceboard.ca/hcp/details/society/gender-income-gap.aspx, retrieved March 26, 2015.

35. Matthew McClearn, "Mind the Gap," *Canadian Business,* November 5, 2007, pp. 21–22.

36. Sarah Schmidt, "Report Says Male Profs Paid More Than Females," *Winnipeg Free Press,* July 17, 2004, p. A11.

37. Ibid.

38. Canadian Human Rights Commission, "2007 Annual Report," p. 6, www.chrc-ccdp.ca/publication/ar_2007_ra/page6-en .asp#41, retrieved April 14, 2008.

39. Vanessa Lu, "Canada Post Says 10,000 Have Received Pay Equity Cheques," *The Toronto Star,* January 13, 2015, www.thestar.com, retrieved March 26, 2015; "Canada Post Pay Equity Decision," *Canada Post website,* www.canadapostpayequity.ca, retrieved March 26, 2015; and "Supreme Court to Hear Landmark Canada Post Pay-Equity Case, December 16, 2010, www.theglobeandmail.com, retrieved March 26, 2015.

40. "Privacy Commissioner of Canada: A Guide for Canadians," www.privcom.gc.ca/information, retrieved March 21, 2004.

41. "OH&S Legislation in Canada—Basic Responsibilities," *Canadian Centre for Occupational Health and Safety,* www.ccohs.ca/oshanswers/legisl/responsi.html, retrieved March 29, 2015.

42. www.labour.gov.on.ca/english/hs/, retrieved March 23, 2012.

43. www.ccohs.ca/oshanswers/legisl/ire.htm, retrieved February 25, 2004.

44. "Workplace Health and Safety Committees—Pamphlet 6B: Information on Occupational Health and Safety," *Government of Canada website,* www.labour.gc.ca/eng/health_safety/pubs_hs/committee.shtml, retrieved March 29, 2015.

45. "OH&S Legislation in Canada—Basic Responsibilities," *Canadian Centre for Occupational Health and Safety,* www.ccohs.ca/oshanswers/legisl/responsi.html, retrieved March 29, 2015.

46. Russel Zinn, "Driving Under Influence—of a Cellphone," *Canadian HR Reporter,* February 25, 2008, p. 5.

47. "Distracted Driving," *The Ontario Ministry of Labour,* www.mto.gov.on.ca/english/safety/distracted-driving.shtml, retrieved April 1, 2015.

48. Mari-Len De Guzman, "Distracted Drivers to Distracted Workers: Tips for Developing Workplace Cellphone Policy," *Canadian Occupational Safety*, April 23, 2013, www.cos-mag.com/safety/safety-stories/distracted-drivers-to-distracted-workers-tips-for-developing-workplace-cellphone-policy.html, retrieved April 1, 2015.

49. "OH&S Legislation in Canada—Basic Responsibilities," *Canadian Centre for Occupational Health and Safety*, www.ccohs.ca/oshanswers/legisl/responsi.html, retrieved March 29, 2015.

50. Ibid.

51. Ibid.

52. Andy Shaw, "Slow Evolution from WHMIS to GHS," *Canadian HR Reporter*, March 10, 2008, p. 11.

53. "Environmental and Workplace Health—WHMIS 2015," *Health Canada*, www.hc-sc.gc.ca/ewh-semt/occup-travail/whmis-simdut/ghs-sgh/index-eng.php, retrieved March 29, 2015.

54. Ann Perry, "Workplace Safety Gets a Boost," *Toronto Star*, March 27, 2004, p. D10.

55. "OSH Answers Fact Sheets: Violence in the Workplace," *Canadian Centre for Occupational Health and Safety*, www.ccohs.ca/oshanswers/psychosocial/violence.html, retrieved March 31, 2015.

56. "OSH Answers Fact Sheets: Violence in the Workplace," *Canadian Centre for Occupational Health and Safety*, www.ccohs.ca/oshanswers/psychosocial/violence.html, retrieved March 31, 2015.

57. Sarah Dobson, "Paramedics Facing Abuse on the Job," *Canadian HR Reporter*, January 30, 2012, p. 7.

58. L. Chénier, C. Hoganson, and K. Thorpe, "Making the Business Case for Investments in Workplace Health & Wellness," *Conference Board of Canada*, June 2012, p. 4.

59. Gerry Bellet, "Harassed Woman Awarded $950,000," *Leader-Post*, January 24, 2006, p. A3.

60. J. Roughton, "Managing a Safety Program Through Job Hazard Analysis," *Professional Safety* 37 (1992), pp. 28–31.

61. Roughton, ibid.

62. R. G. Hallock and D. A. Weaver, "Controlling Losses and Enhancing Management Systems with TOR Analysis," *Professional Safety* 35 (1990), pp. 24–26.

63. Field ID, "McShane Construction Selects Field ID to Enhance Worksite Safety and Quality Assurance," news release, October 11, 2011, www.fieldid.com; Field ID, "What Is Field ID?" www.fieldid.com, accessed February 21, 2012.

64. "Young/New Workers," Canadian Centre of Occupational Health and Safety, www.ccohs.ca/topics/workers/youngnew/, retrieved March 30, 2015.

65. "Young Workers Zone," Canadian Centre of Occupational Health and Safety, www.ccohs.ca/products/posters/youngworkers.html, retrieved March 30, 2015.

66. Amanda Silliker, "Shift Workers' Poor Diet a Health Hazard," *Canadian HR Reporter*, February 13, 2012, p. 1, 12.

67. T. Markus, "How to Set Up a Safety Awareness Program," *Supervision* 51 (1990), pp. 14–16.

68. J. Agnew and A. J. Saruda, "Age and Fatal Work-Related Falls," *Human Factors* 35, no. 4 (1994), pp. 731–736.

69. R. King, "Active Safety Programs, Education Can Help Prevent Back Injuries," *Occupational Health and Safety* 60 (1991), pp. 49–52.

70. "Eye Safety at Work," *CNIB website*, www.cnib.ca/en/your-eyes/safety/at-work/Pages/default.aspx, retrieved March 30, 2015.

71. "2014 Responsible Canadian Energy Awards," *Canadian Association of Petroleum Producers website*, May 21, 2014, www.capp.ca, retrieved March 30, 2015.

72. Shannon Klie, "Do Incentives Help Change Behaviour?," *Canadian HR Reporter*, April 21, 2008, www.hrreporter.com, retrieved May 7, 2008.

73. Nikki Pavlov, "A Healthy Workplace Means Recognizing Stress Is the Enemy," *Canadian HR Reporter*, April 9, 2001, www.hrreporter.com, retrieved September 29, 2004.

74. "Wellness Metrics in Action—Desjardins Group: Impressive Return on Investments in Wellness," *Conference Board of Canada*, August 15, 2012, p. 3.

75. J. C. Erfurt, A. Foote, and M. A. Heirich, "The Cost-Effectiveness of Work Site Wellness Programs for Hypertension Control, Weight Loss, Smoking Cessation and Exercise," *Personnel Psychology* 45 (1992), pp. 5–27.

76. "Case Study: Wellness Metrics in Action—Town of Conception Bay South: Reducing Absenteeism," *Conference Board of Canada*, August 2012, pp. 1–3.

77. "OSH Answers Fact Sheet—Employee Assistance Programs (EAP)," *Canadian Centre for Occupational Health and Safety*, www.ccohs.ca/oshanswers/hsprograms/eap.html, *retrieved March 31, 2015.*

78. Brian Lindenberg, "Choosing the Right EAP," *Canadian HR Reporter*, March 24, 2008, pp. 22, 27.

79. Amanda Silliker, "Employers in Best Position to Fight Depression," *Canadian HR Reporter*, January 30, 2012, p. 3, 8.

80. M. Janssens, J. M. Brett, and E J. Smith, "Confirmatory Cross-Cultural Research: Testing the Viability of a Corporation-wide Safety Policy," *Academy of Management Journal* 38 (1995), pp. 364–82.

81. E. Sage-Gavin and P. Wright, "Corporate Social Responsibility at Gap, Inc.: An Interview with Eva Sage-Gavin," *Human Resource Planning* 30, mar. 1, (2007), pp. 45–48.

CHAPTER 3

1. J. Barrett, "Good Job/Bad Job: How We Judge Work Limits Our Ability to Find Meaning i It," *Montreal Gazette*, November 3, 2014, p. A7; A. Taube and S. Gould, "The 10 Best Jobs for People in Their 20s," *Business Insider*, September 12, 2014, www.businessinsider.com/best-jobs-for-people-in-their-20s-2014-9C, retrieved January 17, 2015; Kapel, "Would You Keep Working If You Won the Lottery?" *Canadian, HR Reporter*, September 2, 2014, www.hrreporter.com/blog/compensation-rewards/archive/2014/09/02/would-you-keep-working-if-you-won-the-lottery, retrieved January 17, 2015; "Half of U.S. Workers Would Keep Working if They Won the Lottery," *careerbuilder*, www.careerbuilder.ca/share/aboutus/pressreleasesdetail.aspx?sd=7%2F17%2F2014&id=pr832&ed=12%2F31%2F2014r, July 17, 2014, retrieved January 17, 2015; "U.S. News Ranks the Best Jobs," http://money.usnews.com/money/careers/articles/2014/01/22/about-the-us-news-best-jobs-ranking-methodology, retrieved January 17, 2015.

2. Bill Gregar, "Midwest Firms: Jobs Exist, Skills Scarce," *Plastics News*, October 17, 2011, Business & Company Resource Center, galenet.galegroup.com; Timothy Aeppel, "Man vs. Machine, a Jobless Recovery," *The Wall Street Journal*, January 17, 2012, online.wsj.com.

3. J. R. Hollenbeck, H. Moon, A. Ellis, et al., "Structural Contingency Theory and Individual Differences: Examination of External and Internal Person-Team Fit," *Journal of Applied Psychology* 87 (2002), pp. 599–606.

4. W. Cascio, *Applied Psychology in Personnel Management,* 4th ed. (Englewood Cliffs, NJ: Prentice Hall, 1991).

5. P. Wright and K. Wexley, "How to Choose the Kind of Job Analysis You Really Need," *Personnel,* May 1985, pp. 51–55.

6. Canadian Human Rights Commission website, www.ccrc-ccdp.ca/discrimination/barrier_free-en.asp, retrieved April 3, 2004.

7. M. K. Lindell, C. S. Clause, C. J. Brandt, and R. S. Landis, "Relationship between Organizational Context and Job Analysis Ratings," *Journal of Applied Psychology* 83 (1998), pp. 769–76.

8. Oliver W. Cummings, "What Do Manufacturing Supervisors Really Do on the Job?" *Industry Week,* February 2010, p. 53.

9. "Middle Management Competency Profile," www.canadascapital.gc.ca/sites/default/files/pubs/ncc_middle_management_competency_profile_0.pdf, retrieved March 10, 2012.

10. A. O'Reilly, "Skill Requirements: Supervisor-Subordinate Conflict," *Personnel Psychology* 26 (1973), pp. 75–80; J. Hazel, J. Madden, and R. Christal, "Agreement between Worker-Supervisor Descriptions of the Worker's Job," *Journal of Industrial Psychology* 2 (1964), pp. 71–79; and A. K. Weyman, "Investigating the Influence of Organizational Role on Perceptions of Risk in Deep Coal Mines," *Journal of Applied Psychology* 88 (2003), pp. 404–12.

11. L. E. Baranowski and L. E. Anderson, "Examining Rater Source Variation in Work Behavior to KSA Linkages," *Personnel Psychology* 58 (2005), pp. 1041–54.

12. PAQ Newsletter, August 1989; and E. C. Dierdorff and M. A. Wilson, "A Meta-analysis of Job Analysis Reliability," *Journal of Applied Psychology* 88 (2003), pp. 635–46.

13. E. Fleishman and M. Reilly, *Handbook of Human Abilities* (Palo Alto, CA: Consulting Psychologists Press, 1992); E. Fleishman and M. Mumford, "The Ability Requirements Scales," in *The Job Analysis Handbook for Business, Industry, and Government,* ed. S. Gael (New York: Wiley), pp. 917–35.

14. R. Hackman and G. Oldham, *Work Redesign* (Boston: Addison-Wesley, 1980).

15. W. E. Byrnes, "Making the Job Meaningful All the Way Down the Line," *BusinessWeek,* May 1, 2006, p. 60.

16. F. W. Bond, P. E. Flaxman, and D. Bunce, "The Influence of Psychological Flexibility on Work Redesign: Mediated Moderation of a Work Reorganization Intervention," *Journal of Applied Psychology* 93 (2008), pp. 645–654.

17. M. A. Campion, G. J. Medsker, and A. C. Higgs, "Relations Between Work Group Characteristics and Effectiveness: Implications for Designing Effective Work Groups," *Personnel Psychology* 46 (1993), pp. 823–50.

18. "A Few Facts About Distributed Work," *Canadian HR Reporter,* August 14, 2006, p. 21.

19. Andrea Ozias, ed., "Telework 2011: A WorldatWork Special Report," WorldatWork, July 2011, www.worldatwork.org.

20. Uyen Vu, "A Variety of Options Gives Boost to Remote Work," *Canadian HR Reporter,* August 14, 2006, p. 15.

21. "Evolution of the Workplace: The Growing Demand for Distributed Work," *SuiteWorks,* www.suiteworks.ca/pdfs/Revolution@Work%20SuiteWorks.pdf, retrieved March 23, 2008.

22. See, for example, S. Sonnentag and F. R. H. Zijistra, "Job Characteristics and Off-the-Job Activities as Predictors of Need for Recovery, Well-Being, and Fatigue," *Journal of Applied Psychology* 91 (2006), pp. 330–350.

23. D. May and C. Schwoerer, "Employee Health by Design: Using Employee Involvement Teams in Ergonomic Job Redesign," *Personnel Psychology* 47 (1994), pp. 861–86.

24. Franklin Tessler, "The Hidden Danger of Touchscreens," *InfoWorld.com,* January 11, 2012, Business & Company Resource Center, http://galenet.galegroup.com.

25. Peter Budnick and Rachel Michael, "What Is Cognitive Ergonomics?," *Ergonomics Today,* www.ergoweb.com/news/detail.cfm?id=352, retrieved March 25, 2008.

26. N. W. Van Yperen and M. Hagerdoom, "Do High Job Demands Increase Intrinsic Motivation or Fatigue or Both? The Role of Job Support and Social Control," *Academy of Management Journal* 46 (2003), pp. 339–348; and N. W. Van Yperen and O Janseen, "Fatigued and Dissatisfied or Fatigued but Satisfied? Goal Orientations and Responses to High Job Demands," *Academy of Management Journal* 45 (2002) pp. 1161–1171.

27. Jonathan Spira, "Information Overload: None Are Immune," *Information Management,* September/October 2011, p. 32.

CHAPTER 4

1. www.canadastop100.com/national/, www.canadastop100.com/diversity/, www.canadastop100.com/young_people/, www.canadastop100.com/environmental/, retrieved February 7, 2015; "The Willow Bean Café is Moving Full Steam Ahead with Development," May 24, 2012, http://vancouver-burnaby.cmha.bc.ca/get-informed/e-news/article-120524-willow-bean-café, retrieved February 7, 2015; and http://ca.sodexo.com/caen/default.aspx, retrieved February 7, 2015.

2. I. Brat, "Where Have All the Welders Gone, as Manufacturing and Repair Boom?" *Wall Street Journal,* August 15, 2006, pp. B2–B3.

3. Ben Dummett, "BlackBerry Tells Employees It is Finished with Layoffs," *Wall Street Journal,* August 5, 2014, retrieved January 28, 2015, www.wsj.com/articles/blackberry-tells-employees-it-is-finished-with-layoffs-1407261457; "BlackBerry Timeline: A Tech Titan's Roller Coaster Ride," March 17, 2014, retrieved January 28, 2015 www.cbc.ca/news2/interactives/timeline-rim/; "BlackBerry Lays Off 120 Workers in Waterloo, Ont." March 17, 2014, retrieved January 28, 2014 www.cbc.ca/news/canada/kitchener-waterloo/blackberry-lays-off-120-workers-in-waterloo-ont-1.2575718.

4. J. P. Guthrie, "Dumb and Dumber: The Impact of Downsizing on Firm Performance as Moderated by Industry Conditions," *Organization Science* 19 (2008), pp. 108–123; and J. McGregor, A. McConnon, and D. Kiley, "Customer Service in a Shrinking Economy," *BusinessWeek,* February 19, 2009, pp. 34–35.

5. C. D. Zatzick and R. D. Iverson, "High-Involvement Management and Workforce Reduction: Competitive Advantage or Disadvantage?" *Academy of Management Journal* 49 (2006), pp. 101–112.

6. P. P. Shaw, "Network Destruction: The Structural Implications of Downsizing," *Academy of Management Journal* 43 (2000), pp. 101–12.

7. Brenda Kowske, Kyle Lundby, and Rena Rasch, "Turning 'Survive' into 'Thrive': Managing Survivor Engagement in a Downsized Organization," *People & Strategy 32,* no. (4), (2009), pp. 48–56.

8. Justin Lahart, "Even in a Recovery, Some Jobs Won't Return," *Wall Street Journal,* January 12, 2010, onlinewsj.com; and Sarah E. Needleman, "Entrepreneurs Prefer to Keep Staffs Lean," *Wall Street Journal,* March 2, 2010, online.wsj.com.

9. Olga Kharif, "The Rise of the Four-Day Work Week?" *BusinessWeek,* December 18, 2008, www.businessweek.com.

10. CareerBuilder, "Retirement May Be a Thing of the Past, New CareerBuilder Survey Finds," news release, February 16, 2012, www.careerbuilder.com.

11. S. Kim and D. Feldman, "Healthy, Wealthy, or Wise: Predicting Actual Acceptances of Early Retirement Incentives at Three Points in Time," *Personnel Psychology* 51 (1998), pp. 623–42.

12. D. Fandray, "Gray Matters," *Workforce,* July 2000, pp. 27–32.

13. P. Engardio, "Let's Offshore the Lawyers," *BusinessWeek,* September 18, 2006, pp. 42–43.

14. Steve Minter, "Moving Sourcing Closer to Home," *Industry Week,* September 2009, Business & Company Resource Center, http://galenet.galegroup.com; and Josh Hyatt, "The New Calculus of Offshoring," *CFO,* October 2009, pp. 58–62.

15. A. Tiwana, Does Firm Modularity Complement Ignorance? A Field Study of Software Outsourcing Alliances," *Strategic Management Journal* 29 (2008), pp. 1241–1252.

16. Kelley Hunsberger, "The Risk of Outsourcing," PM Network, November 2011, EBSCOhost, http://web.ebscohost.com; "The Trouble with Outsourcing," The Economist, July 30, 2011, EBSCOhost, http://web.ebscohost.com.

17. P. Engardio, "The Future of Outsourcing," *BusinessWeek,* January 30, 2006, pp. 50–58.

18. W. J Rothwell, *Effective Succession Planning,* 2nd ed. (New York: AMACOM, 2001).

19. B. E. Dowell, "Succession Planning," in *Implementing Organizational Interventions,* ed. J. Hedge and E. D. Pulakos (San Francisco: Jossey-Bass, 2002), pp. 78–109.

20. B. Derr, C. Jones, and E. L. Toomey, "Managing High-Potential Employees: Current Practices in Thirty-Three U.S. Corporations," *Human Resource Management* 27 (1988), pp. 273–90; K. M. Nowack, "The Secrets of Succession," *Training and Development* 48 (1994), pp. 49–54; W. J. Rothwell, *Effective Succession Planning,* 4th ed. (New York: AMACOM, 2010).

21. A. E. Barber, *Recruiting Employees* (Thousand Oaks, CA: Sage, 1998).

22. C. K. Stevens, "Antecedents of Interview Interactions, Interviewers' Ratings, and Applicants' Reactions," *Personnel Psychology 51* (1998), pp. 55–85; A. E. Barber, J. R. Hollenbeck, S. L. Tower, and J. M. Phillips, "The Effects of Interview Focus on Recruitment Effectiveness: A Field Experiment," *Journal of Applied Psychology 79* (1994), pp. 886–96; and D. S. Chapman and D. I. Zweig, "Developing a Nomological Network for Interview Structure: Antecedents and Consequences of the Structured Selection Interview," *Personnel Psychology* 58 (2005), pp. 673–702.

23. J. D. Olian and S. L. Rynes, "Organizational Staffing: Integrating Practice with Strategy," *Industrial Relations* 23 (1984), pp. 170–83.

24. Kim Peters, "Employment Branding Best Way to Reach Untapped Talent," *HR Voice,* November 1, 2007, www.hrvoice.org/story, retrieved March 18, 2008.

25. Kim Peters, "Passive Jobseekers Solution to Labour Woes," *Canadian HR Reporter,* July 16, 2007, p. 18.

26. Carolyn Brandon, "Truth in Recruitment Branding," *HR Magazine* 50, no. 11 (November 2005), pp. 89–96.

27. Patrick J. Kiger, "Burnishing Your Employment Brand," *Workforce Management,* October 22, 2007, web.eboscost.com, retrieved March 18, 2008.

28. Judith MacBride-King, "Governments, Start Your Recruitment Campaigns," *Canadian HR Reporter,* October 8, 2007, p. 18.

29. "Nova Scotia Job Centre Overview", http://novascotia.ca/psc/jobCentre/; and "Manitoba Government Job Opportunities," http://gov.mb.ca/govjobs/, retrieved February 1, 2015.

30. M. A. Conrad and S. D. Ashworth, "Recruiting Source Effectiveness: A Meta-Analysis and Reexamination of Two Rival Hypotheses," paper presented at annual meeting of Society of Industrial/Organizational Psychology, Chicago, 1986.

31. J. A. Breaugh, *Recruitment: Science and Practice* (Boston: PWS-Kent, 1992).

32. Taleo Corporation, "Intercontinental Hotels Group Mobilizes Internal Talent with Taleo in Biggest Ever Recruitment Drive," news release, February 6, 2012, ir.taleo.com.

33. Breaugh, *Recruitment,* pp. 113–114.

34. R. S. Schuler and S. E. Jackson, "Linking Competitive Strategies with Human Resource Management Practices," *Academy of Management Executive* 1 (1987), pp. 207–19.

35. G. Colvin, "How to Manage Your Business in a Recession," *Fortune,* January 19, 2009, pp. 88–93; M. Orey, "Hang the Recession, Let's Bulk Up," *BusinessWeek,* February 2, 2009, pp. 80–81; and J. Collin, "How Great Companies Turn Chris into Opportunity," *Fortune,* February 2, 2009, p. 49.

36. Gerry Crispin and Mark Mehler, "Career Xroads Source of Hire Report 2014," September 2014, www.careerxroads.com.

37. C. R. Wanberg, R. Kanfer, and J. T. Banas, "Predictors and Outcomes of Networking Intensity among Job Seekers," *Journal of Applied Psychology* 85 (2000), pp. 491–503.

38. Sarah Fister Gale, "Social Media: Transforms the Recruiting Software Industry," *Workforce Management,* June 2014, p. 24.

39. Amanda Silliker, "Recruiters Connect via LinkedIn," *Canadian HR Reporter,* September 26, 2011, p. 2.

40. Gillian Livingston, "Half of Working Canadians Use LinkedIn, Site Reports," *The Globe and Mail,* November 1, 2014, p. B17.

41. B. Dineen and R. A. Noe, "Effects of Customization on Applicant Decisions and Applicant Pool Characteristics in a Web-Based Recruiting Context," *Journal of Applied Psychology* 94 (2009), pp. 224–234.

42. P. Smith, "Sources Used by Employers When Hiring College Grads," *Personnel Journal,* February 1995, p. 25.

43. J. W. Boudreau and S. L. Rynes, "Role of Recruitment in Staffing Utility Analysis," *Journal of Applied Psychology* 70 (1985), pp. 354–66.

44. B. Hundley, "On-Campus Recruiting that Resonates with Top Students," *HR Professional,* January 2015, p. 56.

45. R. Hawk, *The Recruitment Function* (New York: American Management Association, 1967).

46. Sarah Fister Gale, "Social Media: Transforms the Recruiting Software Industry," *Workforce Management,* June 2014, p. 24.

47. C. K. Stevens, "Effects of Preinterview Beliefs on Applicants' Reactions to Campus Interviews," *Academy of Management Journal* 40 (1997), pp. 947–66.

48. C. Collins, "The Interactive Effects of Recruitment Practices and Product Awareness on Job Seekers' Employer Knowledge and Application Behaviors," *Journal of Applied Psychology* 92 (2007), pp. 180–190.

49. M. S. Taylor and T. J. Bergman, "Organizational Recruitment Activities and Applicants' Reactions at Different Stages of the Recruitment Process," *Personnel Psychology* 40 (1984), pp. 261–285; and C. D. Fisher, D. R. Ilgen, and W. D. Hoyer, "Source Credibility, Information Favorability, and Job Offer Acceptance," *Academy of Management Journal* 22 (1979), pp. 94–103.

50. L. M. Graves and G. N. Powell, "The Effect of Sex Similarity on Recruiters' Evaluation of Actual Applicants: A Test of the Similarity-Attraction Paradigm," *Personnel Psychology* 48 (1995), pp. 85–98.

51. R. D. Tretz and T. A. Judge, "Realistic Job Previews: A Test of the Adverse Self-Selection Hypothesis," *Journal of Applied Psychology* 83 (1998), pp. 330–337.

52. P. Hom, R. W. Griffeth, L. E. Palich, and J. S. Bracker, "An Exploratory Investigation into Theoretical Mechanisms Underlying Realistic Job Previews," *Personnel Psychology* 51 (1998), pp. 421–451.

53. G. M. McEvoy and W. F. Cascio, "Strategies for Reducing Employee Turnover: A Meta-Analysis," *Journal of Applied Psychology* 70 (1985), pp. 342–353; and S. L. Premack and J P. Wanous, "A Meta-Analysis of Realistic Job Preview Experiments," *Journal of Applied Psychology* 70 (1985), pp. 706–719.

54. P. G. Irving and J. P. Meyer, "Reexamination of the Met-Expectations Hypothesis: A Longitudinal Analysis," *Journal of Applied Psychology* 79 (1995), pp. 937–949.

55. R. W. Walters, "It's Time We Become Pros," *Journal of College Placement* 12 (1985), pp. 30–33.

56. S. L. Rynes, R. D. Bretz, and B. Gerhart, "The Importance of Recruitment in Job Choice: A Different Way of Looking," *Personnel Psychology* 44 (1991), pp. 487–522.

CHAPTER 5

1. Murad Hemmadi, "The End of Bad Hiring Decisions," *Canadian Business,* January 2015, p. 12; Nathan R. Kuncel, David M. Klieger, & Deniz S. Ones, "In Hiring, Algorithms Beat Instinct," *Harvard Business Review,* May 2014, p 32; Vivian Giang, "Why New Hiring Algorithms Are More Efficient," *Business Insider,* October 31, 2013, www.businessinsider.com/why-its-ok-that-employers-filter-out-qualified-candidates-2013–10, retrieved February 10, 2015; Jessica Miller-Merrell, "Hiring by Algorithm. The New Self-Checkout of HR," https://prod.smartrecruiters.com/blog/hiring-by-algorithim-the-new-self-checkout-of-hr-2/, retrieved February 10, 2015; and Joseph Walker, "Meet the New Boss: Big Data; Companies Trade in Hunch-Based Hiring for Computer Modeling," *Wall Street Journal (Online),* September 19, 2012, www.wsj.com, retrieved February 10, 2015.

2. Lauren Weber, "Angry Job Applicants Can Hurt Bottom Line," *The Wall Street Journal,* March 13, 2012, http://online.wsj.com; Lauren Weber, "Your Résumé vs. Oblivion," *The Wall Street Journal,* January 24, 2012, http://online.wsj.com.

3. J. C. Nunnally, *Psychometric Theory* (New York: McGraw-Hill, 1978).

4. N. Schmitt, R. Z. Gooding, R. A. Noe, and M. Kirsch, "Meta-Analysis of Validity Studies Published Between 1964 and 1982 and the Investigation of Study Characteristics," *Personnel Psychology* 37 (1984), pp. 407–22.

5. D. D. Robinson, "Content-Oriented Personnel Selection in a Small Business Setting," *Personnel Psychology* 34 (1981), pp. 77–87.

6. M. V. Rafter, "Assessment Providers Scoring Well," *Workforce Management,* January 19, 2009, pp. 24–25.

7. F. L. Schmidt and J. E. Hunter, "The Future of Criterion-Related Validity," *Personnel Psychology* 33 (1980), pp. 41–60; F. L. Schmidt, J. E. Hunter, and K. Pearlman, "Task Differences as Moderators of Aptitude Test Validity: A Red Herring," *Journal of Applied Psychology* 66 (1982), pp. 166–85; R. L. Gutenberg, R. D. Arvey, H. G. Osburn, and R. P. Jeanneret, "Moderating Effects of Decision-Making/Information Processing Dimensions on Test Validities," *Journal of Applied Psychology* 68 (1983), pp. 600–08.

8. www.chrc-ccdp.ca/publications/screening_employment-eng.aspx, retrieved April 1, 2012.

9. T. W Dougherty, D. B. Turban, and J. C. Callender, "Confirming First Impressions in the Employment Interview: A Field Study of Interviewer Behavior," *Journal of Applied Psychology* 79 (1994), pp. 659–65.

10. Edwin, Jansen, "How to Bust Interview Liars," *Canadian Business,* March 2014, p. 23.

11. Alice Snell, "Using Technology in Sourcing Talent," *Canadian HR Reporter,* January 20, 2007, www.hrreporter.com, retrieved April 6, 2008.

12. Judy Greenwald, "Layoffs May Spark Defamation Suits," *Business Insurance,* June 1, 2009, Business & Company Resource Center, galenet.galegroup.com.

13. "Guide to Screening and Selection in Employment," May 2007, www.chrc-ccdp.ca/publications/screening_employment-eng.aspx, retrieved April 1, 2012.

14. A. Ryan and M. Lasek, "Negligent Hiring and Defamation: Areas of Liability Related to Preemployment Inquiries," *Personnel Psychology* 44 (1991), pp. 293–319.

15. A. Long, "Addressing the Cloud over Employee References: A Survey of Recently Enacted State Legislation," *William and Mary Law Review* 39 (October 1997), pp. 177–228.

16. Clarence Bennett, "Stop Fighting Over Reference Letters," *Canadian HR Reporter,* December 1, 2014, p. 15.

17. Lynne Van Buskirk "Can I Get a Reference?" *Canadian HR Reporter,* March 10, 2008, www.hrreporter.com, retrieved April 3, 2008.

18. Ann Zimmerman, "Wal-Mart to Probe Job Applicants," *The Wall Street Journal,* August 12, 2004, pp. A3, A6.

19. "Corporate Testimonials," http://backcheck.net/testimonials.htm#scotiabank, retrieved April 1, 2012; http://backcheck.net/background-check-solutions-and-services.htm, retrieved April 1, 2012.

20. Jim Middlemiss, "Didn't You Check?" *National Post,* January 31, 2007, p. WK3.

21. Shannon Klie, "Weeding Out the Fakes," *Canadian HR Reporter,* May 7, 2007, www.hrreporter.com, retrieved April 6, 2008.

22. "Be Careful Who You Google," *Investment Executive,* March 1, 2012; "Pitfalls of Social Media in Background Checks," *24 Hours Toronto,* March 19, 2012; Amanda Silliker, "Tread Carefully with Social Media Checks," *Canadian HR Reporter,* January 30, 2012, p. 1, 11.

23. Public Service Commission of Canada, "Office Skills Test," July 7, 2007, www.psc-cfp.gc.ca/ppc/assessment_pg2_ba_e.htm, retrieved April 6, 2008.

24. L. C. Buffardi, E. A. Fleishman, R. A. Morath, and P. M. McCarthy, "Relationships Between Ability Requirements and Human Errors in Job Tasks," *Journal of Applied Psychology* 85 (2000), pp. 551–64; J. Hogan, "Structure of Physical Performance in Occupational Tasks," *Journal of Applied Psychology* 76 (1991), pp. 495–507.

25. "RCMP Fact Sheets—Recruitment," www.rcmp-grc.gc.ca/factsheets/fact_recruit_e.htm, retrieved April 6, 2008.

26. "PSC Tests by level," *Public Service Commission of Canada,* www.psc-cfp.gc.ca/ppc-cpp/psc-tests-cfp/index-eng.htm, retrieved February 11, 2015.

27. M. J. Ree, J. A. Earles, and M. S. Teachout, "Predicting Job Performance: Not Much More Than *g,*" *Journal of Applied Psychology* 79 (1994), pp. 518–24; L. S. Gottfredson, "The *g* Factor in Employment," *Journal of Vocational Behavior* 29 (1986), pp. 293–96; J. E. Hunter and R. H. Hunter, "Validity and Utility of Alternative Predictors of Job Performance," *Psychological Bulletin* 96 (1984), pp. 72–98; Gutenberg et al., "Moderating Effects"; F. L. Schmidt, J. G. Berner, and J. E. Hunter, "Racial Differences in Validity of Employment Tests: Reality or Illusion," *Journal of Applied Psychology* 58 (1974), pp. 5–6; J. A. LePine, J. A. Colquitt, and A. Erez, "Adaptability to Changing Task Contexts: Effects of General Cognitive Ability, Conscientiousness, and Openness to Experience," *Personnel Psychology* 53 (2000), pp. 563–93.

28. George Anders, "The Rare Find," *Bloomberg Businessweek,* October 17, 2011, EBSCOhost, web. ebscohost.com.

29. "Human Resources Consultant Simulation Exercise," www.psc-cfp.gc.ca/ppc-cpp/psc-tests-cfp/sim-410-eng.htm, retrieved April 4, 2012.

30. D. J Schleiger, V. Venkataramani, F. P. Morgeson, and M. A. Campion, "So You Didn't Get the Job . . . Now What Do You Think? Examining Opportunity to Perform Fairness Perceptions," *Personnel Psychology* 59 (2006), pp. 559–90.

31. F. L. Schmidt and J. E. Hunter, "The Validity and Utility of Selection Methods in Personnel Psychology: Practical and Theoretical Implications of 85 Years of Research Findings," *Psychological Bulletin* 124 (1998), pp. 262–74.

32. W. Arthur, E. A. Day, T. L. McNelly, and P. S. Edens, "Meta-Analysis of the Criterion-Related Validity of Assessment Center Dimensions," *Personnel Psychology* 56 (2003), pp. 125–54; C. E. Lance, T. A. Lambert, A. G. Gewin, F. Lievens, and J. M. Conway, "Revised Estimates of Dimension and Exercise Variance Components in Assessment Center Postexercise Dimension Ratings," *Journal of Applied Psychology* 89 (2004), pp. 377–85.

33. N. M. Dudley, K. A. Orvis, J. E. Lebieki, and J. M. Cortina, "A Meta-analytic Investigation of Conscientiousness in the Prediction of Job Performance: Examining the Intercorrelation and the Incremental Validity of Narrow Traits," *Journal of Applied Psychology* 91 (2006), pp. 40–57; W. S. Dunn, M. K. Mount, M. R. Barrick, and D. S. Ones, "Relative Importance of Personality and General Mental Ability on Managers' Judgments of Applicant Qualifications," *Journal of Applied Psychology* 79 (1995), pp. 500–509; P. M. Wright, K. M. Kacmar, G. C. McMahan, and K. Deleeuw, "P=f (M × A): Cognitive Ability as a Moderator of the Relationship between Personality and Job Performance," *Journal of Management* 21 (1995), pp. 1129–1139.

34. M. Mount, M. R. Barrick, and J. P. Strauss, "Validity of Observer Ratings of the Big Five Personality Factors," *Journal of Applied Psychology* 79 (1994), pp. 272–280.

35. L. A. Witt and G. R. Ferris, "Social Skill as Moderator of the Conscientiousness-Performance Relationship: Convergent Results across Four Studies," *Journal of Applied Psychology* 88 (2003), pp. 809–820.

36. N. Schmitt and F. L. Oswald, "The Impact of Corrections for Faking on the Validity of Non-cognitive Measures in Selection Contexts," *Journal of Applied Psychology* (2006), pp. 613–621.

37. S. A. Birkland, T. M. Manson, J. L. Kisamore, M. T. Brannick, and M. A. Smith, "Faking on Personality Measures," *International Journal of Selection and Assessment* 14 (December 2006), pp. 317–335.

38. C. H. Van Iddekinge, P. H. Raymark, and P. L Rother, "Assessing Personality with a Structured Employment Interview: Construct-Related Validity and Susceptibility to Response Inflation," *Journal of Applied Psychology* 90 (2005), pp. 536–552; R. Mueller-Hanson, E. D. Heggestad, and G. C. Thornton, "Faking and Selection: Considering the Use of Personality from Select-In and Select-Out Perspectives," *Journal of Applied Psychology* 88 (2003), pp. 348–355; and N. L. Vasilopoulos, J. M. Cucina, and J.M. McElreath, "Do Warnings of Response Verification Moderate the Relationship between Personality and Cognitive Ability?" *Journal of Applied Psychology* 90 (2005), pp. 306–322.

39. E. Freudenheim, "Personality Testing Controversial, but Poised to Take Off," *Workforce Management,* August 14, 2006, p. 38.

40. V. Knight, "Personality Tests as Hiring Tools," *Wall Street Journal,* March 15, 2006, p. B1; G. L. Stewards, I. S. Fulmer, and M. R. Barrick, "An Exploration of Member Roles as a Multilevel Linking Mechanism for Individual Traits and Team Outcomes," *Personnel Psychology* 58 (2005), pp. 343–365; and M. Mount, R. Ilies, and E. Johnson, "Relationship of Personality Traits and Counterproductive Work Behaviors: The Mediation Effects of Job Satisfaction," *Personnel Psychology* 59 (2006), pp. 591–622.

41. A. Hedger, "Employee Screening: Common Challenges, Smart Solutions," *Workforce Management,* March 17, 2008, pp. 39–46; and J. Welch and S. Welch, "Team Building: Right and Wrong," *BusinessWeek,* November 24, 2008, p. 130.

42. D. S. One, C. Viswesvaran, and E. L. Schmidt, "Comprehensive Meta-Analysis of Integrity Test Validities: Findings and Implications for Personnel Selection and Theories of Job Performance," *Journal of Applied Psychology* 78 (1993), pp. 679–703; H. J. Bernardin and D. K. Cooke, "Validity of an Honesty Test in Predicting Theft Among Convenience Store Employees," *Academy of Management Journal* 36 (1993), pp. 1079–1106.

43. www.chrc-ccdp.caflegislation, retrieved May 31, 2004.

44. "Canadian Human Rights Commission's Policy on Alcohol and Drug Testing," October 2009, p. 10, www.chrc-ccdp.gc.ca/sites/default/files/padt_pdda_eng_2.pdf, retrieved February 11, 2015.

45. Duncan, Marsden, "Drug and Alcohol Testing: A Divided Nation?" *Canadian HR Reporter,* October 5, 2009, pp. 5-6; Todd Humber, "Pre-employment Drug Tests Dealt Blow," *Canadian HR Reporter,* July 17, 2006, www.hrreporter.com, retrieved April 8, 2008.

46. M. A. McDaniel, E. P. Morgeson, E. G. Finnegan, M. A. Campion, and E. P. Braverman, "Use of Situational Judgment Tests to Predict Job Performance: A Clarification of the Literature," *Journal of Applied Psychology* 86 (2001), pp. 730–740; J. Clavenger, G. M. Perreira, D. Weichmann, N. Schmitt, and V. S. Harvey, "Incremental Validity of Situational Judgment Tests," *Journal of Applied Psychology* 86 (2001), pp. 410–417.

47. M. A. Campion, J. E. Campion, and J. P. Hudson, "Structured Interviewing: A Note of Incremental Validity and Alternative Question Types," *Journal of Applied Psychology* 79 (1994), pp. 998–1002; E. D. Pulakos and N. Schmitt, "Experience-Based and Situational Interview Questions: Studies of Validity," *Personnel Psychology* 48 (1995), pp. 289–308; and A. P. J. Wllis, B. J. West, A. M. Ryan, and R. P DeShon, "The Use of Impression Management Tactics in Structured Interviews: A Function of Question Type?" *Journal of Applied Psychology* 87 (2002), pp. 1200–1208.

48. Todd Humber, "How BMO Financial Selects Employees," *Canadian HR Reporter,* December 6, 2004, p. G2.

49. N. Schmitt, F. L. Oswald, B. H. Kim, M. A. Gillespie, L. J. Ramsey, and T. Y Yoo, "The Impact of Elaboration on Socially Desirable Responding and the Validity of Biodata Measures," *Journal of Applied Psychology* 88 (2003), pp. 979–88; N. Schmitt and C. Kunce, "The Effects of Required Elaboration of Answers to Biodata Questions," *Personnel Psychology* 55 (2002), pp. 569–87.

50. Hunter and Hunter, "Validity and Utility of Alternative Predictors of Job Performance."

51. R. Pingitore, B. L. Dugoni, R. S. Tindale, and B. Spring, "Bias Against Overweight Job Applicants in a Simulated Interview," *Journal of Applied Psychology* 79 (1994), pp. 184–190.

52. M. A. McDaniel, D. L. Whetzel, F. L. Schmidt, and S. D. Maurer, "The Validity of Employment Interviews: A Comprehensive Review and Meta-Analysis," *Journal of Applied Psychology* 79 (1994), pp. 599–616; A. I. Huffcutt and W. A. Arthur, "Hunter and Hunter (1984) Revisited: Interview Validity for Entry-Level Jobs," *Journal of Applied Psychology* 79 (1994), pp. 184–190.

53. Y. Ganzach, A. N. Kluger, and N. Klayman, "Making Decisions from an Interview: Expert Measurement and Mechanical Combination," *Personnel Psychology* 53(2000), pp. 1–21; G. Stasser and W. Titus, "Effects of Information Load and Percentage of Shared Information on the Dissemination of Unshared Information During Group Discussion," *Journal of Personality and Social Psychology* 53 (1987), pp. 81–93.

54. Liz Bernier, "Hiring Managers a Thorn in HR's Side," *Canadian HR Reporter,* September 8, 2014, p. 1, 12.

CHAPTER 6

1. "Our Culture," http://newsroom.fb.com/company-info/, retrieved March 8, 2015; Robert Jeffery, "We've Already Got All The Skills We Need," *People Management,* April 2014, pp. 30–31; Justin Brusino, "The Long View: Stuart Crabb," *T+D,* January 2012, pp. 64–65; Kellye Whitney, "Facebook 'Likes' Learning," *Chief Learning Officer,* November 2011, pp. 22–25.

2. *Merriam-Webster Dictionary,"* www.merriam-webster.com/dictionary/learning, retrieved March 1, 2015.

3. "Developing Skills in the Canadian Workplace," *Canadian Workplace Gazette* 2, no. 1, p. 98, http://labour-travail.hrdc-drhc.gc.ca.

4. Jon Younger, Norm Smallwood, and Dave Ulrich, "Developing Your Organization's Brand as a Talent Developer," *HR: Human Resource Planning* 30, no. 2 (2007), p. 21.

5. Colin Hall, "Learning and Development Outlook, 12th Edition: Strong Learning Organizations, Strong Leadership" (Ottawa: The Conference Board of Canada, February 2014), p. 14. Based on data from International Institute for Management Development, *World Competitiveness Yearbook 2013, 2012, and 2008* (Lausanne, Switzerland).

6. Colin Hall, "Learning and Development Outlook, 12th Edition: Strong Learning Organizations, Strong Leadership" (Ottawa: The Conference Board of Canada, February 2014), p. iii.

7. Colin Hall, "Learning and Development Outlook, 12th Edition: Strong Learning Organizations, Strong Leadership" (Ottawa: The Conference Board of Canada, February 2014), pp. 8–9. Based on data from International Institute for Management Development, *World Competitiveness Yearbook 2013, 2012, and 2008* (Lausanne, Switzerland).

8. R. Noe, *Employee Training and Development,* 4th ed. (New York: Irwin/McGraw-Hill, 2008).

9. Ryann K. Ellis, *A Field Guide to Learning Management Systems,* Learning Circuits (American Society for Training & Development, 2009), accessed at www.astd.org.

10. I. L. Goldstein, E. P. Braverman, and H. Goldstein, "Needs Assessment," in *Developing Human Resources,* ed. K. N. Wexley (Washington, DC: Bureau of National Affairs, 1991), pp. 5–35–5–75.

11. J. Z. Rouillier and I. L. Goldstein, "Determinants of the Climate for Transfer of Training" (presented at Society of Industrial/Organizational Psychology meetings, St. Louis, MO, 1991); J. S. Russell, J. R. Terborg, and M. L. Powers, "Organizational Performance and Organizational Level Training and Support," *Personnel Psychology* 38 (1985), pp. 849–63; H. Baumgartel, G. J. Sullivan, and L. E. Dunn, "How Organizational Climate and Personality Affect the Payoff from Advanced Management Training Sessions," *Kansas Business Review* 5 (1978), pp. 1–10.

12. Jull Casner-Lotto et al., *Are They Really Ready to Work?* (New York: Conference Board; Washington, DC: Corporate Voices for Working Families; Tucson, AZ: Partnership for 21st Century Skills; Alexandria, VA: Society for Human Resource Management, (2006)), available at www.infoedge.com; R. Davenport, "Eliminate the Skills Gap," *T+D,* February 2006, pp. 26–34; and M. Schoeff, "Amid Calls to Bolster U.S. Innovation, Experts Lament Paucity of Basic Math Skills," *Workforce Management,* March 2006, pp. 46–49.

13. R. A. Noe, "Trainees' Attributes and Attitudes: Neglected Influences on Training Effectiveness," *Academy of Management Review* 11 (1986), pp. 736–49; T. T. Baldwin, R. T. Magjuka, and B. T. Loher, "The Perils of Participation: Effects of Choice on Trainee Motivation and Learning," *Personnel Psychology* 44 (1991), pp. 51–66; S. L Tannenbaum, J. E. Mathieu, E. Salas, and J. A. Cannon-Bowers, "Meeting Trainees' Expectations: The

Influence of Training Fulfillment on the Development of Commitment, Self-Efficacy, and Motivation," *Journal of Applied Psychology* 76 (1991), pp. 759–69.

14. L. H. Peters, E. J. O'Connor, and J. R. Eulberg, "Situational Constraints: Sources, Consequences, and Future Considerations," in *Research in Personnel and Human Resource Management,* ed. K. M. Rowland and G. R. Ferris (Greenwich, CT: JAI Press, 1985), vol. 3, pp. 79–114; E. J. O'Connor, L. H. Peters, A. Pooyan, J. Weekley, B. Frank, and B. Erenkranz, "Situational Constraints' Effects on Performance, Affective Reactions, and Turnover: A Field Replication and Extension," *Journal of Applied Psychology* 69 (1984), pp. 663–72; D. J. Cohen, "What Motivates Trainees?," *Training and Development Journal,* November 1990, pp. 91–93; Russell, Terborg, and Powers, "Organizational Performance."

15. S. Allen, "Water Cooler Wisdom," *Training,* August 2005, pp. 30–34.

16. B. Mager, *Preparing Instructional Objectives,* 2nd ed. (Belmont, CA: Lake Publishing, 1984); B. J. Smith and B. L. Delahaye, *How to Be an Effective Trainer,* 2nd ed. (New York: Wiley, 1987).

17. Colin Hall, "Learning and Development Outlook, 12th Edition: Strong Learning Organizations, Strong Leadership" (Ottawa: The Conference Board of Canada, February 2014), p. 40.

18. American Society for Training and Development, *Learning Circuits: Glossary,* www.astd.org/LC/glossary. htm, accessed March 16, 2012.

19. Red Seal Program, Human Resources Development Canada, www.red-seal.ca/English/redseal_e.shtml, retrieved March 21, 2004.

20. Ibid.

21. "MBA Internships/Industry Related Partnerships," www. sauder.ubc.ca/Programs/MBA/MBA_Full_Time/Career_ Services/Internships_and_Industry_Projects, retrieved April 7, 2012.

22. www.uregina.ca/coop/students/current/handbook. shtml, retrieved March 11, 2004.

23. W. J. Rothwell and H. C. Kanzanas, "Planned OJT Is Productive OJT," *Training and Development Journal,* October 1990, pp. 53–56.

24. CATSA News, April 2007, p. 6, www.catsa-acsta.gc.ca/ english/media/bulletin/2007-04.pdf, retrieved May 23, 2008.

25. Doug Cameron, "Dreamliner's Here: Now Learn to Fly It," *The Wall Street Journal,* November 1, 2011, online.wsj. com.

26. Pat Galagan, "Second That," *T+D,* February 2008, pp. 4, 34–37.

27. Ryan Ori, "OSF, Medical College Receive $25 Million Donation," *Journal Star (Peoria, Ill.),* February 28, 2010, Business & Company Resource Center, http://galenet. galegroup.com; and "Welding Simulation Software Enhances Training Efforts," *Product News Network,* November 23, 2009, Business & Company Resource Center," http://galenet.galegroup.com.

28. Julie Winkle Giulioni and Karen Voloshin, "A Case for the Mini Case Study," *TD: Talent Development,* November 2014, pp. 27–29.

29. www.stratxsimulations.com/markstrat_online_home. aspx, retrieved May 23, 2008.

30. G. P. Latham and L. M. Saari, "Application of Social Learning Theory to Training Supervisors Through Behavior Modeling," *Journal of Applied Psychology* 64 (1979), pp. 239–46.

31. D. Brown and D. Harvey, *An Experiential Approach to Organizational Development* (Englewood Cliffs, NJ: Prentice Hall, 2000); and Larissa Jogi, review of *The Handbook of Experiential Learning and Management Education,* eds. Michael Reynolds and Russ Vince, *Studies in the Education of Adults* 40 no. 2 (Autumn 2008): pp. 232–234, accessed at OCLC FirstSearch, http://newfirstsearch.oclc.org.

32. J. Cannon-Bowers and C. Bowers, "Team Development and Functioning," in *A Handbook of Industrial and Organizational Psychology,* ed. S. Zedeck, 1: 597–650 (Washington, DC: American Psychological Association, 2011); L. Delise, C. Gorman, A. Brooks, J. Rentsch, and D. Steele-Johnson, "The Effects of Team Training on Team Outcomes: A Meta-analysis," *Performance Improvement Quarterly* 22 (2010): 53–80.

33. Lesley Young, "All in the Family at Toronto Hydro," *Canadian HR Reporter,* March 24, 2008, p. 16.

34. C. E. Schneier, "Training and Development Programs: What Learning Theory and Research Have to Offer," *Personnel Journal,* April 1974, pp. 288–93; M. Knowles, "Adult Learning," in *Training and Development Handbook,* 3rd ed., ed. R. L. Craig (New York: McGraw-Hill, 1987), pp. 168–79; B. J. Smith and B. L. Delahaye, *How to Be an Effective Trainer,* 2nd ed. (New York: Wiley, 1987); and Traci Sitzmann, "Self-Regulating Online Course Engagement," *T+D,* March 2010, Business & Company Resource Center, galenet.galegroup.com.

35. K. A. Smith-Jentsch, F. G. Jentsch, S. C. Payne, and E. Salas, "Can Pretraining Experiences Explain Individual Differences in Learning?," *Journal of Applied Psychology* 81 (1996), pp. 110–16.

36. W. McGehee and P. W. Thayer, *Training in Business and Industry* (New York: Wiley, 1961).

37. R. M. Gagne and K. L. Medsker, *The Condition of Learning* (Fort Worth, TX: Harcourt-Brace, 1996).

38. J. C. Naylor and G. D. Briggs, "The Effects of Task Complexity and Task Organization on the Relative Efficiency of Part and Whole Training Methods," *Journal of Experimental Psychology* 65 (1963), pp. 217–24.

39. Kirkpatrick, Jim D., and Wendy Kayser Kirkpatrick. *Training on Trial: How Workplace Learning Must Reinvent Itself to Remain Relevant* (New York: American Management Association, 2010).

40. Colin Hall, "Learning and Development Outlook, 12th Edition: Strong Learning Organizations, Strong Leadership" (Ottawa: The Conference Board of Canada, February 2014), p. 66.

41. K. Mantyla, *Blended E-Learning* (Alexandria, VA: ASTD, 2001).

42. M. R. Louis, "Surprise and Sense Making: What Newcomers Experience in Entering Unfamiliar Organizational Settings," *Administrative Science Quarterly* 25 (1980), pp. 226–51.

43. Kira Vermond, "Rolling Out the Welcome Mat," *The Globe and Mail,* April 26, 2008, www.theglobeandmail.com, retrieved April 28, 2008.

44. Ibid.

45. Ibid.; and "Bringing New Hires Up to Speed: How Structured Onboarding Can Help," *The Conference Board of Canada,* August 2011, p. 6.

46. Danielle Harder, "Diversity Takes Flight at Air Canada," *Canadian HR Reporter,* May 5, 2008, www.hrreporter. com, retrieved May 23, 2008.

47. S. Rynes and B. Rosen, "What Makes Diversity Programs Work?," *HR Magazine,* October 1994, pp. 67–73; Rynes and Rosen, A Field Survey of Factors

Affecting the Adoption and Perceived Success of Diversity Training," *Personnel Psychology* 48, no. 2 (1995), pp. 247–271; J. Gordon, "Different from What? Diversity as a Performance Issue," *Training,* May 1995, pp. 25–33.

48. M. London, *Managing the Training Enterprise* (San Francisco: Jossey-Bass, 1989) and D. Day, *Developing Leadership Talent* (Alexandria, VA: SHRM Foundation, 2007).

49. R. W. Pace, P. C. Smith, and G. E. Mills, *Human Resource Development* (Englewood Cliffs, NJ: Prentice Hall, 1991); W. Fitzgerald, "Training versus Development," *Training and Development Journal,* May 1992, pp. 81–84; R. A. Noe, S. L. Wilk, E. J. Mullen, and J. E. Wanek, "Employee Development: Issues in Construct Definition and Investigation of Antecedents," in *Improving Training Effectiveness in Work Organizations,* ed. J. K. Ford (Mahwah, NJ: Lawrence Erlbaum, 1997), pp. 153–189.

50. J. H. Greenhaus and G. A. Callanan, *Career Management,* 2nd ed. (Fort Worth, TX: Dryden Press, 1994); and D. Hall, *Careers in and out of Organizations* (Thousand Oaks, CA: Sage, 2002).

51. R. Noe, *Employee Training and Development,* 5th ed. (New York: McGraw-Hill Irwin, 2010).

52. A. Howard and D. W. Bray, *Managerial Lives in Transition: Advancing Age and Changing Times* (New York: Guilford, 1988); J. Bolt, *Executive Development* (New York: Harper Business, 1989); J. R. Hintichs and G. P. Hollenbeck, "Leadership Development," in *Developing Human Resources,* ed. K. N. Wexley 237; and Day, *Developing Leadership Talent.*

53. Joyce Rowlands, "Soft Skills Give Hard Edge," *The Globe and Mail,* June 9, 2004, p. C8.

54. Ibid.

55. A. Thorne and H. Gough, *Portraits of Type* (Palo Alto, CA: Consulting Psychologists Press, 1993).

56. D. Druckman and R. A. Bjork, eds., *In the Mind's Eye: Enhancing Human Performance* (Washington, DC: National Academy Press, 1991); M. H. McCaulley, "The Myers-Briggs Type Indicator and Leadership," in *Measures of Leadership,* eds. K. E. Clark and M. B. Clark (West Orange, NJ: Leadership Library of America, 1990), pp. 381–418.

57. G. C. Thornton III and W. C. Byham, *Assessment Centers and Managerial Performance* (New York: Academic Press, 1982); L. F. Schoenfeldt and J. A. Steger, "Identification and Development of Management Talent," in *Research in Personnel and Human Resource Management,* eds. K. N. Rowland and G. Ferris (Greenwich, CT: JAI Press, 1989), vol. 7, pp. 151–81.

58. Thornton and Byham, *Assessment Centers and Managerial Performance.*

59. P. G. W. Jansen and B. A. M. Stoop, "The Dynamics of Assessment Center Validity: Results of a Seven-Year Study," *Journal of Applied Psychology* 86 (2001), pp. 741–53; and D. Chan, "Criterion and Construct Validation of an Assessment Centre," *Journal of Occupational and Organizational Psychology* 69 (1996), pp. 167–81.

60. R. G. Jones and M. D. Whitmore, "Evaluating Developmental Assessment Centers as Interventions," *Personnel Psychology* 48 (1995), pp. 377–88.

61. C. D. McCauley and M. M. Lombardo, "Benchmarks: An Instrument for Diagnosing Managerial Strengths and Weaknesses," in *Measures of Leadership,* pp. 535–45; and Center for Creative Leadership,

"Benchmarks®—Overview," www.ccl.org, accessed March 28, 2006.

62. C. D. McCauley, M. M. Lombardo, and C. J. Usher, "Diagnosing Management Development Needs: An Instrument Based on How Managers Develop," *Journal of Management* 15 (1989), pp. 389–403.

63. J. F. Brett and L. E. Atwater, "360-Degree Feedback: Accuracy, Reactions, and Perceptions of Usefulness," *Journal of Applied Psychology* 86 (2001), pp. 930–42; Marshall Goldsmith, "How to Increase Your Leadership Effectiveness," *BusinessWeek,* November 20, 2009, www.businessweek.com; and Brenda Bence, "Would You Want to Work for You?" *Supervision,* February 2010, Business & Company Resource Center, http://galenet.galegroup.com.

64. L. Atwater, P. Roush, and A. Fischthal, "The Influence of Upward Feedback on Self- and Follower Ratings of Leadership," *Personnel Psychology* 48 (1995), pp. 35–59; J. F. Hazucha, S. A. Hezlett, and R. J. Schneider, "The Impact of 360-Degree Feedback on Management Skill Development," *Human Resource Management* 32 (1193), pp. 325–351; J. W. Smither, M. London, N. Vasilopoulos, R. R. Reilly, R. E. Millsap, and N. Salvemini, "An Examination of the Effects of an Upward Feedback Program over Time," *Personnel Psychology* 48 (1995), pp. 1–34; J. Smither and A. Walker, "Are the Improvements in Multirater Feedback Ratings Over Time?" *Journal of Applied Psychology* 89 (2004), pp. 575–581; and J. Smither, M. London, and R. Reilly, "Does Performance Improve Following Multisource Feedback? A Theoretical Model, Meta-analysis, and Review of Empirical Findings," *Personnel Psychology* 58 (2005), pp. 33–66.

65. M. W. McCall Jr., *High Flyers* (Boston: Harvard Business School Press, 1998).

66. R. S. Snell, "Congenial Ways of Learning: So Near Yet So Far," *Journal of Management Development* 9 (1990), pp. 17–23.

67. C. D. McCauley, M. N. Ruderman, P. J. Ohlott, and J. E. Morrow, "Assessing the Developmental Components of Managerial Jobs," *Journal of Applied Psychology* 79 (1994), pp. 544–60.

68. Andrew Wahl, "Leaders Wanted," *Canadian Business,* March 1–14, 2004, pp. 33, 34.

69. M. London, *Developing Managers* (San Francisco: Jossey-Bass, 1985); M. A. Camion, L. Cheraskin, and M. J. Stevens, "Career-Related Antecedents and Outcomes of Job Rotation," *Academy of Management Journal* 37 (1994), pp. 1518–42; London, *Managing the Training Enterprise.*

70. Margaret Fiester, "Job Rotation, Total Rewards, Measuring Value," *HR Magazine,* August 2008, Business & Company Resource Centre, http://galenet.galegroup.com; and "Energize and Enhance Employee Value with Job Rotation," *HR Focus,* January 2008, OCLC FirstSearch, http://newfirst search.oclc.org.

71. R. A. Noe, B. D. Steffy, and A. E. Barber, "An Investigation of the Factors Influencing Employees' Willingness to Accept Mobility Opportunities," *Personnel Psychology* 41 (1988), pp. 559–80; S. Gould and L. E. Penley, "A Study of the Correlates of Willingness to Relocate," *Academy of Management Journal* 28 (1984), pp. 472–78; J. Landau and T. H. Hammer, "Clerical Employees' Perceptions of Intraorganizational Career Opportunities," *Academy of Management Journal* 29 (1986), pp. 385–405; J. M. Brett and A. H. Reilly, "On the Road Again: Predicting the Job Transfer Decision," *Journal of Applied Psychology* 73 (1988), pp. 614–20.

72. D. B. Turban and T. W. Dougherty, "Role of Protégé Personality in Receipt of Mentoring and Career Success," *Academy of Management Journal* 37 (1994), pp. 688–702; E. A. Fagenson, "Mentoring: Who Needs It? A Comparison of Protégés' and Non-Protégés' Needs for Power, Achievement, Affiliation, and Autonomy," *Journal of Vocational Behavior* 41 (1992), pp. 48–60.

73. A. H. Geiger, "Measures for Mentors," *Training and Development Journal,* February 1992, pp. 65–67; Lynnie Martin and Tyler Robinson, "Why You Should Get on Board the Mentor Ship," *Public Manager,* Winter 2011, pp. 42–45; "The Payoff," *California CPA,* October 2011, p. 12.

74. K. E. Kram, *Mentoring at Work: Developmental Relationships in Organizational Life* (Glenview, IL: Scott-Foresman, 1985); L. L. Phillips-Jones, "Establishing a Formalized Mentoring Program," *Training and Development Journal* 2 (1983), pp. 38–42; K. Kram, "Phases of the Mentoring Relationship," *Academy of Management Journal* 26 (1983), pp. 608–25; G. T. Chao, P. M. Walz, and P. D. Gardner, "Formal and Informal Mentorships: A Comparison of Mentoring Functions and Contrasts with Nonmentored Counterparts," *Personnel Psychology* 45 (1992), pp. 619–36; and C. Wanberg, E. Welsh, and S. Hezlett, "Mentoring Research: A Review and Dynamic Process Model," in *Research in Personnel and Human Resources Management,* eds. J. Martocchio and G. Ferris (New York: Elsevier Science, 2003), pp. 39–124.

75. Michele Lent Hirsch, "Mentor Makeover," *Psychology Today,* July/August 2011, EBSCOhost, web.ebscohost.com.

76. L. Eby, M. Butts, A. Lockwood, and A. Simon, "Protégés' Negative Mentoring Experiences: Construct Development and Nomological Validation," *Personnel Psychology* 57 (2004), pp. 411–47; R. Emelo, "Conversations with Mentoring Leaders," *T+D,* June 2011, pp. 32–37; M. Weinstein, "Please Don't Go," *Training,* May/June 2011, pp. 38–34; "Training Top 125," *Training,* January/February 2011, pp. 54–93.

77. R. A. Noe, D. B. Greenberger, and S. Wang, "Mentoring: What We Know and Where We Might Go," in *Research in Personnel and Human Resources Management,* eds. G. Ferris and J. Martocchio (New York: Elsevier Science, 2002), vol. 21, pp. 129–74; and T. D. Allen, L. T. Eby, M. L. Poteet, E. Lentz, and L. Lima, "Career Benefits Associated with Mentoring for Protégés: A Meta-Analysis," *Journal of Applied Psychology* 89 (2004), pp. 127–36.

78. Wendy Murphy, "Reverse Mentoring at Work: Fostering Cross Generational Learning and Developing Millennial Leaders," *Human Resource Management,* July–August 2012, p. 549.

79. Ryann Ellis, "Letting Millennial Lead the Way," *T+D,* September 2013, p. 13; C.S. Kulesza and Daniel Smith, "Reverse Mentoring—Something for Everyone!" *Strategic Finance,* April 2013, pp. 21–23, 63; Wendy Murphy, "Reverse Mentoring at Work: Fostering Cross Generational Learning and Developing Millennial Leaders," *Human Resource Management,* July–August 2012, p. 549–574.

80. D. B. Peterson and M. D. Hicks, *Leader as Coach* (Minneapolis: Personnel Decisions, 1996).

81. David Brown, "Mentoring Boosts Retention, *T&D.* But It's a Long-Term Game," *Canadian HR Reporter,* July 12, 2004, p. 7.

82. Sarah McVanel and Christine Burych, "Are You In or Out?" *HR Professional,* March/April 2015, pp. 41–42.

83. J. Smither, M. London, R. Flautt, Y. Vargas, and L. Kucine, "Can Working with an Executive Coach Improve Multisource Ratings over Time? A Quasi-experimental Field Study," *Personnel Psychology* 56 (2003), pp. 23–44.

84. A. Vorro, "Coaching In-House Counsel Helps Perfect Their Game," *Inside Counsel,* Volume 23, Issue 242 (2012), p. 53.

85. Rajiv L. Gupta and Karol M. Wasylyshyn, "Developing World Class Leaders: The Rohm and Haas Story," *People & Strategy,* December 2009, pp. 36–41; and Kathleeen Koster, "This Too Shall Pass," *Employee Benefit News,* July 1, 2009, Business & Company Resource Center, http://galenet.galegroup.com.

86. Claudine Kapel and Catherine Shepherd, "Career Ladders Create Common Language for Defining Jobs," *Canadian HR Reporter,* June 14, 2004, p. 15.

87. "2014 Catalyst Census: Women Board Directors," January 13, 2015 (Data from October 2014), www.catalyst.org/knowledge/2014-catalyst-census-women-board-directors, retrieved March 5, 2015.

88. P. J. Ohlott, M. N. Ruderman, and C. D. McCauley, "Gender Differences in Managers' Developmental Job Experiences," *Academy of Management Journal,* 37 (1994), pp. 46–67; L. A. Mainiero, "Getting Anointed for Advancement: The Case of Executive Women," *Academy of Management Executive* 8 (1994), pp. 53–67; and P. Tharenov, S. Latimer, and D. Conroy, "How Do You Make It to the Top? An Examination of Influences on Women's and Men's Managerial Advancements," *Academy of Management Journal* 37 (1994), pp. 899–931.

89. R. A. Noe, "Women and Mentoring: A Review and Research Agenda," *Academy of Management Review* 13 (1988), pp. 65–78; B. R. Ragins and J. L. Cotton, "Easier Said than Done: Gender Differences in Perceived Barriers to Gaining a Mentor," *Academy of Management Journal* 34 (1991), pp. 939–51; Joann S. Lublin, "Female Directors: Why So Few?" *The Wall Street Journal,* December 27, 2011, http://online.wsj.com; Christine Silva and Nancy Carter, "New Research Busts Myths about the Gender Gap," *Harvard Business Review,* October 6, 2011, http://blogs.hbr.org; Catalyst, "Catalyst Study Explodes Myths about Why Women's Careers Lag Men's," news release, October 13, 2011, www.catalyst.org; "Too Many Suits," *The Economist,* November 26, 2011, EBSCOhost, http://web.ebscohost.com.

90. Alice H. Eagly and Linda L. Carli, "Women and the Labyrinth of Leadership," *Harvard Business Review,* September 2007, pp. 63–71.

91. C. B. Derr, C Jones, and E. L. Toomey, "Managing High-Potential Employees: Current Practices in Thirty-Three U.S. Corporation," *Human Resource Management,* 27 (1988), pp. 273–290; K. M. Nowack, "The Secrets of Succession," *Training and Development* 48 (1994), pp. 49–54; and "2009 Trends in Review: What Do You Know?" *T+D,* December 2009, pp. 33–39.

92. L. W. Hellervik, J. F. Hazucha, and R. J. Schneider, "Behavior Change: Models, Methods, and a Review of Evidence," in *Handbook of Industrial and Organizational Psychology,* 2nd ed., eds. M. D. Dunnette and L. M. Hough (Palo Alto, CA: Consulting Psychologists Press, 1992), vol. 3, pp. 823–899.

93. D. B. Peterson, "Measuring and Evaluating Change in Executive and Managerial Development," paper presented at the annual conference of the Society for Industrial and Organizational Psychology, Miami, 1990.

CHAPTER 7

1. Dean Johnson, "Acklands Grainger," *Globe & Mail,* October 23, 2014, p. B2; Sarah Dobson, "Award-winning Corporate Cultures About Values, Feedback, Communication, *Canadian HR Reporter,* January 28, 2013, p. 26; and "Acklands-Grainger," https://www.acklandsgrainger.com/AGIPortalWeb/WebSource/AboutUs/begin.do, retrieved March 11, 2015.

2. Angelita Becom and David Insler, "Performance Management—A Bad Process or a Broken Promise," *People & Strategy,* Volume 36, Issue 32 (2013), p. 43.

3. Amy Armitage and Donna Parrey, "Reinventing Performance Management: Creating Purpose-Driven Practices," *People & Strategy,* Volume 36, Issue 32 (2013), p. 32; Christopher Collins and Bradford Bell, "The State of the Art in Performance Management," *People & Strategy,* Volume 36, Issue 32 (2013), p. 51.

4. Wallace Immen, "Handling the First 100 Days on the Job," *The Globe and Mail,* March 14, 2008, p. C2.

5. Nicole Stewart and Elyse Lamontagne, "Compensation Planning Outlook 2014" (Ottawa: Conference Board of Canada, October 2013), p. 21.

6. Carolyn Heinze, "Fair Appraisals," *Systems Contractor News,* July 2009, Business & Company Resource Center, http://galenet.galegroup.com.

7. Chris French, "Crowdsourcing the Performance Review," *Canadian HR Reporter,* January 27, 2014, p. 24.

8. M. Parker, "Culture Clash: Performance-managing Culture," *Financial Post,* February 20, 2012, retrieved May 4, 2012 http://business.financialpost.com/2012/02/20/culture-clash-performance-managing-culture/; "Investment in Feedback Pays Off," *National Post,* May 14, 2008, FP14; M. Parker, "It's How You Do Things, Not What You Do: Results From the 2010, Canadian Corporate Culture Study," *The Waterline,* Issue 7, July 13, 2010, retrieved May 2, 2012 www.waterstoneehc.com/news-events/newsletters/issue-7.

9. S. Scullen, P. Bergey, and L. Aiman-Smith, "Forced Choice Distribution Systems and the Improvement of Workforce Potential: A Baseline Simulation," *Personnel Psychology* 47 (1963), pp. 149–155.

10. Nicole Stewart and Elyse Lamontagne, "Compensation Planning Outlook 2014" (Ottawa: Conference Board of Canada, October 2013), p. 22.

11. P. Smith and L. Kendall, "Retranslation of Expectations: An Approach to the Construction of Unambiguous Anchors for Rating Scales," *Journal of Applied Psychology* 47 (1963), pp. 149–55.

12. K. Murphy and J. Constans, "Behavioral Anchors as a Source of Bias in Rating," *Journal of Applied Psychology* 72 (1987), pp. 573–77; M. Piotrowski, J. Bames-Farrel, and F. Estig, "Behaviorally Anchored Bias: A Replication and Extension of Murphy and Constans," *Journal of Applied Psychology* 74 (1989), pp. 823–26.

13. G. Latham and K. Wexley, *Increasing Productivity Through Performance Appraisal* (Boston: Addison-Wesley, 1981).

14. U. Wiersma and G. Latham, "The Practicality of Behavioral Observation Scales, Behavioral Expectation Scales, and Trait Scales," *Personnel Psychology* 39 (1986), pp. 619–28.

15. D. C. Anderson, C. Crowell, J. Sucec, K. Gilligan, and M. Wikoff, "Behavior Management of Client Contacts in a Real Estate Brokerage: Getting Agents to Sell More," *Journal of Organizational Behavior Management* 4 (2001), pp. 580–90; F. Luthans and R. Kreitner,

16. K. L. Langeland, C. M. Jones, and T. C. Mawhinney, "Improving Staff Performance in a Community Mental Health Setting: Job Analysis, Training, Goal Setting, Feedback, and Years of Data," *Journal of Organizational Behavior Management* 18 (1998), pp. 21–43.

17. J. Komaki, R. Collins, and P. Penn, "The Role of Performance Antecedents and Consequences in Work Motivation," *Journal of Applied Psychology* 67 (1982), pp. 334–40.

18. S. Snell, "Control Theory in Strategic Human Resource Management: The Mediating Effect of Administrative Information," *Academy of Management Journal* 35 (1992), pp. 292–327.

19. R. Pritchard, S. Jones, P. Roth, K. Stuebing, and S. Ekeberg, "The Evaluation of an Integrated Approach to Measuring Organizational Productivity," *Personnel Psychology* 42 (1989), pp. 69–115.

20. G. Odiorne, *MBO II: A System of Managerial Leadership for the 80's* (Belmont, CA: Pitman Publishers, 1986).

21. R. Rodgers and J. Hunter, "Impact of Management by Objectives on Organizational Productivity," *Journal of Applied Psychology* 76 (1991), pp. 322–26.

22. P. Wright, J. George, S. Farnsworth, and G. McMahan, "Productivity and Extra-Role Behavior: The Effects of Goals and Incentives on Spontaneous Helping," *Journal of Applied Psychology* 78, no. 3 (1993), pp. 374–81.

23. Christopher Collins and Bradford Bell, "The State of the Art in Performance Management," *People & Strategy,* Volume 36, Issue 2 (2013), p. 52.

24. "What Is a Balanced Scorecard?," www.2gc.co/UK/pdf/2GC-FAQ1.pdf, retrieved July 14, 2004.

25. Cam Scholey, "Alignment—Has Your Organization Got It?," *CMA Management* 81, no. 6, pp. 16–18.

26. Mehrdad Derayeh and Stephane Brutus, "Learning from Others' 360-Degree Experiences," *Canadian HR Reporter,* February 10, 2003, www.hrreporter.com, retrieved February 15, 2005.

27. Patty McCord, "How Netflix Reinvented HR, *Harvard Business Review,* January–February 2014, p. 74.

28. R. Heneman, K. Wexley, and M. Moore, "Performance Rating Accuracy: A Critical Review," *Journal of Business Research* 15 (1987), pp. 431–48.

29. T. Becker and R. Klimoski, "A Field Study of the Relationship Between the Organizational Feedback Environment and Performance," *Personnel Psychology* 42 (1989), pp. 343–58; H. M. Findley, W. F. Giles, K. W. Mossholder, "Performance Appraisal and Systems Facets: Relationships with Contextual Performance," *Journal of Applied Psychology* 85 (2000), pp. 634–40.

30. K. Wexley and R. Klimoski, "Performance Appraisal: An Update," in *Research in Personnel and Human Resource Management,* vol. 2, ed. K. Rowland and G. Ferris (Greenwich, CT: JAI Press, 1984).

31. F. Landy and J. Farr, *The Measurement of Work Performance: Methods, Theory, and Applications* (New York: Academic Press, 1983).

32. G. McEvoy and P. Buller, "User Acceptance of Peer Appraisals in an Industrial Setting," *Personnel Psychology* 40 (1987), pp. 785–97.

33. Joann S. Lublin, "Transparency Pays Off in 360-Degree Reviews," *The Wall Street Journal,* December 8, 2011, online.wsj.com.

34. D. Antonioni, "The Effects of Feedback Accountability on Upward Appraisal Ratings," *Personnel Psychology* 47 (1994), pp. 349–56.

Organizational Behavior Modification and Beyond (Glenview, IL: Scott, Foresman, 1975).

35. Rachel Emma Silverman, "Performance Reviews Lose Steam," *The Wall Street Journal,* December 19, 2011, online.wsj.com.

36. H. Heidemeier and K. Moser, "Self-Other Agreement in Job Performance Rating: A Meta-Analytic Test of a Process Model," *Journal of Applied Psychology* 94 (2008), pp. 353–70.

37. J. Bernardin, C. Hagan, J. Kane, and P. Villanova, "Effective Performance Management: A Focus on Precision, Customers, and Situational Constraints," in *Performance Appraisal: State of the Art in Practice,* pp. 3–48.

38. K. Wexley and W. Nemeroff, "Effects of Racial Prejudice, Race of Applicant, and Biographical Similarity on Interviewer Evaluations of Job Applicants," *Journal of Social and Behavioral Sciences* 20 (1974), pp. 66–78.

39. Nicole Stewart and Elyse Lamontagne, "Compensation Planning Outlook 2014" (Ottawa: Conference Board of Canada, October 2013), p. 22.

40. Phillip L. Hunsaker and Dale Dilamarter, *Training in Management Skills,* Cdn. ed. (Toronto: Pearson Education Canada Inc., 2004), p. 330.

41. Ibid.

42. D. Smith, "Training Programs for Performance Appraisal: A Review," *Academy of Management Review* 11 (1986), pp. 22–40; and G. Latham, K. Wexley, and E. Pursell, "Training Managers to Minimize Rating Errors in the Observation of Behavior," *Journal of Applied Psychology* 60 (1975), pp. 550–55.

43. Rose Mueller-Hanson and Elaine Pulakos, "Rethinking Your Performance Management Training: Increase the Impact by Shifting the Emphasis from Process to People," *T+D,* December 2013, p. 68.

44. E. Pulakos, "A Comparison of Rater Training Programs: Error Training and Accuracy Training," *Journal of Applied Psychology* 69 (1984), pp. 581–88.

45. "Most Large Companies Calibrate Performance Poll Finds," *HR Magazine,* February, 2012, p. 87.

46. J. Sammer, "Calibrating Consistency," *HR Magazine,* January 2008, pp. 73–75; and Fox, "Curing What Ails Performance Reviews," pp. 55–56.

47. S. W. J. Kozlowski, G. T. Chao, and R. F. Morrison, "Games Raters Play: Politics, Strategies, and Impression Management in Performance Appraisal," in *Performance Appraisal: State of the Art in Practice,* pp. 163–205; and C. Rosen, P. Levy, and R. Hall, "Placing Perceptions of Politics in the Context of the Feedback Environment Employee Attitudes, and Job Performance," *Journal of Applied Psychology* 91 (2006), pp. 211–20.

48. Deborah Busser, "Delivering Effective Performance Feedback, *T+D,* April 2012, pp. 323.

49. Malcolm Gabriel and Pierre Robitaille, "Sustaining High Performance with Generation-Y Employees," *Canadian HR Reporter,* January 14, 2008, p. 13.

50. Nicole Stewart and Elyse Lamontagne, "Compensation Planning Outlook 2014" (Ottawa: Conference Board of Canada, October 2013), p. 24 and Emily Huston, "Helping Millennials Help You: Managing Your Young Workplace," *The Conference Board: Executive Action Series,* May 27, 2013, p.4.

51. Ann Pace, "Cultivating a Coaching Culture," *T+D,* February 2012, p. 16; Ann Pace, "A New Era of Performance Management," *T+D,* October 2011, p. 12.

52. "Ceridian Canada and Harris Decima Survey Reveals Surprising Employee Attitudes Towards Performance Reviews and Corporate Training," October 24, 2011, www.ceridian.ca/en/news/2011/1024-pulse-of-talent .html.

53. Wexley, V. Singh, and G. Yukl, "Subordinate Participation in Three Types of Appraisal Interviews," *Journal of Applied Psychology* 58 (1973), pp. 54–57; K. Wexley, "Appraisal Interview," in *Performance Assessment,* ed. R. A. Berk (Baltimore: Johns Hopkins University Press, 1986), pp. 167–85; B. D Cawley, L. M. Keeping, and P. E. Levy, "Participation in the Performance Appraisal Process and Employee Reactions: A Meta-analytic Review and Field Investigations," *Journal of Applied Psychology* 83, no. 3 (1998), pp. 615–63; H. Aguinis, *Performance Management* (Upper Saddle River, NJ: Pearson Prentice-Hall, 2007); and C. Lee, "Feedback, Not Appraisal," *HR Magazine,* November 2006, pp. 111–14.

54. D. Cederblom, "The Performance Appraisal Interview: A Review, Implications, and Suggestions," *Academy of Management Review* 7 (1982), pp. 219–27; B. D. Cawley, L. M. Keeping, and P. E. Levy, "Participation in the Performance Appraisal Process and Employee Reactions: A Meta-analytic Review of Field Investigations," *Journal of Applied Psychology* 83, no. 3 (1998), pp. 615–63; W. Giles and K. Mossholder, "Employee Reactions to Contextual and Session Components of Performance Appraisal," *Journal of Applied Psychology* 75 (1990), pp. 371–77.

55. Kenneth M. Nowack, "Taking the Sting Out of Feedback: Research Reveals that Feedback Really May Be Dangerous to Your Health," *T+D,* August 2014, p. 50.

56. James Heeney, "Personal Harassment Liability Always a Danger for Employers," *Canadian HR Reporter,* October 22, 2007, p. B15; Stuart Rudner, "Psychological Harassment Hurts Employees' Productivity," *Canadian HR Reporter,* October 22, 2007, p. 31; Christopher M. Andree Crawford, "Poor Treatment Is Constructive Dismissal," *Canadian Bar Association,* www.cba.org/CBA/newsletters/lab-2003/18.aspx, retrieved April 27, 2008; "Bullying at Work: Another Form of Workplace Violence," www.emond-harnden.com/publications/feb03/bullies.shtml, retrieved April 27, 2008.

57. James Heeney, "Personal Harassment Liability Always a Danger for Employers," *Canadian HR Reporter,* October 22, 2007, p. B15.

58. Kristina Dell, "A Spy in Every Pocket," *Time,* March 27, 2006, p. 31; http://trackingthe world.com/gps-asset-tracking html, retrieved April 24, 2008.

59. Uyen Vu, "Privacy Law Working Well: Commissioner," *Canadian HR Reporter,* December 18, 2006, p. 1, 13.

CHAPTER 8

1. "Total Rewards at Longo's," www.longos.com/Careers/CompanyOverview.aspx, retrieved May 18, 2015; "Company Overview," www.longos.com/Careers/CompanyOverview.aspxwww.longos.com/, retrieved May 18, 2015; Amanda Silliker, "Longo's Fruitful Communicating Total Rewards," *Canadian HR Reporter,* August 13, 2012, p. 17; and "Human Resources Summit Awards: 2012 Winners," www.hrsummitawards.com/landing-pages/2012-awards.htmlOverview, retrieved May 18, 2015.

2. "World at Work Total Rewards Model," www.worldatwork.org/waw/aboutus/html/aboutus-whatis.html#model, retrieved October 22, 2008.

3. "Strategic Rewards in Canada: Building the Optimal Reward Plan—Watson Wyatt's 2004 Survey of Canadian Strategic Rewards and Pay Practices," in "Why Firms

Develop a Total Rewards Strategy," *Canadian HR Reporter,* February 14, 2005, p. R5.

4. Katie Fleming and Nicole Stewart, "Compensation Planning Outlook 2015" (Ottawa: Conference Board of Canada, October 2014), p. 15.

5. "What Is Total Rewards?," www.worldatwork.org/waw/aboutus/html/aboutus-whatis.html, retrieved October 22, 2008.

6. Gerhart and G. T. Milkovich, "Organizational Differences in Managerial Compensation and Financial Performance," *Academy of Management Journal* 33 (1990), pp. 663–91; E. L. Groshen, "Why Do Wages Vary among Employers?," *Economic Review* 24 (1988), pp. 19–38.

7. J. S. Adams, "Inequity in Social Exchange," in *Advances in Experimental Social Psychology,* ed. L. Berkowitz (New York: Academic Press, 1965); P. S. Goodman, "An Examination of Referents Used in the Evaluation of Pay," *Organizational Behavior and Human Performance* 12 (1974), pp. 170–95; J. B. Miner," *Theories of Organizational Behavior* (Hinsdale, IL: Dryden Press, 1980).

8. J. P. Pfeffer and A. Davis-Blake, "Understanding Organizational Wage Structures: A Resource Dependence Approach," *Academy of Management Journal* 30 (1987), pp. 437–55.

9. This section draws freely on B. Gerhart and R. D. Bretz, "Employee Compensation," in *Organization and Management of Advanced Manufacturing,* ed. W. Karwowski and G. Salvendy (New York: Wiley, 1994), pp. 81–101.

10. E. E. Lawler III, *Strategic Pay* (San Francisco: Jossey-Bass, 1990); G. Ledford, "3 Cases on Skill-Based Pay: An Overview," *Compensation and Benefits Review,* March/April 1991, pp. 11–23; G. E. Ledford, "Paying for the Skills, Knowledge, Competencies of Knowledge Workers," *Compensation and Benefits Review,* July/August 1995, p. 55.

11. B. C. Murray and B. Gerhart, "An Empirical Analysis of a Skill-Based Pay Program and Plant Performance Outcomes," *Academy of Management Journal* 41, no. 1 (1998), pp. 68–78; N. Gupta, D. Jenkins, and W. Curington, "Paying for Knowledge: Myths and Realities," *National Productivity Review,* Spring 1986, pp. 107–23.

12. B. Gerhart and G. T. Milkovich, "Organizational Differences in Managerial Compensation and Financial Performance," *Academy of Management Journal* 33 (1990), pp. 663–91.

13. Katie Fleming and Nicole Stewart, "Compensation Planning Outlook 2015: Table 5—Overall Prevalence of Incentive Plans, By Sector and Employee Group" (Ottawa: Conference Board of Canada, October 2014), p. 9.

14. G. T. Milkovich and A. K. Wigdor, *Pay for Performance* (Washington, DC: National Academy Press, 1991); Gerhart and Bretz, "Employee Compensation"; C. Trevor, B. Gerhart, and J. W. Boudreau, "Voluntary Turnover and Job Performance: Curvilinearity and the Moderating Influences of Salary Growth and Promotions," *Journal of Applied Psychology* 82 (1997), pp. 44–61.

15. Shannon Klie, "New Challenges in Pay for Performance," *Canadian HR Reporter,* April 23, 2007, p. 9.

16. R. D. Bretz, R. A. Ash, and G. F. Dreher, "Do People Make the Place? An Examination of the Attraction-Selection-Attrition Hypothesis," *Personnel Psychology* 42 (1989), pp. 561–81; T. A. Judge and R. D. Bretz, "Effect of Values on Job Choice Decisions," *Journal of Applied Psychology* 77 (1992), pp. 261–71; D. M. Cable and T. A. Judge, "Pay Performance and Job Search Decisions: A Person–Organization Fit Perspective," *Personnel Psychology* 47 (1994), pp. 317–48.

17. R. D. Bretz, G. T. Milkovich, and W. Read, "The Current State of Performance Appraisal Research and Practice," *Journal of Management* 18 (1992), pp. 321–52; R. L. Heneman, "Merit Pay Research," *Research in Personnel and Human Resource Management* 8 (1990), pp. 203–63; Milkovich and Wigdor, *Pay for Performance.*

18. Bretz et al., "The Current State of Performance Appraisal Research and Practice."

19. T. L. Ross and R. A. Ross, "Gainsharing: Sharing Improved Performance," in *The Compensation Handbook,* 3rd ed., ed. M. L. Rock and L. A. Berger (New York: McGraw-Hill, 1991).

20. T. M. Welbourne and L. R. Gomez-Mejia, "Team Incentives in the Workplace," in *The Compensation Handbook,* 3rd ed., ed. M. L. Rock and L. A. Berger (New York: McGraw-Hill, 1991).

21. L. R. Gomez-Mejia and D. B. Balkin, *Compensation, Organizational Strategy, and Firm Performance* (Cincinnati: South-Western, 1992).

22. This idea has been referred to as the "share economy." See M. L. Weitzman, "The Simple Macroeconomics of Profit Sharing," *American Economic Review* 75 (1985), pp. 937–53. For supportive research, see the following studies: J. Chelius and R. S. Smith, "Profit Sharing and Employment Stability," *Industrial and Labor Relations Review* 43 (1990), pp. 256S–73S; B. Gerhart and L. O. Trevor, "Employment Stability Under Different Managerial Compensation Systems," working paper, Cornell University Center for Advanced Human Resource Studies, 1995; D. L. Kruse, "Profit Sharing and Employment Variability: Microeconomic Evidence on the Weitzman Theory," *Industrial and Labor Relations Review* 44 (1991), pp. 437–53.

23. James Thomson, "Rich Pickings: Four Challenges for Facebook's New Millionaires," *Business Spectator,* May 18, 2012, www.businessspectator.com.au/bs.nsf/Article/facebook-ipo-zuckerberg-millionires-billionaires-i-pd20120518-UE5TK?OpenDocument &src=sph&src=rot, retrieved May 18, 2012.

24. https://www.westjet.com/pdf/greatWestJetJobs.pdf, retrieved May 19, 2015.

25. M. A. Conte and J. Svejnar, "The Performance Effects of Employee Ownership Plans," in *Paying for Productivity,* pp. 245–94.

26. B. Gerhart and G. T. Milkovich, "Employee Compensation: Research and Practice," in *Handbook of Industrial and Organizational Psychology,* vol. 3, 2nd ed., eds. M. D. Dunnette and L. M. Hough (Palo Alto, CA: Consulting Psychologists Press, 1992), vol. 3; and J. Swist, "Benefits Communications: Measuring Impact and Values," *Employee Benefit Plan Review,* September 2002, pp. 24–26.

27. "Canadian Employers Rate Health Plans over Cash," *The Globe and Mail,* May 12, 2004, p. C2.

28. Yaldaz Sadakova, "Employees Expect More from Their Benefits," *Benefits Canada,* June 2014, p. 9.

29. Bureau of Labor Statistics, "Employer Costs for Employee Compensation," http://data.bls.gov, accessed April 28, 2010.

30. Erik Sherman, "Four Perks Employees Love," *Inc.,* April 11, 2012, www.inc.com; Robert J. Grossman, "Tough Love at Netflix," *HR Magazine,* April 2010, www.shrm.org.

31. Kathryn M. Werntz, "Business Benefits from Facebook's Egg Freezing to Virgin Unlimited Holidays," *The Guardian,* October 21, 2014, www.theguardian.com/sustainable-business/2014/oct/21/facebook-apple-egg-freezing-virgin-unlimited-holidays-business-benefits, retrieved May 20, 2015

32. "Canada Pension Plan," www.servicecanada.gc.ca/eng/ services/pensions/cpp/index.shtml?utm_source=vanity+URL&utm_medium=print+publication,+ISPB-185,+ISPB-341&utm_term=/CPP&utm_content=Mar+2013,+eng&utm_campaign=OAS+Pension+2013,+Benefits+for+Low+Income+Seniors, retrieved May 19, 2015

33. "Employment Insurance," www.servicecanada.gc.ca/eng/sc/ei/index.shtml, retrieved May 19, 2015.

34. Katie Fleming and Nicole Stewart, "Compensation Planning Outlook 2015" (Ottawa: Conference Board of Canada, October 2014), p. 23.

35. Sarah Beech, "Lifestyle Choices," *Benefits Canada,* March 2008, p. 45.

36. Mary Teresa Bitti, "Alternative Health Plan Benefits Small Firms," *National Post,* March 8, 2004, pp. FE1, FE4.

37. Tammy Burn, "Employers Promoting Healthier Workforce," *Benefits Canada,* May 9, 2012, www.benefitscanada.com/benefits/health-wellness/employers-promoting-healthier-workforce-28660, retrieved May 16, 2012.

38. Shannon Klie, "Do Incentives Help Change Behaviour?," *Canadian HR Reporter,* April 21, 2008, www.hrreporter.com, retrieved May 7, 2008.

39. Brian Lindenberg, "Choosing the Right EAP," *Canadian HR Reporter,* March 24, 2008, pp. 22, 27.

40. Statistics Canada, "Table 1: Registered Pension Plan Membership, by Sector and Type of Plan," *The Daily,* August 28, 2014, www.statcan.gc.ca/daily-quotidien/140828/t140828d001-eng.htm, retrieved May 21, 2015.

41. "Phased Retirement: Aligning Employer Programs with Worker Preferences—2004 Survey Report," www.watsonwyatt.com/research/resrender.asp, retrieved April 21, 2004.

42. Deborah McMillan, "Redefining Retirement," *Benefits Canada,* August 2007, pp. 13, 15, 17.

43. "Pension Plans in Canada, as of January 1, 2013," Statistics Canada, www.statcan.gc.ca/daily-quotidien/140828/dq140828d-eng.htm, retrieved May 21, 2015.

44. Statistics Canada, "Table 1: Registered Pension Plan Membership, by Sector and Type Of Plan," *The Daily,* August 28, 2014, www.statcan.gc.ca/daily-quotidien/140828/t140828d001-eng.htm, retrieved May 21, 2015 and Statistics Canada, "Pension Plans in Canada," *The Daily,* May 9, 2011, www.statcan.gc.ca/daily-quotidien/110509/dq110509a-eng.htm, retrieved May 17, 2012.

45. Tara Perkins, "RBC to Stop Offering Defined Benefit Plan," *Globe and Mail Update,* September 23, 2011, www.theglobeandmail.com/globe-investor/investment-ideas/streetwise/rbc-to-stop-offering-defined-benefit-plan/article2176656/, retrieved May 17, 2012.

46. "Pension Plans in Canada, as of January 1, 2013," Statistics Canada, www.statcan.gc.ca/daily-quotidien/140828/dq140828d-eng.htm, retrieved May 21, 2015.

47. Richard Yerema and Kristina Leung, "Canada's Top Family-Friendly Employers 2012: Ontario Public Service, www.eluta.ca/top-employer-ontario-public-service, and Georgian College, www.eluta.ca/top-employer-georgian-college, retrieved May 18, 2012.

48. Marlene Habib, "'Sandwich Generation' has Smorgasbord of Options," *Globe and Mail Update,* November 20, 2011, www.theglobeandmail.com/globe-investor/personal-finance/financial-road-map/sandwich-generation-has-a-smorgasbord-of-options/article2255328/, retrieved May 18, 2012 and Statistics Canada, "Study: The Sandwich Generation," *The Daily,* September 28, 2004, www.statcan.ca/Daily/English/040928/d040928b.htm, retrieved October 22, 2008.

49. Government of Canada, "Part-Time Work and Family-Friendly Practices in Canadian Workplaces—June 2003," p. 1, www.hrsdc.gc.ca/en/cs/sp/sdc/pkrf/publications/research/2003–000183/page00.shtml, retrieved October 22, 2008.

50. R. Broderick and B. Gerhart, "Nonwage Compensation," in *The Human Resource Management Handbook,* ed. D. Lewin, D.J.B. Mitchell, and M. A. Zadi (San Francisco: JAI Press, 1996).

51. Michael Fradkin, "An Ounce of Prevention Also Can Cut Disability Costs," *National Underwriter Life & Health,* April 21, 2008, Business & Company Resource Center, http://galenet.gale group.com.

52. Sarah Coles, "Package: Scratch Head at Start," *Employee Benefits,* January 14, 2008, Business & Company Resource Center, http://galenet.gale group.com.

53. B. T. Beam Jr. and J. J. McFadden, *Employee Benefits,* 6th ed. (Chicago: Real Estate Education Co., 2001).

54. Cathy O'Bright, "Flex Benefits Drive Culture Change, Contain Costs at Superior Propane," *Canadian HR Reporter,* September 8, 2003, www.hrreporter.com, retrieved March 21, 2004.

55. David Johnston, "Poorly Communicated Plans Worse Than None at All," *Canadian HR Reporter,* February 14, 2005, p. R7.

56. M. Wilson, G. B. Northcraft, and M. A. Neale, "The Perceived Value of Fringe Benefits," *Personnel Psychology* 38 (1985), pp. 309–20; H. W. Hennessey, P. L. Perrewe, and W. A. Hochwarter, "Impact of Benefit Awareness on Employee and Organizational Outcomes: A Longitudinal Field Experiment," *Benefits Quarterly* 8, no. 2 (1992), pp. 90–96.

57. Todd Humber, "The Power to Change," Supplement to *Canadian HR Reporter,* May 31, 2004, pp. G1, G10.

58. Leigh Doyle, "The Growing Role of Social Media," *Benefits Canada,* April 17, 2012, www.benefitscanada.com/pensions/cap/the-growing-role-of-social-media-27688, retrieved May 16, 2012.

59. "Total Rewards Statements Help to Engage Employees," *Benefits Canada,* November 17, 2011, www.benefitscanada.com/benefits/health-benefits/total-rewards-statements-help-to-engage-employees-22892, retrieved May 16, 2012

60. Hugh Mackenzie, "Glory Days: CEO Pay in Canada Soaring to Pre-Recession Heights," Canada's CEO Elite 100," *Canadian Centre for Policy Alternatives,* January 2015, p. 9.

61. Hugh Mackenzie, "Glory Days: CEO Pay in Canada Soaring to Pre-Recession Heights," Canada's CEO Elite 100," *Canadian Centre for Policy Alternatives,* January 2015, p. 6.

62. Stephen O'Byrne, "Assessing Pay for Performance," *The Conference Board,* October 2011, p. 3, www.conferenceboard.org, retrieved May 16, 2012.

63. Andy Holloway, "Change is Good," *Financial Post Magazine,* November 1, 2011, retrieved May 16, 2012, and "CEO Scorecard 2011," www.financial post.com/executive/ceo/scorecard/index.html, retrieved May 20, 2012.

64. Hugh Mackenzie, "Glory Days: CEO Pay in Canada Soaring to Pre-Recession Heights," Canada's CEO Elite 100," *Canadian Centre for Policy Alternatives,* January 2015, p. 6.

65. Ibid.

66. Gerhart and Milkovich, "Organizational Differences in Managerial Compensation"; B. Gerhart, S. L. Rynes, and I. S. Fulmer, "Pay and Performance: Individuals, Groups, and Executives," *Academy of Management Annals* 3 (2009): 251–315.

CHAPTER 9

1. Mike Hensen, "Air Canada Express Pilots Ratify 11-year Tentative Agreement," *Toronto Sun,* January 31, 2015, www.torontosun.com/2015/01/31/air-canada-jazz-pilots-ratify-11-year-tentative-agreement, retrieved April 7, 2015; Ross Marowits, "Jazz to Operate Updated, Smaller Fleet After Deal with Air Canada, Pilots," *The Globe and Mail,* January 13, 2015, www.theglobeandmail.com/report-on-business/jazz-to-operate-updated-smaller-fleet-after-deal-with-air-canada-pilots/article22435588/, retrieved April 7, 2015; Ross Marowits, "Air Canada Pilots Ratify 10-Year Contract with 20% Wage Increase," *The Globe and Mail,* October 31, 2014, www.theglobeandmail.com/report-on-business/air-canada-pilots-ratify-10-year-contract/article21401537/, retrieved April 7, 2015; and Kristine Owram, "Air Canada Strikes Tentative Deal with Pilots for a New 10-Year Contract as Bitter Relations Thaw," *Financial Post,* October 6, 2014, http://business.financialpost.com/news/transportation/air-canada-strikes-tentative-deal-with-pilots-for-a-new-10-year-contract, retrieved April 7, 2015.

2. J.T. Dunlop, *Industrial Relations Systems* (New York: Holt, 1958); and C. Kerr, "Industrial Conflict and Its Mediation," *American Journal of Sociology* 60 (1954), pp. 230–245.

3. T. A. Kochan, *Collective Bargaining and Industrial Relations* (Homewood, IL: Richard D. Irwin, 1980), p. 25; and H. C. Katz and T. A. Kochan, *An Introduction to Collective Bargaining and Industrial Relations,* 3rd ed. (New York: McGraw-Hill, 2004).

4. "About Unifor," www.unifor.org/en/about-unifor, retrieved April 8, 2015.

5. "About PSAC," http://psacunion.ca/about, retrieved April 8, 2015.

6. "Union Coverage in Canada, 2013," June 11, 2014, *Government of Canada,* www.labour.gc.ca/eng/resources/info/publications/union_coverage/union_coverage.shtml, retrieved April 8, 2015.

7. "About the CLC," www.canadianlabour.ca/about-clc, retrieved April 8, 2015.

8. Whether the time the union steward spends on union business is paid for by the employer, the union, or a combination is a matter of negotiation between the employer and the union.

9. "Unionization of the Public Service," *Canadian Museum of History,* www.historymuseum.ca/cmc/exhibitions/hist/labour/labh37e.shtml, retrieved April 8, 2015.

10. James Fix-Morris, "RCMP Officers Have Right to Collective Bargaining, Supreme Court Rules," January 16, 2015, www.cbc.ca/news/politics/rcmp-officers-have-right-to-collective-bargaining-supreme-court-rules-1.2912340, retrieved April 7, 2015.

11. "History of Unions in Canada," www.mapleleafweb.com/old/education/spotlight/issue_51/history.html?q=education/spotlight/issue_51/history.html, retrieved October 22, 2008.

12. Suzanne Payette, "Yesterday and Today: Union Membership," excerpt from the *Workplace Gazette* 5, no. 3 (Fall 2002), www.rhdcc.gc.ca, retrieved November 5, 2004.

13. "Union Coverage in Canada, 2013, *Government of Canada,* June 11, 2014, www.labour.gc.ca/eng/resources/info/publications/union_coverage/union_coverage.shtml, retrieved April 8, 2015.

14. "Work-Unionization Rates," *Employment and Social Development Canada,* www4.hrsdc.gc.ca/.3ndic.1t.4r@-eng.jsp?iid=17, retrieved April 7, 2015 and "Union Coverage in Canada: Unionization Rate Stable Over Past Four Years," *Human Resources and Skills Development Canada,* www.hrsdc.gc.ca/eng/labour/labour_relations/info_analysis/overview/2010/section_6.shtml, retrieved May 16, 2012.

15. Diane Galarneau and Thao Sohn, "Long Term Trends in Unionization; Table 2 Unionization Rates by North American Industry Classification (NAICS) Employed Individuals Aged 17 to 64," November 2013, www.statcan.gc.ca/pub/75-006-x/2013001/article/11878-eng.pdf, retrieved April 7, 2015.

16. Katz and Kochan, *An Introduction to Collective Bargaining,* building on J. Fiorito and C. L. Maranto, "The Contemporary Decline of Union Strength," *Contemporary Policy Issues* 3 (1987), pp. 12–27; G. N. Chaison and J. Rose, "The Macrodeterminants of Union Growth and Decline," in *The State of the Unions,* ed. G. Strauss et al. (Madison, WI: Industrial Relations Research Association, 1991).

17. T. A. Kochan, R. B. McKersie, and J. Chalykoff, "The Effects of Corporate Strategy and Workplace Innovations in Union Representation," *Industrial and Labor Relations Review* 39 (1986), pp. 487–501; Chaison and Rose, "The Macrodeterminants of Union Growth and Decline"; J. Barbash, *Practice of Unionism* (New York: Harper, 1956), p. 210; W. N. Cooke and D. G. Meyer, "Structural and Market Predictors of Corporate Labor Relations Strategies," *Industrial and Labor Relations Review* 43 (1990), pp. 280–93; and T. A. Kochan and P. Capelli, "The Transformation of the Industrial Relations and Personnel Function," in *Internal Labor Markets,* ed. P. Osterman (Cambridge, MA: MIT Press, 1984).

18. Scott Stinson, "The $4B Election Fund: Unions Have A Free Hand to Use Their Billions In Compulsory Dues to Win Elections Key to Maintaining Their Pay Advantage," *National Post,* June 7, 2014, p. A8.

19. Catherine Swift, "High Times for The Public Sector," *Special to Financial Post,* August 28, 2014, http://business.financialpost.com/fp-comment/high-times-for-the-public-sector, retrieved April 8, 2015.

20. Diane Galarneau and Thao Sohn, "Long Term Trends in Unionization; Table 1 Unionization Rates by Sex and Age, Employed Individuals Aged 17–64," *Statistics Canada,* November 2013, p. 4, www.statcan.gc.ca/pub/75-006-x/2013001/article/11878-eng.pdf, retrieved April 8, 2015.

21. "Study: The Union Movement in Transition," *The Daily,* August 31, 2004, www.statcan.ca/Daily/English/040831/d040831b.htm, retrieved November 6, 2004.

22. Diane Galarneau and Thao Sohn, "Long Term Trends in Unionization; Table 1 Unionization Rates by Sex and Age, Employed Individuals Aged 17–64," *Statistics Canada,* November 2013, p. 4, www.statcan.gc.ca/pub/75-006-x/2013001/article/11878-eng.pdf, retrieved April 8, 2015.

23. Christopher Hallamore, "Industrial Relations Outlook 2008" (Ottawa: Conference Board of Canada, January 2008), p. 20.

24. Ibid., p. 21.

25. C. Brewster, "Levels of Analysis in Strategic HRM: Questions Raised by Comparative Research," Conference on Research and Theory in HRM, Cornell University, October 1997.

26. "National Young Workers' Committee," http://cupe.ca/national-young-workers-committee, retrieved April 8, 2015.

27. J. T. Addison and B. T. Hirsch, "Union Effects on Productivity, Profits, and Growth: Has the Long Run Arrived?," *Journal of Labor Economics* 7 (1989), pp. 72–105; and R. B. Freeman and J. L. Medoff, "The Two Faces of Unionism," *Public Interest* 57 (Fall 1979), pp. 69–93.

28. L. Mishel and P. Voos, *Unions and Economic Competitiveness* (Armonk, NY: M. E. Sharpe, 1991); Freeman and Medoff, "Two Faces"; and S. Slichter, J. Healy, and E. R. Livernash, *The Impact of Collective Bargaining on Management* (Washington, DC: Brookings Institution, 1960).

29. A. O. Hirschman, *Exit, Voice, and Loyalty* (Cambridge, MA: Harvard University Press, 1970); and R. Batt, A. J. S. Colvin, and J. Keefe, "Employee Voice, Human Resource Practices, and Quit Rates: Evidence from the Telecommunications Industry," *Industrial and Labor Relations Review* 55 (1970), pp. 573–94.

30. R. B. Freeman and J. L. Medoff, *What Do Unions Do?* (New York: Basic Books, 1984); Addison and Hirsch, "Union Effects on Productivity"; M. Ash and J. A. Seago, "The Effect of Registered Nurses' Unions on Heart-Attack Mortality," *Industrial and Labor Relations Review* 57 (2004), p. 422; and C. Doucouliagos and P. Laroche, "What Do Unions Do to Productivity? A Meta-Analysis," *Industrial Relations* 42 (2003), pp. 650–91.

31. B. E. Becker and C. A. Olson, "Unions and Firm Profits," *Industrial Relations* 31, no. 3 (1992), pp. 395–415; B. T. Hirsch and B. A. Morgan, "Shareholder Risks and Returns in Union and Nonunion Firms," *Industrial and Labor Relations Review* 47, no. 2 (1994), pp. 302–18; and Hristos Doucouliagos and Patrice Laroche, "Unions and Profits: A Meta-Regression Analysis," *Industrial Relations* 48, no. 1 (January 2008), p. 146.

32. "National Apprenticeship & Training Policy for the Construction Industry in Canada, p. 2, www.buildingtrades.ca/sites/default/files/pdf/2007_final_training_policy_document_eng.pdf, retrieved April 12, 2015.

33. "Average Hourly Wages of Employees by Selected Characteristics and Occupation, Unadjusted Data, by Province (Monthly), Canada," *Statistics Canada,* www.statcan.gc.ca/tables-tableaux/sum-som/l01/cst01/labr69a-eng.htm, retrieved April 8, 2015.

34. "Campaigns," *CUPE website,* http://cupe.ca/campaigns, retrieved April 12, 2015.

35. "History and Development of Unions in Canada: The Rand Formula," www.law-faqs.org/nat/un-ran.htm, retrieved October 22, 2008.

36. S. Webb and B. Webb, *Industrial Democracy* (London: Longmans, Green, 1987); J. R. Commons, *Institutional Economics* (New York: Macmillan, 1934).

37. Kathryn May, "Supreme Court Ruling Could Pave Way for Federal Union Challenge on Right to Strike," *Ottawa Citizen,* January 30, 2015, http://ottawacitizen.com, retrieved April 7, 2015 and "Supreme Court Recognizes Constitutional Right to Strike for Canadian Workers," http://cupe.ca/supreme-court-recognizes-constitutional-right-strike-canadian-workers, retrieved April 7, 2015.

38. The Canadian Press, "Canadian National Railway Returns to Bargaining Table with Unifor," www.huffingtonpost.ca/2015/02/23/canadian-national-railway_n_6733758.html, retrieved April 12, 2015; Laura Payton, "Canadian Pacific Railway Strike Leads to 2,000 Layoffs," *CBC News,* May 23, 2012, www.cbc.ca/news/business/story/2012/05/23/canadian-pacific-strike.html, retrieved May 23, 2012; David K. Shepherdson, "Industrial Relations Outlook 2012 Going Sideways, With a Twist," November 2011, *The Conference Board of Canada,* p. 4;; "Air Canada Legislation OK'd by Ottawa," *CBC News,* March 13, 2012, www.cbc.ca/news/business/story/2012/03/13/air-canada-union.html, retrieved May 23, 2012; and "Postal Back-to-work Bill becomes Law," *The Globe and Mail,* June 25, 2011, www.theglobeandmail.com/news/politics/postal-back-to-work-bill-becomes-law-mail-could-resume-tuesday/article2075879/, retrieved May 23, 2012.

39. Adapted from "Publication: Information Circulars No. 5," Canada Industrial Relations Board website, www.cirb-ccri.gc.ca/publications/info/05_eng.asp, retrieved April 8, 2015.

40. "Information Circular No. 07–Application for Certification," *Canada Industrial Relations Board,* www.cirb-ccri.gc.ca/eic/site/047.nsf/vwapj/Information_Circular_No_07.pdf/$file/Information_Circular_No_07.pdf, retrieved April 8, 2015.

41. R. B. Freeman and M. M. Kleiner, "Employer Behavior in the Face of Union Organizing Drives," *Industrial and Labor Relations Review* 43, no. 4 (April 1990), pp. 351–65.

42. "Guide to the Labour Relations Code Province of British Columbia," *Labour Relations Board Province of British Columbia,* www.lrb.bc.ca/codeguide/chapter5.htm, retrieved April 12, 2015.

43. Fossum, *Labor Relations,* p. 262.

44. R. E. Walton and R. B. McKersie, *A Behavioral Theory of Negotiations* (New York: McGraw-Hill, 1965).

45. C. M. Steven, *Strategy and Collective Bargaining Negotiations* (New York: McGraw-Hill, 1963); and Katz and Kochan, *An Introduction to Collective Bargaining.*

46. "Overview of Collective Bargaining in Canada, 2013," *Government of Canada Labour Program,* www.labour.gc.ca/eng/resources/info/publications/collective_bargaining/collective_bargaining.shtml, retrieved April 12, 2015.

47. "Overview of Collective Bargaining in Canada, 2013," *Government of Canada Labour Program,* www.labour.gc.ca/eng/resources/info/publications/collective_bargaining/collective_bargaining.shtml, retrieved April 12, 2015 and Sharanjit Uppal, "Unionization 2011: Component of Statistics Canada Catalogue no. 75-001-X Perspectives on Labour and Income," Table 4, October 26, 2011, p. 11.

48. Kochan, *Collective Bargaining and Industrial Relations,* p. 272.

49. Katz and Kochan, *An Introduction to Collective Bargaining.*
50. Kochan, *Collective Bargaining and Industrial Relations,* p. 386; and John W. Budd and Alexander J.S. Colvin, "Improved Metrics for Workplace Dispute Resolution Procedures: Efficiency, Equity, and Voice," *Industrial Relations 47,* no. 3 (July 2008), p. 460.
51. T. A. Kochan, H. C. Katz, and R. B. McKersie, *The Transformation of American Industrial Relations* (New York: Basic Books, 1986), chap. 6; E. Appelbaum, T. Bailey, and P. Berg, *Manufacturing Advantage: Why High-Performance Work Systems Pay Off* (Ithaca, NY: Cornell University Press, 2000).
52. L. W. Hunter, J. P. MacDuffie, and L. Doucet, "What Makes Teams Take? Employee Reactions to Work Reforms," *Industrial and Labor Relations Review 55* (2002), pp. 448–472.
53. J. B. Arthur, "The Link Between Business Strategy and Industrial Relations Systems in American Steel Minimills," *Industrial and Labor Relations Review 45* (1992), pp. 488–506; M. Schuster, "Union Management Cooperation," in *Employee and Labor Relations,* ed. J. A. Fossum (Washington, DC: Bureau of National Affairs, 1990); E. Cohen-Rosenthal and C. Burton, *Mutual Gains: A Guide to Union–Management Cooperation,* 2nd ed. (Ithaca, NY: ILR Press, 1993); T. A. Kochan and P. Osterman, *The Mutual Gains Enterprise* (Boston: Harvard Business School Press, 1994); and E. Applebaum and R. Batt, *The New American Workplace* (Ithaca, NY: ILR Press, 1994).
54. A. E. Eaton, "Factors Contributing to the Survival of Employee Participation Programs in Unionized Settings," *Industrial and Labor Relations Review 47,* no. 3 (1994), pp. 371–89.
55. "Preventive Mediation: Nova Scotia Industrial Relations Conciliation Services," www.gov.ns.ca/enla/conciliation/prevbro.htm, retrieved March 5, 2005.
56. Judith Lendvay-Zwicki, "The Canadian Industrial Relations System: Current Challenges and Future Options" (Ottawa: Conference Board of Canada, April 2004), www.conferenceboard.ca, retrieved April 19, 2004.

CHAPTER 10

1. Jamie Sturgeon, "Tim Hortons Ready for International Stage, New Owners Say," *Global News,* March 25, 2015, http://globalnews.ca/news/1905606/tim-hortons-ready-for-global-expansion-new-owners-say/, retrieved April 16, 2015; Robert Benzie, "Tim Hortons Tops Menu at Kathleen Wynne Meeting in China," *Toronto Star,* October 27, 2014, www.thestar.com/news/canada/2014/10/27/tim_hortons_tops_menu_at_kathleen_wynne_meeting_in_china.html, retrieved April 16, 2015; Jamie Sturgeon, "With Burger King's Help, Tim Hortons Poised to Go Global," *Global News,* August 25, 2014, http://globalnews.ca/news/1525221/is-tim-hortons-about-to-go-global/, retrieved April 16, 2015; and Bruce Philip, Richard Warmica, "Canada's Top Brands 2014," *Canadian Business,* May 2014, pp. 47–52, 54.
2. Vladimir Pucik, "Human Resources in the Future: An Obstacle or a Champion of Globalization," *Tomorrow's HR Management,* ed. Dave Ulrich, Michael R. Losey, and Gerry Lake (John Wiley & Sons, Inc. New York, 1997), pp. 326–327.
3. Raju Gopalakrishnan, "Bangalore Software Industry Trying to Avoid an Ironic Fate," *Chicago Tribune,* April 17, 2012, sec. 2, p. 3.
4. Lee Berthiaume, "Russia Won't Go 'Begging' for Better Relations with Canada: Ambassador," *Ottawa Citizen,* January 24, 2015, http://ottawacitizen.com/news/politics/russia-wont-go-begging-for-better-relations-with-canada-ambassador, retrieved April 16, 2015.
5. "Moving Back to America," *The Economist,* May 14, 2011, EBSCOhost, http://web.ebscohost.com.
6. Dan Ciuriak, Dmitry Lysenko, and Jiangliang Xiao, "Province-Level Impacts of The Canada-Korea Free Trade Agreement," "Moving Back to America," *Asia Pacific Foundation of Canada, March 4, 2015,* https://www.asiapacific.ca/canada-asia-agenda/province-level-impacts-canada-korea-free-trade-agreement, retrieved April 16, 2015.
7. Phalguni Soni, "Why Lululemon is Looking at a Global Store Footprint," December 16, 2014, http://finance.yahoo.com/news/why-lululemon-looking-global-store-193709512.html, retrieved April 21, 2015.
8. "Professional Development Program," *Canadian Employee Relocation Council website,* www.cerc.ca, retrieved April 21, 2015 and Stephen Cryne, "New Designation Responds to Growing Complexities of Global Mobility," *Canadian HR Reporter,* p. 12, August 12, 2013.
9. L. Kwoh, "Asia's Endangered Species: The Expat," *The Wall Street Journal,* March 28, 2012.
10. Loewen website, www.loewen.com/whyLoewen/aboutUs/companyProfile.html, retrieved May 27, 2012.
11. N. Adler and S. Bartholomew, "Managing Globally Competent People," *The Executive* 6 (1992), pp. 52–65.
12. V. Sathe, *Culture and Related Corporate Realities* (Homewood, IL: Richard D. Irwin, 1985); and M. Rokeach, *Beliefs, Attitudes, and Values* (San Francisco: Jossey-Bass, 1968).
13. N. Adler, *International Dimensions of Organizational Behavior,* 2nd ed. (Boston: PWS-Kent, 1991).
14. "The Hofstede Centre," http://geert-hofstede.com/national-culture.html, retrieved April 19, 2015.
15. Hofstede, "Cultural Constraints in Management Theories."
16. A Ramesh and M. Gelfland, "Will They Stay or Will They Go? The Role of Job Embeddedness in Predicting Turnover in Individualistic and Collectivistic Cultures," *Journal of Applied Psychology* 95, no. 5 (2010): 807–823.
17. W. A. Randolph and M. Sashkin, "Can Organizational Empowerment Work in Multinational Settings?" *Academy of Management Executive* 16, no. 1 (2002), pp. 102–115.
18. B. Gerhart and M. Fang, "National Culture and Human Resource Management: Assumptions and Evidence," *International Journal of Human Resource Management* 16, no. 6 (June 2005); pp. 971–986.
19. National Center for Education Statistics (NCES), "International Comparisons of Education," *Digest of Education Statistics, 2000,* chap. 6, NCES website, http://nces.ed.gov, retrieved September 23, 2002.
20. World Bank, "The State of Education," *EdStats,* www.worldbank.org, accessed May 15, 2012.
21. Chris Parr, "BRICS & Emerging Economies Ranking 2015 Results; China Racing Ahead," December 4, 2014, *Times Higher Education,* www.timeshighereducation.co.uk/news/brics-and-emerging-economies-rankings-2015-results/2017339.article, retrieved April 16, 2015.

22. European Commission, "Rights at Work," http://ec.europa.eu, accessed May 14, 2012; European Union, "Organisation of Working Time (Basic Directive)," http://europa.eu, accessed May 14, 2012.

23. "Saskatchewan Looking to Lure Nurses from Philippines," February 21, 2008, www.cbc.ca/canada/saskatchewan/story/ 2008/02/21/nurses-philippines.html, retrieved June 7, 2008.

24. Gopalakrishnan, "Bangalore Software Industry"; The Economist, "Moving Back to America."

25. Lawrence A. West Jr. and Walter A. Bogumil Jr., "Foreign Knowledge Workers as a Strategic Staffing Option," The Academy of Management Executive, November 2000.

26. "Fact Sheet—Temporary Foreign Worker Program," Government of Canada, www.cic.gc.ca/english/resources/publications/employers/temp-foreign-worker-program.asp, retrieved April 23, 2015.

27. Richard Cuthbertson, "Maritime Seafood Processors Fear Worker Shortage Will Hurt Market," CBC News, April 17, 2015, www.cbc.ca/news/canada/nova-scotia/maritime-seafood-processors-fear-worker-shortage-will-hurt-market-1.3037875, retrieved April 23, 2015.

28. W. A. Arthur Jr. and W. Bennett Jr., "The International Assignee: The Relative Importance of Factors Perceived to Contribute to Success," Personnel Psychology 48 (1995), pp. 99–114; and G. M. Spreitzer, M. W. McCall Jr., and J. D. Mahoney, "Early Identification of International Executive Potential," Journal of Applied Psychology 82 (1997), pp. 6–29.

29. W. "Global Mobility Policy & Practice: 2014 Survey Executive Summary Report," p. 5, http://guidance.cartusrelocation.com/rs/cartus/images/2014_Global_Mobility_Policy_Practices_Survey_Exec_Summary.pdf, retrieved April 19, 2015

30. P. Caligiuri, "The Big Five Personality Characteristics as Predictors of Expatriates' Desire to Terminate the Assignment and Supervisor-Rated Performance," Personnel Psychology 53 (2000), pp. 67–88.

31. Delia Flanja, "Culture Shock in Intercultural Communication," Studia Europaea (October 2009), Business & Company Resource Center, galenet.galegroup.com.

32. J. Flynn, "E-mail, Cell Phones, and Frequent-Flier Miles Let 'Virtual' Expats Work Abroad but Live at Home," The Wall Street Journal, October 25, 1999, p. A26.

33. Liam Dixon and Margaret Sim, "Short-Term Assignments Growing in Popularity," Canadian HR Reporter, March 10, 2008, p. 17.

34. Tim McCarney, "Relocation Policies More About Speed, Dexterity," Canadian HR Reporter, December 5, 2011, p. 20.

35. Stephanie Stephen, "What's Allowed, What's Taboo with Background Checks Outside of Canada," Canadian HR Reporter, pp 13, March 26, 2012.

36. D. M. Gayeski, C. Sanchirico, and J. Anderson, "Designing Training for Global Environments: Knowing What Questions to Ask," Performance Improvement Quarterly 15, no. 2 (2002), pp. 15–31.

37. J. S. Black and M. Mendenhall, "A Practical but Theory-Based Framework for Selecting Cross-Cultural Training Methods," in Readings and Cases in International Human Resource Management, ed. M. Mendenhall and G. Oddou (Boston: PWS-Kent, 1991), pp. 177–204.

38. C. Lachnit, "Low-Cost Tips for Successful Inpatriation," Workforce, August 2001, pp. 42–44, 46–47.

39. Jillian Austin, "Brandon has New Foreign Workers," Winnipeg Free Press," September 1, 2012, www.winnipegfreepress.com/local/brandon-has-new-foreign-workers-168258536.html, retrieved April 19, 2015.

40. D. D. Davis, "International Performance Measurement and Management," in Performance Appraisal: State of the Art in Practice, ed. J. W. Smither (San Francisco: Jossey-Bass, 1998), pp. 95–131.

41. M. Gowan, S. Ibarreche, and C. Lackey, "Doing the Right Things in Mexico," Academy of Management Executive 10 (1996), pp. 74–81.

42. L. S. Chee, "Singapore Airlines: Strategic Human Resource Initiatives," in International Human Resource Management: Think Globally, Act Locally, ed. D. Torrington (Upper Saddle River, NJ: Prentice Hall, 1994), pp. 143–59.

43. "Johnson & Johnson Takes World View on Compensation," Employee Benefits, June 2011, p. 7.

44. "Top Whack: Big Country, Big Pay Cheques," The Economist, January 29, 2011, EBSCOhost, http://web.ebscohost.com.

45. Bureau of Labor Statistics, International Labor Comparisons, "Country at a Glance," www.bls.gov/fls/country.htm, last modified July 20, 2011.

46. See, for example, A. E. Cobet and G. A. Wilson, "Comparing 50 Years of Labor Productivity in U.S. and Foreign Manufacturing," Monthly Labor Review, June 2002, pp. 51–63; Bureau of Labor Statistics, "International Comparisons of Manufacturing Productivity and Labor Cost Trends, 2008," news release, October 22, 2009, www.bls.gov; and Daron Acemoglu and Melissa Dell, "Productivity Differences between and within Countries," American Economic Journal: Macroeconomics 2010 2, no. 1 (2010): 169–88.

47. Stephen Miller, "Grasp Country Difference to Manage Global Pay," Compensation Discipline, March 30, 2010, www.shrm.org.

48. Ann Macaulay, "Scouting the Danger Online," Canadian HR Reporter, September 24, 2007, p. 13.

49. "Employers Compensating Employees in High-Risk Areas," August 5, 2003, www.hrreporter.com, retrieved January 23, 2004.

50. Macaulay, ibid.

51. Craig Malcolm, "Protecting Employees in Danger Zones," Canadian HR Reporter, September 24, 2007, p. 9.

52. P. J. Dowling, D. E. Welch, and R. S. Schuler, International Human Resource Management, 3rd ed. (Cincinnati: South-Western, 1999), pp. 235–36.

53. Dowling, Welch, and Schuler, International Human Resource Management, p. 231.

54. Sharon Terlep, "GM's Mr. Fix-It Tackles Opel Mess," The Wall Street Journal, April 15, 2012, http://online.wsj.com.

55. Eric Bellman, "Seeking Safeguards for Unskilled Workers Abroad," The Wall Street Journal, February 6, 2012, online.wsj.com.

56. J. K. Sebenius, "The Hidden Challenge of Cross-Border Negotiations," Harvard Business Review, March 2002, pp. 76–85.

57. Stephen Cryne, "Avoiding the Perils of Foreign Assignments," Canadian HR Reporter, March 12, 2007, p. 14.

58. Margaret Sim and Liam Dixon, "Number of Women Expats Increasing," Canadian HR Reporter, May 21, 2007, p. 14.

59. E. Krell, "Evaluating Returns on Expatriates," HR Magazine, March 2005, http://web5.infotrac.galegroup.com.

Notes

60. Ibid.; M. Harvey and M. M. Novicevic, "Selecting Expatriates for Increasingly Complex Global Assignments," *Career Development International* 6, no. 2 (2001), pp. 69–86.

61. M. Mendenhall and G. Oddou, "The Dimensions of Expatriate Acculturation," *Academy of Management Review* 10 (1985), pp. 39–47.

62. Arthur and Bennett, "The International Assignee."

63. J. I. Sanchez, P. E. Spector, and C. L. Cooper, "Adapting to a Boundaryless World: A Developmental Expatriate Model," *Academy of Management Executive* 14, no. 2 (2000), pp. 96–106.

64. P. Dowling and R. Schuler, *International Dimensions of Human Resource Management* (Boston: PWS-Kent, 1990).

65. Sanchez, Spector, and Cooper, "Adapting to a Boundaryless World."

66. Catherine Aman, "Horses for Courses," *Corporate Counsel,* December 15, 2008, Business & Company Resource Center, http://galenet.galegroup.com.

67. Andrew L. Molinsky, "Code Switching between Cultures," *Harvard Business Review,* January–February 2012, pp. 140–41.

68. "How Can a Company Manage an Expatriate Employee's Performance?" *SHRM India,* www.shrmindia.org, accessed May 6, 2010.

69. Kwoh, "Asia's Endangered Species."

70. Tim McCarney, "Relocation Policies More About Speed, Dexterity," *Canadian HR Reporter,* December 5, 2011, p. 20.

71. Lynne Molmar, "Addressing Expatriate Tax Issues," *Canadian HR Reporter,* March 13, 2006, p. 15.

72. Amy Maingault, Lesa Albright, and Vicki Neal, "Policy Tips, Repatriation, Safe Harbor Rules," *HR Magazine,* March 2008, p. 34.

73. "Minimizing Expatriate Turnover," *Workforce Management Online,* August 2004, www.workforce.com/section/09/article/23/81/28.html, retrieved March 22, 2005.

74. Adler, *International Dimensions of Organizational Behavior.*

75. L. G. Klaff, "The Right Way to Bring Expats Home," *Workforce,* July 2002, pp. 40–44.

CHAPTER 11

1. Sandy McIntosh, "Work Styles: A View into TELUS's Flexible Work Program," http://blog.telus.com/inside-telus/work-styles-a-view-into-telus-flexible-work-program/, retrieved May 11, 2015; "Working in Style: One Organization Implements a Program Designed to Help Employees Work Whenever and Wherever They Could be Productive," *T+D,* April 2015, p. 112; "New Study Demonstrates Why Canadian Business Should Enhance a Flexible Working Program," September 14, 2014, *Telus website,* http://about.telus.com/community/english/news_centre/news_releases/blog/2014/09/15/new-study-demonstrates-why-canadian-businesses-should-embrace-a-flexible-working-program, retrieved May 11, 2015; Andrea Goertz, "Finding Health Work-Life Balance in a Wireless World," June 22, 2014, www.huffingtonpost.ca/andrea-goertz/work-life-balance_b_5187415.html, retrieved May 11, 2015; "TELUS Sustainability Report 2014," http://csr.telus.com/en/community_investment/employee_experience/work_styles/, retrieved May 11, 2015; "TELUS history," http://about.telus.com/community/english/news_centre/company_overview/company_history, retrieved May 11, 2015.

2. S. Snell and J. Dean, "Integrated Manufacturing and Human Resource Management: A Human Capital Perspective," *Academy of Management Journal* 35 (1992), pp. 467–504.

3. M. A. Huselid, "The Impact of Human Resource Management Practices on Turnover, Productivity, and Corporate Financial Performance," *Academy of Management Journal* 38 (1995), pp. 635–72; U.S. Department of Labor, *High-Performance Work Practices and Firm Performance* (Washington, DC: U.S. Government Printing Office, 1993); and J. Combs, Y. Liu, A. Hall, and D. Ketchen, "How Much Do High-Performance Work Practices Matter? A Meta-Analysis of Their Effects on Organizational Performance," *Personnel Psychology* 59 (2006), p. 501–528.

4. R. N. Ashkenas, "Beyond the Fads: How Leaders Drive Change with Results," *Human Resource Planning* 17 (1994), pp. 25–44; Ronald M. Katz, "OPTimize Your Workforce," *HR Magazine,* October 2009, p. 85; and Luis Echevarria, "Creating Call Center Agents Who Think for Themselves," *Response,* June 2011, p. 45.

5. J. Arthur, "The Link Between Business Strategy and Industrial Relations Systems in American Steel Mini-Mills," *Industrial and Labor Relations Review* 45 (1992), pp. 488–506.

6. J. A. Neal and C. L. Tromley, "From Incremental Change to Retrofit: Creating High-Performance Work Systems," *Academy of Management Executive* 9 (1995), pp. 42–54; and M. A. Huselid, "The Impact of Human Resource Management Practices on Turnover, Productivity, and Corporate Financial Performance," *Academy of Management Journal* 38 (1995), pp. 635–72.

7. T.J. Atchison, "The Employment Relationship: Untied or Re-Tied," *Academy of Management Executive* 5 (1991), pp. 52–62.

8. D. McCann and C. Margerison, "Managing High-Performance Teams," *Training and Development Journal,* November 1989, pp. 52–60.

9. D. Senge, "The Learning Organization Made Plain and Simple," *Training and Development Journal,* October 1991, pp. 37–44.

10. M. A. Gephart, V. J. Marsick, M. E. Van Buren, and M. S. Spiro, "Learning Organizations Come Alive," *Training and Development* 50 (1996), pp. 34–45.

11. T. T. Baldwin, C. Danielson, and W. Wiggenhorn, "The Evolution of Learning Strategies in Organizations: From Employee Development to Business Redefinition," *Academy of Management Executive* 11 (1997), pp. 47–58; J. J. Martocchio and T. T. Baldwin, "The Evolution of Strategic Organizational Training," in *Research in Personnel and Human Resource Management* 15, ed. G. R. Ferris (Greenwich, CT: JAI Press, 1997), pp. 1–46; and "Leveraging HR and Knowledge Management in a Challenging Economy," *HR Magazine,* June 2009, pp. 81–89.

12. H. James Wilson, "Employees, Measure Yourselves," *The Wall Street Journal,* April 2, 2012, http://online.wsj.com.

13. E. A. Locke, "The Nature and Causes of Job Dissatisfaction," in *The Handbook of Industrial & Organizational Psychology,* ed. M. D. Dunnette (Chicago: Rand McNally, 1976), pp. 901–96l.

14. T. A. Judge, C. J. Thoresen, J. E. Bono, and G. K. Patton, "The Job Satisfaction–Job Performance Relationship:

A Qualitative and Quantitative Review," *Psychological Bulletin* 127 (2001), pp. 376–407; and R. A. Katzell, D. E. Thompson, and R. A. Guzzo, "How Job Satisfaction and Job Performance Are and Are Not Linked," *Job Satisfaction,* ed. C. J. Cranny, P. C. Smith, and E. F. Stone (New York: Lexington Books, 1992), pp. 195–217.

15. "Best Employer Studies Canada: What is Employee Engagement," Aon Hewitt website, https://ceplb03. hewitt.com/bestemployers/canada/pages/driving_engagement.htm, retrieved June 11, 2012.

16. For examples see M. Huselid, "The Impact of Human Resource Management Practices on Turnover, Productivity, and Corporate Financial Performance," *Academy of Management Journal* 38 (1995), pp. 635–672; S. Payne and S. Webber, "Effects of Service Provider Attitudes and Employment Status on Citizenship Behaviors and Customers' Attitudes and Loyalty Behavior," *Journal of Applied Psychology* 91 (2006), pp. 365–368; J. Hartner, F. Schmidt, and T. Hayes, "Business-Unit Level Relationship between Employee Satisfaction, Employee Engagement, and Business Outcomes: A Meta-Analysis," *Journal of Applied Psychology* 87 (2002), pp. 268–279; I. Fulmer, B. Gerhart, and K. Scott, "Are the 100 Best Better? An Empirical Investigation of the Relationship Between Being a 'Great Place to Work' and Firm Performance," *Performance Psychology* 56 (2003), pp. 965–993; "Working Today: Understanding What Drives Employee Engagement," *Towers Perrin Talent Report* (2003).

17. Towers Watson, "Employee Engagement to the Power of Three," *Viewpoints,* March 2011, www.towerswatson.com.

18. Aon Hewitt, "Trends in Global Employee Engagement," 2011, www.aon.com.

19. Kathleen Kindle, "Brand Alignment: Getting It Right," www.siegelgate.com/blog, accessed May 30, 2012; Aon Hewitt, "Trends in Global Employee Engagement," 2011, www.aon.com.

20. P. E. Boverie and M. Kroth, *Transforming Work: The Five Keys to Achieving Trust, Commitment, and Passion in the Workplace* (Cambridge, MA: Perseus, 2001), pp. 71–72, 79.

21. R. P. Gephart Jr., "Introduction to the Brave New Workplace: Organizational Behavior in the Electronic Age," *Journal of Organizational Behavior* 23 (2002), pp. 327–44.

22. John Bersin, "Why Companies Fail to Engage Today's Workforce: The Overwhelmed Employee," March 15, 2014, www.forbes.com, retrieved May 11, 2015.

23. Ibid.

24. Ibid.

25. D. W. Baruch, "Why They Terminate," *Journal of Consulting Psychology* 8 (1944), pp. 35–46; J. G. Rosse, "Relations among Lateness, Absence and Turnover: Is There a Progression of Withdrawal?" *Human Relations* 41 (1988), pp. 517–31; C. Hulin, "Adaptation, Persistence and Commitment in Organizations," in *Handbook of Industrial & Organizational Psychology,* 2nd ed., eds. M. D. Dunnette and L. M. Hough (Palo Alto, CA: Consulting Psychologists Press, 1991), pp. 443–50; and E. R. Burris, J. R. Detert, and D. S. Chiaburu, "Quitting before Leaving: The Mediating Effects of Psychological Attachment and Detachment on Voice," *Journal of Applied Psychology* 93 (2008), pp. 912–22.

26. D. A. Harrison, D. A. Newman, and P. L. Roth, "How Important Are Job Attitudes? Meta-analytic Comparisons of Integrative Behavioral Outcomes and

Time Sequences," *Academy of Management Journal* 49 (2006), pp. 305–25.

27. R. P. Quinn and G. L. Staines, *The 1977 Quality of Employment Survey* (Ann Arbor, MI: Survey Research Center, Institute for Social Research, University of Michigan, 1979).

28. T. Judge and T. Welbourne, "A Confirmatory Investigation of the Dimensionality of the Pay Satisfaction Questionnaire," *Journal of Applied Psychology* 79 (1994), pp. 461–66.

29. John Thackray, "Feedback for Real," March 15, 2001, http://gmj.gallup.com/conent/default.asp?ci=811, retrieved November 28, 2004.

30. Ibid.

31. Terence F. Shea, "Getting the Last Word," *HR Magazine,* January 2010, Business & Company Resource Center, http://galenet.galegroup.com; and L. M. Sixel, "Keeping Top Talent Has Employers Worried," *Houston Chronicle,* March 14, 2010, Business & Company Resource Center, http://galenet.galegroup.com.

32. "Stay Interviews," www.bcjobs.ca/re/hr-centre/interview-techniques/human-resource-advice/stay-interviews, retrieved June 11, 2012.

33. Kettler, ibid.

34. M. Lewis Jr., "The Heat is On," *Inside Business,* October 2007, downloaded from General Reference Center Gold, http://find.galegroup.com.

35. B. Becker and M. A. Huselid, "High-Performance Work Systems and Firm Performance: A Synthesis of Research and Managerial Implications," in *Research in Personnel and Human Resource Management* 16, ed. G. R. Ferris (Stamford, CT: JAI Press, 1998), pp. 53–101.

36. B. Becker and B. Gerhart, "The Impact of Human Resource Management on Organizational Performance: Progress and Prospects," *Academy of Management Journal* 39 (1996), pp. 779–801.

37. David Hatch, "Can Apple Polish Lowe's Reputation?" *U.S. News & World Report,* May 15, 2012, http://money.usnews.com.

38. M. Pearson, "Top-Gun Talent Make Ideal Recruiters," *The Globe and Mail,* July 21, 2011, www.theglobeandmail.com/report-on-business/small-business/sb-tools/sb-columnists/top-gun-talent-make-ideal-recruiters/article2103859/, retrieved June 11, 2012.

39. Sarah Dobson, "Project Connects Dots Between T&D, Profit," *Canadian HR Reporter,* April 21, 2008, p. 3.

40. "The Evolving Teller Role: Measuring Performance, Creating Accountability," *TellerVision,* March 2012, pp. 1–3 (interview with Linda Eagle).

41. H. J. Bernardin, C. M. Hagan, J. S. Kane, and P. Villanova, "Effective Performance Management: A Focus on Precision, Customers, and Situational Constraints," in *Performance Appraisal: State of the Art in Practice,* ed. J. W. Smither (San Francisco: Jossey-Bass, 1998), p. 56.

42. Patrick Darling, "Intel Sets 2020 Environmental Goals," Intel newsroom blog, May 17, 2012, http://newsroom.intel.com; Intel, *2011 Corporate Responsibility Report,* www.intel.com, accessed May 18, 2012.

43. L. R. Gomez-Mejia and D. B. Balkin, *Compensation, Organizational Strategy, and Firm Performance* (Cincinnati: South-Western, 1992); and G. D. Jenkins and E. E. Lawler III, "Impact of Employee Participation in Pay Plan Development," *Organizational Behavior and Human Performance* 28 (1981), pp. 111–28.

44. K. M. Kacmer, M. C. Andrews, D. L. Van Rooy, R. C. Steilberg, and S. Cerrone, "Sure Everyone Can Be Replaced . . . But at What Cost? Turnover as a Predictor

of Unit-Level Performance," *Academy of Management Journal* 49 (2006), pp. 133–44; J. D. Shaw, N. Gupta, and J. E. Delery, "Alternative Conceptualizations of the Relationship between Voluntary Turnover and Organizational Performance," *Academy of Management Journal* 48 (2005), pp. 50–68; and J. Lublin, "Keeping Clients by Keeping Workers," *Wall Street Journal,* November 20, 2006, p. B1.

45. Uyen Vu, "What's the Real Cost of Turnover?" *Canadian HR Reporter,* July 14, 2008, www.hrreporter.com, retrieved July 14, 2008.

46. M. M. Le Blanc and K. Kelloway, "Predictors and Outcomes of Workplace Violence and Aggression," *Journal of Applied Psychology,* 87, 2002, pp. 444–53.

47. "Wrongful Dismissal Law in Canada," Duhaime's Employment and Labour Law Centre, www.duhaime. orgfEmployment/ca-wd.aspx, retrieved March 28, 2005.

48. Jeffrey Smith, "Truck Driver Didn't Get the Message," *Canadian HR Reporter,* April 6, 2015, p. 5.

49. K. Karl and C. Sutton, "A Review of Expert Advice on Employment Termination Practices: The Experts Don't Always Agree," in *Dysfunctional Behavior in Organizations,* eds. R. Griffin, A. O'Leary-Kelly, and J. Collins (Stanford, CT: JA1 Press, 1998).

50. Government of Canada, "Corporate Social Responsibility: An Implementation Guide for Canadian Business," 2006, p. 5, www.commdev.org/content/document/detail/1468.

51. Paul Tsaparis, "Social Responsibility Gives Canadian Firms an Edge," *Canadian HR Reporter,* May 23, 2005, p. 18.

52. Ibid.

53. Anthony Watanabe, "From Brown to Green," *HR Professional,* February/March 2008, p. 49.

54. Uyen Vu, "Climate Change Sparks Attitude Shift," *Canadian HR Reporter,* March 26, 2007, p. 11.

55. Adrienne Fox, "Get in the Business of Being Green," *HR Magazine,* June 2008, p. 45.

56. Vancity website, https://www.vancity.com/AboutUs/OurValues/VancityIsCarbonNeutral/, retrieved June 12, 2012; and Shannon Klie, "Credit Union Aims to Be CO_2-Neutral by 2010," *Canadian HR Reporter,* March 26, 2007, p. 12; www.vancity.com, retrieved June 3, 2008.

57. Vancity website, www.vancity.com/AboutUs/OurValues/VancityIsCarbonNeutral/TheJourneyToZero/Transportation/, retrieved June 12, 2012.

58. Beth Tyndall, "Charitable Giving ROI," *HR Professional,* April/May 2007, p. 34.

59. Andrew Wahl et al., "The Best Work Places in Canada 2007," *Canadian Business,* April 23, 2007.

60. "2013 TELUS Corporate Social Responsibility Report," p. 17, sustainability.telus.com//, retrieved May 11, 2015.

61. Wahl, ibid.

62. Nova Scotia Public Service Commission website, www.gov.ns.ca/psc/jobCentre/, retrieved June 12, 2012.

63. Fox, ibid.

64. Wayne F. Cascio and Peter Cappelli, "Lessons from the Financial Services Crisis," *HR Magazine,* January 2009, Business & Company Resource Center, http://galenet.galegroup.com; Chris Petersen, "Thou Shalt Not . . .," *Construction Today,* September 2009, p. 13; and Carolyn Hirschman, "Giving Voice to Employee Concerns," *HR Magazine,* August 2008, pp. 51–53.

65. "Express Scripts Named as a 2014 World's Most Ethical Company by the Ethisphere Institute," March 27, 2014, *Express Scripts website,* www.express-scripts.ca/about/canadian-press/express-scripts-named-2014-worlds-most-ethical-company-ethisphere-institute, retrieved May 12, 2015 and Michael Biskey, "Raising the Bar on Ethical Culture," *Canadian HR Reporter,* February 23, 2015, p. 16.

66. Gwyn Morgan, "'Merger of Equals' Pitch Created EnCana, but It Would Flop Today," *The Globe and Mail,* April 30, 2007, p. B2.

67. Uyen Vu, "HR's Role in Mergers, Acquisitions," *Canadian HR Reporter,* December 4, 2006, p. 17, 21.

68. "Involve HR Early in M&As for Success, Survey Shows," *The Globe and Mail,* December 17, 2004, p. C3.

69. Uyen Vu, ibid.

70. Ibid.

71. S. Shrivastava and J. Shaw, "Liberating HR Through Technology," *Human Resource Management* 42, no. 3 (2003), pp. 201–17.

72. R. Broderick and J. W. Boudreau, "Human Resource Management, Information Technology, and the Competitive Edge," *Academy of Management Executive* 6 (1992), pp. 7–17.

73. Grace Ahrend, Fred Diamond, and Pat Gill Webber, "Virtual Coaching: Using Technology to Boost Performance," *Chief Learning Officer,* July 2010, pp. 44–47.

74. Kim Girard, "A Talent for Talent," *CFO,* May 2011, pp. 27–28.

75. Bob Mosher and Jeremy Smith, "The Case for Performance Support," *Training,* November–December 2011, Business & Company Resource Center, http://galenet.galegroup.com.

76. Matt Charney, "Five Reasons Why Cloud Computing Matters for Recruiting and Hiring," *Monster.com,* http://hiring.monster.com/hr, accessed May 30, 2012; Daniel Shane, "A Human Giant," *Information Age,* www.information-age.com, accessed May 30, 2012.

77. "Hot HR Issues for the Next Two Years" (Ottawa: Conference Board of Canada), September 2004.

78. "CFOs Showing More Interest in HR," *Canadian HR Reporter,* October 25, 2004, p. 4.

79. David Brown, "Measuring Human Capital Crucial, ROI Isn't, Says New Think-Tank Paper," *Canadian HR Reporter,* October 25, 2004, p. 4.

80. Jeff Sanford, "Value for the Money," *Canadian Business,* February 18, 2008, pp. 31–32.

81. Steve Lohr, "The Age of Big Data," *The New York Times,* February 11, 2012, www.nytimes.com.

Glossary

achievement tests Tests that measure a person's existing knowledge and skills.

action learning Training in which teams get an actual problem, work on solving it, commit to an action plan, and are accountable for carrying it out.

adventure learning A teamwork and leadership training program based on the use of challenging, structured physical activities.

alternative work arrangements Methods of staffing other than the traditional hiring of full-time employees (e.g., use of independent contractors, on-call workers, temporary workers, and contract company workers).

applicant tracking system (ATS) A software application that streamlines the flow of information between job seekers, HR staff, and hiring managers.

apprenticeship A work-study training method that teaches job skills through a combination of on-the-job training and classroom training.

aptitude tests Tests that assess how well a person can learn or acquire skills and abilities.

arbitration Conflict resolution procedure in which an arbitrator or arbitration board determines a binding settlement.

assessment Collecting information and providing feedback to employees about their behaviour, communication style, or skills.

assessment centre A wide variety of specific selection programs that use multiple selection methods to rate applicants or job incumbents on their management potential.

avatars Computer depictions of trainees, which the trainees manipulate in an online role-play.

balanced scorecard An organizational approach to performance management that integrates strategic perspectives including financial, customer, internal business processes, and learning and growth.

behavioural interview A structured interview in which the interviewer asks the candidate to describe how he or she handled a type of situation in the past.

behavioural observation scale (BOS) A variation of BARS, which uses all behaviours necessary for effective performance to rate performance at a task.

behaviourally anchored rating scale (BARS) Method of performance measurement that rates behaviour in terms of a scale showing specific statements of behaviour that describe different levels of performance.

benchmarking A procedure in which an organization compares its own practices against those of successful competitors.

Benchmarks A measurement tool that gathers ratings of a manager's use of skills associated with success in managing.

Bill C-45 (Westray Bill) Amendment to the Criminal Code making organizations and anyone who directs the work of others criminally liable for safety offences.

bona fide occupational requirement (BFOR) A necessary (not merely preferred) requirement for performing a job.

brand alignment The process of ensuring that HR policies, practices, and programs support or are congruent with an organization's overall culture (or brand), products, and services.

broadbanding A pay structure that consolidates pay grades into a few "broad bands."

calibration session Meeting at which managers discuss employee performance ratings and provide evidence supporting their ratings with the goal of eliminating the influence of rating errors.

Canada Pension Plan (CPP)/Quebec Pension Plan (QPP) A contributory, mandatory plan that provides retirement pensions, disability benefits, and survivor benefits.

Canadian Labour Congress (CLC) The umbrella organization for dozens of affiliated Canadian and international unions, as well as provincial federations of labour and regional labour councils.

career paths The identified pattern or progression of jobs or roles within an organization.

central tendency Incorrectly rating all employees at or near the middle of a rating scale.

checkoff provision A requirement that the employer, on behalf of the union, automatically deducts union dues from employees' paycheques.

closed shop A union security arrangement under which a person must be a union member before being hired.

coach A peer or manager who works with an employee to provide a source of motivation, help him or her develop skills, and provide reinforcement and feedback.

cognitive ability tests Tests designed to measure such mental abilities as verbal skills, quantitative skills, and reasoning ability.

collective bargaining Negotiation between union representatives and management representatives to arrive at an agreement defining conditions of employment for the term of the agreement and to administer that agreement.

commissions Incentive pay calculated as a percentage of sales.

communities of practice Groups of employees who work together, learn from each other, and develop a common understanding of how to get work accomplished.

compensatory model Process of arriving at a selection decision in which a very high score on one type of assessment can make up for a low score on another.

competencies Knowledge, skills, abilities, and other characteristics associated with effective performance.

competency-based pay systems Pay structures that set pay according to the employees' levels of skill or knowledge and what they are capable of doing.

conciliation Conflict resolution procedure in which a third party to collective bargaining reports the reasons for a dispute, the views and arguments of both sides, and possibly a recommended settlement, which the parties may decline.

concurrent validation Research that consists of administering a test to people who currently hold a job, then comparing their scores to existing measures of job performance.

construct validity Consistency between a high score on a test and a high level of a construct such as intelligence or leadership ability, as well as between mastery of this construct and successful performance on the job.

content validity Consistency between the test items or problems and the kinds of situations or problems that occur on the job.

continuous learning Each employee's and each group's ongoing efforts to gather information and apply the information to their decisions in a learning organization.

contrast error Rating error caused by comparing employee's performance to co-workers rather than to an objective standard.

contributory plan All costs of the plan are funded by employees, employers, and the plan's own investments.

cooperative education A plan of higher education that incorporates paid work experience as an integral part of academic studies.

coordination training Team training that teaches the team how to share information and make decisions to obtain the best team performance.

criterion-related validity A measure of validity based on showing a substantial correlation between test scores and job performance scores.

critical-incident method Method of performance measurement based on managers' records of specific examples of the employee behaving in ways that are either effective or ineffective.

cross-cultural preparation Training to prepare employees and their family members for an assignment in a foreign country.

cross-training Team training in which team members understand and practise each other's skills so that they are prepared to step in and take another member's place.

culture shock Disillusionment and discomfort that occur during the process of adjusting to a new culture.

decision support systems Computer software systems designed to help managers solve problems by showing how results vary when the manager alters assumptions or data.

defined benefit plan A pension plan that defines the benefits to be paid according to a formula stipulated in the plan.

defined contribution plan A retirement plan that specifies the contributions made by the employer as well as the employee and pension benefits are based upon the accumulated contributions and investment returns achieved.

development The acquisition of knowledge, skills, and behaviours that improve an employee's ability to meet the challenges of a variety of new or existing jobs.

differential treatment Differing treatment of individuals where the differences are based on a prohibited ground.

direct applicants People who apply for a vacancy without prompting from the organization.

direct compensation Financial rewards employees receive in exchange for their work.

direct discrimination Policies or practices that clearly make a distinction on the basis of a prohibited ground.

discrimination Treating someone differently, negatively, or adversely because of their race, age, religion, sex, or other prohibited ground.

distributed work A combination of work options, including work from the corporate office, work from home, work from a satellite office, or work from another remote location.

diversity training Training designed to change employee attitudes about diversity and/or develop skills needed to work with a diverse workforce.

downsizing The planned elimination of large numbers of employees with the goal of enhancing the organization's competitiveness.

downward move Assignment of an employee to a position with less responsibility and authority.

duty to accommodate An employer's duty to consider how an employee's characteristic such as disability, religion, or sex can be accommodated and to take action so the employee can perform the job.

e-learning Receiving training via the Internet or the organization's intranet.

electronic human resource management (E-HRM) The processing and transmission of digitized HR information, especially using computer networking and the Internet.

electronic performance support systems (EPSSs) Computer application that provides access to skills training, information, and expert advice as needed.

employee assistance program (EAP) Confidential, short term, counselling service for employees with personal problems that affect their work performance.

employee benefits Compensation in forms other than cash.

employee development The combination of formal education, job experiences, relationships, and assessment of personality and abilities to help employees prepare for the future of their careers.

employee empowerment Giving employees responsibility and authority to make decisions regarding all aspects of product development or customer service.

employee engagement Full involvement in one's work and commitment to one's job and organization.

employee health and wellness program A set of communications, activities, and facilities designed to change health-related behaviours in ways that reduce health risks.

employee stock ownership plan (ESOP) An arrangement in which the organization distributes shares of stock to all its employees by placing it in a trust.

employer branding A strategic approach of attaching a visual, emotional, or cultural brand to an organization.

Employment Insurance (EI) A federally mandated program to provide temporary financial assistance to non-working Canadians.

ergonomics The study of the interface between individuals' physiology and the characteristics of the physical work environment.

ethics The fundamental principles of right and wrong.

evidence-based HR Collecting and using data to show that human resource practices have a positive influence on the company's bottom line or key stakeholders.

exit interview A meeting of a departing employee with the employee's supervisor and/or human resources specialist to discuss the employee's reasons for leaving.

expatriates Employees who take assignments in other countries.

experiential programs Training programs in which participants learn concepts and apply them by simulating behaviours involved and analyzing the activity, connecting it with real-life situations.

expert systems Computer systems that support decision making by incorporating the decision rules used by people who are considered to have expertise in a certain area.

externship Employee development through a full-time temporary position at another organization.

feedback Information employers give employees about their skills and knowledge and where these assets fit into the organization's plans.

Fleishman Job Analysis System Job analysis technique that asks subject-matter experts to evaluate a job in terms of the abilities required to perform the job.

flexible benefits plans Benefits plans that offer employees a set of alternatives from which they can choose the types and amounts of benefits they want.

flextime A scheduling policy in which full-time employees may choose starting and ending times within guidelines specified by the organization.

focus on activities Rating error when employees are assessed on how busy they appear rather than how effective they are in achieving results.

forced-distribution method Method of performance measurement that assigns a certain percentage of employees to each category in a set of categories.

forecasting The attempts to determine the supply of and demand for various types of human resources to predict areas within the organization where there will be labour shortages or surpluses.

gainsharing Team incentive program that measures improvements in productivity and effectiveness and distributes a portion of each gain to employees.

generalizable Valid in other contexts beyond the context in which the selection method was developed.

glass ceiling Circumstances resembling an invisible barrier that keep most women and other members of the employment equity groups from attaining the top jobs in organizations.

global organizations Organizations that choose to locate a facility based on the ability to effectively, efficiently, and flexibly produce a product or service, using cultural differences as an advantage.

graphic rating scale Method of performance measurement that lists attributes and provides a rating scale for each attribute; the employer uses the scale to indicate the extent to which an employee displays each attribute.

grievance procedure The process for resolving union–management conflicts over interpretation or violation of a collective agreement.

halo error Rating error that occurs when the rater reacts to one positive performance aspect by rating the employee positively in all areas of performance.

harassment A form of discrimination that involves any unwanted physical or verbal behaviour that offends or humiliates you.

health and safety committees A committee jointly appointed by the employer and employees at large (or union) to address health and safety issues in a workplace.

health spending account A specific amount of money set aside per employee by the employer to cover health-related costs.

high-performance work system An organization in which technology, organizational structure, people, and processes all work together to give an organization an advantage in the competitive environment.

hiring algorithm Mathematical model that predicts which job candidates are most likely to be high-performers after being hired.

home country The country in which an organization's headquarters is located.

horns error Rating error that occurs when the rater responds to one negative aspect by rating an employee low in other aspects.

host country A country (other than the home country) in which an organization operates a facility.

hourly wage Rate of pay for each hour worked.

HR analytics Type of assessment of HRM effectiveness that involves determining the impact of, or the financial cost and benefits of, a program or practice.

HR dashboard A display of a series of HR measures, showing human resource goals and objectives and progress toward meeting them.

HRM audit A formal review of the outcomes of HRM functions, based on identifying key HRM functions and measures of organizational performance.

human capital An organization's employees, described in terms of their training, experience, judgment, intelligence, relationships, and insight.

human capital analytics The use of quantitative tools and scientific methods to analyze data from human resource databases and other sources to make evidence-based decisions that support business goals.

human resource information system (HRIS) A computer system used to acquire, store, manipulate, analyze, retrieve, and distribute information related to an organization's human resources.

human resource management (HRM) The practices, policies, and systems that influence employees' behaviours, attitudes, and performance.

incentive pay Forms of pay linked to an employee's performance as an individual, group member, or organization member.

indirect compensation The benefits and services employees receive in exchange for their work.

indirect discrimination Policies or practices that appear to be neutral but have an adverse effect on the basis of a prohibited ground.

industrial engineering The study of jobs to find the simplest way to structure work in order to maximize efficiency.

instructional design A process of systematically developing training to meet specified needs.

internal labour force An organization's workers (its employees and the people who work at the organization).

internal responsibility system Philosophy of occupational health and safety whereby employers and employees share responsibility for creating and maintaining safe and healthy work environments.

international organization An organization that sets up one or a few facilities in one or a few foreign countries.

internship On-the-job learning sponsored by an educational institution as a component of an academic program.

involuntary turnover Turnover initiated by an employer (often with employees who would prefer to stay).

job A set of related duties.

job analysis The process of getting detailed information about jobs.

job description A list of the tasks, duties, and responsibilities (TDRs) that a particular job entails.

job design The process of defining the way work will be performed and the tasks that a given job requires.

job enlargement Broadening the types of tasks performed in a job.

job enrichment Engaging workers by adding more decision-making authority to jobs.

job evaluation An administrative procedure for measuring the relative internal worth of the organization's jobs.

job experiences The combination of relationships, problems, demands, tasks, and other features of an employee's job.

job extension Enlarging jobs by combining several relatively simple jobs to form a job with a wider range of tasks.

job hazard analysis technique Safety promotion technique that involves breaking down a job into basic elements, then rating each element for its potential for harm or injury.

job posting The process of communicating information about a job vacancy on company bulletin boards, in employee publications, on corporate intranets, and anywhere else the organization communicates with employees.

job rotation Enlarging jobs by moving employees among several different jobs.

job sharing A work option in which two part-time employees carry out the tasks associated with a single job.

job specification A list of the competencies an individual must have to perform a particular job.

job structure The relative pay for different jobs within the organization.

job withdrawal A set of behaviours with which employees try to avoid the work situation physically, mentally, or emotionally.

knowledge workers Employees whose main contribution to the organization is specialized knowledge, such as knowledge of customers, a process, or a profession.

labour relations A field that emphasizes skills managers and union leaders can use to minimize costly forms of conflict (such as strikes) and seek win-win solutions to disagreements.

Labour Relations Board (LRB) A specialized tribunal with authority to interpret and enforce the labour laws in their jurisdiction.

leaderless group discussion An assessment centre exercise in which a team of five to seven employees is assigned a problem and must work together to solve it within a certain time period.

leading indicators Objective measures that accurately predict future labour demand.

learning An activity or process of gaining knowledge or skills by studying, practising, being taught, or experiencing something.

learning management system (LMS) A computer application that automates the administration, development, and delivery of training and development programs.

learning organization An organization that supports lifelong learning by enabling all employees to acquire and share knowledge.

leniency error Rating error of assigning inaccurately high ratings to all employees.

lockout A closure of a place of employment or refusal of the employer to provide work as a way to compel employees to agree to certain demands or conditions.

long-term disability insurance Insurance that pays a percentage of a disabled employee's salary after an initial period and potentially for the rest of the employee's life.

management by objectives (MBO) A system in which people at each level of the organization set goals in a process that flows from top to bottom, so employees at all levels are contributing to the organization's overall goals; these goals become the standards for evaluating each employee's performance.

mediation Conflict resolution procedure in which a mediator hears the views of both sides and facilitates the negotiation process but has no formal authority to dictate a resolution.

mentor An experienced, productive senior employee who helps develop a less experienced employee (a protégé or mentee).

merit pay A system of linking pay increases to ratings on performance appraisals.

mixed-standard scales Method of performance measurement that uses several statements describing each attribute to produce a final score for that attribute.

multinational company An organization that builds facilities in a number of different countries in an effort to minimize production and distribution costs.

multiple-hurdle model Process of arriving at a selection decision by eliminating some candidates at each stage of the selection process.

Myers-Briggs Type Indicator (MBTI) Psychological test that identifies individuals' preferences for source of energy, means of Information gathering, way of decision making, and lifestyle, providing information for team building and leadership development.

National Occupational Classification (NOC) Tool created by the federal government to provide a standardized source of information about jobs in Canada's labour market.

needs assessment The process of evaluating the organization, individual employees, and employees' tasks to determine what kinds of training, if any, are necessary.

negligent hiring A situation where an employer may be found liable for harm an employee causes to others if references and background checks were not performed adequately at the time of hiring.

nepotism The practice of hiring relatives.

nondirective interview A selection interview in which the interviewer has great discretion in choosing questions to ask each candidate.

offshoring Setting up a business enterprise in another country (e.g., building a factory in China).

on-the-job training (OJT) Training methods in which a person with job experience and skill guides trainees in practising job skills at the workplace.

organization analysis A process for determining the appropriateness of training by evaluating the characteristics of the organization.

organizational behaviour modification (OBM) A plan for managing the behaviour of employees through a formal system of feedback and reinforcement.

orientation Training designed to prepare employees to perform their jobs effectively, learn about their organization, and establish work relationships.

outplacement counselling A service in which professionals try to help dismissed employees manage the transition from one job to another.

outsourcing The practice of having another company (a vendor, third-party provider, or consultant) provide services.

paired-comparison method Method of performance measurement that compares each employee with each other employee to establish rankings.

panel interview Selection interview in which several members of the organization meet to interview each candidate.

passive job seekers Individuals who are not actively seeking a job.

pay equity The concept of "equal pay for work of equal value."

pay grades Sets of jobs having similar worth or content, grouped together to establish rates of pay.

pay level The average amount (including wages, salaries, and bonuses) the organization pays for a particular job.

pay policy line A graphed line showing the mathematical relationship between job evaluation points and pay rate.

pay range A set of possible pay rates defined by a minimum, maximum, and midpoint of pay for employees holding a particular job or a job within a particular pay grade or band.

pay structure The pay policy resulting from job structure and pay-level decisions.

performance improvement plan Summary of performance gaps and includes an action plan mutually agreed to by the employee and supervisor with specific dates to review progress.

performance management The process of ensuring that employees' activities and outputs match the organization's goals.

person analysis A process for determining individuals' needs and readiness for learning.

Personal Information Protection and Electronic Documents Act (PIPEDA) Federal law that sets out ground rules for how private sector organizations may collect, use, or disclose personal information.

phased retirement A gradual transition into full retirement by reducing hours or job responsibility.

piecework rate Rate of pay for each unit produced.

position The set of duties (job) performed by a particular person.

Position Analysis Questionnaire (PAQ) A standardized job analysis questionnaire containing 194 questions about work behaviours, work conditions, and job characteristics that apply to a wide variety of jobs.

predictive validation Research that uses the test scores of all applicants and looks for a relationship between the scores and future performance of the applicants who were hired.

productivity The relationship between an organization's outputs (products, information, or services) and its inputs (e.g., people, facilities, equipment, data, and materials).

profit sharing Incentive pay in which payments are a percentage of the organization's profits and do not become part of the employees' base salary.

progressive discipline A formal discipline process in which the consequences become more serious if the employee repeats the offence.

promotion Assignment of an employee to a position with greater challenges, more responsibility, and more authority than in the previous job, usually accompanied by a pay increase.

protean career A career that frequently changes based on changes in the person's interests, abilities, and values and in the work environment.

psychological contract A description of what an employee expects to contribute in an employment relationship and what the employer will provide the employee in exchange for those contributions.

Rand Formula A union security provision that makes payment of labour union dues mandatory even if the worker is not a member of the union.

readability The difficulty level of written materials.

readiness for training A combination of employee characteristics and positive work environment that permit learning.

realistic job previews Background information about a job's positive and negative qualities.

recency emphasis Rating error that occurs when an annual rating is based only on most recent work performed.

recruiting Any activity carried on by the organization with the primary purpose of identifying and attracting potential employees.

recruitment The process through which the organization seeks applicants for potential employment.

referrals People who apply for a vacancy because someone in the organization prompted them to do so.

reliability The extent to which a measurement generates consistent results, i.e., is free from random error.

repatriation The process of preparing expatriates to return home from a foreign assignment.

reverse mentoring Pairing of a younger, junior employee acting as mentor to share expertise with an older senior colleague, the mentee.

sabbatical A leave of absence from an organization to renew or develop skills.

safety data sheets (SDSs) Detailed hazard information concerning a controlled (hazardous) product.

salary Rate of pay for each week, month, or year worked.

selection The process by which the organization attempts to identify applicants with the necessary knowledge, skills, abilities, and other characteristics that will help the organization achieve its goals.

self-assessment The use of information by employees to determine their career interests, values, aptitudes, behavioural tendencies, and development needs.

self-service System in which employees have online access to information about HR issues and go online to enrol themselves in programs and provide feedback through surveys.

sexual harassment Unwelcome behaviour that is of a sexual nature or is related to a person's sex (gender or gender identity).

short-term disability insurance Insurance that pays a percentage of a disabled employee's salary as benefits to the employee for six months or less.

similar-to-me error Rating error of giving a higher evaluation to people who seem similar to oneself.

simple ranking Method of performance measurement that requires managers to rank employees in their group from the highest to the lowest performer.

simulation A training method that represents a real-life situation, with learners making decisions resulting in outcomes that mirror what would happen on the job.

situational interview A structured interview in which the interviewer describes a situation likely to arise on the job, then asks the candidate what he or she would do in that situation.

social unionism A type of unionism that attempts to influence social and economic policies of government.

stakeholders The parties with an interest in the company's success (typically, shareholders, the community, customers, and employees).

standard hour plan An incentive plan that pays workers extra for work done in less than a preset "standard time."

stay interview A meeting with an employee to explore his or her thoughts and feelings about the job and to uncover issues in the effort to prevent that employee from becoming disgruntled.

stock options Rights to buy a certain number of shares of stock at a specified price.

strictness error Rating error of giving low ratings to all employees, holding them to unreasonably high standards.

strike A collective decision by union members not to work or to slow down until certain demands or conditions are met.

structured interview A selection interview that consists of a predetermined set of questions for the interviewer to ask.

succession planning The process of identifying and tracking high-potential employees who will be able to fill top management positions or other key positions when they become vacant.

sustainability An organization's ability to profit without depleting its resources, including employees, natural resources, and the support of the surrounding community.

talent management A systematic, planned effort to train, develop, and engage the performance of highly skilled employees and managers.

task analysis The process of identifying the tasks, knowledge, skills, and behaviours that training should emphasize.

team leader training Training in the skills necessary for effectively leading the organization's teams.

teamwork The assignment of work to groups of employees with various skills who interact to assemble a product or provide a service.

technic of operations review (TOR) Method of promoting safety by determining which specific element of a job led to a past accident.

360-degree performance appraisal Performance measurement that combines information from the employee's managers, peers, direct reports, self, and customers.

third country A country that is neither the home country nor the host country of an employer.

total compensation All types of financial rewards and tangible benefits and services employees receive as part of their employment.

total rewards A comprehensive approach to compensating and rewarding employees.

training A planned effort to enable employees to learn job-related knowledge, skills, and behaviours.

transaction processing Computations and calculations involved in reviewing and documenting HRM decisions and practices.

transfer Assignment of an employee to a position in a different area of the company, usually in a lateral move.

transfer of learning On-the-job use of knowledge, skills, and behaviours learned in training.

transitional matrix A chart that lists job categories held in one period and shows the proportion of employees in each of those job categories in a future period.

transnational HRM system Type of HRM system that makes decisions from a global perspective, includes managers from many countries, and is based on ideas contributed by people representing a variety of cultures.

trend analysis Constructing and applying statistical models that predict labour demand for the next year, given relatively objective statistics from the previous year.

unfair labour practices Prohibited conduct of an employer, union, or individual under the relevant labour legislation.

union shop A union security arrangement that requires employees to join the union within a certain amount of time after beginning employment.

union steward An employee elected by union members to represent them in ensuring that the terms of the collective agreement are enforced.

unions Organizations formed for the purpose of representing their members' interests in dealing with employers.

utility The extent to which the selection method provides economic value greater than its cost.

validity The extent to which performance on a measure (such as a test score) is related to what the measure is designed to assess (such as job performance).

virtual expatriates Employees who manage an operation abroad without permanently locating in the country.

virtual reality A computer-based technology that provides an interactive, three-dimensional learning experience.

voluntary turnover Turnover initiated by employees (often when the organization would prefer to keep them).

work flow design The process of analyzing the tasks necessary for the production of a product or service.

Workers' Compensation Acts Provincial programs that provide benefits to workers who suffer work-related injuries or illnesses.

workforce planning Identifying the numbers and types of employees the organization will require to meet its objectives.

workforce utilization review A comparison of the proportion of employees in protected groups with the proportion that each group represents in the relevant labour market.

yield ratios A ratio that expresses the percentage of applicants who successfully move from one stage of the recruitment and selection process to the next.

Photo Credits

Chapter 1

p. 1 Blend Images/Getty Images; p. 2 Bloomberg/Getty Images; p. 6 Courtesy of WestJet; p. 23 HR Professional; p. 24 Sean Zaffino, Steam Whistle Brewing; p. 28 © Jose Luis Pelaez, Inc./Corbis; p. 31 © Inti St Clair/Blend Images LLC; p. 34 By permission of Dave Coverly and Creators Syndicate, Inc.; p. 37 Image credit: Virgin.com; p. 42 Reprinted by permission of CRHA.

Chapter 2

p. 45 Photo courtesy of The Willow Bean Café & Sodexo Canada; p. 47 "Canada's Best Diversity Employers" is a trade mark of Mediacorp Canada Inc. and is used with permission. The competition is managed by the Canada's Top 100 Employers project, in partnership with BMO Financial Group and the diversity consulting firm TWI Inc.; p. 52 CORNERED ©2012 Mike Baldwin. Reprinted with permission of UNIVERSAL UCLICK. All rights reserved; p. 53 Adrian Wyld/TCPI/The Canadian Press; p. 65 © LifesizeImages/iStockPhoto; p. 68 Reproduced with permission from the Canadian Centre for Occupational Health & Safety; p. 73 © WorkSafeBC. Used with permission. Copies of the poster, "So you think hearing protection is boring . . . think again" and other workplace health and safety materials are available free of charge at the WorkSafeBC website (WorkSafeBC.com).

Chapter 3

p. 83 Blend Images/Getty Images; p. 84 Michaelpuche/Dreamstime.com/GetStock.com; p. 86 EyeWire Collection/Getty Images; p. 101 Antonio Mo/Getty Images; p. 104 www.CartoonStock.com; p. 106 © biomorph® interactive desks, New York, NY, USA. Design: S.Barlow-Lawson

Chapter 4

p. 114 Jim Ross/Getty Images; p. 117 © Royalty-Free/Corbis/DAL; p. 121 THE CANADIAN PRESS/Chris Young; p. 131 Forest Products Association of Canada, TheGreenestWorkforce; p. 137 Bloomberg/Getty Images; p. 139 Photo by Tibor Kolley, © Copyright The Globe and Mail Inc./CP Photo

Chapter 5

p. 150 Viktor88/Dreamstime.com/GetStock.com; p. 158 © Royalty-Free/Corbis/DAL; p. 165 Image provided by BackCheck, Canada's background checking service and technology leader; p. 170 © Marguerite Reardon/CNET News. 09/29/2008; p. 174 Marconobre/Dreamstime.com

Chapter 6

p. 185 Blend Images/Getty Images; p. 186 Dimitri Otis/Getty Images; p. 197 © The McGraw-Hill Companies, Inc./Lars A. Niki, photographer/DAL; p. 204 © David Pu'u/Corbis; p. 217 © Karen Moskowitz/Getty Images; p. 220 © Jacobs Stock Photography/Getty Images/RF; p. 227 © Manpreet Romano/AFP/Getty Images

Chapter 7

p. 236 Courtesy of Acklands–Grainger; p. 249 kristian sekulic/Getty Images; p. 254 THE CANADIAN PRESS/Jason Franson; p. 263 © Ryan McVay/Getty Images

Chapter 8

p. 279 Blend Images/Getty Images; p. 280 © Anthony Seebaran/iStockPhoto; p. 287 Ron Levine/Getty Images; p. 298 DILBERT © 1995 Scott Adams. Used by permission of UNIVERSAL UCLICK. All rights reserved; p. 299 Adam121/Dreamstime.com/GetStock.com; p. 300 Robert Churchill/Getty Images; p. 311 Denisismagilov/Dreamstime.com/GetStock.com; p. 313 Courtesy of Hill and Knowlton

Chapter 9

p. 326 Blend Images/Getty Images; p. 327 Todd Korol/REUTERS; p. 330 THE CANADIAN PRESS/Ryan Remiorz; p. 336 Photo courtesy of CUPE; p. 347 Jennifer Rowsom/UNIFOR/Newscom; p. 351 The Canadian Press Images/Stephen C. Host

Chapter 10

p. 361 THE CANADIAN PRESS/Pawel Dwulit; p. 364 The Washington Post/Getty Images; p. 368 © Jupiterimages/RF/AP; p. 373 © Paul Almasy/Corbis; p. 375 Courtesy of CERC; p. 376 © Rob Brimson/Getty Images; p. 383 © Patrick Robert/Corbis Sygma

Chapter 11

p. 402 pio3/Shutterstock.com; p. 405 © Peter Beck/Corbis; p. 408 © Getty Images/Photodisc/DAL; p. 414 Wavebreakmediamicro/Dreamstime.com/GetStock.com; p. 427 Wayne Lorentz/Artefaqs Corporation

Subject Index